Canadian Financial Accounting

Principles and Issues

Canadian Financial Accounting

Principles and Issues

L.S. Rosen *York University*
M.H. Granof *University of Texas at Austin*

Prentice-Hall of Canada, Ltd.
Scarborough, Ontario

Canadian Cataloguing in Publication Data

Rosen, Lawrence S., 1935-
Canadian financial accounting

Includes index.

ISBN 0-13-113118-4

1. Accounting—Canada. I. Granof, M.H.
II. Title.

HF5635.R68 657'.0971 C80-094146-2

Prentice-Hall, Inc., Englewood Cliffs, New Jersey
Prentice-Hall International, Inc., London
Prentice-Hall of Australia, Pty., Ltd., Sydney
Prentice-Hall of India Pvt., Ltd., New Delhi
Prentice-Hall of Japan, Inc., Tokyo
Prentice-Hall of Southeast Asia (Pte.) Ltd., Singapore

ISBN 013-113118-4

Design and Cover: Robert Garbutt Productions
Production Editor: Beth Clelland
Typesetting: Howarth and Smith

2 3 4 5 JD 84 83 82 81 80

Contents

Preface

In recent years educators have been able to choose from several Canadian introductory accounting textbooks that emphasize the accounting cycle and what some call "traditional accounting". Few Canadian texts have been available for educators who wish to 1) blend the user and preparer orientations; 2) focus on the why as well as the how-to-do-it; 3) discuss issues currently facing both users and preparers of reports, and their application to Canadian situations; 4) introduce the role of judgment in financial accounting; 5) discuss the foundations and assumptions of accounting measurement and reporting disclosure, and the changing nature of these concepts; and 6) allow students to grapple with realistic, less-directed problem and decision situations, as well as traditional assignment material. This book was written to help accounting educators pursue these six educational themes.

It is hoped that this thematic approach will bring the introductory accounting class closer to those introductory classes of many other university disciplines where the subject is described broadly, the changing nature of the world is taken into account, and thinking is encouraged. Students will then better understand the field of accounting and more intelligently anticipate their possible roles as preparers and users. Preparers will not prepare information relevantly unless they understand the users' needs. Users will not interpret information accurately unless they grasp the thinking and environment of the preparer.

The book allows maximum flexibility to instructors, who can choose topics to fit their own emphases. Issues and discussions in Chapters 11 through 16 are included to serve as a reference book for potential users, as well as a course text; but these chapters can be omitted from study without affecting comprehension of other chapters. Material has been placed in Appendices for assigning whenever the instructor thinks the class is ready. Similarly, parts of Chapter 5 that relate to objectives and key concepts may be assigned at different times. Fundamental themes recur throughout the book; accordingly it may be used in courses of quite different lengths to accomplish various objectives. The student guide, *Self Study Problems for Canadian Financial Accounting,* treats items marked with an asterisk (*) in the "Questions, Problems, and Cases" sections of this text and discusses many other sample problems, cases, and solutions.

L. S. ROSEN
Toronto, Canada

Acknowledgments

Special acknowledgment and gratitude must be expressed to three persons: Joe Bolla of Price, Waterhouse & Co.; Gord Richardson, former Secretary to the Board of Examiners of the Canadian Institute of Chartered Accountants and now a doctoral student at Cornell University; and Lynn Knight. Joe read the manuscript and made many helpful comments, wrote many of the assignment questions, helped with large portions of the instructor's manual, and above all provided encouragement for the new approach adopted in the book. Gord read parts of the manuscript and wrote solutions to many of the assignment questions. Lynn headed a team of efficient secretaries who met the deadlines—a vital task. Members of her team were Bernice Morrison, Sharon Morrison, and Denise Timmons.

Many other organizations and individuals assisted and are also thanked: Bill Wood, David Wishart, Alex Milburn, Brian Jones, and Ron Ellis, all of Clarkson, Gordon & Co.; P. Howard Lyons and Bill King of Deloitte, Haskins & Sells; G. S. Taylor of John Labatt Limited; W. A. Harshaw of The Molson Companies; The Canadian Institute of Chartered Accountants; Canada Permanent Trust Company; Lea B. Hanson and Peter T. Brown of Dominion Securities Limited; Richard D. Falconer and K. McAsey of Wood Gundy Limited; Norm Roth and Bob Patterson of the Toronto Dominion Bank; John Switzer of the Bank of Nova Scotia; Efrim Boritz, a doctoral student at the University of Minnesota; Henry McCandless, of the Office of the Auditor General of Canada; John Dewhirst and Tom Beechy of York University; Al Prentice of the University of Calgary; Bob Crandall of Queen's University; Joe Basu of McMaster University; and several reviewers for Prentice-Hall of Canada, Ltd.

Comments from instructors and students are welcome.

L.S. ROSEN
Toronto, Canada

1 *Introduction*

Accounting: A Dynamic Discipline

Accounting involves the collection, summarization, and reporting of financial information. It is a dynamic discipline in which new principles and procedures are constantly evolving. Evolution is essential because accounting information is continually being judged on its ability to serve the needs of various user groups. Some users may seek information which might aid in prediction; a controller may want reports about the flow of cash in an organization; The Department of National Revenue, or Revenue Canada, may require an organization to file an income tax return; the manager of a company may require special reports. Accounting attempts to serve many masters, a job that is not easy because the needs of one group may conflict with the needs of others. Attitudes change, laws are amended, economic conditions vary, business practices alter, and user education and understanding improves, so accounting must change to meet these conditions.[1]

This text attempts to give students a reasonably sophisticated understanding of financial accounting. It aims to provide an overview of basic accounting principles as well as a familiarity with the significant issues currently facing the accounting profession. Hopefully, by mastering current accounting practices, and understanding why they are so practiced, the student as a future accountant or user will go beyond the present limitations of accounting, find new solutions to old problems, and be able to help resolve emerging problems.

Working accountants are concerned with the description of economic events, with the *measurement* of economic values, and with the determination of periodic changes in such economic values. A brief example can be used to demonstrate the difficulty of establishing precise rules of measurement that can be unanimously agreed upon. The illustration involves concepts and terminology that will be defined or explained in subsequent chapters; a layman's understanding of them should suffice, however, to appreciate why a number of basic accounting issues remain unresolved.

Home Heating Oil Limited was organized on January 1, 19x1. On that date the company sold common shares to individual investors for $1 million cash. The objective of the company was to purchase heating oil from a refinery and to resell and deliver it to residential customers. Upon its formation the company purchased storage tanks, delivery trucks, and other equipment at a total cost of $1 million. The useful life of such *fixed assets* was estimated at 10 years.

The following additional events took place during the company's first year of operations:

> The company purchased 4 million gallons of heating oil at a total cost of $1.6 million (an average cost of $.40 per gallon).
>
> The company sold 3.6 million gallons of oil at a price of $.50 per gallon. Total sales revenue was, therefore, $1.8 million and at the end of the year the firm had in inventory (i.e., goods available for sale in the next year, 19x2) the 400,000 gallons that had not yet been sold.
>
> Total operating expenditures for the year, including labor, advertising, selling and administrative expenditures, amounted to $200,000.

How much profit did the firm earn during its first year of operations? Income, or profit, is regarded by some people as a measure of change in wealth. How much better off was Home Heating Oil Limited at the end of the year than it was at the beginning?

Profit is commonly computed by deducting from sales or other revenues the expenses incurred in the production of such revenues. Thus, for the first year of operations,

Sales revenue (3.6 million gal @ $.50 per gal)		$1,800,000
Less: Costs applicable to revenues:		
Cost of goods sold (3.6 million gal @ $.40 per gal)	$1,440,000	
Other operating expenses	200,000	
Depreciation ($1 million ÷ 10 years)	100,000	1,740,000
Income (ignoring taxes on income)		$ 60,000

The above computation is often called an *income statement*, and is one of several types of reports which comprise financial statements. Some of the other statements are: balance sheet, statement of changes in financial position, and retained earnings statement. These will all be discussed more fully in succeeding chapters. The set of financial statements is accompanied by a number of notes which form an integral part of the financial statement package for an organization.

Sales revenue for the year was $1.8 million. Cost of the heating oil *purchased* (at an *average* price of $.40 per gallon) was $1.6 million, but of the 4 million gallons purchased only 3.6 million gallons, or 90 percent of those purchased, were actually sold. Hence the cost of the oil actually sold was 90 percent of $1.6 million, or $1,440,000. Cost of the remaining 400,000 gallons that were being held in inventory awaiting sale cannot be considered an expense of the first year of operations since the oil has not yet been used and can be assumed to retain its original value.

Operating expenses of the period were $200,000. In addition, the company purchased fixed assets at a cost of $1 million. But the purchase price of such fixed assets cannot be considered to be entirely an expense of the first year of operations. The assets are expected to have a productive life of 10 years, and therefore may be considered to benefit 10 accounting periods of one year duration each. The cost must be spread over, or *allocated* to, each of the 10 periods. Hence depreciation for the period was $1 million ÷ 10 = $100,000.

The "bottom line" of the income statement implies that Home Heating Oil Limited and collectively, the owners of its common shares (commonly called *shareholders*), were $60,000 better off at the end of the first year of operations than they were at the beginning. The computation of net income was governed by "generally accepted accounting principles" — those currently followed by the large majority of accountants and their clients.

But is the company really $60,000 better off at the end of the year than it was at the beginning? Consider some alternative approaches to determining the income of the company. Suppose that the "going" or "market" price for the fixed assets which the company had purchased on January 1 for $1 million had, by year end, increased to $1,150,000. Should $150,000 be added to the revenues ("revenue from appreciation of fixed assets") to reflect the increase in value (thus increasing income to $210,000)? Or should the increase in market value be ignored? Or, might the $150,000 be considered as an increase in wealth but not be included as income? Further discussion of some of these issues occurs in Chapter 16 where we consider the possibility of preparing more than one income computation for different user groups.

Under current generally accepted accounting principles in Canada, the increase in the market price of the fixed assets *generally would not* be reported in financial statements made available to shareholders, creditors, or the general public. But many accountants argue that these current procedures should be modified so that gains from appreciation are recognized in accounting reports.

Suppose also that, of the 4 million gallons of heating oil that were purchased at a total cost of $1.6 million, the first 3.6 million were purchased at a price of $.39 per gallon (a total cost of $1,404,000) and the last 400,000 gallons were purchased at a price of $.49 per gallon (a total cost of $196,000). Should the cost of the 3.6 million gallons sold be computed using the *weighted average* price of oil purchased during the year ($.40, as in the earlier computation), or should it be assumed that the oil that was purchased first was sold first? If the latter assumption is made, then the cost of goods sold would not be $1,440,000 as previously calculated. Instead it would be 3.6 million gallons times $.39 per gallon: $1,404,000. Since the cost of goods sold would then be $36,000 less than before, income would be $36,000 greater: $96,000.

Alternatively, since all oil purchased was mixed together in the same tank, is it logical to assume that the oil purchased *last* was sold first? Cost of goods sold would then be 400,000 times $.49 per gallon + 3.2 million times $.39 per gallon — a total of $1,444,000 — and income would be $4,000 *less* than that originally computed. Conventional practice would permit the company to make any one of the three assumptions regarding the flow of costs: it could assume that the goods sold were purchased at an "average" price, or the first goods purchased were the first sold, or the last goods purchased were the first sold.

Suppose additionally that in the course of the company's first year of operations, inflation was a major problem in the country and that the general consumer price level increased by 10 percent. Was the income of the company still $60,000? Were the shareholders of the company really $60,000 better off at the end of the accounting period than they were at the beginning? When they initially purchased the common shares of Home Heating Oil Limited (on January 1, 19x1) they surrendered $1 million of purchasing power. If after one year they were able to sell their shares for $1,060,000 — original investment plus the income of the period — they would clearly be worse off at the end of the period than they were at the beginning. It would take $1.1 million ($1.0 million plus 10 percent increase in the general consumer price level) on January 1, 19x2 to buy consumer goods that would have cost $1.0 million on January 1, 19x1.

Should the income computation (and financial statements) of Home Heating Oil Limited acknowledge the loss of $100,000 ($1.1 million minus $1.0 million) in general consumer purchasing power? Traditionally, accountants and business managers have not recorded the effects of changes in general purchasing power in financial statements. However, some accountants believe that, at least for large companies, two sets of financial statements should be prepared: one which records the impact of changes in general purchasing power, and one which does not.

The objective of this oversimplified example is to dispel at the very beginning any notion that the study of accounting is merely a matter of learning to apply existing rules and procedures. Unfortunately, there are few definitive answers to questions asked of accountants. The accounting discipline is alive with issues that are currently — and likely to remain forever — unresolved. In reading and studying this text, the *student* should strive not only to understand and be able to apply what is currently being done in practice but also to be able to evaluate available alternatives in light of the objectives of financial reporting.

Students must always remember that accounting is largely the designing of information to aid people who make judgments and decisions. We must always attempt to ascertain the impact of accounting information on the behavior of the users/decision-makers. We must avoid providing misleading information and strive to represent economic events fairly.

Objectives of Accounting

Accounting aims to provide information to facilitate a number of key functions. Among them are

1. *Allocating the resources of our society.* Under any form of economic arrangement, be it capitalistic or socialistic, decisions as to where capital ought to be invested are based on information contained in such sources as financial statements. In a free enterprise system, private investors make judgments about buying, holding or selling shares after considering many factors — the state of the economy, the nature of the industry in which the company is located, the quality of the company's products, and the competence of management. The effects of many of these factors can be found in past financial statements or estimates of future income. Bankers and suppliers of funds investigate many aspects of a company's operations and review its financial statements before loaning money. Revenue Canada and other government agencies use financial statements as a starting point when levying income and other taxes and before giving grants. Labor union executives may also review financial statements of employers when negotiating a new labor contract.

2. *Managing and directing the resources within an organization.* Profit and nonprofit entities alike rely on accounting information to ensure that they maintain effective control over both their human and material resources and to make certain that within their organizations they allocate such resources to the products, sub-units, or functions where they can be most productive.

Accounting information which is prepared for use within an organization, rather than for outsiders such as shareholders and creditors, is usually called managerial or management accounting information. The primary subject matter of this book is financial accounting for outsiders — not management accounting.

3. *Reporting on the custodianship of resources under the command of individuals or organizations.* Individuals, acting either as investors or merely as citizens, entrust resources to professional managers and governmental officials. They expect such managers or officials to provide them with periodic reports by which their performance in office can be evaluated.

4. *Complying with various regulations, requirements or laws, other than income tax and corporate legislation.* School boards, hospitals, charitable institutions, and some profit-seeking organizations are often requested to supply special-purpose reports to a variety of users. Such reports are designed to meet the special needs of the user and are not intended for a general audience. A segment of a university, for example, may be required to furnish information on class sizes, cost per student per semester, expenditures on fixed assets in the previous five years, and similar data, to a potential donor of a large sum of money. Such information may have a major effect on a potential donor's decision, when compared with the donor's preconceptions against figures which indicate the norm.

Accounting focuses on the *measurement and communication* of a wide range of financial and related data. Accountants provide the information required to make decisions as to where to allocate financial resources, and once such decisions are made they provide the data necessary to effectively control such resources. Periodically, as the management process is being carried out, accountants "report the score" — they provide information by which the results of prior decisions can be evaluated.

Standards

Relevancy

If information provided by the accountant is to be useful, then, above all, it must be *relevant* — it must be associated directly with the decisions it is designed to facilitate. Unfortunately, what is relevant for one group of financial statement users may not be relevant for another. For example, businesses which are incorporated under a provincial or a federal Corporations Act — their firm name includes the words Limited (Ltd.), Corporation (Corp.), or Incorporated (Inc.) — are required to prepare a set of financial statements each year. In order to comply with the Act under which they are incorporated, officials of the company may not have to report much information if their sole purpose for reporting is to comply with a Corporations Act. Such an abbreviated set of financial statements would be of little use to a banker — whose main interests may center on the state of the company's inventory and on amounts owing to the company (called *accounts receivable*). A potential investor may have little interest in the abbreviated statements or in inventory and accounts receivable. Instead, the potential investor may want information about sales and cost trends over several years.

As a result it is virtually impossible to prepare a general purpose report which satisfactorily serves the needs of all potential user groups. Yet, in order to comply with various laws, accountants are forced to compile one set of statements for the non-existent general audience. This requirement is a prime cause of some of the controversies which we discuss in succeeding chapters. Sometimes, additional reports can be prepared for specific users, such as Revenue Canada, but even then a procedure adopted for the general purpose financial statements may have to be used as well in computing income taxes. This could result in the company's having to pay income taxes many months earlier than it would prefer.

The notion of relevancy can also be illustrated by an example from management accounting:

MNO Limited manufactures a single product in a plant that it rents. In a given year it produces and sells to its regular customers 1,000 units at a cost of $300 per unit, determined as follows:

Fixed costs: rent, executive salaries, heat, power, administrative costs, etc.	$100,000
Variable costs: labor and materials ($200 per unit produced x 1,000 units)	200,000
Total costs	$300,000
Number of units produced and sold	÷ 1,000 units
Cost per unit	$ 300

The plant is not currently operating at capacity. The federal government has offered to buy 500 units of the product at a price of $250 each. If the company were to accept the offer, its sales to its regular customers would remain unchanged. Should the company sign the contract to sell to the government, even though the selling price is below "cost"?

From the standpoint of an executive of the company, the *relevant* cost to be considered would be $200 per unit, rather than the $300 previously computed. The fixed costs of $100,000 are, of course, fixed. They will remain unchanged whether or not the company accepts the offer of the government. The only additional costs the company would have to incur are the variable costs. If the company accepted the offer of the government, it would earn additional revenue of 500 units times $250 per unit — $125,000 — and incur additional costs of 500 units times $200 — $100,000. Thus, it would be $25,000 better off by accepting the offer.

If the company accepted the offer, then the average cost of each unit produced would be

Fixed costs: rent, executive salaries, heat, power, administrative costs, etc.	$100,000
Variable costs: $200 per unit produced x 1,500 units (the new level of production)	300,000
Total costs	$400,000
Number of units produced	÷ 1,500
Average cost per unit	$ 267

The average cost per unit could be viewed as the relevant cost for the determination of overall income. But for a decision as to whether or not to accept the offer of the government, the relevant cost would be the *incremental* or *marginal* cost — that of producing the additional units required for the government contract.

Objectivity

Accounting information should, ideally, be *objective* and *verifiable*. Qualified individuals working independently of one another should be able, upon examination of the same data or records, to derive similar measures or reach similar conclusions. Insofar as possible, information contained in financial reports should not depend on the subjective judgments of the individual accountant who prepared it.

Herein lies a catch. Information that is most objective may not be relevant to many decisions, and that which is most relevant may not be objective. A few illustrations will highlight this conflict.

1. Should a corporation value land at *historical cost* or *fair market value*? The most objective amount would be *historical cost* — that which the company paid for the land. Such amount is readily verifiable. But of what relevance is it? The company may have bought such land decades ago, and the historical cost provides no indication of what it can be sold for today. Yet any amount other than historical cost — e.g., present market value — would necessarily involve estimates or appraisals and hence be less objective. *Conventional accounting reports are based on historical costs.* Increases in market values are generally not included in the prime figures on the income statement and balance sheet of Canadian companies, but they may be reported elsewhere in the set of financial statements as supplementary information. Some market values, such as for widely-traded securities, tend to be verifiable, and under specified conditions, reductions in such market values might be reported on income statements.

Some accountants advocate the use of replacement costs or selling prices, rather than historical costs, for all assets in computing income and for the other financial statements. Their position is evaluated in later chapters.

2. Should a firm's statement of annual income reflect as revenue earned the potential selling price of inventory (not fixed assets) that the company has produced but not yet sold? Or, alternatively, should the firm defer recognition of such revenue until it has actually sold the items, or even until it has actually collected the full selling price in cash? Income is often said to result from the entire process of production and sale, and since the firm is *usually* able to sell what it produces, financial statements in which income has been reported as soon as goods have been produced would be most relevant for most decision purposes. But such statements would be considerably less objective than those in which profit recognition is delayed until the goods have been formally sold — and hence a firm sales price has been established — or until cash has actually been collected and the full amounts to be received is known with certainty.

3. Should a company's income statement include as current pension expenses only amounts actually paid to retired workers or amounts that will eventually have to be paid to present employees as well? Many companies incur the liability (either legal or moral) to pay their employees pensions in the course of the employees' productive years. The actual cash payment, however, would not have to be made until an employee retires and the actual amount to be paid may depend on the number of years the employee survives after his retirement. Such amount cannot be determined with certainty until after the employee dies. Should the company report an estimate of the pension expense as the employee "earns" the right to his pension (the most relevant time), or should it wait until it actually disburses the cash (when the expense can be objectively determined)?

In Canada, generally accepted accounting principles tend to require the recording of pension expense when the employees earn their pension through weekly or monthly employment. However, because (a) pensions are often based on the employee's years of highest income, which are usually not yet known, (b) some employees leave the company before working the minimum number of years necessary to qualify for a pension, and (c) there can be many other complications, estimates of pension expense are extremely difficult to make, requiring many computations and assumptions by actuaries. As a result it is not uncommon to see criticisms of pension accounting in financial newspapers and magazines. Most of the criticisms seem valid, but finding better methods of accounting is very difficult.

A great many accounting issues can be attributed to the conflicting objectives of relevance and objectivity. Accountants continually face situations in which they must trade the realization of one goal for that of the other. This trade-off can only be made after considering: (a) the different user-groups or the purposes and *objectives* of reporting; (b) the *facts* of the specific situation; and (c) the *constraints* imposed by companies', securities' and similar kinds of legislation. Throughout the book we will be referring to the importance of objectives, facts, and constraints in choosing accounting and reporting methods.

Uniformity and comparability

One might wish that all accounting methods and reports would be the same both within and among organizations. Judgments are made by obtaining at least two pieces of information for comparisons to be drawn and impressions formed.[2] Lay persons tend to expect that if the sales or income figures for one company are compared to those of another, a judgment can be made as to which is the better performer. Unfortunately, such comparisons often cannot be drawn even when the two companies being compared have the same set of reporting objectives, facts and constraints.

It is unlikely that complete uniformity will ever be achieved although some portions of financial statements can be compared from company to company with valid conclusions drawn. Failure to attain uniformity can be ascribed to at least three factors. First, until recently both the professional accounting societies and the government agencies responsible for establishing accounting principles and maintaining accounting standards have allowed individual companies a relatively free hand in selecting among alternative accounting practices. Even today, for example, some firms within the same industry will assume that goods purchased first are sold first, while others will assume that goods purchased first are sold last. Second, the task of prescribing uniform principles that would be appropriate for all companies — or even those within a specific industry — is one that is easier to write about than to accomplish. In the last several decades the range and complexity of business transactions have increased enormously. Accounting procedures designed for one *factual* situation — where the buyer of your goods is a federal government and payment is assured — are often not applicable in a different factual situation — where the buyer is a struggling, young firm which could go bankrupt tomorrow. In addition to differences in facts, constraints may differ because companies may be incorporated under one of several provincial Companies Acts or a federal Act. A few of these Acts may prescribe somewhat different accounting and reporting methods. The number of different combinations of objectives, facts, and constraints is simply too great to prescribe rules for handling each combination.

Third, accountants are not, and cannot be, trained to handle everything which they encounter in a uniform way. Professional judgment is very important in recognizing which objectives of accounting should take priority in a particular situation. Training and attitude differences among accountants can cause major variations in financial statements.

Consistency

For a reader to compare performance in one period with that in another, financial statements must be based on accounting practices that are consistent over time. Thus, although different firms may change their assumptions pertaining to the flow of goods, any one firm would ordinarily base its financial reports on the same assumptions from one year to the next. "A foolish consistency," Emerson pointed out, however, "is the hobgoblin of little minds." In an era of a rapidly changing business environment, accounting practice must necessarily change also. Hence, over a number of years, some degree of consistency must be sacrificed in order for the accountant to achieve his other objectives.

Generally, accountants try to warn readers about major changes in accounting methods and procedures. For example, they tend to restate the prior year's financial statements (whenever two year comparative statements are given to outsiders) using the new accounting procedure. But this would occur only when a change in facts has occurred gradually over several years or when the accounting change was made in accordance with a change in management's attitude toward the situation. Restatement of reports would not occur when an accounting change has been precipitated by a sudden change of facts, beyond management's control. For example, in the case of Home Heating Oil Limited, information about quality of equipment may come to light late in 19x2 which would indicate that the fixed assets will have a life of only three years instead of 10. In this situation, 19x1's financial statements would remain as they previously were reported, whereas in 19x2 a much larger depreciation expense would be reported. In contrast, if management decided to allocate the cost of fixed assets over five instead of 10 years simply because it changed its mind, the prior year's (19x1) depreciation would be restated from $100,000 to $200,000. Depreciation in 19x2 would also be $200,000.

Nonstandards

Lay persons place far greater faith in financial statements than is generally warranted. It is essential, therefore, that the limitations of financial statements be clearly understood.

1. Financial statements are *not accurate* (i.e., precise). This is as true if amounts are carried out to the penny as if they are rounded off to the hundreds or, in the case of many published reports, to the thousands of dollars. Accounting statements are necessarily based on estimates; estimates are inherently inaccurate. In an earlier example it was indicated that the useful life of the fixed assets purchased was 10 years. However, is it possible to predict with any degree of precision how long an asset will last? Why not 9

years, or even 15? If in the example useful life were estimated to be 8 years, instead of 10, then depreciation charges would have increased from $100,000 per year to $125,000. Net income would have decreased from $60,000 to $35,000 — a reduction of over 41 percent!

2. Financial data *cannot be used as the sole measure of managerial accomplishment*. Financial statements of private enterprises generally focus on *profit* or *income*. But profit is by no means a comprehensive measure of performance. Profit tells only a small part of the annual story of a business. Profit for a period of one year can readily be manipulated in order to make an enterprise look good. To the extent that a manager knows that he will be evaluated on the basis of income for a given single year he can readily increase *reported* profit by postponing maintenance and nonessential repairs, cutting back on advertising and research and development costs, and reducing the quality of products or services. The negative impact of such actions is unlikely to be reflected in reported profits until subsequent years.

But profit, even over a longer period of time, may be only a poor indication of management performance. Profit, after all, can be influenced by factors over which a manager has little control. In 1979, for example, oil companies reported unusually high earnings. Yet because of the sudden increase in worldwide oil prices in that year, the managers of a number of individual oil companies would have had to have been downright incompetent not to have led their firms to record earnings. At the same time, managers in firms which were unable to obtain needed petroleum supplies may have suffered declines in income which could have been avoided only by superhuman executive actions. As long as profits are influenced to a considerable extent by forces beyond management control (and such forces do not exert equal pressures on all firms alike — not even those within a given industry) net income by itself may be an inappropriate criterion for management evaluation.

Moreover, managers have goals in addition to that of maximizing profit. Indeed, some writers have suggested that executives in major corporations do not even attempt to maximize profits; instead they seek to achieve "satisfactory" levels of earnings. Many managers would include among their goals improving the environment surrounding company plants; increasing the economic, social, physical, and mental well-being of employees; and increasing the number of minority employees on the corporate payroll. Accountants do not purport that such objectives are taken into account in financial statements.

3. Financial statements are *not neutral*. It is often said that accounting information must be unbiased — that accountants should be disinterested umpires who "call 'em like they see 'em." Accountants may indeed attempt to use an unbiased measuring stick when reporting on economic events. But value judgments enter into the measurement process as ac-

countants determine *what* to measure. Accountants measure income as conventionally defined: revenues less expenses. But they include in their measurements only *selected* revenues and expenses. They do not, for example, include in their financial reports costs of "externalities," such as water or air pollution, employee injuries, or discriminatory hiring practices. Similarly, they fail to give recognition to the benefits received by their efforts to clean up the environment, improve the community welfare, eliminate safety hazards, etc. Indeed several firms have experimented with "social" income statements and balance sheets which are based on nonconventional judgments as to what revenues and costs should be measured and reported.

4. The primary criterion by which the adequacy of financial statements should be judged is *not* whether they minimize the tax liability of the reporting business entity. In the course of this text, numerous alternative accounting procedures will be presented and evaluated. The merits of the alternatives will normally be considered in terms of their objectivity and their relevance to the users of the financial information. Sometimes, unfortunately, a company's choice among alternatives is motivated primarily by income tax considerations, and as a consequence its financial reports are both less objective and less useful to shareholders and potential investors than they might otherwise be.

That is not to say that an accountant should not assist his client in arranging his financial affairs in such a manner as to pay the least amount of taxes required by the Income Tax Act. U.S. Judge Learned Hand has pointed out

> Over and over again courts have said that there is nothing sinister in so arranging one's affairs as to keep taxes as low as possible. Everyone does so, rich and poor; and all do right, for nobody owes any public duty to pay more than the law demands.

Accounting financial statements filed with Revenue Canada in order to comply with the accounting objective or purpose of computing and paying income taxes, may not prove adequate or relevant for decisions that investors, creditors, employees, or managers must make. Taxable income as reported to Revenue Canada is often computed in accordance with specific provisions of the Income Tax Act and Regulations. Such provisions are *not* necessarily consistent with "generally accepted" accounting principles. For example, Income Tax legislation describes in considerable detail the specific way fixed assets have to be depreciated for the purposes of computing taxable income. For this reason alone, taxable income could be quite different from accounting income. In contrast, but with some exceptions, the legislation accepts a wide variety of methods of recognizing revenue on an income statement as long as a firm is consistent in its chosen method from year to year. Often, though, the same revenue recognition method has to be used *both* for reporting to investors and for computing taxable income. The reason is that the income tax legislation in effect states that whatever accounting method is chosen in reports for investors must also be used in computing taxable income. As we shall see later in the book, in circumstances such as the one described, accountants have to choose their one method of accounting for a specific transaction carefully when there may be conflicting objectives such as minimizing income taxes while keeping investors informed. In addition, readers of financial statements must understand these conflicts and the dynamic nature of the subject.

Many companies maintain a separate file or "set of books" for the purposes of computing taxable income. Large companies may in fact have several separate files or "books" in order to be able to compute financial statements for the different user groups or objectives of accounting. Such a practice is neither illegal nor unethical; it is simply reflective of different information needs of different decision makers.

The Accounting Profession

A brief background

Although modern accounting can trace its roots to 1494, when an Italian monk named Fr. Luca Paciolo described a "double-entry" accounting procedure that forms the basis for accounting practice today, public accounting as a profession is relatively new. The development of the profession was spurred primarily by new forms of economic activity associated with the Industrial Revolution. Many of the significant developments in the early stages of the profession's growth can be traced to Great Britain. By the latter half of the eighteenth century, small associations of professional accountants began to develop. In the early part of the twentieth century, the momentum for growth and innovation shifted to the United States. Since 1900, the number of public accountants in the United States has grown exponentially.

Accountants today are employed by *public* accounting firms, corporations, and private business enterprises as well as by government and other non-profit organizations. The term *accountants* is often used to designate persons who provide a wide range of services — from clerks who perform routine clerical functions to corporate vice-presidents who make major financial decisions.

Most commonly, however, the professional accountant is associated with the practice of public accounting (i.e., offering a variety of services to the general public). In Canada there is a wide variation in laws from province to province as to who may practice as a public accountant. The three main federal bodies of accountants in Canada are: Canadian Certified General

Accountants' Association (which grants the designation CGA to its members); The Canadian Institute of Chartered Accountants (designation is CA); and The Society of Management Accountants of Canada (designation is RIA). Members of each of the three bodies belong to one or more provincial groups as well as to the national or federal group. In some provinces, members of all three bodies, as well as others, may practice as public accountants. In other provinces there are restrictions which in essence may limit the practice of public accounting to CAs. Laws affecting public accounting are often in a state of flux.

Members of each of the three bodies are required to pass one or more sets of national examinations. Students aspiring to become chartered accounts (CAs) generally have to obtain a bachelor's degree first. Leaders of all three bodies are recognizing more and more the need for potential members to have a broad exposure to behavioral sciences, economics, quantitative methods, logic, communications, and many other disciplines. A good accountant must understand what makes a company successful, how decisions are made, and a variety of other factors. The prestige of accountants depends upon their ability to influence judgments and decisions — and this requires a broad knowledge base.

Outside of Canada the two most common accounting designations are Certified Public Accountant (CPA), which is used in the United States, and Chartered Accountant (CA), which is used in England and Wales. There are many other designations in other countries for both public accountants and those who specialize as management accountants. In Canada, the RIAs are primarily, but not exclusively, management accountants.

Ask people what public accountants do, and they will probably think of income taxes. Actually, many public accountants are associated with four primary functions: auditing and financial reporting, management advisory services, financial administration and bankruptcy, and tax advice. The auditing function is unique to, and most characteristic of, the public accounting profession.

Public accountants

- *Auditing and financial reporting*

The purpose of the audit function is to lend credibility to financial reports. Persons who rely upon these reports want assurance that they present fairly the results of the economic activities that they describe.

Audits are required in order to comply with various pieces of legislation, and are also requested by a variety of people and groups. For example, when a company decides to sell some of its ownership shares to the general public, the services of an underwriter are usually obtained. The underwriter asks that prospective buyers be provided with audited financial statements. Similarly, banks, insurance companies and other lenders tend to ask for audited financial statements when large sums of money are involved.

In performing an audit (often referred to as the attest function), the public accountant is concerned with *external* financial statements — those given to users outside of the company being reported upon. The division of the accounting discipline dealing with external reports is known as *financial accounting. Internal* financial reports, on the other hand, are those given to managers within a firm to facilitate planning and control. Since such reports are directed to specific users they can be tailor-made to provide information most relevant to the decisions at hand.

Although corporate management is responsible for preparing external financial reports, the auditor plays an important role in ensuring that these reports are suitable under the circumstances. The auditor does not, of course, verify each of the transactions underlying the financial statements. In a large corporation the number of transactions in a year would make that an impossible task. The auditor does, however, review the accounting systems used to accumulate and summarize the underlying data, test check some of the transactions or effects — often using statistical and quantitative techniques — and, most importantly, makes certain that the financial statements have been prepared in accordance with generally accepted accounting principles and any legislation affecting the company.

The end product of an independent auditor's examination is the auditor's report or opinion on the financial statements. Typically, it might appear as shown in Exhibit 1-1. The first paragraph is called the *scope* paragraph wherein the auditor explains in general terms what he has investigated. The second paragraph is the *opinion* paragraph, which sets out what the auditor is willing to support. Although there has been some recent discussion in the U.S. about changing the auditor's reporting format, in Canada the wording is somewhat standardized. The auditor says that the financial statements "present fairly . . . in accordance with generally accepted accounting principles." The concept of fairness is thus tied to Canadian accounting principles, and unless readers know what these principles state, they could read too much into the word "fairly." Throughout this book we must keep asking ourselves: Fair to whom? Fair for which objective or purpose?

If the auditor does not agree that the financial statements "present fairly . . . in accordance with generally accepted accounting principles" (commonly called GAAP), the auditor's report may be "qualified." There are many grounds for qualifying the report, and these would be set forth by the auditor in a paragraph or more between the scope and opinion paragraphs. Generally the auditor tries to influence his client to conform the statements to GAAP. A qualification is a last resort step whenever the client does not

EXHIBIT 1-1

Auditors' Report

To the Shareholders of John Labatt Limited.

We have examined the consolidated balance sheet of John Labatt Limited as at April 30, 1978 and the consolidated statements of earnings, retained earnings and changes in financial position for the year then ended. Our examination of the financial statements of John Labatt Limited and the financial statements of those subsidiaries and partly-owned businesses of which we are the auditors was made in accordance with generally accepted auditing standards, and accordingly included such tests and other procedures as we considered necessary in the circumstances. We have relied on the reports of the auditors who have examined the financial statements of the other subsidiaries and partly-owned businesses.

In our opinion, these consolidated financial statements present fairly the financial position of John Labatt Limited as at April 30, 1978 and the results of its operations and the changes in its financial position for the year then ended in accordance with generally accepted accounting principles applied on a basis consistent with that of the preceding year.

London, Canada.
June 6, 1978.

Clarkson, Gordon & Co.
Chartered Accountants.

wish to agree with the auditor. Most clients try to avoid a qualified audit report because it may affect their reputation, ability to borrow, and related matters. Sometimes a qualified report is unavoidable because the company's financial condition is uncertain, and can only be clarified sometime in the future.

In recent years the accounting profession in the U.S., and to a much lesser extent in Canada, has been severely criticized for its alleged failure to conscientiously fulfill its audit responsibilities. To a great extent such criticism has been the result of a number of corporate bankruptcies. It has been charged that the financial reports of the bankrupt companies which were issued prior to the time that their financial difficulties became publicly known were false and misleading in that they failed to reveal the dubious financial condition of the companies. In most of the cases, the auditors were accused of either allowing their clients to employ inappropriate accounting principles or misapplying acceptable accounting principles. In a number of widely publicized U.S. cases auditors have successfully been sued by shareholders and others who suffered losses attributable to their reliance upon the financial reports. In other cases auditors have been charged with criminal fraud for actions associated with statements that were allegedly false and misleading. In most instances the financial reports in question were said to have artificially inflated company earnings and correspondingly overstated the values of assets or understated the values of liabilities. A key objective of this text is to explore the difficulties faced by management and auditors in selecting among and applying "generally accepted accounting principles" and to highlight resulting limitations of financial reports.

Generally accepted accounting principles

What are "generally accepted accounting principles?" Who decides what is, and what should be, generally accepted? To a large extent what is generally accepted is what has been done over a large number of years. Hence, tradition and widespread use are the major determinants of what is generally accepted.

But in an effort to make practice more uniform, as well as to eliminate obvious abuses in financial reporting, the accounting profession in Canada has formed a series of committees since 1946 to give advice to managers and accountants. The most prestigious group in Canada is the *Accounting Research Committee (ARC)* of The Canadian Institute of Chartered Accountants (CICA). Although the majority of members of the ARC are chartered accountants, there is representation from the CGAs, RIAs, financial analysts, and other groups. The members of ARC in effect are volunteers who cannot devote all their time to the pronouncement process (i.e., issuing recommendations on accounting methods applicable under different circumstances). Often, as a result, Canada tends to lag behind the U.S. and may not have comprehensive, or any, pronouncements on some topics. This means that Canadian accountants sometimes must look to the American and to a lesser extent the British profession for advice. On other occasions the practitioner must rely exclusively on his professional judgment, after conducting some practical research.

Until the early 1970s, the predecessor groups to the ARC in essence issued pronouncements under self-appointed authority. Although there was some indirect support by governments, pronouncements were issued chiefly when it was thought that they would receive the backing of business and accountants. Under such circumstances progress was slow because delicate topics had to be treated gently, if at all. In the past 10 years, the ARC's recommendations on accounting practice have received the support of government agencies. Several Companies or Corporations Acts and provincial securities administrators now require adherence to the *CICA Handbook*, which contains the latest pronouncements by ARC.

Government acceptance could influence the ARC in at least two ways. First, it could empower the ARC to deal with delicate, previously avoided topics. Secondly, it could demand a more thorough performance from ARC. If ARC failed in its attempts to improve accounting practice and the public became aroused, governments might be forced to take over the pronouncement process. In many circles this thought is viewed with alarm because of fears that a government could impose rules that are not workable in several situations. There might be a tendency to force one method on companies and to ignore differing objectives, facts, and constraints.

The pronouncement process in other countries differs in varying degrees from that which exists in Canada. The U.S. is the leader in placing resources into the study of accountancy, primarily because their growth and philosophy have depended greatly on the ability to attract sufficient capital to build large organizations. Until 1973, the U.S. had a series of bodies in the public accounting sector engaged in issuing pronouncements. In 1973, Americans formed a full-time group, the *Financial Accounting Standards Board* (FASB), to overcome the lack of independence and speed in the pronouncement process that was criticized in predecessor groups.

Larger companies that wish to borrow money from the public in the U.S. (and this includes Canadian companies) must adhere to the accounting practices and disclosure policies of the *Securities and Exchange Commission* (SEC). The SEC is a federal group, unlike the situation in Canada where securities regulation is a provincial matter. The FASB (a private sector body) and the SEC (a federal government body) have been trying to work together in improving practice, but occasionally proceed in different directions for short periods. Accounting practitioners therefore have to be fully aware of the latest thinking of both.

The U.K., Australia, and some other members of the Commonwealth have accounting pronouncements which may differ from Canadian and U.S. methods. This lack of uniformity can be a cause for concern by multinational organizations. Attempts have been made to obtain international agreement on pronouncements, but this is difficult because of differing tax and corporate law, and business methods.

Many other accounting organizations strive to improve quality. For example, the members of The Canadian Academic Accounting Association (CAAA) and the American Accounting Association (AAA) are primarily teachers, and researchers examining a variety of current and probable problem areas.

• *Management advisory services*

Most public accountants serve as financial advisors to their clients. Large firms have separate management consulting divisions which provide a wide range of services to both industry and government. Although some consulting engagements are related to accounting and reporting systems (such as aid in installing a computer), many are in such diverse fields as marketing, production management and capital expenditure management. Large firms tend to hire engineers, economists, and a wide range of professional consultants.

In recent years public accounting firms have come under fire for the potential incompatibility of some of their consulting activities with the attest function. Critics argue that the public accountant, whose firm recommends a system or new initiative, will lack independence when he later has to audit it and assess it. Accordingly, public accounting firms have been rethinking their practices and some changes may result.

- *Financial administration and bankruptcy*

  Large public accounting firms and some small ones have special groups, often incorporated separately because of the risk involved, which help clients who get into financial difficulty. Such financial problems might be caused by a poor management decision, by expanding quickly without adequate sources of cash, or by a sudden loss of a key manager. Sometimes the company is forced into bankruptcy, and the specially trained public accountant (called a licensed trustee in bankruptcy) provides for the orderly disposition of assets among creditors. In other circumstances the trustee might successfully propose that creditors accept 50 cents now instead of $1 many years later, and thereby reorganize the company into a fresh start. Trustees work with the courts, bankruptcy legislation, many legal documents, and unhappy creditors, in performing their duties. Canada had some famous major bankruptcies in the 1960s and early 1970s that caused shock waves throughout the financial community, and brought forth some changes in legislation and accounting procedures.

- *Tax services*

  Although Canada has had federal income tax legislation since 1917, major changes became effective in January 1972. Since then companies have had to give extra attention to the income tax implications of business transactions. In addition, some provinces levy a provincial income tax; there are various sales taxes; and many other forms of taxation, direct and hidden, exist. As a result of these and personal income taxes, most public accountants have to employ tax specialists to serve the needs of clients.

Accountants in industry

Many accountants are employed by private business enterprises. Normally they work in financial areas of their companies, but they hold a number of diverse positions. Among those commonly held by accountants are financial vice-president; treasurer, controller (the difference between treasurer and controller functions varies from firm to firm, but in general the treasurer is more concerned with relationships between the firm and bankers, shareholders, and creditors and the controller with internal control and performance evaluation); internal auditor; budget analyst; tax accountant; electronic data processing supervisor. Moreover, many chief executive officers are accountants.

Accountants in nonprofit organizations

Government and other nonprofit (or, more properly, not for profit) organizations are unconcerned with the computation of net income; they are interested in public service, not profit. Yet financial budgets, accounting controls, and quantitative measures of performance are as necessary in nonprofit as in profit-making organizations. Unfortunately, many nonprofit organizations have been slow in realizing the importance of adequate accounting systems and reports. Today, however, they are attempting to make rapid reforms in the area of financial management, and as a result job opportunities in such organizations are abundant.

Nonprofit accounting is an especially challenging field. Administrators of nonprofit organizations require the same types of information as their counterparts in private industry to carry out effectively the functions of management. On a day-to-day basis, problems of planning, controlling, and evaluating performance in nonprofit organizations are remarkably similar to those in industry. The manager of a government-owned electric power company must make the same types of decisions as does one in a private utility. Supervisors of motor pools, mail rooms, clerical departments, and maintenance staffs in government are equally as concerned with reducing costs and increasing output as are those who hold similar positions in private industry.

Accounting in the public sector can be distinguished from that in the private sector by the absence of profit as a primary measure of organizational performance. In the private sector, accountants focus on profit as an indicator of how much better off a company is at the end of an accounting period than it was at the start. In the public sector, managers are not interested in how much better off an organization is; instead they are concerned with how much service or benefit it has provided to the community in relation to costs incurred. Unfortunately, such benefits and costs may be exceedingly difficult to identify, let alone measure.

Suppose, for example, that a local government official requested information that would enable him to determine which of two school districts, each of which received the same amount of funds, was more effectively managed. What data should the accountant provide him with? There are numerous possibilities: number of students attending schools, number of graduates, number of graduates who were able to find jobs, average reading level of students at various grade levels, average change in reading level over a period of several years, etc. None of the measures, either individually or cumulatively, is likely to be a satisfactory indicator of administrative performance. Accountants, experienced in the art of measurement, can play a major role in helping organizations to more clearly define their objectives and appraise the progress they have made in achieving them.

Government auditing

Many accountants are employed by governments at all levels — federal to municipal. Revenue Canada uses accountants as income tax assessors, and in customs and excise assessment. Accountants are employed in departments of finance to help prepare and evaluate federal and provincial budgets, and as controllers of many government departments. Some accountants have been elected to parliament.

Yet, changing rapidly in Canada and gaining greater importance every year is the field of government auditing. The traditional role of auditing was greatly expanded in the late 1970s through public demands for changes in federal, and some provincial, government attitudes and legislation. In 1977 Federal Parliament passed a new *Auditor General Act.* Sections 7(2)(d) and (e) of this Act give the following powers:

> Each (usually annual) report of the Auditor General . . . shall call attention to anything that he considers to be of significance and of a nature that should be brought to the attention of the House of Commons, including any cases in which he has observed that . . .
> (d) money has been expended without due regard to economy or efficiency; or
> (e) satisfactory procedures have not been established to measure and report the effectiveness of programs . . .

Traditionally, auditors in Canada have not concentrated on economy, efficiency, and effectiveness. Economy and efficiency, as used above, are measures of whether value is being received for money which has been spent by government. In short, has the government conducted its affairs in a way which minimizes cost or maximizes revenue? Effectiveness is a measure of success: Does the program work? For example, a government may introduce changes in unemployment insurance procedures or legislation. Yet, the procedures may be inefficient and waste money (i.e., not having "due regard to efficiency"). Or, new unemployment insurance offices may be leased instead of bought and this could result in excessive expenditures (i.e., not having "due regard to economy" in the purchase of fixed assets). Effectiveness is generally harder to measure in government programs because it is difficult to know the full purpose of unemployment insurance (Temporary relief? Welfare?), and many other social programs. Hence, the Auditor General is asked to ascertain whether systems established by government attempt to measure effectiveness; he is not asked for a personal opinion on the success of a program.

As a result of this new legislation, which has also been adopted in several provinces, an audit team in government requires engineers, behavioral scientists, economists and many others to bring their talents to the task of checking actions by government managers. It is impossible, and probably inefficient, to audit every major program. However, a sufficient number must be checked to ensure that managers avoid uneconomic, and inefficient personal behavior patterns, and indirectly that Parliament passes legislation only after due consideration has been given to the question of effectiveness.

If economy, efficiency, effectiveness (often called "value for money") auditing is eventually adopted by private industry, a major new avenue of prestige and importance will open for accountants. This will place greater stress on the need for accountants to have adequate backgrounds in other disciplines, so that they can converse and work well with other specialists. They will have to know their own discipline well so that they can explain it to others. As we have mentioned many times, an understanding of the strengths and limitations of accounting is a prime objective of this book. Students will find such knowledge valuable whether they are majoring in economics, behavioral science, general business, accounting, or several other disciplines.

Summary

The primary purpose of this introductory chapter has been to dispel any notion that an understanding of accounting involves little more than a familiarity with the more widely adhered to practices and procedures. The chapter has placed considerable emphasis on the limitations of accounting reports: they are not based on universally accepted principles; they are not "accurate," in that they are a function of numerous estimates and judgmental determinations; they cannot be used as the sole measure of managerial accomplishment; they are not neutral; they cannot always serve as a basis for comparing financial position or income of one company to that of another. The decision to stress the negative was made at some risk; a student may be misled into questioning whether the efforts required to understand such a seemingly limited discipline are commensurate with the benefits to be derived.

The intent of the approach is to emphasize the dynamic nature of accounting. Accounting information serves a variety of functions and is used by parties with different interests and goals. As a consequence, there can never be any single "correct" means of reporting an economic event or quantifying an economic value. The principles upon which a particular accounting report is based must necessarily represent compromises among the various objectives (sometimes conflicting) of financial reporting. The balance among objectives that is appropriate for one company at a particular time may be inappropriate either for another or for the same company at some other time.

This chapter suggests that people see things differently because of their backgrounds and education. The artist, the environmentalist, the logger, the developer, and the cost accountant may view a tree from quite different perspectives. The same concept applies in accounting because of potentially differing objectives, facts, and constraints, as well as people's attitudes and backgrounds.

A considerable amount of information has been conveyed in this chapter and few students are likely to grasp everything from a first reading. You probably will benefit greatly if you refer to portions of this chapter from time to time as you continue through the book — especially from Chapter 5 onward.

In summary, two basic themes are:

1. The number of different combinations of (a) objectives or purposes of accounting, (b) facts or circumstances about a situation and (c) constraints do not permit accountants to have rules for each combination. As a result judgment must be developed in order to prepare and interpret financial statements.
2. To be consistent with a university-level approach to education, we intend to examine current practice (which is evolving), alternative treatments which show promise, and other developing ideas which may affect financial accounting. We want to identify the assumptions on which accounting is based and evaluate the applicability of these assumptions in a changing world. An accounting practice may quickly become obsolete if it is based on a few biases or assumptions which are subject to rapid change and which may not apply tomorrow.

Notes

[1]For an elaboration see R.M. Skinner, *Accounting Principles: A Canadian Viewpoint* (Toronto: The Canadian Institute of Chartered Accountants, 1972).

[2]See R. Mattessich, "On the Perennial Misunderstanding of Asset Measurement by Means of 'Present Value' ", *Cost and Management* (March-April 1970), pp. 29-31.

Questions, Problems, and Cases

Questions

*1-1 "Accounting attempts to serve many masters, a job that is not easy because the needs of one group may conflict with the needs of others."

Required:

a. Identify potential users of the financial statements.
b. Describe the decision(s) that each user must make.
c. For each user's decision(s) describe what information might be helpful and why.
d. Indicate potential conflicts among the needs of various users as discussed above.
e. As a preparer of accounting information, how would conflicts between users' needs influence your accounting recommendations?

1-2 What are some objectives, purposes of, or reasons for financial accounting?

1-3 "The artist, the environmentalist, the logger, the developer, and the cost accountant may view a tree from quite different perspectives. The same concept applies in accounting because of potentially different objectives, facts, and constraints . . ."

Required:

Explain the above quotation. Give concrete examples of how accounting recommendations may be influenced by the situation and perspective that you take.

1-4 It has been suggested that accounting standards be legislated by a government agency in the same manner as meat or drug standards are.

Required:

a. Identify who you believe might be the major proponents of this view.
b. What advantages and disadvantages do you see in the recommendation?

1-5 Gas and Electric Co. Ltd., of Ontario, recently submitted statements of income to shareholders, to the Department of National Revenue and to the Ontario Energy Board. Different incomes were reported in each report even though the period covered by the reports was identical. Is it possible for all these reports to be correct? Why?

1-6 In the opinion paragraph of the auditor's report on the financial statements of a company, the auditor says that the financial statements "present fairly . . . in accordance with generally accepted accounting principles."

Required:

a. How would you, as an auditor, determine whether the accounts "present fairly"?
b. Define the term "generally accepted accounting principles."
c. How would you, as an auditor, determine what is "generally accepted"? (Hint: Would you ask your neighbor or look in the dictionary . . .?)
d. Identify the benefits and limitations of the information communicated in the auditor's opinion (eg. Does the auditor's report make the financial statements more accurate?).

*1-7 A business which is incorporated under a provincial or a federal Corporations Act may be required to prepare accounting information for

(1) a loan officer of a bank, (2) the Department of National Revenue, (3) a shareholder and (4) a long-term creditor of the company.

Required:

a. Describe how the accounting information presented to each of these users might differ and why.

b. Identify other information which might assist each user in arriving at a decision.

c. How would an auditor's report on the information provided influence each of the users? Why?

1-8 "Accounting is a dynamic discipline in which new principles and procedures are constantly evolving."

Required:

a. Identify some of the factors which make accounting a dynamic discipline.

b. Identify significant issues currently facing the accounting profession which were mentioned in Chapter 1.

1-9 In preparing a financial statement to accompany his loan application to a local bank, Steve Johnson was uncertain as to whether he should report his home as having a value of $25,000 or $60,000. Johnson purchased his house 25 years ago at a price of $25,000; similar homes in his neighborhood have recently been sold for between $55,000 and $65,000. Which amount do you think would be more useful to the bank? Which amount is more objective? Why?

1-10 The accounting reports of one company are unlikely to be readily comparable with those of another. Why has it not been considered feasible to develop a set of accounting rules by which all companies must abide?

1-11 "An audited income statement is an exact and unbiased measure of how much 'better off' a company is at the end of the year than it was at the beginning."

Required:

Do you agree with the quotation? Why? Be specific and use examples to support your position.

1-12 "Computers can now do calculations more quickly and accurately than accountants. The rapid development of computer technology and EDP information systems is making the accountant obsolete."

Required:

Based on your knowledge of accounting, do you agree with the quotation? Why? Be specific!

1-13 List the similarities and differences between accounting for a nonprofit organization and a profit-seeking organization.

Problems

P1-1 Artcraft Co. Ltd. manufactures costume-jewelry rings. The firm has three employees, each of whom earns $10,000 per year. It rents its plant and equipment at an annual cost of $10,000. Materials used in the production of the rings cost $4 per ring.

The company has been manufacturing 5,000 rings per year. It has sold all of them for $15 each.

The company was recently approached by the manager of a large department store. He offered to purchase 1,000 rings at a cost of $7 per ring. If the company were to accept the offer, its other sales would not be affected. Since the company has not been operating at capacity, it would not have to add additional employees, space or equipment.

Required:

a. Prepare an income statement for Artcraft Co. Ltd. at the present operating level of production and sales of 5,000 rings.
b. Who might use this statement? For what purpose(s) might it be used?
c. Should the company accept the offer? What is the relevant cost to be considered in making the decision whether to accept the offer?
d. How would a fact that the company was operating at capacity influence your decision to accept or reject the offer?
e. Assuming the company accepts the offer made by the large department store, prepare a projected income statement for Artcraft Ltd. at the operating level of production and sales of 6,000 rings.

P1-2 The Quick-Cut Lawnmower Co. Ltd. began operations in January 19x1. In its first month of operations the company manufactured 200 lawnmowers at a cost of $60 each. Although it completed all 200 mowers by the end of the month, it had not yet sold any of the mowers.

In February the company produced 300 mowers. It sold and delivered to customers both the 200 mowers manufactured in January and the 300 mowers manufactured in February. Selling price of the mowers was $100 each.

Required:

a. Determine income for each of the months January and February. Explain your reasoning.
b. Assume instead that on January 2 the company signed a noncancellable contract to sell 500 mowers at $100 each to a major chain of department stores. The contract called for delivery in February. The company completed but did not deliver 200 of the mowers by January 31. It completed the remainder and delivered all 500 by February 28. Determine income for each of the two months. Explain your reasoning. What impact does your income calculation have on the users of the company's financial statements?

P1-3 Cross Canada Airline Ltd. owns and operates 10 passenger jet planes. Each plane had cost the airline $6 million. The company's income statement for 19x5 reported the following:

Revenue from passenger fares		$30,000,000
Operating expenses (including salaries, maintenance costs, terminal expenses, etc.)	$22,000,000	
Depreciation of planes	5,000,000	27,000,000
Income before income taxes		$ 3,000,000

Each plane has an estimated useful life of 12 years. The $5 million depreciation charge was calculated by dividing the cost of each plant ($6 million) by its useful life (12 years). The result ($500,000) was multipled by the number of planes owned (10).

Required:

a. Suppose that the useful life of each plane was 8 years rather than 12 years. Determine income before income taxes for 19x5. By what percent is income less than that computed above?

b. Suppose that the useful life of each plane was 15 years. Determine income before income taxes for 19x5. By what percent is income greater than that originally computed?

c. Given that the assumption about the estimated life of an airplane has a significant impact on income before income taxes, how would you, as an auditor, determine the reasonableness of the estimate made by the company?

d. How might your decision about the estimated useful life of an airplane be influenced if you were the president of the company?

e. It is sometimes said that accountants must be concerned that financial statements are accurate to the penny. Do you agree? Why?

P1-4 The Discount Used Car Co. Ltd. purchased four cars in the month of June and sold three cars. Purchase prices and sale prices are indicated below:

	Purchase Price	*Sale Price*
Car 1	$600	$1,000
Car 2	700	1,100
Car 3	800	1,200
Car 4	900	—

The Natural Foods Grocery Store purchased 300 pounds of sugar in the month of June and sold 200 pounds. The sugar is not prepackaged. Instead, as the sugar is purchased it is added to a single barrel; as it is sold, it is scooped out and given to the customer in a paper bag. During June 100 pounds of sugar were purchased on each of three separate dates. Purchase prices, in sequence, were $.50, $.70, and $.80 per pound. All sugar was sold at $1.00 per pound.

Required:

a. Determine the income of the two merchants for the month of June. (Ignore other costs not indicated.)

b. Explain your reasoning.

c. What conclusion with respect to uniformity of accounting methods can be drawn from your computations.

P1-5 Larry Chapman sells greeting cards. Operating out of a garage that he rents for $1,000 per year, he purchases greeting cards from a wholesaler and distributes them door to door. In 19x5, he sold 1,000 boxes of cards at $3 per box. The cost of the cards from the wholesaler was $1 per box.

In 19x6, Chapman decided to expand his product line to include candy. In that year he sold 300 boxes of candy for $5 per box. The candy cost him $4 per box. By making efficient use of his garage, he found that he was able to store his inventory of cards in one half of the garage; thus he could use the other half for his candy. His sale of cards neither benefited nor suffered as the result of the new product. Sales in 19x6 were the same as in 19x5.

At the conclusion of 19x6, Chapman had to decide whether to continue selling candy or to return to selling cards only. His friend, Fulton, an occasional accountant, prepared the following report for him:

Sales of candy (300 boxes @ $5)		$1,500
Less costs:		
Cost of candy sold (300 boxes @ $4)	$ 1,200	
Rent (½ of $1,000)	500	1,700
Net loss on sale of candy		$(200)

On the basis of the report, Chapman decided to abandon his line of candy.

Required:

a. Do you agree with his decision? Explain.

b. Prepare a report comparing the total income of Chapman in 19x5 with that of 19x6.

c. What conclusion can be drawn concerning the use of accounting information?

Cases

C1-1 Accountants measure income as conventionally defined: revenues less expenses. But they include in their measurement only selected revenues and expenses. They do not account for certain "social" benefits provided and costs incurred. Some firms on an experimental basis have prepared a "socioeconomic operating statement." The statement might take the following form:

Social benefits		
Improvement in the environment	$xxxx	
Minority hiring program	xxxx	
Day-care center	xxxx	
Staff services donated to hospitals	xxxx	$xxxx
Social costs		
Damage to the environment	xxxx	
Work-related injuries and illness	xxxx	
Failure to install recommended safety equipment	xxxx	xxxx
Social surplus (deficit) for the year		$xxxx

Required:

a. Identify the primary users of this statement.

b. How might they use this report?

c. Identify potential measurement problems in preparing the statement.

d. Why might accountants be reluctant to include social benefits and costs in their definition of income?

e. What factors would contribute to this type of reporting becoming a part of conventional accounting reports?

C1-2 The president and sole owner of the Blue Mountain Brewery Ltd. asked his auditor to express an opinion on the fairness of the financial statements of his company. The audited financial statements had been requested by a local bank in order to facilitate review of the company's application for a loan.

The controller of the company, who had actually prepared the statements, included among the firm's assets "Land — $3,000,000." According to the controller, the land was reported at a value of $3 million since the company had recently received offers of approximately that amount from several potential purchasers.

After reviewing the land account, the auditor told the president that he could not express the usual "unqualified" opinion on the financial statements so long as land was valued at $3 million. Instead, he would have to express an "adverse" opinion (i.e., "the financial statements do not fairly present . . .") unless that land were valued at $150,000, the amount the company had actually paid for it.

The president was dumbfounded. The land, he told the auditor, was purchased 50 years ago and was located in the downtown section of a major city.

Required:

a. Assume the role of the local banker. Outline your major considerations in arriving at a decision to make a loan to the company. Which amount is likely to be more relevant to your decision? How objective is this information?

b. Which amount should be reported if the statements are to be prepared in accordance with generally accepted accounting principles?

c. If you were the auditor of the company what recommendation would you make to the president?

d. In your opinion, does the adherence to generally accepted accounting principles ensure fairness of the financial statements?

C1-3 Dave Richardson, president of Reliable Foundation Ltd., a construction company, was concerned about the poor performance of his company in the first 11 months of the year. If the company continued at its present pace, reported profits for the year would be down $20,000 from those of the previous year. Thinking of ways to increase reported earnings, he hit upon what he considered to be an ingenious scheme. Two years earlier the company had purchased a crane at a cost of $100,000. Since the crane was now 2 years old and had an estimated useful life of 10 years, it was currently reported on the company's books at eight-tenths of $100,000: $80,000. Prices of cranes had increased substantially in the last 2 years, and the crane could be sold for $120,000. The president suggested that the company sell the crane on the last day of the year for $120,000 and thereby realize a gain on the sale of $40,000 ($120,000 less the book value of $80,000). Of course, the company would have to buy a new crane next year — and new cranes were currently selling for $160,000 — but the cost of the new crane could be spread out over its useful life of 10 years. In future years, the president realized, "depreciation" charges would increase from $10,000 on the old crane ($100,000 divided by 10) to $16,000 on the new ($160,000 divided by 10), but in the current year, the company would report a gain of $40,000. Hence, reported income would go from $20,000 less than that in the previous year to $20,000 more.

Required:

a. Identify the potential users of the company's financial statements and their needs or decisions.

b. The scheme of the president is, in fact, consistent with generally accepted accounting principles. Do you think, however, that the company is really $40,000 better off if it sold the old crane and purchased a new one than if it held on to the old one? Comment.

c. What impact would this accounting treatment have on each of the users of the financial statements?

d. Assume that generally accepted accounting principles requires that "fixed assets," such as the crane, be reported on corporate books at the price at which it could currently be sold — i.e., $120,000. Would the scheme of the president accomplish its desired results? Why do you suppose generally accepted accounting principles do not require that such assets be valued at the prices at which they could be sold?

2 A Look at Financial Statements

Accountants report on the results of operations and on the current status of a business enterprise by means of two basic financial statements, the *balance sheet* and the *income statement*. A third statement, the *statement of changes in financial position* (sometimes called the funds or funds flow statement) has been gaining importance in recent years because it provides a different perspective than the balance sheet and income statement. Some annual financial reports of companies include a fourth statement, changes in *retained earnings*, or even a fifth or more, such as a statement of changes in *contributed surplus*. Nearly all financial reports are accompanied by a set of notes or footnotes, which is an integral part of the financial statement package.

The Balance Sheet

The balance sheet reports the status of the enterprise at a *specific point in time*. It describes the enterprise *as of* the close of business on a specific date. In contrast, the income statement reports the history of a business for a period of time, e.g., income for the month of June, income for the year ended December 31, 19x1.

The balance sheet, or *statement of financial position* (as it is less frequently but more descriptively called), indicates the financial resources (assets) available to the firm to carry out its economic activities as well as the claims against such resources. These resources may be either tangible (of a physical nature) such as buildings, equipment, land, and motor vehicles, or intangible (characterized by legal rights) such as amounts owed by customers (accounts receivable), patents, and bank deposits. They represent *future* benefits or service potentials.

The claims against the enterprise are referred to as *equities* (meaning "rights to or claims against"). There are two primary categories of equities: liabilities and owners' equity.

Liabilities are the claims against the business by creditors. They are amounts to be paid in the *future*. They include amounts owed to employees, suppliers, banks, bondholders, and government agencies. Owners' equity represents the "residual" interests of the owners. It includes the amounts that they contributed to the business either at the time of formation or when additional funds were needed for expansion as well as the earnings accumulated over the years. Owners' equity may be viewed as the resources that would be left over for the owners if all the creditors were paid.

Assets: Economic resources of an enterprise that are recognized and measured in conformity with generally accepted accounting principles; future benefits or service potentials.

Liabilities: Economic obligations of an enterprise that are recognized and measured in conformity with generally accepted accounting principles; obligations to pay definite or reasonably certain amounts at a time in the future.

Owners' equity: The interest of owners in an enterprise; its assets less its liabilities.

An abbreviated balance sheet is indicated in Exhibit 2-1.

EXHIBIT 2-1

Douglas Stores Limited
Balance Sheet
March 31, 19x1

Assets		*Equities*	
Cash	$ 15,000	Liabilities	
Accounts receivable	80,000	Accounts payable	$ 90,000
Merchandise inventory	60,000	Wages payable	20,000
Equipment	110,000	Bonds payable	250,000
Buildings	330,000		
Patents and copyrights	25,000	Total liabilities	360,000
		Owners' equity	260,000
	$620,000		$620,000

As illustrated, the equities, i.e., the claims against the assets, including the residual interests of the owners, *must* be equal to the assets themselves. Thus, in general form,

$$\text{Assets} = \text{Equities}.$$

Or, in a slightly more specific form,

$$\text{Assets} = \text{Liabilities} + \text{Owners' Equity}.$$

In Exhibit 2-1

$$\$620,000 = \$360,000 + \$260,000.$$

The basic accounting equation, assets = liabilities + owners' equity, serves as the foundation for the *double-entry* record-keeping process on which modern accounting is based. Any *transaction* (financial event) which increases or decreases the left-hand side of the equation (assets) must, by definition of the terms of the equation, increase or decrease the right side of the equation (the claims against such assets) by an identical amount.

Consider, for example, several transactions in which an enterprise might engage. The titles beneath the amounts indicate the specific accounts or types of assets or equities that would be affected.

	Assets	=	*Liabilities*	+	*Owners' equity*
Owners contribute $100,000 cash to form a business.	+100,000 (cash)	=			+100,000 (contribution of owners)
The new firm borrows $50,000 from a bank.	+50,000 (cash)	=	+50,000 (notes payable)		
The firm purchases equipment for $10,000, giving a note for the full amount.	+10,000 (equipment)	=	+10,000 (notes payable)		
The firm purchases supplies for $8,000 cash.[a]	+8,000 (supplies) −8,000 (cash)				
The firm pays $3,000 of the amount it borrowed from the bank.	−3,000 (cash)	=	−3,000 (notes payable)		
The firm purchases merchandise inventory for $15,000; it pays $5,000 cash and receives the remaining $10,000 of goods "on account."[b]	+15,000 (merchandise inventory) −5,000 (cash)	=	+10,000 (accounts payable)		
The firm sells merchandise which originally cost $15,000 for $20,000 cash.[c]	+20,000 (cash) −15,000 (merchandise inventory)	=			+5,000 (retained earnings)

[a] Note that some transactions may affect only one side of the equation.

[b] Note that one transaction may affect more than two accounts; note also that the liability account affected is referred to as "accounts payable" rather than "notes payable" since no formal written note was presented to the supplier.

[c] Note that as the result of this transaction the firm has "earned" $5,000. The firm gave up assets of $15,000 in exchange for those of $20,000. As a result, the claims of the owners against the business are $5,000 greater than they were previously. The owners' equity account affected is commonly referred to as retained earnings when the enterprise is incorporated, or as owners' capital, e.g., J. Smith, capital, if the firm is a partnership or proprietorship.

The basic accounting equation can be expressed in a slightly altered form:

$$\text{Assets} - \text{Liabilities} = \text{Owners' equity}.$$

This equation is the mathematical equivalent of the one previously illustrated, but the latter expression, by isolating owners' equity on one side of the equation, focuses more directly on the interests of the owners of the business. As a general rule the equity of the owners will increase as the result of two types of events:

1. The owners make a direct contribution to the firm. Such a contribution of cash is almost always made in return for the right to share in the profits of the firm. If the firm is a corporation, evidence of an ownership interest is provided by a share certificate indicating the number of "shares" owned. If the firm is a partnership, then the partnership agreement indicates the proportionate interest in the enterprise of each of the owners.
2. The firm earns income. The net assets (assets less liabilities) of the firm will be greater than they were previously; hence the residual interest of the owners will also be greater.

Conversely, the equity of the owners will decrease as the result of two opposite types of events:

1. The owners make withdrawals from the firm. The firm pays out a portion of its assets to the owners. In a limited company or corporation such withdrawals are known as *dividends*. The effect is to reduce the assets of the firm and to reduce the remaining equity of the owners — that is, to reduce the size of the asset pool in which the owners are entitled to share. In a partnership, withdrawals are called *drawings*, which are usually in the form of cash or goods.
2. The company incurs a loss. The net assets (assets less liabilities) of the firm are reduced; hence the residual interest of the owners is also reduced.

The Income Statement

The accounting equation and the balance sheet indicate net assets (assets less liabilities) and the owners' claim against such net assets at a given *point* in time. The income statement, on the other hand, indicates changes in owners' equity (and thus changes in net assets) over a given *period* of time resulting from the operations of the business, *excluding* contributions or withdrawals on the part of the owners. (Such changes might be indicated for some forms of business organization in a statement of changes in owners' equity.) The income statement indicates the revenues of the period and the expenses incurred in earning such revenues.

Revenues are the inflows of cash or other assets attributable to the goods or services provided by the enterprise. Most commonly, revenues result from the sale of the company's product or service, but they could also result from interest earned on loans to outsiders, dividends received on shares of stock of other companies, royalties earned on patents or licences, or rent earned from properties owned.

Expenses are the outflows of cash or other assets attributable to the profit-directed activities of an enterprise. Expenses are a measure of the effort exerted on the part of the enterprise in its attempt to "realize" (to obtain) revenues.

An income statement, in condensed form, is illustrated in Exhibit 2-2.

EXHIBIT 2-2

Douglas Stores Limited
Income Statement
For the Year Ended March 31, 19x2

Revenue from sales			$120,000
Cost of merchandise sold	$70,000		
Wages and salaries	15,000		
Advertising	3,000		
Rent	4,000	$92,000	
Taxes		12,000	104,000
Net income			$ 16,000

Contrast the manner in which the date appears on the income statement with that on the balance sheet. The income statement is *for the year ended* March 31, 19x2 — it describes what has happened over a one-year period. The balance sheet is *as of* the close of business on March 31, 19x2 — it describes the financial state as of a particular *moment* in time.

The relationship between the balance sheet and the income statement can be explained with reference to a household bathtub filled with water. The water in the bathtub is comparable to the owners' equity — or, alternatively, to the net assets (assets less liabilities) — of the firm. In describing the level of water in the tub one could say that at a given moment the tub contains *x* gallons of water. Similarly, one could describe a firm as having a particular level of net assets. Indeed, the balance sheet of a firm does exactly that. It indicates, and describes, the level of assets, of liabilities, and of the difference between the two — owners' equity.

Suppose, however, that water is entering the tub through the faucets and at the same time it is leaving through the drain. It would still be possible — and indeed necessary if comprehensive information is to be presented — to describe the level of water in the tub. One could say, for example, that at 11:03 p.m. there were 10 gallons of water in the tub. But such information would hardly constitute a very complete description of activity in the tub. Also needed would be a description of the rate at which the water level is rising or falling. More complete information might be as follows: Water is entering the tub at the *rate* of 3 gallons per minute; it is leaving at the rate of 2 gallons per minute; hence it is rising at the *rate* of 1 gallon per minute.

So also with the firm. Information is required as to the rate at which the equity of the owners is increasing or decreasing. The water entering the tub might be compared to revenues; the water leaving, to expenses; and the difference between the two, to income. Thus it might be said that net assets are entering the firm at the *rate* of $3 million per year (i.e., revenues for the year are $3 million), that net assets are leaving the firm at the *rate* of $2 million per year (i.e., expenses for the year are $2 million), and that the change in net assets (owners' equity) for the year is $1 million (i.e., income for the year is $1 million).

If the amount of water in the bathtub at 11:03 P.M. were 10 gallons and it were increasing at the rate of 1 gallon per minute, then the amount at the end of the minute would be 11 gallons. The beginning amount plus the amount added during the period would equal the ending amount.

So too with the firm. If the owners equity at January 1, 19x8 were $10 million and if income for the year were $1 million, then owners' equity at the end of the year would be $11 million.

The balance sheet indicates the equity that the owners have in the firm at any given *point* in time. Such point of time is usually the end of a month or the end of a year. The balance sheet also indicates the assets and the liabilities which result in the particular level of owners' equity.

The income statement indicates the *rate* at which the equity of the owners is changing. It reveals the revenues, the expenses, and the resultant income for the period. Assuming that no assets or liabilities entered or left the firm from other sources (e.g., the owners neither contributed nor withdrew assets), then owners' equity at the beginning of the period per the balance sheet plus income for the period (per the income statement) must equal owners' equity at the end of the period (per the new balance sheet):

Owners' equity, beginning of period ± Income or loss (± owners' additional contributions or withdrawals) = Owners' equity, end of period

The owners' equity of the Douglas Stores Limited as of March 31, 19x2 (per Exhibit 2-1) is $260,000 and the net income for the year ended March 31, 19x2 (per Exhibit 2-2) is $16,000. If $12,000 had been withdrawn during the year ending March 31, 19x2 as dividends to the owners, what would the owners' equity have been at the *beginning* of the year (April 1, 19x1)?

$$\$260{,}000 + \$12{,}000 - \$16{,}000 = \$256{,}000$$

Owners' equity at end of year + dividends − net income = owners' equity at beginning of year.

The Balance Sheet — A More Detailed Examination

Exhibits 2-3 through 2-6 illustrate the financial statements of the Mercury Truck Manufacturing Corporation for the year ended December 31, 19x3. The balance sheet in Exhibit 2-3 is divided not only into the major categories of assets, liabilities, and owners' (shareholders') equity but several subcategories or accounts as well.

EXHIBIT 2-3

Mercury Truck Manufacturing Corporation
Balance Sheet
December 31, 19x3

Assets

Current assets		
Cash		$ 1,042,954
Marketable securities		380,000
Accounts receivable	$9,083,414	
Less allowance for doubtful accounts	100,000	8,983,414
Inventories		10,958,103
Prepaid expenses		331,115
Total current assets		21,695,586
Noncurrent assets		
Property, plant, and equipment		
Land		918,649
Buildings	4,805,401	
Less accumulated depreciation	1,207,021	3,598,380
Machinery and equipment	9,835,027	
Less accumulated depreciation	2,414,042	7,420,985
Net property, plant, and equipment		11,938,014
Investment and other assets		
Investment in subsidiary		6,211,284
Notes receivable		3,682,487
Unamortized organization costs		1,000

EXHIBIT 2-3 (continued)

Mercury Truck Manufacturing Corporation
Balance Sheet
December 31, 19x3 (continued)

Assets

Patents and trademarks	34,000
Interest on long-term debt paid in advance	33,111
Total investment and other assets	9,961,882
Total noncurrent assets	21,899,896
Total assets	$43,595,482

Liabilities and Shareholders' Equity

Current liabilities	
Accounts payable	$ 5,515,469
Notes payable	4,152,249
Salaries and wages payable	1,938,795
Taxes payable	1,662,171
Interest payable	82,157
Total current liabilities	13,350,841
Noncurrent liabilities	
Advances from customers	87,218
Notes payable	3,057,679
Bonds payable	10,048,075
Total noncurrent liabilities	13,192,972
Total liabilities	26,543,813
Shareholders' equity	
Preferred shares, 10% dividend	96,655
Common shares (no par value, 625,773 shares issued and outstanding)	625,773
Retained earnings	16,329,241
Total shareholders' equity	17,051,669
Total liabilities and shareholders' equity	$43,595,482

Current assets

Current assets include cash and such other assets that will either be transformed into cash or will be sold or consumed within one year or within the *normal operating cycle* of the business if longer than one year. For most businesses the normal operating cycle is one year or less, but for some (such as those in the tobacco or distilling industries where the products must be stored for a period of several years) it may be a longer period.

Cash includes not only currency but savings bank or commercial bank deposits (after deducting outstanding cheques) as well. When it is said that a company disburses "cash" there is no necessary implication that it is making a payment in currency. The term could readily (and most commonly does) apply to payments by cheque.

Marketable securities include shares of ownership in other companies and other securities held by the firm for a short period of time (usually less than one year). In Canada such securities are ordinarily reported at original cost, with market values being shown in brackets:

Marketable securities, at cost (market value $384,500)	$380,000

If the market value were much less than $380,000 (say $305,000) the carrying value ($380,000 in Exhibit 2-3) would be reduced to $305,000 and the $75,000 difference would be included on the income statement as an expense. When market values exceed cost, Canadian accountants do not increase the carrying value on the balance sheet. This is primarily because of the accountant's tendency to be conservative in asset valuation and revenue recognition. (The concept of conservatism is discussed in later chapters. In view of differing accounting objectives and interpretations of facts, what is conservative to one person or in one situation, may not be conservative to another person or in another situation.)

There are already some situations in Canada where the objectives of accounting are such that it makes sense to record marketable securities at market value. Open-ended mutual funds (companies whose assets are almost exclusively comprised of the shares of other companies, and who are continually buying and selling common shares in themselves from and to individual investors) sell their shares to the general public on the basis of the market value per share of the mutual fund's net assets. Since such shareholders are interested in market values — not original cost — it is wise to report to them on this basis.

Accounts receivable — the amounts due from customers — represent those amounts that can be expected to be collected within the operating cycle (those that cannot are included among noncurrent assets). Deducted from accounts receivable is an "*allowance for doubtful accounts*" — an estimate of the amounts owed to the company that will be uncollectible. Thus, the net amount of accounts receivable represents not the total amount owed to the firm but only the amount that it estimates will actually be collectible.

Inventories include both items available for sale to customers and raw materials, parts, and supplies to be used in production. Inventories are ordinarily reported at original cost of either purchase or production, but in the event that the cost of replacing such items has declined, then the inventories may be "written down" to reflect the decline in value. As with marketable securities, increases in value are not ordinarily given similar accounting recognition.

Prepaid expenses represent services or rights to services purchased but not yet consumed. As they are consumed they will be "charged off" as actual expenses. A firm might, for example, purchase a one-year insurance policy for $120 ($10 per month). At the time of purchase it would probably record the policy as a current asset, prepaid insurance — $120. Each month it would reduce the asset by one twelfth of the original amount ($10) and would charge insurance expense with the same amount. Thus, after eight months, the balance in the prepaid insurance account would be only $40 (four months remaining times $10 per month). Other common prepaid expense accounts are prepaid interest, prepaid advertising, and prepaid rent. Prepaid expenses are one type of *deferred charge* — outlays made in one period to benefit future periods.

Noncurrent assets

Noncurrent assets are those assets that cannot be expected to be sold or consumed within one year or within a normal operating cycle of the business if longer than one year. Noncurrent assets are usually considered to be *long-lived* assets, and plant assets in particular are often referred to as *fixed* assets.

Property, plant, and equipment are recorded on the balance sheet at original cost. Deducted from each of the assets other than land, is accumulated depreciation — an allowance to reflect the fact that the assets are being "consumed" over time, by wear and tear as well as by technological obsolescence. Depreciation on each individual asset or group of similar assets is computed separately, and the total amount accumulated is a function of the age and expected useful life of the asset. No depreciation is provided for land since it is not consumed over time and seldom declines in utility.

The classification *investments and other assets* includes amounts that are not used up for at least either one year or one operating cycle if greater than one year, and amounts that the company has invested in other companies. If, for example, a company owns 30 percent of another company, such interest would ordinarily be included among investments and other assets. An interest in another company, however, may be classified as "marketable securities," a current asset, or as "investments in subsidiaries," a noncurrent asset. The decision as to how the interest should be classified depends to a large extent on the *intent* of the company's management. If it intends to maintain its interest for a relatively long period of time and views ownership as a long-term investment, then the amounts owned should be classified as a noncurrent asset. If, on the other hand, the company purchases the interest with the intention of selling it as soon as additional cash might be needed (for example, if it purchases a few hundred common shares of Canadian Pacific as a temporary investment with no intention of buying more and trying to exercise significant control or influence over the company), then the amount owned would be classified as marketable securities, a current asset.

Noncurrent assets may occasionally include *deferred charges* such as prepaid expenses as well. If, for example, a company purchased an insurance policy or a license that had more than a one-year life, then the percentage of original cost representing the unexpired portion of such insurance policy or license might be included among noncurrent assets.

Some deferred charges represent outlays that will benefit future accounting periods but for which both the number of such periods and the value of the benefits are exceedingly difficult to measure. Consider the costs incurred to organize a corporation: the legal fees required to draw up the documents of incorporation, the costs of printing the shares to be issued, and the fees paid to the government upon filing for a corporate charter. Such costs — like those of buildings and equipment — were incurred to benefit the business over a long period of time. Just as income of a single year of operations would be understated if the entire cost of a building were charged as an expense at the time it was purchased, income would also be distorted if the costs of organizing the corporation were charged as an expense in the first or second year after incorporation. As a result, in practice, organizational costs may be reported as an asset for a few years until the company grows to a size that the organization costs may be expensed because, on a relative basis, they are trivial.

Other common examples of deferred charges are interest paid in advance (often in connection with bonds payable issues) and amounts paid to acquire new businesses in excess of the value of the specific assets acquired (i.e., goodwill).

Deferred charges representing benefits which will accrue to the firm over a long period of time in the future are often a source of confusion to shareholders. Deferred charges, unlike most other assets, are intangible and frequently have no market value. Amounts spent as organizational costs, for example, cannot readily be transferred to any other business entity; they cannot be sold to outsiders. How, then, can such amounts be considered assets?

The question must be answered in terms of the nature of all assets. Assets can be defined as future services to be received in money or benefits convertible into money. They can readily be viewed as "bundles of services" available for use or sale by a particular entity. The determination of service potential is made with respect to the business entity issuing the financial reports — not with respect to the world at large.

In accordance with currently employed practices of valuation (alternative practices will be discussed in subsequent chapters), assets are measured and recorded at the time they are acquired at the price paid for them. As their service potential declines over time (e.g., as the assets are consumed) the reported value is reduced *proportionately* through the process of depreciation or amortization. If one third of the services has been consumed, then the asset is reported at two thirds its original cost. As long as the asset is not intended for sale to outsiders, market value seldom enters into the determination of the amount at which an asset is reported. Indeed, an automobile owned by a business might be reported at an amount either greater or less than the price at which similar used cars are being traded.

The outlay for organizational costs will benefit many accounting periods. To the extent that it has "future service potential" (the corporation would not exist without it) it can properly be considered an asset.

Current liabilities

Liabilities are also categorized as either current or noncurrent. *Current liabilities* are those expected to be satisfied out of current assets (or through the creation of other current liabilities) or to be satisfied within a relatively short period of time, usually one year or one operating cycle of the business if greater than one year. Most common categories of current liabilities are amounts owed to employees for wages and salaries; to suppliers for services, supplies, and raw materials purchased (conventionally called trade accounts, or simply accounts payable); to the government for taxes (taxes payable); and to banks or other lenders for amounts borrowed (notes payable) and for interest on such amounts (interest payable) that is payable within one year or one business cycle if greater than one year.

Noncurrent liabilities

Noncurrent liabilities include all other amounts owed. They include long-term (for a period greater than one year) notes as well as bonds payable. Bonds are similar to long-term notes but differ in that the promise to pay is usually included in a more formal legal instrument and in that the term of the loan is often longer. The same bond or note may be classified as both a current and a noncurrent liability. The portion that is due within one year would be considered current; the portion due beyond one year would be noncurrent.

Just as amounts that a company pays in advance to receive goods or services in the future are considered assets of the company, so too the amounts that others pay to the company for goods and services to be provided by the company are considered liabilities of the company. Supose that Air Canada sells a ticket for a trip which the traveler intends to take a month after his purchase. At the time of sale the airline receives an asset (cash or accounts receivable) equal to the price of the ticket. At the time of sale it incurs an obligation to provide services (i.e., one airline trip) to the customer. To be sure, the obligation is not a liability in the usual sense in that the airline has no monetary debt outstanding to the customer. But it is an obligation nonetheless. Such amounts are reported among the liabilities and may be labeled as appropriate: "advances from customers," "revenues received but not yet earned," or, less descriptively but more generally, "deferred credits." They are classified as current if the obligation is likely to be satisfied within one year; otherwise they are classified as noncurrent.

"Nonassets and nonliabilities"

Not all amounts that a firm will have to pay to others if it continues in business are recorded as liabilities, nor are all amounts that it can be expected to receive recorded as assets. If a firm signs a three-year contract with a new president, for example, and promises to pay him $100,000 per year, the firm may be legally liable for the full $300,000 as long as the new president is willing to provide the required services. The firm would not, however, record the full amount as a liability. Only as the president "earns" his salary — i.e., as he performs his side of the bargain — would the firm record as a liability amounts earned but not paid. This is also the case if a firm borrows $1,000 from a bank at a 12 percent rate of interest and gives the bank a one-year note. At the end of the one-year period, the firm will owe the bank $1,120 — the principal of $1,000 plus interest of $120. At the time the note is signed, however, the only liability that would be recorded is the $1,000 actually borrowed. Each month, as the company has use of the borrowed funds, an additional $10 interest for one month will be recorded as a liability. The bank, for its part, would record as an asset a note for $1,000. It, too, would recognize an asset, "interest receivable," only as it earns the interest revenue with the passage of time.

In general, assets and liabilities arising out of *"executory" contracts* (those contingent upon the mutual performance of the two sides to the contract) are recorded only to the extent that one of the parties has fulfilled its contractual obligations. The reason for such limited accounting recognition of assets and liabilities will become considerably clearer as the relationship between balance sheet and income statement accounts is discussed more fully in subsequent chapters.

Owners' equity

The shareholders' equity section of the corporate balance sheet is divided into at least two main subsections. The first indicates the capital contributed by shareholders — either at the time the corporation was formed or when additional shares were issued in the course of the corporation's existence. Corporations may issue several different types of shares. *Common shares* generally give their owners the right to vote for members of the corporation's board of directors as well as on numerous other corporate matters and the right to share in corporate profits whenever dividends are declared by the board of directors. *Preferred shares*, on the other hand, generally do *not* carry voting rights, but do ordinarily guarantee the owner that he will receive dividends of at least a minimum amount each year. The dividend rate is fixed at the time the share is issued. Some provincial Corporations or Companies Acts in Canada allow a company to assign a par value (e.g., $10 per share) to their common and any preferred shares. Such values have legal, but little economic, significance, and shares are commonly issued for amounts above (and sometimes below) these arbitrary par values. Amounts which the company receives in excess of par value are included on the balance sheet as "contributed surplus" — and shown as part of shareholders' equity.

The second subsection, retained earnings, indicates the accumulated earnings of the business. Retained earnings will be commented on in greater detail later in this chapter.

If the firm is not a corporation, that is, if it is a *sole proprietorship* (a firm owned by a single individual) or a *partnership* (a firm owned by two or more parties), then the owners' equity section of the balance sheet may take a somewhat different form. Since such enterprises do not issue shares and are not bound by many of the legal restrictions that apply to firms which do, it is generally most useful to readers of the financial reports to indicate the entire closing equity balance of each owner on a separate line. If Mercury Truck Manufacturing Corporation were owned by two partners, John Switzer and William King, the shareholders' equity section of the balance sheet would appear as:

Partners' capital:	
John Switzer, capital	$ 9,525,347
William King, capital	7,526,322
	$17,051,669

The term "corporation" would not be part of the title of the firm if it were a partnership.

The Income Statement — A Closer Look

Statements of income are presented in a variety of formats, but virtually all are based on the fundamental relationship

$$\text{Revenues} - \text{Expenses} = \text{Net Income}.$$

Although the income statement illustrated in Exhibit 2-4 is that of a manufacturing concern, there are no costs of either labor or raw materials listed among the expenses. The company would, of course, maintain separate accounts for labor, materials and other factors of production, but to avoid inundating the reader with detail such costs are grouped together in one account, *cost of goods sold*. Cost of goods sold may not represent the actual costs of labor, material, and other factors of production incurred during the reporting period. Adjustment must be made for those costs applicable to goods that may have been produced but not yet sold (i.e., retained in inventory) and those goods that have been sold but were produced in prior periods.

EXHIBIT 2-4

Mercury Truck Manufacturing Corporation
Income Statement
Year Ended December 31, 19x3

Revenues	
Sales	$32,904,468
Rents received from leased equipment	3,464,491
Miscellaneous revenue	1,209,975
	37,578,934
Expenses	
Cost of goods sold	28,691,473
Selling and administrative expenses	2,319,231
Depreciation expense	1,704,621
Property and other taxes*	823,347
Interest expense	1,221,896
	34,760,568
Income before income taxes and extraordinary items	2,818,366
Taxes on income	1,245,000
	1,573,366
Extraordinary gain received upon settlement of legal action, less applicable income taxes of $276,923	300,000
Net income	$ 1,873,366

*This line excludes taxes on income, which are shown below.

Occasionally firms engage in transactions or are affected by events that are highly unusual and are unlikely to be repeated. Examples of such events might be losses from natural disasters or from government expropriation of a company's plant in another country. Unless such gains or losses are segregated from income derived from the normal operations of the firm, the income statement will not serve as a meaningful instrument of comparison among financial performances of various years. Moreover, the income of the year in which such events or transactions occurred will provide little insight into earnings potential for the future. As a consequence, such *extraordinary items* — those which are exceptional in nature and infrequent in occurrence — are reported separately in the income statement. And since these events are likely to have a major impact on the income taxes of the firm, the applicable taxes are also reported separately.

The Statement of Retained Earnings

The statement of retained earnings (Exhibit 2-5) serves as the link between the income statement and the balance sheet. The basic accounting equation for incorporated companies can readily be expanded as follows:

$$\text{Assets} - \text{Liabilities} = \text{Capital contributed by owners} + \text{Retained earnings.}$$

Retained earnings represent the sum of the earnings of each accounting period that the company has been in existence less the amounts paid as dividends to shareholders. The retained earnings per the balance sheet at the beginning of the period (which of course must be identical to that at the end of the previous period), plus the income for that period per the income statement, less any dividends declared during the period, equals the retained earnings at the end of the period:

$$\text{Retained earnings, balance at beginning of year} + \text{Income} - \text{Dividends declared} = \text{Retained earnings balance at end of year.}$$

The statement of retained earnings, by indicating both dividends declared during the year and the income for the year, provides a reconciliation of the retained earnings at the beginning of the year with that at the end.

EXHIBIT 2-5

Mercury Truck Manufacturing Corporation
Retained Earnings Statement
Year Ended December 31, 19x3

Balance, January 1, 19x3	$15,210,861
Net income for the year	1,873,366
	17,084,227
Less dividends	754,986
Balance, December 31, 19x3	$16,329,241

Retained earnings, it cannot be overemphasized, *is not cash* or some other asset or resource of the firm. It is a residual figure in the double entry system, representing a portion of owners' equity. In a similar vein, earnings *per se* cannot be distributed to shareholders; earnings cannot be used to purchase goods or services. Only cash or other assets are generally accepted in exchange for other goods or services. Retained earnings represent nothing more than a *claim* against the assets of the enterprise — the claims of the owners attributable to the income earned by the firm over the course of one or more years. Although assets must be equal to the claims against those assets (claims of owners as well as creditors), *there is generally no specific relationship between particular assets and particular claims.*

Dividends are distributions of the assets of the incorporated enterprise to its owners. The asset distributed most often is cash, but it could, in fact, be any asset of the firm. As the assets of the firm are reduced upon distribution to the owners, so also are the claims of the owners against such assets. Assume, for example, that several individuals contribute $1,000 to form a corporation. During the first year of operations the firm earns $200. Its position, at the end of the first year, as indicated by the accounting equation might appear as follows:

Assets =	Liabilities +	Capital contributed by owners +	Retained earnings
$1,200 =	$0 +	$1,000 +	$200

If the firm declared and paid a dividend of $100, then the position of the company after the $100 in assets had been distributed would appear as

$1,100 =	$0 +	$1,000 +	$100

The statement of retained earnings is not included in the financial reports of all corporations. A few companies indicate the dividends distributed to shareholders directly beneath the net income figure on the income statement and omit the reconciliation between beginning-of-year and end-of-year retained earnings.

The Statement of Changes in Financial Position

The statement of changes in financial position (SCFP) has been in existence for over 100 years but has gained prominence only in the last 10 years. Large companies that sell shares to the public are required to include the SCFP in their financial reports filed with Provincial Securities Commissions. However, in some other situations the SCFP may not be required in order for the financial statement package to be in accordance with contemporary reporting "principles." Chapter 14 discusses this aspect of the topic in more detail. The SCFP is gaining greater acceptance year after year; and no doubt will be a required statement under GAAP in a few years.

The SCFP has a flexible design because its purpose is to focus either: (1) on changes in liquidity (such as cash), or (2) on important transactions which are not disclosed, or disclosed well, bv a balance sheet and income statement. The SCFP may therefore be in balanced form, like a balance sheet, or highlight a change in one or more accounts by using the income statement design, which stresses the "bottom line." In some situations it may be possible to highlight both liquidity changes and important transactions during a period, but often it is not possible to accomplish both with one financial statement design. We therefore have to apply our judgment.

Exhibit 2-7 contains the financial statements of John Labatt Limited, a large Canadian company. Their SCFP (page 55) focuses on *working capital* (which is another name for current assets minus current liabilities). In some companies a change in liquidity is measured best by viewing movements in the *cash* position. In other companies, cash, accounts receivable, inventory and accounts payable may change so quickly that they should be part of liquid funds. Liquidity is a somewhat elusive concept which broadly describes the net resources which the company can call upon to pay for expected and unexpected expenditures. A bank, for example, may measure its liquidity in terms of cash on hand plus cash which it will receive shortly. A grocery store may include inventory in its definition of liquidity because it could sell off some of its inventory at reduced prices if it had unexpected cash needs. John Labatt Limited may have chosen working capital as its liquidity measure, or it may feel that the working capital design helps to focus on important transactions. Another possibility is that working capital may be a reasonable compromise between liquidity and important transactions during its year ended April 30, 1978.

In contrast to Exhibit 2-7, Exhibit 2-6 uses a balanced format of SCFP to portray important transactions and results for Mercury Truck Manufacturing Corporation. By employing the balanced format there is no "bottom line" of liquidity changes, and attention is thereby shifted to several larger amounts in the statement. Sometimes, a "bottom line" format is used to focus on major nonliquid transactions (for instance, major expenditures on fixed assets by a public utility company). However, Mercury Truck did not have any major transactions which dwarfed other activities during the year. Hence, the balanced format seems appropriate for this year's events.

Whereas Exhibit 2-7's SCFP is fairly traditional, Exhibit 2-6's is more consistent with recent Canadian pronouncements which advocate flexible formats, grouping similar items (for example, dividends to shareholders are subtracted from income, and proceeds on sale of equipment are shown with additions), and a greater stress on disclosing important financing and investing activities. Roughly speaking, financing activities are those which affect the liability and equity side of the balance sheet. Investing activities are primarily concerned with the asset side of the balance sheet. Inventory is separately reported (instead of being part of working capital) because it is a major item, and presumably because some users of the financial statements want to know about such changes and are entitled (by law or for other reasons) to this information.

EXHIBIT 2-6

Mercury Truck Manufacturing Corporation
Statement of Changes in Financial Position
Year ended December 31, 19x3

Financing activities:	
From regular operations:	
Net income before extraordinary gain	$ 1,573,366
Add operating items not affecting funds	1,704,621
	3,277,987
Less dividends	754,986
	2,823,001
Settlement of lawsuit	300,000
Issue of common shares	4,960,519
Issue of long-term debt	1,000,000
	$ 8,783,520
Investing activities:	
Additions to property, plant and equipment	$ 3,511,819
Less proceeds of disposals of equipment	500,000
	3,011,819
Addition to inventory $6,000,000 less $2,900,000 goods sold	3,100,000
Investments and other assets acquired	254,735
Reduction of long-term debt	2,207,656
Increase in working capital, excluding inventory	209,310
	$ 8,783,520

Further discussion of the SCFP is deferred until Chapter 14. However, it is important to bear in mind that Canadian practice seems to be lagging behind professional pronouncements which are advocating more effective use of the SCFP. The formats of Exhibits 2-6 and 2-7, and the essence of their differences, may be difficult to comprehend at this point in the book. It is probably wise to refer to them from time to time as Chapters 3 to 13 are completed; otherwise, Chapter 14 may prove difficult. Our basic theme is that the design and content of the SCFP is dependent on the objectives or purposes of financial accounting and reporting, the facts (types of transactions encountered during the period), and any legal restrictions or constraints.

A Financial Report Illustrated

John Labatt Limited's financial statements for their 1978 year have been reproduced in their entirety in Exhibit 2-7. Financial statements are provided annually to shareholders and other interested parties. The company also issues quarterly statements in an abbreviated form to shareholders and others.

Over three quarters of the company's "income" (normally called revenue) comes from sales of beer in several countries but Labatt's has diversified and is continuing to do so into a variety of consumer and non-consumer products. The following companies, among others, are fully or partly owned by Labatt's: the Toronto Blue Jays (of the American Baseball League); Laura Secord; Casabello Wines Ltd; McGavin Foods Limited; Chateau Gai Wines; Catelli Foods; and Ogilvie Flour Mills. The financial statements are described as being *consolidated* because the assets, liabilities, sales and expenses of *all* companies in which Labatt's has over 50 percent ownership are included in the financial statement package. Companies which are not consolidated are shown on the consolidated balance sheet as "investments" and any income therefrom is included under "equity in net earnings of partly-owned businesses" on the consolidated statement of earnings.

Terminology can be troublesome when one is learning a new subject. Observe that Labatt's calls the *income statement* (exhibit 2-4) a "consolidated statement of earnings"; both terms are used in practice. However, Labatt's unfortunately uses the category "income" (which is an old term, in less common use) whereas in this book we use the conventional term "revenue" or "sales" for the top section of the income statement. Also Labatt's refers to "operating costs" whereas the conventional term is "operating expenses" or "expenses". *Revenue less expenses equals income.* Overall, though, Labatt's has an excellent annual report and financial statement package and has won awards in Canada for its annual report presentation.

Corporate legislation and generally accepted accounting principles (GAAP) in Canada call for the use of comparative statements. This enables readers to form a quick impression about how the current year compares with the previous one. Many companies, including Labatt's, also provide readers of the annual report with a five or ten-year condensed financial summary elsewhere in the annual report. (Labatt's 1978 annual report amounted to 38 pages; the financial statements covered 11 pages; the balance was devoted to descriptions of the company's activities and results.) Consistent application of accounting principles and five to ten-year summaries help potential investors and creditors to establish informed judgments about a company.

Labatt's financial statement package consists of five related parts: the

EXHIBIT 2-7

Consolidated Statement of Earnings

For the Year Ended April 30, 1978
(with comparative amounts for the year ended April 30, 1977)

	1978	1977
Income		
Gross sales	**$997,263,000**	$922,194,000
Less excise and sale taxes	**158,240,000**	151,898,000
	839,023,000	770,296,000
Operating costs		
Cost of products sold	**529,408,000**	500,872,000
Selling and administrative expenses	**229,732,000**	195,299,000
Depreciation	**17,471,000**	16,340,000
Interest – long term	**12,646,000**	12,894,000
– short term	**1,853,000**	482,000
	791,110,000	725,887,000
Operating income	**47,913,000**	44,409,000
Investment and sundry income	**4,267,000**	2,408,000
Income before taxes	**52,180,000**	46,817,000
Income taxes – current	**13,319,000**	13,287,000
– deferred	**6,410,000**	7,213,000
	19,729,000	20,500,000
Earnings before the following	**32,451,000**	26,317,000
Equity in net earnings of partly-owned businesses	**1,534,000**	1,850,000
Minority interest	**(90,000)**	(102,000)
	1,444,000	1,748,000
Net earnings	**$ 33,895,000**	$ 28,065,000
Earnings per common share	**$2.89**	$2.45
Fully diluted earnings per common share	**$2.53**	$2.12

See accompanying notes

Consolidated Balance Sheet

April 30, 1978
(with comparative amounts as at April 30, 1977)

ASSETS

	1978	1977
Current		
Cash	**$ 2,245,000**	$ 1,743,000
Marketable securities at cost (which approximates market value)	**8,998,000**	8,693,000
Accounts receivable	**73,271,000**	69,320,000
Inventories	**116,672,000**	91,661,000
Prepaid expenses	**15,701,000**	13,086,000
	216,887,000	184,503,000
Investments and other assets		
Investment in partly-owned businesses	**30,434,000**	25,425,000
Investment in other companies	**3,477,000**	3,895,000
Mortgages, loans and advances	**3,413,000**	4,130,000
Due from trustees and employees under share purchase and option plans	**434,000**	586,000
	37,758,000	34,036,000
Fixed at cost		
Land	**12,192,000**	10,899,000
Buildings and equipment	**352,304,000**	322,709,000
	364,496,000	333,608,000
Less accumulated depreciation	**163,162,000**	150,294,000
	201,334,000	183,314,000
Unamortized debt financing expense	**2,041,000**	2,178,000
Goodwill, store licences and trademarks	**60,977,000**	59,110,000
	$518,997,000	$463,141,000

See accompanying notes

LIABILITIES

	1978	1977
Current		
Bank advances and short term notes	**$ 33,053,000**	$ 9,565,000
Accounts payable	**70,077,000**	61,854,000
Taxes payable	**11,536,000**	12,696,000
Dividends payable	**335,000**	244,000
Long term debt due within one year	**2,834,000**	1,160,000
	117,835,000	85,519,000
Deferred income taxes	**42,271,000**	35,653,000
Long term debt	**142,146,000**	145,985,000
Minority interest in subsidiary companies	**1,174,000**	1,175,000
SHAREHOLDERS' EQUITY		
Share capital		
Authorized		
4,000,000 preferred shares		
Class A convertible common shares of no par value in unlimited amount		
Class B convertible common shares of no par value in unlimited amount		
Issued and outstanding		
605,080 Series A preferred shares (828,173 – 1977)	**10,892,000**	14,907,000
11,111,354 Class A common shares (10,821,717 – 1977)		
471,255 Class B common shares (499,441 – 1977)	**63,412,000**	58,741,000
	74,304,000	73,648,000
Retained earnings	**141,267,000**	121,161,000
	215,571,000	194,809,000
	$518,997,000	$463,141,000

On behalf of the Board

P.N.T. Widdrington, Director

J.H. Moore, Director

Consolidated Statement of Changes in Financial Position

For the Year Ended April 30, 1978
(with comparative amounts for the year ended April 30, 1977)

	1978	1977
Sources of working capital		
From operations		
Net earnings	**$33,895,000**	$28,065,000
Net charges to earnings which do not reduce working capital	**22,618,000**	22,795,000
	56,513,000	50,860,000
Sale of properties and other assets	**4,044,000**	1,044,000
Reduction in mortgages, loans and advances	**2,322,000**	2,341,000
Proceeds on sale of partly-owned businesses	**892,000**	
Shares issued under share purchase and option plans	**808,000**	801,000
Reduction in investment in other companies	**418,000**	
	64,997,000	55,046,000
Uses of working capital		
Dividends – preferred	**695,000**	1,147,000
– common	**13,094,000**	12,237,000
Land, buildings and equipment	**36,506,000**	22,926,000
Investment in partly-owned businesses	**5,121,000**	8,175,000
Acquisition of Casabello Wines Ltd.		
(net of working capital deficit $601,000)	**3,726,000**	
Reduction in long term debt	**3,839,000**	965,000
Increase in mortgages, loans and advances	**1,605,000**	682,000
Acquisition of additional shares of subsidiary companies		461,000
Goodwill, store licences and trademarks	**165,000**	319,000
Other	**178,000**	142,000
	64,929,000	47,054,000
Increase in working capital	**68,000**	7,992,000
Working capital, beginning of year	**98,984,000**	90,992,000
Working capital, end of year	**$99,052,000**	$98,984,000

See accompanying notes

Consolidated Statement of Retained Earnings

For the Year Ended April 30, 1978
(with comparative amounts for the year ended April 30, 1977)

	1978	1977
Balance, beginning of year	**$121,161,000**	$106,480,000
Net earnings	**33,895,000**	28,065,000
	155,056,000	134,545,000
Dividends		
– preferred ($1.00 per share 1978 and 1977)	**695,000**	1,147,000
– common ($1.14 per share 1978; $1.09 per share 1977)	**13,094,000**	12,237,000
	13,789,000	13,384,000
Balance, end of year	**$141,267,000**	$121,161,000

See accompanying notes

Notes to the Consolidated Financial Statements

April 30, 1978

1. ACCOUNTING POLICIES

The company follows generally accepted accounting principles, the most significant of which are as follows:

Principles of consolidation

The consolidated financial statements include the accounts of all subsidiary companies. The results of operations of subsidiaries acquired or sold during the year are included from or to their respective dates of acquisition or sale.

Foreign currency translation

Foreign currency assets and liabilities are translated into Canadian dollars on the following basis:

Monetary current assets and current liabilities	– at rates of exchange in effect at the balance sheet date
Inventories, prepaid expenses, fixed and other long term assets, long term debt and depreciation provisions	– at historical rates of exchange
Income and operating costs and expenses	– at average exchange rates prevailing during the year

Gains and losses arising on the translation of foreign currencies are included in earnings.

Long term debt denominated in foreign currency, including the company's share of long term debt of partly-owned businesses, translated at historical rates of exchange amounted to $21,535,000, but if translated at the rates of exchange in effect at the balance sheet date would have amounted to $23,747,000.

Earnings per common share

Earnings per common share have been calculated using the weighted monthly average number of shares outstanding during the year.

Earnings per common share on a fully diluted basis have been calculated on the assumption that all the preferred shares and all the convertible subordinated debentures outstanding at the end of the year had been converted to common shares at the beginning of the year and that all common share options outstanding had been exercised at the beginning of the year.

Inventories

Inventories, other than containers, are valued at the lower of cost, determined on a FIFO basis, and net realizable value. Containers are valued at redemption price or at estimated value not exceeding replacement cost. Inventory values are as follows:

	1978	1977
Finished and in process	**$ 72,741,000**	$56,276,000
Materials and supplies	**31,787,000**	23,445,000
Containers	**12,144,000**	11,940,000
	$116,672,000	$91,661,000

Investment in partly-owned businesses

Partly-owned businesses are companies and partnerships for which the equity method of accounting is appropriate. Under this method, the company's share of earnings of partly-owned businesses, net of applicable income taxes, is included in consolidated net earnings. The investments are carried in the consolidated balance sheet at cost plus the company's share of undistributed earnings since acquisition.

Investment in other companies

Investments in other companies are carried at cost and income is recognized when dividends are received. These investments include partly-owned businesses where income remittance uncertainties exist.

Fixed assets

Buildings, machinery and equipment are initially recorded at cost. Normal maintenance and repair expenditures are expensed as incurred. Gains or losses arising on the disposal of individual assets are recognized in income in the year of disposal.

Depreciation

Depreciation generally is provided on a straight line basis over the estimated useful lives of assets at annual rates of 2½% for buildings and 10% for equipment. Where appropriate, maximum capital cost allowance is claimed for income tax purposes and a related provision is made for deferred income taxes.

Unamortized debt financing expense

Debt financing expenses are amortized over the term of the issue to which they relate.

Goodwill, store licences and trademarks

Goodwill, store licences and trademarks acquired prior to May 1, 1974 are being carried in the accounts at cost without amortization.

Goodwill and other intangible assets acquired after April 30, 1974 are being amortized by charges to earnings over periods not exceeding forty years (1978 – $321,000; 1977 – $296,000). The excess of the purchase price over the net book value of assets acquired after April 30, 1974 is allocated first to land, buildings and equipment and other identifiable net assets with any remainder being allocated to goodwill. Depreciation has been charged on amounts allocated to depreciable assets.

The amount of goodwill, store licences and trademarks (of which $7,256,000 acquired after April 30, 1974 is subject to amortization) consists of:

	1978	1977
Store licences and trademarks	**$ 2,937,000**	$ 2,937,000
Purchased goodwill	**8,248,000**	8,049,000
Excess of purchase price of shares of certain subsidiary companies over net book value of assets acquired	**50,649,000**	48,660,000
	61,834,000	59,646,000
Less accumulated amortization	**857,000**	536,000
	$60,977,000	$59,110,000

Income taxes

In accordance with generally accepted accounting principles the company follows the deferral method of tax allocation. Under this method the provision for income taxes is determined from the earnings reported in the statement of earnings rather than from the company's income for tax purposes. Deferred income taxes on the balance sheet result principally from depreciation allowable for tax purposes being in excess of that included in costs and expenses. In future years, when the amounts allowable for tax purposes will be less than those reflected in the statement of earnings, the applicable income taxes will be paid and the deferred tax balance reduced accordingly.

Under this method future income tax recoveries relating to losses are provided for only where it is virtually certain, in the loss year, that earnings in future years will be sufficient to make such recoveries possible.

The 3 per cent inventory tax credit enacted by the Federal government in December, 1977 but effective from April 1, 1977, resulted in a reduction in current income taxes in the amount of $1,200,000.

2. PARTLY-OWNED BUSINESSES

These investments include McGavin Foods Limited (formerly McGavin ToastMaster Bakeries Limited); Canada Malting Co., Limited; Toronto Blue Jays Baseball Club; Cervejarias Reunidas Skol-Caracu S/A, Brazil; Catelli-Primo Limited, Trinidad and Nana-Manning's, United States of America.

	1978	1977
Investment at cost	**$23,705,000**	$18,680,000
Accumulated equity in undistributed earnings since acquisition	**6,729,000**	6,745,000
	$30,434,000	$25,425,000

During the year the company disposed of its investment in H.E. Saunders and Sons Limited, entered into a partnership with Nana Regional Corporation in Alaska and increased its investment in Cervejarias Reunidas Skol-Caracu S/A.

3. LONG TERM DEBT

Particulars of debentures payable and other long term debt are as follows:

	1978	1977
Sinking fund debentures		
6% Series B to mature January 2, 1979	**$ 186,000**	$ 445,000
6¼% Series C to mature May 15, 1981	**1,048,000**	1,283,000
6¼% Series D to mature June 15, 1987	**4,071,000**	4,253,000
6¼% Series E to mature October 1, 1989	**3,366,000**	3,366,000
7⅛% Series F to mature April 15, 1992	**4,850,000**	5,075,000
9¼% Series G to mature September 1, 1990	**26,875,000**	27,825,000
8¼% Series H to mature March 1, 1993	**29,325,000**	30,000,000
9% Series I to mature March 15, 1994	**30,000,000**	30,000,000
9½% Convertible Subordinated Debentures to mature June 1, 1995	**32,938,000**	33,000,000
Term bank loan repayable May 1, 1978 to 1982	**7,000,000**	7,000,000
	139,659,000	142,247,000
Advances, mortgages and other long term liabilities	**5,321,000**	4,898,000
	144,980,000	147,145,000
Less portion due within one year included in current liabilities	**2,834,000**	1,160,000
	$142,146,000	$145,985,000

The 9½% Convertible Subordinated Debentures are convertible on or before June 1, 1985 at the holder's option into Class A common shares of the company at a conversion price of $18.25 per share.

Maturities and sinking fund requirements for the years 1979 through 1983 are $2,834,000; $5,902,000; $6,786,000; $7,040,000 and $6,158,000 respectively.

At April 30, 1978 the company had satisfied all of the covenants under the trust deed relating to the debentures.

4. SHARE CAPITAL

The company has elected for continuation under the Canada Business Corporations Act. Through the enactment of a by-law the company is a constrained share corporation whereby the total number of voting shares outstanding to be held by non-residents is restricted to 20% and the number to be held by any single non-resident is restricted to 10%.

Common Shares

Under the provisions of the Canada Business Corporations Act and the company's by-laws, the company's authorized common share capital is unlimited as to the number of shares which may be issued.

The two classes of common shares are interchangeable one to another and are subject to the same rights and conditions except in respect of dividends. Dividends paid on the Class A and Class B shares are identical in amount but result in a different tax treatment when received by shareholders. After December 31, 1978, dividends received by shareholders on the Class B shares will not be entitled to this different tax treatment.

Preferred Shares

Of the 4,000,000 authorized preferred shares 605,080 shares are outstanding as Series A preferred shares. The balance of 3,394,920 shares are available for future issue with conditions and preferences as determined by the Board of Directors. Series A preferred shares have a par value of $18 each, are redeemable at par, are non-voting (unless four quarterly dividends are in arrears) and are entitled to cumulative annual dividends of $1 per share.

Each Series A preferred share is convertible to one Class A common share of John Labatt at any time up to the close of business on February 15, 1980 or to the close of business on the date immediately prior to the date fixed for redemption, whichever is earlier. At April 30, 1978 none of these shares had been called for redemption. Of the 3,063,590 Series A preferred shares which were originally issued, there have been 2,458,510 converted to common shares.

Share Purchase and Option Plans

From time to time the company has established various share purchase and option plans. The following schedule sets out details of amounts due from trustees and employees under these plans:

	1978	1977
Due from trustees under the issued share option plan (1978 – nil shares; 1977 – 5,150 shares)		$ 75,000
Due from employees under share purchase plans (1978 – 34,067 shares; 1977 – 36,367 shares)		
Officers	**$ 96,000**	124,000
Other employees	**338,000**	387,000
	$434,000	$586,000

Issued Share Option Plan

During 1967 the company established an issued share option plan. The trustees of this plan acquired 33,500 common shares for future sale to employees and granted options on these shares exercisable at $14.50 per share up to September, 1977. Options covering 32,950 shares have been exercised, fully paid for and the shares transferred to employees. The trustees have sold the issued shares relating to unexercised options and returned the proceeds to the company.

Share Purchase Plans

In certain prior years the company established various employee share purchase plans. Under these plans, the individuals are entitled to purchase the shares and pay for them over periods of up to 15 years.

Shares Available for Share Purchase and Option Plans

During 1975 the company enacted a by-law which made available 750,000 unissued Class A common shares for allotment to employees under share purchase or option plans. At April 30, 1978 these shares were allocated as follows:

Under option	207,850
Reserved for employee share purchase plan maturing in June, 1979	56,912
Issued	33,962
Available for future issuance or option to employees	451,276
Total	750,000

Under the provisions of the by-law the Board of Directors is not restricted with respect to any allotment of these shares.

Details of shares under option to employees (207,850 allotted under this by-law and 7,875 allotted under a previous by-law), as of April 30, 1978 are as follows:

Plan	Number of shares	Price per share	Expiry Date
1974 Share option	7,875	$12.85	December 1984
1975 Share option	80,350	19.00	December 1979
1975 Share option	29,750	19.00	June 1981
1975 Share option	97,750	19.00	December 1983
	215,725		

Of the 215,725 shares under option there are 95,750 under option to officers of the company.

Shares Converted and Issued During the Year

During 1978 changes in the company's issued shares were as follows:

	Series A Preferred Shares	Class A and Class B Common Shares
Issued and outstanding at April 30, 1977	828,173	11,321,158
Conversions	(223,093)	223,093
Issued under employee share purchase and option plans for a cash consideration of $594,000.		34,962
Issued as a result of conversions of the 9½% convertible subordinated debenture at $18.25 per share		3,396
Issued and outstanding at April 30, 1978	605,080	11,582,609

Principal Shareholder

To the knowledge of the directors and officers of the company, Brascan Limited is the only shareholder who beneficially owns, directly or indirectly through a wholly-owned subsidiary, shares carrying more than 10% of the votes attached to shares of the company. Brascan Limited beneficially owns, controls or directs, 2,960,100 Class A shares of the company representing approximately 25.56% of the aggregate outstanding common shares.

5. LEASES, COMMITMENTS AND GUARANTEES

Leases

The company has entered into or guaranteed long term leases substantially all of which will be discharged within 16 years. Fixed rental expense for 1978 was $4,360,000. Approximate future annual fixed rental payments are as follows:

1979	$ 4,571,000
1980	4,174,000
1981	3,664,000
1982	3,102,000
1983	2,426,000
	$17,937,000

Fixed rental payments for subsequent years and guarantees amount to $16,716,000.

Certain store leases require payments related to sales and/or additional charges for increased costs. The amount of such additional rental expense for 1978, not included in the amount above, was approximately $975,000.

In addition to the above, under the terms of vehicle leases, rentals for the next 3 years will amount to approximately $6,000,000 per annum.

Commitments

During 1979 the company plans capital expenditures of approximately $38,384,000. Of this amount $5,090,000 was represented by commitments at April 30, 1978.

During the year the company and Redpath Industries Limited announced their intention to investigate the economic feasibility of constructing a $60 million plant in Southwestern Ontario to produce high fructose syrup from corn for Canada's food industry. This project is still in the study stage and has not been included in the above planned capital expenditures. If the partners decide to proceed with this project, the company's share of the construction costs will be an additional $30,000,000 over the next two years.

Also the company has initiated a feasibility study of a world scale wheat starch and gluten facility to be constructed in Aiken County, South Carolina. If the project proceeds to construction, the company will incur $23,000,000 for additional capital expenditures over the next two years.

The company has a commitment to provide financing, if required, to complete the purchase of its interest in Cervejarias Reunidas Skol-Caracu S/A in the years 1979 and 1980 of approximately $1,383,000 and $1,356,000 respectively.

Guarantees

The company has guaranteed various loans and payments amounting to approximately $4,700,000 in aggregate.

6. PENSIONS

During the year the company made revisions to certain of its pension plans providing for increased benefits. As a result, based on the most recent actuarial valuations, the company's unfunded obligations at December 31, 1977 were $10,686,000.

Past service costs relating to improved benefits are funded and charged to operations over periods not exceeding 15 years. Current service costs are funded and charged to operations as they accrue.

7. ANTI-INFLATION LEGISLATION

As of May 1, 1978, the company and its Canadian subsidiaries are no longer subject to the federal government's anti-inflation legislation relating to the control of prices and profit margins. However, the company and its Canadian subsidiaries will continue to remain subject to the restrictions relative to dividends until October 13, 1978 and to the restrictions controlling levels of employee compensation to varying dates up to December 31, 1978.

8. ACQUISITIONS AND DISPOSITIONS

Effective September 1, 1977, the company acquired 100% of the outstanding shares of Casabello Wines Ltd. Details of net assets acquired, accounted for under the purchase method, are as follows:

Assets acquired at book value	$4,235,000
Less liabilities assumed	3,403,000
Net tangible assets acquired	832,000
Allocated to fixed assets	304,000
Allocated to goodwill (including contingent consideration of $317,000)	1,989,000
Purchase Price	$3,125,000

Under the terms of the Option and Voting Trust Agreement entered into between the company and the shareholders of Casabello in 1972 the purchase price of the shares has been calculated annually by the auditors of Casabello and has been sent by Casabello to its shareholders who have had an annual right to require the company to purchase their shares at the calculated price. During 1977 a difference arose between the company's representative and the shareholders on the board of Casabello as to the proper method of calculating the purchase price. While this difference could not be resolved the parties did agree that if the purchase price was calculated using the same method as had been used in each of the previous four years the purchase price would be $2,808,000 but that if the different method was used, as advocated by the Casabello shareholders, the purchase price would be increased by $317,000. In order to avoid delay the company deposited this additional amount with the depositary under the Option and Voting Trust Agreement and took delivery of the shares. The dispute was referred to arbitration; the arbitration hearing has been held and the decision is expected during the summer. If the company is successful, the additional amount of $317,000 will be returned to it.

During the year the company disposed of its soft-drink operation in Newfoundland and also disposed of its dry livestock feed operation in Quebec and in each case the total cash consideration approximated the net book value of the assets sold.

9. REMUNERATION OF DIRECTORS AND OFFICERS

During 1978 the total remuneration paid to thirteen of the company's eighteen directors, as directors, was $133,500 and to four of these directors as directors of subsidiary companies was $13,100.

The company's twenty officers received remuneration totalling $1,630,000. The five officers who served as directors received no additional remuneration as directors.

10. CLASSES OF BUSINESS

The directors have determined at a meeting of directors and have recorded in the minutes thereof the classes of business in accordance with Section 47 of the Canada Business Corporations Regulations, based upon the functional and managerial organization of the company. The following is a summary of the gross sales, contribution from, and assets employed in the classes:

in thousands of dollars	**1978** Gross Sales	**1978** Percentage	1977 Gross Sales	1977 Percentage
Brewing	**$512,351**	**51.4%**	$479,367	52.0%
Consumer Products	**256,739**	**25.7%**	213,077	23.1%
Agri Products	**228,173**	**22.9%**	229,750	24.9%
	$997,263	**100.0%**	$922,194	100.0%
	Contribution	**Assets Employed**	Contribution	Assets Employed
Brewing	**$46,946**	**$189,092**	$44,028	$170,394
Consumer Products	**7,749**	**136,423**	5,146	112,425
Agri Products	**11,984**	**78,266**	11,019	78,943
	66,679	**$403,781**	60,193	$361,762
Interest	**14,499**		13,376	
Income before taxes	**$52,180**		$46,817	

11. THE COMPANIES ACT (BRITISH COLUMBIA)

The Companies Act (British Columbia) requires consolidated financial statements to include the names of every subsidiary company but permits the circulation within the province of statements which do not so comply.

These consolidated financial statements include the accounts of all subsidiary companies. A list of all of the subsidiaries of the company is available for inspection at the company's registered office in British Columbia.

12. SUBSEQUENT EVENTS

The company has agreed in principle to acquire all of the operating assets of Bear Mountain Winery of Bakersfield, California. Consideration for the winery's assets will be the assumption of substantially all of its liabilities. Bear Mountain Winery is a grower co-operative and the transaction is subject to the approval of the grower – members and appropriate regulatory authorities.

The company has also agreed in principle to acquire for cash all of the outstanding shares of Beurrerie Lafreniere / Laiterie Dallaire, a dairy and an industrial milk processor in north-western Quebec, effective May 31, 1978.

four financial statements mentioned earlier in the chapter (consolidated statement of earnings; consolidated balance sheet; consolidated statement of changes in financial position; and consolidated statement of retained earnings) plus 12 "Notes to the Consolidated Financial Statements." The auditors' report (reproduced in Exhibit 1-1, page 17) accompanies the financial statement package and reports whether or not the statements present fairly in accordance with generally accepted accounting principles.

Measurement and disclosure

The use of notes to financial statements has increased dramatically in the past 15 years in Canada. For many decades accountants were concerned with measurement and the figures on either or both of the income statement and balance sheet. In the late 1800s and portions of the 1920s and 1930s, the balance sheet was important because potential creditors wanted to know what and how much security existed for any loans which they may have wished to make.

In 1917 the first Income Tax Act was introduced in Canada; this obviously put greater pressure on accountants to measure a concept called income. Later, investors used the income statement to assess success. In short, more and more users with somewhat different needs began to look to accounting statements for assistance.

In the 1900s (especially after 1950), research into the efficiency of share-trading on stock markets brought forth considerable evidence about the ability of investors to evaluate financial statements. For example, prior to this, some people believed that changes in net income would cause a *direct* effect on the company's share price as soon as the financial statements were made available to the public. However, the evidence for companies which were widely traded on large stock exchanges indicated that people could "see through" accounting figures. That is, the figures were assessed for reliability and credibility before investors chose to reflect effects in share prices. Sometimes investors believed the accounting figures; sometimes they did not. *If* new information was provided in the financial statements it was quickly reflected in share prices by investors who bought and sold.

Evidence also showed that potential creditors and investors wanted *more* financial information about a company. Since much of the desired information could not be captured by the conventional balance sheet and income statement (which were primarily concerned with *measurement*) the logical step became one of providing notes which give greater *disclosure*. The importance of *measurement* and *disclosure*, and the relative significance of each in different situations is discussed from time to time throughout the book. Together with market efficiency research, the implications of measurement and disclosure are extremely important for persons interested in accounting — either as preparers or users, or as both.

Stock market reaction

Chapter 15 examines the use of financial statements for various investment decisions. In preparation for discussions which precede Chapter 15, we ought to look at some interesting background material about a company such as Labatt's. The shareholders' equity section of the balance sheet shows that three different types of shares of Labatt's are held by persons, and one or more companies. Note 4 provides further information.

Labatt's shares are "listed" for trading on the Toronto Stock Exchange (TSE). Listing facilitates share-trading; a student, for instance, could easily buy shares of Labatt's by using the TSE's services to stockbrokers. In order to become listed for trading, a company must comply with the rules of the exchange. Some of these rules pertain to disclosure of financial information, and the need to give "timely" or prompt disclosure. Because Labatt's shares are traded publicly, the company also has to comply with securities legislation. In total, Labatt's statements and disclosure must be in accordance with the wishes of many authorities.

During 1978 and 1979 prices per share of Labatt's shares ranged as follows on the TSE:

	High	*Low*
Series A Preferred shares	$25½	$18
Class A Common	26⅜	18
Class B Common	22⅜	19¾

We can check to see what the *current* prices of Labatt's shares are by examining the financial section of most large Canadian daily newspapers. If we multiply the number of shares outstanding by the share price, we can *approximate* (not determine precisely) a market value for the company. For example, at a price of $21 times the number of shares outstanding in early 1979, Labatt's market value would be around $250 million. This is considerably higher than the shareholders' equity of $215 million as reported by the balance sheet.

Some of the reasons for the $35 million ($250 – $215) difference have been explained previously; for example, the balance sheet reports historical cost. Another is that accounting reports do not measure everything which investors might consider important in a company. For instance, accounting statements generally do not measure the worth of people, and good managers may be the prime reason for the success of some companies. Also, financial statements (which tend to report on the past and present) may not reflect the future prospects for a company; market prices are estimates of future success. Other reasons are given throughout the book.

The figure of $250 million may not reflect a market price if 100 percent of the company's shares were sold *as a group*. The $21 price per share might only represent the price (excluding commissions to brokers) at which a few shares could be bought. A few shares carry little power and authority because the holder is not entitled to manage the company. However, when a large block of shares is acquired, and the owner of the block could take over management of the company, an extra sum might have to be paid — perhaps as much as $25 to $30 per share. That is, a premium might have to paid to acquire a *control block*.

Earnings per share

Investment analysts sometimes use ratios when they compare companies for possible investment of clients' funds. The earnings per share statistic is one such ratio, and is designed, as its name indicates, to show how much net income has been earned for each share held by investors or owners of the company. Until the late 1960s, analysts employed many different ways of computing earnings (net income) per share. This lack of consistency obviously hampered a person's ability to make quick, informative comparisons. Consequently, the Canadian accounting profession decided to simplify the methods of computation in the 1970s, settling on five basic approaches to the most common objective of accounting and sets of facts.

Labatt's Consolidated Statement of Earnings provides two earnings per share ratios for 1978: $2.89 and $2.53. The $2.89 figure — labelled "earnings per common share" — is also known technically as "*basic* earnings per share." It is computed by dividing net earnings by the *average* number of common shares outstanding during the period. In Labatt's case, the preferred shareholders received a dividend of $695,000 (see the Consolidated Statement of Retained Earnings) which is not available to common shareholders. The basic earnings per share for Labatt's thus is:

$$\frac{\text{Net earnings} - \text{preferred dividend}}{\text{Average number of common shares outstanding}}$$

$$= \frac{\$33{,}895{,}000 - \$695{,}000}{11{,}488{,}000} = \$2.89 \text{ per share}$$

The figure of 11,488,000 shares is not available in Labatt's financial statements. However, it can be approximated by averaging the figures noted under "share capital" on the Consolidated Balance Sheet. The year-end figure of 11,582,609 (11,111,354 class A plus 471,255 class B common shares) and opening sum of 11,321,158 when averaged come close to 11,488,000. The difference results from common shares' being issued at various dates during the year.

Labatt's $2.53 figure, "fully diluted earnings per common share," recognizes that employees and others hold options to purchase Labatt's shares at low prices. Whenever these people choose to buy shares at the low prices this will increase the number of common shares outstanding and have the effect of lowering the $2.89 to $2.53. The fully diluted figure therefore is based on the *current* year's earnings but takes into account *some* possible (*future*) situations which will increase the number of outstanding common shares (denominator) held by investors.

We will return to the technical aspects of this topic later. However, at this point it is important to observe that different earnings per share computations exist to meet the needs of different users and to suit different factual situations. For example, basic earnings per share is based on more facts (e.g., the number of shares outstanding) than is the fully diluted computation (which uses estimates of the number of shares outstanding in the future). Basic earnings are therefore more *objective*. For those who wish information about the future, though, the fully diluted figure is more *relevant*.

Some people have considerable difficulty recognizing that accounting must be tailored to differences in objectives, facts and constraints. This difficulty can often be traced to false impressions repeatedly provided by others about the degree of precision in accounting. At the risk of boring some readers, the authors must emphasize the "tailoring theme." Its importance will become clearer as we proceed. Those who are having difficulty at this point should not be concerned, because we return to most of the technical topics at various points in the book. Once the broad themes have been grasped, it becomes easier to explain the mechanical and technical features. It also becomes easier to point out strengths and limitations of different accounting methods for different situations that people tend to encounter in their careers.

Price/earnings ratio

Financial analysts and stock (share) brokers frequently tend to compare companies using various economic and statistical techniques and ratio analysis. The *value* or *worth* today of a company is dependent upon its *future earnings*, and other factors such as risk (or the degree to which the earnings might vary from one's prediction of what they might be). Prediction of future earnings is an important exercise in the financial community.

Estimates of future earnings are presumably incorporated into current share prices. When one divides the current price per share by earnings per share, a ratio with rough implications results. In the case of Labatt's, the price/earnings ratio might be:

$$\frac{\text{Price per common share}}{\text{Earnings per common share}} = \frac{\$21}{\$2.89} = 7.3 \text{ times}$$

In a literal sense, if no changes occur, investors are paying for 7.3 years of presumably future earnings when they pay $21 per share, and the *basic* earnings per share figure is used in computations. Observe that for convenience we have assumed that future earnings per share will be $2.89.

The price/earnings ratio has some tricky effects. If earnings are expected to increase substantially in the future, the price/earnings ratio is likely to be quite high — possibly in the 30 to 40 or more range. This arises because market price (the numerator) reflects future earnings but earnings per share (the denominator) is based on current earnings. The ratio therefore tends to be a rough guide to the relationship between current earnings and expected future earnings. It also tends to reflect *risk*, or variability in earnings. For example, a company subject to considerable earnings variability (perhaps an oil drilling company) might have a low price/earnings ratio until it strikes oil, causing an increase in the market price of its common shares. Then, for a few years the price/earnings ratio could be quite high. Once the oil flows and produces stable earnings for the company the ratio would drop because current and expected earnings would be approximately the same. Finally, the ratio varies considerably with major changes in the stock market. An economic depression, high inflation, and many other factors affect *general* market prices, causing changes in share prices of individual companies. In summary, the price/earnings ratio must be used with great care because of its crudeness.

Return on investment

For an investor, return on investment usually is expressed as the percentage of net income to investment. For example, the return on investment on a Canada Savings Bond may be 9 percent. The investor might buy a $1,000 savings bond and receive $90 in interest every November 1. Or, the investor might buy $1,000 worth of shares in Labatt's and receive $45 per year in cash dividends — a return of 4.5 percent. If Labatt's share prices rise, the investor could include share-price increases in the numerator of the computation. This would raise the return on investment.

Return on investment can also be calculated for the entire company. As mentioned in Chapter 1, there are different valuations which might be used in the calculations. If we choose to employ accounting financial statement figures, the return on investment (ROI) for Labatt's common and preferred shareholders is:

$$\text{Return on Investment (ROI)} = \frac{\text{Net Income or Earnings}}{\text{Investment (such as Shareholders' Equity)}}$$

$$= \frac{\$33{,}895{,}000}{215{,}571{,}000} = 15.7\%$$

We could easily obtain other ROIs (sometimes called yields) by using current valuations. All ratios must be used with care, and ROI is no exception. Chapter 15 covers investment analysis in greater depth.

Summary

In this chapter we have presented an overview of the three primary financial statements — the balance sheet (statement of financial position), the income statement, and the statement of changes in financial position — as well as a secondary statement, the statement of changes in retained earnings. The chapter was intended to familiarize the reader with the purposes of each statement, with its underlying nature, with its basic format, and with the terminology conventionally employed.

This chapter also noted the importance of *disclosure* as well as *measurement*. Notes to financial statements can convey information which is not readily packaged in typical financial statements. Notes (1) help accountants and managers to cater to a variety of *objectives* or users of financial statements, and (2) help to clarify for readers that *factual situations* may actually not be that clear, and (3) help to respond to different *constraints*. Labatt's, for example, has to adhere to regulations or constraints of the Canada Business Corporations Act and Regulations, Securities Acts, and the Toronto Stock Exchange.

Accounting must be tailored to specific situations, where possible. From a learning standpoint we must focus on what type of accounting makes sense under different objectives-facts-constraints. Whenever we learn about an accounting procedure or technique (such as the earnings per share statistic), we must understand the situations where the technique applies and where it does not. Otherwise, we fail to meet our prime objective of learning how to become good users (managers, investors, etc.) and preparers (vice-president of finance, controller, etc.). If we learn the techniques and nothing else we become bookkeepers, and little more. The techniques can easily change as environmental factors which affect business and accounting change.

The next few chapters move us away from the overview and purposes of accounting into procedures and techniques. Although we will have our hands full during this period with the "how-to-do-it", we must rise above the "how" from time to time to learn the "why."

Questions, Problems and Cases

Questions

2-1 Explain the purpose(s) of the
(i) balance sheet
(ii) income statement
(iii) statement of changes in financial position
(iv) statement of retained earnings
(v) notes to the financial statements.

2-2 Define the following terms: assets, liabilities, owners' equity, revenues, and expenses.
Explain the limitation(s) of each of the above definitions. Be specific and use examples to support your position.

2-3 A bookkeeper recently totaled up the recorded assets of a firm and found that they came to $1,398,576. The total liabilities came to $600,000 and the total owners' equity to $800,000. Are such totals possible in the context of the double-entry bookkeeping process unless an error has been made? Suppose instead that the total assets were equal to liabilities plus owners' equity. Do such totals ensure that no accounting errors have been made? Give examples to support your position.

2-4 What is meant by a *current asset*? How is it possible that the common shares of XYZ Limited, owned by another company, may be recorded as a noncurrent asset? What is (are) the purpose(s) of segregating current and noncurrent assets?

2-5 Included among a firm's noncurrent assets are "unamortized corporate organization costs, $25,000." What is this item? How would you justify reporting this item as an asset? Is there an alternative treatment? How might you justify it?

2-6 The same firm has recorded among its current liabilities "advances from customers, $3,000." Why is this amount a liability? What impact did receipt of the $3,000 have on the accounting equation?

2-7 A company reported substantial earnings for the last several years, yet it is about to file for bankruptcy. How is such a situation possible?

2-8 A firm recently received a cheque from a customer for $10,000, yet it did not record such amount as "revenue." What are two possible reasons for its not doing so?

2-9 A firm recently purchased equipment for $80,000 yet did not record an expense. How would this accounting treatment be justified? Will the amount paid ever be recorded as an expense? When?

2-10 What is meant by *owners' equity*? Why is owners' equity not necessarily indicative of the amount of cash that would be returned to the owners if the assets of the business were to be sold and the creditors paid the amounts owed to them?

2-11 What is meant by *preferred shares*? What preferences do preferred shareholders have over common shareholders? What rights do common shareholders have that preferred shareholders generally do not have?

2-12 What are *extraordinary items*? Why are they reported on the income statement apart from ordinary operating revenues and expenses?

2-13 Is it possible for a firm to have a substantial balance in retained earnings and still be unable to declare a cash dividend? Why?

2-14 A company has assets of $3 million and liabilities of $2 million. There are 100,000 common shares outstanding. Net income for the year was $150,000. The common shares of the company are being traded on a major stock exchange at $30 per share. Compute the return on investment (ROI) and the price/earnings ratio. What is the purpose of these measures?

2-15 The statement of changes in financial position may be in balance form or highlight a change in one or more accounts by using a design which stresses the bottom line. How would you decide on an appropriate design for a statement of changes in financial position for a company?

2-16 Different earnings per share computations exist to meet the needs of different users and to suit different factual situations. Explain.

2-17 What are the implications of market-efficiency research for financial reporting in Canada?

2-18 It is sometimes said that the usefulness of accounting information in making intelligent decisions (by shareholders, managers, etc.) is severely limited both by the inherent limitations of accounting as an information resource and by the human characteristics of the decision-makers themselves, who are seldom, if ever, the "rational men" of economic theory.

Required:

What are the "inherent limitations of accounting" and "human characteristics of decision-makers" to which the above statement refers?

(CICA 1974)

Problems

P2-1 Indicate the nature (i.e., descriptive account title) of the assets and liabilities (if any) that would receive accounting recognition on the books of the Utica Company Ltd. as a result of the following events or transactions:

a. Utica employs six men to perform routine maintenance work at a rate of $5 per hour. The men work a total of 200 hours.
b. Utica signs a three-year contract with a security company. The security company will provide guard service for Utica at a cost of $200 per month.
c. The security company performs one month's services as promised.
d. Utica orders machinery and equipment at a cost of $10,000.
e. The machinery and equipment previously ordered are received and installed as agreed upon by the manufacturer.
f. A customer orders 300 units of Utica's product at a price of $2 per unit.
g. Utica ships the merchandise previously ordered.
h. Utica borrows $40,000 at an interest rate of 10 percent per year. It gives the bank a four-year note.
i. One year elapses, and Utica has paid the bank neither principal nor interest on the note.

j. Utica guarantees to repair any defective products. During the year it sells 10,000 units of product. It estimates from previous experience that 5 percent of such units will be returned for repair work. It estimates also that the cost of such repairs will be $1 per unit.

P2-2 Arrange a sheet of paper into three columns, each corresponding to a term in the accounting equation:

Assets = Liabilities + Owners' equity

Required:

a. Indicate the impact of each of the following transactions on the accounting equation. Suggest titles for the specific accounts that would be affected. Indicate which of the accounts are current and which are noncurrent.
   (i) A company purchases equipment for $7,000 cash.
   (ii) A company borrows $3,000 and issues a sixty-day note.
   (iii) A company borrows $5,000 and issues a three-year note.
   (iv) A company purchases inventory for $1,000 and promises to pay within thirty days.
   (v) A company purchases inventory for $600 cash.
   (vi) A company purchases a building for $100,000 and issues ten-year bonds for the same amount.
   (vii) A company repays a five-year note for $1,790.
   (viii) A company collects $5,000 that was owed by its customers.
   (ix) A company declares and pays a dividend of $10,000.

b. How does the segregation of assets and liabilities into current and noncurrent categories assist the users of the financial statements?

P2-3 Arrange a sheet of paper into three columns, each corresponding to a term in the accounting equation:

Assets = Liabilities + Owners' equity

Required:

a. Indicate the impact that each of the following transactions would have on the accounting equation. Suggest titles for the specific accounts that would be affected.
   (i) Whitman and Farrel form a corporation. It issues 500 common shares to each of the two founders for $3 per share.
   (ii) The corporation borrows $3,000 from a bank, giving the bank a one-year note.
   (iii) The corporation purchases furniture and fixtures for $5,000. It pays $1,000 cash and gives a six-month note for the balance.
   (iv) The corporation rents a building. It pays, in advance, the first month's rent of $700.
   (v) The corporation purchases office supplies for $400 cash.
   (vi) The corporation purchases inventory for future sale to customers for $1,200 cash.

b. Compute the closing "balance" in each of the accounts. Summarize the balances in the form of a balance sheet.

c. What use(s) might be made of this balance sheet?

d. What possible adjustments could be made to this balance sheet? Explain your reasoning.

P2-4 The following account balances are taken from the records of the Mintz Company, a sole proprietorship, as of December 31, 19x8.

Cash	$18,000
H. Mintz, capital	51,600
Sales	72,000
Cost of goods sold	52,000
Prepaid insurance	1,000
Advances from customers	3,000
Patents	8,000
Depreciation expense	2,500
Insurance expense	2,000
Interest revenue	500
Interest expense	900
Prepaid interest	200
Interest payable	600
Accounts receivable	10,000
Inventory	9,000
Rent expense	6,000
Advertising expense	5,000
Notes payable (due in 3 years)	8,000
Buildings and equipment	26,000
Notes receivable	10,000
Accounts payable	19,000

Required:

a. Prepare an income statement and a balance sheet. Title and date the statements as appropriate, and, insofar as the information permits, separate assets and liabilities into current and noncurrent classifications.

b. Assume the role of a short-term creditor, indicate the information you would use from the statements in deciding whether to loan the company money. Why? What additional information would you require?

P2-5 The Lemon Company was organized as a partnership on January 2, 19x5. Each of its two owners contributed $10,000 in cash to start the business. At December 31, 19x5 the company had on hand the following assets: cash, $18,000; accounts receivable, $3,000; inventory available for sale, $10,000; furniture and fixtures, $25,000.

The company owed suppliers (i.e., accounts payable) $8,000 and had notes outstanding to a bank (due in 19x8) of $16,000.

Required:

a. Prepare a balance sheet as of December 31, 19x5.

b. Assuming that the owners neither made additional contributions of capital to the business nor made any withdrawals, compute income for 19x5.

c. Assume instead that the owners withdrew $4,000 from the business. Compute income for 19x5.

d. Why would it be useful to disclose in the financial statements that the notes outstanding to the bank are due in 19x8?

P2-6 The balance sheets and income statements of the Flicker Co. Ltd. for the years 19x2 through 19x5 are indicated below. Also indicated are dividends paid during those years. Some critical figures, however, have been omitted.

	19x2	*19x3*	*19x4*	*19x5*
		Balance sheet December 31		
		Assets		
Cash	$100	$200	$?	$300
Accounts receivable	200	100	300	100
Inventory	350	?	100	100
Building and equipment	600	900	800	400
		Liabilities and owners' equity		
Accounts payable	$200	$100	$200	$300
Notes payable	?	600	300	100
Common shares	200	200	200	300
Retained earnings	100	400	?	?
		Income statement		
Sales	$?	$1,000	$?	$1,200
Cost of goods sold and other operating expenses	500	?	600	?
Net income	?	?	400	300
Dividends paid	$ 0	$ 150	$200	$?

Required:

a. Assuming the Flicker Co. Ltd. began operations on January 1, 19x2, provide the missing figures.

b. Assume the role of a shareholder of the Flicker Co. Ltd. How would you use the above information to evaluate the performance of the managers? What additional information would you require?

P2-7 Many balance sheet accounts have a direct relationship to those on the income statement.

a. The 1/1/19x8 balance sheet of a firm reported "prepaid insurance, $1,200." During the course of the year the firm purchased an additional $1,400 worth of insurance. The income statement of the firm for the year indicated that insurance expense for the year was $1,300 (i.e., that $1,300 of insurance had been "used up"). How much "prepaid insurance" should be reported on the 12/31/19x8 balance sheet?

b. The balance sheet of 1/1/19x8 also reported "prepaid rent, $200." During the course of the year the firm made rent payments of $800. Since the monthly rent on the premises occupied is $100 per month, rent expense per the income statement was $1,200. How much "rent liability" (or "accrued rent payable," as it is often called) should be reported on the 12/31/19x8 balance sheet?

c. The balance sheet of 1/1/19x8 reported "interest liability" of $200 representing two months' interest on a note outstanding. During the year the firm made interest payments of $1,100. The year-end balance sheet reported "interest liability" of $300. How much "interest expense" should be reported on the 19x8 income statement?

d. As of 1/1/19x8, the firm had inventory on hand of $3,000. At the end of the year the inventory on hand was $2,000. During the year the firm purchased new merchandise of $20,000. What was the cost of the merchandise sold during the year?

e. Assume instead that the firm had inventory on hand at the beginning of the year at $1,000. During the year it sold merchandise that had originally cost $18,000. At the end of the year it had inventory on hand of $3,000. How much inventory did it purchase during the year?

P2-8 Arrange a sheet of paper into three columns, each corresponding to a term in the accounting equation:

Assets = Liabilities + Owners' equity

Required:

Indicate the impact that each of the following transactions would have on the accounting equation. Suggest titles for each of the specific accounts that would be affected.

a. Interior Products Co. Ltd. purchases furniture and fixtures for $30,000, giving a five-year note as payment.

b. The firm purchases merchandise inventory for $15,000 "on account".

c. The firm, realizing that it had purchased an excessive amount of furniture, sells a portion of it. It sells for $3,000 cash, furniture that had initially cost $3,000.

d. The firm sells an additional amount of furniture. It sells for $5,000 cash, furniture that had initially cost $2,000. (Has the "level" of net assets increased as the result of this transaction?)

e. The firm sells for $800 "on account" merchandise inventory that had been purchased for $600.

f. The firm purchases supplies for $300 on account.

g. The firm uses supplies that had originally cost $200.

h. The firm collects $600 of the amount owed to it by customers.

i. The firm pays one month's rent in advance, $400.

j. After the end of the one month, the firm wishes to give accounting recognition to the fact that it had occupied the rented premises for the one month for which it had paid in advance.

P2-9 Indicated below are balance sheets of the Murray Company, a sole proprietorship, as of December 31, 19x3, and 19x4. Also provided is information pertaining to financial events that took place during 19x4.

	December 31, 19x3	*December 31,* 19x4
Assets		
Current assets		
Cash	$ 30,000	$ 20,000
Accounts receivable	40,000	70,000
Inventory	39,000	44,000
Prepaid rent	5,000	5,000
	114,000	139,000

Noncurrent assets		
Land	50,000	40,000
Building	160,000	150,000
Equipment	15,000	45,000
	225,000	235,000
Total assets	$339,000	$374,000
Liabilities and owner's equity		
Current liabilities		
Accounts payable	$ 71,000	$ 68,000
Wages payable	5,000	4,000
Interest payable	3,000	2,000
	79,000	74,000
Noncurrent liabilities		
Notes payable	60,000	75,000
Owner's equity	200,000	225,000
Total liabilities and owner's equity	$339,000	$374,000

Additional Information:

1. The company had income in 19x4 of $37,000. Working capital provided by operations was actually $52,000, since $15,000 of the expenses deducted from revenues did not involve an outlay of current assets or an increase in current liabilities—i.e., depreciation expense involved a reduction in buildings and equipment (a noncurrent asset).
2. The company purchased equipment (for cash) at a cost of $35,000.
3. The company sold a parcel of land that had cost $10,000 for $10,000 (cash).
4. The company borrowed from the bank an additional $15,000 and agreed to repay the loan in full in five years.
5. Mr. Murray the owner of the company made cash withdrawals totaling $12,000.

Required:

a. Compute working capital as of December 31, 19x3.
b. Compute working capital as of December 31, 19x4.
c. Compute the increase or decrease in working capital during the year 19x4.
d. Prepare a statement of changes in financial position for the year ended December 31, 19x4. Use the following format:
   Sources of working capital:
   Applications of working capital:
   Net increase (decrease) in working capital for the year.
e. Professional judgment is required in selecting an appropriate design for the statement of changes in financial position. Outline the conditions when you recommend the use of a working capital design for the statement of changes in financial position.
f. Assume the role of a creditor. How would you use the statement of

changes in financial position which you have prepared? Specifically indicate the information which you would use and why.

P2-10 Refer to the financial statements of John Labatt Limited contained in Exhibit 2-7.

a. With respect to the income statement of John Labatt Limited:
   (i) Why are net earnings divided into the following three sources: operating income, investment and sundry income, and equity in net earnings of partly-owned businesses?
   (ii) Assume the role of a shareholder of the company. How would you use the information in the statement of earnings to evaluate the performance of John Labatt Limited?
   (iii) Is there sufficient information in the statement of earnings to determine the amount that the company earned in each of the following activities: brewing, consumer products and agricultural products? How would you determine this? Why is information on particular segments of company activity useful?

b. With respect to the balance sheet of John Labatt Limited:
   (i) Calculate the current ratio (current assets divided by current liabilities) for April 30, 1978 and for April 30, 1977. Is the company more or less liquid than it was in 1977? For what purpose would you use the current ratio of the company?
   (ii) Accounts receivable and inventories at April 30, 1978 have increased significantly from April 30, 1977. Why?
   (iii) Did the company grant any new mortgages, loans and advances during the year?
   (iv) Why did the preferred shares issued and outstanding decline from 828,173 at April 30, 1977 to 605,080 at April 30, 1978?
   (v) Who is the principal shareholder of John Labatt Limited? Why may it be important to know this?

c. With respect to the statement of changes in financial position:
   (i) List some examples of charges to earnings which do not reduce working capital.
   (ii) How much did the company pay for the acquisition of Casabello Wines Ltd.? What was the book value of the net tangible assets acquired? Why did John Labatt Limited pay more than the book value of the net assets for Casabello? Will John Labatt Limited have to pay the entire purchase price which it recorded for Casabello?
   (iii) Why does the statement of changes in financial position indicate both the increase and the reduction in mortgages, loans and advances for the year?

d. With respect to the notes to the financial statements:
   (i) Why does John Labatt Limited disclose its accounting policies?
   (ii) What is the purpose of disclosing information about leases, commitments and guarantees?
   (iii) What is the purpose of disclosing information about the subsequent events of the company?

e. The fiscal year of John Labatt Limited ends April 30, 1978. Why do you suspect that John Labatt Limited has elected to base its financial reports on a fiscal year that does not coincide with the calendar year?

f. Compare "return on investment" in 1978 with that in 1977. What have you chosen as your investment base? Why?

g. Assume the role of a potential shareholder of John Labatt Limited. How would you decide whether to invest in this company?

Cases

*C2-1 The following data relates to W. Entry Co. Ltd.

	September 30 *19x1*	*19x2*
Cash	$ 5,000	$10,000
Accounts receivable	45,000	80,000
Inventory	15,000	25,000
Plant, property and equipment (net after deduction of depreciation)	100,000	90,000
Mortgage payable (secured by plant, property and equipment)	40,000	40,000

Additional information:

1. Cash received from customers during the year amounted to $60,000.
2. Payments made to suppliers for merchandise during the year amounted to $35,000.

Required:

Compute sales revenue, cost of goods sold, net income and shareholders' equity (9/30/19x2) from the above information. Indicate the assumptions that you have made.

C2-2 As of December 31, 19x8, the balance sheet of Dough Company Ltd. appeared as follows:

Cash	$ 85,000
Other current assets	75,000
Other assets, including buildings, land, and equipment	670,000
Total assets	$830,000
Liabilities	$220,000
Common shares (10,000 issued and outstanding)	10,000
Retained earnings	600,000
Total equities	$830,000

In 19x8, Dough Company Ltd. had earnings of $40,000. Since there were 10,000 common shares outstanding (par value per share, $1.00) earnings per share were $4. In 19x8, the company declared no dividends since the directors claimed funds were needed for expansion.

Shortly after the close of the year, the president of the company received a letter from a shareholder protesting the company's refusal to declare a dividend. The letter said in part: "When I studied accounting 'retained earnings' were called 'surplus.' No amount of name-changing can obscure the fact that the company has $600,000 available for distribution to shareholders."

Required:

a. Assume the role of the president of Dough Company Ltd. Prepare a report to the shareholder in response to his protest.

b. Suppose that instead of earnings of $40,000 the company had a loss of $10,000. The company nevertheless declared a dividend of $2.00 per share. A disgruntled shareholder questioned the decision and wrote to the president:

"Dividends are supposed to be distributions of earnings. How is it possible to pay a dividend in a year in which there were no earnings?" How would you respond to his question?

C2-3 Rod Skinner made a contract with a farmer to purchase a quantity of Christmas trees, which he trucked to the city and offered for sale on a rented lot. By December 20th he had sold half of his trees.

Rod often bargains with his customers over the selling price of a tree. Thus prices tend to drop towards Christmas day in order to clear all the trees off the lot. The tree inventory is financed by a loan from the bank.

A friend passing by asked Rod how much profit he had made on the trees already sold. Rod threw up his hands, explaining: "I don't know. My accountant looks after all my bookkeeping and she tells me that it is pointless to determine profit until Christmas day."

Required:

a. Assume the role of Rod's accountant. Explain why you have told Rod to wait until Christmas day to determine profit.

b. As Rod's accountant what information can you give Rod at this time (December 20) to aid in evaluating his position and success?

c. Assume the bank has just called (December 20) and wants a report on how Rod is doing. What accounting information can be given to the banker?

d. What value would you assign to the inventory of trees on December 26th?

Adapted from R.M. Skinner, *Accounting Principles* (Toronto: CICA, 1972)

C2-4 A student has just been informed that she is the recipient of an unusual inheritance. She is to be given a choice of being the sole owner of either Company A, Company B or Company C (or receive nothing), and has been given 24 hours to decide which company to choose. The only information she has about the companies is noted below:

(1) Each company commenced business at the beginning of this year with $1,000,000 cash. Each is in the steel warehousing business wherein they buy from steel mills and sell to many small users of steel.

(2) Each company entered into the same transactions during the year — several purchases and one sale of steel.

(3) The partial income statements of each company are:

	Company A	*Company B*	*Company C*
Revenue	$100,000	$100,000	$100,000
Cost of goods sold	70,000	80,000	90,000
Gross profit	$30,000	$20,000	$10,000

(4) All three companies are located in Canada.
(5) Each company is managed by a skilled manager.
(6) The student is not allowed to interview any employees.

Required:
Which company would you advise her to choose? Why?

3 *The Recording Process*

This chapter will serve to introduce the means by which transactions are recorded and also the *accounting cycle* — the procedures that lead from the initial recognition of a financial event to the preparation of financial statements. Although this text is not primarily directed to practices of maintaining books and records, a familiarity with them will likely facilitate an understanding of the issues to be discussed in subsequent chapters.

Ledger Accounts

The basic accounting equation — assets = liabilities + owners' equity — or the slightly expanded equation — assets = liabilities + capital contributed by owners + retained earnings — serves as the basis for all accounting transactions. Conceivably, all financial events that affect a business and are deemed worthy of accounting recognition could be recorded in a single ledger (or book of accounts), derived from the basic equation. Changes in assets would be indicated on the left-hand side of the page; changes in liabilities or owners' equity would be indicated on the right.

EXAMPLE

1. The CDE Company Limited issues shares for $25,000 cash. (An asset, cash, is increased; owner's equity, common shares, is increased.)
2. The company purchases furniture and fixtures for $10,000 on account.

(An asset, furniture and fixtures, is increased; a liability, accounts payable, is increased.)

3. The company purchases merchandise for $7,000 cash. (An asset, merchandise, is increased; an asset, cash, is decreased.)
4. The company pays $5,000 of the amount it owes on account. (An asset, cash, is decreased; a liability, accounts payable, is decreased.)

CDE Company Limited
"General Ledger"

Assets		*Liabilities and owners' equity*	
1. Cash (asset +)	+$25,000	1. Common shares (owners' equity +)	+$25,000
2. Furniture and fixtures (asset +)	+ 10,000	2. Accounts payable (liability +)	+ 10,000
3. Merchandise (asset +)	+ 7,000		
Cash (asset −)	− 7,000		
4. Cash (asset −)	− 5,000	4. Accounts payable (liability −)	− 5,000
	$30,000		$30,000

The ledger indicates that after the fourth transaction the firm has assets of $30,000 and liabilities and owners' equity of the same amount. The ledger reveals that the accounts are "in balance" (they would have to be unless an error was made), and it indicates the total assets and the total liabilities and owners' equity. But by itself it provides little information that would be useful to either management or owners. Since each side of the ledger page combines changes in a great variety of accounts, the balance in any particular account is not readily available. To find the amount of cash on hand, for example, it would be necessary to search the entire page (or entire book insofar as there were numerous transactions) for all entries affecting cash. How much more convenient it would be if a separate page were provided for each account. Thus,

CDE Company Limited
General Ledger

Assets

Cash

(1)	25,000	(3)	7,000
		(4)	5,000

Liabilities and owners' equity

Accounts Payable

(4)	5,000	(2)	10,000

CDE Company Limited
General Ledger (Continued)

Assets			*Liabilities and owners' equity*		
	Furniture & fixtures			**Common shares**	
(2)	10,000			(1)	25,000
	Merchandise				
(3)	7,000				

In the illustration each of the "T"s represents (for instructional purposes) a separate page in the ledger or book of accounts. Thus, there is a separate page or "T account" for cash, for furniture and fixtures, for accounts payable, etc.

An increase in an *asset* account is recorded on the *left* side of the ledger page or T account; a *decrease* in an asset account is recorded on the *right* side. Conversely, an *increase* in a *liability* or *owners' equity* account is recorded on the *right* side of the ledger page or T account; a *decrease* in a *liability or owners' equity* account is recorded on the *left* side. The balance in an account at any particular time can be determined by subtracting the amounts recorded on one side from those recorded on the other. The convention of recording increases in assets on the left side of the account and increases in liabilities and owners' equity on the right may be related directly to the accounting equation (assets = liabilities + owners' equity) in which assets appear to the left of the equal sign and liabilities and owners' equity to the right.

Debits and Credits

In accounting terminology, any entry to the left side of an account is referred to as a *debit* and any entry to the right side as a *credit*. The term *charge* is often used interchangeably with *debit*.

Debits are used to signify *increases in assets* or *decreases in liabilities or owners' equities*. Credits are used to represent *decreases in assets* or *increases in liabilities or owners' equities*. If a company purchases merchandise for cash, the accountant would *debit* the merchandise account and *credit* the cash account. At any given point in time it would ordinarily be expected that asset accounts would show a *debit* balance (that is, the entries on the left side of the account would exceed in dollar amount those on the right) and liabilities and owners' equity accounts a *credit* balance.

Debits and credits are often a source of confusion to an individual who has had dealings with either a bank or a department store. Should a person deposit funds in the bank, the bank would ordinarily *credit* his account. Should he withdraw funds or "bounce" a check, the bank might send him a *debit* (debt) memo. Similarly, when a person returns merchandise to a store, the store credits his account; it advises him that his liability to the store has been reduced. Does it not appear that *credits* are associated with increases in assets and *debits* with increases in liabilities? Bear in mind, however, that both the bank and the department store maintain their records from their own points of view, not those of their customers. Thus, when a customer deposits money in the bank, the liability of the bank to the customer is increased. Hence the bank *credits* his account on its books. (If the customer maintained a set of books, then he would *debit* his account, "cash in bank," to reflect the debt of the bank to him.) Similarly, when the department store accepts returned merchandise from a customer the accounts receivable of the store have been decreased; thus the store *credits* the account on its books that represents the amount owed by the customer.

Journal Entries

Each T account represents a separate page in a book of accounts. Such a book is often referred to as a *general ledger*. Since a transaction normally affects two or more accounts, each transaction necessitates entries on two or more pages. No one page will contain a complete record of the transaction; at best it will indicate only one half of the transaction. To maintain a comprehensive history of all transactions that affect the various accounts, accountants conventionally maintain a *journal* — a book which serves as the source of many of the entries to the various accounts. The purchase of merchandise for cash ($7,000) necessitates that a debit entry be made in the merchandise account and a credit entry be made in the cash account. The journal is a convenient place to indicate both accounts affected by the transaction. At the time of purchase, the accountant would record the following in the journal:

Debit: Merchandise	$7,000	
Credit: Cash		$7,000

More commonly, the words debit and credit are omitted from the entry, and the accountant indicates a debit or credit by placement of the account title and the amounts. The account to be debited is placed along the left-hand margin, and that to be credited is indented approximately one-half inch. Similarly, the amount to be debited is shown approximately one-half inch to the left of that to be credited. A brief explanation is often indicated beneath the entry, and the entry is numbered or lettered to facilitate referencing. Thus,

(1)		
Merchandise	$7,000	
Cash		$7,000
To record the purchase of merchandise.		

The amounts indicated in the journal would be posted to or recorded in the appropriate ledger account either at the time the transaction is recorded in the journal or, if more convenient, after a number of transactions have been recorded. A cross-referencing system between the journal and ledger is set forth by noting the journal entry number in each ledger account.

Some simple transactions can be used to illustrate the relationship between entries in the journal and those in the various ledger accounts. In this and in several subsequent examples the nature of the account (asset, liability, owners' equity) and whether it has increased (+) or decreased (−) will sometimes be indicated in parentheses next to each journal entry.

B. Heller decides to establish a television repair service.

1. He signs a lease on a small store.
2. He takes $10,000 of his personal funds and deposits them in a chequing account in the name of "Heller TV Repair Service."
3. He purchases tools and test equipment for $5,000. He gives a two-year note for the full amount.
4. He purchases parts for $3,000. He pays $2,000 cash and receives 30 days' credit for the balance.
5. He pays rent in advance for the first three months, $200 per month.

Required Journal Entries

January 2, 19x2:

(1)		
Cash in bank (assets +)	$10,000	
B. Heller, invested capital (owner's equity +)		$10,000
To record the initial contribution of cash.		

(2)		
Tools and equipment (asset +)	$5,000	
Notes payable (liability +)		$5,000
To record the purchase of tools and equipment.		

(3)

	Debit	Credit
Parts inventory (asset +)	$3,000	
Cash (asset −)		$2,000
Accounts payable (liability +)		1,000

To record the purchase of the parts. (Note that a journal entry can combine more than one debit or credit. The account "notes payable" is used to record a liability when a written note is given by the borrower. When short-term trade credit is accepted the liability is recorded as an "account payable.")

(4)

	Debit	Credit
Prepaid rent (asset +)	$600	
Cash (asset −)		$600

To record the rent paid in advance. ("Prepaid rent" represents the right to use the store for three months. It is a current asset — one that will be "written off" or *amortized* as it expires over the three-month period.)

The journal entries would be *posted* to the various ledger accounts:

Assets

Cash in bank

Debit		Credit	
(1)	10,000	(3)	2,000
		(4)	600

Tools and equipment

Debit		Credit	
(2)	5,000		

Parts inventory

Debit		Credit	
(3)	3,000		

Prepaid rent

Debit		Credit	
(4)	600		

Liabilities + owners' equity

Notes payable

Debit		Credit	
		(2)	5,000

Accounts payable

Debit		Credit	
		(3)	1,000

B. Heller, invested capital

Debit		Credit	
		(1)	10,000

If Heller decided to prepare a balance sheet, after the four transactions had been journalized and posted, then it would be necessary to determine and summarize the balances in each account. The balance in each account can readily be calculated by subtracting the total credits from the total debits. Thus, the balance in the cash in bank account is $10,000 minus the sum of $2,000 and $600: $7,400.

The balance sheet separates current from noncurrent assets and liabilities. In the example, the note payable is classified as a noncurrent liability since it will not be due for over one year. Similarly, the tools and equipment are classified as noncurrent assets, because they are expected to have a useful life greater than one year. Prepaid rent, the parts inventory, and the cash in bank are all expected either to be used up or to "turn over" (be replaced by like assets) within a one-year period, so they are classified as current assets.

Heller TV Repair Service
Balance Sheet
January 2, 19x2

Assets			*Liabilities and owner's equity*		
Current			Current liabilities		
Cash in bank	$7,400		Accounts payable	$1,000	
Parts inventory	3,000		Noncurrent liabilities		
Prepaid rent	600	$11,000	Notes payable	5,000	$ 6,000
Noncurrent			Owner's equity		
Tools and equipment		5,000	B. Heller, invested capital		10,000
		$16,000			$16,000

An additional example may serve to illustrate an accounting treatment which is given to other types of financial events. Prentice Limited is organized on June 1, 19x5. The following events occur during the company's first month of operation:

Date				
		(1)		
6/1	The company issues 10,000 shares to its two co-founders for $50 per share, which is received in cash.	Cash (asset +)	$500,000	
		Common shares (owners' equity +)		$500,000
		To record the sale of common shares.		
		(2)		
6/1	The firm issues $100,000 of long-term bonds, payable on June 1, 19x9, with interest payable semi-annually at the rate of 9% per annum.	Cash (asset +)	$100,000	
		Bonds payable (liability +)		$100,000
		To record the issue of long-term bonds.		

		(3)		
6/2	The company purchases a building for $300,000. It gives a down payment of $100,000 and a ten-year note for the balance.	Building (asset +) Cash (asset −) Notes payable (liability +) To record the purchase of the building.	$300,000	$100,000 200,000

		(4)		
6/3	The company purchases equipment for $100,000 and incurs installation and transportation costs of $20,000. The equipment is purchased "on sale." The salesman informs the purchaser that it normally sells for $130,000.	Equipment (asset +) Cash (asset −) To record the purchase of equipment.	$120,000	$120,000

(Note that the installation and transportation costs are necessary to bring the equipment to a *serviceable* condition; hence they are added to the cost of the equipment. The alleged discount of $30,000 is ignored. Except in highly unusual circumstances, an asset is recorded at the amount which is actually to be paid as long as the transaction is "at arm's length" — that is, between two independent parties. Such amount represents the fair market values of the assets both received and surrendered by the purchaser.)

		(5)		
6/27	The firm decides to rent out a portion of its building. The company acquires a lessee, and a five-year lease is signed. Rent is to be $1,000 per month, and three months' rent must be paid in advance. Occupancy is to begin July 1.	Cash (asset +) Rent received in advance (liability +) To record three months' rent received in advance.	$3,000	$3,000

(The company has received the cash. It is still obligated to provide services to the lessee.)

		(6)		
6/28	The company receives an invoice (a bill) from its attorneys — $5,000 — for services performed in incorporating the company.	Organization costs (asset +) Accounts payable (liability +) To record the costs of organizing the corporation.	$5,000	$5,000

(The organization costs, just like the cost of equipment or the prepaid rent, were incurred in order to benefit future accounting periods. Although they are "intangible" — they cannot be seen or felt — they are nevertheless *assets* of the company. Accounts payable, rather than cash, has been credited, because the company has not yet paid the invoice.)

6/28 The company hires J. Pringle as president. The two parties sign a two-year employment contract requiring the firm to compensate Pringle at a salary of $35,000 per year.

No entry is required.
Although the firm seemingly has incurred a liability of $70,000, the president has not yet performed any services for the company. As indicated previously, accountants generally record liabilities resulting from contracts only to the extent that services have been performed or cash has been paid. Thus, after Pringle has been employed for one month, the company will, at that time, record a liability of one twelfth of $35,000, or $2,917.

(7)

6/28 The company purchases merchandise for $60,000. The company is granted a "trade discount" (available to all commercial customers) of 10 percent.

	Debit	Credit
Merchandise inventory (asset +)	$54,000	
Accounts payable (liability +)		$54,000

To record the purchase of merchandise. (The firm will be required to pay $54,000; that is the "fair market" value of both the goods received and the consideration to be paid.)

(8)

6/28 The company purchases 300 shares of Labatt's at a cost of $6,100.

	Debit	Credit
Marketable securities (asset +)	$6,100	
Cash (asset −)		$6,100

To record the purchase of 300 shares of John Labatt Limited.

(9)

6/28 The company pays $5,000 of the amount it owes to its supplier.

	Debit	Credit
Accounts payable (liability −)	$5,000	
Cash (asset −)		$5,000

To record the payment to the supplier.

(10)

6/28 The company returns merchandise that is defective to the supplier. The merchandise cost $7,000 after taking into account the discount. The supplier gives the company credit for the merchandise returned.

	Debit	Credit
Accounts payable (liability −)	$7,000	
Merchandise inventory (asset −)		$7,000

To record the return of merchandise.

Date	Transaction	Entry
6/29	The company's officials read in the *Globe and Mail* that the price of 300 Labatt's shares has increased to $6,300.	No entry necessary. Increases in the market value of assets are generally not recorded in the accounts in Canada. This approach reflects a belief that market prices are not sufficiently objective for some traditional preparers of financial statements. Market values may be reported in notes to the financial statements. (See comments in Chapter 1.)

(11)

Date	Transaction	Entry	Debit	Credit
6/30	The market price of 300 Labatt's shares drops to $6,100 and one half are sold.	Cash (asset +)	$3,050	
		Marketable securities (asset −)		$3,050
		To record the sale of 150 Labatt's shares at original cost, resulting in no gain or loss.		

As before, the journal entries must be posted to ledger or T accounts so that the balances in the accounts can be summarized in a statement of position.

Assets

Cash

	Debit		Credit
(1)	500,000	(3)	100,000
(2)	100,000	(4)	120,000
(5)	3,000	(8)	6,100
(11)	3,050	(9)	5,000
	374,950		

Organization costs

	Debit		Credit
(6)	5,000		
	5,000		

Equipment

	Debit		Credit
(4)	120,000		
	120,000		

Merchandise inventory

	Debit		Credit
(7)	54,000	(10)	7,000
	47,000		

Liabilities and owners' equity

Accounts payable

	Debit		Credit
(9)	5,000	(6)	5,000
(10)	7,000	(7)	54,000
			47,000

Bonds payable

	Debit		Credit
		(2)	100,000
			100,000

Rent received in advance

	Debit		Credit
		(5)	3,000
			3,000

Notes payable

	Debit		Credit
		(3)	200,000
			200,000

Assets			
	Building		
(3)	300,000		
	300,000		

Liabilities and owners' equity			
	Common shares		
		(1)	500,000
			500,000

	Marketable securities		
(8)	6,100	(11)	3,050
	3,050		

To facilitate the process of summarizing the end-of-period balances, double lines have been drawn beneath the recorded debits and credits. The difference between the sums of the debits and credits has been indicated on the appropriate side of the T account. Such amount represents not only the balance at the close of one accounting period but also the balance at the beginning of the next accounting period. For example, if $374,950 is the cash balance at June 30, 19x5, it must also be the balance at July 1, 19x5. Thus, the same account — the same ledger sheet — that was used in June could also be used in July. The entries for the latter month would simply be recorded beneath the end-of-old-month (beginning-of-new-month) balances.

Prentice Limited
Balance Sheet
June 30, 19x5

Assets			*Liabilities and owners' equity*		
Current assets			Current liabilities		
Cash	$374,950		Accounts payable	$ 47,000	
Marketable securities	3,050		Rent received in advance	3,000	$ 50,000
Merchandise inventory	47,000	$425,000			
			Noncurrent liabilities		
Noncurrent assets			Notes payable	200,000	
Building	300,000		Bonds payable	100,000	300,000
Equipment	120,000				
Organization costs	5,000	425,000	Total liabilities		350,000
			Owners' equity		
			Common shares — issued and outstanding: 10,000 shares without par value		500,000
		$850,000			$850,000

The $850,000 represents a total only — either total assets, or total liabilities and owners' equity. As we shall see later, the total has very little significance for users of financial statements.

Revenues and Expenses

Up to this point in the chapter, the illustrated transactions, with few exceptions, involved only exchanges among asset and liability accounts. Goods or services were received in exchange for other assets or for the firm's promise to pay in the future. Increases or decreases in liabilities were offset by concurrent increases or decreases in asset accounts. As a result, the level of *net* assets — that is, assets less liabilities (which is equal, by definition, to owners' equity) — remained the same. To refer back to the bathtub analogy used in the previous chapter, the level of water in the tub never changed as a consequence of the transactions illustrated. Owners' equity only changed when owners made their initial investment in the business.

Since the differences between assets and liabilities stayed constant once the owners made their initial contribution to form their companies, the subsequent transactions could not possibly have left them any better or worse off than they were at the very start of business. There were no inflows or outflows of net assets to the business, no revenues, and no expenses and hence no profits or earnings that could be retained in the business.

How does the accountant record those transactions that do, in fact, result in increases or decreases in the equity of the owners of a business? Assuming that the firm has not previously incurred losses which have reduced the equity of the owners below their original contribution, any transaction in which assets received or liabilities reduced are greater than assets surrendered or liabilities incurred must increase the earnings being retained by the firm. Take, for example, a merchandise transaction. A firm sells for $100 goods that it had previously purchased for $70. The firm receives an asset of $100; it surrenders an asset of $70. Assets have increased by $30, so the owners of the business are $30 better off than they were previously. Income as a result of the transaction is $30, and hence *retained earnings* (an account title within the owners' equity section of the balance sheet) must have increased by $30.

The net effect of $30 is recorded in a retained earnings account rather than an owners' equity account in order to separate original investment from subsequent profit or income. This separation is a requirement of provincial or federal Companies Acts and is discussed further in Chapters 11 and 12. However, we often use several account titles instead of a few because different users or readers want the information kept separate for their decision-making needs.

To view the transaction in two steps: The receipt of cash resulted in an increase of $100 in both cash and retained earnings. An appropriate journal entry would be

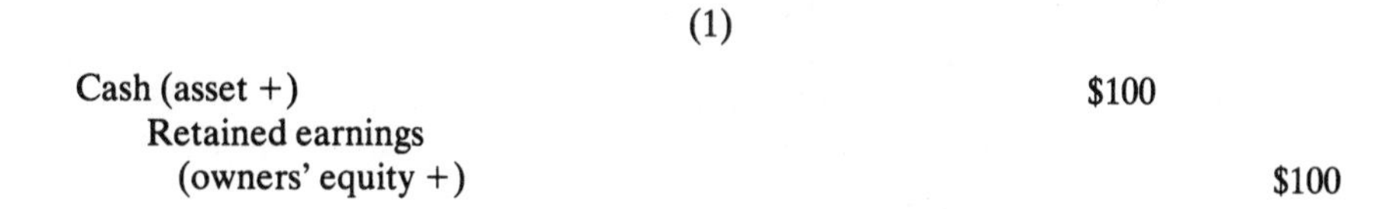

(1)

Cash (asset +)	$100	
Retained earnings (owners' equity +)		$100

The transfer of goods to the new owners resulted in a decrease in both merchandise and retained earnings:

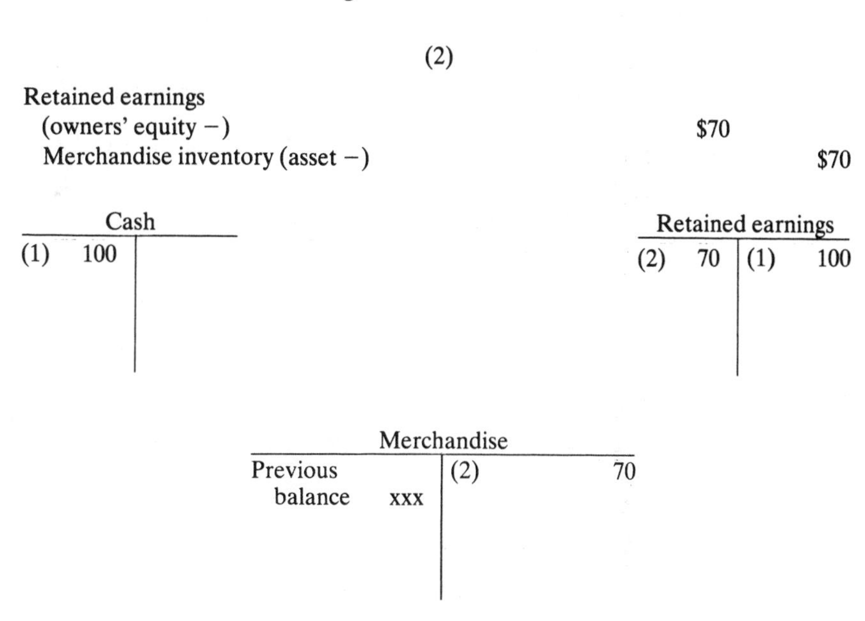

(2)

Retained earnings (owners' equity −)	$70	
Merchandise inventory (asset −)		$70

Cash

(1) 100	

Retained earnings

(2) 70	(1) 100

Merchandise

Previous balance xxx	(2) 70

As a consequence of the transaction, it could be said that the firm had *revenues* of $100 and *expenses* of $70. That is, we have split the net effect on retained earnings into two categories — revenues, and expenses — so that we can better determine the causes of the $30 effect on retained earnings.

Revenue: The *inflow* of assets into the firm as a result of production or delivery of goods and/or the rendering of services.

Expense: The *outflow* of assets in the course of the profit-directed activities of the firm.

Income: The *excess* of revenues over expenses.

ILLUSTRATION A series of simple transactions can further illustrate the relationships among revenues, expenses, and retained earnings.

J. Post starts a newspaper route. He puts $200 into the business. He expects the business to last for two weeks. During the first week,
He purchases a cart for $20.
He buys newspapers for $80.
He prints and distributes advertising circulars; cost, $10.
He pays rent for a garage in which to store his cart and newspapers; cost, $5 per week.
He makes several telephone calls; cost, $5.
He sells newspapers on account for $150.
He collects $145; the remaining $5 he deems uncollectible.
All costs are paid in cash.

The following journal entries would be appropriate:

(1)

Cash (asset +)	$200	
J. Post, invested capital (owner's equity +)		$200
To record the initial cash contribution.		

(2)

Equipment (asset +)	$20	
Cash (asset −)		$20
To record the purchase of the cart.		

(3)

Merchandise inventory (asset +)	$80	
Cash (asset −)		$80
To record the purchase of newspapers.		

(4)

Retained earnings (owner's equity −; advertising expense)	$10	
Cash (asset −)		$10
To record the costs of advertising.		

(5)

Retained earnings (owner's equity −; rent expense)	$5	
Cash (asset −)		$5
To record the cost of one week's rent.		

(6)

Retained earnings (owner's equity −; telephone expense)	$5	
Cash (asset −)		$5

To record the cost of the telephone calls.

(7)

Accounts receivable (asset +)	$150	
Retained earnings (owner's equity +; sales revenue)		$150

To record the sale of newspapers.

(8)

Retained earnings (owner's equity −; cost of goods sold)	$80	
Merchandise inventory (asset −)		$80

To record the original cost of the newspapers that were sold.

(9)

Cash (asset +)	$145	
Accounts receivable (asset −)		$145

To record the collection of cash from customers who previously had purchased newspapers on account.

(10)

Retained earnings (owner's equity −; bad debt expense)	$5	
Accounts receivable (asset −)		$5

To record the loss on accounts which cannot be collected.

(11)

Retained earnings (owner's equity −; depreciation expense)	$10	
Equipment (asset −)		$10

To record one week's depreciation on the cart. (The business is expected to last for only two weeks, and it is assumed that the cart has a useful life of only two weeks. The cart originally cost $20; the cost per week is therefore $10. At the end of the first week an entry is necessary to record the fact that one half of the services expected out of the cart have been used up or "depreciated." Usually an "allowance for depreciation" rather than the asset itself is credited for the amount of depreciation charged, but explanation of such "contra accounts" will be deferred to the next chapter.)

Most commonly, when a business is not a corporation, no distinction is made in the owners' equity accounts between original capital contribution and retained earnings. A single account, J. Post, capital, for example, is maintained to account for both the owner's contributions and earnings which have not been distributed to him. There is no theoretical reason two accounts could not be maintained, as they are in the example, if the additional information provided is deemed useful for judgments which have to be made by the owner.

The journal entries can be posted to ledger accounts. For simplicity we are using T accounts. To highlight the impact of the transactions on the equity of the owner, a brief explanation is included beside each of the entries to the retained earnings account.

Assets

Cash

	Debit		Credit
(1)	200	(2)	20
(9)	145	(3)	80
		(4)	10
		(5)	5
		(6)	5
	225		

Equipment

	Debit		Credit
(2)	20	(11)	10
	10		

Merchandise inventory

	Debit		Credit
(3)	80	(8)	80

Accounts receivable

	Debit		Credit
(7)	150	(9)	145
		(10)	5

Liabilities and owner's equity

J. Post, capital

	Debit		Credit
		(1)	200
			200

Retained earnings

		Debit		Credit	
Advertising expense	(4)	10	(7)	150	Sales revenue
Rent expense	(5)	5		35	
Telephone expense	(6)	5			
Cost of goods sold	(8)	80			
Bad debt expense	(10)	5			
Depreciation expense	(11)	10			

At the end of the first week of operation the position of the newspaper business can be reported as follows:

J. Post, Newspaper Route
Balance Sheet as at the End of the First Week

Assets		*Liabilities and owner's equity*	
Cash	$225	J. Post, capital	$200
Equipment	10	Retained earnings	35
	$235		$235

Since retained earnings are now $35, it is apparent that the equity of J. Post has increased by that amount and that the earnings of the one-week accounting period were also $35. J. Post is $35 "better off" at the end of the first week than he was at the beginning. His income for the period is therefore $35.

If the owners of a business made no withdrawals from their business, then income can be determined by subtracting retained earnings at the beginning of the period from those at the end. But both owners and managers of a business need far more information than income alone. They need to know *how* that income was derived: What were the sources of revenue? What were the expenses? In the example at hand, a statement of income can readily be derived from the entries in the retained earnings account:

J. Post, Newspaper Route
Statement of Income for the First Week of Operation

Sales revenue		$150
Less: Expenses		
Cost of goods sold	$80	
Advertising expense	10	
Rent expense	5	
Bad debt expense	5	
Telephone expense	5	
Depreciation expense	10	115
Income		$ 35

Suppose, however, that there were not six entries which affected retained earnings but that instead there were several hundred. The task at the end of the accounting period of classifying the various entries into a manageable number of revenue and expense categories and of summarizing them into a statement of income would be enormous. Would it not make more sense to divide the retained earnings account into several subaccounts, each of which would represent a particular type of revenue or expense?

Retained earnings

Debit			Credit		
Advertising	(4)	10	(7)	150	Sales revenue
Rent expense	(5)	5			
Telephone expense	(6)	5			
Cost of goods sold	(8)	80			
Bad debt expense	(10)	5			
Depreciation expense	(11)	10			
		35			

Retained earnings

Advertising expense

Debit	Credit
(4) 10	

Sales revenue

Debit	Credit
	(7) 150

Rent expense

Debit	Credit
(5) 5	

Telephone expense

Debit	Credit
(6) 5	

Cost of goods sold

Debit	Credit
(8) 80	

Bad debt expense

Debit	Credit
(10) 5	

Depreciation expense

Debit	Credit
(11) 10	

The retained earnings subaccounts would have but one purpose. They would be used to accumulate data necessary to prepare the periodic statements of income. As soon as the last business day of the accounting period (generally this means a *year* in real life, but for teaching purposes in the text we may use one week or one month) is complete and all entries to subaccounts have been made, the balances in those accounts would be transferred to the overall retained earnings account. The subaccounts could be viewed as serving a very temporary function. They would be used to accumulate, by category, the revenues earned and the expenses incurred for one accounting period only. Seldom do users of financial statements demand knowledge of total revenues and expenses, by category, since the inception of the company, because such information would bear upon few decisions that they are required to make. Instead they want the information on a period-by-period basis. As a result, each subaccount — the revenue and expense accounts — will be terminated (closed) at the end of each accounting period. New revenue and expense accounts will be established for the next accounting period. Returning to the accounts of the J. Post newspaper route, the revised journal entries (including only those that affected retained earnings) would appear as

	Debit	Credit
(4)		
Advertising expense	$ 10	
Cash		$ 10
To record the costs of advertising.		
(5)		
Rent expense	$ 5	
Cash		$ 5
To record the cost of one week's rent.		
(6)		
Telephone expense	$ 5	
Cash		$ 5
To record the cost of the telephone calls.		
(7)		
Accounts receivable	$150	
Sales revenue		$150
To record the sale of newspapers.		
(8)		
Cost of goods sold	$ 80	
Merchandise inventory		$ 80
To record the cost of newspapers that were sold.		
(10)		
Bad debt expense	$ 5	
Accounts receivable		$ 5
To record the loss on accounts which could not be collected.		
(11)		
Depreciation expense	$ 10	
Equipment		$ 10
To record one week's depreciation on the cart.		

Closing Entries

At the end of the accounting period the balances in the revenue and expense accounts would be transferred to the overall retained earnings account. Normally, revenue accounts would have a credit balance; expense accounts would have a debit balance.

Entries to "Close" Revenue and Expense Accounts

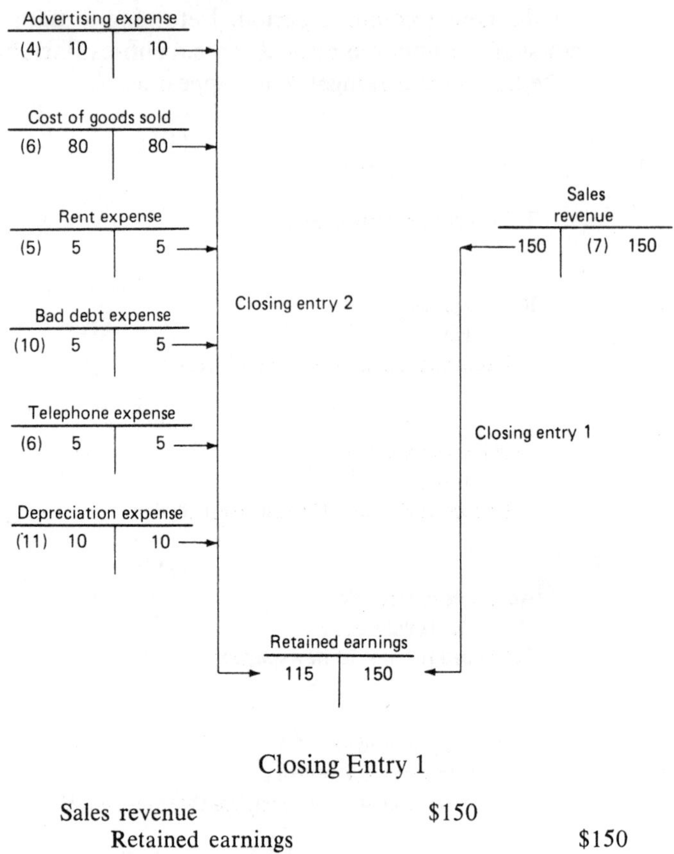

Closing Entry 1

Sales revenue	$150	
Retained earnings		$150
To close revenue account.		

Closing Entry 2

Retained earnings	$115	
Advertising expense		$10
Rent expense		5
Telephone expense		5
Cost of goods sold		80
Bad debt expense		5
Depreciation expense		10
To close expense accounts.		

The transfer can be made by two simple journal entries. First, a journal entry is made in which each revenue account is debited with an amount equal to the balance in the account, and retained earnings is credited with the total of such amounts. Second, a similar journal entry is made in which each expense account is credited with the balance in the account and retained earnings is debited. If the company had a profit, then the net effect of the two entries would be to increase the balance in retained earnings, and if a loss, then to decrease the balance.

After the closing entries have been made and posted to the individual revenue and expense accounts, the balances in those accounts must be zero. The company would then be ready to open new revenue and expense accounts (subaccounts of retained earnings) to accumulate data for the statement of income for the following accounting period.

It must be emphasized that only the revenue and expense accounts need be "closed" at week end. The balance in the J. Post newspaper route *cash* account was $225 at the end of the first week of operations. It will necessarily be $225 at the beginning of the second week. Asset and liability accounts describe the position of a business at a given point of time. Revenue and expense accounts describe inflows and outflows per a given period of time (a week, a month, a year). Once that period of time has elapsed, new accounts must be established to meter the flows of the next accounting period.

Some accountants use an intermediate account, called by names such as "Income Summary" or "Profit and Loss," to minimize the number of debits and credits to retained earnings and thereby (as we shall see later) simplify preparation of the retained earnings statement. Closing entry 1 above would appear as follows:

Sales revenue	$150	
Income summary		$150

Closing entry 2 would be:

Income summary	$115	
Advertising expense		$ 10
Rent expense		5
Telephone expense		5
Cost of goods sold		80
Bad debt expense		5
Depreciation expense		10

We would then need closing entry 3 to close out the *net* balance in the income summary to retained earnings:

Income summary	$ 35	
Retained earnings		$ 35

Although our journal entries have tended to place dollar signs in front of the amounts opposite the ledger accounts, the normal practice is to delete the dollar signs. We are noting the signs from time to time to avoid possible confusion with quantities — which can be troublesome in later accounting courses.

The Complete Accounting Cycle Demonstrated

To demonstrate the complete accounting cycle for an entire accounting period, we shall assume that Davis's Disco Limited, a restaurant and night club, has been in business for one month. Its financial position as of June 30, 19x5, is described by a balance sheet prepared as of that date.

Most firms complete an accounting cycle once a year. That is, once a year they close their books, prepare a complete set of financial statements, and open new revenue and expense accounts. There is no conceptual reason, however, that a firm cannot complete an accounting cycle more frequently than once a year. For purposes of illustration it may be assumed that Davis's Disco Limited closes its books at the end of each month.

It is clear from the owners' equity section that the company is organized as a corporation, since only corporations and not partnerships or proprietorships have shareholders.

Davis's Disco Limited
Balance Sheet
June 30, 19x5

Assets

Current assets		
Cash in bank	$ 6,530	
Inventory of beverages	3,000	
Inventory of food	300	
Inventory of supplies	1,500	
Prepaid rent	1,400	$12,730
Noncurrent assets		
Furniture and fixtures	5,900	
Kitchen equipment	11,800	17,700
Total assets		$30,430

Liabilities and owners' equity

Current liabilities		
Accounts payable		$ 3,750
Noncurrent liabilities		

Notes payable	7,500
Total liabilities	11,250
Owners' equity	
Common shares	17,000
Retained earnings	2,180
Total owners' equity	19,180
Total liabilities and owners' equity	$30,430

It is also obvious from the owners' equity section that the corporation earned a profit during its first month of operations. This is indicated by the positive balance in the retained earnings account. There is, however, no way to be sure *how much* profit was earned during the first month. The firm earned at least $2,180, but it may have earned considerably more than that. If the company decided to distribute the earnings to its shareholders in the form of a cash dividend, then the balance in the retained earnings account would be equal to the first-month earnings of the company less the dividends paid to shareholders. In paying the dividends to shareholders the firm would have recorded the following (or a similar) journal entry:

Retained earnings (owners' equity −)	xxxxx	
Cash (asset −)		xxxxx
To record the declaration and payment of a dividend.		

The distribution of the cash would have reduced both the assets and the retained earnings.

Assume that the events reported below take place during the month of July 19x5. Many of the transactions are summaries of several individual transactions — for example, the sales indicated were by no means made to a single customer in a single evening.

	(1)		
1. The club purchases glassware and other supplies on account for $500.	Inventory of supplies	$500	
	Accounts payable		$500
	To record the purchase, on account, of supplies.		

	(2)		
2. Advertising costs for the month amount to $1,300. As of the end of the month, the bill for the advertising has not yet been paid.	Advertising expense	$1,300	
	Accounts payable		$1,300
	To record advertising costs.		

3. Utilities expense for the month amounts to $150. The entire amount is paid in cash.

(3)

Utility expense	$150	
Cash		$150

To record the cost of utilities.

4. The club pays the salaries of bartenders, waiters, and kitchen employees, a total of $4,000.

(4)

Salary expense	$4,000	
Cash		$4,000

To record the cost of employee salaries.

5. The club purchases beverages (cost $4,000) and food (cost $1,000).

(5)

Inventory of beverages	$4,000	
Inventory of food	1,000	
Accounts payable		$5,000

To record the purchase, on account, of beverages and food.

6. The club makes payments of $4,500 to creditors from whom it had purchased goods or services on account.

(6)

Accounts payable	$4,500	
Cash		$4,500

To record payments to suppliers and other creditors.

7. Sales of beverages for the month total $15,000; those of food $3,000.

(7)

Cash	$18,000	
Sales revenue—food		$ 3,000
Sales revenue—beverages		15,000

To record sales of food and drink.

8. The club rents its premises for $700 per month. Upon signing the lease on June 1, the company paid three months' rent in advance. No rent payments were made during the month of July.

(8)

Rent expense	$700	
Prepaid rent		$700

To record the cost of rent for the month of July and the corresponding reduction of the asset, prepaid rent.

9. The note payable indicated on the June 30 balance sheet bears interest at the rate of 12 percent

(9)

Interest expense	$75	
Interest payable		$75

To record the cost of using borrowed

per year. Interest is payable monthly but at the month's end the company had not yet made its July payment.

funds for the month of July: one twelfth of 12 percent of $7,500.

10. The club estimates that both the furniture and fixtures and the kitchen equipment have a useful life of 5 years (60 months). The furniture and fixtures originally cost $6,000; the kitchen equipment cost $12,000 (the difference between original cost and the amount shown on the balance sheet represents depreciation recorded for the first month of operation).

(10a)

Depreciation expense	$100	
Furniture and fixtures		$100

(10b)

Depreciation expense	$200	
Kitchen equipment		$200

To record depreciation (one-sixtieth of original cost) for the month of July. (The entries could, of course, have been combined into one).

11. An inventory taken at the month's end indicates the following balance of beverages, food, and supplies to be on hand:

Beverages	$1,000
Food	100
Supplies	900

Since the accounts indicate the balances on hand at the beginning of the month and the purchases during the month, the amounts sold or used during the month can readily be derived (assuming, of course, no theft or other misuse).

(11)

Cost of beverages sold (expense)	$6,000	
Cost of food sold (expense)	1,200	
Cost of supplies used (expense)	1,100	
Inventory of beverages		$6,000
Inventory of food		1,200
Inventory of supplies		1,100

To record the cost of the sale or use of beverages, food, and supplies and to reduce the balance in the beverage, food, and supplies inventory accounts to those indicated by the physical count.

	Beverages	*Food*	*Supplies*
Balance on hand, July 1	$3,000	$ 300	$1,500
Add: Purchases in July	4,000	1,000	500
Amounts available for sale or use	7,000	1,300	2,000
Less: Balance on hand, July 31	1,000	100	900
Amount sold or used in July	$6,000	$1,200	$1,100

Cash in bank

	Debit		Credit
Bal. 7/1	6,530	(3)	150
(7)	18,000	(4)	4,000
Bal. 8/1	15,880	(6)	4,500

Accounts payable

	Debit		Credit
(6)	4,500	Bal. 7/1	3,750
		(1)	500
		(2)	1,300
		(5)	5,000
		Bal. 8/1	6,050

Advertising expense

	Debit		Credit
(2)	1,300		

Salary expense

	Debit		Credit
(4)	4,000		

Inventory of supplies

	Debit		Credit
Bal. 7/1	1,500	(11)	1,100
(1)	500		
Bal. 8/1	900		

Notes payable

	Debit		Credit
		Bal. 7/1	7,500
		Bal. 8/1	7,500

Utility expense

	Debit		Credit
(3)	150		

Furniture and fixtures

	Debit		Credit
Bal. 7/1	5,900	(10a)	100
Bal. 8/1	5,800		

Interest payable

	Debit		Credit
		(9)	75
		Bal. 8/1	75

Rent expense

	Debit		Credit
(8)	700		

Inventory of food

	Debit		Credit
Bal. 7/1	300	(11)	1,200
(5)	1,000		
Bal. 8/1	100		

Common shares

	Debit		Credit
		Bal. 7/1	17,000
		Bal. 8/1	17,000

Depreciation expense

	Debit		Credit
(10a)	100		
(10b)	200		
	300		

Inventory of beverages

	Debit		Credit
Bal. 7/1	3,000	(11)	6,000
(5)	4,000		
Bal. 8/1	1,000		

Retained earnings

	Debit		Credit
		Bal. 7/1	2,180

Interest expense

	Debit		Credit
(9)	75		

Cost of beverages sold

	Debit		Credit
(11)	6,000		

Kitchen equipment

	Debit		Credit
Bal. 7/1	11,800	(10b)	200
Bal. 8/1	11,600		

Sales revenue — beverages

	Debit		Credit
		(7)	15,000

Cost of food sold

	Debit		Credit
(11)	1,200		

Prepaid rent

	Debit		Credit
Bal. 7/1	1,400	(8)	700
Bal. 8/1	700		

Sales revenue — food

	Debit		Credit
		(7)	3,000

Cost of supplies used

	Debit		Credit
(11)	1,100		

After the journal entries have been posted to the individual accounts, it is possible to take a *trial balance* of the accounts. A trial balance is nothing more than a complete listing of the balances in each of the accounts. Naturally, the total debit balances must be exactly equal to the total credit balances. If they are not, an error has been made, and the accountant or bookkeeper must read the individual accounts and retrace each of the postings back to the journal entries. Cross-referencing of the journal entry number (or journal page) to each ledger account aids in checking postings and locating errors.

Unfortunately, the equality of the total debit balances to total credit balances is only a necessary condition for the accounts to be in order; it is by no means a sufficient condition. For even if in the trial balance total debit balances are equal to total credit balances, the financial records may still be in error. Transactions may have been recorded using incorrect dollar amounts or may not have been recorded at all; journal entries may have been posted to improper ledger accounts.

A trial balance may be taken at any time. One taken before the closing entries (those which transfer the balances in the revenue and expense accounts to retained earnings) are made is referred to as a *preclosing* trial balance; one taken after the closing entries have been made is called a *postclosing* trial balance.

The trial balance indicated below is a preclosing trial balance.

Davis's Disco Limited
Preclosing Trial Balance
July 31, 19x5

	Debit balances	*Credit balances*
Cash in bank	$15,880	
Inventory of beverages	1,000	
Inventory of food	100	
Inventory of supplies	900	
Prepaid rent	700	
Furniture and fixtures	5,800	
Kitchen equipment	11,600	
Accounts payable		$ 6,050
Interest payable		75
Notes payable		7,500
Common shares		17,000
Retained earnings		2,180
Sales revenue — beverages		15,000
Sales revenue — food		3,000
Advertising expense	1,300	
Utility expense	150	
Salary expense	4,000	
Rent expense	700	
Depreciation expense	300	
Interest expense	75	
Cost of beverages sold	6,000	
Cost of food sold	1,200	
Cost of supplies used	1,100	
	$50,805	$50,805

It is possible to prepare a statement of income directly from the preclosing trial balance.

Davis's Disco Limited
Income Statement
Month Ended July 31, 19x5

Revenues		
From sales of beverages	$15,000	
From sales of food	3,000	$18,000
Expenses		
Advertising	1,300	
Utility	150	
Salary	4,000	
Depreciation	300	
Rent	700	
Interest	75	
Cost of beverages sold	6,000	
Cost of food sold	1,200	
Cost of supplies used	1,100	14,825
Net income		$3,175

Similarly the preclosing trial balance can be used to prepare a balance sheet, but one critical adjustment must first be made. *The balance in the retained earnings account represents that sum at the end of the previous period.* Until the closing entries have been made, earnings of the current period have not been added to retained earnings. Therefore, if the balance sheet is to be prepared from the preclosing trial balance, it is necessary to add to retained earnings the income of the current period. In the example, the adjusted retained earnings would be $2,180 (per the trial balance) plus $3,175 (income for the period) — a total of $5,355. Obviously, if financial statements are to be prepared from the preclosing trial balance, it is essential that the income statement be prepared before the balance sheet in order that income for the period — the amount to be added to retained earnings — can be determined.

Davis's Disco Limited
Balance Sheet
July 31, 19x5

Assets

Current assets		
Cash in bank	$15,880	
Inventory of beverages	1,000	

Inventory of food	100	
Inventory of supplies	900	
Prepaid rent	700	$18,580
Noncurrent assets		
Furniture and fixtures	5,800	
Kitchen equipment	11,600	17,400
Total assets		$35,980

Liabilities and owners' equity

Current liabilities		
Accounts payable	$ 6,050	
Interest payable	75	$ 6,125
Noncurrent liabilities		
Notes payable		7,500
Total liabilities		13,625
Owners' equity		
Common shares		17,000
Retained earnings		5,355
Total owners' equity		22,355
Total liabilities and owners' equity		$35,980

The entries necessary to close the revenue and expense accounts can also be made from the data contained in the preclosing trial balance.

Closing Entry 1

Sales revenue — beverages	$15,000	
Sales revenue — food	3,000	
Retained earnings		$18,000
To close revenue accounts.		

Closing Entry 2

Retained earnings	$14,825	
Advertising expense		$1,300
Utility expense		150
Salary expense		4,000
Depreciation expense		300
Rent expense		700
Interest expense		75
Cost of beverages sold		6,000
Cost of food sold		1,200
Cost of supplies used		1,100
To close expense accounts.		

Advertising expense			
(2)	1,300	(C2)	1,300

Utility expense			
(3)	150	(C2)	150

Salary expense			
(4)	4,000	(C2)	4,000

Rent expense			
(8)	700	(C2)	700

Depreciation expense			
(10a)	100	(C2)	300
(10b)	200		

Interest expense			
(9)	75	(C2)	75

Cost of beverages sold			
(11)	6,000	(C2)	6,000

Cost of food sold			
(11)	1,200	(C2)	1,200

Cost of supplies used			
(11)	1,100	(C2)	1,100

Sales revenue — beverages			
(C1)	15,000	(7)	15,000

Retained earnings			
(C2)	14,825	Bal. 7/1	2,180
		(C1)	18,000
		Bal. 8/1	5,355

Sales revenue — food			
(C1)	3,000	(7)	3,000

Davis's Disco Limited
Postclosing Trial Balance
July 31, 19x5

	Debit balances	*Credit balances*
Cash in bank	$15,880	
Inventory of beverages	1,000	
Inventory of food	100	
Inventory of supplies	900	
Prepaid rent	700	
Furniture and fixtures	5,800	
Kitchen equipment	11,600	
Accounts payable		$ 6,050
Interest payable		75
Notes payable		7,500
Common shares		17,000
Retained earnings		5,355
	$35,980	$35,980

The postclosing trial balance would, of course, consist only of asset, liability, and owners' equity accounts. All revenue and expense accounts would have zero balances. The postclosing trial balance would indicate the opening position of the company at the start of the next accounting period.

Summary

The accounting equation, assets = liabilities + owners' equity, serves as the basis for recording all transactions worthy of accounting recognition and for maintaining the basic books of account. The fundamental accounting cycle may be summarized in six steps:

1. Transactions are recorded in journals in the form of journal entries.
2. The component parts of the journal entries (the individual debits and credits) are posted (recorded) in appropriate ledger accounts.
3. At the end of an accounting period, the entries to each ledger account are summarized by determining the sum of the beginning balance plus the difference between the total debit entries and the total credit entries.
4. The balances in various accounts are summarized in a trial balance. The sum of the accounts that have debit balances must be equal to that of the accounts that have credit balances; otherwise an error has been made.
5. Based on the balances in the trial balance, first an income statement and then a balance sheet are prepared. In the preparation of the balance sheet, the balance in the retained earnings account, per the trial balance, must be adjusted to give consideration to earnings for the period, per the statement of income.
6. Journal entries are made to "close" the revenue and expense accounts — that is, to transfer the balances in the revenue and expense accounts to retained earnings.

In Chapter 4, the explanation of the accounting cycle will be refined to take into account additional types of transactions and financial events.

Questions, Problems, and Cases

Questions

3-1 What is a general ledger? What is a general journal? What is the purpose of each of these records?

3-2 What is a debit? What is a credit? (Relate your definition to the basic accounting equation.)

3-3 When a customer returns merchandise to a department store he is given *credit* — an increase in a liability or a decrease in an asset — on his account when it would appear as if his liability to the store has been decreased. How would you explain this?

3-4 "All accounting transactions can be recorded directly to balance sheet accounts. There is no real reason to maintain income statement accounts." Do you agree? Explain.

3-5 What is the purpose of *closing entries*? Why must revenue and expense accounts have a zero balance at the start of each accounting period? Why aren't balance sheet accounts "closed" at the end of each accounting period?

3-6 If, prior to the end of an accounting period (before closing entries have been made), one were to take a trial balance of all balance sheet accounts (assets, liabilities, owners' equity), the debits would probably not equal the credits. Why not?

3-7 The retained earnings account is generally one of the least active on the balance sheet. What types of transactions or financial events generally require an entry directly to the retained earnings account?

3-8 (a) If at the end of an accounting period the trial balance is not in balance (the debits do not equal the credits), then an accounting error has been made. (b) If at the end of an accounting period the trial balance is in balance, then an accounting error has not been made. Do you agree with either or both of these statements? Explain.

3-9 A retail store purchases merchandise priced at $50,000. The company is allowed a trade discount of 20 percent ($10,000) but incurs shipping costs of $2,000, taxes and duties of $500, and insurance of $750. At what value should the goods be recorded on the books of the company? What general rule governs the value at which assets, such as merchandise inventory or plant equipment, should be initially recorded? Prepare the journal entry to record the transaction.

3-10 What accounting recognition would be given to each of the following financial events on the books of International Electric Co. Ltd.? Explain your reasoning.

a. International Electric Co. Ltd. owns 3,000 common shares of Ford Motor Co. Limited. In the course of a year, the market price of Ford increases from $50 per share to $60.

b. International Electric Co. Ltd. has outstanding 20,000 of its own common shares. In the course of a year, the market price increases from $45 per share to $50.

c. William Barefield sells 100 shares of International Electric Co. Ltd. to Jack Ableson for $45 per share.

3-11 Distinguish among the following terms: expenditure, asset and expense.

3-12 Bookkeeping is only one aspect of accounting. Explain.

3-13 "Computers can do calculations more quickly and accurately than humans. The rapid development of computer technology and EDP information systems will reduce the bookkeeping role of accountants and increase their analytical problem solving role." Do you agree with this quotation? Why? Be specific!

3-14 In designing a record-keeping system for a company, what are some of the factors you would consider? How would the company's accounting objectives and facts affect your recommendation?

Problems

P3-1 An accounting transaction, when analyzed in terms of the basic accounting equation, can have only nine possible effects. They are summarized below. Analyze each of the financial events listed, and indicate by number which of the nine effects is best described. Base your answer on the assumption that each transaction is being entered directly into balance sheet accounts (i.e., bypassing the income statement), but indicate (i) which of the transactions would, in fact, ordinarily be reported on the income statement, and (ii) any assumptions which you have made.

1. Asset +; asset −.
2. Asset +; liability +.
3. Asset +; owners' equity +.
4. Asset −; liability −.
5. Asset −; owners' equity −.
6. Liability +; liability −.
7. Liability −; owners' equity +.
8. Liability +; owners' equity −.
9. Owners' equity +; owners' equity −.

a. Collection of an account receivable.
b. Purchase of merchandise on account.
c. Sale of merchandise on account.
d. Recognition of the cost of goods that have been sold.
e. Declaration (but not payment) of a dividend.
f. Payment of a dividend that had previously been declared.
g. Recognition of one year's depreciation on a company-owned truck.
h. Payment of one month's rent on a truck that the company leases from a "rent-a-truck" agency.
i. Issuance of 1,000 of the company's own common shares in exchange for forgiveness on a $100,000 note payable.
j. Exchange of 1,000 common shares for 2,000 preferred shares.

P3-2 The following data relates to Bookkeeping Co. Ltd.:

	December 31 *19x8*	*19x9*
Cash	$10,000	$15,000
Accounts receivable	8,000	5,000
Inventory	16,000	20,000
Accounts payable for merchandise	12,000	14,000
Furniture and fixtures (net after deduction of depreciation)	9,000	8,000

Additional information:

1. Cash received from customers during the year amounted to $48,000.
2. Payments made to suppliers for merchandise during the year amounted to $40,000.
3. The company issued an additional 100 shares for $2,000 cash during the year.

Required:

Compute sales revenue, cost of goods sold, net income and shareholders' equity (12/31/19x9) from the above information. Indicate the assumptions you have made.

P3-3 Prepare journal entries to reflect the following transactions. Be certain to indicate the nature of each account affected and any assumptions you have made.

a. A company purchases supplies for $500 cash.
b. The company uses $300 of the supplies.
c. The company purchases merchandise for $3,000 on account.
d. The company pays $1,500 of the $3,000 owed to suppliers.
e. The company sells for $4,000, on account, merchandise that had initially cost $3,000. (Two entries are required.)
f. The company collects the $4,000 from its customers.
g. It borrows $10,000 at 6 percent annual interest.
h. The company pays one year's interest.
i. The company purchases a machine for $6,000 cash. The machine has an estimated useful life of three years.
j. The company gives accounting recognition to the use of the machine for one year.

P3-4 Prepare journal entries (as necessary) to reflect the following financial events pertaining to the Allen Co. Ltd. in the month of June, 19x7. Indicate any assumptions which you have made and the reasoning underlying your accounting treatment.

a. The company issues $300,000 in long-term bonds. The bonds provide for the payment of interest twice each year at an annual rate of 8 percent. The bonds are payable 10 years from date of issue.
b. The company purchases a new typewriter. Normal selling price of the typewriter is $400, but because the machine is on sale, the company pays cash of only $320.

c. The company signs a contract with the Watchdog Security Service to provide guard service for the period July 1, 19x6 to June 30, 19x7. The contract calls for payment of $2,000 per month, payable 15 days after the close of the month in which the service is provided.

d. The firm receives a cheque for $5,000 from one of its customers for payment on merchandise that was delivered in January. The amount owed is included among the company's accounts receivable.

e. The firm purchases 100 common shares of Exxon for $84 per share.

f. The *Wall Street Journal* reports that the price of Exxon shares has increased to $88 per share.

g. The company purchases manufacturing equipment for $86,000. The company pays cash of $20,000 and gives a three-year note for the balance. In addition, the company incurs costs (paid in cash) of $2,000 to install the equipment.

h. The company issues 10,000 of its common shares for $12 per share. The common shares have a par value of $10 per share.

i. The company pays $600 rent on its office space. The rent is applicable to the month of May and had previously been recorded as a liability, "accrued rent payable."

j. The company returns to the manufacturer raw materials that it deems defective. The company had been billed $900 for such materials and had recorded the amount as a liability.

P3-5 Prepare journal entries to reflect the following events on the books of both Wholesale Ltd. and Retail Ltd.

a. Wholesale Ltd. sells, for $5,000 on account to Retail Ltd., merchandise that had cost Wholesale Ltd. $4,000.

b. Upon discovering that some of the merchandise did not meet its specifications, Retail Ltd. returns it to Wholesale Ltd. The returned merchandise had been sold to Retail for $1,000 and had cost Wholesale $800.

c. Retail Ltd. pays the balance due on its account.

P3-6 Assume that a company maintains only four accounts: (1) assets, (2) liabilities, (3) invested capital, and (4) retained earnings. The following transactions occurred during its first month of operations:

1. The owners of the company contributed a total of $100,000 to establish the business.
2. The company issued bonds for $50,000.
3. The company purchased equipment, $60,000, giving the seller a note for the full amount.
4. The company purchased merchandise for cash, $40,000.
5. The company had sales of $30,000. Cash sales were $25,000, and those on account, $5,000.
6. The company paid $2,000 rent for the current month.
7. The company paid one month's interest on the bonds, $250.
8. The company recognized one month's depreciation on the equipment purchased. The estimated useful life of the equipment is 60 months.
9. The company paid insurance premiums for two months — the current month and the following month — $300 per month.

10. The company collected $2,000 of the amount sold to customers on account.
11. The company learned that $500 of the amount owed by customers would not be collectible owing to the bankruptcy of one customer.
12. The company determined that of the merchandise purchased $22,000 remained on hand, unsold, at the end of the month.

Required:

a. Establish T accounts for each of the four accounts. Prepare a journal entry to record each of the transactions, and post the entries to the appropriate T accounts. Compute end-of-month balances in each account.
b. Determine income for the month.
c. Suppose that the company had paid a dividend of $2,000 to its owners. How would that affect the balance in the retained earnings account? How would it affect income for the month?
d. Why it is useful to record transactions in journal form and also maintain a general ledger?
e. What are the benefits and limitations of an accounting system such as this which has only four accounts?

P3-7 The Heavy Wire Co. Ltd. had a balance in retained earnings as of January 1, 19x6, of $2.5 million. The following events, which affected the company, occurred in 19x6:

1. The firm had operating revenues of $3.8 million and operating expenses of $2.6 million.
2. The company suffered an extraordinary loss, not included in operating expenses, of $600,000 attributable to the expropriation of foreign properties.
3. In January 19x6, the company paid dividends of $3 per share on 100,000 common shares outstanding. The dividend had been declared in December 19x5 and had been properly accounted for at that time.
4. The market price of the company's common shares was $60 per share on January 1, 19x6. On December 31, 19x6, it was $55 per share.
5. In June 19x6 the company issued 10,000 additional common shares. The shares had a par value of $1 per share and were issued at a price of $58 per share.
6. In July 19x6 the company settled a claim against Revenue Canada. Revenue Canada returned to the company $1.5 million in previously paid taxes, which the company contended were improperly assessed. The company had recorded the $1.5 million as an expense in 19x3. It accounted for the $1.5 million as a "prior period adjustment" (i.e., a correction of income reported in 19x3) in 19x6.
7. In December 19x6 the company declared a common share dividend of $4 per share on 110,000 shares outstanding and a preferred share dividend of $1 per share on 200,000 shares outstanding.

Required:

a. Indicate the impact of each of the events on retained earnings.
b. Determine the December 31, 19x6 balance in retained earnings.
c. Explain the reasoning for not including the expropriation of foreign properties as part of operating expenses.

d. For those events which have an impact on retained earnings identify those that would be recorded directly to retained earnings and those that would be closed to retained earnings (i.e., would first appear in a revenue or expense account).

P3-8 Arrange a sheet of paper as indicated below. Leave room for additional accounts that might be required. The first column indicates balances as of January 1.

Account	*Balance*	*Transactions in January*		*Income statement for January*		*Balance sheet 1/31*	
		Dr	*Cr*	*Dr*	*Cr*	*Dr*	*Cr*
	(1)	*(2)*	*(3)*	*(4)*	*(5)*	*(6)*	*(7)*
Cash	$20,000						
Accounts receivable	50,000						
Merchandise inventory	15,000						
Fixed assets	60,000						
Accounts payable	30,000						
Notes payable	25,000						
Common shares	2,000						
Retained earnings	88,000						

Required:

a. Record the effect of the transactions described, all of which occurred in the month of January, in columns 2 and 3. Indicate the month-end balances in the accounts in columns 4 through 7 as appropriate. Record the total of each column.

1. Sales for the month, all on credit, were $70,000.
2. Collections from customers totaled $80,000.
3. Purchases of merchandise intended for sale were $45,000. All purchases were "on account."
4. Goods on hand at the month's end totaled $5,000.
5. Other operating expenses were $15,000. They were paid in cash.
6. Depreciation expense, in addition to other operating expenses, was based on an estimated useful life of 5 years (60 months) for all fixed assets.

b. Why doesn't the balance sheet balance after all transactions have been posted?

c. Prepare a journal entry to close accounts as necessary.

d. If the revenue and expense accounts were closed to retained earnings at the end of each month how would you determine the revenue and expense amounts for the year?

P3-9 A bookkeeper made several errors as described below. For each, indicate whether, for the period in which they were made, they would cause a misstatement of (1) the balance sheet only, (2) the income statement only, or (3) both the balance sheet and the income statement.

a. Failed to record a sale of $300 on account to a customer.
b. Failed to record the collection of $200 owed by a customer for a purchase he had made several weeks earlier.
c. Incorrectly recorded the issuance of 1,000 common shares at $2 per share; made the following journal entry:

Cash	$2,000	
Marketable securities		$2,000

d. Recorded the purchase of a new carburetor for a company-owned vehicle as an addition to fixed assets rather than as a repair.
e. Recorded funds given a salesman to entertain customers as a miscellaneous expense rather than a sales expense.
f. Failed to record the purchase of a new truck.
g. Failed to record depreciation of a company-owned car.
h. Incorrectly counted merchandise inventory on hand at year end.
i. Failed to record repayment of the company's loan from a bank.
j. Failed to record payment of interest on the same loan.

P3-10 Indicated below is the December 31, 19x8, preclosing trial balance of Babbington Co. Ltd.:

	Debits	*Credits*
Cash	$10,000	
Accounts receivable	12,000	
Inventory	5,000	
Supplies	1,000	
Prepaid rent	800	
Accounts payable		$ 3,000
Accrued interest payable		200
Notes payable		2,000
Common shares		1,000
Retained earnings		23,600
Sales revenue		48,000
Cost of goods sold	35,000	
Supplies expense	4,000	
Rent expense	9,600	
Interest expense	400	
	$77,800	$77,800

Required:

a. Prepare an income statement and a balance sheet.
b. Prepare required year-end closing entries.

P3-11 Typewriter Rental Service Ltd. began operations on January 1, 19x4. During its first month of operations, the following events took place:

1. The company issued 200 common shares at $100 per share.
2. The company rented a store for $200 per month. It paid the first month's rent.
3. The company purchased 20 typewriters at a price of $500 each. The company paid cash of $4,000 and promised to pay the balance within 60 days.

4. The company purchased, on account, supplies for $500.
5. The company rented the typewriters. Total revenues for the month were $800. Of this amount $200 was collected in cash.
6. The company paid $150 cash to cover other operating expenses.
7. A count at month end indicated that $450 of supplies remained on hand.
8. At month end the company gave accounting recognition to the depreciation of 1 month on its typewriters. The useful life of the typewriters is estimated at 36 months.

Required:

a. Prepare journal entries to recognize the above transactions. (Indicate any assumptions which you have made).
b. Post the journal entries to T accounts.
c. Prepare a preclosing trial balance.
d. Prepare an income statement and a statement of position (balance sheet).

P3-12 Upon receiving a gift of $4,000, Perry Keats decides to enter the copy business. During the first month of operations, the following events took place:

1. Keats places the entire $4,000 in a bank account in the name of "Fast-Copy Co."
2. He signs a three-year lease on a store. Rent is to be at the rate of $400 per month. Keats pays three months' rent at the time he signs the lease, $400 for the current month and $800 in advance.
3. He purchases furniture and fixtures for $1,500. He pays $500 at the time of purchase and promises to pay the balance within 60 days.
4. He signs a rental agreement with a manufacturer of copy equipment. The agreement stipulates that Keats will pay $200 per month plus $.02 per each copy made.
5. He places advertisements in the local newspapers. The cost of the ads is $600, payable in cash.
6. He purchases paper and other supplies for $800 on account.
7. He makes his first copies for customers. He sells 30,000 copies at $.05 each. Customers pay cash for all copies.
8. He takes an end-of-month inventory and finds $200 of supplies on hand.
9. He withdraws $200 from the business to meet personal expenses.
10. He pays the amount due the manufacturer of the copy equipment for the first month's operations.
11. He gives accounting recognition to the use of the furniture and fixtures for one month. The furniture and fixtures have an estimated useful life of five years.

Required:

a. Prepare journal entries to record the transactions of the first month of operations. (Indicate any assumptions which you have made.)
b. Post them to T accounts.
c. Prepare an income statement for the month.
d. Prepare any closing entries that would be necessary *if* the books were to be closed at the end of the month (ordinarily books would be closed only at the end of a full accounting period, usually one year).
e. Prepare a statement of position (a balance sheet).

Cases

*C3-1 Recently you have been approached by a man carrying a very large shoebox and asked if you would straighten out his accounts. He explains to you that he incorporated a company, Imperial Soil Limited (ISL) one month ago and since that time he has been doing a booming business. Unfortunately he has been so busy that he has neglected the accounting function of his business. Now, because of a mysterious shortage of cash ISL must acquire outside financing in order to continue its day-to-day operations. Someone told him that accounting information would be useful in securing a loan. For this reason, he has asked you to prepare a set of financial statements for the one-month period his company has been in operation. You agreed to accept this engagement whereupon he turned over to you the large shoebox which represented his accounting records for the past month.

A review of the contents of the shoebox (cheques, invoices, scratch pieces of paper, an old ham sandwich, etc.) indicated that the following transactions had taken place:

Sept. 1: R. Moss, the stranger with the shoebox, incorporated ISL to operate as an enriched soil supplier.

Sept. 1: Moss contributed land originally costing $25,000 (current value $50,000), a tractor originally costing $10,000 (replacement cost $5,000) and $35,000 cash in exchange for 100,000 common shares in the company.

Sept. 2: Paid $10,000 cash for a prefabricated building with an estimated life of 5 years.

Sept. 3: Received a bill from a firm of lawyers in the amount of $5,000 — $4,000 of which related to Moss's divorce and $1,000 to incorporating ISL.

Sept. 4: Bought office equipment for $8,000 cash.

Sept. 5: Purchased on account $10,000 of sales invoices specially printed with Imperial Soil Limited letterhead.

Sept. 6: Received first shipment of enriched soil costing $15,000 of which $10,000 was paid immediately in cash to the farmer.

Sept. 8: Paid $5,000 cash for supplies bought on credit.

Sept. 10: Placed following ad in the Toronto *Sun*: "Enriched soil is good for plants and is cheap to use."
This ad was syndicated across Canada and cost the company $1,500 on account.

Sept. 13: Hired two employees at a rate of $10 each per day.

Sept. 15: Paid lawyer's bill.

Sept. 20: Received $5,000 cash on deposit from a customer for enriched soil to be delivered April 15th.

Sept. 22: Paid $5,000 cash for invoices bought on account on Sept. 5.

Sept. 25: Sold a batch of enriched soil for $6,000 of which $1,000 was received in cash.

Sept. 27: Paid the two employees for the previous two weeks' work.

Sept. 29: Sold one quarter of land for $30,000 on credit.

Sept. 30: A piece of paper bearing the date September 30th had the following scratches:

Supplies inventory at month end	$9,900
Enriched soil inventory	$13,000
Meet Lynn at bar.	

Required:

a. Assume the role of an accounting advisor:
   (i) What are the needs of the users of ISL's financial statements?
   (ii) Which financial statements would you recommend be prepared for ISL? Explain your reasoning.
   (iii) Design a record keeping system for ISL. Explain your reasoning.

b. Assume the role of a bookkeeper:
   (i) Prepare journal entries to record the transactions of the first month of operations. Indicate any assumptions you have made.
   (ii) Post the journal entries to T accounts.
   (iii) Prepare an income statement and balance sheet.

c. Assume the role of an accounting advisor:
   (i) Explain to R. Moss why ISL is experiencing a shortage of cash despite profitable operations.
   (ii) What additional information would you supply, by way of a special report, to assist creditors in deciding whether to make a loan to ISL?
   (iii) What important operating decisions is Moss likely to make? Can accounting assist? How?

C3-2 J. Benny had been actively employed as an appliance and furniture salesman for Interiors Limited. Unfortunately, Interiors Limited went into bankruptcy and J. Benny was forced to seek a livelihood elsewhere. He decided that his experience in the appliance business could be best put to use by creating his own company.

The following data relates to the company's first month of activity:

Dec. 31, 19x3: J. Benny started as a sole proprietorship, a retail appliance store called Bargain Benny's Basement and contributed $25,000 in cash as his initial investment.

Dec. 31, 19x3: The company purchased a building (cost $15,000) and land (cost $10,000), paying $5,000 in cash and obtaining a $20,000 first mortgage at 12 percent interest per annum. Repayment of $1,000 principal and interest is due January 31, 19x4. The balance of principal is to be paid in equal instalments of $1,000 per year commencing January 31, 19x5.

Jan. 4, 19x4: Purchased $5,000 of store equipment and $2,000 of office supplies on credit.

Jan. 7, 19x4: Paid $10,000 in cash for appliances to stock the store.

Jan. 15, 19x4: J. Benny purchased a boat for his own use for $5,000 cash.

Jan. 15, 19x4: Sold $5,000 of appliances for $7,000 on credit.

Jan. 21, 19x4: Customers paid $5,000 of amounts outstanding.

Jan. 30, 19x4: J. Benny withdrew $500 from the company.

Jan. 31, 19x4: Paid principal and interest on the mortgage.

Jan. 31, 19x4: Paid the following bills pertaining to the month of January in cash:

Salaries	$2,500
Telephone	200
Heat	350
Water	50
Taxes	400
	$3,500

Required:

a. For what purposes will Benny require financial accounting?
b. What are some of the accounting problems facing Bargain Benny's Basement? How would you resolve them?
c. Prepare journal entries to record the transactions of the first month of operations. Indicate any assumptions that you have made.
d. Post the journal entries to T accounts.
e. Prepare an income statement and balance sheet.
f. Assume that J. Benny has approached you with the offer to become his partner. What factors would you consider? Specifically, how would you use the income statement and balance sheet? What additional information would you require?

C3-3 Maiden Tywand Co. Ltd. ("MTCL" or the company) has just completed its first year of operation. It is a closely held company and the owners do not take an active part in the management of the company.

The company presently operates a gift shop. However this is only the beginning of its planned activities. When it was created the owners envisaged it being eventually involved in the importing and manufacture of merchandise for sale in both their own and other gift shops.

All operating decisions were left up to Cathy Richardson, a seasoned merchandiser and buyer. Ms. Richardson had several years' experience with a large retailer, Conception Bay Co. Ltd., and had learned that the key to success is volume purchasing.

Ms. Richardson was intrigued by the glamour of buying merchandise and promoting the store. However she was not fond of accounting. She had taken a few accounting courses in high school and university but found them dull and preoccupied with debits and credits.

For this reason, she has asked you to look after the accounting for MTCL. Through a series of interviews you determine the company had the following major financial events in its first year of operations:

1. The owners purchased 1,000 common shares at a price of $100 per share.
2. The company leased a store in a major shopping center. Monthly rent was $3,000. During the year, rent payments of $36,000 were made. The space being rented was twice as big as the company now required because MTCL was expected to grow quickly.
3. The company purchased furniture and fixtures for the store at a cost of $60,000. The company paid $40,000 and gave a one-year note on the balance. The estimated useful life of the furniture and fixtures was 15 years.

4. In the course of the year the company purchased merchandise at a cost of $340,000 which it intended to resell. Ms. Richardson's main criterion for purchasing was to order large quantities from suppliers in order to obtain volume discounts. The company paid $210,000 cash for the merchandise; as of year end the balance was owed.
5. The company had sales of $300,000. Sales were made for both cash and credit. As of the year end, the company had outstanding receivables from customers of $100,000.
6. The company paid salaries of $40,000.
7. The company had incurred and paid other operating costs of $15,000.
8. As of the year end, the company had $170,000 of merchandise still on hand.

Before you have had an opportunity to prepare MTCL's financial statements, you receive a telephone call from the company's bank manager requesting a meeting with you and Ms. Richardson in two days. You inform Ms. Richardson of this meeting and she replies "Oh good, the bank probably wants to give us some more money because of our excellent performance in the first year of operation."

Ms. Richardson then instructs you to prepare an income statement as soon as possible. She wants to send it to the owners of the company to assure them that the company is performing well. In addition, she is eager to receive her bonus which is based on income.

Required:

a. Prepare journal entries to reflect the financial events of the company's first year of operations.
b. Prepare an income statement.
c. What other information do you feel the owners require to assess the performance of the company?
d. Why do you think the bank manager requested the meeting? What information would you present to the bank manager during your meeting?
e. Prepare a balance sheet and an analysis of the cash account. Indicate the sources of cash and how it was used.
f. What would you recommend that the company do?

C3-4 Midnight Auto Parts began operations at the beginning of 19x6. According to the records maintained by the proprietor, Mr. Ipoff, sales for 19x6, the first year of operation, were $98,000. The company made sales both for cash and on credit. At the end of each day Mr. Ipoff recorded the day's sales in a book he called a "sales journal." The single figure recorded each day was a sum of the sales for cash, the sales for credit and the subsequent cash collections on previous sales for credit. At the beginning of 19x6 the company had accounts receivable of $8,000 from customers; at the end of 19x6 the amount receivable from customers had increased to $10,000. During 19x6, $22,000 had been collected from customers who made purchases on credit.

On December 31, 19x6, the company's year end, a count of the parts on hand revealed that the company had an inventory of parts that cost $25,000. A similar count on December 31, 19x5 indicated an inventory of $15,000. During 19x6 the company had purchased from suppliers parts that cost a total of $65,000. Other cash operating expenses for the year were $23,000.

Mr. Ipoff had designed the company's accounting system. He believed that it had two strengths — he could understand it and it met his needs. Recently, at a cocktail party, one of his friends raved about the work that a student studying introductory accounting had done for him. Mr. Ipoff decided that it might be advantageous for him to have a student of accounting look at his accounts.

He has approached you and asked you if you would review his accounting system and make any recommendations that you feel are warranted. He is especially concerned about his start-up costs in the amount of $1,000. This represents the first month's rent for his premises. He set this up as an asset because he had no business in the first month of operations and at December 31, 19x6 he is still showing this as an asset.

Required:

Assume the role of an accounting advisor. Prepare a report addressed to Mr. Ipoff outlining your recommendations, the reasoning underlying them and any implications that your recommendations may have. Include an income statement in your report so that Mr. Ipoff can evaluate the performance of his company.

4 Accruing Revenues and Expenses

The primary objective of this chapter is to examine the accrual concept and to discover its impact on the recording process. An overview of the basic books of account will also be presented.

The Accrual Concept

ILLUSTRATION Vertigan Furniture Stores (a proprietorship) commenced business January 2, 19x1 with $10,000 cash, promises of additional cash from a local bank and several potential customers waiting for a new line of merchandise to be released for sale. During January the company entered into the following transactions:

(1) Rented a warehouse and showroom for $2,000 per month and paid for three months' rent in advance.

(2) Bought $200,000 of furniture from suppliers who gave the company until March 15 to pay for the inventory.

(3) Sold inventory costing $160,000 for $180,000. Customers paid $80,000 in cash and promised to pay the balance over the next 12 months.

(4) Bought supplies costing $1,500 cash, which are expected to last for two months.

(5) Computed January wages and commissions of staff and sales personnel, $18,500, and told them that they would be paid on February 5, 19x1.

How successful has Vertigan Furniture Stores been? If we use the *cash basis* (sometimes inappropriately called the single entry basis) of computing success, we arrive at the following conclusion:

Owner's cash, $10,000 — ignored because it is capital or investment and does not indicate success in January, 19x1.	
Cash received from customers	$80,000 +
Showroom rental (3 months x $2,000)	6,000 –
Supplies bought	1,500 –
Excess of cash received over that disbursed	$72,500 +

The increase in cash of $72,500 gives us the impression that the business has been very successful.

However, if we use accrual accounting procedures and try to match the revenues and expenses by periods (i.e., in this case the month of January is our prime concern) we arrive at the following:

Revenues		$180,000
Expenses:		
Cost of the inventory which was sold	$160,000	
Rental of warehouse — showroom	2,000	
Supplies used (one half of $1,500)	750	
Wages and commissions	18,500	181,250
Net *loss*		$ 1,250

The accrual basis and cash basis give a substantially different picture of success. Which is the so-called true picture? We shall see as we progress with the material that in accounting there is no such concept as "truth." Both the cash and accrual bases have their strengths and weaknesses. In financial accounting, as we note hereunder, the accrual basis is widely used.

The notion that revenues and expenses should be reported on an accrual basis is central to modern-day accounting. The effects of transactions and other financial events on the assets and liabilities of an enterprise should be accorded accounting recognition at the time that they have their primary economic impact, *not necessarily when cash is received or disbursed.* Revenues should be assigned to the period in which they are *earned*. Revenues are said to be *realized* at the point when they are earned. Costs are charged as expenses in the period in which they provide their expected services in an effort to generate revenues.

Under the accrual concept, costs which are intended to provide future services are *capitalized* or recorded as assets (bundles of "prepaid" expenses) until such time as the services are actually provided. Such services might be provided before or after the related cash disbursement. The services to be provided by office supplies are, at the time the supplies are purchased, recorded as an asset, "supplies inventory." The cost of the supplies is not recorded as an expense until the supplies are actually consumed. The supplies could be consumed either before or after the supplies are paid for.

Similarly, the cost of services provided by an office clerk is generally recorded as an expense during the period in which the firm benefits from his services even though his pay cheque may be delivered in a subsequent (or even a previous) accounting period.

In practice revenue can be recorded in the accounts at different points in time, which should be determined after carefully weighing the firm's objectives of accounting, facts, and constraints. Accountants strive for a uniform accounting treatment of the *same set of objectives-facts-constraints*. But in practice this is not always attained because of educational and judgmental differences. Traditionally accountants have tried to choose an *objective* point for recognizing revenue — which means a point when the revenues and many costs associated with the sale are known with a high degree of certainty. A sale to the federal government, for example, might be recorded when a contract is signed rather than when the cash is received (perhaps 60 - 90 days later). This is because the revenue and eventual cash receipt are known with a high degree of certainty. In contrast, a sale to an unreliable brother-in-law may not be recorded until the cash is received. Or, if it is recorded as a sale when goods are shipped, a notation might be made that the account receivable from the brother-in-law may not be a good asset.

Probably the most frequently used point in time for recording revenue occurs when goods are shipped. The illustrations in this chapter are generally based on such a point; in later chapters we tie the recording more closely to specific objectives-facts-constraints.

Several series of events and the appropriate journal entries can be used to illustrate the accrual concept. The more common accruals are:

1. EXPENSE/ASSET — Over time the asset is used up and becomes an expense.

2. EXPENSE/LIABILITY — The services are performed (thereby an expense is incurred) but they have not yet been paid for.

3. LIABILITY/REVENUE — The customer paid in advance and a liability account was credited at that prior time. Now the service has been rendered (thereby generating revenue); hence, the liability can be debited.

4. ASSET/REVENUE — Revenue is earned because a service has been performed; but, because cash was not received, another asset (eg. accounts receivable) is debited.

5. OWNERS' EQUITY/ LIABILITY — Sometimes the debit or charge does not go to an expense account but rather is what is called "a capital transaction." An example would be a dividend to owners of the business.

EXAMPLE 1 A company purchases supplies but does not pay for them until after they are consumed. (EXPENSE/ASSET EXAMPLE)

(a)

January 3 19x1		
Supplies inventory (asset +)	$300	
Accounts payable (liability +)		$300
To record the purchase of $300 of supplies on account. (No expense is "charged" — which means "debited.")		

(b)

January 31 19x1		
Supplies expense (expense +)	$200	
Supplies inventory (asset −)		$200
To record the use of $200 of the supplies previously purchased.		

(c)

February 5 19x1		
Accounts payable (liability −)	$300	
Cash (asset −)		$300
To record payment of the $300 owed for the supplies. (No expense is charged.)		

An expense is charged when the supplies are *consumed* — not when supplies are received or paid for. The *use* of the supplies is the critical economic event.

Occasionally a term such as *supplies* is used to refer to both an asset, "supplies inventory," and an expense, "supplies expense." Accountants allow themselves considerable flexibility in the titles that they ascribe to accounts. To avoid confusion, however, titles that *clearly* indicate the *nature* of the account (asset, liability, revenue, expense) should always be employed. In the case of supplies the asset is generally referred to as prepaid supplies or supplies inventory whereas the expense includes the word "expense."

EXAMPLE 2 A company benefits from the services of salaried employees in one accounting period but does not pay them until the next. (EXPENSE/LIABILITY EXAMPLE)

(a)

December 31 19x2 (Friday)		
Salaries expense (expense +)	$14,000	
Accrued salaries payable (liability +)		$14,000
To record one week's salaries. Salaries are paid each Tuesday for the week ending the previous Friday.		

(b)

January 4 19x3 (Tuesday)		
Accrued salaries payable (liability −)	$14,000	
Cash (asset −)		$14,000
To record payment of $14,000 owed for salaries.		

The expense is charged in the accounting period in which the work is performed — regardless of when cash payment is actually made.

EXAMPLE 3 A firm receives payment in one accounting period for merchandise that it delivered to a customer in a subsequent accounting period. (LIABILITY/REVENUE EXAMPLE)

(a)

January 15 19x2		
Cash (asset +)	$25,000	
Advances from customers (liability +)		$25,000
To record advance payment from a customer for merchandise to be delivered in the following period.		

(b)

February 22 19x2		
Advances from customers (liability −)	$25,000	
Sales revenue (revenue +)		$25,000
To record the sale of merchandise to the customer.		

(c)

February 22 19x2		
Cost of goods sold (expense +)	$18,000	
Merchandise inventory (asset −)		$18,000
To record the cost of the goods delivered to the customer as part of the sales transaction recorded in entry (b).		

The significant event in a merchandise transaction is usually considered to be the transfer of goods to the customer. Therefore, at the time of transfer, both sales revenue and the related cost of the goods sold should be recognized.

EXAMPLE 4 A company delivers merchandise in one period but receives payment in a subsequent period. (ASSET/REVENUE EXAMPLE)

(a)

February 15 19x1		
Accounts receivable (asset +)	$46,000	
Sales revenue (revenue +)		$46,000
To record the sale of merchandise to a customer.		

(b)

February 15 19x1		
Cost of goods sold (expense +)	$33,000	
Merchandise inventory (asset −)		$33,000
To record the cost of the goods delivered to the customer as part of the sales transaction recorded in entry (a).		

(c)

March 7 19x1		
Cash (asset +)	$46,000	
Accounts receivable (asset −)		$46,000
To record the receipt of the amount previously billed.		

As in the previous example, both revenue and the related expense are recorded at the time the merchandise is delivered to the customer — not when the cash payment is received.

EXAMPLE 5 A company declares (announces its intention to pay) a dividend in one accounting period but does not pay it until the next period. For example, on November 28, 19x1, a company declares a dividend of $1.00 per share payable to shareholders on January 15, 19x2; there are 50,000 shares outstanding (i.e., held by shareholders). (OWNERS' EQUITY/LIABILITY EXAMPLE)

(a)

November 28 19x1		
Dividends (cannot properly be classified as revenue, expense, asset, or liability; represents a reduction of owners' equity owing to a distribution of assets to shareholders)	$50,000	
Dividends payable (liability +)		$50,000
To record the declaration of the dividend.		

(b)

January 15 19x2		
Dividends payable (liability −)	$50,000	
Cash asset −)		$50,000
To record the payment of the dividend.		

On December 31, 19x1 when year-end financial statements are prepared the "dividends" account (like revenue and expense accounts) would be "closed" to retained earnings:

December 31 19x1		
Retained earnings	$50,000	
Dividends		$50,000
To close the dividend account.		

As a consequence, the dividend will have its critical impact on the financial statements (i.e., will result in the decrease of owners' equity) in the year in which it is declared, rather than when it is actually paid. It is upon the *date of declaration* of the dividend that the company establishes its obligation to distribute assets (usually cash) to shareholders.

Periodic adjusting entries

Updating entries

Some expenses are incurred and some revenues are earned on a continuous basis. Buildings depreciate over time. Rent, insurance, and interest expenses, are also incurred as a function of time. Similarly, electricity and heating costs are often incurred without interruption. Revenues, such as interest revenue, rent revenue, and insurance premium revenue (from the standpoint of an insurance company), are also continuously being earned. To the extent that the accrual concept requires that accounting recognition be given to expenses as they are incurred and to revenues as they are earned, a firm's bookkeeper would have to be making entries around the clock to keep the accounting records current.

Although the accrual concept need not be adhered to around the clock, accounts must be updated whenever a set of financial statements is to be issued — which may be monthly, quarterly, or annually. These "updating entries" are commonly called *adjusting entries* and normally are entered in the firm's journals only at the year end. In order to prepare monthly or quarterly figures any adjusting entries needed are recorded on spread sheets or work sheets that serve as temporary journals. The use of work sheets minimizes the number of direct entries in the journals.

Several "updating" entries are indicated in the examples that follow. Common to all is the fact that the credits to revenues or the debits to expenses are made for all entries regardless of whether or not there has been a receipt or disbursement of cash.

The four illustrations which follow assume for teaching purposes that the accounts are adjusted at the end of each month. Adjusting entries merely amend or correct the balances in the ledger accounts to the amount which should exist at the date of preparation of financial statements. The logical process is:

1. How much *is* the account balance now (unadjusted)?
2. How much *should be* in the account?
3. Do I debit or credit to adjust from "what is" to "what should be"?

Adjusting entries (or correcting entries as some types are called) correct for all sorts of limitations in *original transaction entries*, as described in the previous chapter. Appendix 4-A delves into adjustments in much greater detail. Four types of adjusting entries are described at this point:

Example 1: EXPENSE/LIABILITY recorded at each month end.
Example 2: LIABILITY/REVENUE recorded at each month end. The second half of this example is an ASSET/REVENUE situation.
Example 3: EXPENSE/ASSET CONTRA record at each month end.
Example 4: EXPENSE/ASSET recorded at each month end.

EXAMPLE 1 On January 1 a firm borrows $3,000 for two months at an annual rate of interest of 12 percent.

January 1		
19x1		
Cash (asset +)	$3,000	
Notes payable (liability +)		$3,000
To record the receipt of cash and the corresponding liability.		

January 31 19x1		
Interest expense (expense +)	$30	
Accrued interest payable (liability +)		$30
To record both interest expense for one month and the corresponding liability. The term "accrued" is frequently used to reflect the fact that the related expense or revenue has been earned or incurred but the asset or liability is not yet *legally* receivable or due. For simplicity we have rounded off the interest expense to $30 per month.		

February 28 19x1		
Interest expense (expense +)	$30	
Accrued interest payable (liability +)		$30
To record the interest expense for the second month.		

February 28 19x1		
Accrued interest payable (liability −)	$ 60	
Notes payable (liability −)	3,000	
Cash (asset −)		$3,060
To record the subsequent payment of both the interest and the principal due.		

The two entries at February 28 could have readily been combined as follows:

February 28 19x1		
Interest expense (expense +)	$ 30	
Accrued interest payable (liability −)	30	
Notes payable (liability −)	3,000	
Cash (asset −)		$3,060

EXAMPLE 2 On June 15, 19x1 Basu Limited leases a residential house to a tenant. Rent is $400 per month, and the lease is for a one-year period beginning July 1.

June 15 19x1		
Cash (asset +)	$400	
Unearned rent (liability +)		$400
To record both the receipt of one month's rent in advance and the corresponding "liability" — in this instance a "deferred credit" or obligation to provide services to the tenant.		

	Debit	Credit
July 31		
19x1		
Unearned rent (liability −)	$400	
Rental revenues (revenue +)		$400
To give accounting recognition to both the revenue earned in July and the satisfaction of the related liability.		

	Debit	Credit
August 31		
19x1		
Rent receivable (asset +)	$400	
Rental revenues (revenue +)		$400
To give accounting recognition to the revenue earned in August. (Assume that the tenant has failed to make his required payment for August.)		

	Debit	Credit
September 30		
19x1		
Cash (asset +)	$1,200	
Rent receivable (asset −)		$400
Rental revenue (revenue +)		400
Unearned rent (liability +)		400
To record $1,200 cash received from tenant. The amount received represents rent for August, which was due the previous month; rent for September, which is currently due; and rent for October, paid in advance.		

EXAMPLE 3 On January 2, 19x1, a firm purchases a bookkeeping machine for $12,000. The estimated useful life of the machine is ten years, after which it will have negligible scrap or resale value.

	Debit	Credit
January 2		
19x1		
Office equipment (asset +)	$12,000	
Cash (asset −)		$12,000
To record purchase of the machine.		

	Debit	Credit
January 31		
19x1		
Depreciation expense (expense +)	$ 100	
Accumulated depreciation – office equipment (contra asset +)		$ 100
To record depreciation for the first month. An identical entry would be made each month for the 10 year period.		

In Example 3, it was necessary, at the end of the first accounting period, to give accounting recognition to the depletion by one month's use of the "bundle of future services" represented by the asset, office equipment. The credit in the journal entry was not made directly to "office equipment"; instead it was made to "Accumulated depreciation — office equipment" The latter account is known as a *contra* (meaning *against* or *opposite*) or *offset* account, and its balance is always reported directly beneath that of the account with which it is associated. If the contra account is associated with an asset account, then the asset account would always have a debit balance, and the contra account would always have a credit balance. The asset account would indicate the original cost of the equipment; the contra account would indicate the expired portion of the cost.

The reasons why accountants record and report both the asset and its contra instead of just the net balance may vary but they tend to adhere to the needs of preparers and users. Two ledger accounts instead of one may be maintained to facilitate compliance with income tax legislation, which requires the separation of original cost from figures such as the net balance. Also, some people are skeptical of estimates in the contra account and want to see both figures instead of a net one on a balance sheet. They may compute their own contra. The use of two accounts may also have an educational effect in that it stresses the fact that *original cost* is recorded and not some current price.

The difference between the asset account and its contra reflects the unexpired cost (i.e., its *net book value*). At the end of the second month after acquisition of the asset, the office equipment and related contra account would appear as follows:

Office equipment		
January 2 19x1	12,000	

Accumulated depreciation — office equipment		
	January 31 19x1	100
	February 28 19x1	100
		200

At February 28, 19x1, the two accounts would appear on the balance sheet as follows:

Office equipment, at cost	$12,000	
Less accumulated depreciation	200	$11,800

The account which was debited (depreciation expense) when accumulated depreciation was credited appears on the income statement and is closed to the income summary (or retained earnings) account. Thus, the expense remains relatively small each period compared to accumulated depreciation which is a total "accumulation" for the asset since its purchase.

Should the assets be removed from the books, it would also be necessary to remove the related accumulated depreciation from the contra account. Assume that immediately after the second month the office equipment described above was sold for $11,150. The net book value at the time of sale was $11,800 (original cost $12,000 less $200 accumulated depreciation). Hence, the loss was $650. The following journal entry would be appropriate:

Cash (asset +)	$11,150	
Accumulated depreciation – office equipment (contra asset −)	200	
Loss on sale of office equipment (expense +)	650	
Office equipment (asset −)		$12,000

It should be noted that the expression "allowance for" depreciation is sometimes used in place of "accumulated" depreciation.

EXAMPLE 4 Suppose that at the beginning of an accounting period a company has on hand $1,000 in supplies. During the accounting period the company purchases for cash $4,000 of supplies and consumes $2,000. The correct ending balance in the supplies account would therefore be $3,000; supplies expense for the period would be $2,000 (the amount consumed).

Balance, supplies inventory, 1/1	$1,000	
Purchases, 1/1–12/31	4,000	$5,000
Supplies used (expense), 1/1–12/31		2,000
Balance, supplies inventory, 12/31		$3,000

The most direct means of accounting for supplies would be to increment the supplies inventory account each time supplies were purchased and to relieve the account each time supplies were withdrawn and presumably used. Thus,

(a)

Various Dates

Supplies inventory (asset +)	$4,000	
Cash (asset −)		$4,000

To record the purchase of supplies. (If the $4,000 of supplies represents the sum of several purchases, then similar journal entries would be made for each purchase.)

(b)

Various Dates

Supplies expense (expense +)	$2,000	
Supplies inventory (asset −)		$2,000

To record the use of $2,000 of supplies.

At the end of the year the accounts would appear as follows:

Supplies inventory

Bal. 1/1	1,000		
(a) various dates	4,000	(b) various dates	2,000
Ending	3,000		

Supplies expense

(b) various dates	2,000		

Cash

Bal. 1/1	xxx		
		(a) various dates	4,000

The accounts correctly reflect that ending inventory is $3,000 and that supplies expense for the period was $2,000. No adjusting entries are required. It is necessary only to "close" the supplies expense account. But as supplies are withdrawn in small amounts at frequent intervals, record keeping in the course of the year may tend to become burdensome since a separate entry must be made for each purchase and each withdrawal.

Alternatively, a company can avoid making an accounting entry each time supplies are *withdrawn* from the storeroom. Instead of recording both the purchase and the use of supplies, it would record only the purchase. In the course of the year, the supplies inventory account would be debited only — never credited. At the end of the year, however, the firm would take a *physical inventory* (by counting the supplies and multiplying each item by its cost) to determine the actual amount of supplies on hand. The company would assume that all supplies purchased plus those on hand at the beginning of the year must have been used during the year if they are not physically present at the conclusion of the year. It would adjust the accounts by crediting inventory with the amount required to reduce supplies inventory to reflect the inventory actually on hand and by debiting supplies expense with the same amount — the amount presumably used during the year. Thus,

(a)

Various Dates

Supplies inventory (asset +)	$4,000	
Cash (asset −)		$4,000
To record the purchase of supplies throughout the year.		

At the end of the year, prior to the physical inventory, the accounts would show the following:

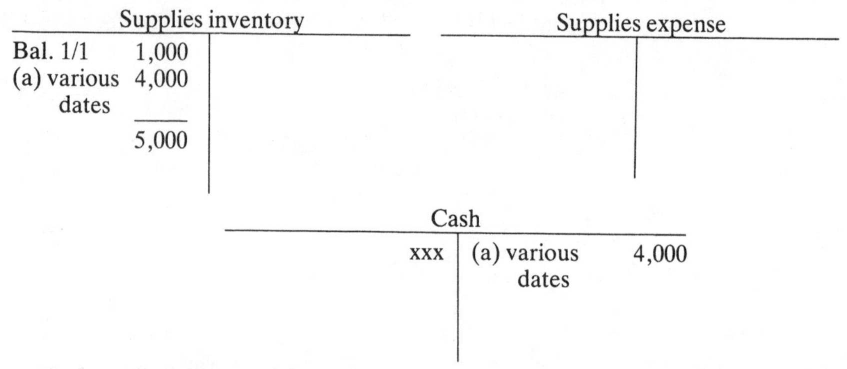

If a physical count at year end reveals supplies on hand of $3,000, then $2,000 of supplies ($5,000 per the accounts less $3,000 on hand) must have been consumed. The appropriate adjusting journal entry would be:

(b)

	Debit	Credit
12/31		
Supplies expense (expense +)	$2,000	
Supplies inventory (asset −)		$2,000
To adjust the accounts at year end to reflect the physical count of supplies.		

Supplies inventory

Debit		Credit	
Bal. 1/1	1,000		
(a) various dates	4,000	(b) 12/31	2,000
	$3,000		

Supplies expense

Debit		Credit
(b) 12/31	2,000	

Once the adjusting entries have been posted, the account balances would be identical to those derived from the procedure illustrated previously. The former approach is often referred to as a *perpetual* method, since the inventory account always reflects the actual quantity on hand, and the latter approach as a *periodic* method, since periodic counts bring the inventory account up to date.

The same results could also be obtained by a third procedure, which is also widely used. A company, instead of charging (debiting) all purchases of supplies to supplies inventory, could charge them to supplies expense. Then, as it would do if it followed the second procedure, it would make a year-end count of supplies on hand. To adjust the inventory account to reflect the actual inventory on hand, the balance in the supplies inventory account (which would represent supplies on hand at the *beginning* of the year) would be debited (increased) *or* credited (decreased) with the amount required to correspond with the quantity indicated by the physical count. The corresponding credit or debit would be made to supplies expense. If more supplies were purchased than were actually used, then the amount in the supplies expense account would have to be reduced (credited); if more were used than purchased (i.e., beginning inventory reduced), then supplies expense would have to be increased (debited).

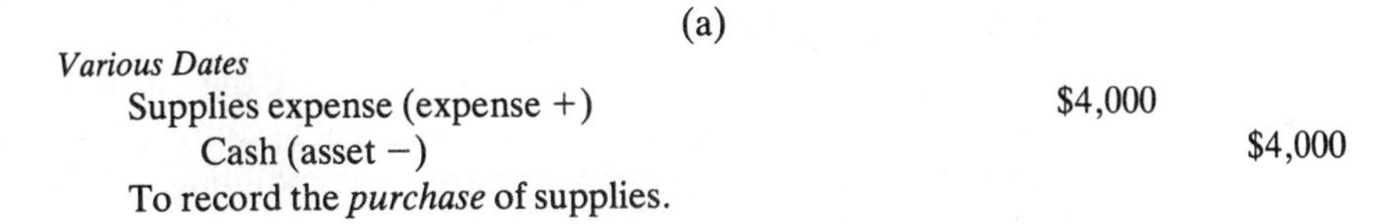

(a)

Various Dates		
Supplies expense (expense +)	$4,000	
Cash (asset −)		$4,000
To record the *purchase* of supplies.		

At the end of the year, prior to adjusting entries, the accounts would appear as follows:

Supplies inventory

Bal. 1/1	1,000	

Supplies expense

(a) various dates	4,000	

Cash

xxx	(a) various dates	4,000

If the physical count at year end revealed $3,000 of supplies on hand, then supplies inventory would be understated by $2,000. Correspondingly, supplies expense would be overstated by that same amount. The required adjusting entry would therefore be

(b)

12/31		
Supplies inventory (asset +)	$2,000	
Supplies expense (expense −)		$2,000
To adjust the inventory and expense accounts for the excess of the physical count over the balance in the inventory account.		

Supplies inventory

Bal. 1/1	1,000	
(b)	2,000	
12/31	3,000	

Supplies expense

(a) various dates	4,000	(b) 12/31	2,000
	2,000		

The adjusted balances would, of course, be in accord with those derived by the other two methods.

The three alternatives are of significance for two primary reasons. First, they are illustrative of the flexibility of the double-entry system. Identical events can be accounted for in a variety of ways. If a firm deems it too inconvenient or costly to keep its books and records perpetually up to date — that is, to record immediately every financial event that is worthy of accounting recognition — it can readily make periodic adjustments whenever current information is needed.

Second, the three alternatives demonstrate the intrinsic relationships between balance sheet and income statement accounts. For almost all income statement (*flow*) accounts there are corresponding balance sheet (*storage*) accounts. Among the expenses, cost of goods sold is related to inventory; interest expense is related to either prepaid interest (an asset) or accrued interest payable (a liability). Depreciation is related to fixed assets such as buildings or equipment. Similarly, among the revenues, sales revenue is related to either accounts receivable or to "unearned" or "deferred" revenue (e.g., airline tickets sold but services not yet provided); rent revenue is related to either rent receivable or to "unearned" rent (i.e., rent received in advance).

A warning

In either updating or adjusting entries, neophyte accountants are often unsure of the accounts to be adjusted. Although it may be obvious to them that one account must be corrected, they are unsure of the corresponding half of the entry. There is a temptation, in the face of uncertainty, to debit or credit either "cash" or "retained earnings." In fact, neither is likely to be affected by periodic adjustments. "Cash" needs to be debited or credited only upon the actual receipt or disbursement of cash. Unless the student can actually envision a transfer of cash — by cheque, in currency, or by notification of credits or charges by the bank — he can be reasonably certain that it is not "cash" that should be debited or credited. Similarly, retained earnings in the ordinary course of business are affected directly by only two types of events: the declaration of a dividend and the posting of year-end closing entries. Most updating or adjusting entries affect either an asset or liability account and its related revenue or expense account.

Year-end Adjustments — an example

Exhibit 4-1 indicates the December 31, 19x2 trial balance of Baxter Appliances Limited, a retail store, before year-end adjustments have been made. Available to the accountant in charge of preparing annual financial statements is the additional information described below which requires accounting recognition.

Unexpired insurance

The prepaid insurance indicated on the trial balance represents the unexpired portion of a three-year policy purchased in 19x1. No insurance expense ($2,000 per year) has yet been charged for 19x2.

(a)

Insurance expense	$2,000	
Prepaid insurance		$2,000
To record the expiration of one-third of a three-year policy.		

EXHIBIT 4-1

Baxter Appliances Limited
Trial Balance
December 31, 19x2

	Debits	*Credits*
Cash	$ 10,500	
Accounts receivable	43,750	
Allowance for uncollectible accounts		$ 4,500
Merchandise inventory	65,200	
Prepaid insurance	4,000	
Supplies	500	
Land	10,000	
Building	45,000	
Accumulated depreciation — building		11,000
Furniture and Fixtures	4,700	
Accumulated depreciation — furniture and fixtures		1,410
Notes receivable	2,000	
Accounts payable		17,000
Sales taxes payable		200
Advances from customers		500
Dividends payable		1,200
Common shares		25,000
Retained earnings		87,365
Sales revenue		330,200
Gain on sale of furniture and fixtures		1,200
Cost of goods sold	217,900	
Wages and salaries	56,700	
Delivery and shipping charges	3,350	
Depreciation expense	1,285	
Property taxes	180	
Supplies expense	940	
Other expenses	3,570	
Income taxes	10,000	
	$479,575	$479,575

Depreciation

The company charges depreciation semiannually, June 30 and December 31. Depreciation for the second half of the year has not been recorded in Exhibit 4-1. The building, which originally cost $45,000, is being depreciated over a thirty-year period; furniture and fixtures, which originally cost $4,700, are being depreciated over a ten-year period. Depreciation charges for a full year would be $1,500 and $470, respectively — for a half-year, $750 and $235. Note that the amount to be charged for the second half of the year is less than that charged for the first ($1,285 per "depreciation expense" on the trial balance). As indicated by the account "gain on sale of furniture and fixtures," some furniture assets must have been sold during the first half of the year.

(b)

Depreciation expense	$985	
Accumulated depreciation — building		$750
Accumulated depreciation — furniture and fixtures		235
To record depreciation for the second half of the year.		

Interest earned

The note receivable, $2,000, is a one-year note and was received from a customer on November 1, 19x2. The note bears a rate of interest of 12 percent. Interest is payable at the expiration of the note. Accounting recognition must, however, be given to interest earned in the two months in 19x2 during which the company held the note. Interest earned would be two twelfths of 12 percent of $2,000 = $40.

(c)

Accrued interest receivable	$40	
Interest revenue		$40
To record the interest earned but not yet collected.		

Property taxes

The company makes property tax payments once a year, on January 31. Total taxes payable on January 31, 19x3 will be $2,280. Accounting recognition must be given to that portion — eleven twelfths — of the total amount payable applicable to the current year. Tax expense for 19x2, to be added to the expense applicable to January 19x2 which was recorded when the previous tax bill was paid, is, therefore, $2,090.

(d)

Property taxes (expense)	$2,090	
Accrued property taxes payable		$2,090
To record the portion of property taxes due in 19x3 applicable to 19x2.		

Supplies

A physical count indicated supplies on hand of $300. Supplies purchased during the year were charged entirely to supplies expense. The supplies inventory account must be credited for $200 to reflect the difference between the current balance in the account ($500) and actual supplies in stock.

(e)		
Supplies expense	$200	
Supplies inventory		$200
To adjust the accounts to reflect the physical count of supplies on hand.		

Wages and salaries

The company pays its employees every two weeks. At year end employees had worked four days for which they will not be paid until the first payday of the new year. Wages and salaries applicable to the four-day period totaled $1,090.

(f)		
Wages and salaries (expense)	$1,090	
Accrued wages and salaries payable		$1,090
To record wages and salaries earned by employees but not yet paid.		

Inventory shortage

The company maintains its merchandise inventory on a *perpetual* basis. Each time an item is sold an entry is made in which merchandise inventory is relieved of the cost of the item sold, and cost of goods sold is charged for the same amount. Thus, at year end, the amount recorded in the accounts should be in agreement with that actually on hand. However, an actual count of merchandise on hand revealed an unexplained shortage of $600. The shortage, of course, requires accounting recognition.

(g)		
Inventory shortage (expense)	$600	
Merchandise inventory		$600
To adjust the accounts to reflect the physical count of merchandise on hand.		

Income taxes

Based on a preliminary computation, income taxes for the year will total $15,500. To date, the company has, in compliance with the law, made payments of $10,000. The company now estimates that additional payments of $5,500 will be required. Although such payments need not be made until February 28, 19x3, they represent an expense of the current year 19x2.

(h)

Income taxes (expense)	$5,500	
Accrued income taxes payable		$5,500
To record additional income tax expense based on preliminary computation.		

Exhibit 4-2 depicts the affected accounts of the company after the above transactions have been posted. Exhibit 4-3 depicts a trial balance derived from the adjusted accounts; Exhibit 4-4 illustrates the income statement and balance sheet developed from the adjusted trial balance. Notice, however, that the retained earnings indicated on the balance sheet are those per the adjusted trial balance *plus* income for the year. Until the closing

EXHIBIT 4-2

General Ledger Accounts (Only Those Affected by Adjusting Entries)

Accrued interest receivable

Debit	Credit
(c) 40	
(40)	

Prepaid insurance

Debit	Credit
Bal. 4,000	2,000 (a)
(2,000)	

Supplies inventory

Debit	Credit
Bal. 500	200 (e)
(300)	

Merchandise inventory

Debit	Credit
Bal. 65,200	600 (g)
(64,600)	

Accumulated depreciation—building

Debit	Credit
	11,000 Bal.
	750 (b)
	(11,750)

Accumulated depreciation—furniture & fixtures

Debit	Credit
	1,410 Bal.
	235 (b)
	(1,645)

Accrued wages & salaries payable

Debit	Credit
	1,090 (f)
	(1,090)

Accrued income taxes payable

Debit	Credit
	5,500 (h)
	(5,500)

Accrued property taxes payable

Debit	Credit
	2,090 (d)
	(2,090)

Interest revenue

Debit	Credit
	40 (c)
	(40)

Inventory shortage expense

(g)	600	
	(600)	

Income taxes expense

	10,000	
(h)	5,500	
	(15,500)	

Insurance expense

(a)	2,000	

Depreciation expense

Bal.	1,285	
(b)	985	
	(2,270)	

Property taxes expense

Bal.	180	
(d)	2,090	
	(2,270)	

Supplies expense

Bal.	940	
(e)	200	
	(1,140)	

Wages & salaries expense

Bal.	56,700	
(f)	1,090	
	(57,790)	

EXHIBIT 4-3

Baxter Appliances Limited
Adjusted Trial Balance
December 31, 19x2

	Debits	*Credits*
Cash	$ 10,500	
Accounts receivable	43,750	
Allowance for uncollectible accounts		$ 4,500
Accrued interest receivable	40	
Merchandise inventory	64,600	
Prepaid insurance	2,000	
Supplies inventory	300	
Land	10,000	
Building	45,000	
Accumulated depreciation — building		11,750
Furniture and fixture	4,700	
Accumulated depreciation — furniture and fixtures		1,645
Notes receivable	2,000	

Accounts payable		17,000
Sales taxes payable		200
Advances from customers		500
Accrued property taxes payable		2,090
Accrued wages and salaries payable		1,090
Accrued income taxes payable		5,500
Dividends payable		1,200
Common shares		25,000
Retained earnings		87,365
Sales revenue		330,200
Interest revenue		40
Gain on sale of furniture and fixtures		1,200
Cost of goods sold	217,900	
Wages and salaries expense	57,790	
Delivery shipping charges	3,350	
Depreciation expense	2,270	
Property taxes	2,270	
Supplies expense	1,140	
Insurance expense	2,000	
Inventory shortage	600	
Income taxes expense	15,500	
Other expenses	3,570	
	$489,280	$489,280

EXHIBIT 4-4

Baxter Appliances Limited
Income Statement
Year Ended December 31, 19x2

Revenues		
Sales		$330,200
Interest		40
Gain on sale of furniture and fixtures		1,200
Total revenue		331,440
Expenses		
Cost of goods sold	$217,900	
Wages and salaries expense	57,790	
Delivery and shipping charges	3,350	
Depreciation	2,270	
Property tax	2,270	
Supplies	1,140	
Insurance	2,000	
Inventory shortage	600	
Other	3,570	
Total expenses		290,890
Income before taxes		40,550
Income taxes		15,500
Net income		$ 25,050

Baxter Appliances Limited
Balance Sheet
December 31, 19x2

Assets			*Liabilities and Shareholders' Equity*	
Current assets			Current liabilities	
Cash		$ 10,500	Accounts payable	$ 17,000
Accounts receivable	$43,750		Sales taxes payable	200
Less allowance for uncollectible accounts	4,500	39,250	Advances from customers	500
Accrued interest receivable		40	Accrued property taxes payable	2,090
Merchandise inventory		64,600	Accrued wages and salaries payable	1,090
Supplies inventory		300	Accrued income taxes payable	5,500
Prepaid insurance		2,000	Dividends payable	1,200
		116,690		27,580
Noncurrent assets				
Notes receivable		2,000		
Land		10,000		
Building	45,000		Shareholders' equity	
Less accumulated depreciation	11,750	33,250	Common shares	25,000
			Retained earnings	112,415
Furniture and fixtures	4,700			137,415
Less accumulated depreciation	1,645	3,055		
		48,305		
		$164,995		$164,995

entries are prepared and posted, the balance in the retained earnings account indicates only the beginning balance, less any dividends declared during the year that might have served to reduce retained earnings directly.

The closing entries transfer amounts in the revenue and expense accounts to their *parent* account, retained earnings. Conceptually, they cannot be made until after the income statement has been prepared; otherwise the balances in all revenue and expense accounts would be zero. Appropriate closing entries of Baxter Appliances Limited would be

Sales revenue	$330,200	
Gain on sale of furniture and fixtures	1,200	
Interest revenue	40	
Retained earnings		$331,440
To close the revenue accounts.		

Retained earnings	$306,390	
Cost of goods sold		$217,900
Wages and salaries expense		57,790
Delivery and shipping charges		3,350
Depreciation		2,270
Property taxes		2,270
Supplies expense		1,140
Other expenses		3,570
Income taxes expense		15,500
Inventory shortage		600
Insurance expense		2,000
To close the expense accounts.		

A trial balance struck after the closing entries had been posted would, of course, be composed entirely of balance sheet accounts.

Errors and Omissions

Accountants do, unfortunately, make errors. An examination of some common types of errors and their impact on financial reports provides additional insight into the accounting process.

Some errors are readily detectable. If an entry to a journal is made in which the debits do not equal the credits, or if incorrect amounts are posted to the ledger accounts, when a trial balance is struck the sum of the general ledger debits may not equal the sum of the credits.

Other errors, particularly those related to updating or adjusting entries, are not as readily detectable and are likely to impinge on both balance sheet and income statement accounts. Many such errors are, however, *self-correcting* over time. They will automatically be eliminated either upon the liquidation of the offending asset or liability or when other routine adjustments to the accounts are made. Unfortunately, the errors may affect the financial reports of one or more intervening accounting periods, and for parties who relied upon the erroneous statements all that ends well may not, in fact, *be* well.

Consider a firm that maintains its inventory records on a periodic basis. The firm physically counts merchandise on hand at the end of each fiscal year. During the year it maintains accurate records of all purchases. In determining the cost of the goods sold for the year, it computes goods available for sale (beginning inventory plus purchases during the year) and subtracts goods that remained unsold at the end of the year (ending inventory). If beginning inventory were $3,000, purchases were $30,000, and ending inventory were $6,000, then cost of goods sold during the year would be $27,000:

Beginning inventory	$ 3,000	
Purchases	30,000	$33,000
Ending inventory		(6,000)
Cost of goods sold		$27,000

If, in the following year, purchases were $35,000 and ending inventory were $2,000, then cost of goods sold would be $39,000:

Beginning inventory (same as ending inventory of previous year)	$ 6,000	
Purchases	35,000	$41,000
Ending inventory		2,000
Cost of goods sold		$39,000

Suppose, however, that at the end of the first year the firm miscounted its inventory. Instead of $6,000, the firm counted goods on hand of $5,000. As a result of the miscount, cost of goods sold during the first year would have been reported as $28,000 — *overstated* by $1,000. In the second year, the *beginning inventory* would have been understated by $1,000. As a result, cost of goods sold for the second year (assuming a correct count at the end of the second year) would have been reported at $38,000 — *understated* by $1,000.

	Year 1		*Year 2*	
Beginning inventory	$ 3,000		$ 5,000	
Purchases	30,000	$33,000	35,000	$40,000
Ending inventory		(5,000)		(2,000)
Cost of goods sold		$28,000		$38,000

Cost of goods sold — and thus income — would be correctly stated for the two-year period combined but incorrectly stated for each of the two individual periods. Both current assets (inventory) and retained earnings would be in error after the first year, but correct after the second. Error correction is discussed later in the book.

Basic Books of Account

The basic accounting information processing system is simple and straightforward. Relatively few books and records need to be maintained or prepared — regardless of the size of the business enterprise and of the accounting system, be it manual or electronic.

The fundamental means of giving accounting recognition to financial events or transactions is the journal entry. Journal entries, as their name implies, are transcribed in journals, or books appropriately ruled and designed to facilitate two-sided entries of the type illustrated throughout the text. Journal entries are prepared from source documents, such as invoices (bills), payment vouchers (internal documents authorizing disbursements), receiving or shipping reports, remittance advices (documents indicating the receipt of cash), and credit memoranda (documents authorizing that a customer be given credit for merchandise damaged or returned or for special allowances or discounts to which he may be entitled).

Journal entries are *posted* to the *general ledger*, a book in which the current status of all balance sheet and income statement accounts are maintained. General ledger accounts are represented in this text by T accounts. Posting involves transcribing the entries from the journals to the appropriate accounts.

In a manual (or non-computerized) accounting system the general ledger would not be a T account, but would have a column for the net balance of the debits and credits:

General Ledger

Cash

Date	*Reference*	*Debit*	*Credit*	*Balance*	*Dr. or Cr.*
January 3	GJ 1	1,000.00		1,000.00	Dr.
31	SJ 1	9,235.65		10,235.65	Dr.
31	CD 1		6,480.59	3,755.06	Dr.

The ledger would also have a reference column indicating the name (abbreviated) and page number of the source journal. For instance:

GJ 1 = General Journal, page 1
SJ 1 = Sales Journal, page 1
CD 1 = Cash Disbursements, page 1

Periodically, the balances in the general ledger accounts are summarized in the form of a *trial balance*, a listing of all the account balances. From the trial balance the income statement, the balance sheet, and selected other financial reports are prepared. The flow of information is depicted graphically in Exhibit 4-5.

Although conceptually only a single or *general* journal is needed in which to record transactions, in practice, most firms find that record keeping is facilitated by several supplementary journals. Since a firm may enter into numerous transactions which affect identical accounts, it is relatively easy to combine such transactions into a single journal entry and supple-

EXHIBIT 4-5

Flow of Information

Source documents →	*Journals* →	*Ledgers* →	*Trial balance* →	*Financial statements*
Journalizing	*Posting*	*Summarizing*	*Classifying*	
Such as:	General journal and/or specialized journals such as:	General ledger supported by subsidiary ledgers such as:		Income statement
Invoices	Sales journal	Accounts receivable ledger		Balance sheet
Sales tickets	Cash receipts journal	Fixed asset ledger		Statement of changes in financial position
Remittance advices	Cash disbursements journal	Accounts payable ledger		Statement of changes in retained earnings
Factory labor reports				

mentary or special journals enable the firm to do so. They also permit a division of work which can speed up accounting, and assist in strengthening the firm's *internal control* in order to reduce errors and potential fraud. Most firms, for example, maintain a sales journal. The sales journal may be designed as follows:

Sales Journal

Date	*Purchaser*	*Sales (Cr)*	*Cash. (Dr)*	*Accounts receivable (Dr)*

As each sale is made, the accounting clerk enters the name of the customer to whom the sale is made; enters the amount of the sale in the column "Sales (Credit)"; the amount of cash received, if any, in the column "Cash (Debit)"; and enters the difference between the amount of sale and the amount of cash received in the column "Accounts Receivable (Debit)." At the end of each month, the columns are totaled. Then either the following entry is made in the general journal or the amounts are posted directly to the appropriate general ledger accounts:

Cash	xxxx	
Accounts receivable	xxxx	
Sales		xxxx

Similarly, the firm might maintain a cash receipts book (also a journal). One column indicates the amount of cash received; other columns are reserved for the accounts that are credited most frequently when cash is received — e.g., accounts receivable, advances from customers, etc. One column, labeled miscellaneous, usually serves as a catchall for accounts that must be credited other than the ones for which specific columns have been established. Room must be left so that the name of the specific account to be credited can be indicated. As with the sales journal, the columns are periodically totaled and either a single summary entry is made in the general journal or the totals are posted directly to the general ledger accounts affected.

Cash Receipts Book

Date	*Reference*	*Cash (Dr)*	*Accounts receivable (Cr)*	*Advances from customers (Cr)*	*Other accounts*	
					Title	*Amount (Cr)*

The cash disbursements book provides a similar function in consolidating entries that result from cash payments. Ordinarily, there is a column for cash, the account to be credited, and several for the accounts most frequently debited.

Cash Disbursements Journal

Date	Reference	Cash (Cr)	Merchandise inventory (Dr)	Freightout (Dr)	Other accounts Title	Other accounts Amount (Dr)

Subsidiary ledgers

A firm almost always finds it necessary to keep records of each customer from whom it holds a receivable, each fixed asset owned, each supplier to whom it is indebted, and often (under a *perpetual* system) each major type of inventory item which it holds. This would obviously necessitate a general ledger of massive proportions if separate accounts were maintained for each customer, supplier, or fixed asset. Instead, most firms maintain, in the general ledger, *control accounts* that summarize the numerous individual accounts. Control accounts might be maintained for accounts receivable, accounts payable, and fixed assets. The individual accounts would be maintained in *subsidiary ledgers*. Obviously the sum of the balances in a subsidiary ledger must equal the balance in the general ledger control account for which the subsidiary ledger provides support. Each time an entry is made to the general ledger control account, one or more entries which sum to the amount debited or credited to the control account must be made to the subsidiary accounts.

Suppose, for example, that during the month of May, sales, on account, are made as follows:

Jones	$100
Smith	50
Hanson	75
	$225

When the sales are made, the names of each of the three customers and the amount of their sales would be entered in the appropriate columns of the *sales journal*. At the same time, the accounts of each of the three customers in the *accounts receivable subsidiary* ledger would be debited for the amount of the sale. At the end of the month, the following entry would be made to the general ledger, based on totals in the sales journal:

Accounts receivable	$225	
Sales revenue		$225
To record, in summary form, sales of the month.		

Ignoring accounts of other customers and previous sales to the customers to whom sales were made in the current month, the accounts receivable subsidiary ledger would have three accounts, each with a debit balance, the total of which was $225.

As customers paid their accounts, the initial cash receipts would be recorded in both the cash receipts journal and the accounts receivable subsidiary ledger. At the end of the month, an entry summarizing the receipts would be made to the general ledger accounts, cash, and accounts receivable.

Insofar as an enterprise maintains a computerized accounting system, the journals or ledgers may not take the precise form illustrated. They would, however, serve the same function and be designed to accommodate the same information.

Additional Technical Matters

This chapter contains three appendices:

1. 4-A Adjusting and Correcting Journal Entries
2. 4-B Recognizing Expense in a Manufacturing Operation
3. 4-C Product versus Period Costs

Appendix 4-A should be read only after the material in Chapter 4 is fairly well grasped. Reading of Appendices 4-B and 4-C can be postponed for a chapter or two but should be covered before commencing Chapter 8.

Summary

The primary purpose of this chapter has been to explain the accrual concept and to demonstrate some of its many ramifications for accounting practice. The accrual concept requires that the effect of transactions and other financial events on the assets and liabilities of an enterprise be accorded accounting recognition at the time that they have their primary economic impact, not necessarily when cash is received or disbursed. Revenues should be assigned to the periods in which they are earned. Costs should be matched to the revenues that they serve to generate and should be charged as expenses in the periods in which accounting recognition is given to such revenues.

The services associated with a cost may be both acquired and paid for in periods other than those in which the revenues to which they must be matched are given accounting recognition. The services provided by supplies, for example, may be acquired (purchased) in one period, consumed in a second, and paid for in a third. The double-entry accounting system provides that costs applicable to services that will benefit periods in the future may be *stored* in asset accounts and charged as expenses only as the revenues with which they are associated are recognized. Similarly, the obligation for the payment may be maintained in a liability account until such time as the required cash disbursement is actually made.

In order that a measure of bookkeeping convenience may be achieved, accounting records are not always kept up to date. Sometimes, as in the case of supplies, it is more convenient to record the use of supplies periodically rather than each time supplies are consumed. Or, as in the case of rent or interest revenue, the benefits received accrue over time; it would be physically impractical to update the books on an around-the-clock basis. As a consequence, firms must periodically bring the records to a current status by means of updating and adjusting entries.

The manner in which costs are accounted for in a manufacturing operation (covered in Appendix 4-B) is another manifestation of the accrual concept and the related principle of matching. All manufacturing costs are maintained in asset accounts (e.g., raw materials, labor, work in process, finished goods) until that period in which they might be matched to revenues from the sale of the product and charged as an expense (cost of goods sold).

Conventionally, not all costs are matched directly with specific revenues. (See Appendix 4-C.) When the relationships between some costs and revenues are sufficiently indirect, accountants do not attempt to match certain costs with particular revenues, because they could not do so with any degree of objectivity acceptable to users of the financial statements. These costs, often referred to as *period* costs, are charged as expenses in the periods in which they are incurred, regardless of the amount of revenues recognized in that particular period.

A secondary objective of this chapter has been to provide an overview of the major types of books and records maintained by most business enterprises. Firms conventionally maintain two basic books of account: the general journal and the general ledger. Transactions are recorded in the general journal; they are then posted to the accounts that they affect, which are maintained in the general ledger. To facilitate the processing of large numbers of transactions and the maintenance of large numbers of accounts, most firms employ additional journals and ledgers to support and supplement entries in the general journals and ledgers. These are referred to as specialized or subsidiary journals and ledgers.

Chapter 4 discussed the accounting cycle, which can be summarized as follows:

1. Transaction or event requiring accounting recognition occurs.

ORIGINAL TRANSACTION ENTRIES
2. Event in 1. is recorded in a journal.
3. The journal entry is posted to ledgers.
4. After a batch of posting occurs, a trial balance is prepared (to help catch some types of errors).

When financial statements are desired, adjusting entries would be needed.

ADJUSTING ENTRIES
5. Adjusting journal entries are journalized.
6. The adjusting entries are posted to ledger accounts.
7. A post-adjusting trial balance might be prepared.

8. Financial statements can be prepared.

CLOSING ENTRIES
9. Closing entries are prepared and journalized.
10. Closing entries are posted to the ledgers.
11. An after-closing trial balance is prepared.

In summary, there are in effect three types of journal entries: original transaction, adjusting, and closing. The first two are similar in that, together, they record transactions on an accrual basis. As the brackets indicate, journalizing tends to be part of a three-step process: journalize, post to ledgers, and prepare a trial balance.

Chapter 5 expands on the accrual concept by considering appropriate differences in the timing or dating of revenue recognition for specific objectives of accounting, facts, or constraints. Ideally, *like accounting for like objectives-facts-constraints* will best aid users of financial statements.

Questions, Problems, and Cases

Questions

4-1 What is meant by the accrual method of accounting? How does it differ from the cash method?

4-2 What are adjusting entries? Why are they necessary?

4-3 Before making adjusting entries what must be known?

4-4 What are *contra accounts*? Why are they used? Where are they reported on the balance sheet?

4-5 A company charges all purchases of merchandise intended for sale to customers to "cost of goods sold." Is such practice acceptable? What year-end adjusting entry would be necessary to "correct" the account?

4-6 A bookkeeper incorrectly charges a prepayment of January 19x2 rent to "rent expense" in 19x1. What would be the impact of such an error on the financial statements of the year ended December 19x1 and that ended December 19x2? What action would you take to correct this error assuming it was discovered in 19x2?

4-7 A manager of a manufacturing company noticed that the account "labor cost" was included in the general ledger among the asset accounts. Since he was unable to visually inspect labor costs he wondered how they could possibly be considered an asset. How would you answer him?

4-8 What is meant by the *matching principle*? If a company were to recognize sales upon the collection of cash from the customer rather than upon the delivery of goods, when would you recommend that the cost of the goods sold be charged as an expense? What conditions would be necessary to justify the recognition of sales upon the collection of cash?

4-9 Distinguish between product costs and period costs. How would you defend the position of accountants that depreciation can sometimes be considered a product cost and sometimes a period cost?

4-10 Suppose that in a particular accounting period a company sells the same number of goods that it produces. Would it make any difference as far as net income is concerned if depreciation on office equipment used in the factory were considered a product or a period cost? What if the company sold only a portion of the goods that it produced?

4-11 Give an example of a subsidiary ledger. Why do companies maintain subsidiary ledgers rather than include all accounts in the general ledger? What is meant by a specialized journal? Give examples of several commonly used specialized journals. Why do companies maintain specialized journals?

4-12 An accountant attempted to prepare both an income statement and a balance sheet from the adjusted trial balance. Closing entries had not yet been made. He was unable, however, to get his balance sheet to balance. Assets exceed liabilities plus owners' equity by an amount exactly equal to income for the year. Which account is most likely in error? Why?

4-13 As you are getting ready to prepare year-end financial statements you learn that your company has not yet received invoices (bills) for services it received in December. The company estimates that in January it will receive invoices as follows, relating to December:

From the telephone company	$130
From the gas and electric company	327
From the outside maintenance service	100

Required:

a. Prepare any journal entries that you would consider necessary.

b. Suppose that you failed to make such journal entries. What effect would such failure have on income of the year, income of the following year, and current liabilities?

c. Who would be affected by a failure to record the journal entries in December? Why?

4-14 On December 13, 19x1, the board of directors of a company declared a dividend of $.75 per common share. The dividend will be payable on January 18, 19x2 to the "shareholders of record" (i.e., to those who owned shares on a particular date) of January 10, 19x2. The company has 100,000 common shares outstanding.

Required:

a. Prepare an appropriate journal entry to record the declaration of the dividend.

b. Prepare an appropriate closing entry as of December 31, 19x1.

c. Prepare an appropriate journal entry to record payment of the dividend.

d. Explain the reasoning underlying your entries.

4-15 A dance studio offers customers a "One-Year-Learn-To-Dance Special." Customers pay $120 at the time they sign a contract and are entitled to four lessons per month for one year.

In November, 10 customers signed contracts and paid for the series of lessons. In December, each of the customers took four lessons.

Required:

a. Prepare a journal entry to record the sales of the contracts and the collection of the cash.

b. Prepare any entries that would be appropriate when the customers took their first four lessons in December. (Ignore expenses incurred in connection with the lessons.)

c. Prepare any *closing* entries that might be necessary at December 31.

4-16 Examination of a company's general ledger as of the year end reveals the following account balances (both debit balances) pertaining to merchandise inventory:

Inventory	$100,000
Purchases	600,000

Upon inquiry, you learn that the balance in inventory represents that at the *beginning* of the year. No entries were made to that account during the year. All purchases during the year were debited to purchases. You also learn that a physical count at the end of the year revealed goods on hand of $60,000.

Required:

What adjusting entry would you propose assuming that you want to eliminate the balance in the purchases account, to have the inventory account reflect the correct balance of goods on hand at year end, and to have a cost of goods sold account reveal the cost of merchandise sold during the year?

4-17 Differentiate between the cash basis of accounting and the accrual basis of accounting. Which would you recommend? Why? Explain thoroughly by stating the assumptions that you have made.

4-18 "There is considerable flexibility in selecting the number and type of records a company maintains and the original journal entry it makes for certain transactions."

Required:

a. Give examples supporting the above quotation.

b. Before recommending to a company the type of records it should maintain and the original journal entries it should make what factors would you consider? Explain your logic by referring to the objectives, facts and constraints of the company.

4-19 Differentiate between the periodic and perpetual inventory method. Which would you recommend? Why? Explain thoroughly by clearly stating the assumptions that you have made.

Problems

P4-1 During the first three years of its existence, Bravo Company's manufacturing costs, end-of-year inventories, and sales were as follows:

Year	*Manufacturing costs*	*End-of-year inventories*	*Sales*
1	$80,000	$ 80,000	None
2	90,000	130,000	$ 60,000
3	30,000	None	250,000

Required:
Ignoring all other costs or revenues, determine the income of Bravo Company for each of the three years. Explain your reasoning.

P4-2 The December 31, 19x1 balance sheet of a company reported accrued interest payable of $3,000 in connection with bonds outstanding of $100,000. Interest, at a rate of 12 percent, is payable semiannually on April 1 and October 1.

Required:

a. Prepare all required journal entries for the next year, including year-end adjusting entries, assuming that cash payments are made when due, if alternatively:
   (i) The company makes appropriate *accrual* entries every three months.
   (ii) The company debits "interest expense" with the full amount of each cash payment.
   (iii) The company debits "accrued interest payable" with the full amount of each cash payment.

b. If you were the company's bookkeeper which of the above alternatives would you select? Why?

P4-3 In each of the following *independent* situations, prepare any necessary journal entries that would be required either to adjust a company's books or to bring them up to date in order to prepare year-end December 31 financial statements. Assume that closing entries have not yet been made.

Required:

a. Property taxes, which amount to $15,000 annually, are payable on the last day of the city's fiscal year, which ends April 30. No property tax accruals have yet been made.
b. Employees are paid each Monday for wages earned during the previous week. December 31 falls on a Wednesday. Weekly payroll (for a five-day work week) is $3,000.
c. As heating oil was purchased it was debited to "fuel expense." As of the end of the year, heating oil which had cost $300 was still on hand.
d. On March 1, the company purchased a one-year fire insurance policy at a cost of $3,600 paid in cash. The entire cost of the policy was charged to "insurance expense."
e. The company is on a periodic inventory basis. After taking year-end inventory and making appropriate adjustments to its accounts it discovered that $400 of inventory was incorrectly omitted from the count.
f. The company is on a periodic inventory basis. After taking year-end inventory and making appropriate adjustments to its accounts it discovered that goods which had cost $1,000 had just recently been purchased. No accounting recognition, however, had been given to either the pur-

chase or the corresponding liability for payment. (Note that since the adjustment to the accounts resulting from the physical inventory count had already been made, the inventory account is *properly* stated.)

g. The company ran an advertisement in the December 30th edition of the local newspaper. The company has not yet received a bill for such advertisement or given it any accounting recognition. The cost of the advertisement was $250.

h. The company is on a periodic inventory basis. After taking year-end inventory and making appropriate adjustments to its accounts it discovered that a purchase of equipment was incorrectly debited to "inventory" rather than to "equipment." The cost of the equipment was $2,100. (The *physical* count was correctly taken.)

i. On June 1 the company borrowed $10,000 from a bank. It paid the entire interest for one year ($1,200) in advance at the time it signed the note. The advance payment of interest was properly recorded, but no entries pertaining to the interest have been made since the date of payment.

j. On November 1 customers placed orders for merchandise with a selling price of $15,000. The customers paid in advance, and their payment was properly recorded. The goods were delivered on December 29, but no accounting recognition has been given to the delivery. The company uses a periodic inventory method, and the goods were not included in the December 31 inventory count.

P4-4 Prepare journal entries to record the following events:

a. A company purchases two trucks for $15,000 cash each. The estimated useful life of a truck is five years, after which it has negligible scrap or resale value.

b. The company records first-year depreciation on the trucks.

c. At the beginning of the second year, the company sells one of the trucks for $13,000 cash.

d. The company records second-year depreciation on the remaining truck.

e. At the beginning of the third year, the company sells the second truck for $8,000 cash.

P4-5 As you were about to prepare year-end financial statements, the journal entries indicated below, which were made by an inexperienced bookkeeper, came to your attention. You are to make the journal entries that would be required to correct the errors. (*Hint:* First determine the entry that should have been made; then determine the most efficient means of eliminating the incorrect, and adding the correct, amounts.)

a. A customer made a payment to reduce the balance in his account.

Cash	$75	
Sales revenue		$75

b. The company sold for $300 a machine that had originally cost $400 when purchased three years earlier. Accumulated depreciation on the asset amounted to $200.

Cash	$300	
Sales revenue		$300

c. In January the company paid rent for the previous December. Before preparing the year-end financial statements as of December 31 the company had correctly accrued rent for December.

Rent expense	$500	
Cash		$500

d. The company charged depreciation of one year on equipment that had cost $6,000 and had a useful life of three years with no salvage value.

Allowance for depreciation	$2,000	
Depreciation expense		$2,000

e. The company paid a bill received from its advertising agency for an ad that it had run the previous year. The company had properly accounted for the ad at the time it was run.

Advertising expense	$675	
Cash		$675

f. The company paid $130 to Cooks Auto Service for repairs to one of its trucks. It had given no previous accounting recognition to the repair costs.

Fixed assets — autos and trucks	$130	
Accounts receivable		$130

P4-6 Give adjusting journal entries at May 31, 19x1, for each of the following unrelated 19x1 situations. State your assumptions clearly:

a. Cash of $4,500 was received on May 1 from a tenant who has rented an office for three months.
b. A fixed asset costing $12,000 and having a life of five years was acquired on May 1 and the sum was charged to maintenance expense.
c. $2,000 was received on May 30 for goods to be completed and delivered in June.
d. Cash of $3,500 was received on May 31 for goods sold on account earlier in May.
e. Employee's wages of $950 had not been paid by May 31.
f. Cash of $2,700 was paid on May 1 for equipment to be rented for May, June and July.

P4-7 The president of a corporation is uncertain as to whether certain administrative, transportation, and depreciation costs should be classified as *product* or *period* costs. Such costs average approximately $120,000 per year. He asks your advice as to the significance over the next two years of his decision. Labor and material costs are estimated at $6 per unit. Selling price of the product is $10 per unit.

Required:

a. Suppose that in both year 1 and year 2 the company expects to produce and sell 40,000 units per year. What would be the resulting differences in (i) income, (ii) ending inventory, and (iii) retained earnings for (or after) each of the two years if the company classified the costs as period rather than product costs?

b. Suppose instead that the company expected in year 1 to produce 40,000 units but sell only 30,000 units and in year 2 to produce 30,000 units and sell 40,000 units. What would be the resultant differences in (i) income, (ii) ending inventory, and (iii) retained earnings for (or after) each of the two years if the company classified the costs as period rather than product costs?

c. What criteria would you use in deciding whether the costs should be classified as product or period costs?

P4-8 Suppose that a company was organized on January 1, 19x2. In each of the next 10 years it had sales of $100,000; the costs of the goods sold were $80,000 per year. In each year, the company collected in cash 75 percent of the sales of that year plus 25 percent of the sales of the previous year. Similarly, in each year the company paid in cash 75 percent of the costs incurred in that year plus 25 percent of the costs incurred in the previous year. The company ceased operations at the end of year 10. It remained in business in year 11 only to collect outstanding receivables and to liquidate remaining debts.

Required:

a. Assuming that the company maintained its accounts on an *accrual* basis, compute total income for the 11-year period. Determine income for each of the 11 individual years.

b. Assume instead that the company maintained its accounts on a cash basis — i.e., recognized revenues and expenses as cash was received or disbursed. Determine total income for the 11-year period as well as income for each of the 11 individual years.

c. Based on your calculations in parts a. and b., does it matter whether you use the accrual basis or cash basis of accounting? Why?

P4-9 Indicated below is information taken from the ledger accounts of the Wright Manufacturing Co. The figures reported are the total amounts debited or credited to the various accounts during the year 19x5. The figures do *not* represent ending balances and do *not* include beginning balances. Some amounts have been omitted. Based on your knowledge of the accounting flow in a manufacturing operation, you are to fill in the missing amounts. That is, you are to determine which accounts are normally associated with debits or credits to other accounts. (For example, by knowing the amount *credited* to accounts payable, you can determine the amount *debited* to raw materials inventory.) No closing entries have yet been made.

	Debits	*Credits*
Allowance for depreciation (factory)	0	$ 17,000
Depreciation cost (factory)	?	?
Raw materials inventory	?	95,000
Factory labor cost	$107,000	107,000
Work in process	?	?
Finished goods	212,000	?
Cost of goods sold	197,000	0
Factory wages payable	105,000	?
Accounts payable[a]	85,000	110,000

[a]Includes only amounts owed in connection with purchases of raw materials.

P4-10 On December 31, at the end of the 19x3 annual accounting period, a bookkeeper made the following errors:

a. He failed to record $90 of accrued salaries.

b. A portion of the company's warehouse was rented on December 1, 19x3 at $150 per month to a tenant who paid his December, January, and February rent in advance. The bookkeeper did not make an adjustment for the unearned rent on December 31, which had been credited on receipt of the cash.

c. Through an oversight the bookkeeper failed to record $245 of depreciation on store equipment. The equipment had a useful life of an additional five years. Depreciation was properly recorded in 19x4, and no equipment was sold in 19x4.

d. The bookkeeper failed to accrue one-half year's interest on a note receivable. The $1,000 note was received on July 1, 19x2, and was due on June 30, 19x4. Interest was at the rate of 6 percent per year, payable each year on June 30.

e. The bookkeeper made an error in adding the amounts on the year-end inventory sheets which caused a $75 understatement in the merchandise inventory. (Inventory on December 31, 19x4, was properly stated.)

f. On January 2, 19x3, the company purchased a two-year fire insurance policy for $800. The bookkeeper charged the entire amount to "insurance expense."

g. On December 31, 19x3, the company declared a dividend of $6,000 payable on January 15, 19x4. The bookkeeper failed to record the declaration.

h. The company owned 1,000 common shares of General Motors. On December 20, the company received notification from Gooder and Co., the firm's stockbroker, that General Motors had declared and paid a dividend of $1.20 per share. Since Gooder and Co. holds in its own name the shares owned by the company, it credited the company's account for $1,200. The bookkeeper first recorded the dividend in January 19x4 when the cash was forwarded to the company.

Required:

Under the assumption that none of the errors were explicitly discovered and corrected in 19x4 but that some of the errors would automatically be corrected if normal accounting procedures were followed, indicate the effect of each error on the financial statements. In each case, indicate the amount of the overstatement or understatement the error would cause in the assets, liabilities, owners' equity, revenues, expenses, and net income. If the error would have no effect on an item, then so state. The first one is done for you as an example.

	19x3 Income Statement			*December 31,* 19x3 *Balance Sheet*			19x4 *Income Statement*		
Error	*Revenues*	*Expense*	*Net income*	*Assets*	*Liabilities*	*Owners' equity*	*Revenues*	*Expense*	*Net income*
a	None	Under $90	Over $90	None	Under $90	Over $90	None	Over $90	Under $90

P4-11 Presented below is the unadjusted trial balance of the Coronet Company Ltd. as of December 31, 19x9 as well as selected other information.

Coronet Company Ltd.
Unadjusted Trial Balance
12/31/19x9

Cash	$ 3,000	
Accounts receivable	5,000	
Merchandise inventory	155,000	
Prepaid rent	1,500	
Furniture and fixtures	15,000	
Accumulated depreciation		$ 6,000
Accounts payable		9,000
Notes payable		6,000
Sales revenue		220,000
Selling expenses	55,000	
General expenses	18,000	
Interest expense	800	
Tax expense	3,500	
Capital received from shareholders		6,000
Retained earnings		9,800
	$256,800	$256,800

Other information:

1. Interest on the note, at a rate of 12 percent, is due semiannually, April 30 and October 31.
2. Useful life of the furniture and fixtures is five years, with no salvage value. No depreciation has yet been recorded for the year.
3. The company employs a periodic inventory system. A physical count at year end indicates merchandise on hand of $24,000.
4. The company last paid its rent on December 1. Such payment was intended to cover the month of December. (Rent expense is included among "general expenses"; the payment was properly recorded.)
5. On December 31, the board of directors declared a cash dividend, payable January 12, of $4,000.
6. $700 of advertising costs were incorrectly charged to "general expenses" rather than "selling expenses."
7. Estimated taxes for the year are $8,500. Of these only $3,500 have been paid.

Required:

a. Prepare all necessary updating or adjusting entries.
b. Post such entries to T accounts.
c. Prepare a year-end income statement, balance sheet, and statement of changes in retained earnings.

P4-12 This problem is designed to illustrate a year-end *work sheet*, a device useful for the preparation of reports from an unadjusted trial balance.

The end-of-year *unadjusted* trial balance of the Columbia Flying Service Ltd. is indicated below. The following additional information has come to your attention:

1. Instructor salaries for the last week of the month have not yet been recorded. They will be payable the first week of the new year. Salaries for the one week are $1,350.
2. In the course of the previous two weeks, lessons were given that had been paid for in advance. The retail value of such lessons was $650.
3. No depreciation has been recorded in 19x6. The useful life of the planes is estimated at 10 years (no salvage value) and that of the equipment at 7 years (also no salvage value).
4. Rent for December, $100, has not yet been paid.
5. The company purchases a one-year insurance policy each year which takes effect on July 1. The entire cost of the current year's policy has been charged to "insurance expense." The 12/31/19x6 balance in "prepaid insurance" is the same as that on 1/1/19x6. No entries to the account have been made during the year.
6. Interest on the $6,000 note outstanding is payable twice each year, April 1 and October 1. The annual rate of interest is 8 percent. The note was issued on April 1, 19x6; the amount in interest expense represents the first interest payment, which was made on October 1.
7. A physical count of parts on hand indicated an unexplained shortage of parts that had cost $200. No adjustment to inventory has yet been made.
8. All purchases of supplies are charged (debited) to "supplies expense." The balance in "supplies inventory" represents supplies on hand at the beginning of the year. A physical count on December 31, 19x5 indicated supplies currently on hand of $400.
9. On December 30, the company flew a charter for which it has not yet billed the customer and which it has not yet recorded in the accounts. The customer will be charged $680.
10. Based on preliminary computations, the firm estimates that income taxes for the year will be $2,200.

Columbia Flying Service Ltd.
Unadjusted Trial Balance
December 31, 19x6

Cash	$ 3,750	
Accounts receivable	4,500	
Supplies inventory	200	
Parts inventory	2,400	
Equipment	4,200	
Equipment — accumulated depreciation		$ 600
Planes	21,600	
Planes — accumulated depreciation		7,100
Prepaid insurance	1,500	
Accounts payable		800
Lessons paid for but not yet given		2,800
Notes payable		6,000
Common shares		1,000
Retained earnings		7,810

Revenues from lessons		89,500
Revenues from charters		15,600
Salaries	62,300	
Fuel expense	18,900	
Maintenance expense	5,100	
Supplies expense	600	
Insurance expense	3,400	
Advertising expense	1,300	
Rent expense	1,100	
Interest expense	240	
Licenses and fees	120	
	$131,210	$131,210

Required:

a. Prepare all journal entries that would be necessary to adjust and bring the accounts up to date. (Add any additional account titles that you believe to be necessary.)

b. On a 10-column sheet of accounting paper, copy the trial balance as it appears above. Leave an additional six or seven lines between the last account balance and the totals to accommodate accounts to be added by the adjusting entries. Use two columns for the account titles and two for the unadjusted account balances. Label the next two columns "Adjustments" (debits and credits), the next two "Income Statement" (debits and credits), and the last two "Balance Sheet" (debits and credits).

c. Instead of posting the journal entries to T accounts, post them to the appropriate accounts in the column "Adjustments." When you have finished posting the entries, sum the two columns and make certain that the totals of debits and credits are equal.

d. Add (or subtract, as required) across the columns, and indicate the total of each account in the appropriate column under the income statement or balance sheet. Take care. Remember that credits have to be subtracted from debits. Make certain that amounts are transferred to the proper column; it is easy to make an error.

e. Add each of the four income statement and balance sheet columns. The difference between the debit and credit columns of the income statement should be the net income for the year. The difference between the debit and credit columns of the balance sheet should also be the income for the year. If the two differences are not equal, then an error has been made. Why shouldn't the balance sheet balance; i.e., why shouldn't the debits of the balance sheet equal the credits? Look carefully at the balance indicated for retained earnings. Is such balance the before or after "closing balance"? Does it include income of the current year?

f. From the work sheet, prepare in good form both an income statement and a balance sheet. Remember that retained earnings have to be adjusted to take into account income for the current year.

Cases

C4-1 Captain Smith recently incorporated a company, Toronto Tours Limited ("TTL" or the company), to provide tours between Toronto harbor and Niagara-on-the-Lake. In the mid-1920s these trips had been very popular. However, in recent times, trips of this nature were not being offered. Captain Smith was confident that these tours would again become successful. He observed more tourists coming to Toronto and more people interested in the Shaw Festival at Niagara-on-the-Lake. In addition to providing tours, he intended to charter his boat on a per hour basis to special groups. During the month of September the company engaged in the following transactions:

Sept. 1: TTL was incorporated and Captain Smith contributed $35,000 in cash in exchange for 10,000 common shares in the company.

Sept. 1: Signed a five year lease for a boat house calling for a monthly rent of $200. Paid $400 in cash.

Bought a boat at an auction for $25,000 (replacement cost $40,000). Paid $20,000 in cash and signed a 12 percent promissory note payable in two years for the remainder.

Sept. 6: Purchased the following items on credit:
i) fuel – $5,000
ii) life preservers – $200

Sept. 7: Paid $1,000 in cash for a liquor licence.

Sept. 12: Paid for fuel previously purchased on credit.

Sept. 14: Paid $5,000 in cash for wood to be used in the construction of Mr. Smith's cottage.

Sept. 28: Received $1,000 as a deposit from a customer wishing to charter the boat on October 4.

Sept. 29: Declared a dividend of $1,000 payable on October 2.

Sept. 1–30: A summary of charters for the month is as follows:
Charters made to customers who paid cash $6,000.
Charters made to customers on credit $2,000.

Sept. 1 - 30: Collected a total of $500 on charters made to customers on credit.

Sept. 30: Paid the crew's salary of $600 in cash. This $600 represented $500 for the month of September and $100 for the first four days of October.

Additional information:

1. A review of the accounts receivable subsidiary ledger indicates that $200 is likely to be uncollectible.
2. The value of fuel in the storage tanks at the end of the month is $3,000.
3. During September, Captain Smith stood on a busy street corner handing out coupons for free trips of Toronto harbor in the month of October.
4. On October 6, Captain Smith received an invoice in the amount of $500 from his lawyer for incorporating the company.

Required:

a. Assume the role of the controller:
   (i) What are the accounting problems?
   (ii) Which financial statements would you recommend be prepared? Why?
   (iii) Account for the above transactions indicating why you consider each of your entries to be appropriate.

(iv) Prepare an income statement and balance sheet.

b. Assume the role of the banker.

(i) What questions would you raise with Captain Smith in assessing the company's financial statements?

(ii) Would you make a loan to the company? Why?

*C4-2 Good Boy Limited ("GBL" or, the company) was incorporated several years ago by Mr. Oaster. Since its incorporation the company has been moderately successful. Its operations consist of three retail appliance stores located in Southwestern Ontario. The company's fiscal year end is August 31.

The success of the appliance business is directly related to the state of the economy. More specifically, appliance sales improve as the number of housing starts increase, the unemployment rate reduces and disposable incomes increase.

Mr. Oaster has been in the appliance business for thirty-five years and he loves it. He would like to expand GBL's operations. At present, he is the president and only shareholder of the company. Unfortunately, his wife would prefer him to retire and move to Florida together with their two dogs.

Mr. Oaster has managed to appease his wife by promising that he will retire within three years. However, before he retires he would like to see his company grow to be one of the largest retail operations in Ontario. However, growth requires capital and Mr. Oaster has little personal savings. Therefore the only options that appear to be available are to sell additional shares or borrow money from a creditor.

Recently, Mr. Oaster has had offers from individuals who are interested in purchasing the property upon which his stores are situated. In addition he has been approached by large retail operations wishing to acquire his appliance operations. Both of these courses of action were rejected by Mr. Oaster.

However, in order that he might better assess his company's future, he would like a set of financial statements prepared. Therefore, Mr. Oaster has provided you with the following unadjusted trial balance and additional information as at August 31, 19x7:

	Debit	*Credit*
Cash	$ 1,000	$
Accounts receivable	150,000	
Inventory	200,000	
Unexpired insurance	5,000	
Property, plant and equipment	200,000	
Accumulated depreciation		60,000
Accounts payable		150,000
Notes payable (bearing interest at 12%)		200,000
Common shares		30,000
Retained earnings		55,000
Sales		510,000
Cost of goods sold	240,000	
Salaries expense	80,000	
Office expenses	32,000	

Heat, light and power expense	10,000	
Selling expense	75,000	
Interest expense	12,000	
	$1,005,000	$1,005,000

Additional data:

1. A review of the accounts receivable subsidiary ledger indicates that $12,000 is likely to be uncollectible.
2. At year-end unexpired insurance is $1,400.
3. Salaries payable at August 31 total $1,500.
4. Interest on the 12 percent notes payable at August 31, is $4,000. The notes payable are due on December 31, 19x7.
5. Estimated electricity expense for August is $800.
6. A physical count of inventory at year end revealed that merchandise costing $185,000 was on hand.

Required:

a. Assume the role of an accounting advisor and
   (i) Prepare the adjusting journal entries at August 31, 19x7 which you feel are appropriate.
   (ii) Prepare a balance sheet and an income statement together with the notes to the financial statements which you feel are appropriate.
   (iii) What would you recommend that Mr. Oaster do? Why?

b. Assume the role of a potential creditor. What additional information do you require? Would you loan the company money? Why?

c. Assume the role of a potential investor. What additional information do you require? Would you invest in the company? Why?

C4-3 The ABC Doll Co. Ltd. manufactures dolls. The shares of the company are closely held but the owners do not take an active role in managing the company. Business has been good but the company does have capacity to produce 50,000 dolls and sales in recent years have never exceeded 40,000 dolls.

The sales price per doll is $10. The company has had orders for dolls at lower prices but has refused these because it wants to make a "reasonable profit." Presently a customer has offered to buy 15,000 dolls at $7.50 each.

Each doll requires $2 of raw materials and $4 of factory labor to produce. In addition the company estimates that depreciation costs on the factory building and equipment as well as other *fixed* factory costs total $60,000 per year. ("Fixed" factory costs, although at times considered product costs, do not vary with the number of units produced. They would be the same in total regardless of whether the company produced 10,000 or 50,000 dolls per year.)

Last year, 19x7, the company produced 40,000 dolls but sold 20,000 dolls. It is now June 30, 19x8. To date the company has produced 10,000 dolls and sold 20,000 dolls. Projected sales for the remainder of 19x8 are 15,000 dolls.

The company plans to issue additional common shares in January 19x9. The company controller thinks it is important that the firm impress potential purchasers with a significant growth in earnings in 19x8. However, he is not sure how the company can generate this earnings growth. Therefore, he has approached you for advice.

Required:

Write a report to the controller outlining your recommendations. Include in your report an analysis of alternatives and the reasoning underlying your recommendations.

C4-4 Costing Ltd. (or the company) was incorporated January 2, 19x1. The company is owned by brothers who perform many duties on behalf of the company ranging from helping on the production line to marketing the company's products. Costing Ltd. manufactures lamps. The manufacturing process consists of two operations — machining and assembly.

While the brothers know a lot about the lamp business, they are not very knowledgeable when it comes to accounting.

Therefore, they have approached you for some advice. Fortunately they have kept all the documents, invoices and so forth that relate to the company. A review of these records has provided the following information:

1. On January 2 the owners of the company contributed $25,000 in cash to start the business.
2. The company borrowed $10,000 from a local bank. It agreed to make annual interest payments at a rate of 12 percent and to repay the loan in its entirety at the end of three years.
3. The company rented manufacturing space. It paid three months' rent in advance. Rent is $400 per month.
4. The company purchased manufacturing equipment at a cost of $36,000 and office furniture and equipment at a cost of $4,800. Both purchases were made on account.
5. The firm purchased raw materials at a cost of $7,000 cash. Of these, raw materials that cost $6,000 were placed in production.
6. The firm hired and paid factory workers, $6,000, and office workers, $1,500, in cash.
7. Factory maintenance costs incurred during the month were $450; factory utility costs were $600. Neither cost had yet been paid.
8. The company recorded depreciation for the month; manufacturing equipment, $1,000; office furniture and equipment $100.
9. The company gave accounting recognition to interest and rent costs for the month. (See events 2 and 3 above.) Seventy-five percent of rent costs were allocated to the factory and twenty-five percent to the office.
10. The company completed and transferred to finished goods inventory products that had cost $14,000 to manufacture.
11. The company sold for $20,000 (on account) goods that had cost $13,000 to manufacture.
12. Selling and other administrative costs paid in cash were $1,000.

Required:

a. Discuss the advantages and disadvantages of accrual vs cash accounting system for the company.
b. Which of Costing Ltd.'s costs would you classify as products costs? Why?
c. Design a record-keeping system for the company (i.e., indicate the subsidiary records which are required and why).
d. Prepare journal entries to reflect the events that took place in January.
e. Post the journal entries to T accounts.
f. Prepare a month-end income statement and balance sheet.
g. Evaluate the company's first month of operations.

Appendix 4-A

Adjusting and Correcting Journal Entries

Internal control

In order to protect a company against fraud and error, its accountants set up a system of *internal control*. Such a system attempts to divide up warehouse, plant, and office work procedures so that a person acting alone is less likely to cause serious errors and fraud.

Often internal control can be strengthened by selecting one accounting procedure over another. Consider a situation where a company pays $3,600 in advance for 36 months of insurance. The transaction may be recorded in at least two ways:

1. Prepaid (or unexpired) insurance (asset +)	$3,600	
Cash (asset −)		$3,600
2. Insurance expense (expense +)	$3,600	
Cash (asset −)		$3,600

Entry 1 is preferred when internal control is an important objective of accounting: companies usually have far greater controls placed on a balance sheet account than on an income statement account and the prepaid insurance account would be analyzed and controlled more carefully than an expense account. Consequently, internal control is usually strengthened when the offsetting debits or credits to cash receipts and payments are made to balance sheet accounts, rather than income statement accounts.

Understanding adjustments

There is a tendency in introductory accounting classes to memorize without understanding the subject, particularly adjusting journal entries. In order to minimize this danger, we are providing an additional exercise to aid in understanding. Some of the original entries following are unusual and contrary to a good system of internal control; but we are using them to teach adjusting journal entries, which are needed to measure income. This should be carefully noted as we proceed.

The theme of adjusting and correcting entries is simple. Adjusting entries amend each of the ledger accounts from its current balance before adjustment to the required amount at statement preparation dates. The *error* which *must be avoided* is failing to ask oneself: "What is the current balance before adjustment?"

Asset/expense example

To illustrate, let us refer to the two journal entries which we might have made for the thirty-six-month $3,600 insurance purchase. The *adjusting* entry after one month, *assuming* the *original* debit was to prepaid insurance would be:

Insurance expense (expense +)	$100	
Prepaid insurance (asset −)		$100

In contrast, if the original debit of $3,600 was to insurance expense, the adjusting entry at the end of the first month would be:

Prepaid insurance (asset +)	$3,500	
Insurance expense (expense −)		$3,500

The variations can be depicted as follows:

If the original transaction entry is:			*The adjusting entry would be:*		
January 1, 19x1:			January 31, 19x1:		
(1) Prepaid insurance (asset +)	$3,600		(1) Insurance expense (expense +)	$100	
Cash (asset −)		$3,600	Prepaid insurance (asset −)		$ 100
(2) Insurance expense (expense +)	$3,600		(2) Prepaid insurance (asset +)	$3,500	
Cash (asset −)		$3,600	Insurance expense (expense −)		$3,500
(3) Insurance expense (expense +)	$ 100		(3) No entry required.		
Prepaid insurance (asset +)	3,500				
Cash (asset −)		$3,600			

In (3) above, we ask ourselves the basic questions:

A. What are the balances in the accounts before adjustment?
B. What should the balances be after adjustment?
C. How do I get from (A) to (B)?

At the end of January the figures for (3) are:

Account	*What is now before adjustment*	*What ought to be after adjustment*	*Adjustment needed*
Insurance expense	$ 100 Debit	$ 100 Debit	None
Prepaid insurance	$3,500 Debit	$3,500 Debit	None

Liability/revenue example

Suppose you were given the following facts and asked for *adjusting* journal entries on January 31, 19x1 for a magazine publisher: "$72,000 was received on January 1, 19x1 for magazine subscriptions extending to the next thirty-six months; the magazine is published monthly at mid-month."

Clearly, it is not possible to provide an adjusting entry without first *making an assumption* about the original transaction journal entry. The variations are:

If the original transaction entry is:			*Then, the adjusting entry would be:*		
January 1:			January 31:		
(1) Cash (asset +)	$72,000		(1) Unearned revenue (liability −)	$ 2,000	
Unearned revenue (liability +)		$72,000	Revenue (revenue +)		$ 2,000
(2) Cash (asset +)	$72,000		(2) Revenue (revenue −)	$70,000	
Revenue (revenue +)		$72,000	Unearned revenue (liability +)		70,000
(3) Cash (asset +)	$72,000		(3) No entry needed		
Revenue (revenue +)		$ 2,000			
Unearned revenue (liability +)		70,000			

The ability of students to recognize that different original transaction entries require different adjusting entries distinguishes those who understand the accounting cycle and adjustments from those who memorize one way of handling adjustments. A complete answer should be worded somewhat as follows: "*If* the original transaction entry was ________ then the adjusting journal entry would be ________."

Using (2) for illustrative purposes:

Revenue			*Unearned Revenue*		
	Balance before adjustment	$72,000		Balance before adjustment	$ 0
	Balance needed after adjustment	2,000		Balance needed after adjustment	70,000

Adjusting entry needed:

Account	Debit	Credit
Revenue (revenue −)	70,000	
Unearned revenue (liability+)		70,000

Observe that on *February 28*, assuming that the correct adjustments were made on January 31, all of (1), (2) and (3) would require the same *adjusting* entry:

Account	Debit	Credit
Unearned revenue (liability −)	$ 2,000	
Revenue (revenue +)		$ 2,000

Complex example

Adjusting entries can affect, in addition to the above two examples, expense/liability, expense/asset contra, and some other combinations of accounts. Sometimes complex adjusting entries are required. For instance, suppose that a fixed asset costing $60,000 and having a life of five years is inadvertently charged to a "maintenance expense" account on January 1, 19x2. The *adjusting* (and correcting) journal entry at January 31, 19x2 would have to be:

Account	Debit	Credit
Asset (asset +)	$60,000	
Depreciation expense (expense +)	1,000	
Maintenance expense (expense −)		$60,000
Accumulated depreciation (asset contra +)		1,000

The journal entry could be split into two parts: (a) debiting the fixed asset and crediting the expense in order to correct the error; and (b) recognizing depreciation on the newly recorded asset. Part (b) can easily be missed unless one considers the consequences of all previous adjusting entries.

Summary

Before preparing an adjusting entry one must know: (1) what *is* currently showing as the account balance and; (2) what should or *ought to be* in the account. The remainder of one's effort is addition or subtraction as long as the double entry mechanism and related accounts are kept in mind. For example, an expense generally *decreases* only when an asset increases, a liability decreases, and another expense increases. Adjusting entries rarely affect cash. Most often, in fact, the purpose of the adjusting entry is to move away from cash accounting to accrual basis accounting.

Appendix 4-B

Recognizing Expense in a Manufacturing Operation

It has been previously pointed out that, in accordance with the accrual concept, costs are *capitalized* as assets until the intended services are actually provided. But what are such services, and when are they provided? In a business enterprise, costs are incurred in order to generate revenues. Hence costs should be recognized as expenses at the same time that the benefits that they produce are recognized as revenues. In other words, costs should be *matched* with revenues.

In a retail sales operation the major cost incurred in the production of revenue is that of the goods to be sold. As the goods to be sold are received, their cost is *stored* in an asset account, "merchandise inventory." Only when they are actually sold, and when sales revenue is recognized, is the cost of the goods sold charged as an expense. At the time of sale (or if a periodic inventory method is followed, then at least in the period of sale) the following entry is made:

Cost of goods sold (expense)	xxxx	
Merchandise inventory (asset)		xxxx

It follows that in a manufacturing operation all the costs of producing the goods intended for sale should also be stored as assets until the goods are actually sold. This means that not only should costs of raw materials be capitalized as assets, but so too must costs of labor, maintenance, machines used (i.e., depreciation), and all other costs that can readily be identified with the production process.

When raw materials are purchased, their cost is charged initially to an asset account, "raw materials." As they are placed in production, their cost is transferred to "work in process," another asset account, and when the goods are completed their cost is transferred to "finished goods," also an asset account.

This is also true with labor. Although labor, unlike raw materials, cannot be physically stored, the *cost* of labor, like the cost of raw materials, *can* be stored in an asset *account*. Labor costs are conventionally recorded initially in an asset account, "labor," and then transferred immediately (since labor cannot be physically stored) to "work in process." The labor account, although perhaps unnecessary since the costs are transferred immediately to work in process, is ordinarily maintained inasmuch as it facilitates cost control by providing management with a record of labor costs incurred.

So also with other manufacturing costs. Even that portion of manufacturing equipment considered to be consumed in the accounting period must be capitalized as part of the cost of the goods produced. The equipment serves to benefit the periods in which the goods that have been used to produce are actually sold. Costs of using up the equipment (i.e., depreciation) must be added to work in process (an asset account) and thereby included in the cost of the finished goods. They will be charged as an expense (as part of cost of goods sold) when the finished goods are actually sold.

EXHIBIT 4B-1

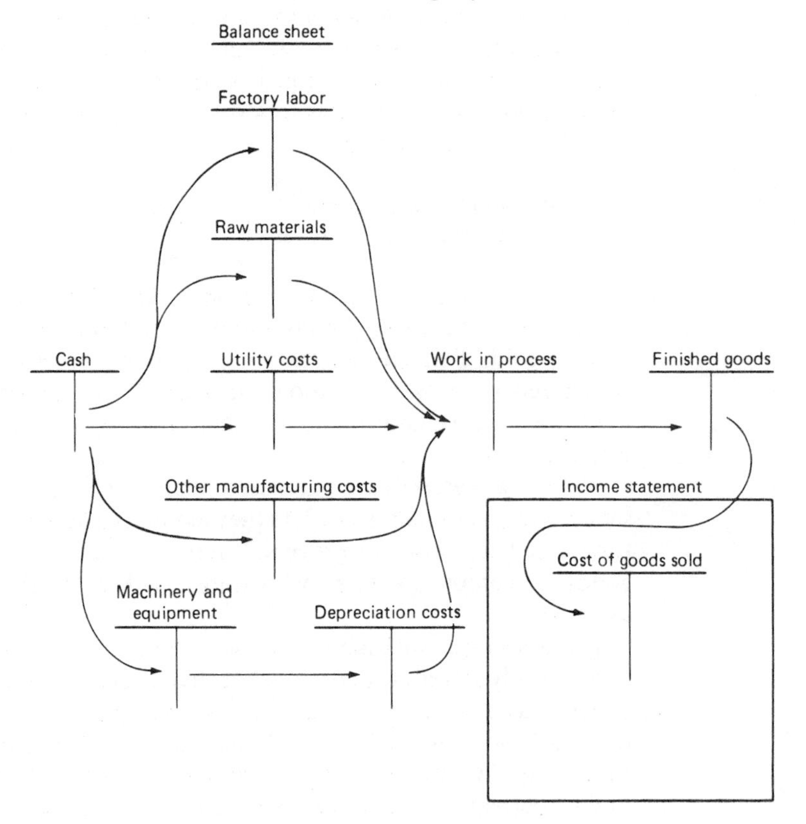

The manufacturing cycle is depicted graphically in Exhibit 4B-1.

EXAMPLE

In its first period of operations the ABC Manufacturing Co. purchased 1,200 units of raw materials at $1 per unit and placed into production 1,000 such units. Labor costs for the period were $2,000; utility costs were $400; depreciation charges on manufacturing equipment were $100. Of the units placed into production all were completed and 800 were sold at a price of $5.00 per unit. The following journal entries would be appropriate:

(a)

Raw materials inventory (asset)	$1,200	
Accounts payable		$1,200
To record the purchase of 1,200 units of raw materials at $1 per unit.		

(b)

Work in process (asset)	$1,000	
Raw materials inventory		$1,000
To record the transfer of 1,000 units of raw materials at $1 per unit.		

(c)

Labor costs (asset)	$2,000	
Wages payable		$2,000
To record the wages of manufacturing personnel. The labor costs are not yet considered to be an expense since the goods to the production of which the employees contributed have not yet been sold; the costs still have "future service value."		

(d)

Work in process (asset)	$2,000	
Labor costs		$2,000
To add applicable labor costs to the costs of production.		

(e)

Utility costs (asset)	$400	
Accounts payable		$400
To record utility costs. Although utility services cannot physically be stored, they are capitalized as an asset (a *deferred* expense) since the costs will benefit the period in which the goods produced using utilities are actually sold.		

(f)

Work in process (asset)	$400	
Utility costs		$400
To add applicable utility costs to the costs of production.		

(g)

	Debit	Credit
Depreciation costs (asset)	$100	
Machinery and equipment — accumulated depreciation		$100

To record depreciation costs. This entry has the effect of transferring costs from one asset, "machinery and equipment," to another, "depreciation costs."

(h)

	Debit	Credit
Work in process (asset +)	$100	
Depreciation costs		$100

To add applicable depreciation charges to the costs of production. (The goods have not been sold; hence, depreciation was incurred in producing an asset — inventory of work in process).

(i)

	Debit	Credit
Finished goods inventory (asset)	$3,500	
Work in process		$3,500

To record the completion of the manufacturing process and the transfer of all costs from "work in process" to "finished goods inventory." The entry, like the previous ones, involves only balance sheet, not income statement, accounts.

(j)

	Debit	Credit
Accounts receivable (asset)	$4,000	
Sales (revenue)		$4,000

To record the sale of 800 units at $5 per unit.

(k)

	Debit	Credit
Cost of goods sold (expense)	$2,800	
Finished goods inventory		$2,800

To record the expense related to the realization of sales revenue. 1,000 units of product, at a total cost of $3,500, were transferred from "work in process" to "finished goods inventory." The cost per unit, therefore, equals $3,500 divided by the 1,000 units — $3.50 per unit. 800 units × $3.50 = $2,800.

Entries (j) and (k) are the critical ones from the standpoint of the enterprise. The previous entries involved nothing more than exchanges among asset and liability accounts. The company was no better off after such exchanges than it was before — at least to the extent that the equity of the owners remained unchanged. Entry (j) recorded the increase in the level of owners' equity attributable to sale of the company's product; entry (k) recorded the decrease in the level of owners' equity attributable to the surrender of assets — the labor, the raw materials, the equipment, and the utility services consumed — which generated the revenues. Exhibit 4B-2 summarizes the journal entries in T account format.

EXHIBIT 4B-2

Example of Manufacturing Cycle

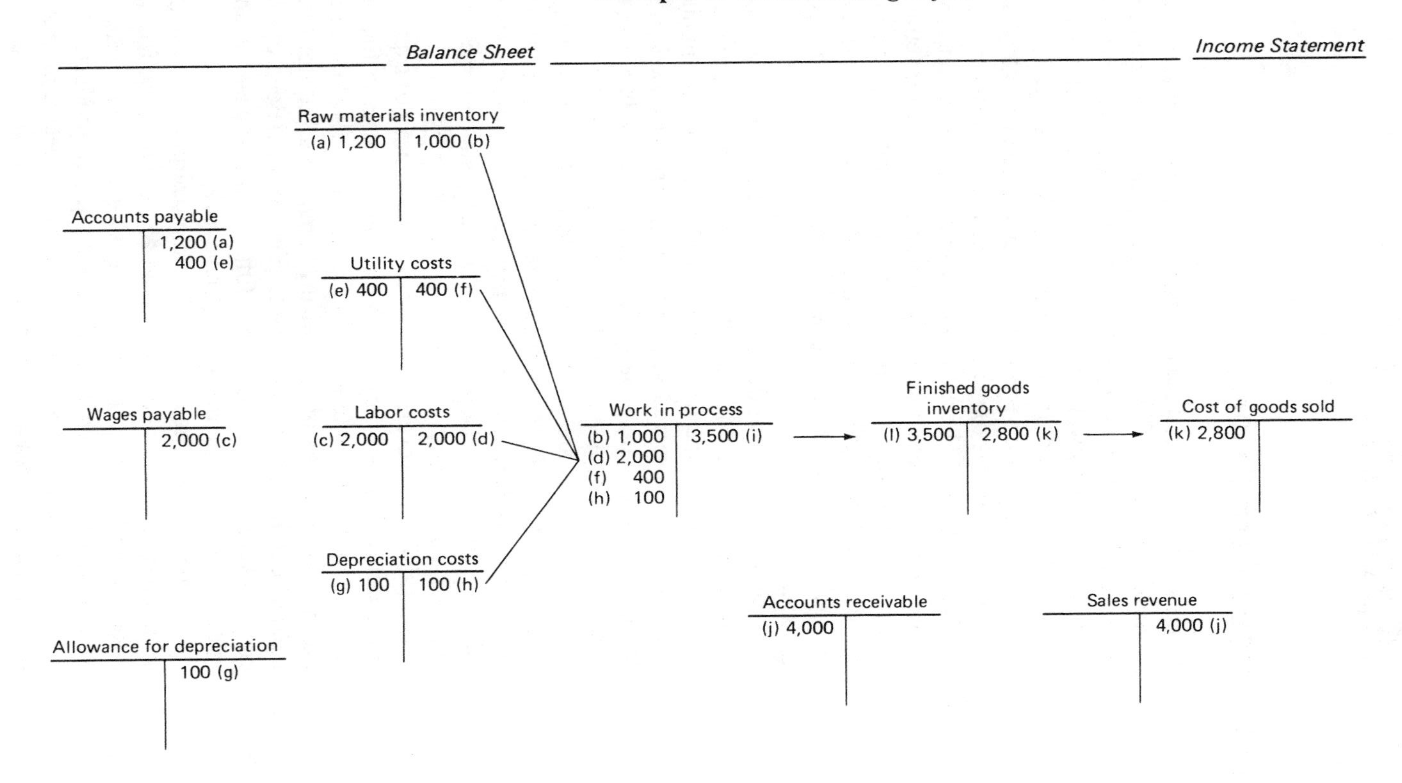

Appendix 4-C

Product Versus Period Costs

Some users of financial statements are interested in accountants' computations of net income. These users might include creditors (especially those who have loaned the company money for twenty or more years) who expect net income to well exceed interest payments to them. Net income is also the starting point in calculating income subject to income taxes.

In computing their version of net income accountants make frequent reference to a *principle of matching* — one that provides that as much as practical all costs should be associated with particular revenues and recorded as expenses in the same periods in which the related revenues are given accounting recognition. Costs that are associated with revenues to be recognized in the future are to be maintained in asset accounts until such time as recognition is accorded the revenues and the costs can properly be charged as expenses.

Expenses have been defined as the goods or services consumed in the creation of revenue. Indeed, *all* expenses are incurred in the hope of generating revenue. If the accountant's objective of determining periodic income is to be best served, then all costs incurred by the firm should be capitalized as assets — i.e., charged initially to "work in process" or otherwise added to the cost of goods held in inventory — and recorded as expenses only as the goods are actually sold. Costs of administering a head office, and selling the products contribute as much to the generation of revenue as those of manufacturing the product. Logically, such costs should also be added to the cost of the product *if* it were possible to trace the link between the costs and revenue.

In practice, however, many types of costs are not capitalized as part of the product. Instead they are charged as expenses in the period in which they are incurred, regardless of when the products of the firm are sold. The logical inconsistency of capitalizing some costs but not others has by no means been lost upon accountants. They have yielded to practical exigencies, however. It is simply too difficult to associate meaningfully — to match — certain expenses with specific revenues.

Consider, for example, costs of administration — the salaries of officers, secretaries, computer operators, and accountants; the fees paid to outside attorneys and auditors; the costs of renting office space and equipment. If a firm manufactured numerous different types of products, it would be difficult, to say the least, to *allocate* such costs to specific products. Or consider sales costs. A salesman might make numerous calls on customers before he receives an order. Is it possible, in any meaningful way, to associate costs of the unsuccessful calls with specific revenues to be generated in the future?

To reduce the need to make knotty allocation decisions, accountants have adopted certain conventions as to which types of costs should be added to the cost of the product and which should be charged off as expenses in the period in which they are incurred. Although there is by no means universal agreement on the conventions, as a general rule, *direct* manufacturing costs, such as factory labor and raw materials, are always charged to the product (i.e., included in "work in process"). So also are several types of *indirect* costs such as depreciation on manufacturing equipment, factory utility costs, rent on the factory building, and salaries of employees who are directly concerned with manufacturing operations. On the other hand, costs of selling, advertising and promotion, interest, employee health and recreational facilities, most taxes, and most other "home office" costs are ordinarily considered to be *period* costs, which are charged as expenses as incurred.

The widely followed conventions do not, by any means, eliminate the need to allocate common costs to specific products. *Factory overhead* costs (those which cannot readily be identified with specific products), such as those for supervision, utilities, maintenance, and rent, must still be assigned on the basis of the best judgment of accountants. And, as a consequence of the conventions, seemingly similar types of costs are sometimes accorded different accounting treatment. Depreciation on tables or chairs in a factory are considered to be product costs; that on tables or chairs in the home office are considered to be period costs; salaries of accounting clerks who are concerned specifically with factory-related accounts are included among product costs; those of accounting clerks who deal with other types of accounts are excluded as period costs. Exhibit 4C-1 compares the recognition of depreciation as a period cost with that of a product cost.

In evaluating whether to include a specific cost as a product or a period cost, one relevant question must always be raised: What would be the impact on both the income statement and the balance sheet of alternative classifications?

If within a given accounting period the enterprise sells the *same* number of goods that it produces (assuming no change in per unit costs from one period to the next), then it makes no difference whether a cost is classified as a product or a period cost. Suppose, for example, the salary of an accounting clerk were $12,000 in a given year. During the year the firm produces and sells 12,000 units. If the salary were considered a period cost, then $12,000 would be reported as an expense among "administrative" expenses; if it were considered a product cost, then $12,000 would first be capitalized as "work in process," then transferred to "finished goods inven-

EXHIBIT 4C-1

Depreciation as a Product Cost Versus Depreciation as a Period Cost

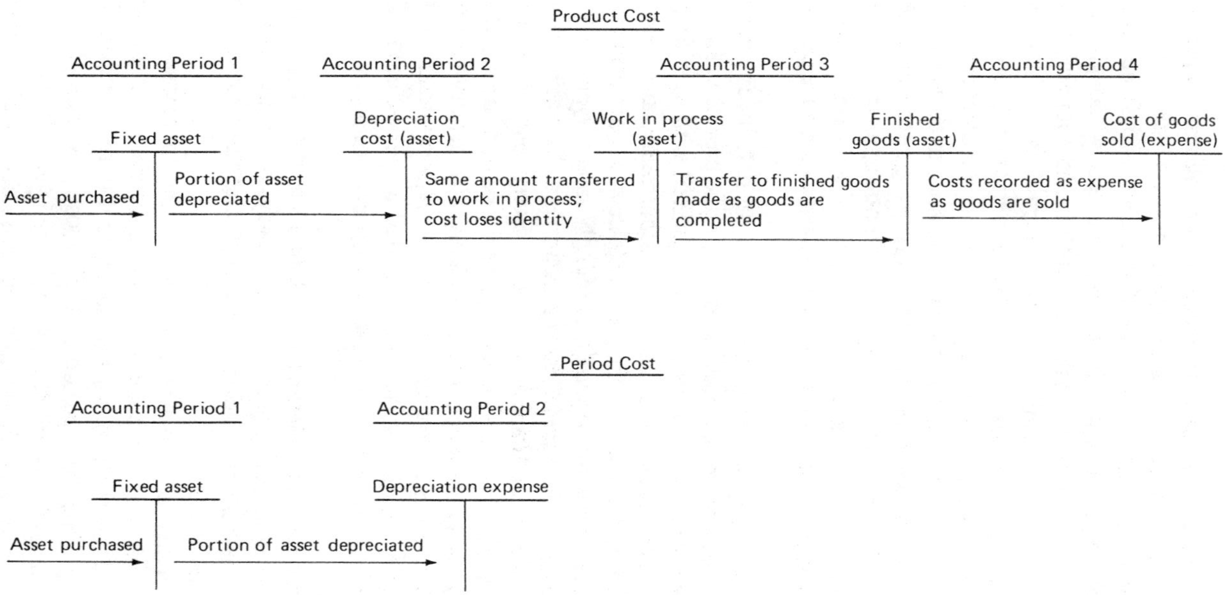

Product Cost

Accounting Period 1

Fixed asset

Asset purchased →

Portion of asset depreciated →

Accounting Period 2

Depreciation cost (asset)

Same amount transferred to work in process; cost loses identity →

Accounting Period 3

Work in process (asset)

Transfer to finished goods made as goods are completed →

Finished goods (asset)

Accounting Period 4

Costs recorded as expense as goods are sold →

Cost of goods sold (expense)

Period Cost

Accounting Period 1

Fixed asset

Asset purchased →

Portion of asset depreciated →

Accounting Period 2

Depreciation expense

Note: Accounting periods need not necessarily be consecutive accounting periods, and more than one transfer can take place in the same accounting period tory" and finally reported as an expense, in the same period, "cost of goods sold."

If the enterprise sells *fewer* goods than it produces, then reported expenses would be *greater* if the costs were categorized as period costs than if they were treated as product costs. Assume the same firm produces 12,000 units but sells only 10,000 units. If the $12,000 salary of the accounting clerk were classified as a period cost, then the full $12,000 would be charged off as an expense. If, however, it were classified as a product cost, then $1 ($12,000 divided by the number of units produced) would be added to the cost of each unit produced. Since 10,000 units were sold, only $10,000 would be included among cost of goods sold. The remaining $2,000 would be *stored* on the balance sheet, included among "finished goods inventory." Hence current assets, specifically inventory, would be $2,000 greater than if the salary were accounted for as a period cost.

If the enterprise sells more goods than it produces, then the reverse would be true. Reported expenses would be less if certain costs were treated as period rather than as product costs. Assume that in the following year the firm produces 12,000 units but sells 14,000 units, taking the additional 2,000 units from inventory. If the accounting clerk's salary were treated as a period cost, then, as previously, the $12,000 would be reported as an expense. But if it were treated as a product cost, $14,000 of salary costs would be charged off as expense — $1 per unit produced and sold in the current period (12,000 units) plus $1 per unit of the goods sold in the current period but produced in the previous period (2,000 units).

5 *Revenues and Expenses*

Objectives of Financial Accounting

We have mentioned that an ideal state for accounting would be to have "*like accounting in like situations*." We have also said that situations differ because of different objectives of accounting, facts, and constraints (mainly legal). Thus, our ideal is to use the *same accounting* procedure or disclosure *when objectives — facts — constraints are the same*.

It is time to take a closer look at what we mean by objectives or purposes of accounting. We will look at facts and constraints in later chapters. Objectives of accounting are broader than objectives of financial statements or financial *reporting*.[1] The listing which follows is that for objectives of financial accounting.

Does the list appear to be complete? As you proceed through it try to think of different types of organizations. What are their objectives of financial accounting?

1. *Internal control* — Some organizations such as charities, which do not pay income tax, want only the bookkeeping benefits of double entry accounting so that errors can be reduced. They may use cash basis accounting for statements rather than statements based on accrual accounting.

2. *Income taxation* — Some smaller businesses need accounting records

only to prepare their income tax returns for the Department of National Revenue. Accounting principles based on GAAP (generally accepted accounting principles) differ somewhat from those accepted under the Income Tax Act. Owners of some smaller businesses therefore may use income tax accounting methods which could be at variance with GAAP in Canada. They are willing to depart from GAAP because their only need is for an income tax return, usually accompanied by a few financial statements in any one of several forms and approaches (GAAP and non-GAAP).

More commonly in Canada, business-owners try to find GAAP procedures which are also acceptable for income tax needs. Professional accountants must frequently deal with organizations whose multiple accounting objectives require a choice, and sometimes a compromise, of accounting procedures.

Those who aspire to be financial analysts or business managers must become fully aware of these conflicts. Those who wish to be professional accountants must learn to judge wisely in view of conflicts. Many Canadian businesses are not incorporated under a Provincial or Federal Companies Act (and do not have the words limited or corporation in their name). Thus, their owners usually do not prepare the lengthy and comprehensive financial statements required for John Labatt Limited. The extensive disclosure employed by Labatt's often enables a company to have one set of financial statements which can satisfy the needs of more than one user group.

3. *Special purpose reports* — Organizations such as hospitals, school boards, and some insurance companies, which are the result of special federal or provincial legislation (eg., Farm Marketing Board) are often required to prepare financial reports for a specific user. These reports vary considerably in design and content and may or may not be in accordance with GAAP. In addition, some merchandising or manufacturing firms have demands for special purpose reports. For example, a report may be prepared to set out losses resulting from a fire. A special report may be requested by a potential major creditor who desires extensive information about large customers and suppliers, and details about inventory and fixed assets.

   The requirements of special purpose reports do not often conflict with regular reporting. However, occasionally a piece of legislation dictates a special type of non-GAAP report and states that reports to owners/shareholders must be based on the specified non-GAAP approach. A few years ago, insurance company accounting was primarily prescribed by legislation which varied with GAAP. Many insurance companies were not allowed by their governing legislation to show *fixed* assets such as furniture and equipment on their balance sheets.

The insurance law requested a balance sheet of *liquid* assets, which could be used on demand to pay off policyholders and other creditors. Insurance law accounting clearly conflicted with needs of owners and other groups. Although some improvements have been made in tailoring insurance company statements to a wider audience, more must still be accomplished.

4. *Stewardship reporting* — Many Canadian companies whose managers are not the owners or creditors and which have borrowed large sums of money are required to prepare "stewardship" financial statements. The basic idea assumes that the managers ("stewards") must report back to the owners/creditors concerning their management of the enterprise and the status of the funds invested. In a narrow sense, your bank book or monthly bank statement is a stewardship report. It shows interest credited to you alongside deposits and withdrawals.

   Unfortunately, stewardship reporting in the 1980s is somewhat nebulous. Three reasons for this are:

   A. Changes in laws, the state of the economy, and shareholder — manager relations have obscured over time the nature and obligations of a manager/steward, and the penalties for incomplete reporting. Various lawsuits in the next decade may clarify the responsibilities of "stewards" in a reporting environment.
   B. In Canada, corporate law permits stewards to prepare reports on themselves. Obviously this poses fairness problems because a person who is reporting on himself may only describe the favorable side of a situation to his owners/creditors. Some control does exist from having auditors check the financial statements; however, auditors may be restricted to reporting on the accounting procedures chosen by the managers. Auditors *do not* pick the company's specific accounting principles and procedures.
   C. When one is trying to satisfy a request it would seem logical to find out clearly what the other person wants. Accountants should therefore ask users such as creditors, financial analysts, and shareholders what they want to see reported. Often users are not sure what they want. The result is that groups such as financial analysts ask for virtually everything. Why? The analysts do not have to pay for accounting preparation costs; accounting information is *free* to them. Under these circumstances, wouldn't you ask for everything? But this attitude hinders accountants in their search for good principles.

   This nebulous state of stewardship reporting will continue to confuse, because "stewardship" involves quite different ideas for different people. In addition, little recent progress has been made in narrowing these differences in thought. In order to proceed we must choose one definition, even though many people will probably disagree with it.

The definition of stewardship to be used in this book is narrow: stewardship accounting and reporting are the *minimum* required to comply with GAAP and any constraints (such as Companies and Securities Acts). Under this definition, objectivity is favored over relevance in many situations.

Broader definitions of stewardship may include items 5 and 6 which follow. Some say that all forms of accounting together constitute stewardship.

Nevertheless, we need a name for objectives of companies which follow minimum disclosure under GAAP and the law. In this book minimum disclosure can be regarded as synonymous with a stewardship objective of accounting. By following such a definition we can give special attention to 5 and 6 below.

5. *Cash flow prediction* — Investors establish the current worth of a business by attempting to ascertain the *present value of cash flows* which may appear in the *future*. The concept of present value is explained in Chapter 6, but a brief comment is necessary now.

   Which would you prefer: \$2,000 received today? or \$2,000 to be received in one year? If we ignore inflation and its effect on the purchasing power of a dollar, we would prefer the \$2,000 received today. Why? The \$2,000 received today could be invested at 10 percent interest per annum and be worth \$2,200 (\$2,000 + (10 percent x 2,000)) in one year. Whereas the period of one year hence might be thought of as *future value*, the concept of present value means, *value today*. Observe that we cannot compare the above choice (\$2,000 today vs. \$2,000 in one year) unless we have both in the *same* time frame — either future value or present value. Since decisions are made at the current time, people tend to compare using *present value*.

   Using present value terms and a 10 percent interest rate:

	Present Value is
\$2,000 received today	\$2,000
\$2,000 to be received in one year:	
$\$2{,}000 \times \frac{100}{110} =$	\$1,818

   On a present value basis, the \$2,000 received today is worth \$182 more.

   Where did we get the fraction 100/110 from? The 100 is the present time, and the 110 is one year hence:

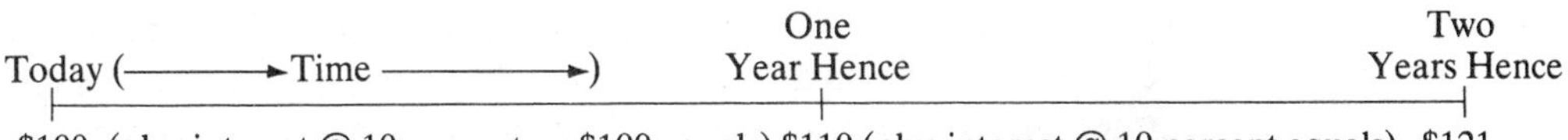

To convert at 10 percent interest per annum from one year hence to today we would have to multiply by 100/110. To convert from two years hence to today we would multiply by 100/121. The Appendix at the back of the book converts the fractions to decimals for easier computation.

Investors would establish the current worth of $1,000 to be received in one year as $909 (assuming a 10 percent interest rate is used) ($1000 × 100/110). They would also establish the current worth at $200 of these amounts: $110 to be received in one year and $121 to be received two years hence:

$$\$110 : \frac{100}{110} = \$100$$

$$121 : \frac{100}{121} = \underline{100}$$

$$\underline{\underline{\$200}}$$

Naturally, when one tries to establish the present value or current worth of an ongoing business one would have to look many years into the future. It is important to remember that to many investors, present worth means future *cash* flows discounted at an interest rate to arrive at today's present value.

Can financial accounting aid in establishing the *amount* and *timing* of cash flows which may occur in the future? Obviously some people think that financial accounting reports *are* helpful in predicting cash flows and tend to request accounting information. This accounting information may be different from that used for income tax or stewardship objectives. Yet, if the company needs money in the future for expansion it must satisfy potential investors by providing extensive information about itself to aid in the prediction of the amount and timing of cash flows. Company managers would not usually report *their* guesses about the future cash flows and earnings of their company, because this is often illegal. Hence, investors are left on their own to make predictions about the future success of a company. They use economic, political, legal, foreign affairs, and other information besides accounting in trying to estimate future cash flows of a company.

For large companies in Canada, the preparation of accounting statements for investors who wish to predict future cash flows is no doubt important. But it is vital to remember that prediction is only one of several objectives and may be of little importance in many medium or small-sized Canadian companies where owners have access to other sources of information. Accounting researchers have recently spent considerable time and effort on the prediction objective, and many current articles exist on the subject — perhaps to the exclusion of a fair treatment of other objectives. Students who read accounting journals should remember to put the prediction objective in perspective for Canada: It pertains mainly to the larger corporations which also have other accounting objectives.

6. *Evaluation of management by outside creditors and investors* — Unfortunately, this objective is as vague as some of the previous ones. It is a close associate of the prediction objective because evaluations of management are an intermediate step in attempting to predict (future) cash flows of an enterprise. Supporters of this objective reason as follows: *If* (1) good and bad luck can be separated from good and bad management; *and* (2) actions and results attributable to the current management can be separated from those of previous managements; *and* (3) good management actions of the past will somehow be repeated in the future; *then* accounting reports which separate factors such as good management and good luck, might be a powerful tool to predict (future) cash flows. Ideally, the information would reflect management actions of the *current* year. This is asking a great deal from accounting reports.

   Suppose that 50 years ago Green Forest Products Corporation bought a parcel of land (#101) and rights to harvest the timber for $500,000. This year it bought an adjoining parcel of land (#102) with the same acreage and quality of timber for $10,000,000. If management wishes to log one of the two parcels this year, which would it choose? If the two parcels are identical presumably it would not matter to operating managers which is logged. However, the effect on income before income taxes would be huge! Assuming that there is no residual value to land which has been logged, the cost of goods sold could be as much as $9,500,000 higher for parcel #102! Should accounting reports explain the effect of one management decision versus another? They probably could not.

   Supporters of the "evaluation of management" objective advocate showing the $9,500,000 difference as attributable to management actions of a previous period, and possibly to current management's actions in a prior year. Hindsight tells us that (1) the purchase of parcel #101, and (2) annual decisions to hold onto parcel #101, were wise. Was this good management or good luck? Can you tell by looking at Labatt's financial statements which income effects resulted from good management?

   Those persons who continue to study accounting seriously will observe many accounting procedures which appear to be designed to evaluate management's actions *of the current year*. Other procedures (to be discussed mainly in Chapters 8 and 16) will attempt to evaluate management's actions over the past few years as a group, somewhat like the stewardship objective which is closely related to evaluation of management. Whenever one encounters attempts at this type of accounting the questions to ask are:

1. Am I able to distinguish good luck from good management? Or, doesn't this matter?
2. Given that management prepares its own reports on itself, gives them to outsiders, who in turn use them to evaluate this same management, can I believe what I see in the reports?

The management of Green Forest Products could make itself look good simply by cutting timber from parcel #101 instead of #102.

In summary, there are several current objectives of accounting, and some of them conflict. For instance, the main purpose of the income tax objective is to *postpone* paying income tax — the company can save interest while it might otherwise have to borrow from a bank or other creditor to pay income taxes. In contrast, someone interested in prediction wants up-to-date information — that has not been purposely delayed — in order to meet the income tax objective. Other objectives, especially 4, 5, and 6, tend to overlap. In addition to these six, other objectives will be noted in later discussion. Overall, objectives are important because:

1. It is difficult to interpret financial statements fairly unless we know which objectives were in the mind of the preparer. If a company had four objectives (income tax, stewardship, prediction, and management evaluation), which was considered most important? As we shall see later, accounting differences can be significant when one chooses one objective over another.
2. Sometimes it is virtually impossible to prepare financial statements when objectives are not clear.

Additional Considerations

Some research has been directed toward using accounting information for specific decisions, but a large portion of good accounting and reporting is based on feelings, professional judgment, impressions and experience concerning such matters as: (1) what the users appear to want; (2) what the managers of the company want to tell readers (they may not want to report information which may help a competitor); and (3) what the laws and regulations (of, say, the Vancouver Stock Exchange) require. Unless people grasp the possible objectives of accounting and how they differ, accounting reports cannot be prepared well — and certainly will not be interpreted well.

Recent research into accounting objectives and user needs has raised some very interesting issues. Some of these are: (1) Should accounting reports be geared to those who have limited access to information? (Large creditors may be able to use other sources to judge the credit-worthiness of a loan application.) (2) Who should pay for accounting statements: Investors? Creditors? The company? (3) If investors buy *portfolios* of investments (shares and bonds from several different companies) in order to lessen their chances of investment failure, should accounting statements give more information about *risk* of loss in various parts of the business? Accountants tend to record *one* figure or amount for each asset, liability, and expense, instead of giving ranges or probabilities. Using one figure can have severe limitations. A weather forecaster may predict a 50 percent chance of rain tomorrow, without stating the extremes: "no rain" or "rain." Accountants face much the same circumstances when they make the numerous estimates which are required to prepare financial statements for large companies (such as Labatt's). If there is a 50 percent chance of losing a $10,000,000 lawsuit, what should the company's financial statements say?

The authors certainly do not expect persons who are being exposed to accounting for the first time to grasp the full significance of the issues raised in this section on objectives. However, it is important to understand that accounting is not an exact science. Accounting deals with a changing environment, changing attitudes, and circumstances which require judgment.

Statement of the Problem

The previous chapter emphasized that revenues should be *realized* (accorded accounting recognition and considered to result in an increase in net assets) when *earned*, not necessarily when the related cash is received. Omitted, however, was a discussion of when revenues should be considered to be "earned." In the illustrations, up to this point in the text, revenue has been recognized either with the passage of time (when earned as rent or interest) or when goods or services have been delivered to the customer (when earned in connection with sales transactions). Relatively few types of revenues can appropriately be considered earned with the passage of time, since relatively few types of goods or services are provided uniformly over time. Moreover, recognition of revenue at the time that goods or services are delivered to the customer may, for many types of business transactions, result in financial statements that are misleading to both management and investors. Consider, for example, two situations.

SITUATION 1: D Limited signed a contract with the federal government in 19x1 to produce several icebreakers for the Atlantic region. In 19x2 D Limited commenced building a special new shipyard for the construction of the vessels. The shipyard was completed in 19x3 and work commenced on the first two icebreakers. They were completed in

19x4 and tested late in the year. Both were turned over to the federal government in 19x5 and cash was received for their purchase 90 days later. A warranty accompanying each vessel expires in late 19x6.

When is revenue earned? We have already said that the so-called answer depends upon objectives, facts and constraints. If our objective is stewardship accounting we would probably be interested in maximizing objectivity in our measurements. We would want to be sure that the revenue was reasonably assured before we recognized revenue in the financial statements.

If D reported all revenue at the time of sale (19x5) there would be no profit from the icebreakers in 19x1, 19x2, 19x3, 19x4, and 19x6. Costs incurred in 19x1 through to the date of sale would be *capitalized* in a type of inventory account, perhaps called "Icebreakers under construction." Any costs expected to be incurred in 19x6 would be accrued in 19x5 and credited to a liability account. In brief, all costs would be expensed in 19x5 and all revenues reported in 19x5. Is this fair reporting?

Clearly, some effort was expended in each of the years 19x1 through to 19x6. Yet, if our objective is stewardship reporting we would wait until the costs and revenues associated with the two icebreakers were reasonably known. In 19x5 we do not know what the warranty costs might be; hence, we have two choices: (1) wait until 19x6 when they are known, or (2) estimate them in 19x5 and accrue a liability. If we can estimate the costs accurately (maybe they are the costs of one inspection) we could reasonably record revenue in 19x5. Thus, for stewardship purposes we could say that such income reporting is fair, because we stressed objectivity.

Is such accounting fair to those outsiders interested in cash flow prediction and evaluation of management? It depends on what else is reported. To some, note disclosure (as in Labatt's statements in Chapter 2) is as satisfactory as measurements incorporated into financial statements. Hence, if the financial statements for 19x1 through to 19x4 disclosed the existence of the contract, the amounts involved, and such other *facts* as the name of the buyer, investors interested in prediction would probably regard the statements as fair or "fairer" for their particular judgments. In Canada today, few companies report details of major contracts in the financial statements.

If *no* disclosure of the contract existed in 19x1 to 19x4 — either through financial statements or other means — some investors could quite possibly be badly treated. In the extreme case a shareholder might sell shares in D Limited in late 19x4 when the market was not aware of huge potential profits in 19x5. Once the information became known D's share price would rise (because discounted cash receipts in D would rise). This of course is an extreme case because the stock market often gathers information from various sources. The market *anticipates* until information on its "guesses" is published. Then, it corrects share prices for incomplete estimates. If information about the contracts were known in 19x1, prices of D's common shares would rise through to 19x5 as work was completed, and costs, and net cash flow or income effects became known.

What harm occurs from misleading investors? Some countries' economies rely heavily on funds from capital markets (investors) to build huge projects which the citizens desire in order to improve their standard of living. Misleading investors may ultimately result in funds being attracted to undesired projects. When this occurs the "wrong" projects may prove idle or unproductive. Meanwhile, because of a shortage of funds, other needed projects cannot be commenced. In short, a *misallocation of resources occurs*. A prime purpose of accounting is to minimize such misallocations.

In a narrower sense, people who mislead investors could be successfully sued by those investors who were injured (suffered losses of money). These persons could also be jailed for fraud.

SITUATION 2: N Limited sells furniture on the *installment* plan. Customers make a small down payment and have up to three years to pay the balance of the purchase price. The company sells to poor credit risks. As a consequence, it is unable to make meaningful estimates of the amount it will be able to collect and exerts far more effort (in both time and cost) in collecting its accounts than in making initial sales. In 19x2 the company had "sales" of $100,000 but collected only $20,000 in cash. The cost of the merchandise sold was $40,000. Other operating costs were $15,000.

If N Limited were to report revenues at the time of sale, then in 19x2 it would report revenue of $100,000, cost of goods sold of $40,000, and other operating expenses of $15,000: an income of $45,000.

But how much confidence could a shareholder place in the reported income? Of the $100,000 of reported revenues, only $20,000 has been collected in cash. How much of the remaining $80,000 will be collected is uncertain and cannot readily be estimated. Moreover, although the company has sold and delivered the merchandise to its customers, a major part of its economic effort — the collection of its accounts — has yet to be exerted. Can it really be said, therefore, that the company is $45,000 better off at the end of 19x2 than it was at the beginning? Might not the interests of investors be better served if recognition of the sales revenue were deferred until ultimate collection became more certain and a greater portion of economic activity had been exerted?

Observe that in Situation 2 the prime consideration is one of *fact* (as opposed to objectives or constraints): *How much* of the $100,000 will be collected in cash? *When*? Compared to Situation 1 where the buyer is reliable, Situation 2 is risky and somewhat unpredictable. Presumably, officials of N are clever enough to avoid the *very* poor risks. Past experience may even be able to tell the officials that, say, 75 percent of the revenue will be collected in cash. Thus, we might recognize $100,000 of revenue in 19x2 *if* we also accrue a loss of $25,000 ($100,000 − $75,000) for uncollected revenue *and if* we are satisfied that the $25,000 is not far out, *and if* investors are content to live with an error of, say, ±20 percent in the $25,000 estimate. Obviously, if the foregoing *facts* are not clear we may wait and recognize revenue as cash is collected, or choose some other method.

A combination of objectives, facts, and constraints must be kept in mind. Under the stewardship objective, where objectivity or verifiability of measurement is important, the facts of Situation 2 may be sufficiently unclear that revenue recognition is delayed. However, under a prediction objective — where predictions are bound to err — we could be sufficiently content with an error of $2,500 or far more (say up to $15,000).

Students sometimes forget that government and business officials are always making major decisions on the basis of whatever information they are able to gather about the future. Such people are accustomed to large differences between estimated and actual cost or revenue. These people therefore have much different tolerance levels than someone who seeks a stewardship report.

How do accountants tend to handle these differences in tolerances and objectives? Sometimes both or all groups can be accommodated through various kinds of disclosure. However, when this is not possible the views of one of the groups are given priority and a note may tell what was done in the financial statements. But the note may not give adequate information to convert the figures to what all of the other groups may wish to see.

The problem of determining when and how much revenue has, in fact, been earned exists only because investors and other users of financial information insist on receiving *periodic* reports of income. If they were content to receive a single report of profit or loss *after* the enterprise had completed its operations and was ready to return to shareholders their original investment plus any accumulated earnings, then determination of income would be a simple matter: Subtract from the total amount either available or already distributed to shareholders the amount of their total contributions to the firm. The difference would be income over the life of the enterprise. Indeed, in the sixteenth and seventeenth centuries, companies were frequently formed with an expected useful life of only a few years — perhaps to carry out a specific mission, such as the charter of a ship for a single voyage. Investors in such companies were satisfied to wait until the companies were liquidated to get reports of their earnings.

The term "single venture accounting" has been coined for this type of accounting which looks at finite (separate) events such as a single voyage. In later chapters we will see several situations in which accountants and business managers cling to single venture thinking in spite of facts which render the idea highly questionable.

Most companies today have indeterminate lives, and both owners and managers demand periodic reports of economic progress. Since many transactions are not completed in the same accounting period in which they are started, accountants are forced to make determinations of when and how much revenue should be assigned to specific periods.

Impact Upon Related Accounts

The issue of revenue realization does not, of course, impact solely upon revenue accounts. Directly affected also are both expense accounts and, equally significantly, balance sheet accounts. As pointed out previously, because the accountant computes income by *matching* expenses and revenues, the question of when to recognize *expenses* is inherently tied to that of when to recognize revenues. To the extent that specific costs can be associated with the revenues they generate, they are *matched* to and charged as expenses in the *same accounting period* in which recognition is given to the revenues. If the costs cannot be directly associated with specific revenues, then they are considered *period* costs and charged as incurred. Insofar as costs *can* be matched to specific revenues, they may be charged as expenses in an accounting period either before or after they have actually been incurred. In Appendix 4-C, for example, it was emphasized that costs of production may be incurred in one period but not be reported as expenses (cost of goods sold) until a later period, when the goods are actually sold. Many situations occur, however, in which costs should properly be reported as expenses in a period earlier than that in which they are incurred. Suppose a company, in year 1, sells and delivers manufacturing equipment to a customer. The company guarantees to provide maintenance service on the machines for one year after sale. The cost of providing the maintenance service is a cost that can be directly associated with the revenue generated by the sale of the equipment. It follows, therefore, that it should be *matched* with the sales revenue and charged as an expense (even if an estimate of the actual cost has to be made) in the same accounting period as that in which the related revenue is recognized. The journal entries required to implement this matching approach will be illustrated later in this chapter.

The valuation of assets, liabilities, and owners' equity is also related to the recognition of revenue. Revenue has been defined as an inflow of cash or other assets attributable to the goods or services provided by the firm. When recognition is given to revenue, so also it must be given to the resultant increase in assets or decrease in liabilities. Indeed, recognition of revenue is equivalent to the recognition of an increase of owners' equity (i.e., in retained earnings). An increase of owners' equity must be accompanied by an increase in assets or a decrease in liabilities.

Exhibit 5-1 illustrates a typical operating cycle of a business. The enterprise starts with an asset, generally cash, and continuously transforms it into other assets — first to materials, equipment, and labor and then to work in process, to finished goods, to accounts receivable, and eventually back to cash. If the company earns a profit, then ending cash is greater than beginning cash. The critical question facing the accountant is at which point in the production cycle should the increase in the "size" of the asset

EXHIBIT 5-1 **Operating Cycle of a Business**

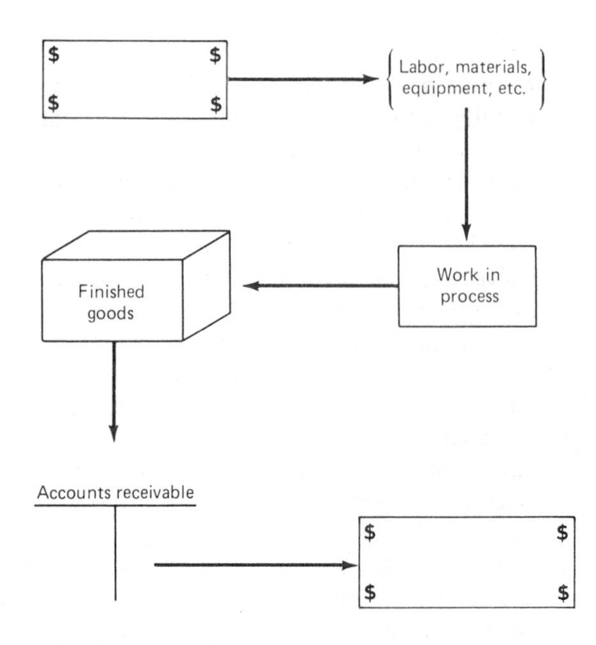

package be recognized; at what point in time is the enterprise "better off" than it was before.

Most commonly, especially in a manufacturing or retail operation, the accountant recognizes the increase in value of the assets at time of sale — when goods or services are delivered or shipped to customers. Because many external financial reports are based on stewardship, and perhaps management evaluation objectives of accounting, the concept of *objective/ verifiable figures* is thought to be important. At the time of sale *most* of the costs and revenues are known. (Some revenue adjustment may be needed if not all of it is collected in cash. Also, aside from delivery costs, which are usually considered period costs, and perhaps a warranty cost, other costs to manufacture and sell are already known). The margin of error between estimates and eventual actual cost is probably small at the date of shipment to customers for *many, but not all*, merchandising and small manufacturing businesses.

By selecting that date, however, the accountant implicitly ignores the value to the firm of the entire production cycle up to that point. He asserts that all previous transactions involved nothing more than exchanges of assets and liabilities of equal magnitude — that the level of net assets remained unchanged. He is also stating that all subsequent transactions (e.g., collection of cash, fulfillment of warranty obligations, etc.) will also involve nothing more than exchanges of assets and liabilities of equal (though greater than prior to recognition) magnitude and that such exchanges will have no effect on the new level of net assets.

The use of the shipment date to recognize revenue is inappropriate in situations in which delivery of goods provides little assurance that the amount owed by the customer will be collectible. It may be equally inappropriate where the enterprise has completed a significant portion of its economic activity and eventual collection of cash from a known customer is certain long before the goods are actually delivered to him.

Guidelines for Revenue Recognition

There are, unfortunately, no pervasive principles as to when revenue should be recognized. At least four criteria, however, are cited in the accounting literature and are generally adhered to in practice. Revenue should be recognized under a *stewardship* objective as soon as:

1. The firm has exerted a substantial portion of its production and sales effort;
2. The revenue can be objectively measured;
3. The major portion of costs have been incurred, and the remaining costs can be estimated with reasonable reliability and precision; and
4. Eventual collection of cash can reasonably be assured.

However, different criteria might be applied under different objectives. For example, owners of many small businesses who have only the *income tax* objective in mind would tend to postpone revenue recognition as long as possible so that income, and income taxes, are postponed. Obviously any postponement of revenue recognition has to be consistent with the facts of when cash receipts can be estimated satisfactorily. For instance, if the buyer is a reliable company and has agreed to pay within 30 days, revenue recognition would tend to occur now, and not up to as late as 30 days later. (In practice a company tends to have *one* revenue recognition principle for each type of product or warehouse — and not one for each customer. In setting this principle, the average or typical set of facts is kept in mind).

If the prime users of financial statements are investors and the *prediction* objective is of greatest importance, revenue (and accompanying expenses) might be recorded when a buyer orally agrees to acquire goods — which may be weeks before actual shipment date. Public accountants and auditors are reluctant to depart from stewardship and objectivity, and in some cases may object to revenue recognition prior to the existence of a written purchase order from a customer, or something of equivalent reliability. But this is because of current laws concerning the legal liability of accountants who might provide false information. Recent attempts have been made in the U.S. to overcome legal liability fears, and it is possible that such changes may appear in Canada. The authors therefore feel that it is important to teach and explain more than current practice, and more than stewardship accounting.

In situations where revenue is recognized prior to shipment, the costs of the goods which *will be* shipped are charged to cost of goods sold on the same date revenue is recognized. If the goods are not yet completed, revenue recognition would probably await completion of the goods — unless completion costs were well known.

In summary, the guidelines for revenue recognition are general: always bear objectives-facts-constraints in mind. The following situations may aid understanding.

Recognition at Time of Sale

For most manufacturing and retail concerns, the four criteria of revenue recognition are first satisfied at the so-called "point of sale" — frequently the date of shipment of goods. At that time the firm has exerted a major portion of its economic activity, including its sales efforts. A firm price has been established. Most of the costs have been incurred, even though there might be additional costs, such as those pertaining to product warranties, guaranteed maintenance, and collection of receivables that might have to be incurred in the future. Collection of cash usually can reasonably be assured, although the firm may have to estimate and make allowances for merchandise that will be returned and customers who default on their accounts.

From time to time accountants reason that the passage of legal title to goods should be used as the point at which revenue should be recognized. That is, if commercial law in a province states, for example, that the legal ownership of goods transfers to the buyer at the point of loading goods into the buyer's trucks, then this is the point at which revenue supposedly ought to be recorded. Let us pursue this line of reasoning for a moment to see what is implied about objectives, facts, and constraints. Clearly, there is an assumption about facts — that the buyer will either pay cash on receipt of the goods, or that there is high assurance that full cash will eventually be received from the buyer. (If these assumptions did not exist, revenue might be too high because of possible credit losses.) There does not seem to be any assumption with respect to constraints of company law. What about objectives? The passage of legal title approach was popular in some companies at one time when a prime objective of accounting was to check the legality of dividends. Any dividend ought to be deducted from income, and not the owners' original investment. Accountants, at one time, had to be sure in some companies that income was "legally computed" for dividend purposes. Hence, a cornerstone of income measurement — revenue recognition — was based on a legal title change for its so-called point of sale.

What message should we draw from the previous paragraph? The obvious one is that any accounting procedure is based on assumptions with respect to objectives, facts and constraints (OFCs). The key to understanding accounting is to identify these assumptions — and to test your suggested accounting treatment for reasonableness of assumptions in each situation which you face. Are you inadvertently applying a procedure which was designed for another set of OFCs?

Recognition During Production

For some firms, especially those which provide goods or services under long-term contracts, revenue may be recognized as production takes place rather than waiting until point of delivery. Recognition of revenue during the entire production process enables firms to avoid the erratic — and often misleading — pattern of income that may result from point of delivery revenue recognition (as was illustrated earlier in Situation 1.)

A widely used means of recognizing revenue throughout the entire production process is known as the *percentage of completion method.* On any given contract, the proportion of total contract price to be recognized as revenue in each accounting period is the percentage of the total project completed during that period. If 20 percent of the project is completed in a particular year, then 20 percent of the expected total revenue from the project would be recognized during that year.

The percentage of completion or any other production-oriented means of revenue recognition is appropriate only when total costs of completing the project can be estimated with reasonable reliability and precision, the contract price is fixed and certain to be collected (as is often the case when the contract is with a governmental agency or major corporation), and there can be no question about the ability of the firm to complete the project and to have it accepted by the other party to the contract.

Another example of a situation in which revenue could be recognized in the course of production would be that in which a management consulting firm undertakes to advise a client on the installation of a new accounting system. Assuming that the consulting firm bills its client on the basis of number of hours of service rendered, then each of the four criteria would be reasonably satisfied as the consulting engagement progresses.

Recognition at Completion of Production

For those companies that face ready markets and stable prices for their products, the four basic criteria can often be satisfied at the completion of the production process. Prior to 1972, the U.S. government guaranteed to purchase all gold offered to it at a price of $35 per ounce. From the standpoint of a gold mining company, as soon as its production process was complete, its revenue could be objectively determined; it would have few remaining expenses (storage and transportation), all of which could be readily estimated; and sale of product and collectibility of cash would be assured. Not only would the accounting interests of objectivity and relevance be best served by recognizing revenue as soon as the mining process was complete, but delay of recognition until actual sale would, by valuing gold at its cost to acquire rather than at the amount at which it was certain to be sold, understate the assets of the company.

Few situations today are as well defined as that of the pre-1972 gold mining company (the U.S. government presently purchases gold only as needed and at fluctuating higher prices). Nevertheless, recognition of revenue at completion of the productive process is appropriate for those mining and agricultural concerns which have negligible marketing costs, face stable prices, and can readily sell all commodities that they produce, since they can reasonably satisfy the four criteria of revenue recognition at such time.

It is important to note that the above applies when the company desires its financial statements to show figures containing a combination of relevance (for those who are interested in management evaluation and prediction) and objectivity. In contrast, if the company has only stewardship and income tax objectives in mind it might choose to delay revenue recognition as long as possible.

Some accountants become very upset when a company delays revenue recognition and thereby ignores what they call "the underlying economic reality." At one time accountants referred to this as ignoring "the underlying truth." However, it eventually became clearer that "truth was in the eye of the beholder" and that different people saw different versions of "the underlying truth." Unfortunately, the word "truth" seems to have been replaced with "economic reality," but it too is subject to different interpretations by people from different backgrounds, experience, and so forth. Who is correct? Do you know the truth or the underlying economic reality, whereas your neighbor does not?

Accountants are frequently trying to identify criteria which separate one situation from others, and to give guidance as to a suitable accounting treatment. But, for years accounting was anchored to an economic base and many accountants were trained in "applied economics." It is not surprising from time to time to encounter phrases such as "underlying economic reality" and to discover a rejection of some aspects of the behavioral (user) side. Accounting is a blend of economics, behavioral sciences, quantitative methods, politics, and many other subjects. We must reject the temptation to make the subject so simple that it is totally irrelevant. Somehow, in this introductory text we must:

1. Inform you about current accounting practice and business procedures.
2. Critically analyze statement 1 to point out strengths and shortcomings.
3. Alert you to possible changes which you may see in practice in a few years.

This chapter is particularly heavy because of rapid changes which are occurring in the subject.

Recognition Upon Collection of Cash

In some situations, the four criteria will not be satisfied until the production and sale processes are complete *and* cash has been collected. In those cases it is necessary to delay recognition of revenue until cash is actually in hand. In the previous installment-sales illustration, for example, the company sold to customers with poor credit ratings and from whom the company had no assurance that it would be able to collect its accounts receivable. Prudence dictates that no revenue be recognized until the company is certain that its customer receivables can be transformed into cash.

Obviously every company takes a risk when it sells on credit. In most situations, however, the extent of bad debt losses can reasonably be estimated at time of sale. Only when such losses cannot be estimated would users of financial statements interested in stewardship be adequately served by delaying the recognition of revenue. If recognition were delayed, the related assets would be valued at their cost to produce or acquire rather than at the amount that the firm will eventually realize when it actually collects the cash.

The cash collection or *installment* basis of revenue recognition is not widely used today to account for routine merchandise sales — not even those in which the customer pays "on time" or on the "installment plan" — since it is generally possible to make reasonable estimates of credit losses. It is, however, widely used to account for certain types of real estate or other property transactions in which the collectibility of the receivable held by the seller is questionable. A builder, for example, might sell a recently constructed shopping center to a group of investors. The builder accepts from the investors a note for a portion of the selling price with the understanding that the investors will be able to make payments on the note only insofar as they are able to rent the stores in the shopping center. If there is uncertainty as to whether sufficient space in the shopping center can be rented to enable the investors to make payments on their note, the builder would delay recognition of revenue on the sale of the property until cash is actually in hand.

In evaluating the alternative means of revenue recognition to account for specific types of transactions, it is helpful to keep in mind the standards of reporting set forth in Chapter 1. Accounting information should be both relevant and objective if it is to be useful to as wide an audience of users as is possible. However, it may not be possible in some situations to cater to all user groups. The cash basis of revenue recognition generally provides the most objective or verifiable information. By the time revenue is recognized, eventual realization is virtually certain as cash is already in hand. The methods which recognize revenue at an earlier stage in the earning process are less objective since doubts may remain as to whether all or most cash will in fact be collected. But insofar as they provide a better indication of a company's economic effort and the rewards that will *most probably* accrue from that effort, they may result in reports that are more relevant to users interested in cash prediction and management evaluation.

Analysis of Transactions

The impact of the alternative bases of revenue recognition on revenues and expenses as well as on assets and liabilities can readily be seen when transactions are analyzed in journal entry form. The journal entry process may sometimes appear a bit tricky, but it can be simplified if a few guidelines are kept in mind:

1. In those periods in which revenue is to be recognized (and *only* in such periods) a revenue account must be credited. Since recognition of revenue implies an inflow or increase of net assets, a corresponding debit must be made to an asset or liability account.

2. In the periods in which revenue is recognized (and *only* in such periods) an expense account must be debited to give recognition to the related costs. The proportion of total expected costs that is charged as an expense in any particular period would be equal to the proportion of total anticipated revenues that is recognized in that period. Since recognition of expenses implies an outflow of net assets, a corresponding credit must be made to either an asset or liability account. (This guideline gives effect to the *matching* principle, which holds that expenses must be matched to the revenues with which they can be associated.)

3. In all periods in which revenue is *not* recognized, transactions involve *only* exchanges of assets and liabilities; hence, only asset and liability accounts should be debited or credited. Some examples will serve to illustrate these guidelines.

EXAMPLE 1

Recognition of Revenue at Time of Sale — Warranty Obligation Outstanding

Lanfranconi Equipment Limited, in 19x4, purchases equipment intended for resale for $50,000 cash. In 19x5 it sells the equipment for $80,000 on account, giving the buyer a one-year warranty against defects. The company estimates that its cost of making repairs under the warranty will be $5,000. In 19x6 the company collects the full sales price from the purchaser and incurs $5,000 in repair costs prior to the expiration of the warranty.

19x4

(a)

Merchandise inventory (asset +)	$50,000	
Cash (asset −)		$50,000
To record the purchase of equipment.		

19x5

(b)

Accounts receivable (asset +)	$80,000	
Sales revenue (revenue +)		$80,000
To record the sale of the equipment.		

(c)

Cost of goods sold (expense +)	$50,000	
Warranty expense (expense +)	5,000	
Merchandise inventory (asset −)		$50,000
Warranty liability (liability +)		5,000
To record the expenses associated with the revenue recognized.		

The warranty expense charged and the warranty liability credited represent an *estimate* of costs to be incurred in the future. Since such costs can be directly related to the sales revenue, and can be "accurately" estimated, they should be recorded in the same accounting period in which the revenue is recorded, in order to fulfill the stewardship objective or purpose of accounting.

19x6

(d)

Cash (asset +)	$80,000	
Accounts receivable (asset −)		$80,000
To record customer payment.		

(e)

Warranty liability (liability −)	$ 5,000	
Cash (asset −)		$ 5,000
To record costs incurred to fulfill the warranty obligations.		

The costs incurred to make repairs required under the warranty are *charged* (debited) against the liability that was established at the time the costs were charged as an expense. In the event that the original estimate of costs proves incorrect, then an adjustment can be made as soon as the error becomes known, which may be a year or so after the initial sale. Thus, if costs were greater than $5,000, the additional amount would be charged as an expense as incurred. If less, then at the expiration of the warranty the warranty liability account would be debited (decreased) and the warranty expense account credited (decreased) for the difference. (The credit to the warranty expense account will have the effect of reducing warranty expenses in a year subsequent to that in which the initial sale was made.)

EXAMPLE 2

Recognition of Revenue During Production

The construction of an asset such as the icebreakers described earlier can be used to illustrate the approach to recognizing revenue in which the amount of revenue recognized in any given period is based on the percentage of the entire project completed in that period. We will choose another company for illustrative purposes. Suppose that M Limited contracts to build two icebreakers at a price of $100 million. It estimates that total construction costs will be $90 million. In 19x5 it begins construction and incurs $30 million in costs; in 19x6 it incurs $42 million more, and in 19x7 it incurs $18 million and completes the project. In 19x7 the company collects the full contract price from the government. (This example is oversimplified for purposes of illustration. In practice, the government would probably make periodic cash payments to the contractor during construction of the vessel. The timing of the cash collections, however, would have no impact upon the timing of the revenue recognition.)

19x5

(a)

Construction in progress, at cost (asset +)	$30,000,000	
Cash (asset −)		$30,000,000
To record costs incurred in construction of the icebreakers.		

(b)

Long-term receivable (asset +)	$33,333,333	
Revenue (revenue +)		$33,333,333

To record revenue based on one-third completion of the estimated costs; and to debit a long-term receivable for sums not due until 19x7.

(c)

Expenses (accompanying revenue from construction) (expense +)	$30,000,000	
Construction in progress at cost (asset −)		$30,000,000

To record expenses incurred to earn the revenue of $33,333,333.

In the above illustration the company has completed one third of the project, assuming that percentage of completion is based on costs incurred to expected total costs (i.e., $30,000,000 incurred of an expected $90,000,000). It is therefore appropriate to recognize one third of both estimated revenues and expenses, resulting in a profit of $3,333,333.

19x6

The entries for 19x6 are similar to those for 19x5:

(d)

Construction in progress, at cost (asset +)	$42,000,000	
Cash (asset −)		$42,000,000

To record costs incurred in construction of the icebreakers.

(e)

Long-term receivable (asset +) (A portion of this may be a current asset)	$46,666,667	
Revenue (revenue +)		$46,666,667

To record revenue of 42/90 x $100,000,000 and receivable due in 19x7.

(f)

Expenses (accompanying revenue from construction) (expense +)	$42,000,000	
Construction in progress, at cost (asset −)		$42,000,000

To record expenses incurred in earning the construction revenue.

In 19x6 a further 42/90 of the cost is incurred, and an additional 42/90 of the estimated profit of $10,000,000 ($100,000,000 − $90,000,000) has been reported ($46,666,667 − $42,000,000 = $4,666,667) in 19x6.

19x7

The entries are similar to 19x6 but an additional one is needed to record the current receivable from the government.

(g)

Construction in progress, at cost (asset +)	$18,000,000	
Cash (asset −)		$18,000,000
To record costs incurred in construction of the ice-breakers.		

(h)

Long term receivable (asset +)	$20,000,000	
(A portion of this may be a current asset.)		
Revenue (revenue +)		$20,000,000
To record revenue of 18/90 of $100,000,000.		

(i)

Expenses (accompanying revenue from construction) (expense +)	$18,000,000	
Construction in progress (asset −)		$18,000,000
To record balance of construction costs.		

(j)

Accounts receivable (asset +)	$100,000,000	
Long-term receivable (asset −)		$100,000,000
To record current receivable from government.		

Summarizing, the annual and total effects are:

	19x5	*19x6*	*19x7*	*Total*
Revenue	$33,333,333	$46,666,667	$20,000,000	$100,000,000
Costs incurred to earn revenue	30,000,000	42,000,000	18,000,000	90,000,000
Gross profit	$ 3,333,333	$ 4,666,667	$ 2,000,000	$ 10,000,000

There are many other ways of accounting for long-term construction contracts. As well, many complications arise when actual revenue and cost do not coincide with estimated revenue and cost. Traditionally such technical complications are covered in intermediate-level accounting courses.

EXAMPLE 3

Recognition of Revenue at Completion of Production

In 19x1 Hanna Limited receives an order from a major electronics manufacturer to produce 10,000 units of a part used in the production of television sets. The purchaser agrees to pay $10 a unit for the part, but under the terms of the contract the seller is to store and retain title to the goods until they are needed by the purchaser. Payment is certain and is to be made upon delivery of the goods. The cost of producing the part is $6 per unit. Hanna elects to recognize revenue upon completion of production, which occurs in 19x2. At that time the four criteria of the stewardship objective are satisfied; revenue can be objectively measured, all major costs have been incurred (storage costs are considered to be negligible), the major part of productive effort has been exerted, and collection of cash is virtually certain.

During Production — 19x1 and 19x2

(a)

Work in process (asset +)	$60,000	
Cash (asset −)		$60,000
To record costs of production. (This entry summarizes several entries which would be made as production progresses.)		

At Completion of Production — 19x2

(b)

Finished goods at cost (asset +)	$60,000	
Work in process (asset −)		$60,000
To record completion of goods produced.		

(c)

Finished goods at selling price (asset +)	$100,000	
Manufacturing revenue (revenue +)		$100,000
To recognize revenue upon completion of goods manufactured.		

(d)

Cost of goods manufactured (expense +)	$60,000	
Finished goods at cost (asset −)		$60,000
To record the expense pertaining to the manufacture of the goods.		

The pattern of entries is similar to those made in Example 2. At the time revenue is recognized, related expenses are also recognized. The realization of revenue is accompanied by an increase in an asset; however, in this example the carrying value of the goods produced (i.e., the finished goods) increased from cost to market value, the amount of the increase being the income earned on the transaction.

At Time of Delivery — 19x2

(e)

Accounts receivable (asset +)	$100,000	
Finished goods at selling price (asset −)		$100,000
To record the delivery of goods.		

As in the previous examples, events in periods prior or subsequent to those in which revenues and expenses are recognized involve only exchanges among assets and/or liabilities.

EXAMPLE 4

Recognition of Revenue upon Collection of Cash (the Installment Basis)

In 19x2 a company sells a parcel of land to a developer for $200,000. The original cost of the land to the company was $150,000. Under the terms of the sales contract, the seller is to receive 5 percent of the selling price at the time of closing and transfer of title, 60 percent at the end of 19x3, and the remaining 35 percent at the end of 19x4. Because the company views ultimate collectibility as being highly uncertain, it has decided to recognize revenue only upon actual receipt of cash. (In this example, recognition of revenue upon receipt of cash would be consistent with the pronouncements in the U.S. of the American Institute of Certified Public Accountants (AICPA) contained in an industry audit guide, *Accounting for Profit Recognition on Sales of Real Estate.* In Canada, Securities' legislation tends to stipulate that revenue should not be recognized until 15 percent cash has been received. Hence, no revenue would be recognized in 19x2, and that deferred from 19x2 could be included in 19x3.)

At Time of Sale and Collection of First Payment — 19x2

(a)

Company interest in land sold (asset +)	$150,000	
Land (asset −)		$150,000
To record the sale of the land.		

The purpose of this entry is simply to reclassify the property sold — to distinguish between land to which the company actually holds title and that in which it has merely an accounting interest.

(b)

Cash (asset +)	$10,000	
Revenue from sale of land (revenue +)		$10,000
To record collection of 5 percent of the selling price and to recognize 5 percent of the anticipated revenue.		

(c)

Cost of land sold (expense +)	$7,500	
Company interest in land sold (asset −)		$7,500
To record 5 percent of expenses applicable to the sale of land. (The original cost of the land to the company was $150,000; 5 percent of $150,000 = $7,500.)		

The latter two entries recognize a portion of the total revenue to be realized on the sale and an identical portion of the related expense.

At Time of Collection of Second Payment — 19x3

(d)

Cash (asset +)	$120,000	
Revenue from sale of land (revenue +)		$120,000
To record collection of 60 percent of the selling price and to recognize 60 percent of the anticipated revenue.		

(e)

Cost of land sold (expense +)	$90,000	
Company interest in land sold (asset −)		$90,000
To record 60 percent of the expense applicable to the sale of the land.		

At Time of Collection of Third Payment — 19x4

(f)

Cash (asset +)	$70,000	
Revenue from sale of land (revenue +)		$70,000
To record collection of 35 percent of the selling price and to recognize the remaining 35 percent of the revenue.		

(g)

Cost of land sold (expense +)	$52,500	
Company interest in land sold (asset −)		$52,500
To record 35 percent of the expense applicable to the sale of the land.		

By the time the final payment has been made, the company will have recorded revenues of $200,000, expenses of $150,000, and income of $50,000. It will report on the balance sheet an increase in cash of $200,000 and a decrease in land of $150,000.

Although the journal entries illustrated lead to a "correct" statement of both income and assets, they are deficient in that the amount due from the customer — i.e., an account receivable — is never incorporated into the accounts. This deficiency results from the nature of the revenue recognition process. Sales revenue is recorded only upon the receipt of cash; hence the increase in assets associated with recognition of revenue can be reflected only upon the receipt of cash. The deficiency can readily be remedied, however, by establishing two related accounts, "accounts receivable" and "accounts receivable — contra." When a contract is first signed, the following entry could be made:

Accounts receivable (asset)	$200,000	
Accounts receivable — contra (asset, contra)		$200,000

Then as each payment of cash is received, the entry would be "reversed":

Accounts receivable — contra	$10,000	
Accounts receivable		$10,000

The balance in the two accounts, both of which are balance sheet accounts, will always *net* to zero. The accounts will, however, provide a measure of control over amounts due from customers and indicate the anticipated cash collections (and hence, help to accomplish the internal control objective of accounting).

Examples From Current Practice

In order to provide information which might prove helpful to a variety of users of financial statements, the Canadian Institute of Chartered Accountants (CICA) has recommended to its members that certain accounting principles or policies which are being followed by a company be disclosed in the annual financial statements:

> "As a minimum, disclosure of information on accounting policies should be provided in the following situations:
> (i) where a selection has been made from alternative acceptable accounting principles, methods and procedures;
> (ii) where there are accounting principles, methods and procedures used which are peculiar to an industry in which an enterprise operates, even if such accounting principles, methods and procedures are predominantly followed in that industry."

We have indicated that revenue recognition would be one of those situations where both conditions (a) and (b) might apply, in different companies. Some examples of disclosure by Canadian companies follows:

Sales of franchises

Rights to use a company's name, its production processes, and its management and advertising philosophy are frequently sold to private business persons (*franchisees*). Examples are Kentucky Fried Chicken and other fast-food outlets, and the many muffler- or transmission-repair shops. Different companies have different types of contracts (i.e., a difference in *facts* may exist for accounting purposes) under which they sell franchise rights. Most franchisers require an initial down payment from the business person plus periodic fees (a) in payment for franchise rights, and (b) for the franchisee's share of overall annual administration, advertising, etc. However, amounts involved and terms of contracts can differ substantially with each franchiser. The accounting question of interest is how one should recognize revenue on the sale of the franchiser's idea (e.g., recipe, cooking process and ingredients for fried chicken) and franchise rights. Generally, the franchisee's payments for (b) above are offset against costs incurred by the franchiser, who, overall, often makes a profit on (b). However, amounts received and receivable under (a) can be very large in relation to the net effect of (b), and could be a major portion of the franchiser's revenue.

Here is the accounting treatment given by four Canadian companies:

The Becker Milk Company Limited (1977):
"Franchise fees are taken into income over the term of the franchise agreement."
(This tells you that they do not accrue the entire fee in the year in which the franchise agreement is signed or the first year of operation of the franchisee. However, they do not say if the fee is accrued evenly or unevenly over the period of the agreement.)

Silverwood Industries Limited (1978):
"Franchise fees are taken into income over the term of the franchise agreement on a straight line basis."
(This company also tells you that the fee is accrued evenly. Silverwood's Mac's Milk Stores compete with Becker's Milk Stores in parts of Canada.)

Foodcorp Limited (1977):
"The company records income on the sale of franchises on a cash basis as deposits and balances receivable are collected. Under certain circumstances, the company may be required to repurchase franchises. A provision is made for possible future repurchases."

Koffler Stores Limited (1977):
"Franchise fees are based on a variable percentage of retail store sales and are recorded as earned."
(Kofflers has operated or sold franchises for Shoppers Drug Mart Stores.)

How do the above illustrations relate to our course theme that, where possible, accounting in practice is tailored to specific objectives, facts and constraints? In an *ideal* situation we might be able to cater to all objectives of accounting by following two broad criteria: accounting figures ought to be *objective* as well as *relevant*. But *people* prepare and use accounting data, and their attitudes, education, and understanding affect their judgment. This makes the task of uniformity (even for like objectives, facts, and constraints) of accounting treatment difficult to pursue.

We are *not* saying that the pursuit of like accounting for like objectives, facts and constraints is pointless. University and college courses ought to indicate paths to improvement. But, we *are* saying that we ought *not to delude ourselves* by covering only ideal states. By the end of this book readers must be allowed the chance to understand main issues affecting the past, present and future of accounting.

The four examples showed that companies do not always disclose sufficient information about their accounting treatment to enable us to be certain about our analysis. It is possible that Beckers is using straight-line amortization, but maybe not. If not, is this because the facts differ, or because of undisclosed personal preferences of management? Similarly, is Foodcorp extra-cautious in its policy, or do the facts (some financially shaky franchises?) warrant a delay? What is the effect of this on various users?

In short, we must focus on the limitations of current financial reports and current practice; otherwise, we could convey a misleading impression about the accounting and business world of today. Sometimes differences in accounting treatment arise because of different objectives, facts and contraints. Sometimes differences might be caused by many other factors, including ignorance, intended deceit, and unusual personal beliefs. We must remain alert to reasons for differences, and their implications for our decisions.

Construction Revenue

Bridge and Tank Company of Canada Limited (1977):

"The company recognizes revenue from contracts generally on the percentage of completion basis, determined by the ratio of costs incurred to management's estimates of total anticipated costs. If estimated total costs on any contract indicate a loss, the company provides currently for the total loss anticipated on the contract."
(Observe use of the word "generally" in the first sentence.)

Ronyx Corporation Limited (1977):

"Gross profit on contracts . . . is recorded as follows:
(i) On manufacturing contracts or programs extending over one year billable at a fixed price per unit, the proportion of total estimated gross profit for the entire contract or program applicable to the number of

units shipped based on the average unit cost for each program estimated to final completion.

(ii) On other manufacturing contracts completed within the year the actual gross profit applicable to units shipped.

(iii) On real estate construction contracts, the percentage of completion method. Gross profit on speculative housing construction is recorded as sales are completed.

Estimated losses on contracts are recorded when they become known. In the case of contracts extending over one year revisions in cost and profit estimates are reflected in the accounting period in which the relevant facts become known."

Ronyx therefore has different revenue recognition bases for different factual situations. Both companies are trying to be as objective as possible despite the uncertainty which exists in the construction business.

Timing of Expenses

This chapter has emphasized that costs should be charged as expenses in the same period in which the revenues to which they are related are recognized. Net income should be determined by subtracting from revenues the expenses which were incurred to generate the revenues. Indeed, insofar as possible, expenses and revenues should be reported as if a cause and effect relationship exists between them. Regrettably, a cause and effect relationship is not always readily apparent.

As pointed out in the previous chapter, factory costs that can be directly associated with the manufacture of specific products are *capitalized* as assets and charged as expenses in the period in which the goods manufactured are sold. But other costs, such as sales and administrative costs, cannot easily be associated with specific sales and, therefore, out of practical necessity, are charged off in the period in which they are incurred.

There are many additional types of costs for which cause and effect relationships with specific revenues are also unclear. For these costs, accountants may do their best to match them with appropriate revenues, but in the absence of specific rules set forth by authoritative professional or governmental bodies, the determination as to when the costs should be charged as expenses must, in large measure, rest with the *judgment* of the individual accountant. As a result, similar types of costs are often accorded dissimilar treatment by firms even within a single industry.

Consider, for example, costs incurred by advertising agencies. A primary source of an agency's revenues is its commissions on advertising placed in the media. An agency will develop and produce advertisements for a client. Its fee for providing the service is a percentage of the cost of running the ad in a publication or on the air. Most advertising agencies recognize *revenue* at the time they bill their clients — that is, as the ads are published or broadcast.

An advertising agency incurs some costs that can readily be associated with revenues earned. But, in addition, it incurs substantial costs in acquiring new clients, studying clients' products, analyzing markets in which they expect to sell, and developing advertising objectives and strategies. These costs cannot be identified directly with specific advertisements. In light of the uncertain benefits derived from such *start-up* costs, persuasive arguments can be made for either charging them to expenses as incurred or for capitalizing them as assets and charging them off over the period in which they will *most likely* be identified with revenues earned.

Similarly, consider costs, such as those of site selection, rent, stocking the shelves, and advertising, incurred by a retailer prior to the opening of a new store. With the revenues of which accounting periods should such costs be associated? Should they be charged off as incurred (in a period in which the store might generate zero revenues), in the period in which the store opens, or in several periods subsequent to the opening of the store? It is doubtful that the method of expense recognition used by one firm or the others provides information that is inherently more useful or objective. Of utmost importance, however, is that the financial analyst be aware of the differences and of their impact on reported income as well as on assets and liabilities. Therefore, where alternative accounting treatments exist, it is useful to specify, as a minimum, which accounting policy is being employed.

Impact of Timing Differences

As a consequence of the recurring nature of many revenues and expenses, the choice of a basis of revenue and expense recognition may have less impact on reported *income* than is at first apparent. To the extent that a particular source of revenue or cost is constant over time, the effect of one basis as opposed to another will generally be insignificant, since the over- or understatements of current year's earnings are offset by "corrections" of over- or understatements of prior years' earnings. Insofar as income is concerned, the impact of choice of basis on earnings is generally most critical when a firm is either expanding or contracting.

In evaluating alternative means of revenue and expense recognition, however, the accountant or financial analyst must also consider their impact upon balance sheet accounts. The effect on balance sheet accounts, retained earnings in particular, may sometimes be substantially greater than that on income.

Consider, for example, a firm that constructs bridges. Each bridge takes three years to complete, and construction work is spread evenly over the three years. The contract price of each bridge is $3 million. In the period from 19x3 to 19x6 the firm begins and completes construction of one bridge each year. At the start of 19x3, however, it had one bridge one third complete and another two thirds complete. Revenue for the period, if recognized upon the *completion* of a bridge, would be as follows:

Revenue Recognized on Completed Contract Basis[a]

	Revenue (000 omitted).		
	19x3	19x4	19x5
Bridge 1 (19x1)	$3,000		
Bridge 2 (19x2)		$3,000	
Bridge 3 (19x3)			$3,000
Bridge 4 (19x4)			
Bridge 5 (19x5)			
Total revenue recognized	$3,000	$3,000	$3,000

[a]Dates in parentheses indicate year in which construction was begun.

Revenue, if recognized on the *percentage of completion basis*, would be the same $3 million per year, since each year the company would be constructing one third of each of three bridges:

Revenue Recognized on Percentage of Completion Basis

	Revenue (000 omitted)		
	19x3	19x4	19x5
Bridge 1 (19x1)*	$1,000		
Bridge 2 (19x2)*	1,000	$1,000	
Bridge 3 (19x3)	1,000	1,000	$1,000
Bridge 4 (19x4)		1,000	1,000
Bridge 5 (19x5)			1,000
Total revenue recognized	$3,000	$3,000	$3,000

*Note that on the bridge begun in 19x1, $1 million in revenue would have been recognized previously in both 19x1 and 19x2; on that begun in 19x2, $1 million would have been recognized in 19x2.

But if the company were to have recognized revenue on the percentage of completion basis, then at the end of any given year it would have recognized a total of $3 million more revenue *to date* than on the completed contract basis: $1 million on the bridge that is one third complete, and $2 million on the bridge that is two thirds complete. As of the end of 19x3, using the percentage of completion method, $2 million in revenue would have been recognized on the bridge started in 19x2; $1 million in revenue would have been recognized on that started in 19x3. By contrast, using the completed contract method, no revenue would have been recognized on either bridge. This $3 million lag in recognition of revenue under the completed contract method will remain in the accounts for as long as the company continues to construct the equivalent of one bridge each year. To the extent that at any given time total revenue recognized to date is $3 million greater under the percentage of completion basis than under the completed contract basis, then (ignoring any offsetting increases in total expenses recognized) retained earnings must also be $3 million greater. And if retained earnings were $3 million greater, then, in accordance with the basic accounting equation, so too must be net assets. Hence, even though the choice of method of revenue recognition may have a negligible effect on reported income in a particular year, it may have a sizable impact on both retained earnings and net assets. This effect could be very important, as we shall see later in the book, when what are called *restrictive covenants* on long-term debts restrict dividend payments to common shareholders unless the retained earnings after payment of the dividend is so many dollars.

If the company were to begin building two bridges each year commencing with 19x6, then periodic revenue, in addition to the related balance sheet accounts, would differ substantially under each of the two methods of revenue recognition. Under the percentage of completion method, the construction of the additional bridges would have an impact on revenues in the year in which they are begun. Under the completed contract method, the impact would be delayed until the bridges have been completed.

Revenue Recognized on Completed Contract Basis[a]

	Revenue (000 omitted)		
	19x6	19x7	19x8
Bridge 4 (19x4)	$3,000		
Bridge 5 (19x5)		$3,000	
Bridges 6&7 (19x6)			$6,000
Bridges 8&9 (19x7)			
Bridges 10&11 (19x8)			
Total revenue recognized	$3,000	$3,000	$6,000

[a]Dates in parentheses indicate year in which construction was begun.

Revenue Recognized on Percentage of Completion Basis

	Revenue (000 omitted)		
	19x6	19x7	19x8
Bridge 4 (19x4)	$1,000		
Bridge 5 (19x5)	1,000	$1,000	
Bridges 6&7 (19x6)	2,000	2,000	$2,000
Bridges 8&9 (19x7)		2,000	2,000
Bridges 10&11 (19x8)			2,000
Total revenue recognized	$4,000	$5,000	$6,000

In addition, the difference between retained earnings and net assets would increase from $3 million at the end of 19x5 to $4 million at the end of 19x6 to $6 million at the end of 19x7 — the increments being equal to the accumulated differences between reported revenues.

Revenue and Expense Recognition — an Overview

The issue of when to recognize revenues and expenses is pervasive in accounting. It is intrinsically related to virtually all other accounting questions.

In the remaining chapters a great deal of attention will be directed to questions of asset and liability valuation. But valuation answers must always be viewed with an eye toward their effects on revenues or expenses. After all, income can be defined as the change in net assets between two points in time. To take but a few examples: The question of whether a firm should report marketable securities, such as shares, at the price the firm paid for them or the price at which they are currently being sold is also an issue of revenue recognition — that is, should the company recognize gains or losses from market price-changes as the selling price of the shares increases or decreases over time, or should it delay recognition until it actually sells the shares?

The question of whether inventories should be reported at cost to produce them or the price at which they will eventually be sold can also be expressed in terms of whether revenue should be recognized at point of sale or at various points throughout the production process. Disputes over whether or not a firm should report seemingly valueless assets such as "organizational costs," "deferred store opening costs," or "deferred research and development costs" are also conflicts over when such costs should be charged off as expenses. It is vital, therefore, that every accounting question be analyzed in terms of its effect on *both* the income statement *and* the balance sheet.

Key Accounting Concepts

From time to time we have mentioned a few of the basic concepts which underlie accountants' reasoning processes. Let us now try to pull many of these together in one place and add a few which may help our further study of accounting. Most of what follows relates to the *stewardship objective* of accounting. Those who wish to continue their studies of accounting must realize that the explanations are restricted primarily to stewardship and are not all-purpose definitions. In order to accomplish, say, a management evaluation or prediction objective, the concepts and definitions might have to be quite different!

Entity

An entity can be a limited liability company or corporation, a proprietorship (one owner), a partnership, a cooperative, a charitable institution, or a union. For accounting purposes, we "build a fence around the entity" and then account for it (using journals, ledgers, etc.). In practical terms we define our entity based on our decision needs. For example, suppose that Ms. Macrae has the following:

— 50 percent ownership interest in a partnership which sells clothes.
— 1,000 common shares of Dominion Stores Limited.
— a consulting office which she operates as a proprietorship.
— a part-time position with a large corporation.

How many entities are there? The partnership = 1; Dominion Stores' shares = 2; the proprietorship = 3; the part-time position = 4; and of all of them = 5.

Would Ms. Macrae need five different "sets of accounting books"? The answer depends upon her decision needs, including legal requirements. For income tax purposes she would need an overall "set of books," no matter how roughly maintained, because her salary, Dominion Stores' dividend and income from the proprietorship and partnership are taxable and she would have to show income from these on her income tax return. She may also need a "set of books" for her proprietorship entity so that she could make some judgments such as whether to continue it or sell it. The partnership probably needs a "set of books" to help the owners keep track of assets and liabilities and divide up net income. It is unlikely that she would need "books" for her shares in Dominion Stores and her part-time position.

The importance of defining an entity carefully can be observed when a person is engaged in several activities. An example would be a proprietor who manages the business and also owns the building which is rented by the business. Someone careless might prepare the following income statement for the proprietorship:

Revenue		$450,000
Cost of goods sold		285,000
Gross profit		165,000
Expenses:		
Salary	$90,000	
Rent	60,000	
Other	52,000	202,000
Loss		$ 37,000

Someone looking at the $37,000 loss might ask whether the business should be closed or sold. Further investigation, however, may indicate that $70,000 of the $90,000 "salary" really is a bonus to the proprietor, who probably earned only $10,000 of it. Also, a fair rental charge for the premises may be $36,000 and not the $60,000 charged by the proprietor. If fair values were entered, the net loss would change to a profit:

> ($70,000 − $10,000) + ($60,000 − $36,000) − $37,000 loss = $47,000 income (before any income taxes, which are paid by the proprietor and are not normally shown on a proprietorship's income statement.)

On the basis of the revised figures, the proprietorship seems to be profitable. However, we may need a "set of books" to check on the financial health of the building "entity." Maybe it costs $60,000 to operate but generates rental revenue (at fair value) of only $36,000. Possibly the building should be sold, and the proprietorship moved to a new location.

We have stretched the illustration to make a point. Often, in practice, only one set of books actually exists. However, our thinking must overcome the deficiencies of "one entity" financial statements and focus on multiple entities when separate decisions should be made. Management accounting courses stress the multiple-entity theme.

Arm's-length-status

Those associated with you through blood, marriage, or adoption are often deemed people with whom you cannot deal at arm's length for business purposes. The proprietor in the previous illustration could not deal with the proprietorship business at arm's length — and charged an unreasonable salary for himself and as rental for his building. Similarly, a single owner of a limited company might set unrealistic salary and rental charges in non-arm's-length dealings between himself and the limited company. People and businesses not associated through blood, marriage, or adoption bases are viewed as ones which will bargain with you in setting *fair* values.

Accounting concepts often are based on the *implicit* assumption that an arm's-length transaction has occurred. Note, for example, our previous discussions about objectivity. What steps do accountants take when arm's-length status is missing? This subject is currently under study, and it may take years to develop operational guidance. Generally, accountants attempt to disclose that a transaction has not been at arm's length. For example, any salary, rent and interest paid to proprietors and partners ought to be disclosed separately in financial statements.

Sometimes the existence of non-arm's-length transactions are obvious and sometimes they are not. Consider your local automobile dealership. Generally, this dealership sells the products of one automobile manufacturer — perhaps under some type of franchise agreement. Do these people conduct business on a complete arm's-length basis? If the manufacturer exercises extensive authority over the dealer, does arm's-length status disappear? For example, can the dealership refuse to accept some of the manufacturer's products and still remain a dealer? Situations are often fuzzy. Yet, they are critical to a potential lender who is considering a loan to a dealership. The lender needs assurance that the dealer will not lose his connections with the manufacturer as long as the loan is outstanding.

Consider also a small furniture manufacturing company which sells 80 percent of its products to the Bay (Hudson's Bay Company) or Eaton's. Should the financial statements disclose (a) the relationship; (b) the dollar amounts involved; (c) both the relationship and dollars; or (d) nothing? Can accountants assume "let the reader beware"? This situation obviously has to be clarified in an age where non-arm's-length transactions are common.

The Income Tax Act devotes considerable space to non-arm's-length transactions. Business persons often structure contracts and transactions to gain maximum benefit permitted by the Act. Sometimes the Act refuses to accept a non-arm's-length transaction; and, for other circumstances the price used in the exchange may be ignored and replaced by fair market value. The issue is interesting and complicated.

Measuring unit

Selecting a unit of measure is important because the unit has to mean something and be broad enough to include whatever one wishes to measure. Accountants chose, as their lowest common denominator, the dollar. Serious implications result. First, accountants in effect have excluded from their measurement system those facets of an entity which are not easily measured in dollars. People, for example, are not shown as assets (or liabilities in some cases) on the balance sheet. Yet, thousands of dollars could have been spent in training, and would have been expensed. Second, a dollar is a changing unit. The dollar is spent to acquire goods and services — and the amount of such goods and services which can be bought from year to year with a dollar might differ substantially.

Objectivity

Since this has been discussed before, only brief comment is necessary now. What is objective to one person may be subjective to another. Objectivity is a continuum, as follows:

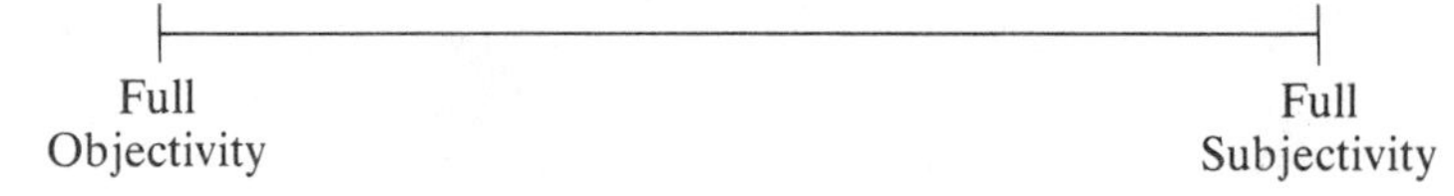

Is anything towards the left side objective? Or is only the extreme left? Accountants interested in a stewardship objective or purpose of accounting sometimes define objectivity as an unchanging concept somewhere close to the extreme left. In their view an amount is objectively measured if outside parties agree with the sum. In the following chapters we shall see many accounting conventions which are considered by some accountants to be objective, but which you may consider subjective. Make a list of them for future use in your career. (The net book value of a depreciable asset, for example, is a mixture of "objective" and "subjective." Original cost may be "objective"; accumulated depreciation is "subjective".)

Materiality

Professional judgment is an extremely important attribute which accountants, financial analysts, and others must acquire. We have advocated the objectives-facts-constraints framework as a starting point until you devise your own scheme on which to attach new ideas, and develop your judgment.

Materiality can be defined in many ways. A common way states that an amount or disclosure is material if awareness of it would tend to alter a person's assessment or judgment. For example, suppose that a firm was being sued for $100,000. Is this material, and should the matter be disclosed in financial statements? If the firm's total assets were $500,000 and net income $50,000 the sum of $100,000 would seem material. If the firm's assets were $10 billion and net income $50 million the $100,000 would not be material. What about amounts between $50,000 and $50 million of net income? We must apply our professional judgment.

What do we consider in exercising our professional judgment with respect to materiality? Our guiding criterion is users' decisions, particularly whether the users would have been misled if they were not made aware of the sum or event. Accountants have tended to translate effects on users' judgments into effects on current and future net income, income trends, and effects on assets and liabilities. Since different accountants apply different materiality guidelines, it would not be surprising to see a lack of uniformity in financial statements.

Consistency/comparability

The terms consistency and comparability are often used interchangeably. In this book we will use consistency for "within company" situations; that is, consistent from year to year for the same company. Comparability will be used for "between company" situations; that is, comparing financial statements of two companies.

Consistency is a major strength of accounting because, despite its limitations, useful trends may be observed from year-to-year comparisons. In Canada, consistency takes on a specific interpretation. A company may decide to change accounting principles (from say completed contract revenue recognition to percentage of completion) if facts change (e.g., the type of contract and riskiness alter) and to a lesser extent, if objectives of accounting change. It is certainly not bound to use the same principles forever. (The same company in fact may have several different revenue recognition methods for different factual situations as long as it is consistent from year to year in its application of the methods.)

The interesting point, when the company changes accounting principles, is the disclosure to be given to the change. Canadian practice differs from the American in that the CICA generally advocates *retroactive* treatment (accompanied by a description of the earnings impact of the change, in the year of change). This means that unless a material change in facts brings about the change in accounting, prior years' financial statements are restated using the *new* accounting principle. It is assumed therefore that the company had always been using the new principle, or method.

In practice, prior years' financial statements are not recalled from the holders. Rather, when comparative data for prior years is disclosed (see Labatt's statements in Chapter 2) the comparative data uses the new principle(s). Current financial statements note that a change has occurred this period.

The retroactive method has limitations because it does not indicate what the current year would look like using the old principles. Despite auditors' objections, a company could possibly decide to switch from the percentage of completion to the completed contract basis in the year in which the contract is completed. *If* most of the eventual profit had already been reported in previous years, a "doubling-up" effect tends to occur.

To illustrate, suppose that the profit was $500,000 on a three-year job, and that 40 percent of the work was done the first year, 50 percent in the second year, and 10 percent in the third year. The figures would appear as follows:

	Percentage of Completion	*Completed Contract*	*Retroactive Change in Principle in 19x3*	*Income as Reported in Financial Statements Previously Issued**
19x1	$200,000	—	—	$200,000
19x2	250,000	—	—	250,000
19x3	50,000	$500,000	$500,000	500,000
Total	$500,000	$500,000	$500,000	$950,000

*Percentage of Completion used in 19x1 and 19x2, and completed contract used in 19x3.

With complete disclosure the change is unlikely to be misinterpreted by readers; they would deduct the $450,000 duplication from 19x3. However, without complete disclosure misinterpretations might arise.

Comparability is somewhat puzzling to describe in a book such as this. In an ideal world with superior education, understanding, and ethics, comparability in accounting might be possible. In Canada today we have only limited comparability; and, the challenge if we are analysts is to know when we have reasonable comparability and when we do not.

Full disclosure

Accounting bodies, such as the CICA, educate their members to strive for full disclosure so that all users' needs are met. But realistically, only limited progress can be made in pursuit of full disclosure. Preparers and users of financial statements often have different objectives, fears and concerns, and are affected by different laws. They all act in accordance with their environment at the time.

Disclosure costs money to prepare the information, to audit it (where applicable), to print and distribute it, and to interpret it. Disclosure can create false impressions. Yet, disclosure — perhaps by footnotes — may be the prime way of catering to users with different needs.

Realization/revenue recognition

This chapter has been concerned with revenue recognition, a subset of the larger question of realization, which deals with write-ups or write-downs of assets and liabilities. Much has already been described, but one interesting point remains.

When a business commences, costs are incurred first, and revenue comes later. Business persons invest and hope for revenue. Accountants reverse this natural sequence. Revenue is recognized first and expenses are matched as much as possible to revenue. Why? Are accountants backward?[2] The traditional reason for this reversal has been that accountants have been concerned (at least in a stewardship sense) with reporting on *actual* events. In particular, was the decision to commence the business a wise one? We have already seen that in an ongoing business a report on the past is not possible, often because some assets are valued on the basis of their future contribution to cash inflow. Yet, under a stewardship objective, attempts are made to isolate sections of the past and measure the results in "objective" terms.

In later chapters, when we examine some other objectives of accounting we will have to reinterpret the realization concept. Less objective measures could be more relevant to some people.

Matching

We have said that income can be measured by matching expired costs (expenses) to revenue. We have also stressed that complete matching is impossible because of the task of tracing expenses to particular revenue. As a result accountants have devised conventional accounting treatments which are often impossible to defend.[3]

Is matching valid today? Over one hundred years ago it may have been possible to match when fewer major assets, long-lasting research programs, and technological changes existed. But, in today's business environment the income figure which results from matching revenues and expenses should be viewed with skepticism. We must learn which parts of a financial statement have greater reliability than others.

Cost

In order to be able to match expired costs with revenue, we obviously must define cost. Suppose that you are a grocer in Canada and have to import grapefruit and oranges from Florida. You pay (1) the grower in Florida, (2) the persons who load the truck and the trucker who brings them to Canada, (3) the persons who unload the truck, and (4) the person who puts the fruit on the grocery shelf. What is cost? If we ignore materiality, all four outlays would become part of "cost," because cost includes all outlays to make the goods *available to earn revenue*. In practice we may expense some of the outlays (especially (4)) because of the difficulty of tracing them to particular revenue items, and because of materiality.

Cost also has traditionally been defined to exclude interest charges. Suppose that you are offered an asset for $100,000 cash or $10,000 per month for twelve months, and because you are currently short of cash decide to pay $10,000 per month for 12 months. What is cost? Accountants say $100,000 is the lowest cash cost. The journal entry would be:

Asset (asset +)	$100,000	
Deferred finance charges (asset +)	20,000	
Liability (liability +)		$120,000

(Some accountants argue that the liability should be $100,000 and the deferred finance charges account should not exist at this point. Their reasoning is that the liability would exist only as the interest expense is incurred over time — and not yet paid.) The deferred finance charges would be charged to expense over one year, the period over which you "borrowed" the money. The reason for this treatment is that accountants concerned with stewardship follow what is called "proprietary accounting" — accounting for the interests of the common shareholders or partners or proprietors. Creditors are not proprietors, and any costs of borrowing from them are viewed as an expense.

Trade-ins also present a problem in cost determination. Suppose that apart from a junk dealer who will pay $50, nobody wants to buy your old car. Yet if you trade it in on a new car you are offered $400. You accept the offer and have to pay the dealer $6,500 in cash (the only cash which changes hands). What is the cost of your *new* automobile? Accountants say $6,550 ($6,500 plus $50 fair market value of the trade-in). They regard the $350 difference (between $400 trade-in allowance and $50 paid by a third party at arm's-length) as sales gimmickry. Accountants would reason that someone without a trade-in would pay $6,550 cash.

Continuity/going concern

Accountants depreciate fixed assets such as automobiles over their useful lives, using the assumption that the business will continue to exist. If the business will not continue, cost is no longer appropriate, and liquidation values should appear on the balance sheet.

In practice the going concern assumption can create difficulties. A typical scene in Canada is the closing down of a mine because metal prices have declined. The ore remains in the ground and the mine remains closed until the selling price of the metal in the ore increases. After a mine has been closed for ten years, and is filled with water and supported by rotting timber, is it still a going concern? Depreciation on underground assets may continue while the mine is closed, but what about other assets above ground?

Auditors face a dilemma. Their declaring a business no longer a going concern may force it into bankruptcy, while it otherwise might have had a good chance of survival. On the other hand, auditors may be sued if they do not indicate that the business faces difficulties.

For the above and other reasons the going concern assumption is interesting. As we shall see in Chapter 16 a reworking of the concept can lead to different definitions of income and approaches to business.

Conservatism

Conservatism in accounting is sometimes explained as "anticipate no profit; provide for all known or estimable losses." Under stewardship accounting and the climate of the 1929 Stock Market Crash and the Depression, it is not surprising that such a concept gained acceptance. In its place with uncertainty and conservative users, it makes sense; but what about its affect on other users?

Unfortunately for its advocates, conservative accounting eventually reverses itself and ultraunconservative accounting might result. For example, if management writes down its inventory of goods for resale, the current year's profit and retained earnings plus the asset "inventory" are "understated" compared to no write-down. But what happens next year, when the goods are sold? With a smaller cost of goods sold, net income is much higher.

	Conservative Accounting Inventory Written Down		*No Inventory Write-Down*	
	19x1	*19x2*	*19x1*	*19x2*
Revenue	$1,000	$1,000	$1,000	$1,000
Cost of goods sold	900*	500	700	700
Gross profit	100	500	300	300
Expenses	100	100	100	100
Income	$ 0	$ 400	$ 200	$ 200

*Comprised of $700 cost of goods sold plus $200 write down.

Have some readers been misled? In the above conservative accounting case they have been misled because $200 was charged through cost of goods sold in 19x1, but selling prices did not decline in 19x2. The effect was $200 extra in 19x2. What conclusions might readers draw about the company's future profitability? In short, conservative accounting can be dangerous to some and beneficial to others. It is something which we must watch for in performing financial statement analysis.

Summary

Chapter 5 is undoubtedly the most important and difficult chapter in the book. Much of what has been said will be repeated throughout the book, by using examples from specific assets, liabilities and equities. Students should not feel overwhelmed at this point. Repetition in the following chapters will make the concepts more understandable. Frequent references back to Chapter 5 will greatly aid your understanding of accounting (as opposed to just bookkeeping).

The sections on "Objectives" and "Key Accounting Concepts" cannot be summarized easily, so no attempt has been made. They are vital and must be reread several times as you progress through the book. In brief, you cannot account and report unless you know what you are trying to accomplish in terms of objectives. Similarly, it may be very difficult to understand accounting procedures used in pursuing the stewardship objective unless you refer to the key accounting concepts which accountants rely on in their reasoning.

Revenues should be realized when earned for several of the objectives of accounting; costs should be charged as expenses at the time the revenues to which they are related are realized. This chapter has addressed the question of when revenues should be considered to be earned and how costs can most meaningfully be related to specific revenues. In this chapter we have not attempted to provide answers; indeed there are no definitive answers. Instead we have explored the nature of the problems and set forth general guidelines for their resolution.

Revenues are commonly recognized (considered to result in an increase in net assets) at time of sale. They may also be recognized, however, during the process of production, at the completion of the process, or after both the completion of the process and the point of sale — that is, upon collection of the cash owing to the sale. As a rule, for the stewardship objective, revenue should be recognized as soon as

1. The firm has exerted a substantial portion of its production and sales effort;
2. The revenue can be objectively measured;
3. The major portion of costs have been incurred, and the remaining costs can be estimated with reasonable reliability and precision; and
4. Eventual collection of cash can reasonably be assured.

Expenses should be matched with and charged against the revenues that they serve to generate. Often, however, a clearly defined cause and effect relationship is not apparent. In the absence of such a relationship the determination of which expenses should be matched to which revenues must be based, in large measure, on the good judgment of business managers and their accountants.

In general, if an enterprise is neither expanding nor contracting, then total reported revenues as well as expenses would be the same regardless of to which specific policies of revenue and expense recognition the firm adhered. If, however, as is most commonly the situation, the firm is either increasing or decreasing the volume of its operations, then the impact of alternative practices on reported earnings may be substantial.

Issues of revenue and expense recognition must never be viewed in isolation from those of asset and liability valuation. They are intrinsically related. Any determination that affects reported income must necessarily affect a related balance sheet account. Questions of asset valuation will be addressed directly, however, commencing in Chapter 6.

Notes

[1]Many publications have recently dealt with some objectives of financial accounting and reporting. A few are: Financial Accounting Standards Board, *Objectives of Financial Reporting by Business Enterprises* (Stamford: FASB, 1978); Report of the Study Group on the Objectives of Financial Statements, *Objectives of Financial Statements* (New York: AICPA, 1973); and the Committee To Prepare a Statement of Basic Accounting Theory, *A Statement of Basic Accounting Theory* (Evanston: AAA, 1966).

[2]A famous Canadian accountant, the late Howard Ross, once remarked that "Accountants stand facing the past. Sometimes they should look over their shoulder at the brilliant future behind them."

[3]For further information see the writings of Arthur L. Thomas, noted in Chapter 9.

Questions, Problems, and Cases

Questions

5-1 What do you consider "reasonable" objectives or purposes of financial accounting? Explain your beliefs thoroughly.

5-2 "It can be virtually impossible to prepare financial statements when objectives of financial accounting are not clear."

Required:

a. Illustrate, by giving specific examples, how different accounting objectives of financial reporting can result in different accounting treatment.

b. How would you decide which objectives of financial accounting or reporting are most important in a given situation? Explain your position clearly by giving specific examples.

5-3 "The main purpose of financial reporting should be stewardship. If we adopt this modest objective, our focus can be sharper and we can be more effective. We can adopt uniform measurement as our guide in setting standards and can gain greater comparability. As a goal reliability can be placed ahead of economic reality."

Required:

Do you agree with the above quotation? Explain your reasoning.

5-4 In order to accomplish the stewardship objective accountants refer to "key accounting concepts" in their reasoning process.

Required:

Identify the limitations of accounting data that result from using these concepts.

5-5 Accounting income is defined as revenue minus expenses.

Required:

a. Explain how revenue and expense recognition is inherently intertwined with that of asset and liability valuation.

b. Identify and explain briefly the key accounting concepts underlying the measurement of revenues and expenses within stewardship accounting.

c. Explain some of the problems which might be encountered in applying these key accounting concepts.

d. Explain some of the limitations of the income figure derived under stewardship accounting.

5-6 Your neighbor, who has no knowledge of accounting has asked you what "generally accepted accounting principles" means. How would you respond?

5-7 It is sometimes pointed out that over the life of an enterprise it matters little on what basis revenues and expenses are recognized; it is only because investors and others demand periodic reports of performance that problems of revenue and expense recognition arise. Do you agree? Explain.

5-8 As soon as it is determined when revenues should be recognized, it should be a simple matter to determine when expenses should be recognized; simply match the expenses to the revenues which they generated. If this is true, how do you account for similar companies' according different accounting treatment to expenses even though they may employ identical methods of revenue recognition?

5-9 "If financial statements are to be truly objective, it is inappropriate to recognize revenue on a transaction until the seller has cash in hand; recognition of revenue at any point prior to collection of cash necessarily involves estimates of the amount of cash that will actually be collected." Do you agree? Why is revenue often recognized before the collection of cash?

5-10 The Evergreen Forest Co. raises trees intended for sale as Christmas trees. Trees are sold approximately ten years after they have been planted. What special problems of income determination does the company face if it is to prepare financial statements?

5-11 The Cresent Co. Ltd. engaged in only one transaction in the current year. It sold for $150,000 land which it had purchased eight years earlier for $100,000. The increase in fair market price of the land could be attributed entirely to the impact of inflation — i.e., goods and services which cost $1.00 eight years ago would cost $1.50 today.

Required:

a. How much income should the company report for the current year under stewardship accounting? Explain your reasoning.
b. How much better off was the company at the end of the year than it was at the beginning?
c. Assuming that your main objectives for financial accounting are management evaluation and cash prediction how might your measurement of income differ from Part a. above?

5-12 Define the following concepts of stewardship accounting:

a. Arm's length
b. Going concern
c. Conservatism

What implications do the above definitions have on financial reporting?

5-13 Is it desirable for accounting information to be both relevant and objective? Give examples of the potential conflict between these two criteria. How would you resolve this conflict?

5-14 Egg producers are guaranteed a price for eggs by an egg marketing board. In late 19x1, an egg producer gathered 1,500 eggs and decided to place them in cold storage rather than immediately selling them to the egg marketing board because he anticipated the board would be increasing its price. However, by the time of the producer's fiscal year end the marketing board had not yet increased the price and the eggs were still in storage unsold.

Required:

How much revenue should be recognized in 19x1? Explain your reasoning.

Problems

*P5-1 At a recent cocktail party you found yourself in a conversation with two businessmen. One was the president of a large public company engaged in the manufacture of steel. The other was an owner-manager of a local men's clothing store.

Required:

How might the objectives or goals of these two people (organizations) differ and what effects might there be on the objectives of accounting and accounting procedures of each? Be specific where possible.

P5-2 The Darville Construction Co. Ltd. agreed to construct six playgrounds for the City of Brantford. Total contract price was $1.2 million. Total estimated costs were $960,000.

The following schedule indicates for the three-year period during which construction took place, the number of playground units completed, the actual costs incurred, and the amount of cash received from the City of Brantford.

		Year	
	19x1	*19x2*	*19x3*
Playgrounds completed	1	2	3
Cost incurred	$480,000	$288,000	$192,000
Cash collected	$240,000	$360,000	$600,000

Required:

a. Determine revenues, expenses, and income for each of the three years under each of the following alternatives:
   (i) Revenue recognized on the basis of the percentage of costs incurred.
   (ii) Revenue recognized as soon as each playground is completed.
   (iii) Revenue recognized upon the collection of cash.

b. What criteria would you use in selecting a revenue recognition point from the above alternatives? Why?

P5-3 On December 31, 19x6, Reliable Roofing Co. Ltd. reported among its liabilities the following balance:

Liability for roof guarantees $4,000

During 19x7 , the company constructed roofs for which it billed customers $300,000. It estimates that, on average, it incurs repair costs, under its two-year guarantee, of 2 percent of the initial contract price of its roofs. In 19x7 the company actually incurred repair costs of $7,500, which were applicable to roofs constructed both in 19x7 and in prior years.

Required:

a. Prepare both the liability and expense accounts pertaining to roof repairs in journal entry and T account form for the year 19x7.

b. How can a company justify charging repair expenses *before* they are actually incurred, based only on an *estimate* of what actual costs will be?

P5-4 The Walton Company Limited sells a parcel of land for $150,000. Terms of the contract require that the seller make a down payment of $30,000 at the time the agreement is signed and pay the remaining balance in two instalments at the end of each of the next two years. In addition, the contract requires the seller to pay interest at a rate of 8 percent on the balance outstanding at the time of each of the two instalment payments.

Walton Company Limited had purchased the land for $90,000.

Required:

a. Identify alternative revenue recognition points.

b. Assuming that the recognition of revenues and expenses is related to the collection of cash, record the sale of land and subsequent receipts of cash.

c. Outline the conditions necessary for using the above revenue recognition point.

P5-5 The Harrison Co. Ltd. manufactures television sets for sale to Save-More Discount Stores, a sole proprietorship. Save-More sells the sets under its own brand name. In 19x1 Harrison Co. Ltd. signed a contract to deliver to Save-More 30,000 sets at a price of $100 per set over the next three years. By the end of 19x1 the company had not yet delivered any sets to Save-More but had 10,000 sets 90 percent complete. In 19x2 the company completed and delivered to Save-More 23,000 sets: The 10,000 sets started in the previous year plus 13,000 sets started in 19x2. In 19x3 the company completed and delivered the remaining 7,000 sets.

Each set cost Harrison Co. Ltd. $75 to manufacture. As agreed upon in the contract, Save-More made cash payments to Harrison Co. Ltd. of $1 million in each of the three years.

Required:

a. Determine revenues, expenses, and income for each of the three years if revenue were to be recognized (1) in the course of production, (2) at time of delivery, (3) at time of cash collection. Are total revenues, expenses, and income the same under each of the three methods?

b. Which basis of revenue recognition do you think results in the most objective measure? Which is the most relevant determination? Why?

P5-6 "The theory of the critical event as the moment at which to recognize profit or loss on a transaction seems very useful. It is a theory based on the fundamental process rather than upon such frequently used rationalizations as convenience, conservatism, certainty, tax timing, legal passage of title. The present status of relying upon many different theories of when to match revenue and expense cannot long stand in a profession."

Required:

a. Evaluate the above quotation. (Do you agree with it?)

b. One of the criteria for revenue recognition under a stewardship objective is: The firm has exerted a substantial portion of its production and sales effort. When do you think this would occur in the following industries:

(i) Merchandising?
(ii) Manufacturing?
(iii) Contracting?
(iv) Publishing?
(v) Lending money?
(vi) Real estate development? And rental?

P5-7 The Haines Co. Ltd. was organized on June 1, 19x7 for the specific purpose of chartering a ship to undertake a three-month, 10,000-mile voyage. On June 1, the founders of the company contributed $600,000 to the company in exchange for common shares. On the same day, the company paid the entire $600,000 to the owners of a ship for the right to use it for a period of three months.

During the three month period the chartered ship made several stops.

Indicated below are the number of miles traveled and the amount of cargo, in terms of dollar billings to customers, that the firm loaded and unloaded. (For example, in June the company loaded cargo for which it billed customers $500,000. During that same month it unloaded $300,000 of that same cargo.)

	Loaded	*Unloaded*	*No. of Miles Traveled*
June	$ 500,000	$ 300,000	4,000
July	300,000	100,000	2,500
August	200,000	600,000	3,500
	$1,000,000	$1,000,000	10,000

Operating expenses, in addition to the charter fee, were $100,000 per month.

The Haines Co. Ltd. was liquidated on August 31, 19x7. At that time all expenses had been paid and all bills collected.

Required:

a. Determine the income of the company over its three-month life.

b. Determine the income of the company during *each* of the three months. Make alternative decisions as to the methods used to recognize revenues and charge expenses. Assume that revenues are recognized (i) when cargo is loaded and (ii) when cargo is unloaded. Assume that the $600,000 is charged as an expense (i) evenly over the three-month period and (ii) in proportion to number of miles traveled.

c. Which methods are preferable? Why?

P5-8 The Clappison Construction Co. Ltd. contracts with the Selby Corporation to construct an office building. The contract price is $50 million. The Clappison Co. Ltd. estimates the building will cost $40 million and will take three years to complete. The contract calls for the Selby Corporation to make cash advances of $10 million during each of the first two years of construction and to make a final payment of $30 million upon completion of the building; these cash advances are to be accounted for on the books of Clappison Construction Co. Ltd. as a liability until the project is completed.

The company elects to recognize revenue on the project on the percentage of completion basis. Actual expenditures over the three-year period are as follows:

19x1	$10,000,000
19x2	25,000,000
19x3	5,000,000

Required:

a. Prepare journal entries to account for the project over the three-year period. Assume that all costs are paid in cash as incurred.

b. Prepare an income statement and a balance sheet for each of the three years. Assume that at the start of the project the only asset of the company is cash of $20 million.

c. Outline the necessary conditions to recognize revenue on the percentage of completion basis.
d. Assume that cash prediction and management evaluation are major financial accounting objectives of the Clappison Construction Co. Ltd. What additional disclosure would you recommend at the end of 19x1? Why?

P5-9 Bob Bryce celebrated Christmas 19x3 by purchasing a new car. In his first year as sales manager of the newly formed industrial equipment division of the Shakespeare Manufacturing Co. Ltd. Bryce and his sales force had generated $750,000 in noncancellable orders for equipment.

Bryce's employment contract provided that he receive an annual bonus equal to 3 percent of his division's profits. He was aware that costs of manufacturing the equipment were approximately 60 percent of sales prices and that the company had budgeted $200,000 for administrative and all other operating costs. He could afford to splurge on a new car since according to his rough calculations, his bonus would total at least $3,000.

In mid-January, Bryce received a bonus cheque for $1,200. Stunned, but confident that a clerical error had been made, he placed an urgent call to the company controller. The controller informed him that no error had been made. Although costs were in line with those budgeted, reported sales were only $600,000.

The equipment produced by the company is special-purpose polishing equipment. Since it must be custom-made, customers must normally wait for delivery at least two months from the date of order.

Required:

a. Demonstrate how the amount of bonus was calculated by *both* Bryce and the company controller. What is the most likely explanation of the difference in their sales figures? What reasoning might they use to support their respective positions?
b. The company president has asked for your recommendations with respect to the bonus plan. Assuming that the objective of the company is to give reasonably prompt recognition to the accomplishments of its sales manager, on what basis do you think revenue should be recognized for the purpose of computing his bonus? Do you think the company should use the same basis for reporting to shareholders? Explain.

P5-10 Starlight Ltd. and Paramour Ltd. both produce short films intended for television exhibition. The cost to produce a typical film is $150,000. The film can be licensed to a television network for $200,000. The license agreement gives exclusive exhibition rights to the network for a period of five years. At the end of the five-year period the films seldom have any commercial value.

Starlight Ltd. recognizes revenue from film productions as soon as it completes a film and signs an agreement with a network. Paramour, on the other hand, recognizes revenue only upon actual collection of license fees. Fees are contractually collectible only upon delivery of a film. Delivery is usually made several months after an agreement is signed.

In 19x1 both companies completed and signed agreements on six films; they collected the license fees on four films.

In 19x2 they completed signed agreements *and* collected the license fees on eight films.

In 19x3 they completed no films but collected the license fees on two films.

Required:

a. Prepare income statements for each of the three years for both Starlight Ltd. and Paramour Ltd.
b. Indicate the assets related to production and licensing of the films (cash, films, license fees receivable, etc.) that would be reported on each of the corresponding balance sheets. Assume all costs of production were paid in cash in the year in which the films were completed and that each of the companies started 19x1 with $100,000 cash.
c. If, at the end of 19x1 the financial statements of Starlight Ltd. and Paramour Ltd. were presented to a potential investor, what impact will the difference in revenue recognition points have on his decision?
d. What additional information would you recommend be disclosed to aid potential shareholders?

Cases

C5-1 Beautiful Person Health Club charges members an annual $240 membership fee. The fee, which is payable in advance, entitles the member to visit the club as many times as he wishes.

Selected membership data for the three-month period January to March 19x1 are indicated below:

	Jan.	*Feb.*	*March*
Number of new memberships sold	20	30	10
Number of renewals	50	20	10
Number of expirations (including members who renewed)	50	40	10
Total number of active members at end of month	600	610	620

Members who renew their contracts must also pay the $240 annual fee in advance of their membership year.

Monthly costs of operating the health facilities are approximately as follows:

Rent	$ 1,000
Salaries	5,000
Advertising and promotion	3,000
Depreciation and other operating costs	1,500
	$10,500

The company controller and the auditor, an independent CA, disagree over the basis on which revenue should be recognized. The CA argues that since members can use the facilities over a 12-month period, revenue from each member should be spread over a 12-month period (i.e., $20 per month per member). The controller, on the other hand, asserts that the entire membership fee should be recognized in the month the member either joins or renews. A major portion of corporate effort, he argues, is exerted *before* and at the time a new member actually joins the club. He points out that the company spends over $3,000 per month in direct advertising and promotion costs, and, in addition, a significant portion of the time of several club employees (whose salaries are included in the $5,000 of salary costs) is directed to promoting new memberships and processing both new applications and renewals.

Required:

What would you recommend? Justify your position by determining the impact on monthly income of alternative accounting treatments and the criteria and concepts you have used.

C5-2 The Fivetran Co. Ltd. developed a series of computer programs designed to simplify the "back office" operations of stock brokerage firms. All costs of developing the programs have been charged to expense accounts as incurred. Although the programs can be readily applied to the operations of all firms in the industry, certain features of the programs must be custom-designed to meet the specific requirements of each customer.

In January 19x7 analysts of Fivetran Co. Ltd. made a preliminary study of the "back office" operations of Conrad, Roy, Atwood, Smith, and Harris (CRASH), a leading brokerage firm. Fivetran Co. Ltd. hoped that as a result of the study it could demonstrate the savings in costs and increases in efficiency that its programs could bring about and that it could thereby sell its programs to CRASH. It was agreed that the total costs of the preliminary study would be borne by Fivetran Co. Ltd. CRASH was under no obligation to either purchase the programs or pay for the preliminary study. Cost of the preliminary study was $10,000.

The preliminary study was successful; on February 2, 19x7, CRASH placed an order with Fivetran Co. Ltd. for its series of programs; the contract price was $150,000.

During February and March, Fivetran Co. Ltd. developed the custom features of the program for CRASH. Costs incurred in February were $8,000, and in March, $12,000. On March 15, 19x7, Fivetran Co. Ltd. delivered the completed series of programs to CRASH, and they were reviewed and accepted by CRASH management.

On April 4, 19x7, Fivetran Co. Ltd. received a cheque for $50,000 plus a two-year, 8 percent note for the balance.

Required:

a. Assume the role of an accounting advisor to Fivetran Co. Ltd. What basis of revenue and expense recognition would you recommend? Why? Indicate any assumptions that you have made.
b. Prepare journal entries to record the events described above.
c. Prepare comparative income statements for the months ending January 31, February 28, March 31 and April 30.

C5-3 Classic Concerts Ltd. ("CCL") is a private, profit-making corporation which presents chamber music concerts in a rented, 483-seat recital hall. The series of concerts which CCL presents is an annual International Series of twenty concerts by international chamber music groups. This series is always completely sold out by advance subscription each year.

The planning of each year's series occurs at least one year in advance. For example, during the 19x5-6 concert season, CCL invites the participating artists for the 19x6-7 series, and all appearances will be firmly contracted (as to date and fee) no later than May 1, 19x6. In May of 19x6, a brochure describing the 19x6-7 series will be mailed to all subscribers, who will have until June 30, 19x6 to renew their subscriptions. Any unrenewed subscriptions will be offered to the general public after July 1, and they always are sold out within a few days because there is a waiting list of people who want to subscribe. The subscribers may pay by cash, money-order, cheque, post-dated cheque (no later than September 1), or credit card, but they must remit payment when they subscribe.

The concerts themselves will take place between September 15, 19x6 and June 30, 19x7. On rare occasions, it is necessary to reschedule a concert due to booking conflicts or ill health. About once every two years, a group will not be able to appear, and CCL must then find a substitute group (which may cost somewhat more or less than the original group). Ticket refunds are never made, although Classic Concerts Ltd.'s box office will resell tickets for subscribers who cannot attend individual concerts. The proceeds of resale are returned to the subscriber, less a one dollar per ticket service charge.

The rental of the hall (including ushers, stagehands, and the house manager) is contracted when the concerts are initially being planned. CCL runs small advertisements in the newspapers for each concert in order to maintain public awareness of the concerts, even though they are sold out (which fact is clearly indicated in the ads). CCL has a small administrative staff throughout the year. Other expenses, such as program printing and hospitality for the artists, are relatively small and can be budgeted fairly accurately.

Required:

The president of Classic Concerts Ltd. has approached you to ask how to account for the revenue and expenses of the corporation for the fiscal year ending December 31, 19x6. He is curious about the financial statement effects of different possible methods of revenue recognition. However, he is concerned about using the "proper" method of revenue recognition and is relying on you to select a method which will be in his best interests and at the same time defensible. What would you recommend?

C5-4 Shifman, Shifman and Shifman ("SSS" or the firm) are chartered accountants who operate as a partnership. The firm has been in existence for several years and presently has five partners, three managers and a staff of about twenty-five. This year one of the partners, S. Shifman, is retiring and one of the managers, M. Mintz, will be admitted to the partnership. The partnership has a January 31 year end.

During the year, the firm moved its office in order to become more centrally located. Previously it was located 25 miles north of the city in a building which it owns. Now it is located 20 miles north of the city in an office which it rents from S. Shifman. The firm decided to retain the building which it owns because property values have increased dramatically since it was purchased twenty years ago. The original cost of the property was $100,000 and recently one of the tenants offered $600,000 for it.

Clients normally are billed at an hourly rate (differing rates exist for different levels of staff) at the completion of a job. Each staff member keeps track of the time he or she spends on a particular client and submits a weekly time report to the accounting office. Periodically, the accounting office summarizes these time reports by client indicating the hours each staff member has spent to date on particular clients. At the completion of a job, the time spent by each employee is accumulated and extended at the employee's hourly rate. This rate includes a (1) wage rate (2) a sum to cover cost of typists, stationary, office rental etc. and (3) an element of profit. The total sum of all employee time and cost is then calculated. The invoice sent to the client may be more than, less than, or equal to this total. When the invoice is sent, the firm records revenue.

Required:

One of the partners of SSS has approached you to provide an independent opinion on when to recognize revenue and how to record the accounting impact of the firm's move. Write a report outlining your recommendations. Your recommendations are particularly important to the firm because they will form the basis of determining how much capital M. Mintz must contribute on admission to the partnership.

C5-5 Financial Statements of the Government of Canada. The financial statements prepared by the Government of Canada differ from those compiled in the private sector (such as those for Labatt's, which are reproduced in Chapter 2). The balance sheet (called a Statement of Assets and Liabilities) shows liabilities, cash and receivables but does not show fixed assets or owner's equity. It is balanced by a large debit amount called "excess of recorded liabilities over net recorded assets". The "income" statement (called a Statement of Revenue and Expenditure) shows tax and other revenue received in cash during the year less cash expenditures for both expenses and fixed assets, and less some expense accruals. The bottom line is called budgetary deficit (*not* net income or loss). The Statement of Changes in Financial Position is in abbreviated form and mainly shows changes in long term liabilities. In addition the activities of some government organizations such as CNR and Air Canada are excluded from the financial statements.

Person A: "Who uses the financial statements of the Government of Canada?"

Person B: "I'm not sure. When the government wants to sell bonds in the world money markets it always tells people what its liabilities are, but no more than this; no financial statements are provided. I guess that some people are concerned about the amount of budgetary deficit and think that the government should try to balance expenditures to the amount of revenues which it collects."

Person A: "Does the budgetary deficit mean the same thing as net income — that is, it measures some form of success or failure?"

Person B: Not really. Fixed assets are expensed; and there is no depreciation accounting. The deficit is not a loss, I think, because some of the cash expenditures are for fixed assets which last much longer than one year. Such expenditures could well exceed any depreciation expense in a year. Also, it's hard to know what the assets owned by the government are currently worth.

Maybe the increase during the year in value of the fixed assets could exceed the budgetary deficit."

Person A: "What else is different about the government situation to lead to reporting which differs from the private sector?"

Person C: "The amount of dollars involved is huge compared to that for most companies. Also, the government can borrow on the basis of its ability to tax individuals and companies. Investors will lend to a government as long as the government can repay the debt from tax receipts. It doesn't have to earn revenue from its fixed assets."

Person A: "Is that why the government doesn't record fixed assets, depreciation, and owner's equity?"

Person D: "Possibly; I'm not sure. The government does not have to worry about disclosure constraints in Companies Acts, Securities Acts and various income tax legislation when it prepares financial statements. Governments have to be concerned with more than a profit motive. For instance, the health of citizens should not be viewed only in quantitative cost-benefit terms. Welfare programs are devised to aid people; not show a profit."

Person E: "But, how do we know whether or not the government is performing well? You imply that the financial statements are of little use in indicating a government's performance."

Person D: "Should and can the government's financial statements be set up to permit people to judge performance? These are tough questions. For example, if the financial statements are organized to permit performance evaluation will they be rendered useless for another judgment or purpose?"

Person B: "Can anyone judge performance from an annual financial statement? Government programs are set up to attain benefits over several years — not immediately. Besides, how do you measure the benefit of police protection, amateur sports programs, or aid to other countries?"

Person A: "I still do not understand what the government's financial statements are used for. How do you know whether the government might be near bankruptcy?"

Person B: "The budgetary deficit is a rough indication of the amount of new cash which the government must borrow in the bond market. If it can borrow it won't go bankrupt."

Person A: "Rough indication? How rough? Revenues seem to be on a cash basis whereas expenses are on a part cash, part accrual basis, excluding expenditures on fixed assets. What does this tell you?"

Person C: "The government doesn't have to borrow all of the budgetary deficit from the bond market. It borrows some of its needs from its employees' pension plans."

Person E: "The more I hear the more I think that the government's financial statements need a major revision."

Person F: "To accomplish what?"

Required:

In your opinion, are the financial statements prepared by the Government of Canada sensible, given the objectives, facts, and constraints which you have identified from the above? Explain your reasoning. What do you recommend?

Appendix 5-A

Less-Directed Questions

Throughout this text we have emphasized that the preparation of accounting information ought to reflect the needs of the various people who use the information as a basis for decision making. For this reason, the methodology underlying the preparation of financial reports is often as important as the information itself. The people who use the information want to know not only how the information is arranged, but why it is presented in a certain way. They want to understand the logic underlying the accountant's approach, especially when there are alternative ways in which the material can be represented with important financial implications for the firm.

Students should be aware that accounting information is designed to help a number of people who must each cope with different situations. Obviously, then, we cannot seek the general and learn the exceptions later. The general is non-existent, and looking for it can easily become bookkeeping. The basics of accounting are communication, analytical reasoning, and knowledge of people and their financial needs — not knowledge of one way of bookkeeping or the accounting cycle.

Nature of direction

A *directed* question leads toward an answer. Directed questions have their place in accounting courses when the purpose of the question is to provide practice in repeating basic techniques, and testing a knowledge of terminology and definitions. But excessive use of such questions mitigates against digging for facts, querying what is read and ascertaining purposes and uses of accounting — all requirements of the accounting profession.

Less-directed questions examine more complex situations, remove important pieces of information from a question, and may provide conflicting data which must be assessed for relevance. Objectives of accounting may not be clear, and it is often necessary to adopt another's point of view to determine financial needs. Such questions demand that logical assumptions be made. Assumptions may vary, and therefore responses could be quite different; as a result, more detailed explanations of logic are required. Why was a particular accounting procedure or disclosure recommended? How does it relate to the objectives, facts and assumptions, and constraints of the situation? Do you know which technique and approach to use in different situations?

The use of less-directed questions is not the only approach to teaching a theme of tailoring accounting needs to objectives-facts-constraints (OFC).

Different students have different needs which is why this discussion appears in an Appendix rather than in the body of the text. It is important that accounting courses maximize the knowledge appropriate for these varying needs.

This Appendix begins to explain a method of handling less-directed financial accounting questions. This method is not simply another way of answering questions; it demonstrates a logical progression from OFC to "suitable" accounting and disclosure methods which are required in a professional situation. As we have said, how an answer is obtained can be more important than the answer itself, especially when someone wants to know on receiving a recommendation, what factors were considered and why.

Examples

Two cases will be presented to illustrate *an* approach which *might* be used. With practice, the logic of answers to less-directed inquiries can be mastered.

Family Furniture Factory

Family Furniture Factory (FFF) is located in a rural district close to a major highway which is used to transport FFF's products to many of its customers, mainly department and specialty furniture stores.

FFF assembles the furniture, which is used in both homes and offices, at its one location using workers from the local community. Labor is usually plentiful because the area's unemployment rate tends to be between 15 and 20 percent much of the year. Fabrics are bought from a variety of suppliers in Canada and the U.S.

The owners could be considered wealthy, having made most of their money in real estate and gold purchases in the past fifteen years. As a result they have no difficulty borrowing money from a bank in order to finance short term needs of FFF.

The president of FFF — one of the founder's two sons — has asked you to review the company's accounting policies. They were set up by the founder many years ago and the president wonders whether they are still appropriate.

FFF sells 3-4 percent of its production directly in the local community for a 20 percent cash down payment plus the balance in monthly payments over 36 months with interest at 18 percent per annum. Revenue on these sales is recognized in the accounts as cash is collected. Another 50-55 percent of production is sold to department stores who pay within 90 days of receipt of the merchandise. Revenue on these items is usually recognized in full on date of shipment because full cash is nearly always received when due. The balance of sales are to large and small furniture specialty stores. The larger stores handle the same type of merchandise as the department stores, and, because payments are received when due, revenue is recognized on shipment, the same as for department stores. A lower quality line of furniture is assembled for smaller furniture stores who sell to lower income families and newlyweds. Revenue from these smaller stores is recognized in the accounts as cash is received.

In all cases cost of goods sold is deferred as necessary to match the period of revenue recognition. Selling and office expenses are treated as period costs and expensed as work is performed.

Required:
Review the company's accounting policies, per the president's request, and advise, giving reasons to support your advice.

A response

This question is primarily concerned with revenue recognition, mainly because we are still at an early stage in the range of subjects in the book. As a result, the response which follows is not fully developed at this time. However, some highlights can be provided along with explanations of our thinking process. Your instructor will probably grade your response by examining the logical assumptions which you have made, not just the quality of your recommendations. Directed questions tend to be graded by viewing the recommendations or so-called answer — and not how you got there. Other directed questions may be graded in broader terms.

Objectives or purposes of accounting

Quite likely we would be safe in assuming that income tax is the major objective of accounting for FFF. We can support this assumption by noting that there seems to be little need to prepare financial statements for creditors such as bankers because the bankers probably (we are not certain, though) lend to the owners on the basis of their general wealth. As a result, the two objectives of prediction and evaluation of management are not important in a situation where neither the owners nor the creditors appear to require financial statements. It might be possible to muster a good argument on behalf of stewardship accounting *if* the four owners do not know what is happening in FFF and rely on the financial statements for information. However, if each of the owners visits FFF's factory and office frequently, a financial statement prepared just to keep the owners informed would not be necessary. Since the case does not tell us a vital piece of information about the closeness of the owners to their company it becomes necessary for us to *state our assumption in writing* about the frequency of visits by the owners and the state of their knowledge about FFF. (This question tests our knowledge and understanding of a situation where vital information is absent. Are we aware that we must gather information about closeness of the owners to the business before proceeding with our analysis?) To summarize, we can safely proceed in FFF with the assumption that our entire set of accounting principles can be selected with the objective of postponing, within limits of the law, income tax payments (which are based on "taxable income", which in turn is partially based on accounting income).

Facts

We have tended to use the word "fact" a little loosely when we refer to the objectives – facts – constraints approach to viewing the subject of financial accounting. The word "fact," according to a dictionary, tends to mean "something known to exist or to have happened, or a truth known by actual experience or observation." Sometimes we can ascertain facts (e.g., a product is manufactured; goods are shipped) which lead to an accounting treatment (such as credit inventory, and debit cost of goods sold). Other times the facts (such as the company being sued) are not much help to us in ascertaining the dollar effect of an event, but can lead to general disclosure in footnotes to financial statements. Situations also exist where it is difficult to separate fact from fiction.

In less-directed questions we purposely leave out some facts to see whether students can recognize that they cannot respond to a question until they find out the missing facts. In order to proceed with their analysis, students must make logical assumptions about what they think the facts would probably be. In practice, we often have to gather proxy or substitute information because we do not know what the facts *might* be. We try to peer into the future in order to estimate such matters as how many customers likely will not pay for their purchases. Our proxy information may be: How many did not pay in the past? Will the future repeat itself or differ? Is the economy better or worse? Are more unemployed? In our analysis of less-directed questions, fact will be used loosely to mean fact, assumption, and proxy information, which is used to guess as best we can at what the facts might be.

What are the important facts — that is, important in deciding upon accounting treatment — in FFF? (Remember, our concern at this point in the course is with revenue recognition.) First, there are three types of customers: department and large stores, small furniture speciality stores, and local residents. The likelihood of receiving cash payment from each might differ substantially because of differences in wealth and probable incomes.

When the facts are absolutely clear, and there is no room for judgment, it is difficult to favor a particular accounting treatment so as to accomplish a particular objective of accounting — such as the postponement of income tax payments. For example, when cash is virtually assured as a result of selling to a large store, revenue probably should be recognized on the date when the goods are ordered for shipment to the store. That is, objectives can be ignored when the facts are powerful and beyond dispute. (A special purpose report might handle matters differently, but in this discussion we are ignoring special purpose reports.) In contrast, considerable doubt exists about the amount and date of receipt of cash when sales are made to local residents. Hence, there is room for judgment, and objectives become very important.

The *relationship between objectives* of accounting *and facts is* a *critical* one. Many instructors teach introductory accounting strictly from a preparer's (of the financial statements) point of view. Often a fictional merchandising store is assumed and "ideal" accounting treatment is recommended. Such instructors may not like financial accounting being tailored (or biased) to particular objectives of accounting — especially income tax — when facts are subject to the interpretation of one's professional judgment. The user point of view must be given equal space because many people take accounting classes in order to understand how to *use* accounting information. Students must be taught that facts are often unclear, that room for judgment often exists, and that judgment has to be exercised — using a model, such as objectives-facts-constraints.

Users must realize that in Canadian practice and elsewhere, accounting treatment results from a *review by the preparer* of objectives of accounting facts of the situation, and any legislation or constraints. Users must therefore interpret what the preparer had in mind — which could very well be quite different from what is taught in some introductory or even advanced financial accounting courses. Small businesses such as FFF could easily have an income tax postponement objective in mind. Major misinterpretations of financial statements could result unless we recognize their objectives.

The enormous challenge for us is to ascertain whether the facts are compatible with the accounting treatment which has been chosen to accomplish particular objectives. In short, are the principles of accounting appropriate or misleading? Both users and auditors have to ask this question. Preparers must be ready to defend the principles which they choose.

We are asked for FFF to review the principles in the light of objectives, facts and constraints. The accounting treatment or principles can be summarized as follows:

Customer	*Accounting Treatment*
(1) Local residents	Recognize revenue on receipt of cash
(2) Department stores	Recognize revenue on date of shipment
(3) Specialty stores	Recognize revenue on date of shipment
(4) Smaller stores	Recognize revenue on receipt of cash

A summary of the facts shows:

(A) Re local residents: high unemployment in the local area; 18 percent interest rate on outstanding balance; represents 4 percent or less of total sales; no evidence of past experience on collections (missing fact); 20 percent cash down payment at time of sale; no information on how revenue is recognized for 18 percent interest charges (missing fact).

(B) Re department and specialty stores: cash receipt reasonably assured; represents majority of sales volume; no evidence to indicate that merchandise is returned.

(C) Re smaller stores: customers of these stores probably have to borrow funds to buy furniture or sign longer-term finance contracts (an assumption); the merchandise is lower quality and therefore may be of little value if it has to be repossessed; it is not clear whether FFF charges interest on receivables which are outstanding for a long period.

Given the company's prime objective of accounting, which is preparing a financial statement which helps postpone income tax payments, it seems to follow that:

(1) The facts of payment on sales to department and specialty stores are consistent with recognizing revenue at the date of shipment. Any delay beyond this point would not seem supportable because both revenue and costs can be objectively measured.

(2) In the case of sales to local residents, a delay of revenue recognition until the point of cash receipt is probably warranted because of the surrounding uncertainty about collecting receivables. (Chapter 7 discusses the alternative of recognizing revenue earlier, but also debiting an expense account for possible losses on uncollected receivables).

(3) Interest receipts on outstanding receivables of local residents pose an interesting problem. Normally, interest is earned through the passage of time. However, this situation has the additional fact that the entire amount which is due may not be collected. At least three options are available:

   (a) Delay or defer revenue recognition on the interest receipts until the customer has paid the entire amount due on the furniture (excluding interest). If this approach is followed it may also be necessary to defer interest paid by FFF to a bank in order to borrow funds needed to "lend" to local residents. When the customer has paid for the furniture (excluding interest), interest revenue would be recognized as cash is received, and interest expenses would be charged. For example, if FFF borrows from a bank at 10 percent and charges the customer 18 percent a gross profit of 8 percent would result as cash is collected. But this effect would be deferred until furniture revenue (excluding interest) had been collected in full.

   (b) Recognize interest revenue as cash is collected and delay revenue recognition on the furniture sale (excluding interest) until any interest which is due has been credited to revenue. For example, if $35 interest was due (through the passage of time) and the local resident paid $40, the full $35 would be credited to interest revenue and only $5 to furniture sales.

(c) Methods (a) and (b) could be combined so that interest expense and cost of furniture sold would be treated as a lump sum, as would interest revenue and furniture revenue. Thus, a gross profit would be recorded on both interest and furniture as cash is received.

Since the question does not tell us which of the three (or other) FFF is using, we might want to recommend one which is consistent with our objectives of accounting and the facts. The most convenient one to use would be (b) because of its simplicity in not having to defer interest costs (which can be difficult to trace) and its being easier for many people to grasp.

Observe that the discussion under point (3) is deeper and more extensive than the technical topic coverage provided to date in the book. At this stage we are not really expecting you to be able to handle a case in such depth. We are using the cases, though, to pass along additional technical information to you as well as to give you practice in logical thinking and in defending your responses.

(4) Given the company's objective of choosing accounting principles which primarily help postpone income taxes, the accounting procedures being used to record revenue on sales to smaller stores seem appropriate — as long as income tax assessors accept the delay in revenue recognition. The facts conflict somewhat; hence, there is room for debate. For example, unless we know from past experience that a number of the smaller stores are slow-paying or do not pay their accounts in full we may have difficulty arguing with an assessor that the criteria for revenue recognition have not been met at the date of shipment to the small store.

Constraints

FFF is not incorporated and therefore does not have to be concerned with corporate legislation, such as the *Canada Business Corporations Act*. It is not borrowing funds from the general public, and therefore does not have to comply with a *Provincial Securities Act.* FFF probably operates as a partnership; and Provincial Partnership Acts do not give any attention to accounting principles and methods. Thus, FFF is free of legislative constraints.

Summary

FFF is probably using appropriate accounting principles, given its objective of preferring to choose principles (within income tax law) which help postpone income tax payments. Naturally, if its objectives or important facts change, it may want to alter accounting procedures, principles and methods.

Although we have implied that the partnership (FFF) would be taxed directly on its income, the income tax legislation calls for directly taxing the owners of a partnership — not the partnership itself. The effect on owners is the same, though, because postponed income at the partnership stage results in postponed income for its owners. In brief, in a partnership, all income is considered to be distributed to the owners even though they may not receive any cash. But in a limited company or corporation the owners do not receive anything unless a dividend is declared.

The owners of FFF probably could save or postpone income taxes if they incorporated, as a limited liability company. This is discussed later in the book.

Perspective

So far we have analyzed one case in a rather wandering fashion. We have tried to respond to likely queries on the spot as they occurred during our analysis. A good student response on an assignment or examination would certainly not give all of the asides and detailed commentary which we provided. A good response should, however, give the logic of how the accounting principles and disclosure which have been recommended connect with objectives, facts, and constraints for the organization which is under review.

Many people arrive at their first course in accounting with preconceptions about the subject's precision, and feel that there is only one way of handling a transaction. Chapter 1 pointed out that such beliefs are grossly incorrect. Misconceptions take time to correct. In studying each chapter, students have to look for the circumstances (objectives, etc.) where each principle or procedure makes sense. Often, answers are not readily apparent. One course cannot make you an expert; but we will try to move quickly. Above all, do not get discouraged or feel that the material is above you. The ideas will begin to fall into place as we progress through the book.

The response to the next case will be brief in order to give a better idea of how to move toward a reply. Observe that although the basic setting is the same — a furniture enterprise — circumstances differ, and result in somewhat different accounting.

Colossal Furniture Corporation

Colossal Furniture Corporation (CFC) was incorporated many years ago under federal corporate legislation. Its common shares are listed on the Toronto Stock Exchange, and are widely held. CFC has been expanding rapidly in recent years and is frequently issuing bonds and shares to the general public to obtain necessary funds. The company also borrows from a bank during peak seasons. At the present time CFC has three furniture factories and six warehouse outlets which retail directly to the public. The warehouse outlets account for 60 percent of CFC's sales.

The warehouse outlets have two types of sales plans. The first requires cash payment from the customer. The second involves a down payment plus monthly payments over 12, 15, 18 or 24 months. Interest at the rate of 18 percent or more per annum is charged. CFC checks credit-worthiness closely.

Approximately 30 percent of sales are to specially-appointed dealers who operate in locations which do not compete with the warehouse outlets. These dealerships stock only CFC merchandise and are owned by each dealer. Terms for purchases from CFC require cash payment 90 days after shipment from the factories.

The remaining 10 percent of sales are special orders for commercial enterprises, such as hotels, nursing homes, motels, government offices, and similar organizations which desire standardized furniture and equipment. Generally, CFC seeks a 10 percent down payment when the goods are ordered; 60-120 days later the items are completed and shipped, and payment is due 30 days thereafter.

CFC produces good quality merchandise and backs it up with a one-year guarantee covering material and labor. Customer acceptance of CFC's goods has shown itself in increasing sales volume each year. The company has good relations with unions, and appears to have reliable suppliers.

CFC recognizes revenue at the time of shipment from the factory (or from warehouse outlets) for all of its goods and types of customers. An asset contra account is credited for estimated uncollectible receivables as the information on uncollectibility becomes known and an expense account is debited. Warranty costs are expensed as they are incurred.

Required:
Assume the role of a financial analyst who is working for a large underwriter/stock broker. Are the company's accounting principles appropriate?

An analysis

For practice we will employ the objectives-facts-constraints framework. Note that this approach is not essential. The important part of the exercise is to explain one's reasoning process.

Objectives or reasons for accounting

CFC would appear to have multiple objectives, such as: stewardship, perhaps; income tax; cash flow prediction; evaluation of management; and quite possibly others such as special purpose reports. Such a company would therefore have to ascertain which objectives are more important than others, and gear their reporting that way. It must also value consistency, and resist changing its principles frequently.

There is plenty of room for debate but we will give top priority to prediction and evaluation of management. (You will recall that the instructor is primarily concerned with the logic used to link objectives and such to recommendations. Thus, although we gain some marks by defending our choice of objectives in a wide-open situation like this, it does not make sense — unless we have unlimited time and space — to engage in a long debate). We reason that the company continually has to sell its bonds or shares, and would therefore have to keep the current and prospective bondholders and shareholders well informed.

Facts and assumptions

We do not have to repeat every fact about the situation; only those which can lead to a difference in our recommendations. The company appears to have quality products and customers. Unfortunately we do not know how much their bad debt losses and warranty costs have been in recent years. As analysts, we may be able to find out these figures by asking officials of the company. But, if we cannot, we have to make an assumption. In view of the quality nature of both the customers and the product, it seems reasonable to assume that such costs are minor.

Constraints

Although the company has to comply with both a Companies Act and Securities Acts, there is no real constraint to be concerned about. Such legislation is silent on revenue recognition and issues such as bad debt losses and accruals of liabilities for estimated warranty expenditures. If an audit of CFC's financial statements by a chartered accountant were desired, GAAP would have to be followed. However, GAAP for revenue recognition is wide open.

Recommendations

The company's accounting principles appear appropriate:

Revenue recognition — Most costs and revenues are known at the date of shipment. (Deposits are not treated as revenue until the goods are shipped). There is a potential non-arm's-length situation between CFC and the dealerships if CFC forces them to buy excessive quantities of merchandise. In the absence of such a situation, the revenue recognition point makes sense.

Bad debt losses — As long as these are accrued when the possibility of potential losses becomes known, investors and bondholders will be kept informed on a timely basis through quarterly and annual reports.

Warranty expenditures — If these become large they should be accrued at the shipment date so that they can be matched to revenue. Since we have assumed that they are minor — not material in amount to a prudent investor — there is no cause for concern.

In summary, the company's accounting seems consistent with its objectives, facts, and constraints — as long as it gives adequate disclosure of its methods in notes to the financial statements. (See Labatt's notes in Chapter 2.)

Concluding Remarks

The two cases and accompanying analyses are provided as illustrations only, and are not the only approaches which could have been followed. For example, in CFC we might have arrived at quite different recommendations (ie., delay revenue recognition; accrue warranty costs for stewardship purposes) if stewardship and income tax were thought to be the most important reasons for accounting.

We are overstressing the objectives-facts-constraints framework in order to combat biases which people tend to bring to accounting courses. A favorite bias is to ask for the "true" way of accounting. We want you to look at differences in accounting treatment and critically evaluate them. Are they sense or nonsense? Both accountants and users must be able to assess the final product. In many respects accounting is like merchandising. If the shopkeeper does not stock merchandise that customers desire, sales are few. Although there are some differences (such as legal) between accountants and shopkeepers, the analogy must not be forgotten.

6 *Valuation of Assets; Cash and Marketable Securities*

PART I Valuation of Assets

The five previous Chapters presented the terminology and basic ideas which are required to understand the following chapters. Chapters 6 to 14 contain applications of objectives of accounting and key concepts, and at times may seem repetitious. However, reinforcement is essential, to delineate the usage of the ideas. As we have seen, there is considerable room for judgment in most applications, and understanding comes only after you grasp the limits of the concepts.

The next several chapters will be directed primarily to questions of asset and liability valuation — that is, to the problems of determining the most informative amounts to be assigned to the various balance sheet accounts. This chapter will be both an overview of the valuation process and a consideration of two specific assets, cash and marketable securities.

Although accountants have been unable to derive a universally accepted definition of an asset, almost all proposed definitions stress the notion that assets represent rights to future services or economic benefits. That is, assets represent a store of wealth which generates income, cash flows or other benefits in the future. An asset's present worth is often determined by the (1) *amount* and (2) *timing* of the cash flows it is expected to generate. The value of an asset such as a famous painting, reflects a combination of the demand for the item by art collectors and the pleasure which the owner derives from viewing and possessing the item.

The question facing the accountant is what "value" or quantitative measure should be assigned to the asset or liability. This requires an examination of objectives, facts and constraints. For example, someone interested in the prediction objective would hope that the asset *value* reflects the present worth of the cash flow which the asset generates. An office building which is rented, for instance, might be "valued" at the present worth of the rental receipts (less maintenance expenditures) furnished by the tenants. In contrast, with a stewardship objective or under current income tax law there would be a tendency to use historic prices, or the original cost of the office building, less depreciation.

The accounting profession has yet to reach a consensus on criteria of valuation. The reason is suggested, in part, by a comparison of alternative definitions of the term *value.* Value, as it relates to financial statements, can have at least three distinctive meanings: (1) an *assigned* or calculated numerical quantity; as in mathematics, the quantity or amount for which a symbol stands; (2) the *worth* of something sold or exchanged; the worth of a thing in money or goods at a certain time; its fair market price; (3) worth in *usefulness* or importance to the possessor; utility or merit. Each of the three definitions suggests differing principles of valuation.

Historical Cost

The first definition, that value is nothing more than an assigned or calculated numerical quantity, implies that value need have nothing to do with inherent worth; it is simply a numerical quantity assigned on a basis that is, presumably, logical and orderly. It is, in fact, this first meaning that is most consistent with current accounting practice.

Financial statements prepared for outsiders (shareholders, creditors) tend to be *cost based*, although there are exceptions such as special purpose reports and reports for special industries (e.g. mutual fund companies). Generally-speaking, assets are initially recorded at the amounts paid for them. Subsequent to date of purchase, assets are, in general (some exceptions will be pointed out later in this chapter), reported at either initial cost or depreciated cost. Depreciated cost is initial cost less that portion of initial cost (often indicated in a contra account) representing the services of the asset already utilized. Land is an example of an asset that is reported at initial cost; plant and equipment are examples of assets that are reported at depreciated cost.

Except at the date assets are purchased, the cost-based amounts reported on a firm's balance sheet do not represent (unless by coincidence) the prices at which they can be either purchased or sold. The reported amounts can be viewed as approximations of neither the fair market value nor the worth of the services which the assets will provide. They designate nothing more than initial cost less that portion of initial cost already absorbed as an expense.

Why do accountants "value" assets at amounts that have nothing to do with either market value or inherent worth? The justification for this practice is two-fold. First, amounts reported on the balance sheet are relatively objective. The amount at which an asset is initially recorded is established by an exchange transaction among independent parties; it is an amount that can be readily verified. Thereafter, the initial recorded amount is reduced in a systematic and orderly manner. Once useful life has been determined (and some additional assumptions, to be discussed in later chapters, are made pertaining to the method of depreciation to be used), the computation of book value is straightforward. It is unaffected by fluctuations of the market price of either the asset itself or the goods which the asset produces.

Second, and perhaps more significantly, historical cost valuations are consistent with many of the concepts of income determination discussed in the previous chapter; that chapter explained traditional accounting practice, which is more concerned with stewardship accounting than, say, cash flow prediction. The cost of an asset is generally charged as an expense as the services associated with the asset are actually provided. The portion of cost that has not yet been charged off as an expense represents the remaining services to be provided and as such must be accorded accounting recognition. The balance sheet is the means of accounting for the unexpired costs of assets. It may be viewed as a statement of *residuals* — costs which have not yet been charged off as expenses and must, resultantly, be carried forward to future accounting periods. The balance sheet (in conjunction with the income statement) provides a measure of accountability over the *initial costs* of assets purchased. It is not purported to indicate the market value of a firm's assets; its limitations should be clearly understood if we wish to use the financial statements for purposes other than those of a stewardship nature.

Market Values

If, instead, accountants were to accept the second definition of value — the worth of a thing in money or goods at a certain time — then they would most logically look to the market place to determine the amount at which an asset should be reported. They would value assets at their "market prices" on the date of the balance sheet.

The term "market price" is too imprecise for our purposes, as we shall particularly observe in Chapters 8 and 16. The following chart provides a more complete listing of the members of the "market price" family:

Buying Market Price (sometimes called entry price, or input price)	*Selling Market Price (sometimes called exit price, or output price)*
·Original or historic cost	·Net realizable value
·Reproduction cost	·Forced sale price
·Replacement cost	·Discounted cash receipts, at selling price

"Market price" can be either in a buying or selling marketplace. Your local supermarket buys eggs from a wholesaler or egg marketing board and pays the buying market price. The eggs are sold to a homemaker in a "selling" market. Ideally, for inventory items, selling market prices exceed buying market prices; the difference is the supermarket's gross profit. From the wholesaler's point of view the selling market price is that sum paid by the supermarket, and the buying market price is the sum paid to the farmer.

Within the buying and selling markets, a few optional measurement bases exist. The three under the "Buying Market Price" heading represent alternative measurements which make sense under different circumstances, and as you would expect, have implications for preparers and users of financial information. A *past* buying market price is often called original or *historic cost*. As noted this is one of the measurements used frequently in traditional stewardship accounting.

Current buying market prices are often represented by reproduction cost or replacement cost. *Reproduction cost* refers to the cost today of making an asset which is *identical* to the one which you acquired months or years ago. For example, what would it cost today to build a house identical in all respects (same size rooms, same building materials, etc.) to the one you bought 10 years ago? In contrast, *replacement cost* is the cost of a similar asset which will perform a roughly equivalent task. Using the house example, replacement cost today of the house which you bought 10 years ago would be measured in terms of equivalent capacity (four bedrooms, two storeys, and general location) but with different building materials if the original kind are no longer being manufactured or are not economical.

"Likes" must be compared to make good judgments. Thus, we would compare replacement cost *new* to historic cost *new*. That is, both are in their undepreciated state. A more common comparison would be historic cost used (or depreciated) with replacement cost used. Such a comparison might tell us, *if* we are a manufacturer or wholesaler and are pricing on the basis of original cost, for example, whether we are pricing our products lower than is needed to maintain the replacement capacity and continuity of the business. Chapters 8 and 16 cover such analysis in greater depth. The theme is that different measurements are needed for different circumstances.

Similarly, optional measurements and implications exist under the selling market category. *Net realizable value* is the price one would expect to receive under normal conditions in the normal selling market. For example, the manufacturer of machinery would normally sell to other manufacturers, who wish to use the machinery, at a particular price as set in negotiations between many buyers and sellers. We see net realizable value used frequently in traditional accounting practice because accounts receivable are usually measured at net realizable value.

Forced sale price would be received under abnormal conditions and markets. A company on the verge of bankruptcy may have to sell its machinery quickly to someone who may use it for a different purpose — perhaps as scrap iron. Chapter 5 indicated that in the absence of continuity (or the going concern nature of the business), liquidation or forced sale values could be appropriate for financial statements, because these are the figures most readers would be interested in seeing.

The concept of *discounted cash receipts* at selling price was discussed briefly in Chapter 5, earlier in this Chapter, and recurs in this chapter and later. The message which you should draw from the exposure which we are giving to the concept is that it is nothing more than *one popular* form of measurement. It is not the only possibility, as we have already observed. But it is a useful one against which to compare other measurements.

Useful judgments are made by comparing TWO or more measures. These measures can be within the same system (eg., sales at historic cost this year versus at historic cost last year) or between or among systems (eg., a grocer might compare net realizable value with replacement cost to see whether the difference, gross profit, is adequate). We should discipline ourselves to identify the "other" measurement we are using in our judgments. It is too easy to slip into a comparison of something today (eg., cost of houses) with another measure which we fail to identify clearly in our mind. If we compare today's net realizable value of a particular house ($100,000) to the price we paid 10 years ago ($40,000) we might think that we could make a profit if we sold our house ($60,000). But, is this a legitimate comparison? If we still need a place to live in, and the replacement cost is $100,000, is there any profit?

Replacement cost	–	Net realizable value	=	?
$100,000	–	$100,000	=	0

Numerous arguments have been advanced for a replacement cost or net realizable value approach to asset valuation. Proponents assert that a balance sheet in which all assets were reported at replacement cost or net realizable value would provide investors and managers with information far more relevant to the decisions that they ordinarily have to make. Replacement cost or net realizable value are sometimes used to approximate *opportunity cost* — the amount that might be earned if the asset were sold and the proceeds used in the best alternative capacity.

Suppose that management was trying to decide whether or not to sell one of its divisions, which made one product. The latest figures for the division showed (as best as we can *estimate* them):

Net historic cost (after depreciation) of its plant and equipment	$5,000,000
Present value (of cash receipts net of expenses) of the product *if* the division were continued until the machinery wore out	$9,500,000
Net realizable value of plant and equipment	$7,000,000
If the $7,000,000 net realizable value were obtained by selling the "old" division and the sum were invested in a new product, the present value of its net cash receipts would be	$10,000,000

Should the old division be sold?

The valid comparison is between the two present values ($10,000,000 versus $9,500,000) which are discussed in more detail under the third definition, in the next section of this Chapter. Assuming the *risk* — that is, the potential for loss of our investment — of the two is the same, we would choose to sell the old plant and invest in the new one. We would be $500,000 ($10,000,000 − $9,500,000) better off if we did. However, if we chose to retain the old division, we would incur an opportunity cost or loss (of a missed opportunity) of $500,000.

Observe that in order to make the decision we needed three pieces of information:

1. Net realizable value of the old division.
2. Net present value of continuing manufacture of the product of the old division.
3. Net present value of our alternative use of the $7,000,000 (our other *opportunity*).

(We also needed information on riskiness of both of the two assets above and our portfolio of assets. But this can be ignored for now.)

This observation reinforces our previous remarks about requiring *two* or more pieces of information to make decisions. The prime comparison is between two present values of net cash receipts. But, in order to obtain the present value of the opportunity investment, we have to know the net realizable value of selling what we now have.

Since the present values have to be estimated, and a great deal of uncertainty and speculation surrounds our estimation process, people use substitute measures as "next best." Replacement cost and net realizable value are sometimes used as substitutes or "next bests." When substitutes are used we have to recall this later when we interpret the figures and assess the conclusions (to sell or not, for example) which the figures point towards. (How close might the substitute be to our desired figure?)

Despite their obvious appeal for some situations and purposes, replacement cost (or reproduction cost in suitable circumstances) and net realizable value have disadvantages for some financial presentation purposes. One potential disadvantage may be the cost of hiring valuation specialists in order to obtain information about replacement costs or net realizable value. Also the reported value of an asset may be determined apart from its utility to its particular owner. For example, if replacement cost accounting is employed (for all assets and liabilities), regardless of whether the firm intends to sell an asset shortly or to continue to use it for several additional years, replacement cost is not necessarily reflective of its utility to the owner. The owner receives the present value of cash receipts, net of expenses, for goods or services produced by the asset. It is also possible that the owner may be using the asset for a different, perhaps more successful, purpose than that represented by current replacement cost of the asset.

Technological advances may quickly cause the replacement cost of a piece of equipment to decline substantially. But such advances may not necessarily reduce the utility of that equipment to its owner. Moreover (particularly if selling market values were used), assets such as nonsalable specialized equipment or intangible assets such as organizational costs or deferred start-up and preoperating costs would not be considered to be assets at all; they would be assigned values corresponding to the prices at which they could be sold — zero.

Even though conventional accounting is primarily cost based, in selected situations accountants do employ selling prices in determining the appropriate asset values to report. In general, whenever revenue is recognized prior to the point of sale, the related asset is reported at either the amount that is expected to be realized or some fraction thereof. For example, when revenue is recognized upon completion of production (e.g., upon the removal of a precious mineral from the ground) the completed products are valued at their anticipated selling price — a current output price. To avoid the distortions in income that would result from delaying recognition of revenue until point of sale, accountants are forced to make estimates of the amount of revenue that will actually be realized. The best indication of the amount to be actually realized is a fixed contract price, or in the absence of such a price, the current selling price of the commodities intended for sale.

The concern of the accountant with conservatism also leads him to report current values whenever the market price of an asset intended for sale falls below its acquisition cost. Following the rule of *lower of cost or market*, the accountant compares the historical cost of an asset — that which the company paid to either purchase or produce it — with what it would cost to *replace* it (a current *input* cost). If the market or replacement price is less than the historical cost, then (in theory but not necessarily in practice) the asset is *written down* to the market price and the corresponding loss recognized on the income statement. The lower of cost or market rule is applied only to assets, primarily inventories and marketable securities, that the firm actually expects to sell in the normal course of business. It is grounded on the assumption that financial statements would be misleading if assets were valued at prices higher than those for which the company expects to sell them. The rule is not ordinarily applied to assets, such as plant and equipment, that are not intended for resale. The lower of cost or market rule will be examined in greater detail in Chapter 8 in connection with a discussion of inventories.

Value to User

The third definition (specifically the net cash receipts portion discussed in conjunction with the second definition) expresses value in terms of worth in usefulness or importance to the individual possessor. It suggests that the value of an asset be determined with respect to the particular firm that owns it. This third concept of value has considerable attraction to accounting theoreticians, but inasmuch as it requires that the future benefits of an asset be specifically identified and measured, it has received relatively little acceptance in practice. Nevertheless, it is of interest for two reasons. First, understanding the worth of an asset to a particular firm or individual offers insight into the nature of assets and into the determination of market prices. Second, in the absence of both a clearly defined exchange transaction and a current market price, accountants are sometimes forced to resort to analysis of the "true" nature of an asset in order to determine an appropriate book value.

The economic benefits associated with an asset ordinarily take the form of cash receipts. An individual invests in the common shares of a major corporation in anticipation of cash receipts greater than the cash disbursement required by the initial purchase. The cash receipts will be derived from either periodic cash dividends paid by the company or from the proceeds resulting from the sale of the shares or both. Similarly, a manufacturer purchases a machine with the expectation that the machine will contribute to the production of goods which when sold will generate cash receipts. The value of an asset to its owner is, therefore, the value of the cash receipts (net of any required disbursements) that the asset is expected to produce. The task of the accountant is first to identify and measure the cash receipts — an obviously difficult task considering that most assets result in cash receipts only when used in conjunction with other assets and that in a world of uncertainty future sales and future costs cannot be readily estimated. And second, it is to determine the value of those cash receipts.

Although it might appear as if the value of expected cash receipts is simply the sum of all anticipated receipts, an analysis of some fundamental concepts of compound interest will demonstrate that this is not so. Since cash may be placed in interest-bearing bank accounts or used to acquire securities that will provide a periodic return, it has a value in time. Funds to be received in years hence may be of less value than those to be received at present.

Compound Interest and Value of Cash Receipts

Future Value

Suppose that an individual deposits $1 in a savings bank. The bank pays interest at the rate of 6 percent per year. Interest is *compounded* (computed) annually at the end of each year. To how much would the deposit have grown at the end of one year?

The accumulated value of the deposit at the end of one year would be $1 X 1.06 = $1.06.
In more general terms,

$$F_n = P(1 + r)^n,$$

where

F_n represents the final accumulation of the initial investment after n interest periods,
P represents the initial investment or deposit, and
r indicates the rate of interest.

As indicated in Exhibit 6-1, after two years the initial deposit would have accumulated to $1.12 — the $1.06 on deposit at the beginning of the second year times 1.06. After three years it would have accumulated to $1.19 — the $1.12 on deposit at the beginning of the third year again times 1.06.

Employing the general formula (and rounding to the nearest penny),

At the end of two years: $F = P(1 + r)^n; F = \$1(1 + .06)^2 = \$1.12.$
At the end of three years: $F = P(1 + r)^n; F = \$1(1 + .06)^3 = \$1.19.$
At the end of six years: $F = P(1 + r)^n; F = \$1(1 + .06)^6 = \$1.42.$

EXHIBIT 6-1

Future Value of $1 Invested Today — 6% Return (rounded to nearest cent)

			Years			
0	*1*	*2*	*3*	*4*	*5*	*6*
$1.00 →	$1.06 →	$1.12 →	$1.19 →	$1.26 →	$1.34 →	$1.42

If an amount other than $1 were deposited, then the amount accumulated could be computed simply by substituting that amount for P in the basic formula. Thus $200 deposited in a bank and earning interest at a rate of 6 percent would grow at the end of six years to $\$200\ (1.06)^6 = \$283.70$.

To facilitate computations of compound interest, series of tables have been developed and are readily available in almost all accounting textbooks as well as numerous books of financial tables. Table 1 in the Appendix of this volume (page 753) indicates the amounts to which $1 will accumulate at various interest rates and at the end of various accounting periods. The number at the intersection of the 6 percent column and the 6 periods row indicates that $1 would accumulate to $1.4185. $200 would accumulate to $200 times that amount — $200 X 1.4185 = $283.70.

Several examples may serve to illustrate the concept of future value.

EXAMPLE 1

A company sells a parcel of land for $50,000. The purchaser requests to be allowed to delay payment for a period of three years. The company agrees to accept a note from the purchaser for $50,000 plus interest at an annual rate of 8 percent. What amount would the purchaser be required to pay at the end of three years?

As indicated in Table 1 (8 percent column, 3 periods row), $1 will grow to $1.2597. Hence, $50,000 will grow to $50,000 times 1.2597 — $62,985. The purchaser would be required to pay $62,985.

EXAMPLE 2

An individual deposits $300 in a savings bank. The bank pays interest at an annual rate of 4 percent compounded semiannually. To what amount will the deposit accumulate at the end of 10 years?

If interest is compounded semiannually and the *annual* rate of interest is 4 percent, then interest is computed *twice* each year at 2 percent — *one half* the annual rate. (Interest is almost always stated at an *annual* rate even when compounded semiannually or quarterly.) Each interest period would be 6 months, rather than a year, so that over a 10 year span there would be *20* interest periods. Table 1 indicates that, at an interest rate of 2 percent, $1 will accumulate to $1.4859 after 20 periods. Hence, $300 will accumulate to $300 times 1.4859 — $445.77. As a general rule, whenever interest is compounded semiannually, the interest rate must be halved and the number of years doubled.

EXAMPLE 3

A corporation invests $10,000 and expects to earn a return of 8 percent compounded annually for the next 60 years. To how much will the $10,000 accumulate over the 60-year period?

Table 1 does not indicate accumulations for 60 years. However, the table does indicate that $1 invested at 8 percent for *50* years would accumulate to $46.9016. Over 50 years $10,000 would accumulate to $469,016. The table also indicates that $1 invested at 8 percent for *10* years would accumulate to $2.1589. If at the end of 50 years $469,016 were invested for an additional 10 years, it would increase in value to 2.1589 times $469,016 — $1,012,558.

EXAMPLE 4

A corporation reached an agreement to sell a warehouse. The purchaser agreed to pay $80,000 for the warehouse but wanted to delay payment for four years. The corporation, however, was in immediate need of cash and agreed to accept a lesser amount if payment were made at time of sale. The corporation estimated that it would otherwise have to borrow the needed funds at a rate of 5 percent. What amount should the corporation be willing to accept if cash payment were made at the time of sale rather than delayed for four years?

The question can be stated in an alternative form. What amount if invested today at a rate of interest of 5 percent would accumulate to $80,000 in four years? From Table 1, it may be seen that $1 invested today would increase to $1.2155. Hence, some amount (x) times 1.2155 would increase to $80,000:

$$1.2155x = \$80{,}000.$$

Solving for x (i.e., dividing $80,000 by 1.2155) indicates that amount to be $65,817. Thus, the company would be equally well off if it accepted payment of $65,817 today as it would be if it waited four years to receive the full $80,000. In other words, $65,817 deposited in a bank today would increase in value to $80,000 after four years *if* the bank credited us with 5 percent interest per annum compounded annually.

Present Value

As implied in Example 4, it is frequently necessary to compute the *present value* of a sum of money to be received in the future. That is, one may want to know the amount which if invested today at a certain rate of return would be the equivalent of a fixed amount to be received in a specific number of years hence.

In simplest terms, an example can be formulated as follows. If a bank pays interest at the rate of 6 percent annually, how much cash would an individual have to deposit today in order to have that amount accumulate to $1 one year from now? Example 4 illustrated one means of computation. In more general terms, the present value of a future sum can be calculated by rearranging the basic equation for future value — $F_n = P(1 + r)^n$. Thus,

$$P = F_n \frac{1}{(1 + r)^n}$$

where, as previously,

F_n represents the final accumulation of the initial investment after n years,
r indicates the rate of interest (which when used in connection with present value situations is often referred to as a *discount* rate, since a future payment will be *discounted* to a present value), and
P indicates the required initial deposit or investment.

$$P = \$1 \frac{1}{(1. + .06)^1} = \$.94$$

The present value of $1 to be received two years in the future would be

$$P = F_n \frac{1}{(1 + r)^n}; \qquad P = \$1 \frac{1}{(1 + .06)^2} = \$.89.$$

The present value of $1 to be received in six years in the future would be

$$P = F_n \frac{1}{(1 + r)^n}; \qquad P = \$1 \frac{1}{(1 + .06)^6} = \$.71.$$

In other words, as illustrated in Exhibit 6-2, $.71 invested today at 6 percent interest compounded annually would increase to $1 at the end of six years.

EXHIBIT 6-2

Present Values of $1 To Be Received in the Future — 6% Return (rounded to nearest cent)

Years

0	1	2	3	4	5	6
$.94 ←	$1					
.89 ←		$1				
.84 ←			$1			
.79 ←				$1		
.75 ←					$1	
.71 ←						$1

As with future value, if an amount other than $1 were to be received, then the present value of such amount could be determined by substituting that amount for F. Thus, if an individual wanted to receive $200 six years from the present, then the amount he would have to invest today at 6 percent interest would be

$$P = \$200 \frac{1}{(1.06)^6} = \$141.$$

Table 2 in the Appendix indicates the present value of $1 for various discount rates and time periods. The present value of $1 to be received six years from today discounted at the rate of 6 percent would be $.7050. The present value of $200 would be $200 times .7050 — $141.

Concepts of present value are demonstrated in the examples that follow.

EXAMPLE 1

Assume the same fact situation as in Example 4 of the previous section. A corporation agreed to sell a warehouse. The purchaser was willing to pay $80,000 four years hence or some lesser amount at time of sale. Assuming that the corporation would have to borrow the needed funds at a rate of 5 percent, what equivalent amount should it be willing to accept if payment were made at time of sale?

Per Table 2, the present value of $1 to be received in 4 years, at an annual rate of 5 percent, is $.8227. The present value of $80,000 is $80,000 x .8227 — $65,816. Save for a $1 rounding difference, the result is identical to that computed in the earlier illustration.

EXAMPLE 2

A rich uncle wishes to give his nephew a gift of the cost of a college education. The nephew will enter college in 6 years. It is estimated that when he enters college, tuition and other charges will be approximately $20,000 for a degree program. The gift will be placed in a bank, which pays interest at an annual rate of 8 percent, compounded *quarterly*. What size gift is required if the full $20,000 is to be available to the nephew at the start of his college career?

Since interest is compounded *quarterly*, the question to be answered is as follows: What is the present value of $20,000 to be received *24* (4 times 6 years) periods away if discounted at a rate of 2 percent per period? Per Table 2, the present value of $1 to be received 24 periods in the future, discounted at a rate of 2 percent, is $.6217. The present value of $20,000 is, therefore, $20,000 times .6217 — $12,434. (*Check*: Per Table 1, the future value of $1 to be received in 24 periods if invested at a rate of 2 percent is $1.6084. $12,434 times 1.6084 is $20,000.)

Future Value of an Annuity

Commercial transactions frequently involve not just a single deposit or future payment but rather a series of equal payments spaced evenly apart. For example, an individual interested in saving for a particular long-range goal would be concerned with the amount that he would be required to deposit during each of a certain number of years to attain that goal. A series of *equal* payments at fixed intervals is known as an *annuity*. An annuity in which the payments are made or received at the *end* of each period is known as an *ordinary annuity* or an *annuity in arrears*. One in which the payments are made or received at the *beginning* of each period is known as an *annuity due* or an *annuity in advance*. Unless otherwise indicated, the examples in this chapter, as well as in the tables in the Appendix, will be based on the assumption that payments are made or received at the *end* of each period.

Suppose that at the *end* of each of four years a person deposits $1 in a savings account. The account pays interest at the rate of 6 percent per year, compounded annually. How much will be available for withdrawal at the end of the fourth year?

EXHIBIT 6-3

Future Value of $1 Invested at the End of each of Four Periods — 6% Return (rounded to nearest cent)

Years

0	*1*	*2*	*3*	*4*
	$1.00 →	$1.06 →	$1.12 →	1.19
		1.00 →	1.06 →	1.12
			1.00 →	1.06
				1.00
Amount available for withdrawal	$1.00	$2.06	$3.18	$4.37

As shown in Exhibit 6-3, the $1 deposited at the end of the first period will accumulate interest for a total of three years. As indicated in Table 1, it will increase in value to $1.19. The deposit at the end of the second year will grow to $1.12, and that at the end of the third year will grow to $1.06. The payment made at the end of the fourth year will not yet have earned any interest. As revealed in the diagram, the series of four $1 payments will be worth $4.37 at the end of the fourth year.

The mathematical expression for the future value (F) of a series of payments of a fixed amount (A) compounded at an interest rate (r) over a given number of years (n) is

$$F = A\left[\frac{(1+r)^n - 1}{r}\right]$$

The value at the end of four years of $1 deposited at the end of each of four years compounded at an annual rate of 6 percent is

$$F = \$1\left[\frac{(1+.06)^4 - 1}{.06}\right] = \$4.37.$$

Table 3 in the Appendix indicates the future values of annuities of $1 for various rates of return. Notice the relationship between Table 3 and Table 1. With slight adjustment, the amounts in the annuity table (Table 3) represent the sum of the amounts in the future value table (Table 1). The slight adjustment is that to the sum of the amounts in the future value table (Table 1) one more period must be taken and 1.00 must be added. Thus, the sum of the first three amounts in the 6 percent column of the future value table is 3.3746. This amount plus 1.00 (i.e., 4.3746) is the same as that in the 6 percent column, *4th* period row of the annuity table. The adjustment takes into account the fact that the annuity table has been compiled on the assumption that each payment is made at the end of a period rather than at the beginning, as assumed in the single-payment table. The next three examples illustrate the concept of an annuity.

EXAMPLE 1

A corporation has agreed to deposit 10 percent of an employee's salary into a retirement fund. The fund will be invested in stocks and bonds that will provide a return of 8 percent annually. How much will be available to the employee upon his retirement in 20 years assuming that the employee earns $30,000 per year?

The future value of an annuity of $1 per year compounded at a rate of 8 percent per year for 20 years is $45.7620. Hence, the future value of an annuity of $3,000 (10 percent of $30,000) is $3,000 times 45.7620 — $137,286.

EXAMPLE 2

An individual invests $1,000 per year in securities that yield 5 percent per year compounded annually. To how much will his investments accumulate at the end of 60 years?

Table 3 does not specifically indicate values for 60 periods. However, per Table 3, $1,000 deposited at the end of 50 periods and compounded at a rate of 5 percent will accumulate to $1,000 times 209.3480 — $209,348. At the end of 50 years, therefore, the individual will have $209,348 invested in securities. Per Table 1, that sum will increase to $209,348 times 1.6289 — $341,007 — by the end of the 10 additional years. The $1,000 deposited at the end of years 51 through 60 — an ordinary annuity for 10 years — will accumulate, per Table 3, to $1,000 times 12.5779 — $12,578. The total amount that will have accumulated over the 60-year period is the sum of the two amounts, $341,007 and $12,578 — $353,585.

EXAMPLE 3

A corporation has an obligation to repay $200,000 in bonds upon their maturity in 20 years. The company wishes to make annual cash payments to a fund to assure that when the bonds are due it will have the necessary cash on hand. The company intends to invest the fund in securities that will yield a return of 8 percent, compounded annually.

$200,000 represents the future value of an annuity. That is, some amount

(x) deposited annually to return 8 percent will accumulate at the end of 20 years to $200,000. From Table 3, it can be seen that $1 invested annually would accumulate in 20 years to $45.7620. Therefore, some amount (x) times $45.7620 would accumulate to $200,000:

$$45.7620x = \$200{,}000,$$

$$x = \frac{\$200{,}000}{45.7620}$$

$$= \$4{,}370.$$

If deposited annually into a fund which earns a return of 8 percent, $4,370 would accumulate in 20 years to $200,000.

Present Value of an Annuity

Just as it is sometimes necessary to know the present value of a single payment to be received sometime in the future, so also there is sometimes concern for the present value of a stream of payments. An investor or creditor may wish to know the amount to be received today that would be the equivalent of a stream of payments to be received in the future.

The present value, discounted at 6 percent, of $1 to be received at the end of each of four periods is depicted diagramatically in Exhibit 6-4.

EXHIBIT 6-4

Present Value of $1 To Be Received at the End of Each of Four Periods — 6% Return (rounded to the nearest cent)

Years

0	*1*	*2*	*3*	*4*
$ .94 ←	1.00			
.89 ←		1.00		
.84 ←			1.00	
.79 ←				1.00
$3.46				

The present value of the stream of receipts, $3.46, is nothing more than the sum of the present values of the individual receipts. The present values of the individual receipts, which are indicated in the left-hand column, could be taken directly from Table 2.

The mathematical formula for the present value (P_A) of an annuity of A dollars per period compounded at a rate of r for n periods is

$$P_A = A\left[\frac{1 - (1 + r)^{-n}}{r}\right].$$

The present value of an annuity of $1 per period for four periods compounded at a rate of 6 percent is

$$P_A = \$1\left[\frac{1-(1+.06)^{-4}}{.06}\right] = \$3.46.$$

Table 4 in the Appendix indicates the present values of annuities in arrears (i.e., payments received at the *end* of each period), at various rates of return. Each amount in Table 4 is simply the sum, up to that period, of the amounts in Table 2.

The application of the concept of the present value of an annuity is demonstrated in the examples that follow.

EXAMPLE 1

An individual wishes to give his nephew a gift of a sum of money such that if he deposits the sum in a bank he would be able to withdraw $8,000 at the end of each of four years in order to meet his college expenses. The bank pays interest at the rate of 5 percent per year compounded annually. What is the single amount that the individual should give his nephew that would be the equivalent of four annual payments of $8,000 each.

The present value of an annuity of $1 per year for four years compounded at a rate of 5 percent is, per Table 4, $3.5460. The present value of an annuity of $8,000 is $8,000 times 3.5460 — $28,368.

The result can be verified as follows:

Initial deposit	$28,368
First-year earnings (5%)	1,418
Balance at end of first year before withdrawal	$29,786
First-year withdrawal	(8,000)
Balance at end of first year	$21,786
Second-year earnings (5%)	1,089
Balance at end of second year before withdrawal	$22,875
Second-year withdrawal	(8,000)
Balance at end of second year	$14,875
Third-year earnings (5%)	744
Balance at end of third year before withdrawal	15,619
Third-year withdrawal	(8,000)
Balance at end of third year	$ 7,619
Fourth-year earnings (5%)	381
Balance at end of fourth year before withdrawal	$ 8,000
Fourth-year withdrawal	(8,000)
Balance at end of fourth year	$ 0

EXAMPLE 2

A corporation has a choice; it can either lease its new plant at an annual rental of $30,000 for 20 years or it can purchase it. Assuming that the company estimates that it could earn 7 percent annually on any funds not invested in the plant, what would be the equivalent cost of purchasing the plant? Assume also that the plant would have no value at the end of 20 years.

The present value of a stream of payments of $1 per year, compounded at a rate of 7 percent, for 20 years is, per Table 4, $10.5940. The present value of a stream of payments of $30,000 is $30,000 times 10.5940 — $317,820. The company would be equally well off if it had rented the plant for $30,000 per year as if it had purchased it for $317,820 (ignoring, of course, both tax and risk factors).

EXAMPLE 3 A major corporation issues a security (e.g., a bond) that contains the following provision: the corporation agrees to pay the purchaser $20,000 every 6 months for 20 years and make an additional single lump-sum payment of $500,000 at the end of the 20-year period. How much would an investor be willing to pay for such a security assuming that if he did not purchase the security he could, alternatively, invest the funds in other securities which would provide an annual return of 10 percent compounded semiannually?

The company promises to pay an annuity of $20,000 per period for *40* 6-month periods. The present value of such an annuity when discounted at a rate of *5 percent* (the *semiannual* alternative rate of return) is, with reference to Table 4,

$$\$20{,}000 \times 17.1591 = \$343{,}182.$$

The present value of a single payment of $500,000, 40 periods hence, discounted at a semiannual rate of 5 percent is, with reference to Table 2,

$$\$500{,}000 \times .1420 = \$71{,}000.$$

The present value of the stream of payments *and* the single lump-sum payment is, therefore, $343,182 plus $71,000 — $414,182. Similar examples will be alluded to again in Chapter 10; they help explain why a bond with a face value of one amount (e.g., $500,000) might sell in the open market at a greater or lesser amount (e.g., $414,182).

EXAMPLE 4 A company wishes to contribute an amount to a pension fund such that each employee will have an annual income of $12,000 upon retirement. The firm's consulting actuary estimates that an average employee will survive 15 years after his retirement and will be employed 20 years prior to his retirement. The company anticipates that it will be able to obtain a return of 6 percent per year on contributions to the fund. How much should the company contribute each year, per employee, to the pension fund?

Upon the retirement of an employee, the company must have in its pension fund an amount equivalent to a stream of payments of $12,000 for 15 years. Per Table 4, the present value of a stream of payments of $1 per year, for 15 years, discounted at a rate of 6 percent is $9.7122. The present value of the stream of $12,000 is $12,000 times 9.7122—$116,546.

The company must, therefore, make equal annual payments of such amount that the accumulated value of the payments after 20 years (the number of years an employee will work prior to his retirement) will be $116,546. According to Table 3, a stream of payments of $1, invested to yield a return of 6 percent, will accumulate to $36.7856 after 20 years. Hence, some amount (x) times 36.7856 will accumulate to $116,546:

$$36.7856x = \$116{,}546$$
$$x = \$3{,}168.$$

The firm would have to make 20 annual payments of $3,168 in order to be able to withdraw $12,000 per year for 15 years.

Discounted Cash Flow as a Means of Determining the Value of Assets

The procedures described in the preceding section in which a stream of future cash flows is *discounted* back to the present can be employed to determine the value to a particular firm of either individual assets or groups of assets.

EXAMPLE 1

A firm is contemplating the purchase of new equipment. The company has determined that a new machine will enable it to reduce out-of-pocket production costs, after taxes, by $8,000 per year. If the machine will have a useful life of five years and the firm demands that it obtain a return of at least 10 percent per year on all invested funds, what is the maximum amount it would be willing to pay for the machine?

The present value of the stream of equal cash savings is (per Table 4) 3.7908 times $8,000 — $30,326. The company would be willing to pay no more than that amount for the new machine.

EXAMPLE 2

A chain of motels wants to add a new unit in a particular city. An existing motel is available for purchase. The executives of the motel have determined that the physical assets (land, buildings, equipment, etc.) of similar types of motels could be purchased or constructed for $1 million and that ordinarily a motel of that type would provide a cash inflow to its owners of $100,000 per year. The available motel, however, because of a high-traffic location as well as an outstanding reputation for quality service, generates an after-tax cash flow of $150,000 per year. The motel chain executives estimate that if they were to purchase the motel its *goodwill* (those intangible factors to which the unusually high return can be attributed) would continue to provide benefits to the new owners for approximately 7 years. The motel chain would expect a return on investment of 10 percent per year on any amounts paid above the replacement cost of the tangible (in this case, the physical) assets. What is the maximum amount the motel chain should be willing to pay for the existing motel?

The motel chain could purchase similar motels for $1 million which would generate an annual cash stream of $100,000. The motel available for sale would provide the chain with an additional cash flow of $50,000 for 7 years. The present value, discounted at 10 percent, of an annuity of $50,000 for seven years, is, with reference to Table 4, $50,000 times 4.8684 — $243,420. The company would, therefore, be willing to pay $1 million (for the physical assets) plus $243,420 for the goodwill.

Although discounted cash flow techniques are frequently incorporated into the analysis of whether a firm should purchase a particular machine or undertake a major construction project, values of assets to be reported in conventional financial reports are based primarily on historical cost — seldom on present value of anticipated cash benefits. In the absence of a meaningful historical cost, the accountant may, however, look to the present value of an asset to determine an appropriate balance sheet value.

Example 2 pertaining to the goodwill of the motel suggests that a business enterprise has a value apart from that of its component assets. The historical cost or even the market value of the individual assets of the enterprise might sum to one amount, yet the assets combined into an operating business may be worth considerably more than that amount. Suppose, for example, that a firm generates a cash flow of $30,000 per year. If investors believe that an investment in such a company should provide them with a return of 8 percent per year and that the $30,000 cash flow will continue *indefinitely*, then the amount that they would be willing to pay can be calculated simply by dividing the expected cash flows by the appropriate rate of return:

$$\frac{\$30{,}000}{.08} = \$375{,}000.$$

To investors the *firm* would have a value of $375,000 — regardless of the market values of its component assets.

Some theoreticians have suggested that the balance sheet should report *both* the historical cost of assets *and* the present value of the business taken as a whole. The difference between the sum of the historical costs and the present value of the business taken as a whole would be considered an intangible asset, goodwill, under rare circumstances. However, under most circumstances — such as on purchase of an entire company by another company — goodwill would be the difference between the *cost* paid for the entire company, and the individual assets and liabilities (excluding goodwill) measured mainly at *replacement cost* or *net realizable value.* The latter concept is discussed in greater depth in Chapter 13.

Suppose, for example, a firm purchased a parcel of land. The firm was to pay the seller $100,000 at the end of each of the next five years — a total of $500,000. The apparent purchase price of $500,000 would be an inflated historical cost and an inappropriate value for the conventional balance sheet. The $500,000 to be paid over the five-year period requires a considerably smaller economic sacrifice than would $500,000 paid at time of purchase. If the firm's applicable rate of interest were 8 percent, then the five annual payments of $100,000 each would be the equivalent (per Table 4, which indicates the present value of annuity) of a single present payment of only $339,270. Viewed in this light, the firm purchased a parcel of land for $339,270. The additional payments of $160,730 represent interest on money borrowed. Looking to the economic substance of the transaction rather than merely to its form, the accountant would record the land on the balance sheet at $339,270.

How do accountants journalize a situation under current accounting practice when they have "valued" an asset at its discounted present value — such as was the case with the parcel of land example of $339,270?

Balance sheet of purchaser, beginning of 19x1 — Land		$399,270
—Account payable		$399,270
Journal entry *end* of 19x1 (when the first payment is made):		
Accounts payable	$68,060	
Interest expense	31,940	
Cash		$100,000

One's first impression about such an entry is disbelief. Let us analyze it. The credit to cash of $100,000 is satisfactory because that's how much we have to pay. The $68,060 is trickier; it represents the decrease in present value of the account payable in the first year. That is, the present value of $100,000 due at the end of each of the next *four* years at 8 percent (Table 4) is $331,210. The difference between $399,270 and $331,210 is $68,060. The difference between $100,000 and $68,060 is $31,940 — with the latter being one year's interest at 8 percent on the beginning of year payable of $399,270 (8 percent x 399,270 = $31,941).

Why does the debit of $31,940 go to interest expense instead of to land? The reason is the cost concept, as set forth in Chapter 5. Interest on borrowings (in this case *implied* borrowings) is expensed under the *proprietary* concept of income measurement, the concept which is used extensively in current practice. (The proprietor is the shareholder; not the creditor plus the shareholder). The cost concept explained in Chapter 5 incorporates the proprietary concept. (These concepts are dealt with in subsequent accounting courses.)

In years beyond 19x1 the same approach would be used. Interest expense would be incurred because of the implied borrowing. The payable would reduce to reflect the revised present value. The total of the two would be the $100,000 cash payment.

Summary of Part I

Current financial accounting practice tends to assign a historic cost to many, but not all, assets. Historic cost is the amount paid to acquire an asset, less that portion of initial cost representing the services of the asset already consumed (i.e., allowance for depreciation or amortization). Such gross amount (that is, excluding the estimation for depreciation) is relatively objective and is consistent with the concept of income determination by which the cost of an asset is charged as an expense as the services associated with it are actually used. The portion of the cost that represents the services that have not yet been consumed is carried forward to future accounting periods and is reported on the balance sheet.

In some cases under current practice, an asset is stated at a "market" value, either buying market or selling market price. The few buying market alternatives which one tends to encounter are reproduction cost and replacement cost. The most common selling market price is net realizable value — that used, for example, for accounts receivable. Buying and selling market prices (except for a few situations such as accounts receivable) are infrequently seen in conventional financial statements designed for stewardship purposes of accounting. As we shall observe when we come to Chapter 16, some people are advocating the use of current market values in supplementary financial statements, designed mainly for persons who wish to make predictions and evaluate management.

In order to make decisions we require at least two pieces of information. Thus, for example, neither replacement cost by itself nor net realizable value by itself will provide all the information which people need to make decisions. It follows that a set of financial statements based entirely on *either* replacement cost *or* net realizable value can be criticized for not being complete. For instance, *if* the company intends to use an assembly line to manufacture a product rather than to sell the assembly equipment for cash, which figures should be reported in financial statements?

Such a question cannot be answered unless we clearly identify *who* is using the information and for *which judgment.* An investor interested in predicting cash flows will not care about either replacement cost or net realizable value *as long as*: (1) the company intends to use the assembly line to manufacture a product; and (2) the company will liquidate itself rather than replace the assembly line when it wears out (that is, replacement cost cash outflow is not applicable). The relevant figure is discounted net present value of the cash flows generated by the products which will be manufactured. Replacement cost or net realizable value would be used as "next best" measures if the desired discounted present value information was not available. Naturally, if the company had not yet made its decision as to whether to keep or scrap the assembly line, different information would be needed by it — that is, by management, a different user making a different decision. An example in the chapter elaborates on this point of requiring different information for different decisions.

The value of an asset could be stated in terms of its utility to a *specific* user. The worth of an asset to a particular user may be defined as the present value of the anticipated cash receipts with which it is associated. The present value of the cash receipts must take into account the "time value of money" — the fact that a dollar received today is worth considerably more than one to be received in the distant future. Determination of the present value of cash flows requires an understanding of the fundamental concepts of compound interest — hence the extended discussion of that topic in this chapter. It is often impractical, however, to determine the present value of a particular asset, since individual assets are not generally associated with specific cash receipts. Thus, conventional financial statements seldom express asset values in terms of worth to the individual possessor. Nevertheless, an understanding of the concepts of present values of cash flows provides an appreciation of the underlying forces that determine the market values of some assets and particularly of businesses taken in their entirety.

In Part II of this chapter, as well as in the next several chapters, we shall deal with problems of valuing specific assets, such as cash, marketable securities, accounts receivable, inventories, and plant and equipment.

PART II Cash and Marketable Securities

Cash

Of all assets and liabilities, cash would appear to present the fewest problems of valuation. Cash is ordinarily measured at face value. Nonetheless, in recent years controversy has arisen over the most appropriate means of classifying and reporting cash balances.

Cash includes currency on hand and funds on deposit in banks that are subject to immediate and unconditional withdrawal (i.e., amounts in chequing accounts). It does not in any strict sense include amounts that may be subject to withdrawal restrictions, such as funds in the form of savings accounts, which may technically require advance notification for withdrawal, or certificates of deposit, although in practice the distinction between the two is often not made. Most companies maintain several general ledger accounts for cash; in statements made available to the public, however, most cash balances are summarized into a single figure.

There are several characteristics of cash that make it a distinctive concern to the accountant and financial analyst. Cash is the most liquid of all assets and is the common medium of exchange in our society. As such, it must be the subject of especially tight safeguards and controls. As a general rule, for example, the number of persons handling currency should be kept to a minimum, all currency should be deposited in a bank as soon as feasible, and accounting recognition should be given immediately to all cash receipts via a cash register tape or a manual listing. The responsibility for particular cash funds should be assigned to particular individuals, and whenever possible, in order to better assure that the payments are made to the parties for whom they are intended, disbursements should be made by cheque rather than with currency. All of these safeguards are designed to accomplish the *internal control* objective of accounting.

Cash is the accepted medium for paying bills and satisfying obligations. As such it is essential that a firm have an adequate amount of cash available to meet its debts as they come due and to make the day-to-day payments required of any operating enterprise. A financial analyst or potential creditor must, therefore, be critically concerned as to whether the firm's available cash — or assets that can readily be turned into cash — is sufficient to meet foreseeable needs.

Cash, however, is basically an unproductive asset. Cash on hand or on deposit in a chequing account earns no interest. Insofar as there is any degree of inflation in the economy, cash continually loses its purchasing power. Unlike many other assets, it produces no goods or services or other return to its owner. As a consequence, it is to the advantage of a firm to keep as little cash as possible either on hand or in chequing accounts. Cash that is needed for a *safety reserve* or is being held for future purchase of other assets, distribution to shareholders, or payment of outstanding obligations should be invested temporarily in common shares, short-term government notes, certificates of deposit, or other interest-bearing securities.

Cash on hand

Cash on hand includes customer receipts that have not yet been deposited, currency necessary to conduct routine business, and *petty cash.* Petty cash represents small amounts of cash maintained to meet disbursements of insufficient size to justify the time and inconvenience of writing a cheque. Petty cash funds are frequently accounted for on an *imprest* basis. That is, the general ledger balance of petty cash will always reflect a fixed amount,

$100, for example. At any given time the fund itself should contain either cash or payment receipts for that amount. Periodically the fund is restored to its original amount by a transfer from general cash, and at that time accounting recognition is given to the particular expenses that have been incurred. The following journal entry might be made to restore $70 to the petty cash fund:

Postage expense	$30	
Entertainment expense	40	
Cash in bank		$70

Cash in bank

The balance of cash indicated by a firm's general ledger is unlikely to be that actually available for withdrawal at a particular point in time. Conventional practice dictates that a firm reduce the general ledger cash balance at the time that it writes a cheque. However, a period of several days or even weeks may elapse before such cheque reaches and clears the firm's bank. During that period, the balance per the records of the bank will be greater, by the amount of the cheque than that per the records of the firm. Similarly, a firm may record deposits at the time it mails them to its bank or places them in a night-deposit box. The bank will credit the firm's account only when it actually receives the cash. As a consequence, the amount of cash that a firm reports may be either greater or less than that actually available for withdrawal per the records of the bank. Periodically, upon receiving a statement of its account from the bank, the firm must *reconcile* its balance with that of the bank — that is, it must add to the balance per its own books the sum of any cheques that are still outstanding and subtract from such balance any deposits *in transit*. The adjusted balance (plus or minus any other *reconciling items* such as customer cheques returned by the bank for insufficient funds but not yet recorded by the firm) should be in agreement with the balance reported by the bank. An example of a bank reconciliation is illustrated in Exhibit 6-5.

Although a student could readily memorize those items that are conventionally added and those which are subtracted in the reconciliation, a more sensible approach is to pose three simple questions with respect to each item:

1. Who "knows" about the item? On whose books — the bank's or the depositor's — has it been recorded?
2. What impact has the item had on the books in which it has been recorded? Has it increased or decreased the balance relative to that on the books on which it has not been recorded?
3. Does such amount have to be added to or subtracted from the balance

EXHIBIT 6-5

ABC Company Limited
Bank Reconciliation

Balance per bank statement, December 31, 19x8			$16,160.30
Add:			
Deposits in transit		$12,176.25	
December bank service charge not yet recorded on books		10.00	
N.S.F. cheque[a]		236.17	12,422.42
			$28,582.72
Subtract:			
Outstanding cheques			
#367	$ 126.69		
392	24.00		
393	6,200.00		
394	125.00		
395	81.50		
396	5.00	6,562.19	
Note collected by bank but not yet recorded on books		2,000.00	8,562.19
Balance per company books, December 31, 19x8			$20,020.53

[a]An N.S.F. cheque is one returned by the bank marked "not sufficient funds." Ordinarily, a bank gives a company credit on its books for all cheques deposited. Subsequently, when it learns that it is unable to collect the full amount of a particular cheque because the person who drew the cheque has insufficient funds in his account, the bank would return the cheque to the depositor (the company) and debit its account. The N.S.F. cheque will be a reconciling item until the company records the return of the cheque.

of the bank so that the balance per the bank would be in agreement with the balance per the books?

In this example the books of the bank reflect a balance of $16,160.30, and those of the company, $20,020.53.

1. The company made a deposit of $12,176.25 that has been recorded on the books of the company but not yet on those of the bank. The company knows of the deposit; the bank does not. The balance of the bank by virtue of the deposit, is $12,176.25 less than that of the company. To reconcile the two balances, $12,176.25 must be *added* to the balance of the bank.
2. The bank has deducted and recorded a $10.00 service charge. The bank knows of the service charge; the company does not. The balance of the bank is thereby $10.00 less than that of the company. To effect the reconciliation, $10.00 must be *added* to the balance of the bank.
3. The bank subtracted $236.17 from the balance of the company when it found that it could not collect a customer cheque for that amount. The

bank knows of the deduction; the company does not. The balance of the bank is $236.17 less than that of the company. To reconcile the two balances, $236.17 must be *added* to the balance of the bank.

4. The company has written a number of cheques which have not yet cleared the bank. The company knows of the cheques and has reduced its balance at the time it wrote the cheques. The bank does not know of the cheques and will not learn about them until after they are deposited by the recipient. The balance of the bank is thus greater than that of the company in the amount of the outstanding cheques, $6,562.19. That amount must be *subtracted* from the balance of the bank in order to bring the two balances into agreement.
5. The bank collected the proceeds of a customer note for the company and has given the company credit for it. The bank knows of the collection, but the company does not; it has not yet recorded the receipt of the cash on its own books. The balance of the bank is thereby $2,000.00 greater than that of the company. The $2,000.00 must be *subtracted* from the balance of the bank.

The reconciliation to this point has served to account for and to explain the differences between the cash balance as reported by the bank and that indicated on the books of the company. But it has also indicated that as of the date of reconciliation, December 31, 19x8, the books of the company were in error. They were in error not because of any avoidable mistakes or carelessness on the part of the company accountants or bookkeepers, but only because they were not up to date. They had not taken into account those transactions which the bank knew about and recorded but which, as of the date of reconciliation, the company did not know about and had not recorded. If financial statements are to be prepared as of the date of reconciliation, then it is necessary to adjust the books and records of the company to take into account those items which should have been recorded as of the reconciliation date but which were not. Such items would be those transactions which the bank knew about but which the company did not. In the illustration they would include the service charge of $10.00, the N.S.F. cheque of $236.17, and the $2,000.00 note collected by the bank. The following entry would give effect to the adjustment:

Cash	$1,753.83	
Bank service charge (expense)	10.00	
Accounts receivable	236.17	
Notes receivable		$2,000.00

To give effect to adjustments indicated by bank reconciliation. (Accounts receivable has been debited by the amount of the N.S.F. cheque since the person who wrote the cheque is now indebted to the company for the amount of such cheque.)

Classification of cash

Cash is ordinarily classified as a current asset. In a sense cash is the ultimate current asset in that current assets are defined as those that will be converted into cash within the operating cycle of a business. Nevertheless there are exceptions. Cash should properly be considered a current asset only where there are no restrictions — either those imposed by contract or by management intent — upon its use as a medium of exchange within a single operating cycle. Suppose, for example, that management establishes a *sinking fund* for the retirement of bonds that will mature in 10 years. A sinking fund consists of cash or other assets segregated in the accounts in order to repay an outstanding debt when it comes due. Although the cash and other assets are normally considered current assets, they should be classified on the balance sheet as *noncurrent* assets since management has earmarked them for a specific, noncurrent purpose. The intent of management should be the key criterion for classification.

Compensating balances provide an additional exception to the rule that cash be classified as a current asset. Compensating balances are of primary interest to the beginning student of accounting because they are illustrative of the importance of evaluating the substance of a business transaction as opposed to merely observing its form.

A compensating balance commonly takes the form of a chequing account deposit — one that pays no interest — maintained by a corporation in connection with a borrowing arrangement with a bank. In return for a loan or a promise to make credit available in the future, a corporation will agree to keep a minimum cash balance on deposit. For example, in return for a loan of $1 million, the company might agree to maintain with the institution granting the credit an interest-free chequing account balance of $100,000. The consequence of the arrangement is to reduce the amount actually borrowed by the company and to increase its effective interest rate. The company would have the use of only $900,000. If the loan agreement set forth an interest rate of 8 percent (8 percent of $1 million is $80,000), then the "true" rate of interest paid by the company would be $80,000/$900,000 or 8.9 percent. Although it may appear more logical for the corporation to actually borrow $900,000, if that is the amount that it needs, at an interest rate of 8.9 percent, if that is the market rate of interest, the compensating balance arrangement provides advantages for both the bank and the company. The arrangement may enable the bank to satisfy regulations governing bank liquidity and reserves *if* such a lending practice is permitted by legislation governing banks (which differs from country to country). Such a practice may also permit the company to give the appearance of having greater "borrowing power" than it in fact has.

If a U.S. bank asks for a compensating balance arrangement on loans to a corporation, the parties may or may not state the matter in writing. If the arrangement is informal and not overly clear, financial statement presentation can be complicated. Should a note be appended to the financial statements? What wording can be used if the arrangement is informal? In substance, though, whenever such cash cannot be used in the current operating cycle it should not be classified as a current asset.

Another problem arises when cash is held in a foreign currency. In this case the cash balance would have to be *translated* to Canadian dollars using the foreign currency exchange rate in existence at the balance sheet date.

The question of compensating balances suggests two key points. First, accountants must make every effort to present in the financial statements the substance, rather than the form, of financial transactions. And second, even assets as seemingly straightforward as cash raise issues of balance sheet presentation.

Marketable Securities

In an effort to obtain a return on what would otherwise be temporarily idle cash, many corporations use such cash to purchase shares, bonds, or commercial paper (short-term certificates of debt). Temporary investments are ordinarily grouped together in the current asset section of the balance sheet under the heading "marketable securities." Marketable securities are distinguished from other corporate investments by their readily marketable nature and by corporate intent. The firm ordinarily expects to hold such securities for a relatively short period of time, until a need for cash arises, and does not anticipate exercising any significant degree of control over the company whose shares it may own. If the company has other intentions with respect to the securities, they should ordinarily be classified as "long-term investments," a noncurrent asset.

As with most other assets, marketable securities are reported on the balance sheet at their original cost. However, because the company is likely to sell them in the near future, the current market value is disclosed parenthetically on the face of the statement. Thus,

Cash	$ 80,000
Marketable securities, at cost (net realizable value, $350,000)	335,000

In the U.S., when net realizable value is less than cost and the marketable security is a current asset, the lower figure would be used. In Canada cost may be used in these circumstances when the loss is not viewed as permanent.

Gains and losses on the sale of individual securities are ordinarily recognized at the time of sale. No recognition is given to fluctuations in market value. Assume, for example, that a company had purchased 100 shares of IBM at $220 per share. The shares would be reported on the balance sheet at $22,000. Should the company sell the shares for $250 per share, it would record the sale as follows:

Cash	$25,000	
Marketable securities		$22,000
Gain on sale of marketable securities		3,000
To record sale of marketable securities.		

In theory, revenue from interest on marketable securities is accrued whenever a financial statement is being prepared. Dividends receivable would be accrued only when they have been declared. In practice, however, in the case of marketable securities, dividends and interest might be recognized on receipt of cash. Thus, had IBM declared and paid a dividend of $4 per share before the company had sold it, the following entry would have been appropriate:

Cash	$400	
Revenue from marketable securities		$400
To record receipt of dividend.		

The one critical exception to the general rule that marketable securities be reported at historical cost exists where the market price of the entire portfolio is less than cost; then the carrying value of the securities should be reduced to the market value, and a corresponding loss should be recognized. The exception represents an application of the guidelines of conservatism. Unfavorable events should be accorded accounting recognition at the earliest possible time.

This "lower of cost or market" rule need not be applied to individual securities; it may be applied to all currently marketable securities taken as a group. Assume, for example, a firm has a portfolio consisting of 100 shares of each of two stocks. Both had been purchased at a cost of $100 per share. The original cost of the portfolio is therefore $20,000. As of year end, the market price of stock A had increased to $150 per share; that of stock B had declined to $80:

	Original Cost	*Market Value*	*Lower of Cost or Market*
Stock A	$10,000	$15,000	$10,000
Stock B	10,000	8,000	8,000
	$20,000	$23,000	$18,000

If the lower of cost or market rule were applied on an item-by-item basis, then the portfolio would be written down to $18,000. The following entry (or one similar) would be appropriate:

Decline in market value of marketable securities (expense +)	$2,000	
Marketable securities (asset −)		$2,000
To record decline in market value of marketable securities.		

If, however, the lower of cost or market rule were applied on the basis of the portfolio taken as a whole, then it need not be written down at all; the original cost of $20,000 is less than overall market value of $23,000.

Valuation of Marketable Securities — an Alternative Approach

The current practice of generally reporting marketable securities at original cost is consistent with that followed in reporting other assets. Some critics, however, maintain that two important characteristics of marketable securities justify an alternative approach. First, the current market value of marketable securities (at any particular point in time) can ordinarily be objectively determined. This is especially true of securities that are widely traded since current prices are readily available either in newspapers or special brokerage service reports. Second, there is always an available market in which to sell the securities. Unlike fixed assets or inventories, marketable securities can be disposed of at the market price by a single telephone call to a stockbroker. As a consequence of these two characteristics, critics of current practice assert that the dual accounting goals of providing information that is both relevant and objective can most effectively be served by valuing securities on the balance sheet at market value rather than at historical costs.

The critics also focus attention on the impact of historical costs on the income statement. Gains or losses from holding a security are given accounting recognition only when the security is actually sold. In an accounting sense, at least, management is neither credited nor censured for holding a security as it increases or decreases in market value until the period of sale. The period of sale may be one subsequent to the one in which the increase or decrease in value actually took place.

To the extent that it has in its portfolio one or more securities that have increased in value since they were purchased, management can readily manipulate reported earnings. If management wishes to improve earnings of the current period, it simply sells those securities that have appreciated in value. If, on the other hand, it wishes to give the earnings of the following year a boost, it delays the sale until then. It is questionable, given the ease by which it can be done, that the sale of a security is of greater economic significance than the changes in its market value while it is being held.

The problem of reporting marketable securities is of special concern to industries, such as mutual funds and insurance companies, in which all or a sizable portion of assets consist of marketable securities. In those industries it is vital that an investor be concerned with any *unrealized* gains or losses (those representing changes in the market price of securities not yet sold). As a consequence, firms in such industries either already give effect to unrealized gains or losses on both the balance sheet and the income statement or otherwise make prominent disclosure in footnotes.

Although the issue of cost versus market values can readily be highlighted in a discussion of marketable securities, it is one that bears upon all assets and liabilities. It will be alluded to again in several subsequent chapters.

Summary of Part II

In Part II of this chapter we have dealt with problems of accounting for and reporting cash and marketable securities, both of which are ordinarily classified as current assets.

Cash includes currency on hand as well as demand deposits in banks. It is the most liquid of all assets and is the common medium of exchange in our society. As such it must be the subject of especially tight safeguards and controls, in order to achieve an internal control objective of accounting.

Cash, although generally classified as a current asset, should be grouped with the noncurrent assets in those situations in which it is subject to restrictions upon its withdrawal, regardless of whether the restrictions are imposed by contract or by management itself. If, for example, a portion of a company's cash is maintained as a *compensating balance* in connection with a loan agreement and the company does not expect to have access to such cash within a year, then such amount should be included among the noncurrent rather than the current assets.

Marketable securities include those securities which a firm holds as temporary investments. The key issue with respect to marketable securities pertains to the value at which they should be reported on the balance sheet and the point at which increases or decreases in value should be recognized on the income statement. Conventionally, marketable securities are reported at cost. Increases or decreases in market value are recognized only upon the sale of a security. An exception is made, however, when the market value of an entire portfolio is less than its cost. In accord with the "lower of cost or market" rule, the portfolio ought to be written down to its overall market value. Alternatively, however, many accountants argue that all changes in the market values of securities should be given accounting recognition and all gains or losses, both *realized* and *unrealized*, should be reflected immediately in enterprise earnings.

Another exception occurs when an organization has special needs or objectives for financial reporting. Some mutual funds, for example, show all securities which they hold (whether or not they intend to dispose of them in the next year or so) at current market prices. This is to accommodate people who invest in the mutual fund and wish to pay whatever the company is currently worth — which is the current market value of the securities held by the mutual fund.

Questions, Problems, and Cases

Questions

6-1 "It bothers me that many people in our profession are striving for one accounting method for all situations . . . . I am convinced that one inflexible set of rules could not deal adequately with the various business situations that are encountered in the complex financial world of today."

Required:

Do you agree with the above statement? Explain your position clearly and logically using examples related to the material covered in this and previous chapters.

6-2 "The question often facing the accountant is what "value" or quantitative measure should be assigned to the asset or liability. This requires an examination of objectives, facts and constraints."

Required:

Explain the above quotation using examples to support your position.

6-3 What is meant by *value* as the term is used in connection with assets reported on the conventional balance sheet?

6-4 Historical cost values of assets are of little relevance for most decisions faced by management, creditors, or investors. Why, then, do accountants resist efforts to convert to a market-value-oriented balance sheet?

6-5 The term market price is too imprecise. Define the different types of market price and give an example of each.

6-6 Differentiate between reproduction cost and replacement cost. What are some of the problems associated with determining these values?

6-7 What are the economic benefits associated with an asset? How can they be quantified?

6-8 Current assets are defined as those which are reasonably expected to be *realized in cash*, sold, or consumed during the normal operating cycle of the business. Yet cash itself is not always classified as a current asset. Why should this be?

6-9 The owner of a small corporation was recently advised by his accounting advisor that he "has too much cash sitting in his account." The company had a chequing account balance of $100,000, and the accounting advisor told the owner that the account was costing the company "about $5,000 per year." The owner of the corporation insisted that this could not be so; the money was deposited in a "no-charge" chequing account. What do you think the accounting advisor had in mind when he made his comment?

6-10 The general managers of two subsidiaries of a large firm each reported that his company in 19x7 had operating earnings, excluding income from the sale of marketable securities, of $100,000. The manager of company A also indicated that on January 5, 19x7, he had purchased but had not yet sold 1,000 common shares of United Mining Co. Ltd. at $15 per share. On December 31, 19x7, United Mining Co. Ltd. was being traded at $45 per share. By contrast, the manager of company B revealed that he had purchased 1,000 common shares of United Mining Co. Ltd. on April 18, at $35 per share and had sold them on November 25 at $38 per share.

Required:

If conventional accounting principles are adhered to, which company would report the higher income? Excluding all other factors than those discussed above, which company do you think had the superior performance in 19x7? How might this be communicated in the financial statements?

6-11 What is meant by the term *compensating balances*? What impact do compensating balances have upon the effective interest rate on a loan? Why might a reader of financial reports be misled if the terms of compensating balance arrangements are not disclosed?

6-12 Trust companies are currently selling five-year guaranteed investment certificates to depositors on two bases: 9 percent interest when interest is paid semiannually to the depositor or 9¼ percent interest when interest is paid annually. Savings account interest is roughly 6-7 percent.

Required:

Which is the better rate of interest? Why?

6-13 Why is it possible to buy a $1,000 Government of Canada bond with an annual interest rate of 8 percent for $982 in the open market?

6-14 Distinguish between the Canadian and U.S. basis for reporting marketable securities on the balance sheet. Which is better? Why?

6-15 What factors would you consider in deciding whether shares held as an investment by a company should be classified as a current asset?

6-16 The Helping Hand Loan Co. Ltd. placed an advertisement in a local newspaper that read in part, "Borrow up to $10,000 for 5 years at our low, low, rate of interest of 6 percent per year." When a customer went to the loan company to borrow the $10,000 he was told that total interest on the five year loan would be $3,000. That is, $600 per year (6 percent of $10,000) for five years. Company practice, he was told, required that interest be paid in full at the time a loan is made and be deducted from the amount given to the customer. Thus, the customer was given only $7,000. The loan was to be repaid in five annual instalments of $2,000.

Required:

Do you think the advertisement was misleading? Compute approximately what you consider to be the "true" rate of interest.

Problems

P6-1 The board of directors of a printing company decided that the company should take advantage of an unusually successful year to place in reserve a sufficient amount of funds to enable it to purchase a new printing press in six years. The company determines that the new press would cost $200,000 and that funds could be invested in securities that would provide a return of 8 percent, compounded annually.

Required:

a. How much should the company place in the fund?

b. Suppose that the return would be compounded quarterly. How much should the company place in the fund?

P6-2 You deposit a fixed amount in a bank. How long will it take for your funds to double if the bank pays interest at a rate of:

a. 4 percent compounded annually?

b. 8 percent compounded annually?

c. 8 percent compounded semiannually?

d. 8 percent compounded quarterly?

P6-3 Indicated below are year-end balances from selected general ledger accounts of the MacPherson Co. Ltd.

Cash — Joyal Bank	$ 50,000
Note payable — Joyal Bank	500,000
Interest (expense)	35,000

The interest represents borrowing charges for one year on the note payable to the Joyal Bank. Per terms of an oral agreement, the company must maintain in a chequing account an amount equal to 10 percent of any loans outstanding to the Joyal Bank.

The controller of the MacPherson Co. Ltd. has proposed to include the following comment among the footnotes to its published financial statements. "As of December 31, 19x6, the company was indebted to the Joyal Bank for $500,000. The company pays interest at the rate of 7 percent per year."

The controller indicated that he intends to classify the cash in the chequing account with Joyal Bank as a current asset.

Required:

Do you agree with the intended presentation of the note payable and the related balance in the chequing account. Would this result in the most informative disclosure? If not, what changes would you make? Why? Demonstrate how your changes might assist the users of the company's financial statements.

P6-4 On December 31, 19x1 the general ledger of the Brennan Company indicated that the cash balance in its chequing account at the Toronto-Dominion Bank was $108,753. A statement received from the bank, however, indicated that the balance in the account was $145,974. Investigation revealed the following:

1. The company had written cheques totaling $53,186, which had not been paid by the bank.
2. The company made a deposit on the evening of December 31 of

$26,102. This deposit was included by the bank in its business of January 2, 19x2.

3. On December 27, 19x1 the company had deposited a cheque given to it by a customer for $103. On December 31, the bank returned the cheque to the company marked N.S.F. (not sufficient funds in customer's account). The company had given no accounting recognition to the return of the cheque.
4. The bank debited the account of the company for a monthly service charge of $10. The company had not yet recorded the charge.
5. On December 31, 19x1 the bank collected a customer's note of $10,250 for the company. The company did not receive notification of the collection until January 4, 19x2.

Required:

a. Prepare a schedule which reconciles the balance per the general ledger with that per the bank statement.
b. Prepare adjusting entries indicated by the bank reconciliation, as of December 31, 19x1.

P6-5 At the request of several of its customers, a heavy equipment manufacturer has decided to lease as well as sell its equipment. The company expects a rate of return of 12 percent on all investments. The useful life of its equipment is eight years. Each lessee (i.e., customer) will pay all operating costs including taxes, insurance, and maintenance.

Required: (Ignore income tax.)

a. The company establishes an annual lease charge of $12,000. What would be the sales price that would leave the company equally well off?
b. The company previously sold the equipment for $75,000. What annual rental charge would leave the company as well off as if it had sold the equipment?
c. Has this change in company policy any implications for the company's financial accounting or reporting?

P6-6 A company wishes to establish a pension plan for its president. The company wants to assure the president or his survivors an income of $40,000 per year for 20 years after his retirement. The president has 15 years to work before he retires. If the company can earn 7 percent per year on the pension fund, how much should it contribute during each working year of the president? Ignore income tax.

P6-7 In anticipation of the need to purchase new equipment, a corporation decided to set aside a special fund.

Required: (Ignore income tax).

a. Assume it set aside $40,000 each year and the amount in the fund could be invested in securities that provide a return of 5 percent per year, how much would the company have available in eight years?
b. Assume instead that the company knew that it would require $500,000 to replace the equipment at the end of eight years. How much should it contribute to the fund each year, assuming an annual return of 5 percent?
c. How would you disclose this special fund in the company's financial statements? Why?

P6-8 Prepare journal entries (as necessary) to record the following transactions and events on the books of the APO Company Ltd. a firm whose fiscal year ends on December 31 (indicate your reasoning and any assumptions):

8/20/19x8 The APO Company Ltd. purchases 100 shares of Reichhold Chemical Co. Ltd. common shares at a price of $12 per share.

8/31/19x8 *The Globe & Mail* reports that Reichhold Chemical Co. Ltd. common shares *closed* the previous day at $13½.

9/30/19x8 The board of directors of Reichhold Chemical Co. Ltd. declares a quarterly dividend of $.15 per share.

10/20/19x8 APO Company Ltd. receives a dividend cheque in the amount of $15.

12/31/19x8 A telephone call to a stockbroker reveals that Reichhold Chemical Co. Ltd. common shares *closed* at $4½.

1/11/19x9 APO Company Ltd. sells 50 shares of Reichhold Chemical Co. Ltd. at $5¼.

*P6-9 At May 31, the bank reconciliation of the Dewhirst Company Ltd. was as follows:

Balance per bank statement, May 31, 19x1		$ 12,000
Add:		
Deposits in transit	$ 2,000	
N.S.F. cheque	500	2,500
		14,500
Subtract:		
Outstanding cheques		4,560
Balance per company books May 31, 19x1		$9,940

During the month of June the following occurred:

	Per Company Books	*Per Bank*
June deposits	$16,800	$15,500
June cheques	19,730	21,420
Note collected by bank in June		2,000
June bank charges		12
Balance, June 30	18,042	19,600

Dewhirst Company Ltd. deposits all its receipts in the bank and makes all payments by cheque.

Required:

a. Determine the deposits in transit and the outstanding cheques as of June 30.

b. Prepare the June 30 bank reconciliation.

c. Prepare adjusting entries indicated by the bank reconciliation.

d. Explain briefly how bank reconciliations facilitate the internal control objective of accounting.

P6-10 The following data was taken from the cash records of the Rich Company Limited for the month of March:

1. Balance per company books, March 1	$15,000
2. Balance per company books, March 31	6,386
3. Balance per bank statement, March 1	16,500
4. Balance per bank statement, March 31	13,300
5. Note collected by bank, including $100 interest (recorded by bank but not by company)	4,100
6. Outstanding cheques	5,300
7. Deposits in transit	1,200
8. Bank charge	30
9. Error by bank (cheque for $459.50 cashed by bank for $495.50)	
10. N.S.F. cheques of customers (not recorded by company)	720
11. Petty cash on hand	500

Required:

a. Prepare the March 31 bank reconciliation.
b. Prepare necessary entries at March 31 (indicate any assumptions that you have made).
c. Will all reconciling items between the books of account and the bank statement disappear over time if no adjusting entries are made by the company? Explain.

P6-11 The following data relates to a machine owned by Blazouske Ltd.:

Net book value (historic cost less accumulated depreciation)	$250,000
Replacement cost — new	350,000
Net realizable value	175,000
Present value (of cash receipts net of expenses) of the product produced by the machine if it continues to be used	300,000

Required:

a. "In order to make decisions we require at least two pieces of information." Explain.
b. What items above are relevant for a decision to retain the above machine or sell it and place the money in securities?
c. What items are relevant for a decision to keep the old machine or buy a new machine?

P6-12 During 19x1, in its first year of operations, the Mann Company Ltd. purchased, for $60 per unit, 1,000 units of product. Of these 800 units were sold at a price of $100 per unit. On December 31, 19x1, the company was notified by its supplier that in the following year the wholesale cost per unit would be increased to $70 per unit. As a consequence of the increase, Mann Company determined that the retail price would increase to $120 per unit.

Required:

a. Ignoring other revenues and expenses, determine the ending inventory balance, and compute income assuming that ending inventories are to be valued at:

i.) Historical cost (generally accepted basis).
ii.) A current market *input* price (a proposed alternative).
iii.) A current market *output* price (another proposed alternative).

In computing income, distinguish between revenue from the actual sale of product and gains from *holding* the product in inventory (include recorded increases in the value of the inventory in the determination of income).

b. Explain the benefits of each of the above valuation bases.

P6-13 Indicated below are the marketable securities (all common shares) owned by the Colorado Co. Ltd. on December 31, 19x6. All securities were purchased within the previous 12 months. Also shown are the original purchase prices and the current market prices.

Securities	*Number of Shares*	*Purchase Price*	*Current Market Price*
Amer. Can.	100	$ 35¼	$ 40
Cerro	200	14½	10
Fuqua	100	6	16
GAC Corp.	50	5½	2
IBM	20	250	240

Required:

a. Prepare a schedule indicating the lower of cost or market value of each security.

b. Prepare a journal entry to apply the lower of cost or market rule.
(i) Assume the rule is to be applied on an individual security basis.
(ii) Assume the rule is to be applied on a portfolio basis.

c. What factors would you consider in deciding whether to apply the lower of cost or market rule on an individual security basis or a portfolio basis.

d. Can you think of an industry where it would be sensible to account for marketable securities on a portfolio or group basis? Explain briefly.

P6-14 The general ledger of the Odessa Co. Ltd. reflected, in summary form, the following balances (there were no material liabilities):

Current assets (accounts receivable, inventory, etc.)	$ 40,000
Equipment	80,000
Building	120,000
Land	60,000

The Geneva Company Ltd. purchased Odessa Ltd. for a total of $400,000 (cash). Immediately after purchase an independent appraiser estimated the value of the individual assets as follows:

Current assets	$ 40,000
Equipment	100,000
Building	160,000
Land	100,000

Required: (Ignore income tax.)

a. Prepare a journal entry to record on the books of the Geneva Company Ltd. its acquisition of Odessa.

b. Assume that instead of $400,000 the Geneva Company Ltd. paid a price such that it will receive an annual return of 12 percent on its investment. The Geneva Company Ltd. estimates that the acquired company will earn $72,000 per year. Prepare a journal entry to record the purchase.

c. Assume that the Geneva Company Ltd. paid an amount such that it will earn a return of 10 percent on the market value of the individual assets ($400,000) plus a return of 12 percent on any amount paid in excess of the market value of the assets. The Geneva Company Ltd. estimates that the earnings of the newly acquired firm will be $50,000 per year for the first five years following the acquisition and $40,000 per year for an indefinite period thereafter. (The Geneva Company Ltd. paid $400,000 plus an amount which will provide a return of 12 percent on the *excess* earnings of $10,000 per year for five years.)

(i) Prepare a journal entry to record the purchase of Odessa Ltd.

(ii) In view of the fact that the amount paid for the excess earnings will benefit the company only for five years, how do you propose it be accounted for over the five year period?

Cases

C6-1 Rusco Mutual Fund Ltd. ("RMFL" or the company) is an open-ended mutual fund incorporated under the Ontario Business Corporations Act. Its common shares are available for purchase by the public at any time. In addition, RMFL must stand ready to buy back any shares that the public may wish to dispose of. RMFL uses the money it receives from the sale of its shares for purchases of publicly-traded Canadian securities. Its managers concentrate on purchasing securities which yield long-run rather than short-run returns. Returns consist of interest and dividends on securities held and capital appreciation (or depreciation) on securities sold.

In order to concentrate on growth the company pays dividends of 40 percent of interest and dividends received minus operating expenses. The other 60 percent plus capital appreciation on securities sold is reinvested by the company. However, if reinvestment opportunities are poor, rather than retain large holdings of cash the company will pay higher dividends which include some of the capital appreciation in securities sold.

Required:

How should RMFL report its financial position and results from operations (i.e. how should it value its assets and liabilities, how should earnings be reported, etc.)?

C6-2 Mr. Jackson is the sole proprietor of a hardware store. He has had the same location for the past twenty years and owns the building in which his store is located. The neighbourhood surrounding his store is well established and since he is the only hardware store for miles, he tends to get all the neighborhood business.

Mr. Jackson enjoys his work but he is wondering whether it is all worthwhile. He started thinking more seriously about quitting when he received an offer from Mr. Mackenzie to buy his business for $250,000. Mr. Jackson had trouble understanding why Mr. Mackenzie's offer was so high because for the past few years the hardware business has lost money. The most recent income statement was as follows:

Sales	$300,000
Cost of goods sold	240,000
Gross Margin	60,000
Selling and administrative expense	61,000*
Loss	$ (1,000)

*This includes a $35,000 salary paid to Mr. Jackson, $12,000 rent for the building and $2,000 depreciation expense.

Mr. Jackson went to his banker to review the offer. He was curious to know what his business was worth. His banker said that the net realizable value of the assets minus liabilities was about $100,000. Upon discovering this Mr. Jackson decided that Mr. Mackenzie's offer was ideal. It was true he would only receive $50,000 now and the rest in three years but this was a lot better than he was doing!

Required:

Assume the role of Mr. Jackson's accounting advisor. What would you recommend? Explain your recommendation in a fashion that would be understandable to Mr. Jackson given his limited accounting knowledge.

C6-3 Faultless Construction Co. Ltd. ("FCCL" or the company) was entirely owned by Mr. K. Rack. It was incorporated on January 1, 19x1 for the sole purpose of constructing four identical buildings on adjacent pieces of property. Mr. Rack borrowed $1,200,000 from his wife. This loan was at an interest rate of 10 percent compounded annually and paid semiannually. The principal is repayable on December 31, 19x3. The project took six months to complete and the total cash costs associated with the purchase of land and the construction of the buildings was as follows:

Land	$ 400,000
Materials	240,000
Labor	260,000
Interest (6 months' interest)	60,000
Other (includes equipment rental, land servicing, property taxes, etc.)	200,000
	$1,160,000

There were no other costs associated with the project. Based on these costs Mr. Rack determined the cost per property to be $290,000 since they were identical in every way including size and quality of land. He decided that he would like to make a 40 percent profit on each property and began to seek out buyers.

On July 1, 19x1 he found three buyers. The first buyer, Mr. S. Stewart, offered $500,000 cash for one of the properties and Mr. Rack accepted immediately. The second buyer, Mr. S. Ruid, offered $325,000 cash. Mr. Rack contemplated the offer and decided that, since he only wanted to make a 40 percent profit overall and the first property sold for $500,000, he would accept. The third buyer, Mr. B. Rowk, offered $450,000. The terms of his offer were $50,000 immediately and $100,000 payable on July 1 for each of the next four years. Mr. Rack quickly accepted this offer. For the next six months Mr. Rack was unsuccessful in his attempts to find a fourth buyer. His only cost during this period was interest on the loan from his wife. Since he needed a building, he decided to keep the fourth property as premises for Faultless Construction Co. Ltd.

Required:

a. Assume that you are the accountant for all four buyer individuals (organizations). At what cost would you record the property which was acquired? Explain your reasoning. How would you split the cost between land and building? How would you decide on a depreciation expense for each of the buildings?

b. Record in the company's books the first payment of $100,000 made on July 1, 19x2 by Mr. B. Rowk.

c. Assume that you are not the accountant for Mr. S. Stewart and that his accountant recorded the property purchased by Mr. Stewart at $500,000 on the company's books. Suppose Mr. Stewart's business went into bankruptcy in the first year and one of the investors who relied on the financial statements is suing the accountant for fraud. If you were an expert witness in the case what would you argue on behalf of the accountant? Why?

d. Based on your answer to Part a, what conclusions about the comparability and objectivity of the historic cost accounting model can be made?

e. What recommendations for financial accounting do you have?

7 *Receivables and Payables*

This chapter will focus on accounts and notes receivable and payable. It will also include a brief section on accounting for payroll transactions.

Receivables represent claims, usually stated in terms of a fixed number of dollars, arising from the sale of goods, from the performance of services, from the lending of funds, or from some other type of transaction which establishes a relationship whereby one party is indebted to another. Claims which result from the sale of goods or services and which are neither supported by a written note nor secured by specific collateral (i.e., the creditor has no rights to specific assets in case the debtor fails to pay) are categorized as *accounts receivable*. They are distinguished from amounts backed by written notes (which may or may not arise out of a sales transaction) called *notes receivable* and those arising out of a myriad of other day-to-day business activities, such as *deposits receivable* (e.g., amounts to be received upon return of containers), *amounts due from officers* (perhaps as a consequence of loans), *dividends receivable, rent receivable*, and *interest receivable*. Accounts receivable do not ordinarily require the payment of interest; notes receivable usually do.

Payables represent the corresponding obligations on the part of the recipient of the goods or services. Many of the questions pertaining to the valuation of payables are mirror images of those relating to receivables. The discussion in this chapter will center largely around receivables, with the expectation that, as appropriate, the reader can generalize to payables.

Receivables and payables that mature within one year (or one operating cycle of the business if such is greater than one year) are classified as current assets or liabilities. Those that mature in a longer period are classified as noncurrent.

Receivables — an Overview

The amount at which a receivable should be reported in the financial statements of an enterprise is by no means obvious. Although the dollar amount of a receivable may be clearly evident from the terms of the sale or other agreement which establishes the receivable, not all receivables, unfortunately, will prove to be collectible. One of the major causes of corporate bankruptcy is the failure to transform outstanding receivables into cash.

Moreover, the face amount of a receivable is not necessarily indicative of its economic value. Occasionally, the face amount of a receivable may include an element of *interest*, which, as will be demonstrated later in this chapter, serves to overstate the value of the receivable.

Issues relating to receivables are fundamental to those of income determination. As emphasized in Chapter 5, recognition of revenue is commonly associated with increases in receivables. Similarly, recognition of expenses — those pertaining to bad debts, for example — may correspond to decreases in receivables. Questions of when to recognize increases or decreases in receivables may be viewed alternatively as ones of when to recognize revenue or expenses.

The basic journal entries to establish and to relieve a receivable account are straightforward. Upon the sales of goods and services for $100, for example, the appropriate journal entry would be:

Accounts receivable	$100	
Sales revenue		$100
To record the sale of goods and services.		

And upon subsequent receipt of customer payment,

Cash	$100	
Accounts receivable		$100
To record the collection of cash.		

Variations in the terms of sales and the nature of the transactions resulting in the creation of the receivable necessitate considerable modification in the basic entries in order to accommodate specific circumstances.

Uncollectible Accounts Receivable

There are two ways of accounting for uncollectible accounts receivable. The first, and less preferable, is the *direct write-off* method. As soon as it becomes obvious that an account receivable is uncollectible, it is *written off*, and a *bad debt expense* is charged. Upon learning, for example, that a customer from whom it held a receivable of $100 is likely to default on its obligation, a company might give accounting recognition to its loss with the following journal entry:

Bad debt expense	$100	
Accounts receivable		$100
To write off an uncollectible account.		

Concurrently, the firm would also credit the account of the individual customer in the accounts receivable subsidiary ledger. The accounts receivable subsidiary ledger is nothing more than a book or card file of the amounts owed by each customer. Each page or card is maintained as a small general ledger account for a specific customer, with debits indicating additional debts incurred by the customer and credits signifying payments received. The sum of the balances due from each customer should, at all times, be equal to the balance in the accounts receivable ledger account (often called the accounts receivable *control* account). Otherwise an error has been made. In other words, the accounts receivable subsidiary ledger provides the support — or the detail — for the general ledger account.

Should the customer exhibit a willingness and ability to make good on his obligation sometime after his account has been written off, his account receivable can be restored readily. Suppose, for example, he sends in a payment of $60, which gives rise to the hope that the remaining $40 can also be recovered. It is necessary to first correct the "error" made in writing off the account prematurely. The best information now available to the company indicates that it acted too hastily in charging bad debt expense with the balance in the customer's account. Once the previous entry has been reversed, collection can be accounted for in the usual manner. Appropriate entries would be

Accounts receivable	$100	
Bad debt expense		$100
To restore the account previously written off.		
Cash	$60	
Accounts receivable		$60
To record the collection of cash.		

Obviously, the accounts receivable subsidiary ledger card of the customer would also have to be adjusted to reflect the likelihood of collecting the remaining $40.

The direct write-off method, however, is inconsistent with the matching concepts discussed in Chapter 5; it may lead to an overstatement of *both* income of the period of sale and accounts receivable in the period of sale as well as in subsequent periods. Consider, for example, a company in the retail furniture industry. To attract business, the company grants credit to relatively poor credit risks. The policy results in extensive losses on uncollectible accounts, but management is nevertheless satisfied with the policy since it generates increased sales volume which more than offsets the losses. Based on several years' experience, management estimates that for every dollar of credit sales 10 cents will be uncollectible. The company vigorously pursues its delinquent debtors and writes off accounts only after it has made every reasonable attempt at recovery. Few accounts are written off until at least a year has elapsed since a customer has made a payment.

Under the circumstances, it would hardly be appropriate for the company to include among its assets the entire balance of accounts receivable. After all, only a portion of such balance is likely to prove collectible. Similarly, and equally significantly, if in 19x2 the company had $500,000 in credit sales, it would not be justified in reporting revenues of $500,000 without making allowance for the $450,000 (90 percent of $500,000) that would, in all probability, be fully realized. The individual accounts related to the sales in 19x2 would not be written off for at least one or two years subsequent to 19x2. But such losses would be the result of decisions — the decisions to sell to customers who prove to be unworthy of credit — made in 19x2. Such losses would relate directly to sales made in 19x2; they should be matched, therefore, with revenues of 19x2.

There are, however, two obstacles to assigning credit losses to the year in which the sales take place. First, the amount of the loss cannot be known with certainty until several years subsequent to the sales. Normally, however, such amount can be estimated with reasonable precision. Based on the historical collection experience of the company — or on that of other firms in the same or related industries — it is possible to predict the approximate amount of receivables that will prove to be uncollectible. The inability to make precise estimates of the anticipated losses can hardly be a justification for making no estimate at all. For even the roughest of estimates is likely to be more accurate than no estimate at all — the equivalent of prediction of zero credit losses.

Second, even though a firm may be able to predict with reasonable precision the overall percentage of bad debts, it most certainly is unable to forecast the *specific* accounts that will be uncollectible. After all, if it knew in advance that a particular individual would be unable to pay his debts, it never would have sold to him in the first place. If a company were to recognize bad debts as expenses and correspondingly reduce its accounts receivable balance, which individual subsidiary ledger accounts would it credit? Since the sum of the balances of the subsidiary ledger accounts must equal the balance in the accounts receivable control account — i.e., the general ledger balance — the firm cannot reduce the balance in the control account without, at the same time, reducing the balances in the accounts of specific individuals.

The accountant circumvents this second obstacle by establishing a *contra account*, "accounts receivable — allowance for uncollectibles." The contra account will normally have a credit balance (the opposite of the accounts receivable balance) and will always be associated with and reported directly beneath that of its *parent* account, accounts or notes receivable. To give accounting recognition to the fact that the full amount of the balance of accounts receivable is unlikely to be collected, the accountant, instead of reducing or crediting accounts receivable directly, will credit "accounts receivable — allowance for uncollectibles."

To illustrate the procedure, continue the assumption that a firm in 19x2 made $500,000 in credit sales. At year end the firm estimates that $50,000 of the outstanding balance will prove to be uncollectible. The following adjusting entry would be appropriate to give accounting recognition to such estimate:

(a)

	Debit	Credit
Bad debt expense	$50,000	
Accounts receivable — allowance for uncollectibles		$50,000
To establish an allowance for uncollectibles.		

(Some accountants believe that the debit should be made not to "bad debt expense" but rather to an account "sales-uncollectibles" and that such account should be reported as a deduction from revenues. They point out that anticipated revenue has been lost; the firm will realize less than originally hoped. The approach in which "bad debt expense" is debited for the estimated losses is illustrated in this text not because it is theoretically preferable but only because it is more commonly adhered to in practice.)

The relevant T accounts would appear as follows:

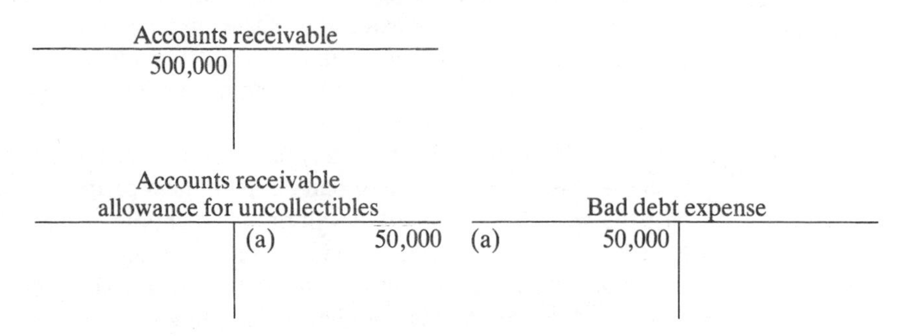

On the balance sheet, accounts receivable (assuming none of the $500,000 has yet been collected) and its related contra account would be reported as:

Accounts receivable	$500,000	
Less: Allowance for uncollectibles	50,000	$450,000

As soon as the company is aware that a specific account cannot be collected it is then able to credit the accounts receivable control account as well as the specific accounts receivable subsidiary ledger account. Since the allowance for uncollectibles had been established for the very purpose of accommodating future bad debts, the offsetting debit would be made to the allowance for uncollectibles contra account.

Assume that in 19x3 accounts totaling $7,000 are determined to be uncollectible. The appropriate entry would be

(b)

Accounts receivable—		
allowance for uncollectibles (asset contra –)	$7,000	
Accounts receivable (asset –)		$7,000
To write off specific accounts.		

At the same time, the specific accounts to be written off would be credited in the accounts receivable subsidiary ledger. It is important to note that at the time specific accounts are written off *no entry is made to "bad debt expense." The effect of the uncollectible accounts on income would already have been recognized in the year the sales were made.* Hence, no further entries to revenue or expense accounts are justified. Moreover, the entry to write off the specific accounts has no effect on current assets or working capital. The *net* accounts receivable (accounts receivable less allowance for uncollectibles) remains unchanged by the entry since both the parent account and the related contra account have been reduced by identical amounts.

Should it turn out that payments are subsequently made on accounts written off, an adjustment would be required only to the accounts receivable account and its contra account. As before, no entry to revenue or expense accounts need be made. Suppose that payment of $1,000 is made on an account which at the time it was written off had a balance of $3,000. The firm determined that payment of the remaining $2,000 was probable. Two entries would be called for: The first reverses the entry in which the account was written off. The second records the collection of the cash.

(c)

Accounts receivable	$3,000	
Accounts receivable—		
allowance for uncollectibles		$3,000
To reverse the entry in which an account was written off. (The individual subsidiary ledger account would be debited for the same amount.)		

(d)

Cash	$1,000	
Accounts receivable		$1,000
To record the collection of $1,000. (The individual subsidiary ledger account would be credited for the same amount.)		

After the entries illustrated above have been posted the ledger accounts would appear as:

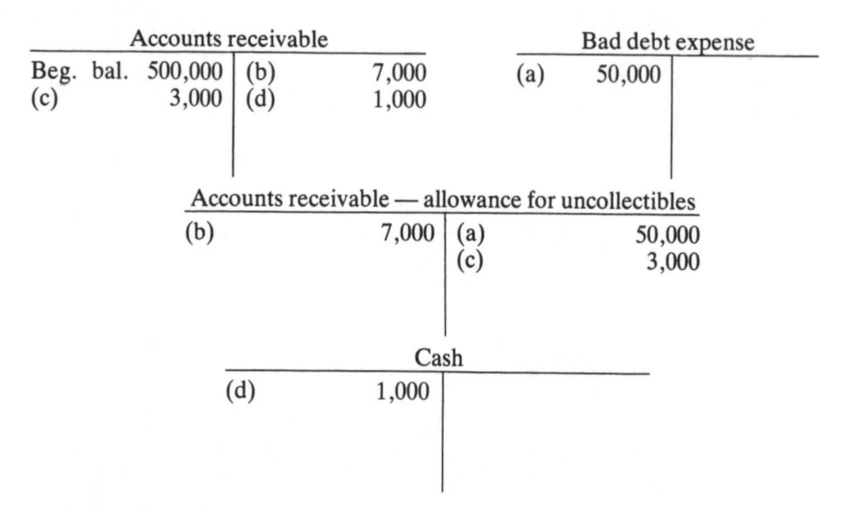

Accounts receivable

Beg. bal.	500,000	(b)	7,000
(c)	3,000	(d)	1,000

Bad debt expense

(a)	50,000		

Accounts receivable — allowance for uncollectibles

(b)	7,000	(a)	50,000
		(c)	3,000

Cash

(d)	1,000		

Generally, a firm creates but a single allowance or contra account for each type of receivable. As a result, the balance in the allowance for uncollectibles account at any given time is comprised of the allowances that have been established in a number of years. Thus, if in 19x3 the company had credit sales of $600,000, 10 percent of which it estimates will be uncollectible, it would make an entry similar to that made in 19x2:

Bad debt expense	$60,000	
Accounts receivable— allowance for uncollectibles		$60,000
To add to the allowance for uncollectibles.		

Methods of Estimating Uncollectibles

There are two widely used methods of determining the charge (debit) to be made each accounting period to "bad debt expense" and the corresponding amount to be added to the allowance for uncollectibles. The first is illustrated above. Based on the collection experience of the company, an estimate is made of the percentage of *sales* (usually taking into account only those made on credit) that will prove uncollectible. Each year, as long as the percentage remains stable, the same percentage is applied to the credit sales of the period, and the resultant amount is added to the allowance.

Alternatively, some firms compute the amount to be added to the allowance with specific reference to the accounts receivable outstanding at the end of the period. Such firms prepare what is known as an ***aging schedule.*** An aging schedule indicates what its name implies — the "age" of each account receivable. That is, it reveals the status of the various accounts — are they current, up to 30 days past due, up to 60 days past due, etc.? An aging schedule is illustrated in Exhibit 7-1.

EXHIBIT 7-1

Aging Schedule as of December 31, 19x2

Customer Name	*Total Balance*	*Number of Days Past Due* *Current*	*0-30*	*31-60*	*61-90*	*Over 90*
J. Faulkner	$ 93,478	$ 93,478				
F. Fitzgerald	60,250	26,139	$ 29,000	$ 5,111		
M. Higgins	100,000	75,000	25,000			
A. Hawthorne	8,222					$8,222
G. Brown	11,650				$11,650	
C. Ryder	92,811	29,206	33,930	26,000	3,675	
D. Deming	37,220		37,220			
G. Hawkins	110,100	110,100				
F. Cohen	116,277	116,277				
	$630,008	$450,200	$125,150	$31,111	$15,325	$8,222

Based on the aging schedule, the firm estimates the dollar amount of accounts that will be uncollectible. Such amount is indicative of the *total* balance required in (not merely the necessary addition to) the allowance for uncollectibles.

As a rule, the longer an account is outstanding — the longer a debtor goes without paying — the less likely the account will be collectible. Thus, a considerably greater proportion of accounts that are 120 days past due than those that are current will in all probability be uncollectible. A larger percentage of the balance of accounts 120 days past due must be added to the allowance for uncollectibles than for accounts that are current. The following summary based on the aging schedule in Exhibit 7-1 reveals the total balance required in the allowance for bad debts:

Summary of Accounts Receivable as of December 31, 19x2

Number of Days Past Due	*Amount*	*Percent Likely To Be Uncollectible*	*Required Provision*
0 (current)	$450,200	2%	$ 9,004
1-30	125,150	8	10,012
31-60	31,111	12	3,733
61-90	15,325	20	3,065
Over 90	8,222	50	4,111
	$630,008		$29,925

The total required provision less the balance that is currently in the account is the amount that must be added to the account. Suppose, for example, that the balance in the allowance for bad debts as of December 31 before adjustment is $7,000. The amount that must be added is $22,925 ($29,925 less $7,000):

Bad debt expense	$22,925	
Allowance for uncollectibles		$22,925
To add to the allowance for uncollectibles.		

The key distinction between the two methods is that under the percentage of sales method the annual addition is determined by multiplying credit sales by a preestablished percentage. The amount of the addition is thereby computed independently of the existing balance in the allowance for uncollectibles account. Under the aging schedule method the annual addition is determined by first estimating the *required* balance in the allowance for uncollectibles account (as revealed by the aging schedule) and then subtracting from such required balance the actual balance in the account.

Which of the methods of determining the amount to be added to the allowance for uncollectibles — the percentage of sales or the aging schedule — is preferable? Insofar as the firm's estimates of either the percentage of sales to be uncollected or the percentages of the various groups of past due accounts are accurate, and uncollectible accounts are written off on a regular basis over time, then both methods will result in approximately equal credits to the allowance and charges to earnings over time. If, however, write offs tend to follow an irregular pattern with few accounts being written off in good years and many accounts being written off in bad years, then the two methods may have differing impacts on earnings. The percentage of sales method will result in a constant percent of (credit) sales being charged to bad debt expense regardless of the number of accounts written off (i.e., debit allowance for uncollectibles; credit accounts receivable) in a particular year. The amount of the charge will be a function of sales volume and not of events affecting the debtor — especially the likelihood that the debtor faces financial difficulty and the account may have to be written off in a few months. The aging schedule approach, on the other hand, will usually result in a more erratic charge to bad debt expense. The amount of the charge will be highly responsive to the number and size of the accounts which eventually may have to be written off and therefore should be provided for in making up the allowance for uncollectibles. To the extent that it is desirable to match the "cost" of the bad debts to the sales to which they are applicable, then the percentage of sales method is preferable. However, oftentimes a firm may misestimate the percentage of sales and as a result the balance in the allowance for bad debts becomes either inadequately low or unnecessarily high. Neither method, therefore, is necessarily preferable. The optimum approach may be to use both methods in conjunction with one another — to make an initial estimate of the charge to bad debt expense by taking a percentage of credit sales and then to test the adequacy of the allowance for bad debts by preparing an aging schedule.

The two cases that follow demonstrate the importance — and the difficulty — of evaluating the collectibility of accounts and notes receivable. The incidents described are by no means intended to malign either the accounting profession or the particular accountants who audited the companies involved. Rather, they are presented to highlight the fact that informative financial reporting is as much dependent on the sound judgment of the accountant as it is on mere mechanical accuracy.

Commercial finance companies

In September, 1970, the *New York Times* reported,

> One of the nation's largest public accounting firms has tentatively agreed to settle for $4.95 million the claims arising from its role in the collapse of the Mill Factors Corporation almost two years ago.
>
> Mill Factors, which today is insolvent, was once considered to be a "Tiffany" among commercial finance companies.[1]

Mill Factors was a publicly owned company, and as a result of its financial debacle, individual investors (shareholders) as well as creditors (lenders) of the firm suffered losses that ran into several million dollars.

The losses of the investors and creditors can in large measure be attributed to the financial statements of the firm, which, until its actual collapse, painted a picture of glowing financial health. In fact, several years earlier, according to a report of CPAs (certified public accountants, who are similar to Canada's chartered accountants or CAs) commissioned especially to investigate the bankruptcy, the true status of the firm's accounts receivable portended a troubled future for the company. Years prior to its collapse, according to the report, the firm should have charged "bad debt expense" for an amount sufficient to bring its allowance for uncollectibles up to between $13 and $19 million to cover potential losses on its $33.6 million commercial loan portfolio. This the company failed to do. Worse yet, according to some observers, the company attempted to cover the errors it had made in making loans to financially dubious borrowers by lending them additional funds. According to one creditor who suffered a large loss,

> A loan officer makes a substantial loan that goes sour. Instead of admitting his mistake, passing on the information to the company's investors and creditors, and possibly risking his reputation and job, he decides to cover up. If the mistake were large enough and were made public, a shadow would be cast over the credit rating of the company. The covering-up process is done by advanc-

> ing more money to the ailing client to enable it to pay interest and principal on the loan, and often to advance more besides. If the client went broke, the cat, of course, would be out of the bag.[2]

The financial statements of Mill Factors were misleading in that they overstated assets (accounts receivable) and understated expenses (bad debt expense). The independent CPAs who attested to their presentation failed to detect the misrepresentation, at least in part, because they were put off by the company's continued advances to borrowers who were known to be in financial difficulty.

Real estate investment trusts

A March 1974 story in *Forbes*, under the headline, "When Is a Lemon a Lemon," began with the exclamation "These accountants burn me up." The story related how the share prices of real estate investment trusts had suffered major declines in recent weeks, attributable, in the words of a disgruntled investor, to the way in which accountants "let a few [firms] run wild with these paper pyramids."[3] It is alleged that some Canadian banks lost large sums of money on U.S. real estate investment trusts.

Real estate investment trusts are generally publicly owned firms which take funds received from shareholders as well as those borrowed from banks and other lending institutions and either purchase real estate directly or lend funds to other purchasers. In 1974, with the real estate industry in a tailspin as the result of inflation, high interest rates, shortages of building materials, and an excessive availability of office space, the real estate investment trusts had difficulty collecting many of their outstanding loans.

The key accounting question raised by the situation in which the real estate investment trusts found themselves was posed by *Forbes* as follows: "At what point does a 'problem loan' — one that is (hopefully) being monitored because payments are late or for some other reason — become a 'bad loan' on which interest should no longer be accrued?" The implications of the question are clear. Firms had not only been failing to write off or provide substantial allowances for bad debts on loans of dubious collectibility but they had also been continuing to accrue interest revenue on such loans even though there was considerable uncertainty as to whether such interest would ever be collected.

The article went on to explain that the question of when a problem loan becomes a bad loan is not susceptible to simple answers:

> Is a loan bad just because it is 30, 60 or 90 days past due? Maybe, maybe not. At times a trust might not mind at all waiting an extra 30 or 60 days for payment. And even a lousy loan can be up to date on its payments. Florida-based builder Walter J. Kassuba, who had borrowed $130 million from REITs (Real Estate Investment Trusts), was up to date on most of his debt service when he

> filed under Chapter 11 (i.e., declared bankruptcy) a few months ago. Everything hinges on how good a handle management has on what's going on in its portfolio.[4]

Nevertheless, the article strongly implied that accountants, despite their generally "conservative" outlook, were not giving the real estate loans the careful scrutiny that they deserved:

> But, we asked the accountants, doesn't management always think, rightly or wrongly, it can "work out" the loan — that is, get it back on schedule without a loss in revenue? Who wants "non-earnings assets," as loans on a non-accrual basis are called? They only spoil the earnings growth and call unwanted attention to the rest of the loan portfolio. Well, the accountants replied, auditors *should* take a closer look at those portfolios in a poor real estate year.[5]

Indeed, the article pointed out that one real estate investment trust continued to accrue interest income on three bankrupt or foreclosed properties because management felt that the loans could be worked out. Such a practice not only overstated the assets of the firm (accounts or notes receivable and accrued interest receivable) but income as well.

Sales Returns

Sales returns involve considerations similar to those of bad debts. Insofar as goods that have been sold are expected to be returned in a subsequent accounting period, accounting recognition must be given in the year in which they are sold. Financial statements which fail to take into account goods to be subsequently returned and refunds to be given to customers would clearly overstate revenues and, hence, earnings. But as with allowances for bad debts, the necessary accounting entries must reflect the fact that until returns are actually made the accountant has no way of knowing either the exact amount of such returns or the specific customers who will make such returns.

The accountant must follow an approach similar to that taken in recording bad debts. He must first make an estimate of anticipated returns (based, perhaps, on previous experience) and then establish an allowance for such returns.

Assume that at year end a firm estimates that merchandise that was sold for $10,000 will be returned in the following year. An appropriate journal entry would be

Sales — returns	$10,000	
Accounts receivable— allowance for returns		$10,000
To record the estimate of sales returns.		

Both of the accounts involved in the entry are *contra accounts*. "Sales — returns" would be reported on the income statement as a reduction of sales. "Accounts receivable — allowance for returns" would be reported on the balance sheet as an additional reduction of accounts receivable along with the allowance for uncollectibles. In practice, both contra accounts would be netted against their "parent" because external users of financial statements tend to not want the detail about returns. Management, however, would seek the detail in financial reports designed for them.

If the merchandise to be returned can be resold, then it is necessary also to give effect to the fact that expenses, i.e., cost of goods sold, in addition to revenues and sales, have been overstated in the year of sale. Assume that the merchandise to be sold had an original cost of $8,000. The required entry to record the anticipated return would be

Merchandise to be returned (asset)	$8,000	
Cost of goods sold (expense)		$8,000
To record the cost of goods to be returned.		

When the merchandise is actually returned, only balance sheet accounts need to be adjusted; the impact on revenues and expenses would have been accounted for in the year of sale:

Accounts receivable — allowance for returns (asset; contra)	$10,000	
Accounts receivable (asset)		$10,000
To give the customer credit for merchandise returned.		
Merchandise inventory (asset)	$8,000	
Merchandise to be returned (asset)		$8,000
To record the receipt of returned merchandise.		

Returns can be a problem in some industries, such as textbook publishing, where large amounts of goods may be returned up to a year after purchase. A professor may assign three or four "recommended" but not required books and order sufficient copies for all students. Students may buy very few of the "recommended" texts. Students may also buy used texts. Problems in estimation are few if the behavior of students and professors is consistent — but it sometimes varies widely.

Cash Discounts

Frequently a seller will offer a customer a discount for prompt payment. A company may, for example, sell under terms 2/10, n/30. The total amount is due within 30 days; however, if payment is made within 10 days, the customer is entitled to a discount of 2 percent. In economic substance it is difficult to view such terms as representing a "true" discount; a more acceptable interpretation is that the customer is subject to a penalty if he fails to make prompt payment. If the customer pays on the thirtieth day following purchase rather than on the tenth day, then he has the use of his funds for an additional 20 days. The use of such funds will have cost him $2 for each $98 of merchandise purchased. His effective interest cost will be at a rate of approximately 37 percent—

$$\frac{360 \text{ days}}{20 \text{ days}} \times \frac{\$2}{\$98}.$$

Only a company with a severely impaired credit rating would be willing to pay such an extraordinarily high rate. An unbiased observer might suspect, therefore, that the merchandise sold had a fair market value not of the stated sales price but rather of the stated sales price less the discount.

The proper accounting for cash discounts is *not* one of the critical issues facing the business community. It is of interest to accounting students primarily because it provides another example of the importance of accounting for substance over form.

Both purchasers and sellers account for cash discounts in either of two basic ways: the net method or the gross method. The *net* method requires that both purchases and sales be recorded at fair market value of the goods traded — that is, sales price *less* the discount — and that payments in excess of the discounted price be recorded separately as a penalty for late payment or as a financing cost. The *gross* method permits purchases and sales to be recorded at the stated price, subject to later adjustment. A simple example can be used to compare the two approaches — first from the standpoint of the purchaser and then from that of the seller.

EXAMPLE

A company purchases on terms 2/10, n/30 merchandise that has a sales price of $100,000:

Net Method			*Gross method*		
Inventory	$98,000		Inventory	$100,000	
Accounts payable		$98,000	Accounts payable		$100,000
To record the purchase of merchandise.					
Accounts payable	$98,000		Accounts payable	$100,000	
Cash		$98,000	Cash		$98,000
			Purchase discounts		2,000
To record payment within the discount period.					

The critical difference up to this point is that under the gross method inventory has been recorded at $100,000 — "overstated" by $2,000. The "error" can be corrected at year end by *closing* the purchase discount account into inventory and cost of goods sold, based on the proportions of goods that have been sold and remain on hand. (The purchase discount account would ordinarily have a credit balance, but its precise classification is a matter of some dispute. The approach taken in this text is that the account should be closed out at year end; hence the question of its proper place in the financial statements is, in large measure, academic.) Suppose, for example, that of the goods purchased during the year, 90 percent have been sold during the year; 10 percent remain in ending inventory. The following entry would eliminate the $2,000 overstatement:

Purchase discounts	$2,000	
Inventory		$ 200
Cost of goods sold		1,800
To eliminate discounts taken from inventory and cost of goods sold.		

In practice few companies would make such an entry. Instead, under the gross method, they would credit the "purchase discounts" of $2,000 to the income statement. Inventory would thus be recorded at $100,000. In contrast, under the net method, inventory would be recorded at $98,000.

(Specific journal entries will vary depending on whether the firm uses the periodic or the perpetual inventory method or whether it initially charges purchases of inventory directly to the inventory account or alternatively to a purchase account.)

Alternatively, if the firm does not pay within 10 days and allows the discount period to lapse, then the following entries would be appropriate:

Net method			*Gross method*		
Accounts payable	$98,000		Accounts payable	$100,000	
Purchase discounts lost (expense)	2,000		Cash		$100,000
Cash		$100,000			

To record payment after the discount period.

The purchase discounts lost account can be interpreted as an expense. Its appearance on an income statement would clearly highlight the cost that the company has incurred by failing to avail itself of the two percent discount. It should put a perceptive financial analyst or investor on notice that the firm may be in a precarious cash position or is being managed inefficiently; it has "borrowed" at an exceedingly high rate of interest. Unfortunately, few companies in Canada seem to use the net method, and even if they did, their books would probably not record the purchase discount lost as a separate line on the income statement prepared for external users.

The entries recording the sales and subsequent collection from the standpoint of the seller would correspond to those of the purchaser:

Net method			*Gross method*		
Accounts receivable	$98,000		Accounts receivable	$100,000	
Sales		$98,000	Sales		$100,000
To record the sale of merchandise.					

Net method			*Gross method*		
Cash	$98,000		Sales discounts	$ 2,000	
			Cash	98,000	
Accounts receivable		$98,000	Accounts receivable		$100,000
To record collection within the discount period.					

Alternatively, if collection were made after the discount period,

Net method			*Gross method*		
Cash	$100,000		Cash	$100,000	
Accounts receivable		$98,000	Accounts receivable		$100,000
Revenue from lapsed discounts		2,000			
To record collections after the discount period.					

Under the gross method, the sales discounts should be interpreted as a reduction of sales. At year end it should either be closed into sales or reported on the income statement *contra* to sales. Significantly, from the standpoint of the investor or analyst, accounts receivable are stated at their gross amount — an amount greater than is likely to be collected. To the extent discounts are relatively high in relation to sales and a large percentage of customers are likely to take advantage of the discount, accounts receivable may be substantially overstated. However, an estimate of discounts which likely would be taken could be accrued.

Non-Arm's Length

The general principle that we disclose as a separate item in the financial statements any information needed by users or readers (as long as the preparer agrees) applies also to the presentation of accounts receivable. Companies' legislation and the *CICA Handbook* (what we have for convenience called potential *constraints* to judgment in this book) request separate disclosure of various types of receivables. Often, but not always, these requirements for *separate* disclosure have resulted from problems caused by transactions with related parties or non-arm's-length transactions. It is assumed that readers are interested in all information about transactions between parties who are somehow related — such as owner-managers, and companies with major investments in another company. As noted in Chapter 5 related parties may, for example, trade on the basis of fair market values, or not be free to engage in some transactions which a competitor may choose.

The *CICA Handbook*, for instance, has the following requirement for financial reporting:

> The amount of any loans made by the company . . . during the company's financial period, other than in the ordinary course of business, to the directors or officers of the company should be disclosed regardless of whether such loans are outstanding at the end of the financial period.[6]

Presumably this requirement might reduce the number and amount of loans granted by officers to themselves, or if loans are made, to ensure that an adequate rate of interest is charged. Interest on loans is discussed in the remainder of this chapter.

Promissory Notes

When a firm extends credit beyond a short period of time (two or three months) or makes a loan, it usually requests formal written documentation of the borrower's obligation to make timely payment. The legal instrument which provides such documentation is known as a *promissory note*. A typical promissory note is illustrated in Exhibit 7-2.

A promissory note, unlike an account receivable, generally provides that the maker (the borrower) of the note agrees to pay a fee, known as interest, for the right to use the funds provided. The promissory note is a legally binding contract. It would specify the following:

The parties involved in the contract — the payor, who is the person or organization that agrees to make the payment, and the payee, who is the person or organization to whom the money is owed (sometimes a note may be drawn to *bearer* — that is, payment is to be made to whomever presents the note to the maker);

EXHIBIT 7-2

Typical Promissory Note

Promissory Note - Non-regulated

Canada Permanent Trust Company
Canada Permanent Mortgage Corporation

the Permanent

Dated this day of 19

Loan number

Full names

Branch Address

Address

Unpaid balance of previous loan(s) $	Security				
Actual proceeds of loan received $					
Official fees and/ or other costs $					Final payment amount *
Principal amount of loan $	First payment due date	Others-same day of each month	Final payment due date		
Cost of borrowing * $	Cost of borrowing Percent per annum.	Monthly payments			
Total amount to be repaid * $	Calculated monthly not in advance	Number	Amount of each $		

* Subject to all payments made on due dates

FOR VALUE RECEIVED I promise to pay to Canada Permanent Trust Company or Canada Permanent Mortgage Corporation, as the case may be, (hereafter called "The Permanent") or order, at the above office of The Permanent the principal amount of $ together with interest thereon at the rate of per cent per annum, calculated monthly, not in advance, payable in consecutive monthly payments of $ commencing on the day of , 19 and on the same day in each succeeding month thereafter until the day of , on which date the balance unpaid shall be due and payable. Each of the payments shall be applied first on account of interest owing to the date thereof and the balance in reduction of the principal amount. Any other payment of money hereunder shall be applied on account of interest owing to the date thereof and to the reduction of the principal amount as the holder at its option may determine. Default in payment in full of any monthly payment hereunder or default under any provision of any mortgage or charge (of land, premises or chattels) or other evidences of indebtedness given by the undersigned, or any one of them, in favour of The Permanent shall, at the option of The Permanent exercisable at any time without notice or demand, render the unpaid principal amount hereof and interest accrued thereon due and payable. Interest at the aforementioned rate shall be payable on any defaulted payment from its due date to and including the date of payment thereof. Any mortgage or charge (of land, premises or chattels) or other evidence of indebtedness given concurrently with this note by the undersigned, or any of them, in favour of The Permanent is concurrent with and also secures the same principal and interest as this promise to pay.

Demand and presentment for payment, notice of non-payment, protest and notice of protest of this note are waived.

I acknowledge receipt of the Statement of Loan.

Signature of witness

Full name (print)

Address of witness

The date the note was issued and the date payment is due (some notes state that payment is due in a specific number of days from the date it was issued);

The *principal* of the note (the amount of credit being extended), often referred to as the *face value* of the note;

The rate of interest;

Any collateral or property that the borrower either pledges or surrenders as security for the note.

Interest on a note is expressed in terms of an annual percentage rate. The formula for translating the percentage rate into the actual dollar amount is

$$\text{Interest} = \text{Principal} \times \text{Rate} \times \frac{\text{Days of loan}}{\text{Total days in one year}}$$

If, for example, a company issues a note for $100,000, that bears interest at a rate of 8 percent and is payable in 91 days, the actual interest that it will be required to pay can be computed as

$$\$100{,}000 \times .08 \times \frac{91}{365} = \$2{,}000 \text{ (approximately).}$$

Notes are generally reported on the balance sheet at their principal or face amount. This convention is a source of confusion to many students since the total obligation of the maker is not only the principal but the interest as well. In the above illustration, for example, the total amount to be paid after 91 days is $100,000 plus $2,000 interest. Yet the note would be recorded on the balance sheet at only $100,000. The logic beyond the convention becomes apparent, however, when the impact of notes and interest on the balance sheet is viewed in conjunction with that on the income statement. Interest is a charge imposed on a borrower for the use of funds over a period of time. From the standpoint of the borrower, therefore, the interest cannot be considered an expense — and hence not a liability — until he has actually used the borrowed funds over a period of time. Over the passage of time, the borrower will recognize the expense associated with the use of funds — interest expense — and at the same time the liability — accrued interest payable. Similarly, the lender will periodically recognize the earnings attributable to the funds that he has provided the debtor and concurrently acknowledge the creation of an asset, interest receivable.

A brief example may make the relationships between income and balance sheet accounts somewhat more clear.

EXAMPLE

On June 1, Echo Co. Limited informs Foxtrot Corporation that it will be unable to make payment on its open account, which on that date has a balance of $20,000. Echo requests that Foxtrot accept instead a 61-day note that will bear interest at the rate of 12 percent. Foxtrot agrees.

Upon accepting the note on June 1, Foxtrot would make the following entry to record the exchange of an account receivable (which does not bear interest and is unsupported by a formal legal instrument) for an interest bearing note receivable:

Notes receivable	$20,000	
Accounts receivable		$20,000
To record acceptance of the note.		

Thereafter, with the passage of time Foxtrot must account for the revenue that it is earning on the note which it holds. Most companies, considering the clerical costs of making frequent journal entries, update their accounts monthly — and the journal entries usually appear on special computer printouts or work sheets, not directly in the journals and ledgers — in order to prepare monthly financial statements, as was stated in Chapters 3 and 4. Assuming that Foxtrot Corporation updates its accounts monthly, the following entry would be appropriate on *June 30*:

Accrued interest receivable	$200	
Interest revenue		$200
To record monthly interest revenue from the note.		

The $200 represents interest for a period of 30 days computed as

$$\$20{,}000 \times .12 \times \frac{30}{365} = \$200 \text{ (approximately).}$$

On July 31 the note would fall due. Assuming that both the note and the interest are paid in full, two entries are required to record collection. The first is identical to that made on June 30; it recognizes the interest earned during the 31-day period since interest revenue was previously recorded:

Accrued interest receivable	$200	
Interest revenue		$200
To record monthly interest revenue from the note.		

The balance in the accrued interest receivable account now stands at $400 and that in the notes receivable account at the original $20,000. Upon collection of both interest and principal, the appropriate entry would be

Cash	$20,400	
Accrued interest receivable		$ 400
Notes receivable		20,000
To record the collection of the note and interest. (Note: this entry has no effect on revenues or expenses.)		

From the standpoint of the payor (Echo) — the maker of the note — the journal entries would be a near mirror image of those of the payee. Summarized briefly, they would be

June 1		
Accounts payable	$20,000	
Notes payable		$20,000
To record the change in status of the liability from an account payable to a note payable.		
June 30		
Interest expense	$200	
Accrued interest payable		$200
To record interest charges on note for the first 30 days.		
July 31		
Interest expense	$200	
Accrued interest payable		$200
To record interest charges on note for the next 31 days.		
Notes payable	$20,000	
Accrued interest payable	400	
Cash		$20,400
To record payment of both principal and interest.		

Notes with Interest Included in Face Value

Frequently a note will not specifically indicate a rate of interest. Instead, the face value of the note will include not only the amount originally borrowed but also the applicable interest charges as well. A borrower, for example, may give to a bank or other creditor a note for $1,000 in exchange for a 91-day loan. The bank, however, would not give the borrower the full $1,000. Instead, if the going interest rate for that type of loan were 12 percent, it would give the borrower only $971. If the annual rate of interest is 12 percent, then the interest on a loan of $971 for 91 days would be

$$\$971 \times .12 \times \frac{91}{365} = \$29.$$

The interest of $29, plus the principal of $971, exactly equals the face value of the note, $1,000.

Regardless of the manner in which the terms of the loan are stated, the difference between the amount actually received by the borrower and the amount that he must eventually repay at the maturity of the note represents the cost of borrowing — i.e., interest. In the present example, the actual amount of the loan as well as the interest could have been readily calculated as follows:

Let x = the actual amount of the loan.

If interest is to be at an annual rate of 12 percent, then interest for the 91-day period, approximately ¼ year, would be a total of 3 percent of the actual amount of the loan. The total amount to be repaid is the actual amount of the loan, x, plus the interest, $.03x$. The total amount to be repaid has been established (the face amount of the note) at $1,000. Hence,

$$\$1{,}000 = x + .03x \quad \text{or}$$
$$\$1{,}000 = 1.03x \quad \text{or}$$
$$x = \frac{\$1{,}000}{1.03} = \$971$$

The interest must be the difference between the face amount of the note and the amount actually borrowed: $1,000 minus $971 or $29.

When the amount actually loaned is less than the face amount of the note — that is, when the face amount includes both principal and interest — the note is known as a discounted note. The journal entries required to record *discounted* notes and the associated interest charges are similar to those for conventional interest-earning instruments.

Assume, for example, that on July 1 a lending institution accepted a three-month note of $1,000 discounted in exchange for an actual cash loan of $971. The entry to record the loan would be:

Notes receivable (at face value)	$1,000	
Cash		$971
Discount on note receivable (asset contra or "deferred credit" — which is a liability account)		29

The overall effect of the entry is to record the asset, notes receivable, at the amount actually loaned. If a balance sheet were to be drawn up immediately after the loan was made, the relevant accounts would be reported on the balance sheet (among current assets) as either:

Notes receivable	$1,000	
Less discount on notes receivable	29	$971

or, for situations where there is a discount, a net figure of $971. Very large finance companies might show the asset as $1,000 and the discount as a "deferred credit" — which in time becomes interest revenue, as the interest is earned. As we have observed previously, the type of financial presentation depends upon the combined views of the preparer and the receiver of the financial statements. For example, from the receiver/user point of view the question to ask is whether the figure for discount is useful in decisions such as cash flow prediction, which you wish to make. If so, ask for separate disclosure of the discount. If not, accept the net figure (of $971). Financial statements are those of the preparer; hence, users might have to lobby or otherwise directly request the information which they wish to see provided by preparers.

As with conventional interest-bearing notes, interest must periodically be taken into account. On July 31, the appropriate entry would be (making the simplifying assumptions that one third of the overall interest charges will be recorded during each of three months regardless of the actual number of days in the month)

Discount on notes receivable	$9.67	
Interest revenue		$9.67
To record interest on the note for one month.		

The effect of this entry is to recognize the interest revenue and also to increase the value of the note (by decreasing the value of the "discount on notes receivable" account) by the amount of revenue recognized. The entry is similar to that which would have been made had the note been one with a stated interest rate. The main difference — a relatively unimportant one — is that with the discounted note the recognition of the interest results in the increase of an asset, notes receivable, whereas with the interest-bearing note it results in the increase of an asset, interest receivable.

On August 31 and on September 30, entries identical to that indicated above would also be made:

Discount on notes receivable	$9.67	
Interest revenue		$9.67
To record interest on the note for one month.		

On September 30, when the note is paid, the balance in the "discount on notes receivable" account would have been reduced to zero. Collection of the note could be recorded as follows:

Cash	$1,000	
Notes receivable — face value		$1,000
To record collection of the note.		

If the period of the loan were greater than one year, present value tables, the use of which was described in Chapter 6, could be conveniently used to determine the amount to be advanced to the borrower.

EXAMPLE

A finance company makes a loan to a customer on a discount basis. The company accepts from the customer a two-year note for $5,000. The actual cash advanced is determined on the basis of a 12 percent annual rate of interest.

Per Table 2, the present value of $5,000 discounted at a rate of 12 percent for two years is

$$\$5{,}000 \times .7972 = \$3{,}986.$$

The finance company would advance the customer $3,986 and record the loan as follows:

Notes receivable	$5,000	
Discount on notes receivable		$1,014
Cash		3,986
To record the loan to the customer.		

Interest revenue for the first year would be 12 percent of the *net* balance of the outstanding customer obligation, that is, 12 percent of $3,986 — $479. An appropriate journal entry after the note has been outstanding for one year (assuming that no entries had been made at the end of each month) would be

Discount on notes receivable	$479	
Interest revenue		$479
To record interest for the first year.		

Since the customer did not actually remit an interest payment, the effective balance of his obligation would increase after the first year by $479. The increase in the effective balance is accounted for by a decrease in the discount. After the first year, the note would be reported as follows:

Notes receivable	$5,000	
Less: Discount on notes receivable	535	$4,465

Interest for the second year would be based on the effective customer obligation at the end of the first year. Thus, it would be 12 percent of $4,465 — $535. The entry after the end of the second year to record both interest revenue and collection of the full $5,000 would be

Cash	$5,000	
Discount on notes receivable	535	
Notes receivable		$5,000
Interest revenue		535
To record second-year interest on the note and collection of the note.		

The interest revenue on a discounted note would increase from year to year, corresponding to an increase in the effective obligation of the customer. Interest must be paid not only on the original amount borrowed but also on any unsatisfied obligations for interest as well. (If the loan is for a relatively short period of time — less than one year — the "interest on the interest" is usually sufficiently immaterial so that it can safely be ignored.)

Non-interest Bearing Notes

Occasionally, a firm will sell on especially generous terms of credit. In fact, sometimes the terms are so generous that they raise serious doubts as to whether the goods are really worth the price at which they are being sold.

Assume, for example, that a company sells a building for $100,000. The company accepts from its customer a five-year *interest-free* note for the full sales price. As emphasized in Chapter 6, $100,000 to be received in five years is worth considerably less than the same amount to be received today. Indeed, per Table 2, the present value of a single payment of $100,000 five years hence, discounted at a rate of 8 percent, is

$$\$100{,}000 \times .6806 = \$68{,}060.$$

It is hardly reasonable to expect a company to provide an interest-free loan to a customer for five years. A more credible interpretation of the transaction states that interest charges are included in the $100,000 selling price. If, indeed, the prevailing rate for similar types of loans is 8 percent, the facts suggest that the "true" selling price of the building is $68,060. The difference between such amount and the stated selling price of $100,000 represents interest on a five-year loan of $68,060.

If accountants are to be concerned with the substance rather than the form of transactions, they must divide the $100,000 into its component parts. They must account separately for the sales price and the interest. If the building had been recorded on the books of the seller at $50,000, then the following entry would be appropriate:

Notes receivable	$100,000	
Building		$50,000
Discount on notes receivable		31,940
Gain on sale of building		18,060
To record the sale of the building.		

During each year that the note was outstanding, the company would accrue interest on the effective balance of the "loan" — the note receivable less the unamortized portion of the discount. Thus, to record interest after one year (assuming no entries had been made at the end of each month):

Discount on note receivable	$5,445	
Interest revenue		$5,445
To record interest for one year on a note of $68,060 at a rate of 8 percent.		

And after the second year,

Discount on note receivable	$5,880	
Interest revenue		$5,880
To record interest for one year on a note of $73,505 at a rate of 8 percent ($73,505 represents the face value of the note less an unamortized discount of $26,495).		

Over the life of the note, the firm will recognize earnings on the transaction of $50,000 — $100,000 received in cash less the recorded value of the building of $50,000 — regardless of how the $100,000 is divided between "true" sales price and interest. If the transaction were accounted for in accordance with its form (selling price of $100,000), then a gain of $50,000 would be realized at time of sale. If accounted for in accordance with substance (selling price of $68,060), then a gain of only $18,060 would be recognized in the year of sale. The remaining $31,940 would be recognized as interest and taken into income over the five-year period of the note.

From the standpoint of the purchaser of the building, if the entire $100,000 is assigned to the cost of the building, then that amount would be subject to depreciation and recognized as an expense over the useful life of the building — perhaps 40 years. If, however, the interest of $31,940 were taken into account, then only $68,060 would be assigned to the cost of the building and expensed as depreciation over its useful life. The interest, $31,940, would be charged as an expense over the five-year period of the note. The manner in which the transaction is accounted for has no effect on *total* earnings of either the purchaser or the seller; it does, however, have a significant impact on the year-to-year timing and classification of such earnings.

Retail Land Sales Companies

The issue of imputed interest is especially important with respect to *retail land sales* companies. Retail land sales companies are those that purchase large tracts of land and subdivide them into small parcels for sale to consumers. Such firms *master-plan* communities; install streets, sewers, and utilities; and sometimes construct *amenities* such as golf courses, club houses, motels, and restaurants. They often engage in extensive promotional efforts (e.g., free dinners or trips to the site) and frequently direct their sales efforts at those who are interested in either a retirement or a vacation home. Retail land sales companies seldom accept interest-free notes. Sometimes, however, they charge relatively low rates of interest. For example, they might charge a purchaser 6 percent interest annually at a time when the *prime rate* (that charged by banks to their most select customers) is 9 percent and the firms' own costs of borrowing are 12 percent.

Until recently, it was standard procedure in the industry to record sales at the face value of the note received. Such practice, however, was criticized on the ground that it overstated sales revenue and understated interest revenue. Since sales revenue is recognized at the time a sales contract is signed and interest revenue is recognized over the term of the note, the effect was to speed up recognition of revenue and, according to critics, to overstate earnings in the year of the sale. Considering that the notes (particularly those of companies in the U.S.) were often for 10 years and that the difference between the rate actually charged and that normally charged for "loans" of a similar type may have been as much as 10 percent, the difference in first-year revenues on a sale of $10,000 could be almost $3,500.

Canadian accounting practice with respect to low interest bearing notes is not entirely clear. Many accountants follow the American position which calls for discounting at the prevailing rate of interest. However, some accountants apparently do not follow such a practice. Thus, from the user's point of view it is necessary to be careful to learn what accounting practice is being employed in preparing financial statements.

EXAMPLE

Eckel Development Corporation sells parcels of land for $10,000. Purchasers must pay $1,000 down and can give a 10-year note, which bears interest at a rate of 4 percent for the balance. The note must be paid in 10 annual installments of $1,110. ($1,110 is the annual payment required to repay a loan of $9,000 in equal installments if interest is charged at a rate of 4 percent per year.)

If the company's customers had attempted to borrow the funds from a traditional lending institution, they would have had to pay the prevailing interest rate of 12 percent.

The present value of the consideration — that is, the "true" selling price of the land — can be determined by discounting *all* required payments (both principal and interest) by the *effective* rate of interest, in this example 12 percent:

Present value of $1,000 down payment	$1,000
Present value of 10 annual payments of $1,110 discounted at a rate of 12 percent: Per Table 4, $1,110 × 5.6502	6,272
	$7,272

As a consequence, the firm would recognize sales revenue of only $7,272. The difference between that amount and $10,000 would be accounted for as interest revenue and reported as such over the 10-year period that the note is outstanding.

Receivables and Revenue in Practice: An Industry Illustration

The relationship between receivables and revenues cannot be overemphasized. The accounting practices of the franchise industry highlight some of the key issues pertaining to the realization of revenue and the valuation of receivables.

Franchisers sell to individual businessmen (franchisees) the right to operate a specific kind of business, to use the name of the franchiser and to provide goods or services associated with the franchiser. Companies such as McDonald's and Holiday Inn are among the best known franchisers, and their establishments appear to have become permanent additions to the North American landscape. But hundreds of other franchise operations, often imitators of the well-known firms, make brief appearances on the North American scene before fading into oblivion and often bankruptcy.

The revenue of a franchiser ordinarily comes from several sources. First, the franchiser sells franchises to the individuals who will operate them. The franchiser receives a small down payment and accepts from the franchisee long-term notes. Second, it generally receives royalties based on the sales volume of the franchisee. Third, it sometimes sells to the franchisee all or a portion of the products that will be sold to the public (e.g., the seasonings for fried chicken).

The source of revenue that presents the most difficult accounting problems is the first — that from the sale of the franchise. Commonly, the franchiser and franchisee will enter into a contractual arrangement many months prior to the time that the franchisee is ready to begin operations. During the intervening period and sometimes for a period subsequent to opening, the franchiser is required to provide services (advertising and management training, for example) to the franchisee. The question arises as to the point at which the revenue from the sale should be recognized and to that at which the related receivable should be recorded as an asset. Consistent with the principle that revenue should be related to productive effort, it could be recognized at the time the contract is signed, when the outlet first commences operations, or in the one or more periods in which various services are performed.

The issue of revenue recognition is compounded, however, by the fact that firms in the industry tend to face a high rate of default on notes received from the franchisees. The collectibility of the notes is directly dependent on the success of the individual franchisees. The franchiser can expect payment only insofar as the operations of a franchisee generate sufficient cash to meet his obligations as they come due.

Because eventual collection of cash cannot always be reasonably assured, it has sometimes been suggested that revenue be recognized only as the notes are actually collected, that is, on the cash collection or installment basis. Such approach would eliminate the possibility that the assets of the franchiser are overstated by the amounts that will prove uncollectible; it would make certain that revenue is not prematurely realized. But it would also be inconsistent with the general accounting practice of recognizing revenue when a transaction is substantially completed (and, as necessary, making appropriate provisions for uncollectible accounts). The installment method of accounting is ordinarily reserved for those exceptional cases where there is no reasonable basis for estimating the degree of collectibility of outstanding receivables.

In the mid-1960s there was an appreciable growth in the franchise industry. Firms followed a variety of different accounting practices, and there were allegations that some firms adopted policies which overstated both earnings and assets. In 1973, to assure greater uniformity of practice, a committee of the American Institute of Certified Public Accountants set forth guidelines for the recognition of revenue.[7] The committee recommended that revenue from the sale of a franchise should be delayed until the franchiser has substantially performed all of the initial services as set forth in the sales agreement. It pointed out that because of a variety of practices in the industry there can be no one specific condition or event that can serve as the sole criterion for recognition of revenue. Substantial performance may occur at different times for different franchisers. Nevertheless, the committee indicated that "conservatism justifies the presumption that commencement of operations by the franchisee is the earliest point at which substantial performance has occurred; recognition of revenue at an earlier point in time carries with it a burden of demonstrating that the presumption has been overcome."

The committee took cognizance of the unusual risks of collection faced by some franchisers. But it recommended that the cash collection basis of revenue recognition be reserved for those exceptional cases where no reasonable basis of estimating the degree of collectibility exists. Instead, it urged that companies establish adequate allowances for uncollectible accounts and periodically review such allowances to make certain that they are sufficient in the light of changed conditions.

Canada (through the CICA) has not issued a pronouncement on the franchise industry. Some Canadian accountants follow the U.S. (AICPA) position.

Payroll Transactions

Although they present few conceptual considerations that have not already been dealt with, payroll expenses and the related payroll liabilities are worthy of discussion because they are of concern to virtually all business and nonprofit organizations and are sometimes of major magnitude.

Accounting for payroll transactions is characterized by the fact that the wage or salary expense pertaining to an individual employee may be considerably greater than that indicated by his wage or salary rate but that the amount actually paid to the employee may be considerably less than that which would be indicated by his rate. The business firm must pay additional payroll charges such as Canada Pension Plan, Workmen's Compensation, and Unemployment Insurance that are levied on the employer and, commonly, must provide for *fringe benefits* in addition to regular wage and salary payments. Moreover, the employer must withhold from each employee's wages and salary the employee's share of income taxes as well as amounts for other designated purposes. Amounts withheld from the employee ordinarily represent a liability of the employer; they must be remitted either to the government or to a specific fund.

EXAMPLE

An employee is paid at the rate of $2,000 per month. From her salary must be withheld (by law, union contract, or otherwise) the following: federal income tax — $350; provincial income tax (applies only in a few Canadian provinces) — nil; unemployment insurance — $20; Canada Pension Plan — $30; health and dental plan — $30; purchase of Canada Savings Bond by employee — $100; contribution to pension plan — $110; disability insurance — $15; and union dues — $20. As a consequence of the deductions *take-home* pay of the employee would be $1,325.

This might be journalized as follows:

(1) Salary expense	$2,000	
Employee income tax deductions payable		$350
Unemployment insurance payable		20
Canada Pension Plan payable		30
Health and dental insurance payable		30
Canada Savings Bond payable		100
Pension plan payable		110
Disability insurance payable		15
Union dues payable		20
Salaries payable, or cash		1,325
To record salary expense for the period.		

Some of the employee deductions noted above may represent only a portion of the cost of the benefit (such as health insurance). The other portion would be paid by the employer. On the assumption that the employer pays an additional sum representing 50% of the total cost (excluding the Canada Savings Bond and union dues deduction), the journal entry would be:

(2) Salary expense	$205	
Unemployment insurance payable		$ 20
Canada Pension Plan payable		30
Health and dental insurance payable		30
Pension plan payable		110
Disability insurance payable		15
To record employer's share of joint costs.		

The $350 represents the sum which employers have to deduct per the Income Tax Act and Regulations.

In addition to the above two journal entries a third would be needed to accrue those costs which are borne entirely by the employer. Two common ones in this category are workmen's compensation insurance and vacation pay, although others such as health, dental and disability insurance could be borne entirely by the employer. Workmen's compensation does not apply to all positions or employment; it is primarily associated with occupations with greater risk of injury to workers (construction, for example) and need for protection by government. Vacation pay is an accrual, needed to cover the outlay which is required when the employee actually takes a vacation. Provincial law stipulates the minimum vacation pay rate; some employers pay more than this.

In the following situation, workmen's compensation is accrued at 2 percent and vacation pay is at 6 percent of gross salary. Based on the $2,000 salary the journal entry would be

(3) Salary expense	$160	
Workmen's compensation provision		$ 40
Provision for vacation pay		120
To recognize costs to be borne entirely by employer.		

Eventually, the Workmen's Compensation Board would assess the company (usually based on a complex formula which recognizes the accident-prone nature of the company's employees and other factors) and seek payment. The journal entry would be:

(4) Workmen's compensation provision	$40	
Cash		$40
To record payment, based on assessment.		

Similarly, when the employee goes on vacation, the entry would be:

(5) Provision for vacation pay	$120	
Salaries payable		$80
Employee income tax deduction payable		25
Other deductions (similar to the first journal entry — (1))		15

Some companies would accrue more than the $120 in the "Provision for vacation pay" account in order to cover the employer's share of costs included in journal entry (2), plus the employer's share of other costs in entry (3), such as workmen's compensation. That is, they would accrue *all* costs of a vacation at the time when the employee is fully working. Other companies do not bother with an accrual if employees are taking vacations at various times during the year, and vacation costs tend to be fairly evenly incurred.

Pension accounting can be more complex than we have described in this section. The subject is covered in greater depth later in the book.

Summary

Three main ideas pervaded the discussion of receivables and payables:

1. Questions of the amounts at which receivables and payables should be stated are directly related to those of when revenues and expenses should be recognized.

If an enterprise grants credit to its customers, it is doubtful that all of its receivables will be transformed into cash. "Losses" on bad debts are an expected deduction from revenues. They should be charged as an expense (or a reduction of sales) in the same accounting period in which the related sales are made. Correspondingly, accounts receivable should be reduced by the amount likely to prove uncollectible.

Similarly, both sales and receivables should be reduced by the amount of expected returns, allowances and discounts of which customers may avail themselves. They should be reduced also by amounts included in the face of the receivable but not yet earned. Notes receivable, for example, often include in the stated value an element of interest to be earned during the period over which the notes will be held — interest not yet earned at the time the note is first received and recorded.

2. The substance of a transaction must take precedence over its form. Accountants must look to the economic rather than the stated values of goods or services exchanged. It is not unusual, for example, for firms to allow customers to delay payments for months or even years and make no explicit charges for interest. Money, however, has a time value, and the right to use funds for an extended period of time is not granted casually. Whenever the sales price of an item is *inflated* by unspecified interest charges, the accountant must impute a fair rate of interest and account for

the revenue from the sale of the item apart from the revenue from the interest.

3. Sensible accounting for receivables and payables is dependent on the good judgment of both managers and accountants. The "correct" value of receivables can never be known with certainty. It is dependent on the number of customers that fail to fulfill their payment obligations, the amount of goods returned, and the amount of cash discounts taken. In determining the amount to report as a receivable as well as the amount of revenue to be considered reálized, such amounts must necessarily be estimated. At best, accounts receivable and the related revenues can never be viewed as being "accurately" presented — only "fairly" presented.

Notes

[1]Quoted in Abraham J. Briloff, *Unaccountable Accounting*. New York: Harper & Row, 1972, p. 128.

[2]*Ibid.*, p. 131.

[3]"When Is a Lemon a Lemon," *Forbes*, Vol. 113, March 15, 1974, p. 63.

[4]*Ibid.*, p. 63.

[5]*Ibid.*, p. 63.

[6]*CICA Handbook*, Section 3020.03.

[7]*Accounting for Franchise Fee Revenue*. American Institute of Certified Public Accountants, 1973.

Questions, Problems, and Cases

Questions

7-1 "At best, accounts receivable and the related revenues can never be viewed as being 'accurately' presented — only 'fairly' presented." Explain.

*7-2 "One of the 'key accounting concepts' is objectivity. Since it is impossible to know in advance which specific account will prove to be uncollectible, no loss should be recognized in the accounts until it is obvious a customer will not pay."

Required:

Do you agree? Explain your position by identifying the key accounting concepts you have used.

7-3 Explain the logic of basing an estimate of uncollectible accounts receivable on:

a. percentage of sales
b. percentage of credit sales
c. percentage of accounts receivable
d. aging analysis of accounts receivable
e. a combination of aging analysis of accounts receivable and percentage of credit sales.

7-4 Differentiate between the net method and the gross method of accounting for cash discounts. Which do you prefer? Why?

7-5 On December 29 a company purchases for $100,000 merchandise intended for resale. The company is granted a 5 percent discount for paying cash within 10 days of purchase. The company records the purchase using the gross method. As of year end the company has not yet paid for the goods purchased but has resold half of them. The company intends to pay within the specified discount period. Assuming that no adjustment to the accounts has been made, in what way is it likely that the financial statements as of year end are misstated? What adjustments, if any, would you make? State any assumptions which you have made.

7-6 A company borrows $1,000 for one year at a rate of interest of 6 percent. The note issued to the lender promises payment of $1,000 plus interest of $60 after one year. Upon borrowing the funds the company recorded a liability for $1,060. Do you agree with such accounting treatment? Explain. How would you record the liability and the subsequent payment of interest?

7-7 A finance company loaned an individual $1,000 on a discount basis. The actual cash given to the borrower was only $940; interest was deducted in advance. At the time of the loan the company recorded its receivable at $1,000, reduced its cash by $940, and recognized revenue of $60. Do you agree with such practice? How would you record the loan? Explain, stating the assumptions which you have made.

7-8 A retail store places the following ad in the paper: "Complete Room of Furniture: $1,000; no money down; take up to 2 years to pay; no interest or finance charges." During a particular month the firm sold 10 sets of the advertised furniture. The company recorded sales of $10,000. If you were the firm's independent auditor, what reservations would you have about the reported sales? What accounting adjustments would you recommend? Explain your position.

7-9 A firm acquires a building at a cost of $200,000 but gives the seller a five-year interest-free note for the entire amount. Assuming that the firm would otherwise have had to borrow the funds at a rate of interest of 10 percent compounded annually, at what amount should the building be recorded? What would be the impact of failing to take into account *imputed* interest on reported earnings of the years during which the note is outstanding as well as on those of the remaining years of the useful life of the building?

7-10 After operating successfully in a single city, the owners of Big Top Ice Cream Parlors Ltd. decide to sell franchises to individual businessmen in other cities. Within one year they sign contracts and receive down payments for 20 franchises. The total sales price of each franchise is $50,000. The required down payment is a small fraction of the total sales price. During the first year only 5 outlets are actually opened. The company reported revenues from sale of franchises of $1 million. Do you agree with this accounting treatment? Explain your position. What would you recommend?

7-11 The supervisor of a large clerical department in a government agency has determined that efficiency in his department seems to drop during the summer months. He determines efficiency by dividing total payroll costs by number of documents processed. Total payroll costs include amounts paid to employees on vacation. The department charges all salaries — both those of workers actually on the job and those on vacation — as an expense in the month paid. Why do you suspect efficiency appears to be low during the summer months? What improvements to the accounting system might you recommend?

7-12 A finance company charges customers 12 percent interest on all balances outstanding. The company continues to accrue interest revenue on outstanding loans (that is, it debits interest receivable and credits interest revenue) even though loan payments might be past due. Only when it writes off a loan does it cease to accrue interest. What "dangers" are suggested by such a practice? Are there any "dangers" in not accruing interest on past due loans?

7-13 Johns Company Ltd. reported accounts receivable of $1 million as of December 31, 19x1. Of that amount $800,000 represents sales of the final 20 days of the year. The company allows its customers to take a cash discount of 4 percent of sales price on all merchandise paid for within 20 days.

The company has consistently accounted for cash discounts by the *gross* method. Annual sales and year-end balances in accounts receivable have remained generally constant over the last several years. Approximately 90 percent of customers take advantage of the cash discount. Comment on whether the firm's sales and accounts receivable are likely to be fairly presented. Indicate the amount of any possible over or understatement.

Problems

P7-1 The Grimm Co. Ltd. purchases all of its merchandise from the Anderson Co. Ltd. Terms of sale are 1/15, n/30. In the month of December the following transactions took place:

12/2 Grimm purchased $80,000 of merchandise on account.
12/10 Grimm remitted payment for the goods purchased.
12/12 Grimm purchased $50,000 of merchandise on account.
12/31 Grimm remitted payment for the goods purchased.

Required:

a. Record the transactions on the books of the Grimm Co. Ltd. using first the net method and then the gross method.
b. Record the transactions on the books of the Anderson Co. Ltd. using first the net method and then the gross method.
c. Comment on the effect of the different methods on year-end financial statements. Assume that all merchandise acquired by Grimm was sold and that all revenue or expense accounts pertaining to discounts were properly closed.

P7-2 The Discount Food Co. Ltd. uses the gross method to record cash discounts for both purchases and sales.

The December 31, 19x8, trial balance of the company contains the following balances:

Inventory, 1/1/19x8	$100,000
Purchases	600,000
Sales discounts	20,000
Accounts receivable	25,000

Purchase discounts	$ 12,000
Sales	875,000
Accounts Payable	50,000

A physical count at year-end indicated inventory on hand, December 31, 19x8, to be $50,000 (at gross prices). Inventory of January 1, 19x8, as recorded in the trial balance, is stated net of cash discounts.

The company takes advantage of all cash discounts granted. It is generally granted a discount of 2 percent on all purchases.

The company allows customers a 3 percent discount for prompt payment. It estimates that discounts will be taken on 80 percent of the accounts receivable outstanding at year-end.

Required:

a. Determine the cost of goods sold for 19x8 and the inventory (stated at an amount that you consider to be most consistent with fair presentation) as of December 31, 19x8. Assume that all goods on hand at the beginning of the year were sold during the year.

b. Determine sales for 19x8 and accounts receivable (also stated at an amount that you consider to be most consistent with fair presentation) as of December 31, 19x8.

P7-3 Compute the opening accounts receivable balance from the following information (state your assumptions):

Accounts receivable — closing	$ 30,000
Cash collection of accounts receivable and receipts credited to unearned revenue	100,000
Unearned (sales) revenue — beginning	8,000
Unearned (sales) revenue — ending	7,835
Allowance for bad debts — beginning	4,000
Allowance for bad debts — ending	4,350
Bad debts expense for year	1,120
Sales revenue	101,000
Cash sales	2,000

P7-4 Wellman Manufacturing Co. has 100 hourly employees, each of whom worked 40 hours in a given week and was paid $6.50 per hour.

Total federal income taxes which the company was required to withhold were $3,900.

The unemployment insurance rate applicable to both employer and employee is 1 percent.

The company is required to pay 2 percent of gross wages into Workmen's Compensation.

The company has a matching pension plan. Employees contribute 5 percent of their wages; the company contributes an equal amount.

The firm is required by union contract to withhold from each employee union dues of $2.50 per week.

Twenty employees have elected to join the Canada Savings Bond program. The cost of a savings bond, $18, is withdrawn from wages each week and used to purchase a Canada Savings Bond.

The company pays medical insurance for each employee. The cost is $8 per week per employee.

Required:

a. Prepare a journal entry to record the weekly payroll.

b. Prepare a journal entry to record disbursement of all required payments to the various government agencies, insurance companies, pension funds, etc.

P7-5 The Schandl Co. Ltd. has an annual payroll of approximately $2,080,000. This amount does *not* include amounts paid to employees while on vacation. The company does not *accrue* vacation pay; it charges it to expense as employees take their vacations. The controller has rejected the suggestions of the company's independent auditor that vacation pay be recognized on a week-by-week basis; the controller claims that such recognition would have no effect on the financial statements; it would only increase clerical costs.

The payroll of the company has remained constant for a number of years. Employees are entitled to three weeks' vacation each year based on work performed in the previous fiscal year, and such vacations must be taken during July and August. Employees receive their regular wages while on vacation, and all employees must be replaced, at the same wage rate, by temporary employees. The company's fiscal year ends June 30.

Required:

a. Is the controller correct in his assertion that accrual of vacation pay would have no impact on the financial statements? Determine the impact of a change in policy on both the income statement and the balance sheet.

b. Suppose the firm were to issue interim financial statements on December 31 for the six months ending on that date. What would be the impact of accruing vacation pay on the income statement and the balance sheet?

P7-6 Transactions involving accounts receivable and related accounts of Williams Department Store for 19x6 and 19x7 can be summarized as follows:

	19x6	*19x7*
Credit sales	$3,000,000	$3,000,000
Cash collection on accounts receivable	2,800,000	3,100,000
Accounts deemed uncollectible and written off	30,000	65,000

The firm estimates that 2 percent of annual credit sales will prove uncollectible.

Included in the $3.1 million of cash collections in 19x7 is $3,000 from customers whose accounts had been written off in 19x6. The balances in the accounts when they were written off totaled $8,000. It is the policy of the company to restore in their entirety accounts previously written off upon collection of a partial payment from a customer since a partial payment is often an indication that payment of the remaining balance will be forthcoming.

Required:

a. Prepare journal entries to record the activity reported above.

b. Compare the impact on reported earnings of credit losses in 19x6 with that of 19x7.

c. Comment briefly on how your answer to Part b would differ if the amount to be added to the allowance for doubtful accounts were based on an aging schedule instead of a flat percentage of sales.

P7-7 The letter of a company president which accompanied the 19x3 financial statements of the Mony Co. Ltd. contained the following:

"*Loss Reserves*

Year	*Amount charged off*	*Recov-eries*	*Net charge-offs as percent of average receivables*	*Reserve at year end*	*Percentage of reserve to notes receivable*
19x3	$16,807,000	$802,000	2.95%	$18,824,000	3.30%
19x2	15,936,000	944,000	2.68	15,501,000	2.69
19x1	15,664,000	870,000	2.80	15,509,000	2.85

Losses from receivables deemed uncollectible or which would require excessive collection expense are charged against reserves created for that purpose. The accompanying table shows reserves together with amounts charged off and the related percentages. The reserve at the end of 19x3 is the highest in the last 10 years." (The company uses the term *reserve* inappropriately to signify its allowance for uncollectibles.)

Required:

a. Determine the bad debt expense in 19x3.

b. Prepare journal entries to record for 19x3 (i) the bad debt expense (ii) the amounts written off, and (iii) the subsequent recovery of amounts written off.

c. Assume the role of a shareholder of the company. How would the information contained in the president's letter affect your decisions?

P7-8 The Melrose Co. Ltd. began operations in January 19x5. The schedule below indicates credit sales and end-of-year balances in accounts receivable for 19x5 through 19x8. The end-of-year balances are broken down by the "age" of the receivables.

		(000 omitted) *End-of-year balance in accounts receivable*				
				Number of days past due		
Year	*Credit sales*	*Total*	*Current*	*1-30*	*31-60*	*Over 60*
19x5	$12,000	$1,080	$ 800	$100	$150	$ 30
19x6	14,000	1,500	1,100	300	50	50
19x7	16,000	1,600	900	400	200	100
19x8	18,000	1,820	1,280	220	200	120

The company estimates that approximately 5 percent of all credit sales will prove to be uncollectible. It has also determined that of its accounts receivable balance at any date the following percentages will likely be uncollectible:

Current	15%
1-30 days past due	40
31-60 days past due	50
Over 60 days past due	60

The balance in the "allowance for uncollectibles" account was zero prior to the adjustment at the end of 19x5. Actual writeoffs of accounts receivable were as follows:

19x5	$260
19x6	580
19x7	815
19x8	893

Required:

a. Determine the bad debt expense for each of the four years assuming first that the company bases its addition to the allowance for uncollectibles on credit sales and alternatively on a schedule of *aged* accounts receivable. (Bear in mind that when the sales method is used the bad debt expense is determined directly. When the aged accounts receivable method is used it is necessary to first determine the required balance in the allowance for uncollectibles account.)

b. Compare total bad debt expense over the combined four-year period under each of the two methods. (They should be the same in this example). Which method results in the more erratic pattern of bad debt expense in this particular example? Why?

c. How would you recommend that Melrose Co. Ltd. calculate its bad debt expense?

P7-9 Division Products Ltd. had gross sales in 19x5 (its first year of operations) of $4 million and in 19x6 of $6 million. As of December 31, 19x5, the company had accounts receivable of $2 million and as of December 31, 19x6, of $3 million. The business of the company is highly seasonal; most of its sales are made in the last three months of the year.

The company follows standard practice in its industry. It permits the retailers with whom it deals to return for full credit any merchandise that they are unable to sell within a reasonable period of time. In January 19x6, the company accepted for return merchandise which it had sold for $400,000 in 19x5. A return rate of 10 percent of sales is typical for the industry. None of the merchandise had yet been paid for by the retailers.

The firm's cost of goods sold is approximately 60 percent of selling price. In financial statements prepared for internal use only (and not in accord with generally accepted accounting principles of reporting to the general public), the firm gives accounting recognition to merchandise returned only when it is actually received; it establishes no year-end allowances.

Required:

a. Determine both for 19x5 and 19x6 the difference in income and assets that would result if the company were to adhere to generally accepted accounting principles and establish an allowance for returned merchandise. Assume first that all goods returned had negligible scrap value, and then, alternatively, that all goods returned could be resold at standard prices.

b. Suppose that the company were in a business, such as toys, in which it is extremely difficult to predict the rate of return from pre-Christmas sales. What warnings would you give to a potential investor or creditor who is likely to rely upon the company's financial statements?

c. How can companies in highly seasonal industries, such as toys, minimize the risk of misestimating sales returns? Why do you suppose that many department stores report on the basis of a fiscal year ending July 31 or January 31?

P7-10 Sunrise Finance Co. Ltd. loaned a customer $10,000 for two years on a discount basis. The customer was to repay $5,000 at the end of each year. The rate of discount (the *effective* rate of interest) was 12 percent.

Required:

a. How much cash would the company actually advance the customer? Prepare a journal entry to record the loan and the receipt by the company of a note for $10,000.

b. How much revenue should the company recognize during the first year of the loan? Prepare a journal entry to record receipt of the first payment of $5,000. At what value will the note be reported (net of discount) after the first year? How much revenue should the company recognize during the second year?

c. Many accountants would argue that a portion of the total revenue to be earned over the two-year period should be recognized at the time the loan is made, without waiting for interest to accrue with the passage of time. What would be the reasoning of these accountants? Would you accept their position? Why?

P7-11 The Allen Co. Ltd. purchased a building from Empire Co. Ltd. The stated selling price of the building was $100,000. Empire Co. Ltd. agreed to accept an interest-free note from Allen Co. Ltd. which was payable in full five years from the date the transaction was closed (i.e., the date the legal title transfers).

The building has an estimated useful life of 20 years and zero salvage value. At time of sale it had been recorded on the books of Empire Co. Ltd. at $40,000. Had Allen Co. Ltd. been required to pay cash for the building it would have had to borrow the funds from a bank at an annual rate of interest of 10 percent.

Required:

a. Prepare a journal entry to record the purchase of the building on the books of Allen Co. Ltd. Be certain that the entry recognizes "substance over form."

b. Prepare any journal entries that would be required after the first year of ownership to recognize both interest expense and depreciation.

c. Determine the difference on Allen Co. Ltd. earnings of the first year that would result from taking into account, as opposed to ignoring, the *imputed interest.*

d. Determine the difference in Empire Co. Ltd. earnings of both the first year and second year that would result from taking into account the *imputed* interest. What would be the total difference in earnings in years 1 through 5? (You should not have to compute earnings in each of the five years to answer this question.)

P7-12 The Davis Land Development Co. Ltd. sells real estate on terms of 10 percent down, the balance to be paid in annual instalments over a three-year period. Customers are not specifically charged interest on their outstanding balances.

During 19x6 the company sold several lots at a stated price of $8,000 each. The original cost to the company of each of the lots was $400. The interest rate on similar "loans" would be 10 percent per year.

Required:

a. How much *income* do you think the company should recognize at time of sale (upon collection of the 10 percent down payment) assuming recognition of all *sales* (but not *interest*) revenue at time of down payment? Prepare a journal entry to record the transaction.

b. How much income should be recognized at the time of each of the three instalment payments? What would be the balance in notes receivable and the related discount account immediately following each payment?

c. How would you disclose the sale of real estate in the 19x6 financial statements of Davis Land Development Co. Ltd.?

Cases

C7-1 Balloon Realty Co. Ltd. ("BRCL" or the Company) is a federally incorporated land development company engaged in virtually all fields of real estate in the United States and Canada. Its shares are widely held and like most real estate companies it is heavily financed by debt.

High inflation, high interest rates, union strikes, and slow processing of development plans by the government have adversely affected the company this year. It had intended to issue additional common shares but its share price has dropped from $12.00 to $7.00 making a share issue unrealistic in the near future. Its earnings this year are extremely low and its cash flows are poor. However it has a good inventory of property most of which was acquired several years ago.

During 19x7, the year just completed, the following major events occurred:

(1) The company sold an office building recorded on its books as land, $2 million; gross fixed assets, $3 million; and accumulated depreciation, $1 million, to Harris Co. Ltd. for $8 million. The terms of the sale were as follows:

a. $500,000 cash upon closing (i.e., transfer of legal title from BRCL to Harris Co. Ltd.)

b. $7,500,000 in the form of a note at 4 percent interest per annum and repayable in 5 equal instalments commencing one year from closing.

c. BRCL was to continue to manage the property for Harris Co. Ltd.

d. Collateral for the note was the office building. Consequently if Harris Co. Ltd. was unable to pay the note, BRCL could recover the building.

(2) The company loaned its officers money at several points throughout the year. At one point the total loan outstanding to officers was $750,000. However at year end no loans were outstanding.

(3) One of BRCL's receivables proved to be uncollectible. On January 1, 19x6, it had sold a piece of property for $1,000,000 of which $250,000 was paid in cash. The remaining $750,000 was to be paid in five annual instalments of $150,000 plus 12 percent interest compounded annually commencing January 1, 19x7. The first payment was not made and it

now appeared unlikely that the purchaser would be in a position to repay the note. Consequently BRCL commenced foreclosure proceedings (i.e., started legal proceedings to recover the property). At the present time the accounting records show a receivable of $840,000 (which includes interest of $90,000 accrued in 19x6. No interest was accrued in 19x7).

Required:

Assume the role of the auditor of BRCL. What accounting treatment of the above events would you recommend? Explain your reasoning.

C7-2 Connone Drum Limited ("CDL" or the company) is a closely held family corporation started by two brothers some years ago. The company primarily manufactures various sizes of drums. However, over the past few years it has gradually been expanding its operations to include the production of other types of containers. The owners, the Leboite brothers, still play an active role in the management of the company.

In order to finance its gradual expansion of operations, CDL borrowed from the bank. The bank loan was secured by the company's inventories and accounts receivable. In addition, the bank required the company to maintain a current ratio position (i.e., current assets to current liabilities) of 1.5 to 1, to keep on deposit $100,000 cash and to have an annual audit.

Mr. T. Ackhurst, the company's controller, was in the process of finalizing the financial statements for the year ending December 31, 19x8. However, he was having difficulty with the following items:

(1) During December, 19x8, a price reduction on a major product line was announced. In response to this announcement the company was swamped with orders. Some very large orders, approximately $500,000 in total sales value, received prior to December 31, 19x8, were not shipped until after CDL's year end because the warehouse staff were too busy filling other orders and taking a physical inventory count. In addition, an order received prior to the year end with a sales value of $400,000 was 80 percent complete by year end; however, because the customer wanted the entire order shipped at the same time, it was held over until January 20, 19x9. Officers of the company want these items included in this year's sales. CDL has an average mark-up of 50 percent on cost.

(2) In order to help a long-time customer, Steadfast Cap Co. Ltd. (SCCL), overcome some liquidity problems, CDL loaned SCCL $300,000 cash and obtained as security 10,000 shares of another company, Cole Aterol Co. Ltd. At the date of the advance, the shares had a market value of $25 per share. The terms of the loan agreement were that if the loan was not repaid by November 30, 19x8, CDL would obtain legal title to shares of Cole Aterol Co. Ltd. SCCL was unable to repay the loan and CDL received legal title to Cole Aterol Co. Ltd.'s shares. At the time of the transfer of legal title the price per share was $20. By December 31, 19x8, the price per share was $18 and on February 16, 19x9 the price per share was $16. The accounts of CDL still show a receivable of $300,000.

(3) At December 31, 19x8, CDL had $50,000 cash on deposit and a term deposit of $75,000 with the bank from which it had the loan and was in an overdraft position of $200,000 with another bank.

Required:

a. Assume the role of the company's auditor. What accounting treatment would you recommend? Why?

b. Assume the role of the controller of the company. What accounting treatment would you recommend? Why? (CICA adapted)

C7-3 Fried Chicken Co. Ltd. after successfully operating a single retail fried chicken outlet for several years, decided in 19x8 to expand its operations. It offered to sell Fried Chicken franchises in several cities for $60,000 each. For that amount, an individual businessman acquired the right to sell under the name "Fried Chicken" and to purchase from the franchiser, chickens, the seasoning for fried chicken and so forth.

The franchisee was required to pay $10,000 upon the opening of his outlet and could pay the balance over the next 10 years. He was to be charged interest at a rate of 10 percent per year on the balance outstanding.

The company estimated that the cost of initial services that it would be required to provide the franchisee prior to the opening of his outlet would be $30,000 for advertising, and business advice.

In 19x8 the company signed sales contracts with 10 franchisees. Of these, six began operations during the year. The company incurred $180,000 in costs in connection with the outlets actually opened and $100,000 in connection with those expected to open in the following year.

In addition, the company had cash sales of merchandise to the outlets of $120,000; the cost of merchandise sold was $80,000.

The company collected $10,000 from each franchisee at the time the outlet began operations. In addition, it collected $10,000 in payments on its notes receivable. It earned and collected $6,000 in interest.

Required:

a. Establish a revenue and expense recognition policy for Fried Chicken Co. Ltd. Explain your position logically.

b. Prepare an income statement for 19x8 to reflect the franchise operations.

c. Assume that the company began the year with $200,000 in cash and shareholders' equity and that all costs were paid in cash. Prepare a balance sheet as of the year end.

d. Draft the notes to the financial statements that you feel are necessary. Explain your reasoning.

8 *Inventories and Cost of Goods Sold*

The term *inventory* refers both to goods that are awaiting sale and to those that are in the various stages of production. It includes the merchandise of a trading concern as well as the finished goods, the work in process, and the raw materials of a manufacturer. In addition, the term embraces goods that will be consumed indirectly as the enterprise manufactures its product or provides its service. Thus, stores of stationery, cleaning supplies, and lubricants would also be categorized as inventories, although some companies may include such items on the balance sheet with prepaid expenses.

Accounting for inventories is critical not only because they often comprise a substantial portion of a firm's assets but also because they relate directly to what is frequently the firm's major expense — the cost of goods sold. The beginning inventory balance plus purchases minus the ending inventory balance equals the cost of goods sold. This chapter will be directed to several key accounting issues pertaining to inventory, some of which are currently at the center of active controversy. Among the questions to be raised are:

What are the objectives of inventory measurement and valuation?
What costs should be included in inventory?
How should inventory quantities be determined?
What assumptions regarding the flow of costs are most appropriate in particular circumstances?
What accounting recognition should be given to changes in the selling or buying market prices of inventories?

Inventories will be discussed in the context of generally accepted accounting principles — how inventories are accounted for in practice. But consideration will also be given to alternatives that have been proposed but which are not presently viewed as acceptable.

It may be worthwhile to review Chapter 5 — especially the Key Concepts and Objectives of Accounting — before proceeding. The cost concept and matching, for example, play major roles in the discussion which follows.

Chapters 6, 7, and 8 cover much of the *working capital* of an enterprise. Working capital is defined as current assets less current liabilities. The flow of working capital in a business is discussed in Chapter 14.

Objectives

The overriding objective of conventional inventory accounting under the stewardship objective is to match the costs of acquiring or producing goods with the revenues that they generate. In a typical operating cycle of a firm, the costs of goods which are either manufactured or purchased are included in inventory and reported as an asset. The costs are not considered expenses; rather they are *stored* on the balance sheet until the goods are sold and the costs can be associated with specific revenues. In the course of a year, a portion of the goods remains on hand; a portion is sold to outsiders. A portion of the costs, therefore, must be assigned to the goods that remain on hand and the rest to the goods that have been sold. That portion of the costs that is assigned to the goods on hand will continue to be carried on the balance sheet, while that assigned to the goods that have been sold will be charged to an expense account, cost of goods sold, and reported on the income statement. The question facing the accountant is, how much of the total costs should be assigned to the goods on hand and how much to the goods that have been sold? Diagramatically the issue can be depicted as shown in Exhibit 8-1.

EXHIBIT 8-1

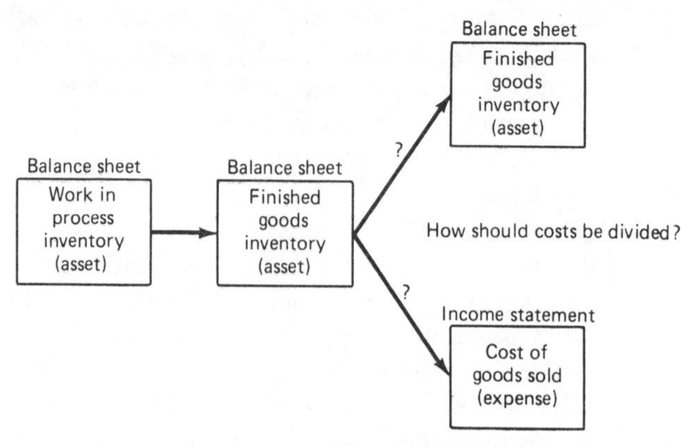

Insofar as a greater value is placed on the goods in inventory, a lesser amount will be charged as an expense. Insofar as a greater amount is charged as a current expense, then smaller amounts will remain on the balance sheet to be charged as expenses in future years.

It is sometimes asserted that another objective of inventory accounting — that is, another objective of accounting — should be to provide investors with information that will enable them to predict the future flows of cash with which inventories are likely to be associated. The arguments in favor of this objective take two forms. First, it is pointed out that inventories on hand will ordinarily be sold within a single operating cycle of the business. The inventories should be valued, it is asserted, in such a way as to provide the best indication of the amount of cash to be obtained by their sale. Logically, proponents of this position contend, inventories should be reported at the amount for which they will eventually be sold (less, of course, any costs that will be incurred to prepare them for sale). That is, selling market prices — specifically, net realizable value — would be used as the basis of valuation.

Unfortunately, the proponents' position that the objective of inventory accounting is to indicate expected cash inflows conflicts with the stewardship objective of accounting — which is still the objective upon which most current accounting practice is based. Supporters of the stewardship objective would contend (1) that there is too much guesswork for their purposes in the use of net realizable value and (2) that under such a measurement all or most revenue would be recognized at the time the goods were purchased (rather than when the goods were sold).

For example, suppose that goods costing $1,000 (in the normal buying market) have a price of $1,325 in the normal selling market. *If* inventory were to be priced at net realizable value, and there were no selling costs, a journal entry would be made shortly after *purchase* of the inventory, as follows:

Inventory	$325	
Revenue — from buying inventory		$325
To record net realizable value of inventory.		

At the date of sale both the inventory and the selling price would be $1,325 and no further profit would result.

Observe that estimated net realizable value provides a sensible basis of valuation for inventories *when* our objective of accounting is to aid in cash flow prediction. A banker, for instance, would be quite interested in net realizable values for inventory because they may indicate whether sufficient cash will exist to repay a bank loan. However, cost seems preferable under a stewardship objective of accounting. Once again, a principal theme reappears — that of different valuations for different objectives, facts, and constraints (in this situation emphasis is placed on different objectives).

Second, it has been observed that inventories on hand will enable the firm to reduce its outlays in future periods to acquire goods that will be sold in such future periods. The amount of the saving will be equal to the amount that would have to be spent to replace the goods that are on hand. It is asserted, therefore, that an objective of inventory accounting should be to indicate to investors the cash outflow that would otherwise be required. The direct implication of this objective is that inventories should be valued at their replacement cost. This form of argument that inventory prices should reflect or predict future cash outflows similarly conflicts with the historical cost (in a sense, stewardship) basis of accounting. It suggests that accounting recognition be given to transactions that are likely to take place in the future as well as to those that have already taken place in the past.

The preceding comments are not intended to suggest that arguments in favor of the alternative objectives of inventory accounting are not without merit. But in evaluating the several choices that are currently available to business enterprises, it is important to appraise them in the context of the historical cost framework of accounting that is "generally accepted" today, so that the student can interpret today's typical financial statements.

In summary, observe that replacement cost for inventory tells us about cash *out*flows (needed to replace what has been sold) and net realizable value tells us about cash *in*flows (what the customer pays). The difference between the two is cash flow "profit" (after deducting "selling" expenses), which, when discounted to the present, helps us to establish the current worth of the business — *if* this is our objective.

Costs Included in Inventory

In current practice, inventories are conventionally stated at historical cost — that of acquisition or production. Cost, as applied to inventories, "means in principle the sum of the applicable expenditures and charges directly or indirectly incurred in bringing an article to its existing condition and location."[1] If goods are purchased from outsiders, then cost would include not only the invoice price but also costs of packaging and transportation. Trade (those given to a special class of customers), cash, or other special discounts or allowances would ordinarily be deducted from the stated price.

As a general rule, all costs that can reasonably be associated with the manufacture or acquisition and with the preparation for sale of goods should be included as part of the cost of such goods. In brief, this is one facet of the *cost concept* which was mentioned in Chapter 5. In determining whether a particular item of cost should be added to the reported value of inventory, the impact of the decision on both the income statement and the balance sheet should be taken into account. Insofar as costs are added to the reported value of goods on hand, they will be charged as expenses (as part of cost of goods sold) in the period in which the merchandise is actually sold. By contrast, if the costs are not assigned to particular items of inventory, then they will be charged as expenses in the periods in which they are incurred, regardless of when the merchandise is sold.

EXAMPLE A company purchased 100 units of product at $20 per unit. It was permitted a trade discount (one granted to all customers in a particular category) of 5 percent but had to pay shipping costs of $300. Cost per unit would be computed as follows:

Base price (100 units @ $20)	$2,000	
Less trade discount (5 percent)	100	$1,900
Plus shipping costs		300
Total cost of 100 units		$2,200
Number of units		÷100 units
Cost per unit		$ 22

If goods are produced by the company itself, the problem of cost determination is considerably more complex. Cost would include charges for labor and materials and any overhead that can be directly associated with the product and may also include those for *overhead* such as rent, maintenance, and utilities that may be common to several products produced in the same plant. To determine the cost of a particular product, a company will have to *allocate* such common charges among the various products. In addition, however, the firm has to decide whether certain costs should be considered *product* costs and thereby added to the carrying value of the goods produced, or *period* costs and thereby charged off as an expense as incurred. The implications of classifying an outlay as a product rather than a period cost were discussed earlier in Appendix 4-C in connection with the discussion of the manufacturing cycle. The entire question of determining the cost of goods manufactured is the focus of a branch of accounting referred to as *cost accounting*.

A Caution

Many *allocations* in accounting are handled on an arbitrary basis. In recent years one writer in particular, Arthur L. Thomas,[2] has analyzed the subject carefully and pointed out serious weaknesses in "allocation," which involves, for example, spreading to each product those costs which are really common to several manufactured products. When reading financial statements we must recognize that allocations (such as with manufacturing overhead, depreciation, etc.) have limitations, and interpret the income or depreciated cost figures with care. Accrual accounting, which includes allocations, definitely has limitations which we must always keep foremost in our minds.

Similarly, we must be alert to the limitations of cash basis accounting, and form versus substance complications. Business people can arrange contracts — such as those calling for franchise fee payments, or for pension payments — to suit their particular needs for cash at particular times. For example, an employer may defer paying pension funds to the administrator of the pension plan until such time as there is an "excess" of cash in the employer company. In order for us to ascertain the effects of postponed cash payments we must employ discounting techniques and determine a present value or present worth. Of course, in order to discount we must choose an interest rate, and it too can be arbitrary — a circle, so to speak.

In essence, we are saying that *many* accounting figures have to be interpreted with care.

Accounting for Quantities on Hand

In Chapter 4 it was pointed out that inventories may be maintained on a perpetual or a periodic basis. A perpetual basis implies that accounting recognition is given to the change in inventories each time a sale is made, supplies are consumed, or raw materials are added to production. When goods are removed from inventory upon a sale, for example, the following journal entry would be made:

Cost of goods sold	xxxx	
Inventory		xxxx

The periodic method, on the other hand, requires that recognition be given to the reduction in inventory resulting from the sale or use of goods only periodically, perhaps once a year. As goods are added to inventory, the inventory account is debited with their cost. As goods are removed however, no entry is made. Throughout the year, therefore, the inventory *account* misstates the cost of the goods actually on hand. At the end of the period, a *physical* count of goods is taken and valued on the basis of acquisition cost, and the inventory account is adjusted to reflect the value of goods actually on hand. If, for example, at year end an inventory account reflects a balance of $10,000 but a physical count reveals inventory on hand of only $500, the following entry would be appropriate (assuming that the difference between the two amounts reflects merchandise sold and not that damaged or pilfered):

Cost of goods sold	$9,500	
Inventory		$9,500
To adjust the year-end inventory account to reflect goods actually on hand.		

(Many firms, as they acquire inventory, debit an account entitled "purchases" rather than the inventory account itself. At year end, they transfer the balance in the purchases account to the inventory account by debiting "inventory" and crediting "purchases.")

Although this text is not primarily directed toward the record-keeping procedures of enterprises, the two alternative methods of accounting for inventories are explained here because they *may* have an impact on the reported value of inventories at year end. The circumstances in which a difference may occur will be identified in the following discussion of the flows of costs.

Exhibit 8-2 summarizes the journal entry differences between the periodic and perpetual methods:

EXHIBIT 8-2

Periodic vs. Perpetual Methods

Transaction	*Periodic Method*			*Perpetual Method*		
(1) Opening inventory balance $10,000	(Journalized the previous period; debit balance in inventory of $10,000.)					
(2) Purchases of $100,000 for cash	Inventory	$100,000		Inventory	$100,000	
	Cash		$100,000	Cash		$100,000
(3) Purchases returned for cash $2,000	Cash	$2,000		Cash	$2,000	
	Inventory		$2,000	Inventory		$2,000
(4) Goods costing $70,000 are sold for $89,995	Accounts receivable	$89,995		Accounts receivable	$89,995	
	Revenue		$89,995	Revenue		$89,995
	No Entry			Cost of goods sold	$70,000	
				Inventory		$70,000
(5) Physical count shows inventory of $36,700 on hand (Per perpetual records, "on hand" balance should be $10,000 + $100,000 − $2,000 − $70,000 or $38,000)	Cost of goods sold	$71,300		Inventory shortage (expense)	$1,300	
	Inventory		$71,300	Inventory		$1,300
(6) Closing entries	Revenue	$89,995		Revenue	$89,995	
	Cost of goods sold		$71,300	Inventory shortage		$ 1,300
	Income summary (to retained earnings)		18,695	Cost of goods sold		70,000
				Income summary (to retained earnings)		18,695

The perpetual method helps achieve the internal control objective or purpose of accounting. It isolates the loss due to spoilage, error, or theft. In contrast, the periodic method is not able to detect an inventory overage or shortage. Observe also that the charge to cost of goods sold occurs only periodically.

Flows of Costs

The critical issue of inventory accounting, that of flows of costs, arises because the acquisition or production costs of goods do not remain constant. As a consequence, it is sometimes necessary to make assumptions as to which goods have been sold and which remain on hand — those with the higher costs or those with the lower. (Recall the example in the first chapter of the text pertaining to the cost of heating oil sold.) In some situations, identification of specific costs with specific goods presents no problem. The goods have sufficiently different characteristics so that they can readily be tagged with specific costs. The costs to retailers of automobiles, appliances, or rare pieces of jewelry, for example, can easily be associated with specific units. Not so, however, with *fungible* (interchangeable) goods such as grains or liquids, purchases of which made at different times are mixed together, or with most small items, such as canned goods or items of clothing for which it is inconvenient to account for each unit independently. Moreover, for reasons to be indicated shortly, accountants sometimes find it desirable to make assumptions regarding the flow of *costs* which are in obvious conflict with known information regarding the flow of *goods*.

Specific Identification

The specific identification inventory method requires the enterprise to keep track of the cost of each individual item bought and sold. Ordinarily a firm would either code the cost directly on the item itself or otherwise tag each item with a control number and maintain a separate record of costs.

EXHIBIT 8-3 **Purchases and Sales of a Particular Item**

Date		*Purchases* *Units*	*Unit cost*	*Total*	*Sales units*	*Balance units*
1/1	(Bal. on hand)	300	$5	$1,500		300
3/2		100	6	600		400
4/20					200	200
5/25		400	8	3,200		600
9/18		200	7	1,400		800
11/8					300	500
	Total	1,000		$6,700	500	

Refer, for example, to the data provided in Exhibit 8-3, which indicates quantities of an item purchased and sold on various dates. Also indicated are the opening balance, the prices at which the various acquisitions were made, and the total cost of each acquisition. Assume that of the 200 items that were sold on 4/20, 100 units were taken from the lot that was on hand on 1/1 and 100 were taken from that purchased on 3/2. Of the 300 items sold on 11/8, 100 were taken from the lot on hand on 1/1 and 200 from that purchased on 5/25. The cost of goods sold would be computed as follows:

Sale of 4/20		
From lot of 1/1	100 @ $5	$ 500
From lot of 3/2	100 @ $6	600
	200	$1,100
Sale of 11/8		
From lot of 1/1	100 @ $5	$ 500
From lot of 5/25	200 @ $8	1,600
	300	$2,100
Cost of goods sold	500	$3,200

Total merchandise costs to be accounted for during the year (initial balance plus purchases) are $6,700. If the cost of goods sold is $3,200, then the balance of the total costs must pertain to the goods still on hand at year end — $6,700 minus $3,200 = $3,500. This amount can be verified by the following tabulation of ending inventory:

From lot of 1/1	100 @ $5	$ 500
From lot of 5/25	200 @ $8	1,600
From lot of 9/18	200 @ $7	1,400
Ending inventory	500	$3,500

The specific identification method is most appropriate for enterprises that sell relatively few items of large unit cost. It becomes burdensome to a firm that sells large quantities of low-cost items. The specific identification method is rational in that it assures that the amounts charged as expenses are the actual costs of the specific goods sold. But at the same time, especially if the goods sold are similar to one another, it permits management the opportunity to manipulate income. If, in the above example, management wanted to report a higher income, it could simply have made certain that the units sold were taken from a lot of lower cost (e.g., the goods sold on 11/8 were taken from the $7 lot of 1/18 rather than from the $8 lot of 5/25).

Auditors express concern when a company uses the specific identification method and sells large quantities of interchangeable items. This especially occurs when replacement prices are changing or are likely to change rapidly. Thus, although the specific identification method looks like an ideal method to achieve a suitable matching of revenue and expenses, in practice, it is not seen much where expensive goods are easily interchangeable. (You will recall the timber example in Chapter 5, page 187.) The auditor tries to persuade the client to adopt a method less subject to manipulation by management.

First In, First Out

Most well-managed businesses attempt to sell goods in the order in which they have been acquired. Exceptions exist, of course. For example, a company which supplies coal to steel mills fills railroad cars from the outside of any huge coal storage piles near the mine. (It is harder, and more expensive to locate the first coal put into the pile, which is somewhere in the middle of the bottom.)

Selling goods in the order in which they were acquired (with exceptions for items such as coal) minimizes losses from spoilage and obsolescence. In the absence of the ability or the willingness to expend the required time and effort to identify the cost of specific units sold, the assumption that goods acquired first are sold first is likely to provide a reasonable approximation of the actual flow of goods. Under the first-in, first-out approach, commonly abbreviated FIFO, the flow of *costs* (that which is of primary concern to the accountant) is presumed to be the same as the usual flow of goods. The FIFO method can readily be demonstrated using the data presented in Exhibit 8-3.

To compute the cost of goods sold, the items sold on 4/20 would be assumed to have come from the lot that was purchased first — that on hand on 1/1. The items sold on 11/8 would be assumed to have come from the balance of the 1/1 lot and the lots of 3/2 and 5/25. Cost of goods sold, therefore, would be $2,900:

Sale of 4/20		
From lot of 1/1	200 @ $5	$1,000
Sale of 11/8		
From lot of 1/1	100 @ $5	$ 500
From lot of 3/2	100 @ $6	600
From lot of 5/25	100 @ $8	800
	300	$1,900
Cost of goods sold	500	$2,900

If 500 units were sold at a cost of $2,900, then still to be accounted for are the remaining 500 units, at a cost of $6,700 minus $2,900 — $3,800. These items — the ones still on hand — would be assumed to be those that were purchased most recently:

From lot of 5/25	300 @ $8	$2,400
From lot of 9/18	200 @ $7	1,400
Ending inventory	500	$3,800

Proponents of the FIFO method point out that not only is the underlying assumption that goods purchased first are sold first in accord with conventional management practice but that the method eliminates the opportunities for income manipulation that are possible if costs are identified with specific units. Regardless of which items are actually sold, for accounting purposes it will be assumed that those purchased first have been sold first. Moreover, FIFO provides a balance sheet value that is comprised of those items purchased last. In most instances the most recent acquisitions are more indicative of current replacement costs than are those purchased earlier. Insofar as current values are of interest to investors and other readers of financial statements, then FIFO provides a more useful balance sheet (but not income statement) valuation than do any of the other original or historic cost-based methods to be discussed.

Weighted Average

The weighted average inventory method assumes that all costs can be aggregated and that the cost to be assigned to any particular unit should be the weighted average of the costs of all the units held during the accounting period. The weighted average method assumes no particular flow of goods. The cost of any unit sold is simply the average of those available for sale — an average that is weighted by the number of units acquired at each particular price.

In the discussion of both the specific identification and FIFO methods no distinction was made between the methods as they would be applied by firms that maintain perpetual inventory records and those which update their records only periodically after taking a physical count of goods on hand. It would make no difference in either cost of goods sold or ending inventory whether the firm followed perpetual or periodic procedures. In applying the weighted average method, however, the results would not be the same. The weighted average cost of goods on hand at the end of the year may differ from those calculated at various times throughout the year. Hence the costs assigned to the various quantities sold would also differ.

To apply the weighted average method on a *periodic* basis, the firm would assign a cost to all goods — both those that were sold and those in inventory at year end — that represents the weighted average of the cost of *all* goods available for sale during the period. The cost of the goods on hand at the beginning of the year as well as those purchased during the year would be considered in the calculation of the average. The weighted average, based on the information in Exhibit 8-3, would be calculated as follows:

Balance 1/1	300 @ $5	$1,500
Lot of 3/2	100 @ $6	600
Lot of 5/25	400 @ $8	3,200
Lot of 9/18	200 @ $7	1,400
	1,000	$6,700

The average cost of goods available for sale would be $\frac{\$6,700}{1,000} = \$6.70.$

Inasmuch as 500 units were sold during the period, the cost of goods sold would be 500 times $6.70 — $3,350. Since, by coincidence, 500 units remain unsold at year end, the closing inventory would also be 500 times $6.70 — $3,350.

The weighted average method can be set forth as representing the physical flow of goods when all goods available for sale are mixed together with one another — as would be the case with liquids or other fungible goods. When applied on a periodic basis, however, such justification becomes tenuous. If goods are purchased subsequent to the last sale of the year, then the cost of those goods will enter into the average cost of the goods sold during the year, even though such goods could not possibly have been sold during the year. Suppose that in the example presented, the firm on 12/1, well after the last sale of the year, acquired 1,000 units at $20 per unit. The 1,000 units at $20 per unit would be included in the computation of the average cost of the units sold, even though it is obvious that none of them were actually sold. The weighted average method, as applied on a periodic basis, owes its popularity to its convenience; insofar as it may result in the inclusion in the cost of goods sold the costs applicable to merchandise purchased after the final sale of the year has been made, it is decidedly lacking in theoretical support.

If the weighted average method were to be applied on a perpetual basis (see Exhibit 8-4), then a new weighted average of the cost of goods available for sale would have to be computed after each purchase at a different price. Such average cost would be assigned to both the goods sold and those that remain in inventory. For example, the average cost of goods available for sale, after the purchase of 3/2, would be calculated as follows:

Cost of goods available for sale on 4/20		
Balance 1/1	300 @ $5	$1,500
Lot of 3/2	100 @ $6	600
	400	$2,100

Average cost of goods available for sale would be $\frac{\$2,100}{400} = \$5.25.$

The cost assigned to the 200 units sold on 4/20 would be 200 times $5.25 — $1,050. That assigned to the 200 units that remain in inventory after the sale of 4/20 would also be $1,050.

The average cost of goods available for the next sale, that of 11/8, would be based on the average cost of goods on hand immediately following the last sale (i.e., 200 units at $5.25 per unit) plus that of the subsequent acquisitions. Thus:

Cost of goods available for sale on 11/8		
Balance 4/20	200 @ $5.25	$1,050
Lot of 5/25	400 @ $8.00	3,200
Lot of 9/18	200 @ $7.00	1,400
	800	$5,650

Average cost of goods available for sale would be $\frac{\$5,650}{800} = \$7.0625.$

EXHIBIT 8-4

Perpetual Inventory Record Weighted Average Method

	Purchases			*Sales*			*Balance*		
Date	*Units*	*Unit cost*	*Total*	*Units*	*Unit cost*	*Total*	*Units*	*Unit cost*	*Total*
1/1							300	$5.00	$1,500.00
3/2	100	$6.00	$ 600				400	5.25	2,100.00
4/20				200	$5.25	$1,050.00	200	5.25	1,050.00
5/25	400	8.00	3,200				600	7.0833	4,250.00
9/18	200	7.00	1,400				800	7.0625	5,650.00
11/8				300	7.0625	2,118.75	500	7.0625	3,531.25

The cost assigned to the 300 units sold on 11/8 would be 300 times $7.0625 — $2,118.75 — and that to the 500 units remaining on hand at year end would be 500 times $7.0625 — $3,531.25 (or $5,650 minus the $2,118.75 assigned to the goods sold). The total cost of goods sold for the year would be the sum of the costs assigned to each of the two lots sold:

Total cost of goods sold during the year	
Goods sold on 4/20	$1,050.00
Goods sold on 11/8	2,118.75
Total	$3,168.75

This compares with $3,350 calculated using the periodic procedures.

Last In, First Out

In recent years the last-in, first-out method has been the focus of accounting controversy pertaining to inventory valuation. As its name implies, the last-in, first-out method (LIFO) assigns to goods sold the costs of those goods that have been purchased last. It assumes that, irrespective of the actual physical flow of goods, the goods sold are those that have been acquired last and the goods that remain on hand are those that have been acquired first. No pretense is made that the flow of costs even approximates the usual flow of goods. (LIFO is sometimes facetiously called FISH; first-in, still here.)

As with the weighted average method, there will be significant differences in the cost of goods sold, as well as in the ending inventory, if a firm follows periodic as opposed to perpetual inventory procedures. If the firm determines ending inventory and cost of goods sold based on a *periodic* (i.e., annual) inventory count, then the cost of the goods sold will be considered to be that of those that were purchased *closest to the year end*. If the firm maintains *perpetual* records, then the cost of the goods sold will be considered to be that of those that were purchased closest to each of the individual sales.

LIFO, assuming periodic procedures, will be illustrated first. As indicated in Exhibit 8-3, the firm sold 500 units during the year. The cost to be assigned to those 500 units will be that of the 500 units purchased most recently, i.e., those purchased on 9/18 and 5/25:

Cost of goods sold		
From lot of 9/18	200 @ $7	$1,400
From lot of 5/25	300 @ $8	2,400
Cost of goods sold	500	$3,800

Since there was a total of 1,000 items available for sale at a total cost of $6,700, the costs that would be assigned to the ending inventory would be $6,700 minus the $3,800 assigned to the goods sold — $2,900. Ending inventory would be composed of the 500 items, including those that were on hand at the beginning of the year, that were purchased first:

Ending inventory		
From lot of 1/1	300 @ $5	$1,500
From lot of 3/2	100 @ $6	600
From lot of 5/25	100 @ $8	800
Ending inventory	500	$2,900

EXHIBIT 8-5

Perpetual Inventory Record
Last In, First Out

	Purchases			*Sales*			*Balance*		
Date	*Units*	*Unit cost*	*Total*	*Units*	*Unit cost*	*Total*	*Units*	*Unit cost*	*Total*
1/1							300	$5.00	$1,500
3/2	100	$6.00	$ 600				300 100	5.00 6.00	1,500 600
4/20				100 100	$6.00 5.00	$ 600 500	200	5.00	1,000
5/25	400	8.00	3,200				400 200	8.00 5.00	3,200 1,000
9/18	200	7.00	1,400				400 200 200	8.00 5.00 7.00	3,200 1,000 1,400
11/8				200 100	7.00 8.00	1,400 800	300 200	8.00 5.00	2,400 1,000

If, on the other hand, a company maintained perpetual inventory records (Exhibit 8-5), then the cost of goods sold would have to be computed after each sale. The sale of 200 items on 4/20 would be assumed to be from the items most recently acquired up to that date — first from the purchases of 3/2 and then, insofar as additional goods are needed, from that of 1/1:

Cost of goods sold on 4/20		
From lot of 3/2	100 @ $6	$600
From lot of 1/1	100 @ $5	500
	200	$1,100

The inventory balance on hand after the sale of 4/20 would be composed of 200 units from the opening balance at $5 per unit.

The sale of the items of 11/8 would be assumed to be from the items most recently acquired up to that time — first from the purchase of 9/18 and then from that of 5/25:

Cost of goods sold on 11/8		
From lot of 9/18	200 @ $7	$1,400
From lot of 5/25	100 @ $8	800
	300	$2,200

The total cost of goods sold for the period would be the sum of those of the two sales:

Total cost of goods sold during the year	
Goods sold on 4/20	$1,100
Goods sold on 11/8	2,200
Total	$3,300

If the total cost of goods sold was $3,300, then ending inventory must be the total cost of goods available for sale, $6,700, minus the cost of the goods sold, $3,300 — $3,400. The ending inventory would be composed of that portion of the lot of 1/1 (200 units) that remained on hand after the sale of 4/20 plus that portion of the lot of 5/25 (300 units) that also remained unsold after the sale of 11/8.

Ending inventory		
From lot of 1/1	200 @ $5	$1,000
From lot of 5/25	300 @ $8	2,400
	500	$3,400

Exhibit 8-6 summarizes the costs of goods sold and the ending inventories under the FIFO, weighted average, and LIFO methods.

EXHIBIT 8-6

Summary of Cost of Goods Sold and Ending Inventory

	Cost of goods sold	*Ending inventory*	*Total costs accounted for*
First in, first out (FIFO)[a]	$2,900.00	$3,800.00	$6,700
Weighted average			
Periodic	3,350.00	3,350.00	6,700
Perpetual	3,168.75	3,531.25	6,700
Last in, first out (LIFO)			
Periodic	3,800.00	2,900.00	6,700
Perpetual	3,300.00	3,400.00	6,700

[a]Cost of goods sold and inventory would be the same regardless of whether inventory records were maintained on a periodic or a perpetual basis.

In practice, the choice of an inventory costing method may be determined after giving consideration to such factors as: replacement cost and selling price changes, speed of inventory turnover, dollars involved, and the materiality of differences among the possible methods.

The Rationale for LIFO

Very few firms sell or use first the goods that they have acquired last. In some situations, a company might indeed store certain commodities in a pile and remove goods as needed from the top of the heap — that portion of total goods which presumably has been added last. Such would be the case in firms maintaining stores of ore or sand. But the use of LIFO is not confined to situations where the physical flow of goods follows a last-in, first-out pattern. It is applied even when there is no question but that the goods acquired first are sold first. The justification for the use of LIFO must be found in reasons other than that it is representative of the physical flow of goods.

The objective of inventory accounting, under the traditional stewardship objective of accounting, it was previously indicated, is to *match* the costs of acquiring or producing goods with the revenues that they generate. The more specific objective of the LIFO method is to match the *current costs* of acquiring or producing the goods with the current revenues from sales. Under LIFO the cost of goods sold is considered to be that of the goods most recently acquired.

Proponents of LIFO point out that a business must maintain a minimum supply of goods on hand. This basic stock of goods is as essential to the firm's continued operations as are its fixed assets, such as machinery and equipment. Under generally accepted accounting principles, accounting recognition is seldom given to increases in the market value of fixed assets. Why, then, should accounting recognition be accorded increases in the market price of inventories? Suppose, for example, that upon forming a business an entrepreneur determines that he must have 100 units of product on hand. He purchases the 100 units at a price of $1,000 each. In the course of his first year in business, he sells the units for $1,200 each. At the end of the year he replenishes his stock by purchasing another 100 units — this time, however, at a cost of $1,200 each. If inventory and cost of goods sold were to be determined on a FIFO basis, then ending inventory would be valued at $1,200 per unit; the cost of goods sold would be $1,000 per unit. The firm would report a profit of $200 per unit — a total of $20,000. Is the firm really $20,000 better off than it was at the beginning of the period?

Since the entrepreneur deemed it necessary to maintain an inventory of 100 units, he would be unable to withdraw any funds from his business without contracting operations. He would be required to use the entire $20,000 gain to replace the goods that he had sold. The $20,000, according to proponents of LIFO, is not a "true" profit; rather it represents an *inventory* profit. The inventory profit indicates nothing more than the difference between the initial cost of acquiring a minimum stock of goods on hand and the current cost of doing so.

Under LIFO, ending inventory would be reported at $1,000 per unit and cost of goods sold at $1,200. Since the items were sold at a price of $1,200 per unit, the firm would report zero profit for the year. Inventory would be valued on the balance sheet at the amount initially invested in the 100 units. The firm would not appear to be $20,000 "better off" when, according to the advocates of LIFO, it is in the identical position at the end of the year that it was at the beginning.

LIFO represents an attempt to reduce distortions in the income statement as a result of changes in the replacement cost of purchased inventory. In a period of stable replacement prices, both inventory and cost of goods sold would be identical under both FIFO and LIFO. In a period of rising prices, LIFO would ordinarily result in a lower reported value for inventory (since goods are being valued at the earliest prices paid) and correspondingly a lower reported income (since the cost of goods sold is being determined on the basis of the most recent purchases — those at the higher prices).

Exhibit 8-7 compares reported cost of goods sold and year-end inventory for a five-year period. It is based on the assumption that at the start of 19x2 a firm had on hand 1,000 units at $100 each. During each of the next five years the firm sold 1,000 units and replaced 1,000 units. The cost of the units purchased increased at a compounded rate of 10 percent per year.

As indicated in Exhibit 8-7, the difference each year in cost of goods sold is equal to the difference between the cost of goods purchased in the previous year and the cost of those purchased in the current year. Under FIFO goods sold in 19x2 are assumed to be purchased in 19x1; under LIFO goods sold in 19x2 are assumed to be purchased in 19x2. Proponents of LIFO argue that because FIFO matches current revenues with the cost of goods acquired in a previous period, it consistently understates the "true" cost of goods sold and as a result overstates income.

The difference in ending inventory is considerably more striking. Under FIFO goods on hand at the end of 19x6 are assumed to have been purchased in 19x6; under LIFO they are assumed to be purchased in 19x1 (each year's sales were assumed to have been taken from the current year's purchases; the stock on hand at the start of 19x2 is assumed to never have been depleted). The difference in ending inventory at the end of 19x6 ($61,050) is the equivalent of the cumulative difference in cost of goods sold for the five-year period ($671,560 versus $610,510).

EXHIBIT 8-7

Five-Year Comparison Between FIFO and LIFO

Table 1: *FIFO*

	Cost of goods purchased	*Cost of goods sold*		*FIFO Ending inventory*	
	Per unit	*Per unit*	*Total (1,000 units)*	*Per unit*	*Total (1,000 units)*
19x2	$110.00	$100.00	$100,000	$110.00	$110,000
19x3	121.00	110.00	110,000	121.00	121,000
19x4	133.10	121.00	121,000	133.10	133,100
19x5	146.41	133.10	133,100	146.41	146,410
19x6	161.05	146.41	146,410	161.05	161,050
Total			$610,510		

Table 2: *LIFO*

	Cost of goods purchased	*Cost of goods sold*		*LIFO ending inventory*	
	Per unit	*Per unit*	*Total (1,000 units)*	*Per unit*	*Total (1,000 units)*
19x2	$110.00	$110.00	$110,000	$100	$100,000
19x3	121.00	121.00	121,000	100	100,000
19x4	133.10	133.10	133,100	100	100,000
19x5	146.41	146.41	146,410	100	100,000
19x6	161.05	161.05	161,050	100	100,000
Total			$671,560		

Table 3: Differences Between *FIFO* and *LIFO*
(Table 1 minus Table 2)

	Cost of goods sold		*Ending inventory*	
	Per unit	*Total (1,000 units)*	*Per unit*	*Total (1,000 units)*
19x2	$10.00	$10,000	$10.00	$10,000
19x3	11.00	11,000	21.00	21,000
19x4	12.10	12,100	33.10	33,100
19x5	13.31	13,310	46.41	46,410
19x6	14.64	14,640	61.05	61,050
Total	$61.05	$61,050		

LIFO — Some Reservations

The effects of LIFO on both the balance sheet and the income statement are, according to some accountants, untenable. LIFO results in a reported inventory that is continually out of date. If the firm never dips into its base stock (for example, in Exhibit 8-7 it never reduced its inventory below 1,000 units), then the reported inventory figure on the balance sheet would be reflective of prices that existed at the time LIFO was first adopted, decades earlier perhaps. The balance sheet, as continually emphasized in this text, is not, under the traditional stewardship objective, purported to be representative of current values. Nevertheless, some accountants feel uncomfortable when values that are hopelessly out of date are assigned to the balance sheet.

More serious, however, is the impact of LIFO on reported income when the firm is required to dip into its base stock. If the firm is required to sell goods that are valued on the balance sheet at decades-old prices, then the cost of goods sold will be based on the same ancient prices. Refer back to Exhibit 8-7. Suppose that in 19x6 the firm was unable to purchase its required 1,000 units. Instead, it sold its goods on hand and thereby reduced its end-of-year inventory to zero. The cost of goods sold would be $100 per unit — the price of the goods on hand when the company first adopted LIFO in 19x2. This is at a time when the current replacement cost of the goods is $146.41 per unit. If the cost of goods sold is misleadingly low, then reported income would, of course, be correspondingly high. Whatever its advantages when the firm is able to meet current sales out of current purchases, LIFO might produce results that are absurd when it becomes necessary to reduce inventory below a level that is historically normal. Many accountants who are opposed to LIFO recognize the need to account for rapid increases in the replacement cost of inventories. They believe, however, that there are ways of doing so that eliminate some of the distortions of LIFO. The issue of accounting for changes in replacement cost (of individual commodities) or accounting for *inflation* (the *average* price change for *all* goods and services in the economy) will be addressed in Chapter 16.

Canadian Practice

GAAP in Canada requires companies to disclose the inventory costing method(s) which they use. This might aid some users in sorting out the effects of different costing methods.

Two hundred and twenty companies' financial statements were analyzed and the results were reported in *Financial Reporting in Canada* (12th edition).[3] The survey showed the following inventory costing methods for 1976:

First-in, first-out (FIFO)	99
Average cost	63
Last-in, first-out (LIFO)	13
Retail method (to be discussed later in Chapter 8)	12
Various other methods	33
	220

Seven of the thirteen companies reporting the use of LIFO in fact applied it in U.S. company situations only.

Few Canadian companies use LIFO because it cannot be applied in the computation of income taxes. In the U.S. it can be used. As a result companies are reluctant (because of the extra accounting cost that would be incurred) to keep two sets of inventory costing records — one for the income tax objective of accounting and the other for the stewardship objective.

The "easiest" approach according to the above figures seems to be to choose FIFO.

Comparability

In previous chapters we mentioned the problems which readers of financial statements have in comparing the results and position of two or more companies. We stated that the ideal accounting would be to have "like accounting under like objectives-facts-constraints." The foregoing discussion and survey indicates that companies have considerable freedom in choosing inventory costing methods. There was little indication in the foregoing "debate" between advocates of the different methods that, for example, FIFO should be used under one set of facts and weighted average would be utilized under another set of facts.

Is there an important message to be extracted from this lengthy discussion of inventory methods? A fairly obvious one suggests that financial comparability among companies probably is not being attained and readers have to be careful which conclusions they draw about the relative success of companies. For example, which *one* of the three companies (A, B, and C) shown below, all of which have *identical* transactions, is the *most* successful?

	Company A	*Company B*	*Company C*
Revenue	$ 11	$ 11	$ 11
Cost of goods sold	7	8	9
Gross profit	4	3	2
Expenses	1	1	1
Net income	$3	$2	$1

The answer is that they are *equally* successful if they have identical transactions. The differences in net income are caused by the use of different inventory costing methods. Suppose, for example, that there was no opening inventory and *each* company purchased three items of inventory: the first item at $7; the second at $8; and the third at $9. Company A could be using FIFO, Company B using weighted average, and Company C using LIFO.

Although the illustration is simple and the message seemingly clear, it is amazing how few students retain this thought; instead they proceed to other courses and use accounting figures as though they are beyond dispute.

A second message suggests that the stock market (that is, investors as a whole trading in that market) may be able to see through inventory accounting methods and adjust for differences among companies. We alluded to this concept briefly in Chapter 2. Various studies have been conducted into what is called the "efficiency" of investors as a whole in incorporating accounting *information* (as provided in portions of a firm's financial statements) into share prices. These studies have mainly been conducted on companies listed on the large stock exchanges (such as the New York Stock Exchange). They show that investors are often able to separate information from noninformation in the case of inventories. Given that companies disclose their method(s) of costing inventories and goods sold, investors can be fairly capable of recognizing the magnitude of net income differences caused by different inventory costing methods. They are not tricked into using "noninformation" — data that gives a false picture of a business. When information is not available in the accounting statements investors attempt to guess at effects on the basis of their knowledge of the company and its industry. Often the desired information is available in part from a variety of sources other than accounting reports (industry output and sales statistics, for example). During a period of rising replacement costs, for instance, investors may be unhappy with the income results which occur from using FIFO. Investors may mentally revise the company's income downward to reflect *replacement* cost of goods sold, which is higher than FIFO.

Are Canadian investors as competent as those who trade on the New York Stock Exchange? This is a difficult question and we cannot respond to it in a precise fashion. One suspects that for large companies listed on the Toronto Stock Exchange (TSE) their investors are probably capable of adjusting for material inventory costing differences. This does not mean that all investors who trade on the TSE are equally capable; there will be some big winners and losers. In an important sense it is the combined information of many investors which leads to a good estimate of the net income effect of inventory costing differences. In contrast, when one "investor," such as a banker, is dealing with the owners of two different, small businesses it would be less likely that the banker could adjust net income for inventory costing differences between the two companies. One would hope that the banker would ask the so-called "right" questions of each owner so that the figures could be adjusted to suit the banker's needs. But, we will leave this for you to discover in your future dealings with bankers and other investors.

From time to time students have interviewed Canadian bankers in order to evaluate the bankers' understanding of financial statements and have typically found that some of them understand well and others understand poorly. The banks recognize this by limiting the lending powers of those who cannot grasp the strengths and weaknesses of financial statements. The manager of a small branch in a shopping center is likely to have authority to grant only small loans. Requests for larger loans would be sent to head office or a regional head office.

Retail Inventory Method

Many large department stores find it inconvenient to maintain records of the cost of all merchandise on hand. Instead, as each unit is received it is tagged with the price at which it will be sold. Periodically, store clerks take a physical count of goods on hand. They record the quantity of each item on hand as well as its selling price. As a consequence, the physical count and subsequent summary results in a determination of the inventory on hand valued at expected retail prices. Since ending inventory is conventionally reported and the cost of goods sold is determined on the basis of acquisition cost, not expected selling prices, it is necessary to *estimate* the costs of the goods which are on hand and those which have been sold.

Insofar as a store has kept accurate records of all purchases, it can use the relationship between purchase prices and selling prices as its means of estimation. Assume that the firm's records provide information as to the merchandise on hand at the beginning of the period, overall quantities purchased and the amounts at which they will be sold, ending inventory at retail prices, and sales for the year (which, of course, are based on retail prices). Ending inventory, at cost, can be estimated as follows:

Estimate of Ending Inventory (at cost)

	Cost	*Retail price*	*Cost as a percentage of retail price*
Merchandise on hand 1/1	$100,000	$150,000	
Purchases during year	500,000	800,000	
Goods available for sale	600,000	950,000	63.15%
Sales during year		700,000	
Merchandise on hand 12/31 @ retail price		$250,000	

If merchandise on hand at year end is $250,000 and the cost of the goods available for sale is approximately 63.15 percent of retail price, then ending inventory at cost can readily be determined:

Merchandise on hand, 12/31 at retail prices	$250,000
Cost as a percentage of retail price	× .6315
Merchandise on hand, 12/31 at cost	$157,875

If $600,000 of goods (at cost) were available for sale during the year, of which $157,875 are still on hand, then the cost of goods sold for the period must be:

Goods available for sale	$600,000
Merchandise on hand, 12/31 (at cost)	157,875
Cost of goods sold	$442,125

The retail inventory method provides an approximation of the weighted average method. Goods on hand at the beginning of the period and those purchased during the period are, for cost purposes, mixed together in a common pool. In determining which goods have been sold and which remain on hand at year end, no distinction is made between goods acquired first and those acquired last. Because the retail method assumes that the ratio between cost and selling price of all goods in the pool is identical, unusually large markups and markdowns on a few selected items may not be properly reflected. As with many accounting procedures based on averages, it sacrifices a measure of accuracy for convenience.

The retail method should not be used on too broad a basis, such as storewide for all departments added together. In some departments "cost as a percentage of retail price" may be around 85 percent (say food) whereas in others (such as jewelry) the percentage may be 50 percent. Unless separate computations are made for each department, some strange results could occur.

The retail method, when arranged well by department or better still by type of product sold, can aid in the *internal control* objective of accounting. In a sense the retail method maintains a perpetual balance at retail price, especially when the cash register is tied into a computer which keeps track of inventory quantities. Hence, at the time of a physical count it may be possible to ascertain how successful the shoplifters have been. Then, if losses are major, corrective action can be taken.

Lower of Cost or Market Rule

Regardless of which of the previously described inventory methods a firm adopts, the application of generally accepted accounting principles requires a departure from cost whenever the utility of the goods on hand has diminished since the date of acquisition. Loss of utility might be the result of physical damage or deterioration, obsolescence, or a general decline in the level of prices. Loss of utility should be given accounting recognition by stating the inventories at *cost or market, whichever is lower*. As used in the expression cost or market, *market* could refer to replacement cost (buying market price), to net realizable value (selling market price), or to some variation of these.

The *CICA Handbook* asks for clarification of the meaning of "market" when it is used in the expression "lower of cost or market," but does not recommend a particular basis. *Financial Reporting in Canada*[4] indicates that for 1976 most companies preferred to use "net realizable value":

Net realizable value, and variations thereof	254
Replacement cost	83
Lower of replacement cost and net realizable value	11
Net realizable value less normal profit margin	9
Other	13
Total number of companies	270

The lower of cost or market rule is grounded in the concept of *conservatism*, which holds that firms should give recognition to losses (but not to gains) as soon as they are reasonably foreseeable. As such it tends to be anchored to the stewardship objective of accounting, and may be rooted in part in the psychology of the Depression in the 1930s.

Suppose that a jewelry merchant purchases a lot of 100 digital watches for $100 each, with the intention of selling them at a price of $125. Prior to sale, however, as a result of manufacturing efficiencies, the wholesale price of the watches drops to $70 and the corresponding retail price to $95. Application of the lower of cost or market rule would require that the stated value of the watches on hand be reduced from original cost of $100 to the current market (in this case let us say net realizable value) price of $95. The following journal entry would be appropriate to record the decline in price:

Loss on inventory (expense)	$500	
Inventory (asset)		$500
To record a loss on 100 digital watches from cost of $100 to net realizable value of $95.		

The lower of cost or market rule may be applied to inventories, just as it can to marketable securities, on an individual (item-by-item) or a group basis. If applied on an individual basis, then the cost of each item in stock is compared with its net realizable value (NRV). If NRV of an item is lower than its original cost, then the item is written down to NRV. If applied on a group basis, then the original cost of the inventory pool (which may be either the entire inventory or a collection of similar items) is compared with its market value, and a reduction in book value is required only if total market value is less than total initial cost. The group basis is likely to result in a considerably higher inventory valuation than the individual basis since it permits the increases in the market prices of some items to offset the decreases in others.

The lower of cost or market rule can also be applied in situations where market is defined as replacement cost. This considerably complicates situations. Such complexities are dealt with in more advanced courses.

An Alternative: Use of Current Values

Numerous accounting theoreticians have proposed that inventories be stated at their *current* values. In this way, they suggest, many of the deficiencies of each of the alternative assumptions regarding flow of costs, as well as the complications of the lower of cost or market rule, can be overcome. Their suggestions are worth attention, not so much because they are likely to be accepted in the foreseeable future — although there is unquestionably a trend in the direction of current value accounting — but rather because they provide an insight into the components of gains or losses attributable to the sale of goods that had been included in inventory.

We must recognize in discussions such as these that proponents of alternative methods will suggest new approaches because (1) they wish to pursue a different objective of accounting than stewardship; or (2) they are thinking of different facts than those on which the method in dispute is based. In short, we are back to our theme of different approaches for different objectives-facts-constraints.

Assume that on September 1, 19x6 a merchant purchases 30 cans of tennis balls at $2.00 per can. In the remainder of 19x6 he sells 20 cans at $3.00 per can, at a time when the replacement cost is $2.50 per can.

On December 31, 19x6, he purchases an additional 20 cans of balls, but now at a higher price, $2.50 per can. As a consequence, he raises the retail price on tennis balls — including that on the 10 cans that were purchased at the lower price — to $3.50 per can. When in 19x7 he sells the 10 cans that were purchased first (assuming a FIFO flow of costs) he will record a gain of $1.50 per can. The $1.50 is composed of two types of gains — a *holding* gain of $.50 and a *trading* gain of $1.00.

The trading gain arises out of the normal business activities of the firm. It represents a return to the merchant for providing the usual services of a retailer — providing customers with the desired quantity of goods at a convenient time and place. The holding gain, on the other hand, can be attributable to the increase in prices between the times the merchant purchased and sold the goods. The magnitude of the holding gain depends on the quantity of goods held in inventory and the size of the price increase. Most merchants are required to maintain a stock of goods adequate to service the needs of their customers — that is, to make certain that they have a sufficient number of goods on hand to minimize the risk of stockouts and to provide customers with an ample choice of styles, sizes, and colors. Some merchants, however, intentionally maintain an inventory greater than that necessary to meet their operating needs. Hoping to take advantage of increases in price, they employ inventory as a means of speculation. Speculative holding gains (and of course losses) are especially common in those industries which deal in commodities — e.g., grains, cocoa, and metals — that are subject to frequent and substantial fluctuations in prices.

Were inventories to be stated at their current values, it would be relatively easy to distinguish — and report separately — the holding gains from the trading gains. And more significantly, the holding gains could be identified with the accounting period in which the increase in prices actually took place, rather than delayed until the period of sale.

The following journal entry would be appropriate to recognize the holding gain of $.50 each on 10 cans of tennis balls that took place between date of purchase and year end:

Inventory	$5	
Holding gains on inventory		$5
To record holding gain on 10 cans of tennis balls that remained on hand at year end.		

When the 10 cans were sold in the following year, the cost of goods sold would be charged, and inventories credited for their adjusted carrying value of $2.50 per can:

Cost of goods sold	$25	
Inventory		$25
To record the cost of goods sold.		

In addition to the treatment of the 10 cans, we have a "holding gain" so to speak on the 20 cans sold in 19x6 when replacement cost was $2.50 per can. The journal entry in 19x6 which recognizes the "holding gain" would be:

Inventory	$10	
Holding gains on inventory		$10
To record holding gain of 50 cents per can on 20 cans sold in 19x6.		

When the 20 cans were sold, the entries (assuming the perpetual method) would be:

Cash	$60	
Revenue		$60
To record the sale of 20 cans @ $3 each.		
Cost of goods sold	$50	
Inventory		$50
To record the sale of 20 cans now carried in inventory @ replacement cost of $2.50 each.		

The $10 difference between revenue of $60 and cost of goods sold of $50 is the trading gain on the 20 cans sold in 19x6. [($3.00 – $2.50) × 20 cans.]

On which financial statement should the credit "holding gains on inventory" be shown? This difficult question is discussed in Chapter 16, but some brief comments are necessary at this point.

The location of the credit (balance sheet-equity capital versus income statement) gets us embroiled in the *capital maintenance* issues mentioned briefly in previous chapters. If we wish to "maintain" only our original capital, and to measure success in terms of original capital, then the credit goes to the income statement. That is, we say that we make a profit whenever we sell for sums in excess of original cost. In contrast, if we wish to measure success in terms of our replacement capital the credit goes to a special section of owner's equity — other than retained earnings.

Our wishes in turn must tie into our intentions for the business. If we wish to stay in business indefinitely, we must preserve our *replacement capital maintenance*. You may recall the question of whether we made a profit when we sold our house. If it cost us $40,000 five years ago and we sell it for $75,000 today, did we make a profit? If we have to buy a similar house to live in which costs us $75,000, most people would say that there was no profit. We simply traded residences — and we will need a residence, forever, so to speak. Our capital maintenance concept in this case is *physical replacement* of a house, which at the moment translates to $75,000 of "replacement capital maintenance".

However, if the house were an "extra" which we bought for speculative or investment purposes (and we lived elsewhere) we *could* say that we made a profit of $35,000 ($75,000 − $40,000). That is, we have assumed that our capital maintenance concept is original cost of $40,000. Anything received in excess of $40,000 could be called profit. The traditional stewardship basis of accounting employs original cost capital maintenance.

Again we see that there is no one "true" profit concept. The different objectives and sets of facts lead to different, suitable approaches.

If we adopt the original cost capital maintenance approach, comparative income statements which give recognition to the sale in 19x6 of 20 cans of tennis balls at $3.00 per can and the sale in 19x7 of 10 cans at $3.50 per can would appear as follows:

	19x6	*19x7*
Sales	$60.00	$35.00
Holding gains (in total, 30 cans @ 50¢ each)	15.00	—
	75.00	
Cost of goods sold:		
20 cans @ $2.50 each	50.00	
10 cans @ $2.50 each		25.00
Income	$25.00	$10.00

However, if we adopt the replacement capital maintenance approach the "holding gains" would not be in income and the net income for 19x6 would be $10 ($60 − $50). Income in 19x7 would remain the same at $10, for a two year total of $20. Where does the "missing" $15 go? It would appear on the balance sheet in the owner's equity section, and be called something such as "capital maintenance adjustment." The "adjustment" and original capital would total "replacement capital" — the sum needed to ensure that the company can remain in business when replacement prices are rising.

In the merchant's case his replacement capital maintenance balance sheet at the end of 19x6 would appear as follows (assuming that he commenced the business with $60 cash, just sufficient to buy 30 cans @ $2 each):

Cash	$ 60	Accounts payable (second purchase)	$ 50
Inventory:		Owner's equity:	
10 @ $2.50 (first purchase)	25	Original capital	60
20 @ $2.50 (second purchase)	50	Capital maintenance adjustment	15
		Retained earnings	10
	$135		$135

The total of "original capital" and "capital maintenance adjustment" is $75. *This represents 30 cans at the current replacement cost of $2.50 each.* We have thus preserved replacement capital (by not showing the $15 as retained earnings, from which dividends may be declared) and have not fooled our financial statement readers into thinking that the only profit in 19x6 was $25.

A balance sheet could be prepared at the end of 19x7 based on the same approach. It would show the same replacement capital maintenance because replacement cost is still $2.50 each.

Which is the "true" profit in 19x6 — $25 or $10? It depends on our personal beliefs and intentions. For example, was the house which you just sold an extra or the one in which you were living? Where are you going to live now? If you need accommodation you ought to think in terms of replacement cost capital maintenance.

Although we have employed replacement cost in illustrating "holding gains" — which are not really gains when we view them in terms of replacement capital maintenance — we could have used other measures. Net realizable value could have been used. Also, we could have used a different capital maintenance concept. Chapter 16 looks at these issues.

Summary

In this chapter we have dealt primarily with accounting issues pertaining to inventory within the traditional historical cost framework. Because of the overriding importance of inventories to most manufacturing and retail companies, selection of accounting alternatives may have a critical impact on both reported assets and earnings.

The primary objective of conventional stewardship accounting is to match the costs of acquiring or producing goods with the revenues that they generate. To realize such objective it is necessary to make assumptions as to the flow of costs — whether the cost of goods acquired first, or last, for example, should be associated with the revenues of a particular period. Powerful arguments can be advanced in favor of or against each of the assumptions, and choice of assumption may have a significant effect on reported cost of goods sold as well as ending inventories.

Regardless of assumption, however, inventories should be restated at the lower of cost or market to reflect declines in their replacement cost, or net realizable value. Although some accountants have suggested that accounting recognition be given to increases in market prices as well as to decreases, current practice favors conservatism over consistency, and gains from holding inventories are considered to be realized only at the time they are sold.

This chapter also expands on how one uses accounting, and how one avoids misinterpreting accounting results. This is a theme that we will continually return to. Although our desire is to find a world where there is "like accounting for like objectives-facts-constraints," we must recognize that there is still a long way to go to achieve this. Hence, we must know about current practice and avoid falling into traps when we read current financial statements.

Notes

[1]*Accounting Research Bulletin No.43.* Committee on Accounting Procedure, American Institute of Certified Public Accountants, 1961.

[2]See for example *The Allocation Problem in Financial Accounting Theory.* (Evanston: American Accounting Association, 1969), and *The Allocation Problem: Part Two.* (Sarasota, Florida: American Accounting Association, 1974). See also Leonard G. Eckel, "Can financial accounting allocations be justified?" *CA magazine* (May 1976), pp. 49 – 53.

[3]Published by the Canadian Institute for Chartered Accountants (CICA) in 1977.

[4]CICA, *Financial Reporting in Canada.* 12th ed. (Toronto: CICA, 1977).

Questions, Problems, and Cases

Questions

8-1 "Inventory measurement and valuation are dependent upon the objective of financial accounting." Explain.

8-2 "In determining the unit cost of inventory for a manufacturing company two problems plague the accountant more than any others. They are (a) distinguishing between product and period costs and (b) the allocation of common product costs." Explain.

8-3 Distinguish between the perpetual and periodic method of maintaining inventory records. Which would you recommend? Why?

8-4 "The reader of the financial statements does not care which inventory costing method (i.e., FIFO, LIFO, or weighted average) a company selects since the same total acquisition costs are incurred regardless of the method used." Comment on this quotation with particular reference to the information needs of statement readers external to the company and the decisions they are likely to make.

8-5 "Accountants make assumptions regarding the flow of goods only because it is costly and inconvenient to keep records of specific items actually sold. The specific identification method is theoretically superior to any of the other methods and eliminates the possibilities of income manipulation associated with them." Do you agree? Comment.

8-6 Very few businesses sell or use first the goods that have been received most recently. How, then, can the use of LIFO be explained? Outline the conditions where you would recommend the use of the LIFO cost method of valuing inventory for a company. Provide an example of a situation in which a company does sell or use first the goods acquired last.

8-7 National Steel Ltd. and Great Supermarkets Ltd. each have annual sales of approximately $10 million and earnings of $300,000. National Steel maintains an inventory equal in value to about 5 percent of cost of goods sold, and Great Supermarkets, about 0.5 percent. In other words, the inventory of National Steel *turns over* approximately 20 times per year, and that of Great Supermarkets, about 200 times a year. For which of the two firms would a shift from FIFO to LIFO have the greater impact on earnings? Explain, stating your assumptions clearly.

8-8 It is sometimes argued that LIFO provides a more meaningful income statement, albeit not necessarily a more meaningful balance sheet. Why does LIFO provide a more meaningful income statement? Does it always? Provide an example of a situation in which it may seriously distort income.

8-9 A businessman made the following statement: "We bought these goods last year before prices went up. This gives us a competitive edge, and we can continue selling these goods at our old prices until we have to start dipping into the stocks we bought this year. Our competitors are on LIFO and can't do that."

Required:

Evaluate this statement. Does the method of inventory costing affect the firm's ability to compete? Does the method of inventory costing affect the firm's ability to attract investors?

8-10 What is meant by the term "market", as it is used in the expression "cost or market, whichever is lower"? The lower of cost or market rule is often cited as an example of the possible conflict between conservatism and consistency. Why? Over a period of several years, is the lower of cost or market rule likely to decrease the overall income of a firm? Explain.

8-11 Outline the conditions under which you would recommend the use of the "lower of FIFO cost or market" as the inventory valuation method for a company. Explain thoroughly.

*8-12 Explain what is meant by "stock market efficiency." What implications does it have for financial reporting in Canada?

8-13 What are the advantages for a large department store of using the retail method of inventory valuation? Under what conditions would this method yield poor results?

8-14 Explain the term "capital maintenance." What impact does the capital maintenance concept have on the determination of income? Give an example to illustrate your response.

8-15 How is capital maintenance measured under traditional stewardship accounting? Explain how different objectives of accounting might be better satisfied by using different measures of capital maintenance.

8-16 Distinguish between a holding gain and a trading gain. Give an example to illustrate your response. How might separate disclosure of these two types of gains assist the users of financial statements?

Problems

P8-1 The ABC Co. ordered 1,000 units of product at $6 per unit. It received an invoice from its supplier for $5,343 determined as follows:

1,000 units @ $6	$6,000	
Less: Trade discount — 20 percent	1,200	$4,800
Plus: Taxes and import duty		543
Amount to be paid		$5,343

In addition, the company received a separate invoice from a freight company for shipping charges of $357 for transporting the goods to ABC's plant and $50 for transporting 200 units to ABC's customer.

Required:

Prepare a journal entry to record the *costs* applicable to a sale of 200 units.

P8-2 As of January 1, 19x1 R. Bell Ltd. had 700 units of product on hand. The stated value was $1,400. During the year the firm had two sales — the first on January 17 of 700 units, and the second on November 11 of 600 units. On March 8 the firm received a shipment of 1,600 units at a cost of $4,800. Assume that the purchases were for cash.

Required:

Prepare those journal entries which would affect inventory assuming that the firm uses

a. Periodic inventory procedures:
   (i) FIFO.
   (ii) LIFO.
b. Perpetual inventory procedures:
   (i) FIFO.
   (ii) LIFO.
c. Compare the total cost of goods sold and the ending inventory under each of the alternatives.

P8-3 During 19x7, C. Trunkfield Ltd. engaged in the following purchases and sales of an item:

	Purchases		Sales
	No. units	Cost per unit	No. units
Jan. 1 (bal.)	400	$5.00	
Feb. 11			150
May 6	200	5.10	
Sept. 8			220
Sept. 30	300	5.20	
Oct. 17			310
Nov. 26	100	5.25	
Dec. 16			50
	1,000		730

Required:
Determine December 31 inventory and cost of goods sold for 19x7 assuming first that the company maintains its inventory on a periodic basis, and then on a perpetual basis. Assume also each of the following flows of costs: FIFO; weighted average; LIFO.

P8-4 Baesal Co. Ltd. existed in business for a period of four years. During that period, purchases and sales were as follows:

	Units Purchased	Units Sold
19x1	12,000	8,000
19x2	14,000	15,000
19x3	9,000	9,000
19x4	10,000	13,000

The selling price per unit throughout this period remained constant at $20.
Required:

a. Assume that the cost per unit was $12 in 19x1, $14 in 19x2, $16 in 19x3 and $18 in 19x4; determine income and year end inventory for each of the four years using first FIFO and then LIFO.
b. Do the same as in Part a, assuming this time that the cost per unit was $18, $16, $14 and $12 in each of the four years.
c. What generalizations can be made regarding the impact of LIFO as compared to FIFO on cost of goods sold and inventories in periods of rising prices versus periods of falling prices?
d. Determine total income for the four year period. Over the life of the business, does it matter which method of costing inventory is used? Why then is the costing method selected by a company important to the users of the financial statements?

P8-5 "In the U.S., unlike in Canada, the LIFO inventory costing method is acceptable for tax purposes. For this reason, more companies use the LIFO inventory costing method in the U.S. than in Canada, especially in this time of rising prices."
Required:

a. Explain the above quotation. Provide an example to illustrate your response.
b. Suppose you were the shareholder of a company that switched its inven-

tory costing method from FIFO to LIFO and as a result its income dropped $2 million. What would be your reaction? Explain thoroughly.

c. What implications does stock market efficiency have for companies contemplating changes in their inventory valuation method?

P8-6 On August 31, 19x7, Silver's Department Store, a sole proprietorship, had on hand merchandise that cost $770,000 and was priced to sell at $1 million. During the fiscal year 19x8, Silver's made purchases of $4.75 million which it marked up to sell at $6 million retail. Sales for 19x8 (at retail) were $6.6 million. A physical count at August 31, 19x8, indicated goods on hand tagged to sell at $400,000.

Required:

a. Determine the cost of goods sold for 19x8 and inventory (at cost) at August 31, 19x8, using the retail inventory method.

b. Under what conditions would your response to Part a be suspect?

P8-7 A fire on June 16, 19x3, destroyed all merchandise of the Pearl Discount Store Ltd. Salvaged records reveal that as of July 31, 19x2, the store had merchandise on hand that had cost $1.5 million and that was marked to sell at $1.76 million. In the period since that date the store had purchased merchandise that cost $7.5 million and was intended to be sold for $9,375,000. Actual sales for the period were $9.2 million.

Required:

a. For the purposes of making an insurance claim how would you value merchandise destroyed in the fire?

b. Assuming that the insurance company will reimburse the company for the historic cost of merchandise destroyed in the fire, for how much should the store submit a claim to its insurance company?

c. Assume the role of an employee of the insurance company. How would you test the reasonableness of the claim submitted by Pearl Discount Store Ltd.?

P8-8 Indicated below is the December 31, 19x8 inventory of the Goodale Co. Ltd. along with current replacement costs and expected selling prices:

Items	*Units*	*Unit cost*	*Replacement cost*	*Expected selling price*
A	6,000	$10	$12	$18
B	4,000	8	6	9
C	12,000	6	4	6
D	2,000	4	2	6

It is the policy of the company to sell at 50 percent above cost, but sometimes market conditions force (or enable) the company to sell at a lower (or higher) price.

Required:

a. What factors would you consider in deciding whether to apply the lower of cost or market rule on an item-by-item basis or on a group basis?

b. What measure of market would you use to apply the lower of cost or market rule? Explain thoroughly.

c. Apply the lower of cost or market rule to determine the value at which

December 31, 19x8 inventory should be stated. Apply the rule first on an item-by-item basis and then on a group basis.

P8-9 In December 19x1, Mr. Bishop established a door-to-door sales company. He invested $10,000 and purchased 2,000 units of inventory at $5 per unit — the minimum number of units required to sustain his business. He made his purchase at a propitious time, for the next day, before he had a chance to make a single sale, the price per unit of his inventory increased to $6.

During 19x2 Mr. Bishop purchased an additional 40,000 units at $6 pei unit and sold 10,000 units at $7 per unit. He withdrew from the business for his personal use *all* cash except that necessary to assure that his inventory was maintained at its minimum level of 2,000 units.

Required:

a. Prepare journal entries to reflect the above transactions. Assume first that Bishop maintained his inventories on a FIFO basis; then assume that he maintained his inventories on a LIFO basis. Prepare income statements and balance sheets comparing results under the two methods.

b. How much cash was Bishop able to withdraw during 19x2? Compare his cash withdrawals with income as determined by both the FIFO and the LIFO methods.

c. What do you suppose that some financial observers mean when they say that in periods of inflation LIFO results in earnings that are of "higher quality"?

P8-10 Loffmark Retailers Ltd. sells only three products. Information about purchases and sales during 19x9 is provided below:

	Products		
	A	*B*	*C*
Balance on hand, 1/1			
Number of units	2,000	10,000	2,000
Cost per unit	$12	$8	$40
Purchases during year excluding one shipment received on December 31			
Number of units	116,000	30,000	7,000
Cost per unit	$12	$8	$40
Purchase of December 31			
Number of units	2,000	10,000	1,000
Cost per unit	$12	$16	$40
Sales during year			
Number of units	119,000	40,000	8,000
Sales price	$15	$10	$80
Balance on hand, 12/31			
Number of units	1,000	10,000	2,000
Expected sales price	$15	$20	$80

Required:

a. Determine ending inventory and cost of goods sold using each of the three following inventory methods:

(i) First-in, first-out (periodic).

(ii) Weighted average (periodic).
(iii) Retail method (applied on a store-wide basis for all products added together).

b. Compare totals under each of the three methods. Comment on the hazards of using inventory methods based on averages. Why are the results under the weighted average and the retail methods distorted?

P8-11 As of January 1, 19x6 Wong Ltd. had 10,000 units of product on hand. Each had a carrying value of $20. In November of that year the president estimated that sales for the year would total 80,000 units. To date, the company had produced 70,000 units, at a cost of $25 per unit. If additional units were to be produced in the remainder of the year, they would cost $26 per unit. The company determines inventory on a *periodic* LIFO basis.

Required:

a. Determine cost of goods sold if
   (i) The president ordered that no additional units be produced during the year.
   (ii) The president ordered that 10,000 additional units be produced.
   (iii) The president ordered that 40,000 additional units be produced.

b. What conclusion can you draw from your calculations in Part a?

c. If the company used a perpetual LIFO basis would the same results occur? Why?

d. Is the periodic LIFO basis of valuing inventory the only one influenced by management decisions? Give an example. Explain your response.

P8-12 T. Metal Co. Ltd. trades in scrap metal. The company purchases the scrap from small dealers and sells it in bulk to the major steel manufacturers. As a matter of policy, the company sells the scrap to the manufacturers for $5 per ton more than the current price it pays the individual dealers. The price of scrap steel is volatile. The following table indicates several price changes that occurred in 19x7 and the transactions engaged in by the T. Metal Co. Ltd. in the periods between the price changes:

Period	*Price paid to dealers*	*Number of tons purchased*	*Number of tons sold*	*Price per ton*
1/1	$ 82	5,000[a]		
1/2 – 3/11	85	16,000	18,000	$ 90
3/12 – 6/4	87	25,000	22,000	92
6/5 – 9/26	93	5,000	9,000	98
9/27 – 12/30	104	17,000	13,000	109
12/31	106	–0–	–0–	
		68,000	62,000	

[a]Opening inventory

During the year the company incurred operating costs of $325,000.

Required:

a. Prepare a conventional income statement in which gains or losses are recognized only upon actual sale of goods. Use the FIFO method of inventory valuation.

b. Prepare an income statement in which gains or losses are recognized upon increases in wholesale prices (paid to dealer). Cost of goods sold should be based on replacement costs applicable at the time the goods are sold. Be sure to indicate holding gains actually realized as well as those applicable to goods still in inventory at year end.
c. On which financial statement should the holding gains be shown? Explain.
d. What additional information about the company's performance do users of the financial statements have when inventory is valued at replacement cost? How does this assist the decisions they make?

P8-13 Gilbert Ltd. manufactures two products on one machine. The following data relates to the two products:

	Products	
	A	*B*
Material	$5/unit	$10/unit
Labor	$8/unit	$ 4/unit

Other relevant data:
1. Annual depreciation of the machine is $20,000.
2. Annual rent of the manufacturing facilities is $12,000.
3. Sales for the year were 4,000 units of A and 6,000 units of B.
4. Production for the year was 6,000 units of A and 10,000 units of B.
5. Product A requires twice as much labor time as product B.

Required:
a. Assuming there were no other costs related to the manufacture of products A and B, determine the cost per unit of each product A and product B. Justify your calculation.
b. Calculate the cost of goods sold and ending inventory.
c. The controller of the company has informed you that the management is giving serious consideration to costing inventory at material and labor cost since these are the only costs directly traceable to the product. In your opinion should the company adopt this method? Why?

Cases

C8-1 Below are three separate situations. In each situation, select the cost flow assumption that you feel is most appropriate. Be sure to indicate the aspects of the company's operations which were most significant in leading to your recommendation.

Situation 1
Prentice Automobile Sales Ltd. is a car dealership. It sells both used and new automobiles as well as providing parts and repair service.

Situation 2
Edible Bits Ltd. is in the food processing business. Its operations consist of buying bulk commodities such as nuts and raisins in world markets, clean-

ing, and packaging them into units which can be marketed at retail, primarily through the major supermarket chains. The commodities involved lose freshness and deteriorate with the passage of time, so the production schedule uses the oldest goods first. Prices in the buying market are subject to the contingencies of crop conditions in various parts of the world and prices in the retail market are tied fairly closely to the annual world price situation.

Situation 3

Tanbar Limited operates a leather tannery, obtaining the hides which are its raw material from the various meatpacking houses, where hide production is a by-product of the slaughtering process. It sells the finished leather to a variety of markets but the majority of sales are to footwear and luggage manufacturers.

Tanbar has little control over either the prices at which it buys hides or those at which it sells finished leather. On the selling side this is because the company's customers view Tanbar's price entitlement as composed of (a) the current cost of hides (adjusted by standard factors for waste, etc.), plus (b) a processing allowance for the tanning operation. On Tanbar's supply side, hides come on the market not because of any factors related to ultimate leather demand but because of the volume of cattle offerings and slaughter directed at meat production that take place at the packing houses. Hide prices can thus vary significantly depending on whether there is a surplus or deficiency of supply relative to ultimate leather demand. Because the processing of leather does take time and this is not allowed for by Tanbar's customers in the prices they offer, the company can find itself gaining or losing on its inventory depending on fluctuations in hide prices.

C8-2 Fun Co. Limited ("FCL", or "the company") is incorporated under the Canada Business Corporations Act and all its shareholders and major creditors are located in Canada. FCL consists of several retail stores which stock a particular line of citizen band radios.

The success of the company depends to a large extent upon sales in the car and truck industry and upon working class incomes. Over the past three years FCL has experienced a dramatic increase in sales and in the current year, 19x5, just ended, sales were 10,000 units or $1,000,000 (i.e. average selling price was $100 per unit).

Much of the company's recent growth has caught it by surprise and it is uncertain about whether it has adequate information to satisfy its needs. At present it is reviewing both its method of costing and controlling inventories and has accumulated the following data from its records:

Inventory, October 31, 19x4	2,000 units @ $90
19x5 purchases:	
January 15	1,000 units @ $80
April 18	2,000 units @ $75
June 22	2,000 units @ $70
September 18	1,000 units @ $70
October 15	6,000 units @ $60

FCL uses a periodic inventory system and a physical inventory taken on

October 31, 19x5 revealed that 3,500 units were on hand. The manufacturer from whom FCL usually makes its purchases quoted a price of $60 per unit on October 31, 19x5 for a lot of 1,000 units. Up until this time FCL had been content with the service which it received from its major supplier, however, as a matter of interest it decided to obtain prices from other suppliers. All suppliers surveyed indicated that their prices were above $60 per unit except for one small supplier who was just starting up in the business. This supplier's price was $55 per unit. Further investigation revealed that this supplier might not be successful and definitely would not be able to supply FCL's entire annual needs. FCL's expected resale price in 19x5 – 19x6 was $85 a unit.

The president (who is not a shareholder) of the company is particularly concerned about adopting a fair method of valuing the company's inventory for the following reasons:

a) Managers of the retail stores receive a bonus based on profits.
b) During the year the company issued an income debenture (that is, the interest on the debenture is 5 percent of net income based upon generally accepted accounting principles).
c) The company's sales price of citizen band radios has declined significantly since the beginning of the year.

The president is aware that there are several acceptable methods of costing inventory and has asked you which is the fairest — first-in, first-out; last-in, first-out; or weighted average. He would also be interested in hearing your opinion on the company's present method of controlling inventory and on the accounting significance of the company's declining sales price.

Required:

What would you recommend? Why? Explain your answer clearly by stating the assumptions which you have made, the calculations you have used (hint: calculate cost of goods sold and inventory figures on a first-in, first-out; last-in, first-out; and weighted average basis), and the logic you have employed.

C8-3 Apple Company (AC) was recently formed by a group of 32 independent apple-orchard owners in order to obtain better profits from their apple harvest. AC is required to buy all the apple output from each orchard owner at the prevailing fair market value. It then sells some fresh apples but also makes bottled apple cider, canned apple juice, and apple sauce. According to the agreement signed by each of the 32 owners, 75 percent of annual net income of AC is to be distributed to the owners in cash within 90 days of the company's March 31 year end. The remaining 25 percent is to be retained for expansion of processing facilities. There are no provisions in the agreement for admitting new owners of AC. If an orchard owner sells his farm, the new owner automatically must become an owner of AC.

On commencement of the business each owner contributed $10,000 of which 80 percent consisted of a 10-year loan bearing interest at 9 percent per annum (the market rate at that time). Each owner also had to give a bank a personal guarantee of $40,000 so that short-term loans could be obtained as needed in order to finance inventories and receivables. No other sources of cash financing are used by the company.

AC leased a building for ten years. It also acquired about $400,000 of processing equipment, trucks, tools, and other necessary assets. Agreements were signed with several large national grocery chains to buy output at prevailing market price. Terms are cash payment within 60 days of delivery to each store. Prices of "finished" products per the agreement are to be a function of supply-demand at the date of sale. Because some inventory could be stored for up to two years, selling prices could be substantially higher or slightly lower than inventory cost (i.e. cost of the apples plus processing, packaging and storing). That is, the market prices are set by the combined action of all buyers and sellers; but AC makes its own decisions as to whether it will sell at prevailing prices, or store, or process fresh apples.

The company's first year end has just passed. The agreement among the owners does not give any guidance as to how net income is to be computed. In the rush to get the company started, officials have not yet paid much attention to the selection of accounting principles and policies. However, they recognize that the company was primarily formed to increase profits of the orchard owners. Also, they know that the owners will be anxious to have their dividend paid before June 30 because each owner's liquid assets will be nearing the low point for the year.

Required:

Assume the role of an accounting adviser to the company, and thoroughly explain which financial accounting policies and principles the company should adopt.

C8-4 The president of S. Rink & Cloth Ltd., Mr. Lee, was disappointed to learn from his controller that the company had suffered a loss of $175,000 in its first year of operations. He was disturbed for the following three reasons:

(1) He received a bonus of 10 percent of profit.

(2) The terms of sale to customers were set by contract. Each year on January 1 the selling price to customers is set at replacement cost plus 25 percent and regardless of any changes which occur in replacement cost subsequent to January 1, no change in selling price is permitted.

(3) In anticipation of replacement cost increases Mr. Lee purposely purchased large quantities of inventory at the beginning of the year. As it turned out, during the year the cost of cloth did rise and he thought he should be rewarded for his astute management of company resources.

The following data related to the company's first year of operations:

	Purchases		*Sales*
	Units	*Unit Cost*	
1/1	600,000	$4.00	
3/15			200,000 (Replacement cost at the time of sale was $4.50/unit)
4/12	300,000	4.50	
5/8			400,000 (Replacement cost at the time of sale was $5.00/unit)
7/12	400,000	5.00	
8/20			300,000 (Replacement cost at the time of sale was $5.50/unit)
9/15	200,000	5.50	
10/2			500,000 (Replacement cost at the time of sale was $6.00/unit)
11/6	300,000	6.00	

During the year the company incurred operating costs of $125,000. A review of the year indicated that the cost per unit had increased dramatically. This was due to a severe shortage of supply which has now been remedied. At December 31, the company's year end, the replacement cost per unit was $6.40 and there was every indication that this cost would remain stable throughout the upcoming year. In addition customer demand is expected to be 1,500,000 units next year.

Required:

Assume the role of an accounting advisor. Evaluate the various alternative inventory costing methods available to the company (including replacement cost) and determine income under each method. Which do you recommend? Why?

9 *Long-Lived Assets*

This chapter will be devoted to long-lived (often referred to as *fixed*) assets of the firm — those that cannot be expected to be consumed within a single operating cycle of the business. Long-lived assets include plant assets (such as land, buildings, and equipment) as well as natural resources (such as minerals) and intangible assets (such as copyrights). Long-lived assets can be thought of as "bundles of services" which the firm will consume over time. Although they may be purchased and paid for in a single year, they will be used to generate revenue over a number of years.

Since a long-lived asset provides services for a span of time longer than one year, its cost must be charged off as an expense over more than one accounting period. The cost of the asset must be matched with the benefits to be provided — with the revenues to be generated. The process of allocating the cost of an asset over a number of accounting periods is referred to as *depreciation* if the asset is plant and equipment; *depletion*, if natural resources; and *amortization*, if intangible.

The basic journal entry to record the acquisition of a long-lived asset, equipment, is (assume the asset to be equipment which cost $10,000)

Equipment	$10,000	
Cash (or accounts payable)		$10,000
To record the purchase of equipment.		

The basic entry to record the periodic allocation of the cost of the asset over its useful life (assume a life of 10 years) is

Depreciation (expense)	$1,000	
Accumulated depreciation — equipment		$1,000
To record periodic depreciation expense.		

Fixed assets are reported on the balance sheet at cost less accumulated depreciation.

The account for accumulated depreciation or amortization (sometimes referred to as *allowance* for depreciation or amortization) is a contra account and is always reported directly beneath the particular group of assets to which it pertains. Use of the contra account enables the firm to provide information that is more complete than if the balance in the asset account was reduced directly. For example, readers of the financial statements may obtain a general indication of the extent to which the company's assets have been used by viewing the ratio of accumulated depreciation to the original cost of the asset. Readers sometimes *may* also be able to form a broad impression of the extent to which additional funds will be needed to replace the assets in the future. However, in order to make either of these judgments the firm would either have to own few assets or accumulated depreciation would have to be reported separately for each major class of assets. (Note Labatt's presentation, in Chapter 2.) Another main advantage to keeping cost and accumulated depreciation separate is that cost is "objective" to those wishing stewardship reports, whereas accumulated depreciation is "arbitrary."

After one year the equipment might be shown on the balance sheet as

Equipment	$10,000	
Less: Accumulated depreciation	1,000	$9,000

Issues of Valuation

The limitations of the historical cost approach to asset valuation — that which is taken in practice today — are particularly pronounced with respect to fixed assets. Fixed assets commonly constitute a major portion of total firm assets, and because they are replaced relatively infrequently, differences between the value based on initial cost and that based on current measures may be especially great. Financial statements in which long-lived assets are reported at historical costs are deficient in that they provide no information as to either the market value of the assets — the price at which they could be sold or which would have to be paid to replace them — or the value of the services to be provided to the particular user.

Market values

The importance of market values may be illustrated by a hypothetical example which assumes that people are naive and unable to "see through" the accounting figures to a more complete picture of events. A publicly held corporation has had meager profits in relation to the book value of its assets for several years. Ownership of the company is dispersed among a large number of shareholders, each of whom has but a small interest in the company and must rely primarily on published annual reports as a source of financial information. The firm's main plant is located on several acres of land in the downtown section of a major metropolitan area. The land on which the plant sits is recorded on the books of the corporation at the price at which it was acquired decades earlier. A group of investors has learned from sources not readily available to the company's shareholders that the land has considerably greater value than that indicated in the financial reports. They offer to purchase all of the firm's common shares at a price several dollars per share higher than the prevailing market price. The unknowing shareholders sell the investors their shares. The new owners, in turn, sell the land for an amount considerably greater than that paid to the previous shareholders for the entire company. They realize a *windfall* profit, one made possible because the financial information provided no information on the current market value of firm assets.

Insofar as the financial reports fail to account for changes in market values, *both* the balance sheet and the income statement are of limited utility to investors. The balance sheet fails to provide information on the total amount of resources available to management and for which it should be held accountable. It serves inadequately, therefore, as a basis on which to determine the return which is being generated by the assets. Corporate performance can be meaningfully measured only in terms of current values — not historical values. Current values provide an indication of the alternative uses to which the assets could be put — the amount for which they could be sold and the proceeds invested in other ventures.

The conventional income statement fails to provide information on the periodic increases in the value of assets (and thus of corporate net worth) over time. If income is to be a measure of how much "better off" a firm is from one period to the next, then changes in the amount for which assets could be bought or sold may be as important in determining income as actual exchange transactions. Decisions as to whether to hold or to sell fixed assets may be critical to the long-run welfare of the company. Since historical cost-based income statements omit consideration of *holding* gains or losses until such time as the assets are sold or retired, they fail to account for an important dimension of corporate performance.

In brief, users of financial statements are often forced to obtain information on replacement cost, net realizable value or discounted cash flows (whenever they desire such figures) from *other* sources. Is this a blow to the prestige of accountants? It is; but, not to the great extent which you might expect, primarily because of current Canadian legislation and the state of public opinion. Accountants (as preparers, auditors of the work of preparers, or users) are "locked in" by a system of disclosure which requires the *issuer* to pay all of the costs of having the financial statements assembled and audited. It would not be surprising, therefore, to find that issuers were reluctant to provide costly information to users other than shareholders who get the data free of charge. If *you* were the president of a large company would *you* report the replacement cost, net realizable value and historic cost of your major assets every year?

Why, then, do some companies report far more information than do others? We cannot provide a simple yet complete response to this question. However, we can relate the question to the role of disclosure in minimizing creditor and shareholder uncertainty. That is, if the issuer expects to have to issue debt or equity in the near future, creditors and investors may be able to set a fairer price for the company's shares in the market place when they have more complete information. When they lack information (such as replacement cost) and are forced to guess, they may attach a higher degree of uncertainty to their guesses or estimates of future cash flows. This means that they discount the cash flow at a *higher* discount rate (to recognize the added uncertainty), which in turn causes a *lower* present value or worth for the company. When creditors, for instance, have all the information which they require they are likely to be more confident of their estimates and ask for a lower interest rate on sums lent to the company. We have oversimplified the explanation; but the general thrust is in place, and is worth remembering.

Under these conditions in Canada is it in the interests of issuers of financial statements to try to fool creditors and investors by providing a too rosy picture of the company's future? Management may through their deceit be able to lower the interest rate from what they would otherwise have to pay to bondholders. But, a few checking mechanisms exist in Canada that help minimize such deceitful behavior by issuers. First, the company's auditors should catch flagrant abuses of disclosure and major measurement errors. Second, provincial Securities Commissions may object to some disclosure or lack thereof, and measurement gimmicks. (When securities are sold to the general public the issuer must prepare a *Prospectus*, which is read and commented upon by accountants and lawyers paid by the Securities Commissions in those provinces in which the securities are offered for sale). Third, the company is not likely to be able to hide the facts forever. Once the facts come to light the issuing company's directors and officers would lose their credibility. They may also be sued if it could be proved that they intentionally deceived people.

Fourth, and an important one from our point of view, is *education*. Many students who initially register for introductory accounting courses do not intend to become accountants. Many also do not recognize on registration that their lives will be affected greatly at times by accounting. The authors of this book have seen fit to repeat important messages every chapter or two. Financial statements must be read carefully with full knowledge of their strengths and limitations. If this message is retained by students it may save them and their employer money and embarrassment at some future date.

Value to Users

Measures of value based on historical costs fail to take into account not only the amounts for which assets could be bought or sold but the benefits to be provided to the particular users as well.

The value of an asset to its user is that of the services that it will provide — the net revenues that it will generate or the cost savings that it will effect. It is a future-oriented measure of earnings potential.

The revenues to be generated or savings to be effected by a long-lived asset will be realized over a period greater than one year. Revenues or savings realized in the future, however, are of considerably less value than those to be realized at the present. The dollar values of services to be provided in the future must be discounted to take into account the time value of money.

Assume, for example, that a firm owns a building which it rents to outsiders. All operating expenses are paid by the tenants. The building has a remaining useful life of five years. The firm receives annual rental payments of $20,000. If the firm requires a rate of return of 8 percent on all assets, then (ignoring taxes) the value of the asset to the firm is the present value of a cash flow of $20,000 for five years. Per Table 4 in the Appendix, which indicates the present value of an annuity, present value (five periods, 8 percent) would be

$$\$20,000 \times 3.9927 = \$79,854.$$

This amount takes into account expected future returns, and is likely to be of far greater utility than historic cost to users of financial statements such as management, investors, and creditors whose objective is to establish the present worth or market value of a firm by discounting the future net cash flows generated by the company's net assets. But this assumes that the computations performed by investors and creditors outside the company have already been calculated by a financial statement preparer and that the preparer (accountants and others within the company) would choose the *same* discount rate as the user. In brief, the question becomes one of value to *which* user? Management's opinion of risk (as reflected in the discount rate) may differ from the estimate of an investor.

For example, suppose that the user *outside* of the company does not agree with the 8 percent rate selected by the preparer, and wishes to use 10 percent. This would occur because the user outside thinks that the cash flows (rental payments) are not as assured or definite as the preparer has assumed, and are likely to be risky. The outside user may figure that some cash rental receipts have a good probability of never being received by the building's owner, and the owner is being far too optimistic. If so, this would affect the present worth of the building asset.

The circuitous reasoning of investment practitioners must be explained more completely. One would think that if there is a risk that not all of the rental receipts would appear, then the most direct approach to recognizing this situation would be to *reduce their amount* for computational purposes, before engaging in the cash flow discounting process. Then, the reduced cash flows could still be discounted at the 8 percent rate. However, it is possible to arrive at approximately the same present worth if, instead, we increase the discount rate and let the cash flows of $20,000 per year remain unchanged.

Using a 10 percent discount rate (see Table 4 in Appendix) the present worth of $20,000 received at the end of each of the next five years would be:

$$\$20{,}000 \times 3.7908 = \$75{,}816.$$

This present worth would be achieved if we used an 8 percent rate and reduced the cash flow per year to roughly $18,990:

$$\$18{,}990 \times 3.9927 = \$75{,}816 \text{ (approximately)}.$$

The $18,990 was "pulled out of the air" just to show that the arithmetic works. Hence, the same result ($75,816) is achieved by either: (1) increasing the discount rate 2 percent (10 percent minus 8 percent); or (2) lowering the annual cash flow for five years by $1,010 ($20,000 – $18,990). Either way the "value to a user" has dropped from $79,854 to $75,816.

Moreover, historical cost-based income statements fail to take into account the economic cost to the firm of the services consumed in the course of an accounting period. The economic sacrifice sustained by the firm is the loss of earnings potential. Such loss can readily be measured by comparing the value of services to be provided by the asset at the beginning of a period with that at the end. In the example of the building, the present value of the services of a building with a five-year useful life was determined to be $79,854. After another year, however, the asset could be expected to generate only four rental payments of $20,000. The present value of four payments of $20,000 discounted at 8 percent is, per Table 4,

$$\$20{,}000 \times 3.3121 = \$66{,}242.$$

The economic loss, with respect to the building, sustained by the firm was therefore

$$\$79{,}854 - \$66{,}242 = \$13{,}612.$$

In journal entry terms for this first year, assuming that the $20,000 annual rental was received in cash:

Cash	$20,000	
Asset		$13,612
Rental income		$ 6,388

To record receipt of cash, decline in the present value of the asset, and an 8% return on the opening asset value of $79,854 ($79,854 × .08 = $6,388).

Observe that this entry is a composite of two elements: (1) so-called "economic depreciation" on the asset; and (2) recognition of (interest) income. In conventional historic cost (often stewardship objective) accounting these two elements are usually reported separately as depreciation expense, and net rental receipts. Depreciation as conventionally determined is based on the cost to acquire an asset; it is past-oriented. It gives no explicit consideration to the loss of earnings potential sustained during the year.

Replacement Cost as an Alternative

One frequently proposed alternative to reporting assets on a historical basis is to state them at *current replacement cost.* Current replacement cost used is the cost of purchasing a similar asset (adjusted for age as well as technological or other factors that make replacement with an identical asset impossible) at the prevailing market price.

The use of current replacement costs would assure that the financial statements reflect at least an approximation of the costs that would have to be incurred if the asset were to be purchased in the current market. It would provide, in most instances, a reasonable estimate of the amount for which the asset could be sold. It would furnish the means to give recognition to *holding gains* attributable to increases in market prices.

Current replacement costs do *not*, however, necessarily indicate the value of the asset to the particular user. The value of an asset to a company that might use it with unusual efficiency might far exceed the price at which it is being traded in currently established markets. Nevertheless, the price that independent purchasers are willing to pay would, in general, be a reasonable approximation of the present value of the services — at buying market prices, not selling market prices — to be provided by the asset. For most companies, replacement cost is likely to be a better indicator of value-in-use than historical cost. In fact, it is seldom feasible to measure directly the service potential of an asset. Most assets, unlike the building used in the previous example, cannot be identified with specific cash flows. They provide services only when used in conjunction with other assets. A piece of equipment used in a manufacturing process, for instance, has value only when used along with other equipment, the plant building, the land on which the plant sits, etc. Replacement cost is, therefore, as good an approximation of value-in-use as a firm could ordinarily expect to obtain.

As indicated in the following example, recognition of increases in replacement cost could readily be effected in the accounts.

EXAMPLE

The Jay Co. Limited owns a building which originally cost $180,000 when purchased 10 years ago. It has an estimated useful life of 40 years and no salvage value. It is currently reflected on the balance sheet as follows:

Building	$180,000	
Less: Accumulated depreciation (10/40 of $180,000)	45,000	$135,000

During each of the 10 years depreciation was recorded with the conventional journal entry

Depreciation	$4,500	
Accumulated depreciation		$4,500
To record annual depreciation expense.		

Replacement cost had remained constant for the first 10 years of asset life.

At the end of the tenth year, however, it was noted that rising construction costs had increased the replacement cost of a new building by $20,000.

The following entry would effect recognition of the increase in replacement cost:

Building	$20,000	
Accumulated depreciation		$ 5,000
"Gain" from appreciation		15,000
To record the increase in replacement cost.		

The necessity for crediting accumulated depreciation for $5,000 may be unclear. It makes sense, however, considering that the useful life of the building has not changed. Thus, 25 percent of the building must still be considered as having been depreciated, regardless of the value placed on the building. The replacement cost of a new building is $200,000; hence 25 percent (10 years worth — $50,000) of replacement cost must be reflected in the accumulated depreciation account.

In each of the following 30 years depreciation would be recorded in the standard manner, except that the charge each year would be 1/40 of $200,000:

Depreciation	$5,000	
Accumulated depreciation		$5,000
To record depreciation expense.		

The credit of $15,000 to " 'gain' from appreciation" may go directly to the income statement or to owners' equity under a replacement cost accounting system. As stated in the previous chapter it all depends on one's view of *capital maintenance* or notion of what capital is. Under a historic cost system in Canada, such write-ups of fixed assets occur from time to time under special circumstances, and credits (of $15,000) usually go directly to owners' equity.

A primary objection to the use of replacement costs is the difficulty of obtaining a reasonable measure of such cost. Many assets must be treated individually and market prices for some of them are not necessarily readily available.

How, for example, would you determine the current replacement cost of a tract of land? In some cases it may be possible to derive a value based on a recent offer to purchase the tract. In others, a reasonable value could be obtained by determining the amount for which similar tracts in the same neighbourhood have recently been sold.

Consider the problem of estimating the value of land in a logging community in British Columbia, such as on Vancouver Island. Some land may have been purchased years ago before the government stopped selling it "in bulk" to forest-product companies and began leasing rights to cut its timber. A logging camp, pulp mill, sawmill, and assorted supporting services located on the land may, in essence, be owned by one company (the "one company town"). A few independent shops and small industrial suppliers may own land adjacent to the company town. What gives the company's land its value? An *operating* camp and mills are what provide the value. If they closed, what would the townsite land be worth? Other buyers may be non-existent because of the geographical isolation of the land, or because the use of the land for further or other commercial purposes is inappropriate. (If new trees were planted, they might not be harvestable for 60 – 80 years). Going-concern nature or continuity, two key concepts explained in Chapter 5, take on special significance in valuing land in this case. If the company has little or no intention of replacing the forests on the land, and the land's net realizable value is zero, historic cost may be as suitable a valuation as any.

If the company land contained trees which would be harvested into lumber, plywood, pulp chips, and other products, then replacement cost would be a useful measurement. An end product, such as lumber, would indeed have to be replaced. Cost of goods sold, at replacement cost, can be useful in assessing current operations. The end products are in contrast to a potential abandoned company town — a ghost town.

Advantages of Historical Costs

The disadvantages of historical costs are obvious. The advantages, however, should not be minimized. Historical costs are objective; the amount paid for an asset can readily be verified. Moreover, financial statements in which assets are stated at acquisition costs (less accumulated depreciation, as appropriate) are transaction based. Assets are initially recorded at the amounts for which they were acquired. The cost of an asset is allocated among the periods in which the service of the asset is provided. The total amount charged as an expense (depreciation) is exactly equal to the actual net cost (cost less salvage value, if any) incurred by the firm. Subjective judgments excluding the depreciation factor are held to a minimum; the financial statements present a historical record based on actual arm's-length exchanges.

It is undeniably true that financial statements based on historical costs do not provide *all* information necessary to make intelligent investment or management decisions. It is questionable whether financial statements prepared on any single basis could do that. The use of historical costs, however, by no means precludes disclosure of current market values of assets as well as other types of data, both of an accounting and nonaccounting nature, that financial statement users would find relevant to the decisions that they must make.

Inventory or Long-Lived Asset?

In practice, it is often not as easy as we have previously indicated to distinguish a long-lived asset from inventory or from a prepaid expense. We generally define items held for resale as "inventory." Let us test this definition. The automobile manufacturers may acquire special "tooling" for the current design of an automobile to be sold in the next two or three automobile model years. Are these acquisitions prepaid expense or long-lived assets? The situation is not clear, and one may expect to see both treatments in financial statements.

Livestock provide an interesting example. A company may be engaged in both breeding and racing horses. Horses such as broodmares and stallions are strictly involved, over a three or more year period, in producing offspring (foals), which will either be sold or kept for racing purposes. Other horses (aged two to eight) are used exclusively for racing purposes, but can be sold during the year, such as when the horse is "claimed" when it is entered in a "claiming race." Would we consider broodmares and stallions to be "long-lived" assets? Racing horses as inventory? The obvious way around the classification difficulty is to show the horses as a separate line on the balance sheet. But where? Any horse, including a broodmare or stallion, may represent a current asset if it is available and intended for sale.

What valuation can be attached to broodmares? To stallions? To foals? To racing horses? If the horse is purchased, we know its cost. But what about a foal? Is the cost zero? In order to overcome the question of when revenue is recognized (and its related issue of when asset values may be changed) some breeders and racers record all their horses at net realizable value — a selling market price. The net realizable value is based on blood lines (were its broodmare and stallion "parents" good racers?) until the horse is ready to race. After it races, its net realizable value can be established from the amount of money the horse is expected to win over its racing years. The value of a stallion may be tied to the likely worth of its future offspring.

Using net realizable value means that the income statement is charged or credited as the asset value of the horse changes. Is this in accordance with the criteria for revenue recognition set forth in Chapter 5? If not, can you find a better way of recording livestock assets?

Similarly complex situations occur in many types of companies. Turkey farming is another interesting example. A farm has these different asset categories: eggs; breeder flocks; growing flocks, for sale at maturity; processed turkeys; plus the usual inventories of supplies. It is possible to compute a cost of eggs if one can establish the cost of upkeep of the breeder flock and egg output (feed and overhead divided by egg production equals cost per egg). Similar cost estimates can be made for the other categories of assets. In some situations (such as processed turkeys) net realizable value may be below cost because of supply being in excess of demand. However, because of the relatively short life of turkeys compared to horses, turkeys would usually be inventory, and current assets (i.e., "inventory of turkeys").

Issues of Ownership

Generally, a firm owns the fixed assets that it uses. But it is not always essential that a firm have formal legal title to the assets in order to record them in its own accounts. Assets are defined by accountants in economic rather than legal terms. Assets, as viewed by the accountant, are the economic resources of the firm; the contractual right to use property may be as much of an economic resource as a certificate of title. The distinction between economic and legal resources is especially important in light of current financial practice. With increasing frequency the rights and obligations of ownership are being contractually assigned to parties other than those which hold legal title.

In a common installment purchase, for example, the seller often retains formal title to the property until the buyer has made final payment of his outstanding obligations. The asset should be accounted for on the books of the purchaser as soon as he first acquires rights to its use. In a more complex financial arrangement, a financial institution might hold title to assets for a major portion of their useful lives. The financial institution leases the property to the party that will use it. The terms of the lease arrangement *may* be such that the annual rental payments approximate what they would have been had the user bought the property outright and borrowed the purchase price from the financial institution. However, leases are often structured in Canada to recognize two important factors: (1) income tax legislation; and (2) cash needs of the parties to the lease. Hence, cash flows can be irregular on some types of leases, such as for leased aircraft, where high rates of depreciation can be used for income tax purposes, and the user is short of cash in early years of the lease. Chapter 10 elaborates on this.

Moreover, the lease contract may specify that the lessee (the user of the property) has to bear all risks and obligations of ownership; that is, he must pay all maintenance and insurance costs and make all required property tax payments, where applicable. Under such an arrangement the user of the property is in substance its owner; the property should, therefore, be accounted for as an asset on the books of the user.

Leasing is common in many industries; the railroad industry is an example of but one. Many freight cars in the U.S. bear notations indicating that they are the property of well-known banks. The banks, obviously, are not in the railroad business. Rather, they have loaned the railroad the cost of the cars and are retaining legal ownership until the railroad has repaid its loan. The loan may, however, take the form of a lease arrangement whereby the railroad rents the car from the bank. After such time as the railroad has made payments equal to the cost of the car (plus interest) the railroad would have the right to purchase the car for a nominal sum, perhaps $1. The railroad is, of course, the constructive owner of the car. The car should be recorded on the books of the railroad as a tangible long-lived asset, whereas the bank would record a receivable from the railroad.

Lease arrangements will be discussed in greater detail in Chapter 10 in connection with long-term liabilities. The point to be emphasized at this time is that the question of whether or not property should be accounted for as an asset must be answered independently of strict legal interpretations or the peculiarities of financing arrangements.

Cost of Plant Assets

As a general rule, plant assets are shown on the balance sheet at original cost, with the accumulated depreciation to date shown in a contra account. Normally, plant assets are said to be valued at "cost less accumulated depreciation." The cost of an asset may not simply be its stated purchase price. It would include all costs that are necessary to bring it to a serviceable condition. Cost would include, in addition to actual purchase price, costs of freight, installation, taxes, and title fees, among others. The costs that are included as a part of the fixed asset are said to be *capitalized.* They were incurred to benefit several periods, not just one; they should be charged as expenses over the useful life of the asset rather than in the year in which they are incurred.

The *sticker* or advertised price of an asset may not always be the relevant purchase price. Oftentimes the stated price of an asset is nothing more than the starting point of the bargaining process. Frequently, dealers give trade discounts (not to be confused with trade-in allowances) to customers of a certain category and cash discounts for prompt payment. Such discounts must be deducted from the originally stated price, since the purchase price must be determined on the basis of value actually surrendered by the buyer and received by the seller.

EXAMPLE

Assume that a firm purchases a machine for $10,000 under terms 2/10, n/30 (the company will receive a 2 percent discount if it pays within 10 days, but, in any event, must pay within 30 days). Transportation costs are $300, and the wages of the two men who install the machine amount to $150. In addition, while the machine is being installed, three employees who work in the vicinity of the new machine are idled for several hours, since power to other machines has to be disconnected. The wages paid to the men while they are idle are $90. The cost of the new machine would be computed as follows:

Purchase price:	$10,000	
Less 2% discount	200	$ 9,800
Freight-in		300
Installation costs		150
Payment for idle time		90
		$10,340

It may appear illogical to add the wages of the idle employees to the cost of the machine. But could the machine have been installed without such loss of time? Was the cost necessary to bring the asset to a serviceable state? If the answer is yes, then such costs have been incurred to benefit future periods, rather than the current period, and should rightfully be capitalized as part of the asset and should be allocated (i.e., depreciated) over the useful life of the new machine. If the answer is no, then the wages of the employees should be charged as an expense entirely in the period of installation. Would we reach the same conclusions if the entire plant has to be shut down for two days? Which costs might then be capitalized?

Purchases of Land

The same general principle applies to purchases of land. If a company purchases a parcel of land on which it intends to erect a new building, then all costs necessary to make the land ready for its intended use should be capitalized as part of the land. Thus, should a firm purchase a plot of land on which stands an old building that must first be torn down before a new building can be constructed, then the demolition costs should be added to the purchase price of the land; they will serve to benefit future accounting periods.

EXAMPLE

A company purchases a plot of land for $100,000, with the intention of constructing a plant. Before construction can begin, however, an old building on the land must be removed. Demolition costs amount to $10,000, but the firm is able to sell scrap from the old building for $3,000. Title and legal fees incurred in connection with the purchase total $1,000. At what value should the land be recorded?

Purchase price		$100,000
Add: Demolition costs	$10,000	
Less sale of scrap	3,000	7,000
Title and legal fees		1,000
Net cost of land		$108,000

Land is somewhat different from other fixed assets in that it does not ordinarily lose either service potential or value with the passage of time. Indeed, most often it *appreciates* in value. Thus the cost of the land should not be depreciated or allocated over time as long as there is no evidence of a decline in its service potential or value. If the land does not decline in value and the firm can, at any time, sell the land for the amount that it originally paid, then there is no real cost to the firm and, thus, no expense need be charged. Land, therefore, is not ordinarily considered a *depreciable* asset.

Construction of Assets

When a firm constructs its own assets the *theoretical* guidelines to determine cost are quite clear. The firm should include in the cost of the asset, all costs necessary to bring it to a serviceable state. Thus, the materials used, as well as the wages of all employees who work on the construction project, should quite clearly be capitalized as part of the asset. It is the *operational* questions that are the most difficult for many firms and their accountants to answer. How should a company account for those costs that are common to a number of activities that are carried out within the firm and cannot be traced either entirely or directly to the construction of the asset? How, for example, should it treat the salary of a general manager who devotes only a portion of his time to supervising the construction project? Or the wages of administrative personnel who maintain records pertaining to both the construction project and other activities of the company? Should such costs be included as part of the asset constructed by the firm or should they be charged to expense as incurred?

The general answer is that the firm should *allocate* such costs between the fixed asset and the other activities. It should make estimates of the proportion of time that the general manager and the administrative personnel performed services relating to the construction project as opposed to the other activities. Only that same proportion of overall costs should be added to the cost of the fixed asset.

EXAMPLE

The cost of constructing a minor addition to a plant might be computed (in oversimplified fashion) as follows:

Wages of employees directly associated with construction	$25,000
Materials and supplies used in project	40,000
Salary of plant supervisor (80 percent of salary for 4 months)	10,000
Wages of administrative personnel (10 percent of wages for 4 months)	600
	$75,600

Decisions as to what proportions of such *joint* (common) costs should be added to the fixed asset are neither trivial nor academic. Costs that are included as part of the fixed asset will be charged as expenses, through the process of depreciation, over the life of the asset. The remaining costs that are allocated to other activities are likely to be charged as expenses in the year in which they are actually incurred. Thus, in the above example, if the decision were made that no portion of the salary of the plant supervisor should be included as part of the asset, then overall company expenses for the year would have been considerably greater, since the entire $10,000 would have been deducted from revenues. As it is, only a small portion of the $10,000 (one year's depreciation) would be charged against this year's revenues; the remainder would be spread over the useful life of the asset.

The decision as to what proportion of joint costs to allocate to a constructed fixed asset and what proportion to allocate to other company activities must to a large extent be based on the good judgment of corporate managers and their accountants. Some companies, especially if they have otherwise had a "bad" year, may attempt to artificially reduce reported expenses by allocating an excessively large portion of joint costs to the fixed asset. Others who wish to minimize their tax liability, may do the reverse — allocate an illegitimately large portion of such costs to other company activities — with the intent of reducing current taxable income.

In brief, companies with different objectives of accounting are likely to differ in their treatment of transactions which are subject to judgment — such as the allocation of the salary of the plant supervisor. Persons who want to see that all companies use the same approach are destined for frustration when they enter the "real world." In areas subject to judgment where there are few concrete criteria providing guidance to accountants, differences of accounting treatment will occur. In what direction? Preparers will favor their own objective(s) of accounting. Nothing short of having the law dictate one method — regardless of objectives and facts — will result in uniform treatment. Naturally, "one method" creates artificial uniformity in accounting if it is applied to different factual situations. Unlikes will be made to look alike.

As stated earlier in the book, the ideal is to have "like accounting under like objectives, facts, and constraints." Shades of differences in facts must be dealt with in accounting pronouncements if we wish to achieve our elusive ideal. For example, if we wanted precision, where would the 80 percent figure for the plant supervisor's time in the foregoing example come from? Obviously, someone would not be keeping minute-by-minute time records of the supervisor's movements. The 80 percent figure is an estimate, and maybe a poor one at that. How precise do we want to be?

The attitude of the readers of the financial statements must be kept in mind. How do they define materiality? Do they want to know precisely or roughly? Does the preparer have an obligation to be precise?

The message here is clear. When one interprets financial statements, and knows that self-construction occurred, the obvious question to ask is, how was the accounting for overhead, such as supervisor's salaries, handled?

At this stage, most students find it helpful to begin to prepare a list of topics where considerable judgment has to be exercised. Such matters as FIFO versus LIFO, and different revenue recognition methods would go on the list, which, when the time comes to interpret financial statements, will be a great help.

Capitalization of Interest

The question of which costs related to the construction of fixed assets should be capitalized is reflected in a long-standing dispute among accountants. When a company has under construction a major fixed asset, such as a new plant, it often has to borrow funds to finance the construction. On the amounts borrowed, it must pay interest. Should the interest be charged as an expense during all the years in which the loan is outstanding or should the interest, like all other costs of construction, be capitalized as part of the fixed asset and charged off, in the form of depreciation, over the life of the asset? Some accountants argue that interest costs are no different from labor costs or material costs. They are a necessary cost of construction and should, therefore, be added to the cost of the asset. Moreover, they assert, the company earns no revenues from the plant while it is under construction; hence the matching principle dictates that it should charge no expenses. The interest costs, they say, will benefit future periods; they should, therefore, be expensed in future periods. Other accountants, however, maintain that interest is a special kind of expense. The firm borrows money, they say, for all sorts of purposes. Just as it is impossible to trace capital contributed by shareholders to specific assets, so also is it impossible to trace the proceeds from the issue of bonds or other instruments of debt to particular assets. Thus, they argue, it would be improper to associate the related interest charges to specific construction projects. Interest, they say, should be expensed in the periods during which the loans are outstanding, regardless of the reason for the borrowing.

In actual practice, relatively few firms capitalize interest costs. Those that do are mostly public utilities, such as gas and electric companies. Interest charges, however, may be substantial in relation to overall income. In comparing the profits of one company that does capitalize interest on construction with one that does not, it is vital that the difference in accounting methods be taken into consideration. Otherwise one company may appear to be considerably more profitable than the other.

The Distinction Between Maintenance or Repairs and Betterments

A frequent question that faces accountants is whether to treat certain costs associated with fixed assets, especially buildings and equipment, as repair (or maintenance) costs or as betterments. The distinction between the two is often unclear, but the accounting implications are significant. In general, repair or maintenance costs are incurred to keep assets in good operating condition. They are recurring costs and do not add to the productivity of the asset or extend its originally estimated useful life. Betterments, on the other hand, enhance an asset's service potential (e.g., extend its useful life or increase its productivity) from what was anticipated when it was first purchased.

Maintenance and repair costs are usually charged off as expenses as they are incurred. Betterments, on the other hand, are added to the original cost of the fixed asset and depreciated over its remaining useful life.

Again, our objectives-facts perspective enters the discussion. If your objective of accounting were to increase net income, and the *facts were unclear*, you would capitalize expenditures. However, if your objective were to minimize income tax payments, and you were not sure whether an outlay were a betterment or a repair, you would "expense" the outlay. But what if you wanted to achieve both objectives, at least temporarily? You would either capitalize some portion and expense the remainder — as a compromise — or decide which objective is more important and journalize accordingly and consistently.

When the *facts are clear* (see Appendix to Chapter 5) it may be difficult to accommodate one particular objective. The general rules as outlined previously would be followed.

Where does all this leave the reader? If the company is audited one would hope that consistency would be adhered to. If the preparer is reliable, consistency would be accommodated. When this is not the case, "let the reader beware". Unless the reader (say a banker) knows the company's reporting objectives and asks about the facts, misleading judgments could be formed.

EXAMPLE

In January 19x7, the C. Clarke Co. Limited expended $500 to air-condition the cab of one of its trucks. At the same time, it spent $75 to replace a wornout clutch. The journal entry to record the repair/betterment combination would be

Trucks (fixed asset)	$500	
Truck — repairs (expense)	75	
Cash		$575
To record repairs and betterments.		

If the remaining useful life of the truck were five years, then during each of the five years, depreciation expense on the truck would be $100 (one fifth of the air conditioning costs) greater than what it was previously.

The "gray" area of maintenance costs involves those costs that recur every few years. Many firms have a policy of repainting their plants every five years. Most of these firms, for the sake of clerical convenience, would record the cost of the paint job (assuming it was done by outside contractors) with the following journal entry:

Maintenance expense	xxxx	
Cash		xxxx

In effect, such firms are obtaining the benefit of the expenditure over a period of five years but charging the cost to one year. It would be considerably more precise to capitalize the cost of the paint job, record it as a separate asset, and allocate the cost to each of the five years to be benefited by the expenditure.

However, accounting must result from the mutual consensus of preparer and user. If expensing could mislead a user and does not seem sensible to a preparer of the statements, then capitalization and subsequent depreciation should occur.

Depreciation

Depreciation under stewardship accounting is the process of allocating (supposedly in a systematic and rational manner) the cost of a tangible asset, less salvage value, if any, over the estimated useful life of the asset. Allocation of cost is necessary if costs are to be matched with the revenues that they help to generate. By salvage value is meant the amount that can be recovered when the asset is either sold, traded in on a new asset, or scrapped. If an asset that originally cost $5,000 could be sold after 10 years (the longest the company expects to use the asset) for $500, then the total amount that must be depreciated, or allocated over useful life of the asset, is $5,000 less $500 — $4,500.

Depreciation in accordance with a historic cost/stewardship objective of accounting is a process of *allocation*, not *valuation*. The original cost of an asset less the accumulated depreciation (the amount of depreciation taken on an asset up to a given time) is often referred to as the *book* value of an asset. Accountants do not purport that the book value of an asset represents the value of the asset on the open market, either buying or selling. The potential for conflict between market values and book value can be demonstrated in a simple example involving an automobile.

A company purchases an automobile for $6,500 with the intention of using it for five years. It estimates that the trade-in value of the auto after that time will be $500. The amount of depreciation to be charged each year can be calculated to be $1,200:

$$\frac{\text{Original cost} - \text{Salvage value}}{\text{Useful life}} = \frac{\$6{,}500 - \$500}{5} = \$1{,}200.$$

Indicated below is a comparison of book values and market values at the end of each of the five years of estimated useful life. The market value represents a "typical" pattern of the decline in value of an automobile.

End of year	*Original cost*	*Depreciation taken to date*	*Cost less accumulated depreciation ("book" value)*	*Estimated net realizable value*
1	$6,500	$1,200	$5,300	$4,600
2	6,500	2,400	4,100	3,100
3	6,500	3,600	2,900	1,900
4	6,500	4,800	1,700	1,100
5	6,500	6,000	500	500

The two patterns of decline in value — book value versus market value — are indicated in Exhibit 9-1.

The fact that the two lines in Exhibit 9-1 do not coincide does not imply that the decision to depreciate the asset at the rate of $1,200 per year was in error. It is *not* the objective of depreciation accounting under stewardship accounting to indicate what the asset could be sold for (net realizable value) at the end of any given year.

It is often said that another objective of the depreciation process is to provide funds with which to replace assets when they must be sold or retired. This remark can be dangerous in a historic cost system. The error about such a proposition is evident by examining the basic journal entry for depreciation:

Depreciation	xxxx	
Accumulated depreciation		xxxx

Cash is neither debited nor credited; it is neither received from outsiders nor removed from one bank account into another. It is not possible for an accountant to assure that a firm will have sufficient cash on hand to purchase a new asset when an old one is retired merely by making an end-of-month or end-of-year adjusting entry.

Only in the most indirect sense can it be said that depreciation accounting provides funds for the future replacement of assets. Depreciation, like other expenses, is deducted from revenues in order to calculate annual income. To the extent that *tax* depreciation reduces income, it also reduces income taxes. Insofar as it reduces income taxes, it enables the firm to save for asset replacement more cash than it would if it had not recorded tax depreciation. In the same vein, the reduction in income attributable to depreciation expense may discourage some firms from declaring cash dividends of the same amount they might have if income were greater. In both cases, the relationship between depreciation and an asset replacement fund is far too removed to permit one to say that depreciation *provides* funds to replace assets. In a period of inflation, such as we have been experiencing in Canada, replacement costs of new automobiles have increased most years and would be well removed in price from a historic cost of five years ago.

EXHIBIT 9-1 **Comparison of Book Value and Market Value: A Typical Automobile**

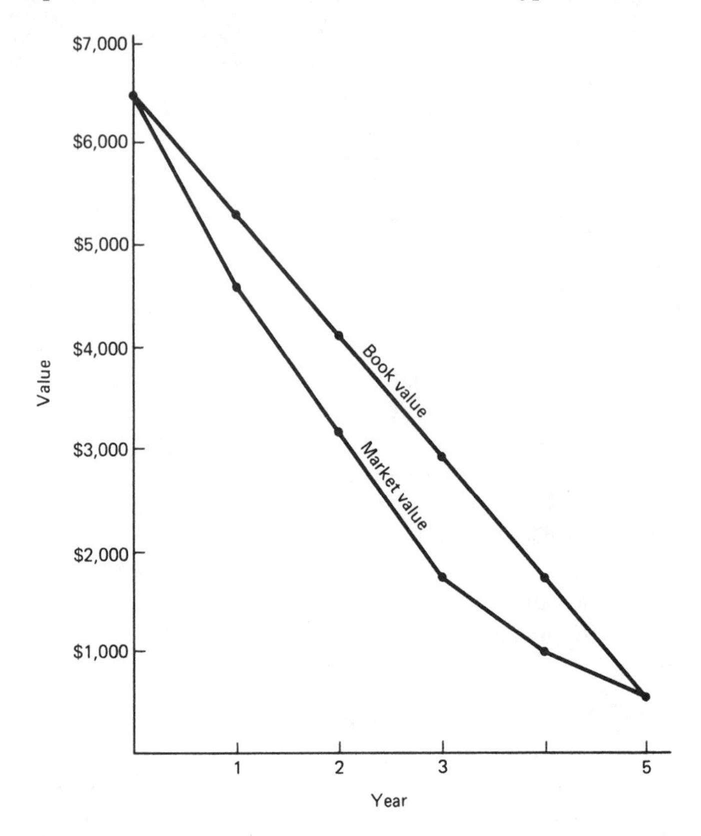

Arbitrary Allocations

Accountants who favor using historic cost because of its "objectivity" and stewardship purposes face a dilemma when they must find a method of depreciation. There is little question that an asset, such as an automobile, wears out. But, what is the pattern of: 1) wear and tear and 2) obsolescence — two important factors, among many, which reduce the usefulness of a long-lived asset?

Can the combined wisdom of the senior management of the company, engineers, economists, accountants and others lead to a so-called "correct" depreciation pattern? Which objectives of accounting are served by depreciation accounting?

Some writers, noteably Arthur L. Thomas, have gone to great lengths to show the arbitrary nature of cost allocations, such as depreciation. The allocation methods of depreciation per Thomas are "incorrigible," a term he chose to convey both amusing alarm and precision. Regarding the latter, "incorrigible" according to a good dictionary can mean "impossible to verify or falsify." Because depreciation patterns to a great extent are at the whim of the preparer of the financial statements, the net income figure which results from the depreciation process must therefore be viewed with caution.

Concerning objectives or purposes of financial accounting Thomas states "no legitimate purpose for financial accounting that has been advanced to date is furthered by making allocations."[1] This is a strong statement; it has received support from others, mainly academic accountants. Why, then, do accountants, on the advice of business managers, allocate asset costs, as we do in historic cost depreciation accounting? Perhaps tradition plays an important role in practice, perhaps accountants have not been educated about the arbitrary nature of depreciation, perhaps practicing accountants do not believe the conclusions of Thomas' studies. The matching concept is still popular practice in Canada, and it requires that an asset which declines in usefulness be expensed; hence, depreciation accounting is practiced. Also, income tax law requires depreciation computations, albeit often computed differently from some traditional accounting methods.

Thomas's alternative to depreciation accounting would be to record the long-lived asset at its net realizable value. Practicing accountants in Canada are not overjoyed with this suggestion because it somewhat changes the nature of their occupation.

Accelerated Depreciation Methods

Up until this point, whenever depreciation has been discussed, the annual depreciation charge has been calculated by dividing the total amount to be depreciated (cost less salvage value, if any) by the number of years that the asset was expected to be in use. The depreciation charges were thereby equal during each year of the asset's life. Such procedure of calculating depreciation is known as the *straight-line* method. There are, however, other means of allocating the cost of an asset to the various periods during which it will be used that result in unequal annual charges.

The most popular form of depreciation method in Canada, next to straightline, is the declining balance method. It is widely used in income tax legislation, both for its administrative convenience for income tax assessors (i.e., the use of a few standard rates simplifies country-wide administration of depreciation write-offs for income tax purposes) and for its flexibility for government policy-making. That is, alterations in income tax payments by Canadian companies can be brought about by changing tax depreciation *rates*, thereby changing income subject to income tax. As a result the economy can be spurred or slowed down somewhat by altering the yields that companies can obtain on investments in new assets. Yields or returns on investments are affected — as we saw in Chapter 6 — by the *timing* and *amount* of cash flows generated by an asset. Income tax can cause a major cash outflow, and its timing can vary depending on the tax depreciation rate in use.

Although there are several varieties of the declining (also called diminishing) balance method, the basic idea is the same for all. The original cost (estimated scrap or salvage is *NOT* deducted from cost) is the base used to commence the computation, and subsequent computations are on cost less depreciation to date. Suppose that a long-lived asset, say a machine, cost $10,000 and a 30 percent declining balance rate of depreciation was selected to recognize the pattern of probable wear and tear and obsolescence of the asset. The first year's depreciation would be $10,000 × 30 percent = $3,000. The second year would be 30 percent × ($10,000 − $3,000) = $2,100.

The full pattern for this asset would be:

Year	*Cost*	*Accumulated Depreciation (beginning of current year)*	*Net Cost*	*Depreciation Expense*	*Accumulated Depreciation (end of current year)*
0	$10,000	—	$10,000	—	—
1	10,000	—	10,000	$3,000	$3,000
2	10,000	$3,000	7,000	2,100	5,100
3	10,000	5,100	4,900	1,470	6,570
4	10,000	6,570	3,430	1,029	7,599
5	10,000	7,599	2,401	720	8,319
6	10,000	8,319	1,681	504	8,823
7	10,000	8,823	1,177	353	9,176
8	10,000	9,176	824	247	9,423
9	10,000	9,423	577	173	9,596
10	10,000	9,596	404	121	9,717
11	10,000	9,717	283 etc.		

Observe that the "net cost" will never reduce to zero as long as 30 percent of the sum is chosen for annual depreciation. This presence of a residual helps to explain why estimated scrap value is not deducted at commencement of the exercise. Roughly speaking, the residual of net cost can serve as an estimate of scrap. For example, at the end of year 8 the net cost of scrap supposedly is $10,000 − $9,423 = $577.

In terms of historic cost and a stewardship objective of accounting, how might we evaluate the declining balance method? We know that the matching concept is a foundation for stewardship-type accounting. We also know that depreciation accounting is an allocation of original cost in order to recognize such factors as wear and tear and likely obsolescence. The latter term is being used broadly to include all those factors (except wear and tear) which limit the usefulness of the asset, such as: inadequate size or capacity; uneconomic operating costs; development or appearance of a newer, cheaper model. Finally, we know that repair and maintenance and other similar expenditures have a bearing on cost incurrence and the matching concept.

For many assets, repair and maintenance costs are likely to increase as the machine gets older. Obviously, there are exceptions to this generalization; for example, some aircraft, such as helicopters, are in effect rebuilt every year and may incur a steady maintenance cost over several years.

Suppose that a manufacturing company had a machine which was likely to require these repair and maintenance costs: year 1: $0; year 2: $900; year 3: $1,530. Using the 30 percent depreciation charge and the $10,000 original cost from the previous illustration, the total costs of operating the machine (excluding labor and power) would be:

Year	*Depreciation*	*Repairs and Maintenance*	*Total cost*
0	$ —	$ —	$ —
1	3,000	—	3,000
2	2,100	900	3,000
3	1,470	1,530	3,000

In this hypothetical example, we have thus been able to combine an increasing repair and maintenance charge with a decreasing depreciation charge and arrive at a stable total cost of the two. Have we matched, per stewardship accounting? We *might* have, *if* there is a stable revenue pattern for the machine's output. That is, the portion, which we might be able to attribute to the machine, of the revenue from sale of the product which is manufactured by the machine is presumed to be fairly constant over several years of the machine's life. If so, have we matched year by year and produced a stable income from this machine? Revenue, for example, may be $5,000, costs are $3,000 and the net is $2,000 per year.

But, have we matched?? What do we mean by matching? In simple terms if we wanted to minimize the effort needed to match we could say that we have matched revenue of $5,000 to expense of $3,000. Stewardship advocates might be content with such an approach, but it is doubtful that other objectives or purposes of accounting would be well served by the idea used.

We know from Chapter 6 that the closer to the present a dollar of cash is received the more it is worth. Hence, our revenue of $5,000 per year is not really an *even* pattern in present value terms. Rather, it is a declining pattern. Further, the $3,000 is not entirely a cash outflow; the portion which is a depreciation charge is merely a cost allocation. (Tax, not accounting, depreciation helps to generate a cash flow by lowering income subject to tax.) Where does all this discussion leave us in terms of matching, if we exclude the income tax effects? It would leave most people confused.

Someone wishing to use financial statements for purposes of prediction or management evaluation would probably want to see *cash flows* matched — and this would exclude depreciation methods which are based on allocations of original cost because they do not involve cash flows. Hence, once again we encounter our theme of different measurements and disclosure for different objectives-facts-constraints. In stewardship terms we can match depreciation charges to revenue, but having matched, what conclusions should we draw? We can't draw particularly valid ones for current and future decision-making.

Income Tax Depreciation

We have indicated that in Canada the Income Tax Act and Regulations thereto outline the method and rate of depreciation which a company must use for a particular type of depreciable asset. We have also noted that the diminishing balance method is used extensively. We now have to describe the system more fully so that matters which come later in the book and in this Chapter can be better understood. (A full description of income tax depreciation may be obtained later by taking an income tax course. The entire subject is too complex to cover in detail at this stage of your learning process).

Generally, assets are depreciated for income tax purposes on a pool or grouped basis which includes all assets of the same type. Income tax depreciation is based on historic cost, not replacement cost or other current value. All automobiles, for example, would use a 30 percent maximum rate applied to the reduced cost balance; all furniture and fixtures have a 20 percent maximum rate. A company having income subject to tax which wishes to lower its income taxes would choose the maximum of 30 percent for automobiles. In contrast, a company with an operating loss may claim no tax depreciation currently, and save the unused tax depreciation for later years when the company might become profitable and would otherwise have to pay income taxes. The taxpayer has the choice of using anywhere up to 30 percent for automobiles, up to 20 percent for furniture and fixtures, and so forth.

Many additional rules exist for applying income tax depreciation; technically it is called *capital cost allowance*. For example, if an asset is sold for a sum in excess of its depreciated cost and it is the only one of its group, any "gain" may have to be divided between (1) gain subject to ordinary income tax rates and (2) gain subject to capital gains tax rates. To illustrate, an asset costing $100,000 which had been depreciated for tax purposes to a net of $60,000 and having been sold for $115,000 would have an income tax gain of $55,000 ($115,000 − $60,000). The sum in excess of original cost of $100,000, that is $15,000, would be subject to capital gains income tax rates. The $40,000 ($100,000 – $60,000) remainder would be subject to ordinary income tax rates. Any losses on sale of depreciable assets are also subject to specific rules.

Our reasons for giving a brief glimpse of income tax depreciation (capital cost allowance) accounting at this point is two-fold: (1) to show that major differences from non-tax objectives of accounting can easily exist; and (2) to warn that in a future chapter we will have to show how the two (income tax versus other objectives of accounting) might be reconciled. Even though a company may have the deferral of income tax as its primary objective of accounting, it might still use one method of depreciation (perhaps straight line) in its accounting records and financial statements and another method (diminishing balance) or rate in its income tax returns which have to be filed with the federal (and some provincial) government(s). This difference can exist because the income tax legislation expressly permits such a practice. In contrast, in other situations (such as many revenue recognition circumstances) whatever method is used for stewardship or prediction accounting purposes also has to be used for income tax purposes.

Some small businesses which are primarily interested in minimizing and deferring income tax use income tax depreciation rates and the diminishing balance method in financial statements prepared for the banker. The banker must be alert to what officials of the company are doing and not assume that the company's assets are depreciating rapidly. That is, income tax depreciation rates are often quite generous in a sense; some rates are as high as 100 percent (one-year write-off). The government has used such high rates applied to historic cost in order to help companies which need modern equipment as well as to lessen the chances that Canadian companies might press for replacement cost depreciation.

Depreciation Based on Productivity

Many other depreciation methods have been devised to accompany historic cost accounting. The *unit charge* or, as it is often called, the *units of output* depreciation method directly takes into account the amount of service that an asset can provide in a given time period. The unit charge method requires that an estimate be made at the time an asset is acquired, not of useful life in terms of years as was required by the other methods, but rather of useful life in terms of units of service. Useful life might be stated in terms of machine-hours, units produced, or some other base. The useful life of an auto, for example, might be expressed as 100,000 miles. The cost of the asset is then allocated to each time period in proportion to the amount of service actually consumed.

EXAMPLE

Assume that an automobile cost $6,500 and that the company has a policy of using the autos for a fixed number of miles — assume 100,000 miles — and then selling them, regardless of how many years an auto has actually been in service. The company estimates that after that many miles the resale value is approximately $500. The following schedule indicates the *actual* number of miles driven in each year and the applicable depreciation charge:

Year	*Miles driven*	*Miles driven as a percent of 100,000*	*Net cost to be depreciated ($6,500 less $500)*	*Depreciation charge*
1	25,000	25%	$6,000	$1,500
2	17,000	17	6,000	1,020
3	18,000	18	6,000	1,080
4	26,000	26	6,000	1,560
5	14,000	14	6,000	840
	100,000	100%		$6,000

Insofar as units of service provided by an asset can be related to the revenue produced by the asset, and obsolescence is not an important consideration, the unit charge method provides a much better match of costs with revenues than do the other depreciation methods. As asset *productivity* increases, so also does the percentage of asset cost charged off as an expense. Unit charge methods of depreciation, however, are not widely used. Their lack of acceptance can be attributed to difficulties of application. For most assets it is very difficult to estimate the number of service units provided. In fact, the useful life of many assets is more a function of time than of physical wear and tear. This is especially true in periods of rapid technological advance when assets tend to become technologically obsolete long before they become physically obsolete.

Depreciation Methods Compared

Although we have analyzed the meaning of matching using accelerated and other depreciation allocation methods, we must be careful to recognize the limits of various criticisms. We have seen the difficulty of matching *inventory* costs to revenue. Sometimes, during periods of rapidly fluctuating replacement costs, the problem of matching can be as difficult as with depreciation. However, there may be other times when matching makes sense for some users. Persons wishing to predict need a form of matched *cash flows* (without cost and revenue "allocations" of common costs) in order to discount at the appropriate time. The criticisms of matching therefore are not as widespread and devastating as one might first suspect. Primarily, the criticisms of matching relate to the use of cost allocations, such as depreciation and amortization accounting.

Nonetheless, many of the comments about declining balance depreciation apply to straight-line depreciation. For instance, in picking a depreciation pattern what are we hoping to accomplish? Under stewardship accounting we wish to match revenue on an *accrual* basis with expense on an accrual basis. In this way we arrive at a net income before income tax which is also on an accrual basis. As we stated earlier in the book, advocates of such a net income before income tax computation hope that it represents a sort of sensible *measure of success* (change in "well offness") of a business.

From time to time we have questioned the logic and conclusions of such advocates; however, the measure in spite of its limitations could be better than some alternatives or not having any measure. For other objectives such as cash prediction or income taxation such accrual matching with allocations seems very questionable. The income tax legislation, for instance, stipulates its own methods of depreciation and some of its own ways of computing taxable income.

Nevertheless, once we accept that our task is to match in accordance with current practice we face the difficult task of choosing a suitable depreciation method. We must fall back on the expertise of engineers, economists, plant personnel and so on to estimate wear and tear, obsolescence, repairs and maintenance and similar costs. Then we have to decide whether we are matching in order to:

1. Provide a stable or even income figure over the life of the asset; or
2. Provide a constant *rate* of return on investment, say 20 percent. (This means that income would be higher in the earlier years when the plant is new and the investment in it is higher.)
3. Accomplish something else.

Ideally, preparers should state their objectives. When this is not done the user/reader will have to assess the method which has been chosen to ascertain whether it adequately recognizes obsolescence, etc. The preparer, for example, may be ultraconservative and try to write off the asset as quickly as possible by using declining balance depreciation and high rates.

Students are often not satisfied after such an explanation of how to choose a depreciation method; this is hardly surprising. Depreciation methods based on the stewardship cost allocation concept have serious limitations. Furthermore, accounting thought on the subject is not clear. This two-fold situation is troublesome. Yet, the situation is challenging. The field of accounting is wide open for bright people who can conduct research and effect needed change.

Changes in Estimates of Asset Life

Estimates of useful life are bound to be unreliable, as they require prescience of several years. The question of the most appropriate means of changing an estimate, as better information becomes available with the passage of time, is illustrative of the needs of the accountant to weigh theoretical against practical considerations.

Suppose that a firm has been depreciating a machine over a five-year period but decides at the end of the third year that, barring an unexpected breakdown, it will continue to use the machine for another four years — a total of seven years in all. The asset cost $3,500, and the firm estimated that it would have no salvage value. Depreciation is being taken on a straight-line basis.

During each of the three years the firm charged depreciation of $700 — a total of $2,100. Had the firm correctly estimated the useful life at the time of acquisition, it would have charged depreciation of $500 ($3,500/7) per year — a total of $1,500. The simplest way of correcting the situation is to change the depreciation schedule to be followed during the remaining life of the asset. At the end of the third year the book value of the asset would be $1,400 (cost of $3,500 less $2,100 in depreciation to date). The remaining useful life would now be estimated to be four years. Depreciation charges for each of the remaining four years would be $1,400 divided by 4 — $350 per year.

Such an approach is straightforward and requires no additional journal entries or corrections of prior years' earnings. At the same time, however, it is not altogether satisfactory. As the result of the original misestimate of useful life depreciation charges for the first three years were overstated by $200 per year, and depreciation charges of the next four years would be *understated* by $150 per year. The error of the first three years would be corrected by making offsetting errors in the next four.

Alternatively, it is *possible* to correct, via a single adjusting entry, the cumulative "error" of the past three years and then proceed during the next four years with what would have been the depreciation charge had the company had perfect foresight and made the correct estimates in the first place. In the example at hand the correcting entry would be

Accumulated depreciation	$600	
Correction of prior years' earnings		$600
To correct for "error" in the estimate of asset life.		

"Correction of prior years' earnings" would be *closed* to retained earnings at the time other year-end closing entries are made.

However, the "correction of prior years' earnings" entry is *not* accepted in Canada. There would appear to be good reasons for the lack of acceptance. Some are:

1. At the time that the estimate of useful life was made, officials of the company were probably using the best information available. Under such circumstances an error could not occur; new information provided through hindsight does not constitute an error in accounting terms.
2. Adjustments of income statements of *prior* years is a questionable practice if a main purpose of accounting is to provide information for *current* and *future* decisions. There is some merit in correcting past financial statements so that users can establish income trend lines over several periods. But, there is some doubt about how consistent many other figures on the income statement are from year to year. As we see, chapter after chapter, accounting is full of judgments and estimates. Frankly, we may be trying for precision which is not attainable. In view of the doubt about the validity of past trend lines for decisions about the future, it seems wise to treat revisions of accounting estimates prospectively (in the future) instead of retroactively (in the past, present and future).

Hence, the net book value of $1,400 would be spread over the four future years.

Retirement of Fixed Assets

Upon the retirement of an asset, either by sale or abandonment, the asset *as well as the related accumulated depreciation* must be removed from the books. If the asset is sold for the amount and at the time originally estimated, then the retirement entry is especially simple.

EXAMPLE

Return once again to the auto which originally cost $6,500 and had an estimated salvage value after five years of $500. At the end of five years (regardless of the choice of depreciation method) the fixed asset account would have a debit balance of $6,500 and the accumulated depreciation account a credit balance of $6,000. If the asset is, in fact, sold for $500, then the appropriate journal entry would be

Cash	$ 500	
Accumulated depreciation — autos	6,000	
Fixed assets — autos		$6,500
To record the sale of the asset.		

If at any time during the life of the asset it is either sold or abandoned for an amount greater or less than its book value at that time, then a gain or loss on retirement would have to be recognized.

EXAMPLE The firm has charged depreciation on the auto using straight-line depreciation. At the end of three years, after $3,600 of depreciation had been charged, the firm sold the auto for $2,000. The book value of the asset at time of sale would have been $2,900 — $6,500 less $3,600. Hence, the firm has suffered a loss of $900.

Cash	$2,000	
Accumulated depreciation — autos	3,600	
Loss on retirement (expense +)	900	
Fixed assets — autos		$6,500
To record the sale of the asset.		

Bear in mind that if an asset is sold anytime before the close of the year, depreciation for the portion of the year which the asset was actually held must first be recorded before any gain or loss can be computed.

An exception to this approach may occur in practice if a company bases its depreciation on the year *end* balances in the depreciable asset accounts. That is, many shortcuts might occur in practice as long as consistency is applied and there are no serious, material errors which might mislead readers to whom the financial statements are addressed.

EXAMPLE The firm sold the auto for $2,050 after it had owned it for four years, three months. The asset subsidiary ledger card indicates that depreciation of $4,800 — four annual entries of $1,200 — had been recorded. Depreciation for the final quarter year has not yet been charged. Two journal entries are thereby necessary to update the depreciation records and to record the sale:

Depreciation	$300	
Accumulated depreciation — autos		$300
To record depreciation for one-fourth year.		

Cash	$2,050	
Accumulated depreciation — autos	5,100	
Fixed assets — autos		$6,500
Gain on retirement (revenue +)		650
To record the sale of the asset.		

The nature of gains or losses on retirement merits comment. Under an environment where replacement costs and net realizable values of assets do not change (that is, this would be a hypothetical situation for Canada in recent years), such gains or losses arise only because a company is unable to have perfect foresight as to the time of retirement and the selling price. (Selling price and scrap value are a function of current market prices; hence, it is necessary to estimate, even under historic cost accounting, future selling market prices. This estimating, of course, is a departure from the degree of objectivity one can obtain from basing accounting on only the purchase invoices for long-lived assets). If it had such foresight, it would have determined its depreciation schedule accordingly and hence there would be no gain or loss upon retirement. In other words, in the previous example the $650 gain on retirement indicates that excess depreciation of $153 per year for the 4¼ years that the asset was held had been charged. Meticulous accounting might therefore dictate that instead of recognizing a gain on retirement the company should correct the prior years' earnings for the excess depreciation charges. In practice, such an approach is virtually never taken, since it would lead to an excessive number of prior period adjustments.

For income tax purposes the $650 gain on retirement might be taxable in the current year. It might also be offset under an approach similar to group depreciation — to be described shortly. Current income tax laws and facts hold the key to current treatment.

Trade-ins

A special problem is presented when a firm *trades in* an old asset for a new one. A firm surrenders an old car, plus cash, for a later model. The most logical way of handling a trade-in is to view it as two separate transactions. In the first, the old asset is sold — not for cash but instead for a *trade-in allowance.* In the second, the new asset is purchased — for cash plus a trade-in allowance. The critical step in implementing such a procedure lies in determining the price for which the old asset was sold. In many instances, the amount that the dealer says he is offering as a trade-in allowance bears no relationship to the actual fair market value of the old asset. In the auto industry, for example, it is common practice for new car dealers to offer unusually high trade-in allowances on the used vehicles of prospective new car purchasers. If the purchaser accepts the high trade-in allowance, he may not be entitled to discounts that are generally granted to purchasers who come without used cars. He may, in effect, have to pay full, or nearly full, *sticker* price for the new car, something he would not ordinarily have to do if he came to the dealer without an old car to trade.

If a meaningful gain or loss on retirement is to be computed it is essential, therefore, that the company determine as accurately as possible the actual fair market value of the asset given up. This can usually be done by consulting industry publications such as the car dealers' "blue " book of used car prices.

EXAMPLE

The auto, which originally cost $6,500 (estimated life of five years, $500 salvage) is traded in for a new car after three years. The dealer grants a trade-in allowance of $3,500, but, according to a book of used car prices, the car is worth no more than $2,600. The sticker price of the new car is $8,500, but, in fact, an astute buyer would not normally pay more than $7,500. In addition to giving up its old car, the company pays cash of $4,900.

The book value of the old car, assuming straight-line depreciation, would at time of trade-in be

Original cost	$6,500
Accumulated depreciation (3 years × $1,200)	3,600
	$2,900

Loss on the sale of the old car would therefore be $2,900 less $2,600 (fair market value of the old car) — $300.

The "sale" of the old car could properly be recorded as follows:

Loss on retirement	$ 300	
Accumulated depreciation — autos	3,600	
Trade-in allowance (a temporary account)	2,600	
Fixed assets — autos		$6,500
To record the "sale" of the asset.		

The entry to record the purchase of the new auto would be

Fixed assets — autos	$7,500	
Cash		$4,900
Trade-in allowance		2,600
To record the purchase of the new asset.		

Clearly, the two entries could be combined (and the trade-in allowance account eliminated). U.S. accountants sometimes prescribe a slightly different method for accounting for trade-in transactions that would otherwise result in a *gain*. Under their method, the new asset would be recorded at the sum of the book value of the old asset and any additional cash paid. No gain on the trade-in would be recognized.

Group Depreciation Methods

Ordinarily, a firm would maintain a separate record of each individual piece of equipment, plot of land, or building owned and would compute separately the depreciation charge for that asset. For accounting purposes, however, the asset need not necessarily be a complete, integrated physical asset. In recording a building, for example, its water heater might be viewed as a separate asset and depreciated over a different useful life than the rest of the building. So, too, as pointed out earlier, could be periodic paint jobs. In the ready-mix concrete industry it is common practice to record the mixer portion of a cement mix truck apart from the engine and chassis.

Sometimes groups of identical assets are recorded as a unit, and depreciation is taken on the group as a whole. The essential characteristic of the *group depreciation method* as compared to the individual depreciation methods discussed so far is that when any one of the units which make up the group is abandoned or sold for an amount either greater or less than its book value at the time, no gain or loss is recognized on the transaction. It is assumed that some members of the group will be sold at an amount above book value; others will be either retired prematurely or sold for an amount below book value. But over time, the gains and losses will even out. Whenever a unit is retired, the asset account is credited for its original cost, and the accumulated depreciation account is debited for the difference between the original cost and the value received (if any) upon retirement.

EXAMPLE

A company purchases 20 desks at a cost of $1,000 each. The desks have a useful life of 10 years, and are depreciated on a straight-line basis, after which time they will be given to charity. At the end of the first year one desk is destroyed. At the end of the second, one is sold for $900. The following entries summarize events for three years with respect to the desks.

Furniture	$20,000	
Cash		$20,000
To record the purchase of the 20 desks.		

Depreciation	$2,000	
Accumulated depreciation — furniture		$2,000
To record first-year depreciation ($100 per desk times 20 desks.)		

Accumulated depreciation — furniture	$1,000	
Furniture		$1,000
To record the destruction of one desk in an accident shortly after the end of the first year.		

Notice that even though only $100 of depreciation had been accumulated to date, no loss on destruction is recorded, and the accumulated depreciation account is debited for $1,000 — the original cost of one desk.

Depreciation	$1,900	
Accumulated depreciation — furniture		$1,900
To record second-year depreciation ($100 per desk times 19 desks).		

Cash	$900	
Accumulated depreciation — furniture	100	
Furniture		$1,000
To record the sale of one desk at the end of the second year for $900 cash.		

Note that even though the *book* value of the desk at time of sale is only $800, no gain is recognized on the sale. The accumulated depreciation account is debited for $100, not withstanding the fact that $200 of depreciation had been accumulated to date.

Depreciation	$1,800	
Accumulated depreciation — furniture		$1,800
To record third-year depreciation ($100 per desk times 18 desks).		

Group depreciation methods add a measure of convenience to the accounting process. But since they are based on assumptions of averages — assumptions that do not always prove realistic — they may also add a measure of distortion.

Natural Resources and Depletion

Natural resources, or *wasting assets*, as they are often referred to, are accounted for in a manner similar to plant and equipment. They are recorded initially at acquisition cost, and the value at which they are reported subsequently is reduced as their service potential declines.

The process of allocating the cost of natural resources over the periods in which they provide benefits is known as *depletion*. The service potential of natural resources can ordinarily be measured more meaningfully in terms of quantity of production (e.g., tons or barrels) than number of years. Hence, depletion is generally charged on a *units of output* basis. As with other types of long-lived assets, the initial cost of a natural resource may be reported on the balance sheet for as long as it is in service. The accumulated depletion may be indicated in a contra account. In practice, however, a contra account is not always used; often the balance in the natural resource account itself is reduced directly by the amount of the accumulated depletion.

EXAMPLE

A firm purchases mining properties for $2 million cash. It estimates that the properties will yield 400,000 usable tons of ore. During the first year of production, the firm mines 5,000 tons.

The following entry would be appropriate to record the purchase of the properties:

Mineral deposits	$2,000,000	
Cash		$2,000,000
To record the purchase of the ore deposit.		

Since the deposit will yield an estimated 400,000 tons of usable ore, cost assignable to each ton is

$$\frac{\$2{,}000{,}000}{400{,}000 \text{ tons}} = \$5 \text{ per ton.}$$

Depletion cost of the first year would be

$$5{,}000 \text{ (tons mined)} \times \$5 \text{ per ton} = \$25{,}000.$$

Depletion	$25,000	
Mineral deposits — accumulated depletion		$25,000
To record first-year depletion.		

After the first year, the mineral deposits would be reported on the balance sheet as

Mineral deposits	$2,000,000
Less: Accumulated depletion	25,000
	$1,975,000

Depletion is a cost of production, to be added along with other production costs (labor, depreciation of equipment, supplies) to the carrying value of the inventory. It will be charged as an expense (cost of minerals sold) in the accounting period in which the inventory is sold and the revenue from the sale is recognized.

Often, a mining or drilling company will have to purchase or build special, immovable equipment or structures that can be used only in connection with the recovery of a specific deposit. If such structures or equipment will be used for as long as the property continues to be "mined," and this period is shorter than the potential life of the equipment or structures, then depreciation charges should logically be determined using the same units of output basis as used to compute depletion. Depreciation, if based on output, is more likely in such circumstances to assure that the cost of equipment or structures is matched with the revenues realized from the sale of the minerals than if based on useful life in terms of time.

Intangible Assets

Intangible assets are those assets characterized by the rights, privileges, and benefits of possession rather than by physical existence. Often, the service potential of intangible assets is uncertain and exceedingly difficult to measure. As a consequence, intangible assets are frequently the subject of controversy. Examples of intangible assets are patents, copyrights, research and development costs, organizational costs, and goodwill. In this section we shall deal specifically with only a few selected intangible assets with the aim of highlighting some key accounting issues. A discussion of goodwill, one of the more controversial intangible assets, will be deferred until the chapter pertaining to ownership interests among corporations, since goodwill generally arises out of the acquisition of one company by another.

Intangibles are considered to be assets either because they represent rights to future benefits or because the expenditures that were made to acquire or develop them will serve to benefit a number of accounting periods in the future. Hence, the costs must be allocated to the periods in which the benefits will be realized.

Intangible assets are recorded initially at the cost to acquire or develop them. Such cost is then amortized over (allocated to) the periods in which the benefits will accrue. Sometimes, when the benefits are expected to accrue over a long period of time, the cost would not be amortized. Examples where amortization would not seem appropriate are: taxi licenses (which grant a right to operate a cab to a *limited* number of taxi owners, who as a group then have exclusive rights to pick up passengers in a designated area; such licenses could be worth $20,000 or more as long as the law does not change); trucking licences (similar to the taxi situation); and some liquor dispensing licenses (in cases where few firms have distribution rights). The general accounting approach to intangibles which are to be amortized may be illustrated using the example of copyrights.

Copyrights

A copyright is an exclusive right, granted by law, to publish, sell, reproduce, or otherwise control a literary, musical, or artistic work. Copyrights are granted for very long periods of time. The cost to secure a copyright from the federal government is minimal; however, the cost to purchase one from its holder on a work that has proven successful — on a best-selling novel or musical recording, for instance — may be substantial.

If a firm were to purchase a copyright, it would record it initially as it would any other asset. Assuming a cost of $20,000, for example, an appropriate journal entry might be

Copyright	$20,000	
Cash		$20,000
To record the purchase of the copyright.		

If the remaining useful life were determined to be 10 years, then the following entry would be appropriate each year to record amortization:

Amortization of copyrights (expense +)	$2,000	
Accumulated amortization — copyrights		$2,000
To record amortization of copyright.		

Accounting practices with respect to copyrights also focus on a question that is raised with respect to many types of intangibles — that of the number of years over which cost should be amortized. Although the legal life of a copyright may be firmly established, the copyright may be of significant economic value for a considerably shorter period of time. Actual useful life may depend on a multitude of factors such as public taste, critical acclaim, or future success of the author, none of which can readily be assessed. As with other long-lived assets, carrying value of the asset as well as amortization charges (the periodic decline in value) must be based, in large measure, on subjective judgments of corporate management and accountants.

Intangible drilling costs

Accounting practices in the oil industry raise another important issue with respect to intangible assets: What is the nature of the costs to be included as part of the asset; how directly must a cost be associated with a future benefit before it should properly be capitalized? Despite highly sophisticated geological survey techniques, it is usually necessary for oil companies, in their search for new reserves, to drill unsuccessfully in several locations before actually striking oil. Obviously the cost of drilling the productive wells should be capitalized and amortized over the years during which oil will be withdrawn from the ground. But what about the costs of drilling the *dry holes*? Should they be written off as incurred, or should they also be capitalized and amortized over the period in which oil is withdrawn from the successful wells? Should they be considered losses (corporate errors, in a sense) or expenditures that are statistically necessary to discover the productive locations? Directly, the dry holes will produce no benefits to the company; indirectly they represent an inevitable cost of finding the productive wells.

Some companies do capitalize "intangible drilling costs"; many do not. Those that capitalize are known as *full-cost* companies; those that do not are *flow-through* (or successful efforts) firms. Either approach is acceptable, although the trend is toward flow-through methods. This is mainly because of pressure from the U.S. accounting bodies and authorities. Flow-through is a response to those criticisms against cost allocation detailed earlier in this chapter, and to other criticisms of full-cost.

To date the accounting profession has given relatively little attention to the question of whether in order for a cost to be capitalized it must be associated directly with benefits to be received, or whether it must merely be a member of a class of costs that will be associated with the benefits.

Research and development costs

Accounting procedures with respect to research and development costs are illustrative of another issue common to intangible assets — to what extent must theoretical concepts of intangible assets be tempered by "practical" considerations? Research and development costs are, by nature, incurred in order to benefit future accounting periods. Expenditures for research and development are made in the expectation that they will lead to new or improved products or processes that will in turn increase revenues or decrease expenses. The matching concept suggests that research and development costs be capitalized as intangible assets and amortized over the periods in which the additional revenues are generated or cost savings effected.

In practice, however, it has proven exceedingly difficult to match specific expenditures for research and development with specific products or processes. Some expenditures are for *basic* research; they are not intended to produce direct benefits. Others produce no benefits at all or result in benefits which could not have been foreseen at the time they were incurred.

The Accounting Research Committee (ARC) of the Canadian Institute of Chartered Accountants (CICA) recently prescribed that expenditures for *some* types of research and development costs must be charged to expense in the year incurred rather than capitalized as intangible assets. The ARC was motivated by the great variety of practice among corporations as to the nature of the costs that were capitalized and the number of periods over which they were amortized. Given almost unlimited flexibility in accounting for research and development, some firms capitalized costs that were unlikely to provide future benefits; others *wrote off* large amounts of previously capitalized costs in carefully selected periods so as to avoid burdening other accounting periods with amortization charges.

The ARC has drawn a distinction between research and development. Their definitions are:

Research is planned investigation undertaken with the hope of gaining new scientific or technical knowledge and understanding. Such investigation may or may not be directed towards a specific practical aim or application.

Development is the translation of research findings or other knowledge into a plan or design for new or substantially improved materials, devices, products, processes, systems or services prior to the commencement or commercial production or use.

The ARC feels that "in most cases, research activities will not produce identifiable benefits in future periods; the amount of future benefits and the period over which they will be received are usually uncertain."

Accordingly, they recommend that "research costs should be charged as an expense of the period in which they are incurred."

With respect to development costs, the ARC states: "Development costs should be charged as an expense of the period in which they are incurred except in the[se] circumstances:

Development costs should be [capitalized or] deferred to future periods if *all* of the following criteria are satisfied:

a) the product or process, is clearly defined and the costs attributable thereto can be identified;
b) the technical feasibility of the product or process has been established;
c) the management of the enterprise has indicated its intention to produce and market, or use, the product or process;
d) the future market for the product or process is clearly defined or, if it is to be used internally rather than sold, its usefulness to the enterprise has been established; and
e) adequate resources exist, or are expected to be available, to complete the project."

For the most part, development costs would tend to be expensed because it is difficult to meet *all* of the five criteria.

The approach of the ARC is inconsistent with the notion that costs should be matched to the revenues with which they are associated. It substitutes a somewhat precise accounting rule for the professional judgment of managers and accountants. It can hardly be viewed as an ideal solution to the accounting problems related to intangibles. But the ARC's approach does represent an attempt to ensure greater comparability of financial statements and to eliminate malfeasance of reporting on the part of at least a few corporations. Unfortunately the ARC's treatment (which is similar but not identical to that adopted in the U.S.), may also make "unlikes in fact look alike."

Write-Downs

Accounting practice in Canada and the theory of stewardship accounting can easily differ. In the case of long-lived assets, the theory is fairly clear when an asset's net realizable value and its value in use (present value to the user) are *below* historic cost less depreciation. A write-down is in order because it is assumed that a loss has occurred.

In practice there may be a reluctance by the preparer of the financial statements to write down a long-lived asset. Presumably people keep hoping that market prices will somehow rise above historic cost less any depreciation. Auditors may press for a write-down but lack evidence to convince their client. The client may say "I know the market price will rise again, very shortly." The auditor can counter with a facetious remark "If *I* knew that the market price (of a particular asset) would rise, I wouldn't be an auditor/accountant. I'd buy the asset, sell it when the price went up, and retire." In summary, readers of financial statements cannot always assume that market prices exceed historic cost, less accumulated depreciation.

Several examples of the above set of facts exist at ay one time in Canada. Variations of the problem also occur. One recent example, which was well known so that there was no deception to anyone, involved Brascan Limited. A large part of its operations consisted of a large electric-generating facility in Brazil. The Brazilian government pressured Brascan for a number of years to sell the facility to them. On Brascan's books the facility was carried at over $800 million. The Brazilian government paid less than half that sum to Brascan, yet until the actual sale took place, Brascan had little idea what the Brazilian government would pay. However, Brascan clearly could have jeopardized its price negotiations with the Brazilian government if the financial statements prepared prior to sale showed a huge write-down. Bookkeeping may be simple; but accounting and auditing can be complex, yet interesting.

Summary

Long-lived assets provide services over a number of accounting periods. Their cost, therefore, in accordance with stewardship objectives, must be allocated over all of the periods benefited.

Long-lived assets are conventionally reported on the balance sheet at their original cost, less the amount assumed to have expired to date. The amount at which they are reported may, however, bear little relationship either to what it would cost to replace them or to their value to their specific users (the present value of the net revenues that they will generate or the cost savings that they will effect).

The process of allocating the cost of a long-lived asset to the accounting periods which will benefit from its services is referred to as depreciation, depletion, or amortization. There are several basic methods of cost allocation. Among them are the straight-line method, various *accelerated* methods, and the units of output method.

Regardless of how a long-lived asset is accounted for — the method of allocation selected, the useful life estimated, or the means of recognizing changes in market value chosen — its accumulated impact on reported income *over its useful life* will be the same. The total cost of an asset — the amount to be charged as an expense — will be the price paid for the asset less the amount for which it can be sold at time of retirement. The manner in which an asset is accounted for may, however, have a significant effect on the earnings of each individual period in which it is used. As a consequence, the issues associated with long-lived assets are of critical concern both to the accounting profession and the financial community at large.

Some practitioners and academics are critical of the cost allocation process because they believe that the approach is fundamentally arbitrary. Others, who are interested in prediction, are critical of cost allocations for depreciable assets because no cash is involved, and it is difficult for financial statement readers to separate the effects on cash from statement totals, which are cash and non-cash.

Years ago some assets had shorter lives and there was less research and development because the economy and industry were less complex. Matching made far more sense then. Today it makes some sense to match cash flow items (such as revenue less selling expenses) but less sense to arbitrarily allocate costs of major assets.

In situations where the facts are vague (should an expenditure be expensed or capitalized? which periods benefit from an outlay for a major new asset?) objectives of accounting take on greater importance. In Canada many small businesses would opt for income tax minimization as their prime objective. As a result outlays which may be betterments become expensed — as long as the business is profitable. Also, income tax depreciation methods may be used. Both of these practices may unduly lower net income. Readers of financial statements have to be aware of the importance of a particular objective of financial accounting to preparers of the statements. Otherwise, serious errors in interpretation may result.

Notes

[1]Arthur L. Thomas, *The Allocation Problem: Part Two.* (Sarasota, Florida: American Accounting Association, 1974), p. 5. See also p. 51 and *The Allocation Problem in Financial Accounting Theory* (Sarasota, Florida: American Accounting Association, 1969).

Questions, Problems, and Cases

Questions

*9-1 "In situations where facts are vague, objectives of accounting take on greater importance." Explain. Use examples relating to long-lived assets to support your position.

9-2 How might separate reporting of the cost and accumulated depreciation for major classes of long-lived assets assist the users of financial statements?

9-3 "Because fixed assets are stated on the *balance sheet* at values that are based on historical costs (in order to satisfy the stewardship objective), the *income statement* is of limited value in evaluating corporate performance." Do you agree? Explain.

9-4 What is the value of an asset to a particular user? Why is it seldom feasible to measure the value of a fixed asset to a particular user? What is often used as a measure of value to a user?

9-5 It is generally agreed that market values of fixed assets are more relevant than other "values" for most decisions that must be made by both investors and managers. Why, then, do accountants persist in reporting historical values? Is this a serious deficiency of accounting?

9-6 Why might some companies report far more information about replacement cost, net realizable values, and cash flows than do others?

9-7 A shareholder recently charged that the financial statements of a corporation in which he owned shares were false and misleading in that included among fixed assets was computer equipment which the company leased from a financial institution but did not actually own. Assuming the assertion to be correct — that leased equipment was included among assets — how might the company respond to charges that the statements were false and misleading?

9-8 A company recently purchased for $350,000 a parcel of land and a building with the intention of razing the building and using the land as a parking lot for employees. The land had an appraised value of $300,000, and the building, $50,000. The company incurred costs of $10,000 to remove the building. The firm recorded the parking lot on its books at $360,000. Can such value be justified?

9-9 "The issue of whether or not interest costs incurred while fixed assets are under construction should be capitalized and added to the stated value of the asset is a trivial one. In the long run (over the life of the asset), the decision as to whether or not to capitalize interest will have no effect on the earnings of the firm." Do you agree? How would you decide on an accounting treatment for interest during construction?

9-10 The term *reserve* for depreciation is occasionally used instead of *accumulated* depreciation. Some businessmen point out that it is essential that firms, through the process of depreciation, make periodic additions to such "reserve" in order to make certain that they have the wherewithal to replace assets when they must be retired. Explain why (or why not) depreciation assures that a firm will have sufficient resources to acquire new assets as old ones wear out.

9-11 "Accelerated methods of depreciation are generally preferable to the straight-line method because most assets decline in market value more rapidly in the early years of useful life than in later years." Do you agree?

9-12 Professional judgment is required in selecting an appropriate method of depreciation. Outline the conditions where you would recommend the use of the straight-line depreciation method.

9-13 Arthur Thomas in his writings seriously questions the wisdom of various allocations, such as depreciation. Why does he? Be specific. Do you agree with him?

9-14 A company incurred $1 million in advertising costs in 19x2 for radio and television advertisements broadcast during the year. It wished to capitalize these costs as an intangible asset and charge them off as expenses over a five-year period. If you were the company's auditor what would you recommend? Why?

9-15 Canadian owned oil companies can presently account for drilling costs on a "full cost" or "flow through" basis. Distinguish between these two methods. Which would you recommend? Why?

Problems

P9-1 Tite Co. Ltd. purchases a small plant for $250,000. The plant has an estimated useful life of 25 years with no salvage value. Included in the plant is a boiler to provide heat and hot water. At the time of purchase the company is aware that the remaining useful life of the boiler is 15 years. The firm estimates the value of the boiler to be $25,000.

Required:

a. Record the purchase of the plant. What assumptions have you made?
b. Record depreciation during the first year. What assumptions have you made?

At the end of 15 years the boiler requires replacement, and the firm purchases a new boiler for $40,000. The useful life of the new boiler is also estimated to be 15 years.

c. Record the replacement of the old boiler with the new.
d. Record depreciation during the sixteenth year.
e. Over how many years did you decide to depreciate the new boiler? What assumptions did you make?

P9-2 Construction Co. Ltd. purchased a crane for $150,000. The company planned to keep it for approximately five years, after which time it believed it could sell the crane for approximately $30,000.

Required:

a. Determine depreciation under each of the following methods for the first four years that the crane is in service:
   (i) Straight-line.
   (ii) Declining balance, using a 40% rate.
b. At the start of the fifth year the company sold the crane for $60,000. Determine the gain under each of the two depreciation methods.
c. Determine for each of the methods the net impact on earnings (total depreciation charges less gain) of using the crane for the four-year period.

P9-3 The Strip Mining Co. Ltd. decides to remove coal from a deposit on property it already owns. The company purchases mining equipment for cash at a cost of $850,000 and constructs a building on the site at a cost of $90,000. The equipment has a useful life of 10 years and an estimated salvage value of $50,000 and can readily be moved to other mining locations. The building has a potential useful life of 12 years but would have to be abandoned when the company ceases operations at the site.

The mine contains approximately 1 million tons of coal, and the company plans to remove it over a four-year period according to the following schedule:

Year 1	400,000
2	250,000
3	250,000
4	100,000

The property will be abandoned at the end of the fourth year.

Required:

a. Record the purchase of the equipment and the construction of the building.

b. Compute depreciation charges for the first year on both the building and equipment. Justify in one or two sentences your choice of depreciation method(s) and lives.

P9-4 You have just been appointed auditor of Miss Co. Ltd. After reviewing the company's financial statements you note that the company has failed to record a depreciation expense on its plant and equipment for the year just ended.

The management of the company informs you that in their opinion no depreciation expense is necessary because:

1. The replacement cost of their plant and equipment has increased such that it now exceeds the value carried on the company's books.
2. They have performed regular repair and maintenance work so the plant and equipment are as good as new.
3. An agreement with one of their creditors prevents their paying a dividend in any year the company incurs a loss. If depreciation is charged then a loss will occur in the year just ended. Shareholders would be very unhappy if they did not receive a dividend.

Required:

Prepare a report to the management of the company outlining your response to their views and your recommendations.

P9-5 In January 19x6 the Vipond Co., a sole proprietorship, purchased a copy machine for $6,000. The machine had an estimated useful life of eight years and an estimated salvage value of $500. The firm used a 25% declining balance method to record depreciation.

In December 19x8 the company decided to trade in the machine for a newer model. The new model had a *list* price of $12,000, but it is common in the industry for purchasers to be given a trade discount off of list price. The manufacturer offered the company a trade-in allowance of $4,000 on its old machine. The company accepted the offer since it was considerably above the several offers of approximately $2,100 that the firm had received from other parties interested in purchasing the machine. The company paid $8,000 in addition to giving up the old machine.

Required:

a. Record the trade-in of the old machine and the purchase of the new. (Assume depreciation had already been recorded for 19x8.)

b. Justify your treatment in Part a.

P9-6 G. Roop Machines Ltd. purchased on January 3, 19x7, 100 electric typewriters at a cost of $400 each. The firm estimated that it would use the machines for three years after which time it would sell them for $100 each.

On January 10, 19x8, 10 machines were stolen from the company. The loss was not covered by insurance.

On January 15, 19x9 the company sold 20 machines at a price of $250 each.

On December 31, 19x9 the company sold the remaining 70 machines at a price of $100 each.

The firm accounts for the machines using the *group* method of depreciation.

Required:

a. Prepare journal entries to record all activity in the typewriter account and related accumulated depreciation account for the three-year period, January 3, 19x7 to December 31, 19x9. (Ignore depreciation for the first few days of January, 19x7.)

b. Determine the ending balances in the two accounts as of the end of 19x9 after the sale of the 70 machines. How could there be a balance in the accumulated depreciation account if all machines have been sold or retired? What recommendation would you make regarding the accumulated depreciation balance?

c. What is the deficiency in using the group depreciation method? When would you use it? Why?

P9-7 On January 2, Evans Co. Ltd. purchased for $10,000 an *option* on a tract of land on which it hoped to construct a plant. The option gave the company the right to purchase the land itself within a given time period and for a fixed price — in this case within 10 months and for $2 million. If the company decided to exercise its option, it would pay the seller an additional $2 million and receive title to the land. If it decided not to purchase the land, then it would allow the option to lapse and would be unable to recover the $10,000. The option arrangement allows the company additional time to decide whether to make the purchase and at the same time compensates the seller for giving the company the exclusive right to purchase the property.

Required:

a. On July 2, Evans Co. Ltd. decided to purchase the tract of land for $2 million. Prepare journal entries to record both the purchase of the option and the subsequent purchase of the land. Should the cost of the option be added to the cost of the land?

b. Suppose instead that on January 2, Evans Co. Ltd. purchased three options — each for $10,000 — on three tracts of land. The company expected to purchase and build on only one of the three tracts; however, it wanted to locate its new plant by the side of a proposed highway, but the exact route of the highway had not yet been announced. The company purchased the three options in order to assure itself that the plant could be built adjacent to the road, regardless of which of three routes under consideration was selected for the highway. On July 2, the company exercised its option on one of the three tracts and purchased the land for $2 million. It allowed the other two options to lapse. Prepare journal entries to record the purchase of the three options, the purchase of the land, and the expiration of two of the options. Consider carefully whether the cost of all three options should be included as part of the cost of the land. Present arguments both for and against including the expired options as part of the cost of the land.

P9-8 The Rhinegold Chemical Co. Ltd. constructed a new plant at a cost of $20 million. The plant had an estimated useful life of 20 years, with no salvage value. After it had used the plant for 4 years, the replacement cost of the plant had increased to $24 million. The company decided to recognize in its accounts the increase in the fair market value of the asset.

Required:

a. Prepare a journal entry to record depreciation for each of the first four years.
b. Prepare an entry to record the revaluation of the plant. (State your assumptions regarding the measurement of capital maintenance. Explain your reasoning.)
c. Prepare an entry to record depreciation in the fifth year, the first year subsequent to the revaluation.
d. At the *start* of the eighth year the company accepted an offer to sell the plant for $19 million. Prepare an entry to record the sale.
e. Suppose the company had not readjusted its accounts after the fourth year to recognize the increase in market value. How much gain would it have recognized upon sale of the plant? Compare total depreciation expense and total gains recognized if the company recognized the increase in market value with those that would have resulted if it adhered to conventional practice and did not recognize the increase.
f. How might valuing the plant at replacement cost assist the users of financial statements? What are the limitations of using replacement cost to value the plant?

P9-9 Mammoth Co. Ltd. recently purchased the land, building, and equipment of Tearful Co. Ltd. On the date of purchase, Mammoth Co. Ltd. gave a cheque for $2 million and a one-year note for $6,360,000. Included in the amount of the note are interest charges, computed at a rate of 6 percent. At the time the cheque was drawn, a company accountant made the following journal entry:

Suspense	$8,360,000	
Cash		$2,000,000
Notes payable		6,360,000

"Suspense" was viewed as a temporary account to be maintained only until final distribution of the purchase price to various fixed asset accounts.

The following additional facts *may* bear on the purchase:

1. An independent appraiser valued the land at $1.5 million, the building at $4 million, and the equipment at $2.5 million.
2. The building was recorded on the books of Tearful Co. Ltd. at a cost of

$4 million, less accumulated depreciation of $3 million; the equipment was recorded at $11 million, less accumulated depreciation of $6 million. The land was recorded at the original cost of $800,000.

3. In making the purchase, the firm incurred legal fees of $25,000 and had to pay $1,000 for a *title search* on the land. The firm has decided to allocate legal fees on a proportionate basis (based on dollar value) among the land, building, and equipment. The legal fees had previously been charged to "legal expenses" and the costs of the title search to "miscellaneous expenses."
4. Immediately after taking possession of the property, Mammoth Co. Ltd. decided to raze an old garage that adjoined the plant. The company has received a bill from the contractor for $2,000, but no entry with respect to the bill has yet been made.
5. Mammoth Co. Ltd. rearranged equipment in the plant. The work was performed by five employees of Mammoth Co. Ltd. who were paid their normal weekly salaries of $300 each. Their salaries had been charged (debited) to "salary expense — direct labor."

Required:

a. Determine the cost of the land, building and equipment. Explain your reasoning. Identify any assumptions that you have made.
b. Prepare journal entries to bring the books of Mammoth Co. Ltd. up to date and correct any entries that have already been made.

P9-10 A company purchases a machine for $1 million cash. The company plans to use the machine for 5 years, after which it believes the machine can be sold for $100,000. The planned production volume for the machine is as follows:

First year	300,000 units
Second year	200,000 units
Third year	150,000 units
Fourth year	150,000 units
Fifth year	100,000 units

Required:

a. Compute depreciation for the first three years under each of the following methods:
   (i) straight-line
   (ii) units of production
   (iii) 10 percent diminishing balance (the rate required for income tax purposes)
b. Which method would you recommend the company use for financial accounting? Which method would you recommend the company use for calculating the taxes it must pay to the government? Explain your reasoning.

P9-11 In 19x8 Hydro Ltd. signed a contract to construct a new plant. The total contract price was $50 million. The plant took two years to construct. Since the company had to make periodic payments to the contractor, it was forced to borrow a considerable amount of funds. Total interest costs incurred during the period of construction were $2 million. The useful life of the plant is estimated to be 40 years with no salvage value.

The rates that Hydro Ltd. is permitted to charge customers are fixed by regulation. The governing regulation stipulates that the rates be calculated as the amount necessary for the company to realize a return on assets, before taxes, of 12 percent per year. That is, the rates will be established so as to permit the company to generate annual revenues in an amount such that revenues less expenses will be equal to 12 percent of the cost of the plant.

The company estimates that once it begins operations, operating expenses, in addition to depreciation, will be $8 million per year.

Required:

a. Determine the annual depreciation charges, on a straight-line basis, that the company would incur if it capitalized interest costs and those that it would incur if it did not. If the company did not capitalize interest, then it would charge the interest as an expense incurred during the period of construction.
b. Determine the income that the regulation would permit the company to earn if interest were capitalized as opposed to if it were not.
c. Determine total revenues that the firm must be permitted to generate if it were to earn the income calculated in Part b.
d. Comment on what you would expect the attitude of public utility executives to be toward capitalization of interest.
e. Does the capitalization of interest make sense from the point of view of the public?

P9-12 Software Co. Ltd. is considering purchasing a new computer that it will be able to rent to a customer for $10,000 per year. The machine has a useful life of four years and no salvage value. The company demands a rate of return of 6 percent on all its assets.

Required:

a. What is the maximum amount the firm would be willing to pay for the machine?
b. Suppose it were able to purchase the machine for that price. It decides to charge depreciation on the basis of what the machine is worth to the company itself at the end of a year as compared to what it was worth at the beginning. How much depreciation should it charge during each of the four years? Determine total depreciation charges for the four-year period.
c. Comment on the trend of charges by this method of depreciation as compared to other methods of depreciation.
d. Suppose instead that at the end of the first year of ownership the firm is able to renegotiate its rental agreements. For the remaining three years of ownership it will be able to lease the machine to its customer for $12,000 per year. How much depreciation should it charge for the first year of ownership?
e. Why is this concept of "economic depreciation" of limited use in practice?

P9-13 How would you classify (i.e., asset or expense) each of the following costs at the time of its incurrence? How would you account for the item subsequent to its incurrence? Give your reasons.

a. Outlays of $1,000,000 incurred by an automobile manufacturer related to the retooling of its equipment to manufacture a new model passenger car.
b. Expenditures of $600,000 incurred by a large oil company related to the test drilling of a new well. Geological reports as yet are inconclusive as to whether sufficient oil reserves exist to make development of this area commercially feasible.
c. Outlays of $250,000 incurred by a chemical company related to research into possible commercial applications of a new chemical.
d. An expenditure of $750,000 paid by a hockey team as a signing bonus to induce a player to play for their team for the next five years at an annual salary of $200,000.
e. An expenditure of $250,000 paid to the Municipal Parking Authority for the right to construct a building without ample parking spaces for the eventual tenants of the property. The Municipal Parking Authority uses funds of this nature to construct parking garages near properties with inadequate parking for their tenants.

Cases

C9-1 Thomas Toys (TT) was recently formed to manufacture and distribute some recent toy inventions of the founder, A. Thomas. Thomas invested a large sum of his own money to commence operations and borrowed about $100,000 from a bank to finance working capital needs.

A special machine costing $40,000 to build, was needed to make one toy, "The Incorrigible." Thomas doubts if he can ever use that machine again for other toys, although some parts worth about $4,000 can be salvaged at any time over the next four years. Estimated production volumes, selling prices, and out-of-pocket costs (excluding depreciation) for "The Incorrigible" are:

	Production & Sales Volume	*Selling Price Per Unit*	*Out-of-Pocket Production and Selling Costs*
Year 1	100,000 units	$ 3.00	$ 0.40
2	100,000 units	2.00	0.40
3	100,000 units	1.00	0.40
4	100,000 units	.50	0.40
5	Zero	Zero	Zero

Thomas has been told that he ought to prepare a set of financial statements to attach to his income tax return, and for the banker. He has heard that he ought to consider a depreciation policy or method — especially for the machine which makes "The Incorrigible" toy. He has come to you for advice.

Required:

What detailed advice would you give Thomas on his accounting problem with the machine that makes "The Incorrigible"? (CICA adapted)

C9-2 Deception Co. Ltd. currently has a loan outstanding from the Gibraltar Insurance Co. Ltd. that requires that Deception Co. Ltd. maintain a *debt/equity ratio* no greater than 1:1. That is, the balance in all liability accounts can be no greater than that in the common share capital and retained earnings accounts. As of December 30, 19x1, Deception Co. Ltd. had total liabilities of $3 million and total common share capital and retained earnings of $3,150,000.

On December 31, 19x1 the vice-president of production of Deception Co. Ltd. wishes to purchase new equipment that would cost $257,710. The equipment would have a three-year useful life and no salvage value and during its life would result in substantial cost savings to the company. Aware that the company is short of cash, the vice-president arranged the following alternatives:

1. The manufacturer of the equipment will lend the company $257,710 at 8 percent interest compounded annually on the unpaid balance. This loan (i.e., notes payable) is repayable in three equal instalments of principal and interest commencing December 31, 19x2.
2. The manufacturer of the equipment will lease the equipment to Deception Co. Ltd. for a three-year period. Annual rent would be $100,000, but Deception Co. Ltd. would have to pay all maintenance and insurance costs. At the expiration of the lease, Deception Co. Ltd. would have an option to purchase the machine for $1.

Required:

a. Assume the role of the controller of Deception Co. Ltd. Which alternative would you recommend? Explain your reasoning. (Note: Include in your analysis a comparison of cash flows and journal entries. Remember to clearly indicate the assumptions that you make.)

b. Assume the role of the creditor. How would you propose Deception Co. Ltd. record the transaction if it decided to lease the equipment? Why?

C9-3 On January 1, 19x7 Blazouske Co. Ltd. ("BCL" or the company) was formed to acquire and operate a gold mining property at Red Lake in northwestern Ontario. A geological report on the property revealed that the ore would yield approximately 25 percent gold. The yield could not be exactly determined until the ore was processed. However, based on the geologist's reports the owners estimated that about 250,000 ounces of gold could be extracted from the mine.

Five engineers own BCL. None of the owners has taken an accounting course. The bank, from which they have borrowed substantial funds, has requested a set of financial statements be prepared in accordance with generally accepted accounting principles. This request has the owners puzzled. They have kept accurate records of cash receipts and disbursements and even prepared a schedule of cash flows for the year. However they are not sure whether this schedule will satisfy the bank's request.

For this reason they have come to you for advice and provide you with the following schedule:

Schedule of Cash Receipts and Disbursements
For Year Ending 19x7

Cash receipts:		
Sales of common shares		$ 7,500,000
Bank loan (Note 1)		7,500,000
Collections from gold sales (10,000 ounces sold at an average price of $200 per ounce)		2,000,000
Total receipts		17,000,000
Cash disbursements:		
Cost of mining properties (Note 2)	$10,000,000	
Building and structures (Note 3)	2,400,000	
Equipment (Note 4)	650,000	
Production costs (Note 5)	2,500,000	
Delivery expenses	75,000	
Administrative expenses	525,000	
Total disbursements		16,150,000
Cash on hand		$ 850,000

Note 1: The bank loan was received on January 1, 19x7. Interest at 12 percent is compounded and payable annually. The first interest payment is due January 1, 19x8.

Note 2: Includes the cost of land, roads, mine shafts and other costs necessary to bring the property to a point of production.

Note 3: The buildings and structures have a useful life of 15 years.

Note 4: Equipment has a useful life of 5 years and a salvage value of $50,000.

Note 5: All production and operating costs incurred were paid during the year.

BCL's production records for 19x7 show the following breakdown in ounces of gold produced:

Sold, delivered and proceeds collected	10,000 ounces
Sold and delivered but proceeds not collected	20,000 ounces
Extracted and refined but not sold or delivered	10,000 ounces
Total production	40,000 ounces

Discussions with the owners indicate that the mining property is located in an area unsuitable for any alternative use and consequently the property has no residual value after the gold deposits are exhausted. In addition, the buildings and structures cannot be economically dismantled and moved to another location at the end of the mine's life. The owners inform you that the price of gold is determined by world supply and demand and at December 31, 19x7 the price of gold was at near record levels of $240 per ounce.

Required:

Assume the role of an accounting advisor. What would you recommend? Thoroughly explain which accounting policies and principles the company should adopt.

C9-4 Brockland Motor Company Limited ("BMCL" or the company) is a public company which manufactures a number of lines of cars and trucks. Until recently the company had an excellent history of earnings. However, the crunch of inflation and unemployment has had a significant effect on this year's profit.

It is now October 19x9 and Mr. Furd, the president of BMCL, is very concerned. Unfortunately he sees no signs of recovery before December 31, the company's year end. This places him in an extremely embarrassing position because in the company's last annual report to shareholders he indicated that there would be an upturn in profits this year.

Therefore, he instructed his controller, Mr. Gibbins, to review the company's accounting principles and policies to ensure that the company's performance is reported in the best possible light. Upon his review, Mr. Gibbins discovered the following:

(1) In February, some of the plant employees were idle. Therefore, the production manager decided to have them construct a small warehouse, to store old parts, behind the plant. The labor and material costs to build the warehouse amounted to $75,000 and $50,000 respectively. Unfortunately one week after the work was completed one of the walls fell in and the company had to hire a construction company to restore the building for $30,000. All these costs were originally expensed. Since the building has future service value the controller decided to now capitalize $155,000 and depreciate it over 25 years.

(2) In May, the plant employees rejected the company's wage offer and went on strike. As a result, the plant was shut down for one month. Depreciation on plant and equipment for May was $250,000. BMCL had originally expensed this amount. However, it did not make sense to the controller that there should be a depreciation charge when the plant and equipment was not used. Therefore he decided to reverse the depreciation charge (i.e., debit accumulated depreciation and credit depreciation expense).

(3) In September the company commenced commercial production of a new line of sports cars. While reviewing the costs related to this new line the controller noticed that the design and testing costs had been inadvertently charged to cost of goods manufactured. While detailed records were not kept for the design and testing of models he estimated that labor (including executive time), materials, and overhead amounted to $1,000,000. He felt these costs should be capitalized and not amortized until the new line begins to make a profit.

Required:

Assume the role of the company's auditor. Discuss the acceptability of the accounting treatment suggested by Mr. Gibbins. What would you recommend?

10 *Liabilities and Related Expenses*

In the preceding four chapters we primarily addressed questions of valuing assets and of reporting the related revenues and expenses. This chapter will be directed to the equally important and controversial issues of valuing liabilities and of measuring their impact upon earnings of the firm.

Throughout the book we have alluded to users of financial statements as being creditors, investors, prospective creditors, prospective investors, union organizers, and governments. Such people might be interested in evaluating the past actions of managements, and might want to predict cash flows of the future. They hope that these processes will enable them to judge the present worth of a company.

This and the next two chapters take a closer look at creditors and investors of the company. Both furnish money to the company, but under different terms. For example, long-term creditors (those who buy bonds) may receive greater pledges of security for their loan than shareholders receive on sums which they furnish. But creditors may receive a lower interest rate than the dividend rate earned by shareholders. Income tax and liquidity (amount of cash and near cash assets) can also play an important role in creditors' decisions. As a result of the difference in terms, the information needs of each group may differ. More will be said about information requirements as we proceed with the remainder of the book.

Note Disclosure

Although a large portion of the chapter is devoted to measurement, note disclosure provides additional information about liabilities and related expenses, which is very important for most readers of financial statements. Those who are interested in evaluating management's success and in cash prediction (amount and timing of cash flows) may obtain a better grasp of corporate activities if note disclosure of cash flows accompanies measurement. (For example, refer to Chapter 2 and the extensive note disclosure by Labatt's.)

This chapter on "liabilities" gives several illustrations (1) where note disclosure is required under GAAP to help various user groups; (2) where disclosure per GAAP is incomplete for the needs of some users (see, for example, lease and pension accounting); and (3) where note disclosure by itself, without measurement, was rejected by accountants (see, for example, accounting for income taxes). Many of the topics covered by this chapter are under constant review; and major changes in accounting practice may occur in the next decade.

Bonds Payable

Corporations, as well as governmental units and nonprofit organizations, borrow funds to finance long-term projects, such as plant and equipment and major public works projects. Conventionally, borrowers provide the lender with evidence of their obligations to repay the funds as well as to make periodic interest payments by issuing notes or bonds. A bond is a more formal certificate of indebtedness than a note. Characteristically bonds are almost always evidence of long-term indebtedness (five years or more), while notes may be issued in connection with short- or long-term borrowing.

Corporate bonds are most commonly issued in denominations of $1,000. The *par* or *face* value of a bond indicates the *principal* amount due at the *maturity* or due date of the bond. Bonds ordinarily carry a stated annual rate of interest, expressed as a percentage of the principal. Most bond *indentures* (agreements which set forth the legal provisions of the bonds) require that interest be paid semiannually. Thus, a corporation which has issued $1,000-denomination bonds that specify an annual rate of interest of 6 percent would pay the holder of a single bond $30 on each of two interest dates six months apart.

Some corporate bonds are *coupon* bonds. Each bond contains a series of coupons which may be clipped and redeemed at six-month intervals for the interest due. Coupon bonds are distinguished from *registered* bonds in that on the latter interest is paid not to the bearer of the coupon but only to a specific party whose name is registered with the borrower.

Corporate bonds may be secured by property, such as a plant, or land. Or they may be unsecured, with the lender relying primarily upon the general unpledged (as security for creditors) assets, good faith and financial integrity of the borrower for repayment. Secured bonds may be categorized by the type of legal instrument used to provide the lien on the property that is pledged — e.g., mortgage bonds and equipment trust bonds. Unsecured bonds are commonly called *debentures*.

Virtually all corporate bonds indicate a specific maturity date. However, many corporate issues provide for the early retirement of the debt at the option of the *borrower* (the corporation). Such a *call provision* ordinarily requires the company to pay the lender (the bond holder) a *call premium*, an amount in addition to the face value of the bond, as a penalty for depriving the lender of his "right" to interest payments for the original term of the loan.

Bonds are generally freely negotiable — they can be bought and sold in the open market subsequent to original issue. An active market for corporate bonds is maintained by Canadian investment dealers. A lender who no longer wishes to have his funds tied up in a loan to the issuer of the bond can sell his bond to an investor who is seeking the type of return provided by that type of bond. The price at which the bond is sold need not be that for which the bond was initially issued. Rather, it would be determined in large measure by interest rates prevalent at time of sale to the other creditor/investor.

The Nature of Bonds

Bonds provide for interest payments of a fixed amount. Ordinarily the more financially sound the borrower, the lower will be the rate of interest. Yet interest rates for securities *within* the same category of risk are determined by the forces of supply and demand — the amount of funds being sought by borrowers, the amount being made available by lenders. Rates of interest that prevail throughout the country fluctuate from day to day and even from hour to hour. Although corporations conventionally set the coupon rate of interest — the amount that will be paid to the lender each interest period — and print it in the bond indentures several weeks prior to the date on which they are to be issued, the actual interest rate is determined at time of sale. The actual interest rate, often referred to as the *yield rate*, is established, not by changing the coupon rate, but rather by adjusting the price at which the bond is sold. Suppose, for example, that a $1,000 bond has a coupon rate of 8 percent — that is, the holder of the bond will be entitled to two payments of $40 each year. At the time of sale, however, the prevailing interest rate for that type of bond is 8¼ percent. Would a purchaser be willing to pay $1,000 for such a bond? Obviously not. He could lend his money to another similar company and receive $82.50 per year rather than $80. Therefore, he would be willing to pay something less than $1,000 for the bond. How much less will be considered in the next section. Similarly if the prevailing interest rate were lower than 8 percent — 7½ percent, for example — a rational buyer would be willing to pay more than $1,000 for the bond. If he were to purchase the bonds of similar companies, he would receive only $75 per year in interest. He would be willing to pay something above $1,000 in order to receive a return of $80 per year. If a purchaser pays less than the face amount for a bond, then the difference between the face amount and what he actually pays is referred to as a bond *discount*. If he pays more than face amount, then the additional payment is referred to as a *premium*.

A rational purchaser would undertake a similar analysis in deciding how much to pay for a bond that had been issued several years earlier, one to be purchased not from the issuing company directly but rather from the current holder of the bond. To the extent that prevailing interest rates are greater than the coupon rate of the bond, he would be willing to pay *less* than the face value of the bond, for he could receive the prevailing rate by purchasing a different bond on which the coupon rate is equal to the prevailing rate. To the extent that prevailing rates are less than the coupon rate, he would be willing to pay more, since the semiannual payments would be greater than what he could obtain elsewhere.

Determination of Discount or Premium

Determination of the amount that a rational purchaser would pay for a bond requires an understanding of the promises inherent in the bond agreement. A somewhat simplified and exaggerated example can be used to illustrate a logical approach to calculating the amount to be paid for a particular bond.[1]

Suppose that on a particular day a corporation seeking to issue bonds requests bids on two bond issues. Bond A bears a coupon rate of 6 percent and bond B a coupon rate of 4 percent. Both bonds will mature in two years. Both pay interest semiannually. The prevailing annual rate of interest is 6 percent.

Both bonds contain a promise to pay the purchaser $1,000 upon maturity after two years — four semiannual periods hence. The present value of a single cash payment four semiannual periods away given an interest rate of 3 percent is, per Table 2 in the Appendix, $1,000 × .8885 — $888.50. The 3 percent rate is one half the annual rate of 6 percent; it reflects the semiannual rather than the annual payment of interest. The 6 percent rate is the *prevailing* rate for bonds of that type, not necessarily the coupon rate on either of the two bonds in question. It is the rate that is relevant to the prospective purchaser since it is that which he could receive if he were to turn to alternative investment possibilities.

Bond A also promises four semiannual payments of $30. The present value of four semiannual payments, discounted at 3 percent per period (one half the *prevailing* annual rate), is, per Table 4, $30 × 3.7171 — $111.50. The total present value of the two promises — the promise to pay principal of $1,000 plus the promise to make semiannual interest payments — discounted at the prevailing rate of 3 percent per semiannual period is ($888.50 plus $111.50) $1,000. The rational buyer would be willing to pay $1,000 — in this instance, the face value — for the bond.

Bond B, on the other hand, promises four semiannual payments of only $20, since the coupon rate is 4 percent per year. The present value of four semiannual payments of $20, discounted at 3 percent is, again per Table 4, $20 × 3.7171 — $74.34. The rate of 3 percent is one half the *prevailing* rate of 6 percent. The *prevailing rate is the one that must be used to evaluate an investment opportunity*, since it (rather than the coupon rate) is indicative of the return that the investor can expect to receive. The present value of the two promises combined is, therefore, $888.50 plus $74.34 — $962.84. The rational purchaser would be willing to pay only $962.84 for the bond with a face value of $1,000. The discount of $37.16 would assure him a *yield* of 6 percent per year, even though the coupon rate is only 4 percent per year. The analysis can be summarized as follows:

	Bond A (6% coupon)	*Bond B (4% coupon)*
Present value of $1,000 to be received at the end of 4 periods, discounted at prevailing rate of 3 percent ($1,000 ×.8885 per Table 2)	$ 888.50	$888.50
Present value of $30 to be received at the end of each of 4 periods, discounted at prevailing rate of 3 percent ($30 × 3.7171 per Table 4)	111.50	
Present value of $20 to be received at the end of each of 4 periods, discounted at prevailing rate of 3 percent ($20 × 3.7171 per Table 4)		74.34
Present value of bond	$1,000.00	$962.84

Diagrammatically, the two bonds can be depicted as in Exhibit 10-1. Both bonds are evaluated at a rate of 3 percent per period — the yield expected by a purchaser. It is assumed that the bonds were sold on January 1, 19x7. All discount factors are per Table 2. Bond A would be issued at face value because its coupon rate is identical to the yield rate. Anytime there is a difference, the bonds would be sold at an amount other than face value.

EXHIBIT 10-1

Bond A
6 percent Coupon; 6 percent Yield

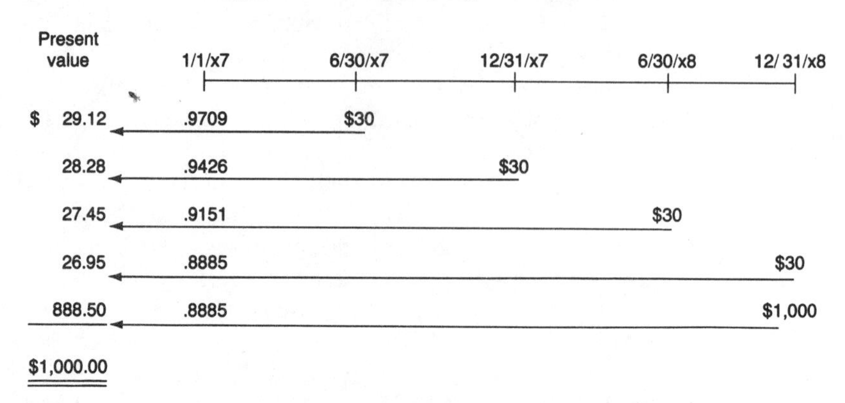

Bond B
4 percent Coupon; 6 percent Yield

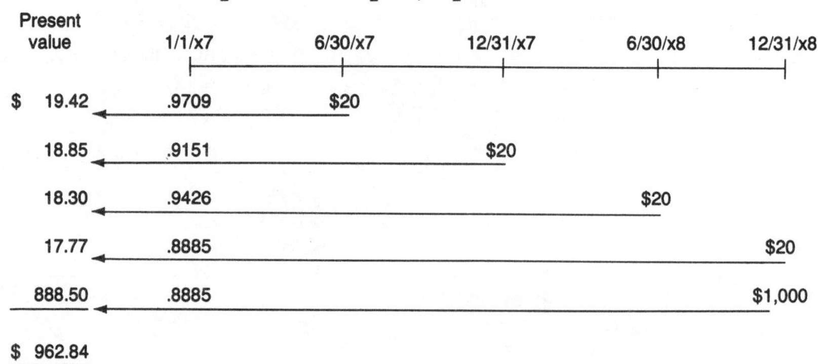

The discount of \$37.16 on bond B can be viewed from a slightly different perspective. If a purchaser desires a yield of 6 percent per year, then from a \$1,000 bond he expects interest payments of \$30 every six months. In fact, bond B will pay him only \$20 per six months. He is losing \$10 per period. The present value of \$10 lost for four periods, discounted at a rate of 3 percent per period (one half the desired yield of 6 percent), is, per Table 4, $\$10 \times \$3.7171 = \$37.16$.

Computation of the bond premium or discount can be facilitated by asking four simple questions:

1. How much interest per period (based on the *coupon rate*) is a purchaser of the bond actually going to receive?
2. How much (based on the *yield rate*) would he like to receive?

3. What is the difference between the two amounts?
4. What is the present value, discounted at the *yield rate*, of such difference?

The present value of the difference between the amount a purchaser would like to receive and what he will actually receive represents either premium or discount.

Recording the Issue of Bonds

The issue of bond B for a price of $962.84 could be recorded by the following journal entry:

Cash (asset)	$962.84	
Discount on bonds (contra account to bonds payable)	37.16	
Bonds payable (liability)		$1,000
To record issuance of the bond.		

Reporting the Issue of Bonds

If financial statements were to be prepared immediately after the sale, the liability would be *reported* as follows:

Bonds payable	$1,000.00	
Less: Discount	37.16	$962.84

As a consequence the *net* liability to be reported would be only $962.84, not the $1,000 face value of the bond. Separate disclosure of the $1,000 face amount of the bonds indicates the eventual cash payment needed on maturity of the bond, and also the amount on which interest payments are based.

Additional note disclosure likely would describe such matters as repayment terms, security for the debt, and any restrictions on further borrowing. (See Labatt's financial statements in Chapter 2.)

Nature of Premium or Discount

The present value of the net liability of the company at the time of sale is only $962.84. This is the amount of cash actually received. It may be argued that the company will have to repay $1,000, the face value of the bond, and that that amount, therefore, is the liability to be reported. The company will, of course, have to pay $1,000 at time of maturity. But if it only borrowed $962.84, then the "extra" $37.16 must represent interest, in addition to the semiannual coupon payments, to be paid to the lender. The additional $37.16 has the effect of increasing the rate of interest paid by the company from 4 percent to 6 percent. Interest is not ordinarily reported as a liability and recorded as an expense until the borrower has had use of the funds. Technically interest accrues daily even though accrual journal entries may be made monthly. Just as the liability for the periodic coupon payments of $20 each will not be recorded until the interest has been earned, neither should that for the additional interest of $37.16 to be paid upon maturity of the bond. Instead, it should be added to the liability account over the remaining life of the bond issue — as the firm has use of the funds borrowed. Similarly, if the bonds were sold at a premium, at a price of $1,020, for example, then the amount borrowed by the company is the amount actually received, $1,020. The company will, of course, have to repay only $1,000. The $20 represents a reduction, over the life of the issue, of the firm's borrowing costs, and should be accounted for as such. (It could, of course, be argued that the company has a legal liability for the full $1,000. However, should the company go bankrupt soon after the sale of the bonds, it may be unusual for a bankruptcy court to award the full $1,000 to a bondholder who recently had loaned the company only $962.84.)

Recording the Payment of Interest

As a consequence of the price adjustments attributable to the premium or discount at which the bonds were sold, the effective rate of interest to be paid by the company is that established not by the coupon rate but rather by the *yield rate* (*the effective rate at time of issue*). The reported interest expense should be based on such yield rate.

In the previous example, the company borrowed $962.84 at an effective interest rate of 6 percent (3 percent per interest period). Each interest date it must pay the bondholder $20. On the first interest date, its effective interest expense is 3 percent of $962.84 — $28.88. $28.88 is $8.88 greater than the actual payment of $20 which it must make to the bondholder. The $8.88 represents the first interest period's share of the $37.16 in additional interest to be paid upon the maturity of the loan. It is, therefore, the amount of the discount that must be amortized and charged as additional interest expense in the first period. The following journal entry would reflect this interpretation of the bond discount:

Interest expense	$28.88	
Cash		$20.00
Discount on bonds		8.88
To record payment of interest.		

As a result of this entry, the unamortized portion of the discount on bonds has been reduced from $37.16 to $28.28. The bond would be reported in the liability section of the balance sheet as follows:

Bonds payable	$1,000.00	
Less: Discount	28.28	$971.72

The *effective* liability of the company has increased from $962.84 to $971.72 because the company now owes not only the original amount borrowed ($962.84) but also a portion of the interest which the bondholder has earned during the first interest period. The additional interest now owed is equal to the effective interest for the period ($28.88) less the amount actually paid ($20.00).

At the end of the second interest period, the interest expense would again be based on the effective interest or yield rate that prevailed at the time the bond was issued. But now the effective liability is not $962.84 as at the end of the first period but rather $971.72, an amount reflective of the amortization of a portion of the original discount. Hence, the effective interest expense is 3 percent of $971.72 — $29.15. As in the first period, the actual payment to the bondholder would be only $20.00. The difference between the two represents the portion of interest earned by the bondholder but not yet paid to him — the amount that must be subtracted from the bond discount and thereby added to the effective liability. The following journal entry would be required on the second interest date:

Interest expense	$29.15	
Cash		$20.00
Discount on bonds		9.15
To record payment of interest.		

As a result of this entry, the unamortized portion of the bond discount has been reduced from $28.28 to $19.13. After the second payment of interest the bond would be reported as follows:

Bonds payable	$1,000.00	
Less: Discount	19.13	$980.87

It is important to observe that the bond may not trade or sell to other investors or long-term creditors for $980.87 as of the date of the second payment of interest. Amortization under stewardship accounting is based on the yield when the bonds are sold (issued) *initially*. Supply/demand for the bonds may have changed subsequent to the initial date of issue and the *current* yield may now have increased or decreased. Hence, if buyers and sellers want a 7 percent yield for such bonds today, the price on the bond market would be below $980.87.

Incidentally, an accounting system based on current market values would handle changing yields on long-term debt differently. A system based on net realizable value probably would report the *current* market price of the bonds payable directly on the balance sheet. The reasoning might be that this is the price for which bonds payable may be repurchased "currently" on the "open market,' or stock exchange.

A history of the bond is summarized in Exhibit 10-2.

EXHIBIT 10-2

$1,000 Bond Issued on January 1, 19x7; Matures on December 31, 19x8; 4 Percent Coupon; Sold to Yield 6 Percent (3 percent per semiannual period)

Date	*Interest (3% of previous liability)*	*Coupon payment*	*Discount*	*Effective liability*
1/1/x7	—	—	$37.16	$ 962.84
6/30/x7	$28.88	($20.00)	(8.88)	8.88
			28.28	971.72
12/31/x7	29.15	(20.00)	(9.15)	9.15
			19.13	980.87
6/30/x8	29.43	(20.00)	(9.43)	9.43
			9.70	990.30
12/31/x8	29.70	(20.00)	(9.70)	9.70
			$ 0.00	$1,000.00

The effective liability, as of any date, can be determined by following the same procedures used to calculate the initial price of the bond. For example, as of 12/31/x7 there are two interest payments of $20 remaining. The present value of such payments discounted at the effective interest or yield rate of 3 percent per period is, per Table 4, $20 × 1.9135 — $38.27. The present value of the $1,000 to be received at maturity is, per Table 2, $1,000 × .9426 — $942.60. The present value of the two sets of payments combined is $38.27 plus $942.60 — $980.87.

The example that follows deals with a bond to be issued at a premium rather than a discount.

EXAMPLE

A company wishes to sell 10-year debentures that bear a coupon rate of 10 percent. At the time of sale, similar bonds are being sold to yield 8 percent.

1. For how much will the company be able to sell each $1,000 bond?

The present value at the effective yield rate of 4 percent per half-year period (8 percent per year) of a single payment of $1,000, 20 periods hence, is, per Table 2, $1,000 × .4564 — $456.40.

The present value of a stream of 20 payments of $50 each (based on the coupon rate discounted at 4 percent per period) is, per Table 4, $50 ×

13.5903 — $679.52. The sum of the two present values is $1,135.92, the amount for which the company will be able to sell the bond.

Present value of $1,000 to be received after 20 periods discounted at prevailing rate of 4 percent per period ($1,000 × .4564 per Table 2)	$ 456.40
Present value of $50 to be received at the end of each of 20 periods, discounted at prevailing rate of 4 percent per period ($50 × 13.5903 per Table 4)	679.52
Present value of bond	$1,135.92

Alternatively, the same result could have been obtained by focusing on the premium. The company is offering the purchaser 20 payments of $50 each. The purchaser, based on the prevailing interest rate of 8 percent would be willing to accept 20 payment of $40 each. The present value of the series of the $10 *bonuses* is, per Table 4, $10 × 13.5903 — $135.90. The latter figure represents the bond premium; hence the sale price would be face value of $1,000 plus a premium of $135.90 — the same (with allowance for rounding discrepancies) $1,135.92 as computed earlier.

2. Prepare a journal entry to record the sale of one bond.

Cash	$1,135.92	
Bonds payable		$1,000.00
Premium on bonds payable		135.92
To record sale of the bond.		

3. How would the bonds be reported on the balance sheet immediately after sale?

Bonds payable	$1,000.00	
Premium	135.92	$1,135.92

4. Prepare a journal entry to record the first interest payment. The total amount borrowed by the company was $1,135.92. The effective rate of interest, the yield rate, was 8 percent. The effective interest rate (on a per period basis) of 4 percent times the outstanding balance of $1,135.92 is $45.43. The amount of interest actually to be paid at the time of the first payment is, based on the coupon rate, $50.

Interest expense	$45.43	
Premium on bonds payable	4.57	
Cash		$50.00
To record payment of interest.		

This entry might be recorded in *two* steps:

(a) Interest expense	$50.00	
Cash		$50.00
To record cash payment.		

(b) Premium on bonds payable	$ 4.57	
Interest expense		$ 4.57
To record amortization of premium on bonds payable in order to reduce the effective interest expense to 8 percent.		

Although the net effect of the two entries is the same as for the one above them, the (b) entry more clearly shows that the amortization has the effect of reducing interest expense to an eight percent yield on the $1,135.92 ($1,135.92 at 8 percent for one-half year = $45.43).

5. How would the bonds be reported immediately after the first payment of interest?

Bonds payable	$1,000.00	
Premium	131.35	$1,131.35

6. Prepare a journal entry to record the second interest payment. The effective liability just prior to the second payment of interest is $1,131.35. Effective interest charges, based on the yield rate at the time of sale, is $1,131.35 × .04 — $45.25.

Interest expense	$45.25	
Premium on bonds payable	4.75	
Cash		$50.00
To record payment of interest.		

The net liability will now be $1,131.35 less that portion ($4.75) of the premium just amortized — $1,126.60.

7. For how much could the bondholder sell the bond immediately after the second payment of interest, *assuming* that prevailing interest rates are still 8 percent?

Present value of $1,000, 18 periods away, discounted at 4 percent, per period (per Table 2), $1,000 × .4936	$ 493.60
Present value of 18 coupon payments of $50 each (per Table 4), $50 × 12.6593	632.97
Price at which bond could be sold	$1,126.57

This amount is the same amount that would be reported on the books of the issuing company as calculated for part 6 of this example (save for a minor rounding discrepancy).

End-of-Year Accruals

If a bond interest date does not occur exactly at year end, it is necessary to accrue interest for the expense incurred from the time of either the issue date or the last payment date. Suppose, for example, that a 6 percent, 20-year coupon bond was sold on December 1, 19x5, for $893.20 — a price that would result in a yield of 7 percent. Interest is payable each year on May 31 and November 30. Interest expense for the first full six-month period would be 3.5 percent of $893.20 — $31.26. That portion of the discount amortized would be the difference between the interest expense of $31.26 and the actual coupon payment of $30.00 — $1.26. The accrual entry on December 31, 19x5 (the company's year end) would reflect one sixth of these amounts:

Interest expense (1/6 of $31.26)	$5.21	
Discount on bonds payable		$ .21
Accrued interest payable		5.00
To record accrual of interest.		

The entry on May 31, 19x6, when the first payment was made would be reflective of the remaining five-sixths (note that the interest expense on May 31 is *not* based on the effective liability at December 31 — after the *partial* amortization of the discount — but rather on that as of December 1):

Interest expense (5/6 of $31.26)	$26.05	
Accrued interest payable	5.00	
Discount on bonds payable (5/6 of $1.26)		$ 1.05
Cash		30.00
To record payment of interest.		

Straight-Line Amortization

Some firms, instead of determining interest charges and amortization of discount or premium as described in the preceding paragraphs, have in the past amortized the premium or discount on a straight-line basis. Total interest charges for the month are calculated by adding to the cash coupon payment (or subtracting from, in the case of a premium) the portion of the discount (premium) amortized. The amount of the discount or premium amortized each period is determined simply by dividing the initial discount or premium by the total number of periods for which the bond will be outstanding. As a consequence, interest charges remain constant over the life of the issue. In the illustration used earlier, a 4 percent coupon bond was issued at a price of $962.84 — a discount of $37.16. Since the bond would be outstanding for four periods, one fourth of $37.16 — $9.29 — would be amortized each period. Total interest costs each period would be $29.29 —

the portion of the discount amortized plus the $20 coupon payment. The straight-line method is convenient; it eliminates the need to recompute interest each period. But it is deficient in that it results in a constantly increasing (or decreasing) *rate* of interest when interest expense is compared to effective liability (face value plus or minus discount or premium). Since, in the example, the effective liability would increase by $9.29 each period, the effective interest rates over the life of the bond (interest expense ÷ effective liability) would be as follows:

$$\frac{29.29}{962.84} = 3.04\%; \quad \frac{29.29}{972.13} = 3.01\%; \quad \frac{29.29}{981.42} = 2.98\%; \quad \frac{29.29}{990.71} = 2.95\%.$$

Canadian practice probably (i.e., concrete evidence is not available) favors straight-line amortization, perhaps on practical grounds (i.e., dollar materiality to readers of financial statements) but also because discounting may be unknown to some accountants who were trained prior to recognition of the importance of interest effects. From a user/reader viewpoint, *if* the amounts involved are large (as might be the case for life or casualty insurance companies) it would be worthwhile to learn what amortization method the company is using. For purchasers of bonds, effects can be minimized, of course, when a company is *continually* buying bonds with discounts (the usual case because of income tax laws) or premiums, and amortizations are smoothened.

Redemption of Bonds

When a firm redeems its bonds outstanding upon their maturity, no special accounting problems are presented. Once the interest expense of the final period is recorded, the discount or premium should have been amortized to zero. Thus, for a single bond, the following entry would be appropriate:

Bonds payable	$1,000.00	
Cash		$1,000.00
To record redemption of the bond.		

If, however, the firm decides to redeem the bonds before they mature, then the accounting questions are more complex.

Assume that a company 20 years earlier had issued 7 percent coupon bonds at a price of $1,025.50 to yield 6.8 percent. With 10 years remaining until maturity, the firm decides to redeem the bonds since it no longer needs the funds that it borrowed. According to the bond indenture agreement, the company has the right to call the issue any time after 15 years at a price of $102. (Bond prices are frequently quoted in terms of $100 even though they are often sold in denominations of $1,000. Thus the company would have to pay $1,020 to redeem a single $1,000 bond.) The bond was originally issued at a price of $1,025.50; if the company had amortized the premium on an effective yield basis, the net value of the bond after 20 years per the corporate books would be $1,007.10. If the company exercised its option to redeem the bond for $1,020.00, the following entry would be appropriate:

Bonds payable	$1,000.00	
Premium on bonds payable	7.10	
Loss on redemption	12.90	
Cash		$1,020.00
To record redemption of the bond.		

The loss should be interpreted with care. It is not a loss in the sense that it is necessarily indicative of a poor management decision. Rather it is reflective of a penalty payment that management has elected to make to the bondholders in return for depriving them of the return which their investment in the bonds was providing them. (Large buyers of bonds, such as insurance companies that continually invest policyholders' money incur some costs for analyzing companies to which they may wish to lend money, secured by bonds. The lenders are therefore not anxious to have their bond holdings redeemed — except when interest rates have increased — because they then have to find another suitable borrower. This is another reason for the existence of redemption premiums such as the $2 per $100 bond.)

A corporation may also realize a gain by redeeming its bond prior to maturity. This is especially true if the company does not officially *call* its outstanding issue but instead purchases its bonds in the open market (i.e., that is, using a broker or bond dealer to acquire bonds from potential sellers). The company would pay the current bondholders the prevailing price for the security. By purchasing the bonds outstanding the company would eliminate its liability to outsiders, and it would recognize as a gain the difference between the book value of the bonds and the purchase price.

Bond prices, as pointed out earlier, are determined by the relationship between the coupon rate and the prevailing return that an investor is able to obtain elsewhere for bonds of the same riskiness. It is commonly believed that bonds are a relatively riskless investment — that bond prices remain reasonably stable. Nothing could be further from the truth. If, for example, prevailing interest rates increase from 6 percent to 7 percent, then the market price on a bond which bears a coupon rate of 6 percent and has 30 years remaining until maturity could be expected to decline from $100.00 to $87.53 — almost a 12½ percent change. If a company had initially issued such a bond at a price to yield 6.1 percent, then the bond would be recorded on its books at a net value of $98.63 (a discount of $1.37

per hundred dollars). The purchase (i.e., the redemption) of a single $1,000 bond at a price of $87.53 per $100 would be recorded as follows:

Bonds payable	$1,000.00	
Cash		$875.30
Discount on bonds payable		13.70
Gain on redemption		111.00
To record redemption of the bond.		

Gains or losses on the redemption of bonds must necessarily be viewed by a financial analyst with a critical eye. Such gains or losses are recognized and reported on the income statement in the year in which the redemption takes place. As a result corporate management could readily time its redemptions in such a manner as to provide a source of discretionary income whenever it is believed that a boost in reported earnings would be helpful.

Remember, some users are interested in evaluating actions taken by management. Is this gain a reflection of good management? Is it related to the current period? Are readers provided with sufficient information in order to judge long-term cash flow implications?

Assume, for example, that in 19x60 a firm issued (at par) $10 million in 5 percent coupon bonds payable in 45 years. In 19x75 the prevailing rate of interest for similar securities was 7 percent. A 5 percent bond with 30 years remaining until maturity would be traded in the open market for approximately $75. The company could purchase the entire issue for $7.5 million and thereby realize a $2.5 million gain. Insofar as management believes that interest rates in the 19x70s to 19x80s will continue to remain substantially above the level of the earlier period, then management is free to select the year in which it redeems the bonds and thereby reports the gain.

One financial columnist for *The New York Times* cynically began an article on opportunities for manipulation inherent in the redemption of bonds as follows:

> Interested in rinky-dink accounting tricks? Best place to look is in the annual reports of ragtag companies, right? Well, perhaps not.
>
> For many years there has been a controversy over the treatment of "profits" arising out of the repurchase and cancellation of debt.
>
> The question has come to the fore recently because of high interest rates, which have forced bonds issued at low rates years ago to sell at deep price discounts.
>
> Such blue-chip companies as Mobil Oil, Tenneco, Borden, American Can and Firestone have retired thousands of bonds, taking the difference between the par value and the price they paid in reacquiring them into profits.[2]

Similar redemptions occurred in the early 1970s in Canada. If the company then issued more bonds at a higher interest rate to finance the cost of the redemption, some companies (possibly at the insistence of their auditors) amortized the "gain." That is, instead of crediting "gain on redemption" and recognizing the total amount as income in the period the companies credited "deferred gain on redemption." The amount in the latter account was then amortized to income (using a technique similar to that described earlier in this chapter) over what would have been the remaining life of the bonds which were redeemed. Unfortunately, not all companies amortized the "gain." Thus, we have encountered another difference in accounting treatment even though the *facts* appear to be the same. Different accounting treatment therefore seems to be the result of different objectives of accounting.

Is Interest Really an Expense?

Throughout the text interest has been accorded the same accounting recognition as other costs to the company. It has been referred to as an *expense* and grouped on the income statement along with other expenses — cost of goods sold, rent, administrative salaries, etc.

From a procedural standpoint it is convenient to account for interest in the same manner as other costs. But whether or not interest is, in fact, an expense is by no means a settled matter among accountants.

A corporation or other business enterprise requires an initial, and sometimes continuing infusion of capital. At least a portion of such capital is provided by shareholders. The corporation grants the shareholders the right to share in the profits of the enterprise and periodically distributes such profits in the form of dividends. Dividends, of course, are not considered an expense of the corporation; they are a distribution of earnings.

In addition, capital may also be provided by individuals or institutions who lend the company funds. This is especially true of bondholders who commit substantial amounts of capital for long periods of time. Indeed, many companies view the amounts obtained through the issuance of long-term bonds as *permanent* capital.

Often it is to the advantage of the company to raise capital by issuing bonds rather than common shares. Interest on bonds, for example, is income tax deductible; dividend payments are not. Whereas an issue of common shares increases the number of shares outstanding, and hence the number of shares among which profits have to be divided, an issue of bonds allows the earnings to remain undiluted (although, of course, substantially diminished by virtue of the interest payments). The specific advantages and disadvantages of issuing bonds as opposed to shares will be dealt with in the following chapter. The point to be emphasized at present, however, is that a company can obtain long-term financing by issuing either debt (bonds) or equity (share) securities. The choice between the two is often dependent on somewhat technical characteristics of the firm's own capital structure as well as existing relationships between prevailing share and bond prices. (The Labatt's balance sheet in Chapter 2, shows — based on book value — $142 million of long-term debt and $216 million of equity (preferred shares, common shares and retained earnings).

In Chapter 5 we referred to the *entity* concept, *cost* concept and *objectives* of accounting and said that the interest expense incurred by the entity was generally excluded from the "cost" of an asset. In Chapter 9 we stated that it might be logical under some conditions to capitalize interest during long construction periods. In this Chapter we have observed that for income tax purposes, interest outlays and accruals are usually treated as an expense. In summary, we have indicated that variety, and not total uniformity, exists.

However, accountants generally treat interest as an expense because this approach frequently suits their objective(s) of accounting. Looking at the matter from a historical or traditional viewpoint, we can observe that one of the major origins of accounting was in the need to report to owners (proprietors or partners; and, in later years to common shareholders). The owners of the entity wanted to know what income remained after paying all costs, one of which was (in their eyes) interest on borrowing, which also was probably for a shorter duration than today. *Constraints*, or corporate legislation of today, require that financial statements of public companies report to owners of the business — the common shareholders. Hence, under this stewardship objective of reporting it makes sense (to the owners) to view interest on debt as an expense, to be subtracted from revenue before reporting to the owners. Bondholders do not require the same legal support from corporate legislation in order to obtain financial information, and hence would not be concerned about such accounting treatment for interest. Bondholders can simply ask for *special* purpose reports designed for them; and if such reports are not forthcoming can always choose not to lend the company additional money.

Different sets of *facts* may nevertheless suggest a different treatment for interest. The "interest during construction" situation presents different facts, which may lead to interest being capitalized when the *materiality* and *matching* concepts are suitably considered by the preparers (management and accountants). Another different factual situation may lead to interest being considered a distribution of income (similar to the treatment of dividends). For example, public utilities in effect are regulated by a type of government board. The board limits the income of the common shareholders and treats them, in a way, like bondholders — whose income is limited by the interest rate. Under these conditions, where telephone rates paid by customers are set by a government board, is there much distinction between bondholders and shareholders? Maybe interest and dividends should be treated the same way. So far in Canada the distinction between interest (an expense) and dividends (distribution of income) still exists. But some day for some sets of facts it may not.

Statement Interpretation

Although treating interest on long-term debt as either an expense or a distribution of income is still somewhat theoretical, there are some practical variations which are worth noting. Until the late 1970s Air Canada and CNR (Canadian National Railways) were both financed for many years in large part by long-term debt held by the federal government. When the government decided to "convert" the debt into shares, net income rose significantly because of the absence of interest expense. Had management improved corporate results?

What do you suppose happened when Air Canada reported these so-called higher profits? Some naive announcers and reporters wrote critical stories about "excess" profit and were upset when the airline asked for increases in air fares to cover increased costs (mainly fuel and wages). It is clear that these reporters had misinterpreted the airline's financial results, because they did not investigate the facts of the situation. Bondholders had become shareholders and now their return on investment took the form of dividends instead of interest. Their position in fact, as chief suppliers of capital, was virtually unchanged. However, because dividends are not an expense whereas interest is, the impact of the "conversion" is an increase in income.

We need at least *two* pieces of information so that we can compare and form judgments. Our comparisions might be between, for example:

1. Two different measurements (e.g., replacement cost vs. net realizable value) for the same company at the same time.
2. Two different figures (e.g., sales for two different years) for the same company.
3. Two different figures (e.g., net income) for two different companies for the same year.

As we have said, item 3 has to be conducted very carefully, especially when we are looking at complex (net figures or composites) concepts such as accounting net income.

Two different companies — one capitalized entirely by equity and the other 90 percent by debt — can have quite different net income figures. Further analysis is needed. For example, given the deductibility of interest expense for income tax purposes, maybe the "all equity" company is not managed well financially. It might be able to borrow at low interest rates, and earn higher income by investing the borrowed funds. Or, it might be subject to high risk and the owners do not want to be burdened by compulsory interest payments. We must investigate and learn the facts.

Leases

In recent years several new methods of financing business growth have been developed and popularized. One financial arrangement that has been of special concern to accountants is *leasing*. In a strict sense a lease involves the right to use land, buildings, equipment, or other property for a specified period of time in return for rent or other compensation. In practice, however, many lease arrangements are the equivalent of installment purchases or other forms of borrowing arrangements.

Suppose that a construction firm needs a piece of earth-moving equipment. The cost of the equipment is $100,000; the estimated useful life is 10 years. Since the company does not have sufficient cash on hand to purchase the equipment, it secures a loan for its full cost. The terms of the loan specify that principal and interest are to be paid in 10 annual installments of equal amount. The amount of each payment is to be determined on the basis of an interest rate of 8 percent. If $100,000 is viewed as the present value of an annuity for 10 periods, discounted at a rate of 8 percent, then the annual payment required to amortize the loan can be determined (per Table 4 of the Appendix) as follows:

$$\$100{,}000 = 6.7101x$$
$$x = \$14{,}903.$$

Upon purchasing the equipment and borrowing the necessary funds, the company would make the following journal entries:

Cash	$100,000	
Note payable		$100,000
To record the loan of $100,000.		

Equipment	$100,000	
Cash		$100,000
To record the purchase of earth-moving equipment.		

Each year the company would make the required payment on the note and would record depreciation on the equipment. The division of the payment between principal and interest would, of course, vary from year to year. As the balance of the loan declines, a smaller portion of the payment would be for interest and a larger portion for reduction of the principal. The entry for the payment of the first year would be

Interest expense (8% × $100,000)	$8,000	
Note payable	6,903	
Cash		$14,903
To record the first payment on the note.		

The entry for depreciation (assuming the straight-line method is being used would be)

Depreciation expense	$10,000	
Allowance for depreciation		$10,000
To record depreciation for one year.		

Suppose instead, however, that the transaction took a slightly different form. The manufacturer of the earth-moving equipment, upon arrangement with the construction company, sold the equipment to a financial institution, such as a bank or an insurance company. The financial institution thereupon leased the equipment to the construction company. The agreement specified that the term of the lease was to be for 10 years, after which time the construction company would have the option to purchase the equipment for $1. Annual rental charges would be $14,903, and the construction company (the lessee) would have to pay all insurance, maintenance costs, and license fees on the equipment. In economic substance all parties are in the identical position in which they would have been had the company purchased the equipment outright and borrowed the required funds from the financial institution. Annual cash payments by the construction company are the same $14,903. Compare, however, the manner in which the lease, as opposed to the borrow/purchase, transaction might be accounted for. At the time the lease agreement was signed no entry would be required. Each year upon payment of the "rent" the following journal entry would be made:

Rent expense	$14,903	
Cash		$14,903
To record payment of rent for one year.		

Depreciation, of course, would not be taken on the equipment, since the equipment itself would never be recorded on the books of the lessee (the construction company).

The fundamental accounting distinction between the transaction as a purchase/borrow arrangement and as a lease is that when considered as a lease the company records on its books neither the asset nor the accompanying liability. From the standpoint of the company, the omission of the liability may represent an important advantage of the lease transaction. Potential creditors and investors may be inclined to view with disfavor excessive amounts of debt appearing on a balance sheet. Moreover, some loan agreements, written by lawyers who are not sufficiently familiar with accounting, specify the maximum amount of debt that a company is permitted to incur. The leasing arrangement would be a convenient means of circumventing such restrictions. In effect it would permit the company to arrange for "off the balance sheet" financing of its equipment acquisitions.

The "success" of "off the balance sheet" financing clearly depends on the sophistication of the readers of the financial statements. A sophisticated user who reads notes to the financial statements very carefully *may* be able to judge the situation based on the cash outlays which are needed in the future to meet lease obligations.

Accounting for Capital Leases

There would be little justification for permitting two transactions, the purchase/borrow arrangement and the lease, which are in economic substance identical, to be accounted for differently. The construction company, as a *lessee*, has the same rights and obligations as it would if it were the legal owner of the equipment. The company bears all risks and has acquired all rights of ownership. Should the equipment last for longer than the estimated 10 years, the company has the option to purchase it for a negligible amount. Should it suffer a major breakdown, the construction company has the obligation to repair it. Moreover, the company has both a legal and a moral obligation to make the specified payments over the life of the lease. The firm that holds title to the equipment, the financial institution, is the owner in name only.

The Accounting Research Committee of the CICA has determined that leases which are clearly in substance purchases of property (*capital leases*) should be recorded as such by the lessee. The acquisition of the construction equipment would be recorded as a purchase. The transaction would be accounted for as the purchase illustrated previously except that appropriately descriptive account titles would be used for both the asset and the liability:

Equipment held under lease	$100,000	
Present value of lease obligations		$100,000
To record acquisition of earth-moving equipment under a lease arrangement. The asset, "equipment held under lease," would be depreciated over the useful life of the equipment; the liability, "present value of lease obligations," would be accounted for as if it were an ordinary interest-bearing note:		

Depreciation expense	$10,000	
Equipment held under lease — allowance for depreciation		$10,000
To record first-year depreciation (straight-line method).		

Interest expense (8% of $100,000)	$8,000	
Present value of lease obligations	6,903	
Cash		$14,903
To record the first lease payment.		

Many lease agreements indicate only the amount of annual payments; they do not reveal either the actual purchase price (i.e., the fair market value) of the property transferred or the interest rate used to determine the required amounts of the annual payments. Insofar as the lease agreement is silent on these points, the accountant has to look for the necessary information in the negotiations leading to the agreement. Almost always, however, he can find some means of estimating the fair market value of the property or an appropriate rate at which to discount the required payments.

From the lessor's (financial institution's) point of view the lease would be recorded as a note receivable (called a financing lease) and interest revenue would be accrued on a yield basis. This approach seems to make sense because the financial institution is in the business of making money through loans.

Accounting for Operating Leases

Not all lease arrangements are the equivalent of purchases. Businesses enter into rental agreements for a variety of reasons: They need property for only a short period of time; they do not wish to accept the risks of ownership; they do not have the cash necessary to make a purchase and are unable or unwilling to incur additional debt; they want the service and maintenance that might be provided by the lessor.

Traditionally, *operating* leases, those which cover merely the right to use property in exchange for periodic rental payments, have been accorded no balance sheet recognition. No entry is made at the time the lease is executed; entries to record the rent expense are made periodically. Many accountants argue, however, that *all* lease agreements (assuming that they are not cancellable) create property rights as well as obligations that deserve to be reported on the balance sheet. A lessee ordinarily has the right to hold and use the property in a manner consistent with the applicable laws, the rights of others, and the provisions of the lease agreement. He often has most of the rights of an owner, with the exception of the right to dispose of the property at his discretion. At the same time, he has the obligation to make rental payments as they come due. The present value of the rights obtained in a lease agreement, according to many accountants, should be *capitalized* and recorded as an asset; the corresponding present value of the obligation should be recorded as a liability. The asset should be amortized (depreciated) over the life of the lease. The stated value of the obligation should be reduced as the periodic rental payments are made. Each rental payment would be considered in part a payment of *principal*; the initial liability being equal to the present value of the property rights, and in part a payment of interest on the unpaid balance of the original obligation.

There are, however, serious obstacles to *capitalizing* (recording as an asset) the value of the property rights inherent in *all* noncancellable lease commitments. It is exceedingly difficult to measure the value of such property rights. Many leases, for example, provide not only for the right to *use* the property but also for services on the part of the lessor. The lessor of an office building, for example, may provide heat, electricity, and janitorial and security services. Consistent with other accounting principles, the rights to receive those types of services are not capitalized as assets — no more than accounting recognition is given to an employment contract at the time it is signed. The task of allocating the lease payments between the right to use the property and the other services provided is likely to be inordinately difficult. Moreover, determination of an appropriate rate at which to discount the lease payments to arrive at their present value is also likely to present difficulties. Whereas in transactions involving purchase-type leases the effective interest rate is often a subject for negotiation, in those pertaining to *operating* (nonpurchase) leases the question of interest may not even be specifically considered.

If the trends of the past continue into the future, it is probable that there will be an increase in the number of types of leases that are recorded on the balance sheet. Unquestionably, the rule-making bodies of the profession will demand increased *footnote disclosure* of the pertinent terms of *all* material noncancellable leases. It is essential that in reviewing financial reports of similar companies an analyst recognize that property rights can be acquired and obligations incurred through lease as well as purchase arrangements. Sometimes the information contained in the footnotes might be used to adjust the financial statements of those companies that do not capitalize lease commitments; however, inadequate information is often provided in order to permit a full adjustment.

Again, we see the important role that note disclosure can play in financial reporting. Many accountants try to overcome limitations of measurement "rules" by giving additional information — about cash payments needed under leases, other than that required by GAAP (which is generally for five future years). But other accountants follow minimum disclosure practices under stewardship accounting. Such financial statements could mislead or be useless to those interested in management evaluation and prediction.

Accounting for Income Taxes

For larger companies in Canada the Department of National Revenue, in particular the income tax branch, owns nearly half of the income-before-income-tax part of the business. That is, income tax rates approach (or may exceed) 50 percent of income before income taxes. Accounting for income tax effects is therefore a serious matter. It is also fairly complicated, and causes much confusion between preparers and users. Some students have great difficulty with this topic; although it appears late in this chapter it merits full concentration.

We have said many times before that in *some* situations whatever accounting principles are selected for a stewardship (or other) objective of accounting are also accepted by income taxation officials. But, we further stressed that sometimes the income tax law prescribes its own principles and that these *could* differ from those chosen for another objective of accounting and incorporated into the firm's external financial statements. Sometimes the differences are *permanent*. For instance, an outlay to a charity outside Canada might be recorded as an expense for accounting purposes, but would *not* be allowed as an expense in arriving at *taxable income*, the figure on which income tax is computed. Other differences are "*timing differences*." This means that in total the expense (or revenue) could be the same over the life of the company under both the income tax and, say, stewardship objectives. However, the amounts involved may be different in *any one* year. Depreciation could be an example of a timing difference if the company used straight-line for stewardship purposes and declining balance for income tax purposes.

Our prime concern is with *timing differences* because these can cause huge swings in income figures. Good income tax planning for situations which create timing differences might vary considerably with our other objectives of accounting and preparing financial reports. Hence, we ought to consider ways of reconciling the figures which result from timing differences and having these different objectives.

The basic issue we are dealing with is actually quite simple. The cure, however, may be worse than the ailment. The issue is: Would you pay the same amount for these two *physically identical* long-lived assets?

1. $1,000,000 can be claimed as capital cost allowance (tax depreciation) thereby saving (on a discounted present value basis) $400,000 in income tax.
2. Zero may be claimed as capital cost allowance.

Obviously you would pay $400,000 more for the one which has capital cost allowance available. To you it is worth more. Agree? Of course you would. How then do you record this *fact* in the accounts and on the financial statements?

Before proceeding with the journal entries and financial statement presentation, we ought to explain the above remarks. In *some* situations (such as when a company invests in common shares of another company) it is necessary to establish a buying or selling price for *each* of the tangible (and perhaps some of the intangible) assets and liabilities. Under these circumstances we must first determine how much of the cost of a long-lived depreciable asset, for example, has already been depreciated for income tax purposes. This is because the tax depreciation, once claimed, is lost forever for this same company; the benefit (of reduced income taxes) was received in a previous year. The purchaser of the shares thus may have an asset which is worth less than one with full tax depreciation available.

In the foregoing illustration the first asset with $1,000,000 of tax depreciation (capital cost allowance) available might be recorded on the financial statements of the purchasing company at $1,000,000. However, the second asset has no capital cost allowance available to reduce income tax. As a result, the second asset is worth much less. How much less that it is worth is a function of income tax rates and when the tax depreciation would otherwise have been claimed.

At a 50 percent income tax rate, if the $1,000,000 of capital cost allowance were claimed immediately, it would reduce income taxes otherwise payable by $500,000 ($1,000,000 at 50 percent):

	No Capital Cost Allowance	*$1,000,000 of Capital Cost Allowance*
Revenue	$5,000,000	$5,000,000
Cost of goods sold*	2,000,000	2,000,000
Gross profit	3,000,000	3,000,000
Expenses (excluding depreciation)	1,200,000	1,200,000
Taxable income before capital cost allowance	1,800,000	1,800,000
Capital cost allowance	0	1,000,000
Taxable income	$1,800,000	$ 800,000
Income tax thereon @ 50%	$ 900,000	$ 400,000

*Does not include depreciation.

Since, under income tax legislation, capital cost allowance is usually not claimed entirely in the first year, something less than the $500,000 benefit would be received. This can be illustrated as follows, using a 10 percent interest rate:

Year	*Capital Cost Allowance Claimed (Figures are artificial)*	*Benefit @ 50% income tax rate*	*Discount Factor @ 10% (end of year)*	*Present Value of Benefit*
1	$ 300,000	$150,000	.909	$136,350
2	250,000	125,000	.826	103,250
3	200,000	100,000	.751	75,100
4	150,000	75,000	.683	51,225
5	100,000	50,000	.621	31,050
	$1,000,000	$500,000		$396,975

Such an asset with no capital cost allowance available would therefore have a value of only $603,025 ($1,000,000 less $396,975) under the above assumptions because the $396,975 could *not* be claimed and would not lower the amount of tax payable.

The asset might be recorded at a net figure of $603,025 on the financial statements of the purchasing company. (The latter treatment is explained in Chapter 13). Or, it might be shown gross at $1,000,000 offset by an asset *contra* account of $396,975. The contra account would be something like accumulated depreciation. A typical account title and statement presentation name is "deferred income taxes." This is a confusing name; its meaning will become a little clearer as we proceed.

In summary, the basic idea that the *absence* of available capital cost allowance *lowers* an asset's value must be kept firmly in mind. The second point to remember is that the decline in income tax value or worth is recorded in an asset contra account with a title such as "deferred income tax."

A Typical Situation

The previous example, though frequently encountered when one company purchases a large block of common shares of another, is not as typical as the occurrence of accounting timing differences within the same company. The usual example involves a timing difference between accounting depreciation and income tax depreciation (capital cost allowance).

Suppose that a company bought an asset costing $10,000,000 which had a life of two years and straight-line depreciation was chosen for stewardship accounting purposes. Suppose also that the entire $10,000,000 could be claimed as capital cost allowance in the first year, and that the company's income before depreciation and income tax expense was $25,000,000 in each of the two years. Finally, assume that the income tax rate was 40 percent each year.

The income tax return (or form) which would be filed with the Department of National Revenue would show the following:

	Year 1	*Year 2*
Income before depreciation and income tax	$25,000,000	$25,000,000
Capital cost allowance	10,000,000	0
Taxable income	$15,000,000	$25,000,000
Income tax payable @ 40% *in cash*	$ 6,000,000	$10,000,000

The income taxes payable of $6,000,000 (year 1) and $10,000,000 (year 2) would actually be paid in cash installments throughout most of each year and shortly thereafter.

If (an important if) income tax expense were based on the *income taxes actually payable in cash*, the income statements prepared for accounting (perhaps stewardship) purposes would be as follows:

	Year 1	*Year 2*	*Two Year Total*
Income before depreciation and income tax	$25,000,000	$25,000,000	$50,000,000
Depreciation expense	5,000,000	5,000,000	10,000,000
Income before income tax	20,000,000	20,000,000	40,000,000
Income tax expense	6,000,000	10,000,000	16,000,000
Net income	$14,000,000	$10,000,000	$24,000,000

Observe that the two years are identical except for the amount of capital cost allowance which was claimed. Observe also that:

1. In year 1 capital cost allowance exceeded depreciation by $5,000,000 ($10,000,000 less $5,000,000). The reverse occurred in year 2.
2. The stewardship "worth" (*not* market value) of the asset dropped by $4,000,000 (the capital cost allowance at the 40 percent income tax rate) plus accounting depreciation (excluding depreciation on the $4,000,000) to a net of $3,000,000 ($10,000,000 less $4,000,000 less one-half depreciation on the remaining $6,000,000).

Does a set of income statements which show a $4,000,000 higher income in year 1 than in year 2 make sense? Note that in year 1 the ratio of income tax expense to income before income tax is 30 percent whereas in year 2 it is 50 percent. Remember, the two years are identical except for the amount of capital cost allowance claimed. (You will recall that capital cost allowance rates are set by government to meet its needs in stimulating the economy, and facilitating administration of the Income Tax Act. These purposes may result in quite different effects from the information sought by users of financial accounting reports.)

How should we acknowledge the decline in "worth" of the asset, caused by claiming $5,000,000 capital cost allowance in excess of depreciation? Our choices (aside from doing nothing) are:

1. Footnote disclosure of the amount of the timing difference: or
2. The use of an asset contra account, such as "deferred income taxes."

The accounting profession in Canada (primarily the CICA with the support of the Provincial Securities Commissions) has chosen the asset contra approach. At one time (shortly after 1954 when many timing differences were first permitted by income tax legislation) footnote disclosure of the amount of timing differences was considered an acceptable alternative. However, public criticisms of existing alternatives which affected the measurement of net income encouraged the CICA to eliminate footnote disclosure. They adopted what is called the "deferred credit to expense" approach. For stewardship objectives of accounting this approach may make sense because it in effect writes down historic cost asset "values" and records expenses; however, for other objectives, such as cash flow prediction, it may have important limitations because it is based on non-cash accrual accounting (technically, called deferral accounting in this type of situation).

Continuing with our previous example we can tabulate these *timing differences*:

	Year 1	*Year 2*	*Two Year Total*
Capital cost allowance	$10,000,000	$ 0	$10,000,000
Depreciation expense	(5,000,000)	(5,000,000)	(10,000,000)
Excess of capital cost allowance, or (excess of depreciation)	$ 5,000,000	$(5,000,000)	0
Tax effect @ 40%	$ 2,000,000	$(2,000,000)	

The journal entries for the deferred income tax approach would be:

Year 1:		
Income tax expense (made up of the amount payable in cash $6,000,000 *plus* the $2,000,000 tax effect in year 1 of the timing difference)	$8,000,000	
Income tax payable		$ 6,000,000
Deferred income tax		2,000,000
To record income tax expense.		
Year 2:		
Income tax expense (made up of the amount payable in cash $10,000,000 *less* the $2,000,000 timing difference effect in year 2)	$8,000,000	
Deferred income tax (reversal of credit from year 1)	2,000,000	
Income tax payable		$10,000,000
To record income tax expense.		

The *credit* to "deferred income tax" in year 1 is computed by multiplying the timing difference of $5,000,000 by the income tax rate of 40 percent, which is the rate in the year in which the difference occurs. The debit in year 2 is computed the same way; but in year 2 depreciation exceeds the capital cost allowance, — hence a *debit* arises. In this simple example, a reversal occurs in the two-year span.

If we view the matter from the asset value side, it is clear that whenever capital cost exceeds depreciation the asset (inclusive of its income tax effect) loses "value." Hence, an asset contra or credit is required.

The two income statements which would be prepared under the deferred (or deferral) income tax method are:

	Year 1	*Year 2*	*Total*
Income before depreciation and income tax	$25,000,000	$25,000,000	$50,000,000
Depreciation expense	5,000,000	5,000,000	10,000,000
Income before income tax	20,000,000	20,000,000	40,000,000
Income tax expense	8,000,000	8,000,000	16,000,000
Net Income	$12,000,000	$12,000,000	$24,000,000

Observe that the ratio of income tax expense to income before income tax is 40 percent in *both* years. (The 40 percent is the income tax rate prescribed in the assumptions of the illustration).

Note that, the two year totals (i.e., $16,000,000) are the same for income tax expense regardless of whether it is based on cash payments of $6,000,000 (year 1) and $10,000,000 (year 2) — called the "taxes payable" or "flow-through" basis — or on the *deferral method* where the $8,000,000 figure exists in each year. But the individual years' net incomes differ depending on whether the flow-through or deferral basis is used. This is obviously caused by the $2,000,000 deferred income tax credit (year 1) or debit (year 2). The net incomes each year are:

	Year 1	*Year 2*	*Total*
Deferral method	$12,000,000	$12,000,000	$24,000,000
Flow-through method	$14,000,000	$10,000,000	$24,000,000

Deferred Income Tax Method Assessed

Three aspects of the "deferral method of tax allocation" (another common name for the issue, or controversy) merit attention. First, the deferral entry *does not involve a flow of cash*. This can be seen more easily when we split the journal entries into two parts:

		Year 1		*Year 2*	
(a) Cash portion	Income tax expense	$6,000,000		$10,000,000	
	Income tax payable		$6,000,000		$10,000,000
(b) Non-cash portion	Income tax expense	$2,000,000			
	Deferred income tax			$ 2,000,000	
	Deferred income tax		$2,000,000		
	Income tax expense				$ 2,000,000

In summary, *cash flows are the same* no matter whether we use the deferral or flow through method. The deferred credit merely records a loss in "value" of the asset, and in a sense is like the accumulated depreciation account.

Second, the deferred income tax method as it presently is practiced in Canada does *not* recognize the time value of money. Note that we merely multiplied the timing difference by the income tax rate which was in effect when the timing difference occurred. We did not try to discount the asset's worth as we previously did in "Accounting For Income Taxes" (page 454).

Third, observe that we have not used a liability method (sometimes called an accrual method) in setting up the asset contra account. That is, if the income tax rate rose from 40 percent in year 1 to 50 percent in year 2, we would *not* accrue the additional 10 percent rate at the end of year 1, as some form of liability.

Of the three comments, the second has received the most attention. Officials of some companies would argue, based on their own forecasts and history, that reversals (appearance of deferred income tax debits) do not occur for many years. This, you will note, is a matter of *fact*. If the reversals are many years away — as would occur in a company which is expanding and buying new long-lived assets every year — the deferral method clearly has serious limitations because it ignores the effects of discounting. The further the amount is away from the present, the less its present value.

Readers of financial statements are therefore warned. As we said a few pages back, some people feel that the accounting cure is worse than the ailment.

Yet, if we accept the basic concept that an asset loses value when capital cost allowance is claimed for it (and we can hardly dispute this point), our accounting problem becomes one of recording and reporting the facts (i.e., the *amount* of capital cost claimed in excess of depreciation, for example). Is footnote disclosure adequate? It might very well be adequate for knowledgeable readers/users because they would be warned that higher cash outlays are needed to pay income tax at some future date. However, less sophisticated readers *may* need the effect recorded for them directly on the balance sheet and income statement. As we have said there are dangers in such a recording approach because the non-cash (not discounted) sums computed under the deferral method may bear little relationship to the additional cash payments which are eventually required (such as when depreciation expense exceeds capital cost allowance).

The accounting profession in Canada clearly faces a dilemma. Ideally, accounting for income taxes ought to be tailored to objectives and *facts* (which could differ from company to company). One company for instance, may be expanding and not expect a timing difference reversal, whereby depreciation exceeds capital cost allowance, for many years. Another company might expect a reversal next year. Readers could follow accounting methods more easily if adequate explanation accompanied the financial statements. Unfortunately, the accounting profession (presumably with support from some Canadian corporations and the Securities Commissions) seems to fear the application of judgment in this situation. Why?

Many accountants feel that too many alternatives (such as FIFO vs. LIFO) already exist in accounting, and that these differences are permitted even under essentially the same conditions or sets of facts. When such extra "freedom" is available accountants (especially those who dictate accounting pronouncements in Canada, and who are for the most part, auditors) feel that manipulation of accounting numbers by preparers is made too easy. A standard joke is that when you ask an accountant what one plus one is, the reply is "What number did you have in mind?" Under these circumstances, some accountants seek some rigid rules for the profession, feeling that such rules would give the profession greater prestige. This runs counter to most definitions of a profession because one characteristic of a professional person is "one who has an ability to choose wisely when confronted with conflicting data." A profession, also by definition, though, deals with an identifiable body of knowledge. Hence, the dilemma occurs. If there is too much variety and many alternatives the boundaries and nature of the professional task become clouded — and questions arise as to whether accounting really is a profession.

Many other timing differences occur between revenue and expense accounts, besides the depreciation versus capital cost allowance example. One other timing difference can occur when a company encounters a net loss for income tax purposes. Although the issue at stake is similar to that just described, accounting treatment can vary. Users/readers of financial statements ought to note this point because they are likely to encounter it sometime in their careers.

Reporting Deferred Income Taxes

Whereas accumulated depreciation is deducted from the asset in balance sheet presentation, deferred income tax credits are shown on the right-hand side of the balance sheet. Whenever a reversal is expected within the operating cycle of a company, the amount involved would be shown as a current liability. Otherwise, the balance is noncurrent. Technically, the amount is not a liability; it is shown separately (see Labatt's presentation in Chapter 2) much like long-term debt.

Employee Pension Plans

Accounting by a company for the annual costs of employee pension plans is another difficult subject which has lately received considerable attention from many sources in Canada. There are two basic types of pension plans: (1) those which are based on *costs*; or amounts contributed by employees and the employer; and (2) those which are based on *benefits* which the employee is entitled to receive on retirement. A *cost-based plan* is relatively easy to account for. The administrator of the plan (usually a person outside the company, employed by an insurance company) receives money paid by the company — perhaps in accordance with a union agreement — and invests it on behalf of the employee. In a simple case, when the employees retire or leave the company, they are entitled to whatever sum has been accumulated (principal plus interest plus or minus any profits or losses on good or bad investments). From the company's viewpoint "pension expense" is debited when the cash is turned over to the administrator of the pension plan, or accrued as stipulated by the administrator. (Other complications can arise but we can ignore these in an introductory course).

Accounting for a *benefit-based plan* can be very complex because of considerable uncertainty involved in matching pension expense with revenue generated for the company by employees' labor. A benefit-based plan is one in which on retirement (or perhaps on leaving) an employee is entitled to a definite sum per year as a pension, such as 60 percent of an average of the employee's five highest-salary years. Since the five highest-salary years might very well be the five years just prior to retirement, what accrual for pension cost should be made, say, in the fifteenth or the eighteenth, or the twentieth year before retirement? Several factors complicate the pension expense and liability computation:

1. Rapid inflation can cause wage rates to increase at a different rate than was forecast by pension administrators or actuaries, and at a rate which differs from investment yields. Hence, accrued liabilities and costs may be far off target on retirement day.
2. More or fewer employees may leave the company before qualifying for a pension than was forecast by the actuary (who is responsible for the mathematics of the plan). (The pension plan may stipulate that no pension is receivable unless at least 10 years of service have been provided to the company. Many employees may leave before this minimum time, and an overaccrual of pension costs might result.) Others may die before attaining the forecast five highest-salary years.
3. The terms of pension plans (e.g., benefits, years of service needed to qualify) may be changed as people's attitudes change.
4. The administrator of the plan may make some exceedingly good or exceedingly bad investments. Whereas under a cost-based plan the employee receives any gain or loss, under the benefit-based plan, the company would generally have to make up for any losses. The focal point of benefit-based plans is always *outputs* (amount of pension to be received by employees) and not the *inputs* (money handed over to pension administrators).

Besides the above complications, there are several caused by the existence of many quite different actuarial methods of *funding* or paying for a plan. Accountants and actuaries in Canada disagree on common objectives because they have different professional responsibilities. Actuaries do not have a clear obligation for external financial reporting.

Suppose that $100,000 is required at age 65 for a particular employee, and the employee is now age 45. As we have seen from Chapter 6 there are many methods of making cash payments that will accumulate to $100,000 twenty years hence. Three are:

1. Give the administrator of the plan $100,000 twenty years from now, just prior to the employee's retirement (called terminal funding). (Pension laws in some provinces do not allow this method; it is shown here for comparative purposes).
2. *If* a "reasonable" rate of interest is 10 percent, a sum could be given *now* to the administrator, and accumulated interest would increase the total to $100,000 in twenty years. From Table 2 in the Appendix the factor for 10 percent and 20 years hence is .1486. The amount which has to be invested now is therefore $100,000 × .1486 = $14,860. (This method is called *initial* funding).
3. A periodic payment plan could be chosen. For instance, a sum could be paid at the end of each of the next twenty years so that at a 10 percent rate of interest per annum it will accumulate to $100,000. From Table 3 in the Appendix the annuity factor for twenty years and 10 percent is 57.2750. Dividing the $100,000 by 57.257 produces our annual payment of $1,746. (This method has various names.)

For simplicity, let us assume that *all* pension costs are being paid by the employer (a non-contributory plan). If so, observe that the three different *funding* (meaning cash payment) methods could bring forth three different annual pension expenses, when the accountant employs cost allocation methods. (Chapter 9 contained some serious criticisms of cost allocations).

1.	Terminal funding: $100,000 allocated evenly over a 20 year period per year is:	$5,000
2.	Initial funding: $14,860 allocated evenly over 20 years; on a per year basis is:	$ 743
3.	Annuity:	$1,746

Which is the so-called best method? Which matches revenue and expenses? The differences above are obviously caused by compound interest; hence, we must consider more than just pension expense when we analyze the problem. For instance, although the terminal funding method's cost is $5,000 per annum, the company *has the use of the funds* (not handed over to the pension administrator) *for twenty years*. Thus, if the company had *NOT* turned over $14,860 (the initial funding amount) but instead had invested it at 10 percent, this sum would accumulate to $100,000 at the end of twenty years. Ignoring income taxes, interest revenue would be $85,140 ($100,000 - $14,860). *If* (and a questionable one) the $85,140 is allocated evenly over twenty years it equals $4,257 per year. When the $4,257 is subtracted from $5,000 we arrive at $743 — exactly the amount of annual cost under the initial funding method.

As a result, when we (1) used a 10 percent interest rate; and (2) allocated on a straight-line basis over 20 years, we merely proved a mathematical "truism." Pension expense less interest revenue on funds not handed over to pension administrators equate all three funding methods under a common 10 percent interest rate assumption. But, only on the surface would all three funding methods turn out to have the same cost per year once interest revenue was considered.

Unfortunately, in real life many variations from our illustration occur. One is caused by changing interest rates. Generally speaking, we would expect that funds would not be handed over to pension administrators if the company could invest them and obtain a higher rate (than 10 percent in the foregoing example). Most Canadian provinces have somewhat loose laws in this respect, but they do force companies to make definite periodic funding payments. Nevertheless, the funding might occur at different times and interest rates could vary widely over a twenty-year period. As well, income tax rates and regulations vary over an extended time-period. Further, actuaries make a variety of other assumptions (such as the average ages of company employees, mortality rates) which affect calculated costs when computing amounts required to be turned over to administrators. In all, the subject of accounting for pension expense is very complex.

Pension Accounting in Perspective

Pension accounting will be under pressure to improve in the next decade. Many different groups (governments, union leaders, company officials, actuaries) besides accountants must act responsibly. On the average the population of Canada is growing older every year; more people will become concerned with the pension problem. Canadian pension plan laws are fairly loose; some day a large number of employees who think that they are protected by a pension plan (called a *vested* plan whereby ownership legally rests with each employee) could find that the company has gone bankrupt and that the pension administrator has not received all the cash needed to invest, because the laws did not require full payment immediately. The public might easily become outraged and demand a tightening of laws.

Union leaders and company officials will have to bargain with an eye on tomorrow, not just on today. It is too easy for companies to give away higher pension benefits in lieu of wages. A union can claim that it received a 9 percent wage increase, when, in reality, it received a 6 percent increase in wages and the effect of 3 percent in pension payments. The company can spread the cost of the 3 percent improvement over the *next* 15 years and the effect on the current year is negligible. Next year the same agreement with the union might be reached. If this happens every year for 15 years some people would reason that the pension cost will be huge. By deferring the costs of pension plans, companies can maintain lower costs for goods. Therefore, today's customers may be receiving a benefit which will have to be paid for in the future.

Actuaries have not seriously addressed the question of which methods are suitable for accounting and financial reporting. Actuaries focus on *cash funding* and try to accommodate (within the law) the cash liquidity needs of their client. Actuaries can be very flexible in their request for funds from clients. Accountants, in contrast, are concerned with such matters as matching and disclosure. Funding payments constitute cash basis accounting, not accrual accounting.

Besides all of this, some actuarial methods do not separate past and current service. Past service funding payments are required from an employer when a pension plan is modified (say, per an agreement with a union) and the employees receive some additional pension credit for the number of years they have already worked for the company. On retirement their pension may be based on the total number of years they have worked for a company, including years prior to the agreement.

An interesting accounting question arises with respect to past service costs. Should costs be charged to past years? To the present year? To future years? Or to some combination of the above? Accountants (including company management) have tended to charge past service costs to as much as the next 10 or 15 or more years, presumably on the questionable assumption that these costs will benefit the company in future years. (That is, management may believe that the employee with a good pension is less tempted to leave and work for a competitor.) A large difference in annual pension expense can therefore result when an outlay is classified as past service, and subject to a different duration of cost spreading or amortization than is current service.

Preparers (accountants, and financial managers of a company) and users of financial statements have to better understand the intricacies of pension plan financing. Some accountants who have not been educated broadly might easily confuse actuarial funding (cash basis) methods with what is needed to meet stewardship accrual accounting objectives. You no doubt have observed that we have avoided journal entry examples in this discussion of pension accounting, because the current state of affairs is deficient — perhaps grossly deficient in some aspects. Disclosure and laws with respect to funding have to be improved so that costs and cash payments are not unduly deferred until some future date. Significant issues have to be debated. To what extent is full payment during the employee's working life necessary? Are there any effects on inflation rates in Canada if companies change their basis of ascertaining costs (which may include pension expense) of goods produced and sold? Will exports of goods be affected if Canada costs its products differently than other countries?

In Chapter 1 we said that accounting is not static and that it must evolve. Pension accounting is a classic example of a topic needing improvements in several respects. "The use of your talents is requested" to help solve these complex issues!

Summary

In this chapter we have reviewed the means by which several types of liabilities — bonds, as well as those relating to leases, income taxes, and pensions — are accounted for. Each of the liabilities is directly related to an expense — interest expense, income tax expense, and pension expense. A central theme of the chapter has been that the amount at which the liability is stated on the balance sheet has a direct impact upon the amount of expense reported on the income statement. As emphasized in each of the chapters pertaining to assets, all questions of balance sheet valuations must necessarily be considered within a context of income determination.

Lease, income tax, and pension accounting are far more complex than we have had space to explain in this chapter. The accounting "rules" with respect to each are short-lived. Readers of financial statements are therefore warned. Information needed for prediction or management evaluation purposes for these types of liabilities may not be noted clearly, or at all, in the financial statements.

In recent years, accountants have used disclosure by way of footnotes to furnish additional information which is not readily discernible in measurements. Such note disclosure is particularly important for subjects mentioned in this and the next two chapters. Sometimes the note disclosure is adequate for users who wish to evaluate management and predict cash flows. However, in many other cases it is not. Some topics are so complex that both measurement and disclosure are needed to convey financial activities and results. Even then an incomplete picture may be described.

Notes

[1]The reader is strongly urged to review the material on compound interest and present value contained in Chapter 6.

[2]Robert Metz, *The New York Times*, May 13, 1973.

Questions, Problems, and Cases

Questions

10-1 List ten different examples drawn from this and previous chapters (example FIFO versus LIFO) of alternative methods of accounting for the same type of transaction (i.e., FIFO versus LIFO are alternative methods of accounting for inventory costs) noting the effects on income and asset-liability valuation of each of the ten. In your opinion is the existence of alternatives good or bad? Explain.

10-2 It is commonly believed that bonds are a riskless investment. However, if someone wished to invest some money for a two- or three-year period then the purchase of long-term bonds, scheduled to mature in 20 years, may not be a safe investment. Explain.

10-3 The account "discount on bonds payable" ordinarily has a debit balance. It has sometimes been argued that bond discount, like most other accounts which have debit balances, should be reported as an asset rather than as *contra* (as an adjustment) to a long-term liability. Considering the nature of bond discounts, do you agree?

10-4 Bond discount or premium can be amortized on an "effective interest" or "straight-line" basis. Distinguish between these two methods. Which would you recommend? Why?

10-5 For many years there has been controversy over the accounting for gains and losses which may arise when a company repurchases or redeems its own bonds at a price different from the value at which they are recorded on its books. Why have some financial observers charged that major corporations have engaged in repurchases or redemptions in order to give an artificial boost to earnings? How is this possible? How do you recommend that companies account for redemptions of their bonds? Why?

10-6 Different objectives of accounting or different sets of facts and constraints may suggest different treatments for interest. Explain. Give specific examples to support your position.

10-7 Distinguish between a "capital" and an "operating" lease. How would you account for each? Why?

10-8 Many lease agreements indicate only the amount of annual payments. They do not reveal either the actual purchase price of the property or the interest rate used to determine the required amounts of the annual payments. In order to record a capital lease, what information do you require? How would you obtain this information if the lease agreement only stipulated annual lease payments?

10-9 Explain the difference in objectives between stewardship accounting and tax law. Give an example of an accounting principle or method selected for a stewardship objective of accounting which differs from that prescribed by tax law (i.e., income tax objective of accounting).

10-10 Accounting principles selected to satisfy a stewardship objective of accounting may differ from those selected to satisfy a tax objective of accounting. Distinguish between "permanent" and "timing" differences. Give an example of each. What impact does each have on the accounting for income taxes?

10-11 Distinguish between a "taxes payable" or "flow-through" method and a "deferred tax allocation" method of accounting for income taxes. Which do you prefer? Why?

10-12 Why do some accountants contend that deferred tax allocation results in an overstatement of liabilities, in that amounts which may never have to be paid are included among reported obligations?

10-13 Distinguish between a "cost-based" and "benefit-based" pension plan. Why is accounting for a "benefit-based" pension plan more complicated?

*10-14 In this chapter most of the discussion about bonds, leases, income taxes, and pensions has been concerned with measurement issues (i.e., how much of the annual lease payments to capitalize). Give two examples of how the cash prediction objective of accounting might be satisfied by the disclosure rather than the measurement of data. Why do you suspect accountants have been preoccupied with measurement rather than disclosure of information?

Problems

P10-1 On January 2, 19x1, the Babiak Co. Ltd. issued 12 percent coupon bonds at a price which provided purchasers with a yield of 10 percent. The bonds paid interest on June 30 and December 31 and were scheduled to mature at December 31, 19x2.

Required:

a. Record the sale of a single $1,000 bond.

b. Determine interest expense for each of the four periods and record the first payment of interest.

c. Record the redemption of the bond (including final interest payment).

P10-2 On May 1, 19x5, the Baltimore Co. Ltd. issued at par (i.e., at a price of $100) $10 million of 8 percent, 20-year coupon bonds. Interest is payable semiannually.

Required:

a. Within two years, prevailing interest rates had increased to 10 percent. At what price could a bondholder sell a single $1,000 bond in the open market? (i.e., what price would you be willing to pay for the bond?)

b. By the fourth year, prevailing interest rates had increased to 12 percent. At what price could a bondholder now sell a single $1,000 bond?

c. What impact would the increase in prevailing interest rates have upon the reported interest expense of the Baltimore Co.?

d. "In comparison to common shares, bonds provide a relatively risk-free investment." Do you agree?

P10-3 The Mallouk Tire Company Ltd. issues 6 percent coupon bonds on January 31, 19x2, to mature in 20 years. The bonds are sold, at par, to yield 6 percent. The bonds require the payment of interest on June 30 and December 31.

Required:

a. What will be the required interest payment on June 30, 19x2, on a single $1,000-denomination bond? (All coupons, including the first, require the payment of the same amount of interest.)

b. Since the bondholder on June 30 would have held the bond for only five months, how much interest would he have earned (i.e., would he actually "deserve" to receive)?

c. Suppose the bondholder agreed to *advance* the company the entire amount of that portion of the first interest payment that he did not actually earn. How much would he advance the company?

d. Prepare a journal entry to record the issue of one bond, assuming that the company received the principal plus the unearned portion of the first interest payment.

e. Prepare a journal entry to record the first interest payment. The interest expense should represent the cost of borrowing funds only for the period during which the company had the use of such funds.

P10-4 The Amernic Drilling Co. issued, in year 1, $100,000 of 6 percent 30-year bonds at par. The bond indenture agreement provided that the company could redeem the bonds any time after year 10 at a price of $102.

In year 15, with 15 years remaining until maturity, the company decided to retire the bonds. Since the prevailing interest rate was 8 percent, the company elected to repurchase the bonds in the open market at the prevailing price.

Required:

a. Determine the price that the company would have to pay for the bonds.

b. Assume instead that the prevailing interest rate in year 15 was 4 percent. Determine the price that the company would have to pay for the bonds. Be sure to consider the maximum price at which the bonds are likely to trade in light of the call provision.

c. Prepare a journal entry to record the retirement of the bonds at the price calculated in Part a. Indicate any assumptions that you have made.

d. Why must "gains" or "losses" on retirement of bonds be interpreted with care by users of the financial statements?

P10-5 In January, Year 1, Thornton Machine Co. Ltd. issued $100,000 of 6 percent, 30-year coupon bonds. The indenture agreement stipulates that the company has the right to *call* (redeem) the bonds at a price of $103 any time after the bonds have been outstanding for 10 years. At December 31, Year 25, the bonds were stated on the company's books at a value of $98,300; there was a reported discount of $1,700.

In January, Year 26, when 5 years remained until maturity, the company controller debated whether or not he should refinance the entire bond issue — that is, whether he should redeem the bonds and reborrow the entire cost of redemption. The prevailing rate of interest at the time he was making his decision was 5 percent. The controller determined that he could borrow the entire $103,000 necessary to call the outstanding issue at that rate.

In Year 26 the company earned a return of 8 percent on all invested capital.

Required:

a. Prepare a journal entry that would be required to record the redemption of the bonds.

b. In view of the fact that the company would have to report a loss on the redemption of the bonds the controller decided against redeeming the bonds. Do you agree with his decision? [*Hint*: Identify all cash flows that would result in the next 5 years (10 semiannual periods) under both of the alternatives. Determine the present value *to the company* of such cash flows. In discounting the cash flows, use the rate that is most appropriate to the company — the rate (8 percent per year or 4 percent per period) that indicates what it could earn on the borrowed funds.]

c. What conclusion can you draw from your calculations in Part b regarding the meaning of "loss on redemption of bonds" to an external reader of financial statements.

P10-6 Suppose a company issues 12 percent coupon bonds at a price which would provide a return to the bondholders of 10 percent. The bonds will mature in 20 years.

Required:

a. Prepare a journal entry to record the issue of a single $1,000 bond.

b. Prepare journal entries to record both the *first* and *last* payments of interest. Assume first that the company uses the effective interest method and second the straight-line method of amortization.

c. Determine the effective rate of interest recorded as an expense under each of the two methods for both the first and the last payments. That is, express the recorded interest expense as a percentage of the reported *gross* liability (bond payable plus premium).

d. What method would you recommend the company use? Why?

P10-7 The managers of Galvin Co. Ltd. are debating whether to buy or to rent a computer. A computer manufacturer has offered the company the opportunity to lease, for a period of 15 years, a machine for $100,000 per year. Alternatively, the company could purchase the machine outright and could borrow the purchase price from a bank at an annual rate of 10 percent. The loan from the bank would be repaid in 15 equal instalments, each instalment representing both a repayment of principal and the payment of interest on the unpaid balance.

Costs of operating the equipment would be the same under either alternative; the salvage value after 15 years would be negligible.

Currently the company has total assets of $5 million and total liabilities of $2 million.

Required:

a. What is the maximum that the company should be willing to pay to purchase the machine?

b. Suppose that the company paid such maximum amount. Compare total expenses that would be reported during the first year if the company purchased the machine as opposed to leasing it (assuming that it accounts for the transaction as an operating lease). The company uses the straight-line method of depreciation.

c. Determine the ratio of total debt to total owners' equity under each of the alternatives.

d. Assume that the company accounts for the lease as a capital lease.

How would it determine the amount to be capitalized and recorded as "equipment held under lease"?

e. If the company recorded the lease as a capital lease then what would the ratio of total debt to total owners' equity be?

P10-8 The indenture agreement associated with the outstanding bonds of the Pollock Machine Co. Ltd. stipulates the maximum amount of debt that the company can incur. The company wishes to expand its plant and purchase new equipment, but has insufficient funds to purchase the equipment outright. Since the company is prohibited by the existing bond indenture from borrowing the needed funds, the controller of the company has suggested that the firm arrange for the manufacturer of the equipment to sell the equipment to a lending institution. The lending institution would, in turn, lease the machine to the company. The lending institution would provide no maintenance or related services, and the company would have responsibility for insuring the equipment. Upon the expiration of the lease, the company would have the option of purchasing the equipment for $1. If the company were to purchase the equipment outright, its cost would be $500,000. If it were to borrow the funds, it would be required to pay interest at the rate of 8 percent per year. The financial institution has agreed to a noncancellable lease with a term of 15 years, a term corresponding to the useful life of the equipment.

Required:

a. If the company decides to lease the equipment, what would be the most probable annual rental payments?

b. How do you suspect the controller intends to account for the acquisition of the equipment? What journal entries do you think he would propose at the time the equipment is acquired? At the time the first payment of rent is made?

c. In your opinion, does this lease meet the criteria of a capital lease? Why?

d. Assuming this lease is recorded as a capital lease, prepare the journal entries at the time the machine is acquired and the first rent payment is made.

e. Accounting attempts to reflect the substance rather than the legal form of transactions. Consequently, in this situation they would measure the equipment acquired at the same value regardless of whether it was purchased outright or leased. However, wouldn't the disclosure of the annual lease payments and the term of the lease in the notes to the financial statements accomplish the same objectives of accounting?

P10-9 As a financial analyst you are reviewing annual reports for the year 19x3 of two chains of discount department stores. The reports indicate that one of the two companies owns all its stores; the other leases them. A footnote to the financial statements of the firm that leases the stores contained the following information:

The company operates principally in leased premises. The basic terms of the leases generally range from 10 to 20 years. These leases are noncancellable and require the company to pay all maintenance, insurance and taxes on the property. Total minimum rental commitments are as follows (in thousands):

19x3–19x8	$30,000 per year
19x9–19x18	$25,000 per year
19x19–19x23	$10,000 per year

An additional note in the financial statements indicates that the company's weighted average cost of borrowing is 8 percent.

Required:

a. Are the financial reports of the two companies comparable? Why?
b. What adjustments would you make to the assets and liabilities of the company that leases its stores to make its financial reports more comparable to those of the company that owns its stores?
c. Are the financial reports of the two companies now comparable? Why?
d. Which objective(s) of accounting does the information contained in the company's footnote satisfy?

P10-10 Suppose that you had the opportunity to buy the following two physically identical long-lived assets:

1. An asset which has $2,000,000 available to be claimed as capital cost allowance (i.e., tax depreciation) on a straight-line basis over a two-year period.
2. An asset which has no available capital cost allowance.

Required:

a. Which asset would you be willing to pay more for? Why?
b. How much more would you be willing to pay? Indicate the assumptions that you have made.
c. How does the deferred tax allocation method reflect the difference in value between asset 1 and asset 2?

P10-11 Beechy Co. Ltd. purchased equipment in 19x1 at a cost of $200,000. The equipment had an estimated useful life of ten years with zero salvage value. The company elected to use straight-line depreciation for general stewardship reporting purposes. However a 20 percent diminishing balance depreciation method (capital cost allowance) is required for tax purposes. In 19x1 the company had income before depreciation expense and taxes of $80,000. The tax rate is 40 percent.

Required:

a. Determine taxable income and taxes for 19x1.
b. Determine reported tax expense and net income for 19x1 under the "deferral method of tax allocation."
c. Prepare the necessary journal entry for Part b.

P10-12 The following relates to Creighton Co. Ltd.:

	19x1	*19x2*
Income before depreciation expense and income taxes	$100,000	$100,000
Permanent differences (deducted to arrive at income before depreciation expense and income taxes above)	10,000	10,000
Depreciation for accounting purposes	30,000	30,000
Capital cost allowance (i.e., depreciation for tax purposes)	50,000	10,000
Income tax rate	40%	40%

Required:

a. Give the journal entries to record the income tax expense for each of the two years using first the "taxes payable" or "flow-through" method and then the "deferral method of tax allocation".
b. What is the total tax expense for the two year period for each method?
c. Why do accountants follow the "deferral method of tax allocation"?
d. If in 19x2 the tax rate changed to 50 percent, would any adjustment to the deferred tax balance at the end of 19x1 be made?
e. Evaluate the "deferral method of tax allocation." What are its strengths and limitations?

P10-13 A company made purchases of fixed assets as follows:

19x1	$ 60,000
19x2	90,000
19x3	120,000
19x4	150,000
19x5	180,000
19x6	210,000

The company uses a straight-line depreciation method for accounting purposes. The useful life of the fixed assets purchased is three years and they have a zero salvage value. The capital cost allowance (i.e., depreciation for tax purposes) is 20 percent diminishing balance. The income tax rate is 40 percent.

Required:

a. Determine, for each of the six years, total depreciation that would be reported on the financial statements and that which would be deductible for tax purposes. Indicate the timing difference each year.
b. Determine the amount that would be reported as a deferred tax "liability" each year. Is the company legally liable for this amount?
c. What conclusion can you draw from your calculations in Part b?
d. What conditions are necessary for the company to actually pay the balance reflected in the deferred tax "liability" account?
e. Why do you suppose some accountants are opposed to the "deferral method of tax allocation"?

P10-14 A major corporation reported on its income statement pension expense of $17 million. Its balance sheet indicated accrued pension costs (liability) of $6 million. A footnote to its financial statements revealed that the company's actual contribution to the pension fund was $14.5 million and that the actuarially computed liability for *unfunded* past service costs was $36 million.

Required:

a. Prepare a journal entry to summarize the pension expense and the cash contribution to the pension fund for the year.
b. Is the company's pension plan "cost-based" or "benefit-based"? Why?
c. What factors influence the pension expense recorded by the company?
d. Distinguish between the liability for accrued pension cost as reported in the balance sheet and that for the unfunded past service costs as reported in the footnotes.
e. As an employee of the company, how would you evaluate the likelihood of receiving the pension benefits promised by the company?

Cases

C10-1 A friend, J. Dewhirst, who knows that you are knowledgeable about financial statements, has asked for some help in deciding on which of the following two companies to invest in:

Opening Balance Sheets, January 1, 19x5

A Ltd.		*B Ltd.*	
Total assets	$100,000	Total assets	$100,000
Long-term debt	$ 10,000	Long-term debt	$ 90,000
Shareholders' equity (9,000 common shares outstanding)	90,000	Shareholders' equity (1,000 common shares outstanding)	10,000
Total liabilities and shareholders' equity	$100,000		$100,000
Net income for 19x5	$ 19,000	Net income for 19x5	$ 11,000

Additional information:

(1) Both companies began operations at the beginning of 19x5 with $100,000 cash.

(2) On December 31, 19x5 both companies paid interest in the amount of 10 percent on the outstanding long-term debt.

(3) On December 31, 19x5 both companies paid dividends of $1 per common share.

(4) Both companies are in the same industry.

J. Dewhirst believed that since both companies started with $100,000 at the beginning of the year, A Ltd. was the better company. Its net income of $19,000 represented a 19 percent return on investment whereas B Ltd. had only an 11 percent return. Given the higher return on investment, Dewhirst felt that A Ltd. had more efficient management and better cash generating ability.

Required:

What advice would you give to J. Dewhirst?

C10-2 While on your way to an accounting class one day you happen to overhear the following conversation:

Introductory accounting Student 1: Pension accounting in Canada is terrible. Companies can do whatever they want. We're supposed to be learning how accounting can assist financial statement readers make decisions. I'd like to know what sort of income figure you get for comparative purposes if each company follows its own system. I'd also like to know how a policy of anything goes assists financial statement users.

Introductory accounting
Student 2: Boy, are you stupid! Haven't you ever heard of the matching concept? Pension expense is just like a lot of other expenses. All you have to do is match the cost to the revenue it generates or the period it benefits. It's just like a salary expense."

Student 1: Really? If you wanted to settle a strike which would you rather give — a salary increase or a pension-benefit increase? The cost of the pension-benefit increase can be spread (i.e., allocated) over a number of future years. Since pension benefits are paid upon retirement, employees are motivated to work harder and remain with the company so that they will be entitled to pension benefits when they retire. Consequently, companies can argue that increases in the cost of pension plans benefit future periods. Therefore only a small fraction of the increased past-service pension cost gets expensed in the current period; whereas, salary increases would be expensed in the current period.

Student 2: It seems to me that you are trying to compare cumquats to camels. An increase in pension benefits is not the same as an increase in salaries. The increase in salaries requires the company to pay more cash in the current period, whereas, the increase in pension benefits requires most of the cash later. What is wrong with showing different expenses depending on the type of employee benefit?

Student 1: At last, I've trapped you. You admit that a company will have to pay out cash some time in the future and yet companies do not even set up a liability for their entire obligation. Haven't you seen the term "unfunded past service costs" in the notes to the financial statements?

Student 3: Both of you have missed the entire point of this year's accounting course. Don't you remember that the market is efficient and therefore you don't need to worry about accounting for pensions at all? No information about pensions need be included in the financial statements.

Required:
Evaluate the arguments presented by each of the students. Give your assessment of the adequacy of pension accounting (as described in this chapter) in Canada, bearing in mind current uses of financial accounting reports.

C10-3 Bernath Company Limited was incorporated thirty years ago. Since that time it has been entirely owned by Mr. Wayne. Mr. Wayne is now sixty-five and has lost interest in taking an active role in the management of the company. He considered hiring a president and becoming a passive owner. However, he decided that it would be impossible for him to take an inactive role in his company. Since he wanted to retire, he decided the best thing to do would be to sell his company.

Mr. Kaiser, a next-door neighbor of Mr. Wayne has offered to purchase the company. This pleases Mr. Wayne because he knows that Mr. Kaiser has the interest and resources to successfully run Bernath Company Limited. They decide that the selling price of the company should be six times the income determined in accordance with generally accepted accounting principles.

You have been hired to prepare the financial statements in accordance with generally accepted accounting principles. In the past, the financial statements were prepared primarily for income tax purposes. Since there were no creditors and Mr. Wayne took an active role in the management of the company there were no other purposes of accounting. Upon reviewing the company's accounting principles you discover the following:

1. The company depreciates its building and equipment at rates permissible for income tax purposes.
2. The company has a benefit-based pension plan and it expenses its pension costs in the year of funding (i.e., when it pays into the pension plan).
3. The company leases some equipment. The lease agreement stipulates that the company is responsible for all maintenance and insurance costs. In addition, it has the option to buy the equipment at the end of the lease for a nominal sum. Presently the company records the lease payments as an expense when paid.
4. The company calculates its tax expense on the taxes payable basis. Its tax rate is 50 percent. Since its income statement reflects taxable income it simply records 50 percent of income before taxes as a tax expense.
5. All other principles adopted by the company are in accordance with generally accepted accounting principles.

Required:
What would you recommend? Justify your position logically.

11 *Capital Accounts, I*

This chapter is the first of two that will be directed primarily to the owners' equity section of the financial statements. In this chapter we shall compare partnerships with corporations and focus on the characteristics of common and preferred shares.

Proprietorships and Partnerships

There are three major types of business enterprises: the individual proprietorship, the partnership, and the corporation. The proprietorship is a business form owned by a single party. The partnership is one owned by two or more parties. The corporation is a separate, legal entity that operates under a grant of authority from one of the provincial governments or the federal government and is owned by one or more shareholders.

The proprietorship is by far the most common type of business enterprise in Canada; however, corporations or limited companies generate well over half the national output.

Limited companies are often thought of as large enterprises, and proprietorships and partnerships are considered to be small. While it is true that most proprietorships and partnerships are smaller businesses, *most* corporations are also relatively small, often family-owned firms. The corporation is associated with a large size because most large businesses — those that account for the major part of industrial output — are corporations. Nevertheless, many large enterprises are organized as partnerships. Service organizations such as law and public accounting firms are commonly organized as partnerships even though they generate hundreds of millions of dollars in annual revenues.

Proprietorships and partnerships are, in a legal sense, extensions of their owners. One or more parties simply establish a business. They purchase or rent whatever equipment or space is needed, acquire supplies or inventory, and obtain any local operating licenses that might be required. No formal federal or provincial certificates are needed. The provinces, however, have partnership legislation which governs some partners' activities *if* the partners do not have a partnership agreement which overrides the legislation.

If the business is to be operated as a partnership, it is generally wise to have an attorney draw up a partnership agreement which specifies the rights and obligations of each partner — how profits will be distributed, who will perform what services, how much each partner must contribute initially, what rights of survivorship will accrue to each partner's estate, what limitations there will be upon the sale of a partner's interest in the business — but such a document is for the protection of the individual partners; it is not ordinarily required by law. Significantly, a proprietor, as well as each partner of a partnership , is usually personally responsible for all obligations of his business. If the enterprise suffers losses, the owners are jointly and severally responsible for all debts incurred. This means that a partner will generally be held liable not only for his share of the debts but, should his partners be unable to meet their share of the claims against the business, for those of his partners as well. As a consequence, few investors are willing to purchase an equity interest in a partnership, such as they might purchase in a corporation. In the event the partnership is liquidated and fellow partners are unable to meet their share of partnership obligations, the personal assets of the investors might be subject to the claims of creditors. Their risk of loss is unlimited, extending beyond their original investment.

There are no limits on the numbers of partners who might compose a partnership. Because of the extended liability to which each partner is subject, most partnerships are small — two or three members. However, many partnerships are considerably larger. Some large public accountancy firms that are organized as partnerships have well over 200 partners.

Neither the proprietorship nor the partnership form of organization provides for the ready transfer of interest from one owner to another. Partners do not individually own or have a share in the ownership of *specific* partnership assets. As with a corporation, property is held in the name of the firm itself. Each partner, like each shareholder, owns a share in *all* partnership property. Nevertheless, most partnership agreements prohibit a partner from freely transferring his interest to a person outside of the partnership. Generally, the agreements stipulate that a partner may sell his interest to an outsider only if all the partners agree to accept the new member. Similarly, the death or the withdrawal of a partner may automatically dissolve the partnership; a partner is not ordinarily free to bequeath his interest to his heirs. In many partnerships, especially those with a large number of partners, special provisions are made to assure the continuity of the business despite the loss of an individual partner. Nevertheless, because of the difficulty of transferring ownership interest, the partnership form of organization is not well-suited to induce casual investors — those who are either unable or unwilling to take an active role in management — to purchase a small interest in a business.

Neither proprietorships nor partnerships are subject to taxes on income. Instead, the tax is assessed on the individual owners. If the organization is a partnership, then each partner is taxed on his share of partnership earnings. The rate of tax is determined by the tax bracket in which the individual partner falls after taking into account his earnings from nonpartnership sources. Each partner is taxed on his share of the entire earnings of the partnership, not just on his withdrawals from the business. Thus, especially if the partnership requires capital for expansion, a partner may be taxed on earnings that are retained in the business, and are not readily available for his discretionary use, as well as on funds actually taken from the business.

A variety of other organizations may operate in a manner close to that of proprietorships and partnerships, and yet be different in some respects. A charitable organization or non-profit enterprise essentially operates as a partnership with people sharing tasks, yet may be incorporated under the Canada Corporations Act. This Act is in contrast to the Canada Business Corporation Act, which, after December 15, 1980, regulates all federally incorporated businesses having share capital. If the charity wants to issue receipts so that donors can deduct their cash contributions for income tax purposes special approval must be obtained from the Department of National Revenue.

Cooperative groceries or similar co-op businesses operate like partnerships and yet must comply with special provisions of laws. A union is much like a partnership but it, too, is regulated by separate laws or sections of government statutes.

In earlier chapters we stressed that non-arm's-length transactions cause measurement and reporting problems. Transactions between proprietors or partners and the business are generally not at arm's-length. As a result GAAP in Canada tends to require separate disclosure of such transactions on financial statements. Unfortunately, GAAP is often not clear for small *limited companies* which engage in the same type of non-arm's-length transactions, such as setting the salary of the owner-manager(s). In short, inconsistencies exist, and these should be noted as we proceed through this and the next chapter. Often the main reasons why a small firm operates as a limited company instead of a proprietorship or partnership are: (1) income tax advantages; and (2) limited liability of owners (to the creditors of the limited liability company).

Corporations

A corporation, by contrast, is a legal entity separate and distinct from its managers. It is a legal "person" created by a government. A corporation is owned by its shareholders, but its shareholders are not compelled to take an active role in its management. In many corporations there is a distinct separation of ownership and operating control, with managers typically holding only a small fraction of total shares outstanding. A corporation has an indefinite life. It continues in existence regardless of the personal fortunes of its owners. Its owners are commonly free to transfer or sell their shares to anyone they wish.

Corporations, unlike proprietorships or partnerships, are creatures of provincial or federal legislation.

A corporation has the right to own property in its own name, and it can sue or be sued. Upon its formation, it must be chartered by a government. Although at one time charters were granted only upon special acts of parliament, today they are routinely issued upon submission of two legal documents which (1) outline the purpose and names of initial directors of the organization, (called "Letters Patent" in some jurisdictions in Canada), and (2) explain the principal means of allocating power to manage the company, and similar considerations (called "By-Laws"). Fees, often based on the amount of corporate share capital desired, have to be paid to the provincial or federal government. These fees, together with legal costs, form the account "Incorporation costs," which was discussed earlier. A certificate of incorporation is issued by the government involved.

After the certificate has been issued the corporation in later years may have to adopt more extensive bylaws, which would govern a number of critical areas of operation besides those by-laws shown to the government on incorporation. For example, the number of directors may have to be increased, the year-end of the company may have to be changed, or more capital may have to be issued. Although there are some differences in terminology and process from jurisdiction to jurisdiction in Canada, the methods of incorporation are similar with the possible exception of Quebec. A small business probably could incorporate at a cost of $1,000 or less; thus, the process is not as complex as one might first suppose.

The single most significant distinction between corporations (not all jurisdictions allow the use of the word "corporation"; a more universal term is "limited company") and proprietorships or partnerships is that the liability of shareholders of a limited company is, as the adjective states, *limited*. That is, creditors of the limited liability company cannot claim any personal assets (such as a house or automobile) of the shareholders, but are restricted to funds invested by way of share capital in the limited company.

Only in rare circumstances — the involvement of corporate shareholders in fraud, for example — is it possible for creditors or others who may have judgments against the corporation to "pierce the corporate veil" and bring a successful legal action against the individual shareholders. Because it is able to protect investors against unlimited loss, the corporation is a vehicle that is well-suited to raise large amounts of capital. Large numbers of persons may be willing to purchase an ownership interest in a company knowing that they can share in the gains of the company to an unlimited extent but that their losses will be limited by the amount of their direct share capital contributions. They need not be overly concerned with the day-to-day operations of their business, since neither the managers nor their fellow owners can so mismanage the business as to put any of their personal assets in jeopardy.

Corporations, like other legal persons, are subject to both federal and provincial income taxes. Earnings of a corporation are taxed, albeit at rates different from those of individuals, regardless of whether or not they are distributed to its owners. The individual owners of the corporation, unlike those of a partnership, are generally not taxed on their share of the earnings that are retained in the business; they are, however, taxed on the earnings as they are distributed to them in the form of dividends. Earnings of a corporation are taxed twice — once when earned by the corporation and again when they are distributed to the shareholders. The Income Tax legislation, however, contains provisions which minimize the burden of double taxation.

Special Incorporations

Banks, and many trust and insurance companies are regulated by separate legislation, such as the Bank Act, Trust Companies Act and Canadian and British Insurance Companies Act. As well, many government-owned companies (called Crown Corporations) such as CNR, and Air Canada have their own incorporating legislation. Accounting for specialized companies — such as banks, trust companies, and insurance companies — can differ from that described to date in this book because of the *constraints* imposed by the separate legislation. Readers of the financial statements of these special companies must be on guard for unique accounting.

For example, the legislation governing insurance companies tends to be concerned with *liquidity* of the enterprise. Will sufficient cash be available to pay insurance claims by policyholders? Special rules therefore exist concerning the type of investments (bonds, shares, et cetera) which may be acquired, how liabilities for losses (insurance claims) are to be calculated, and which assets are considered to be liquid. Under a *liquidity* objective of accounting, "fixed assets" such as furniture are not assets to insurance inspectors or examiners but are called "nonadmissable assets." That is, they do not appear on the balance sheet prepared for insurance examiners. An investor in an insurance company may have another view about what constitutes an asset. In summary, be on your guard when reading financial statements for these special types of enterprises.

Corporations Versus Partnerships: The Distinctions in Perspective

It is easy to overemphasize the distinctions between partnerships and corporations. For some businesses, especially smaller enterprises, the differences may be more of form than of substance. For a small business the corporate form of organization is unlikely to facilitate acquisition of required capital any more than would the partnership form. Small businesses are inherently hazardous, and the corporate form of organization does not measurably enhance prospects for success.

Equally significant, the limited liability feature of the corporate form of organization may actually deter potential suppliers of capital. To a bank or other lending institution, the limitation on owner's liability is an obstacle rather than an inducement to making a loan. The bank, after all, wants assurance that in the event of default it can have access to all the assets of owners, not merely those devoted to the business. As a consequence, many lenders circumvent the limitations on shareholder liability by requiring that the shareholder personally cosign any notes issued by the corporation.

Moreover, the distinction between the corporate and partnership form of organization may be diminished because of a limitation on the liability of certain partners in certain circumstances. As long as there exists one *general* partner whose liability is unlimited, the liability of other partners, (limited partners) particularly those who take no part in the day-to-day management of the enterprise, may be limited.

The advantage of a corporation over a partnership with respect to transferability of shares may also be more illusory than real. Although the shares of major corporations can be sold without difficulty, those of companies that are *closely held* by a small number of shareholders could probably not be sold any more easily than a similar interest in a partnership. Indeed, agreements among shareholders of smaller companies sometimes provide that all sales of shares to outsiders must meet with the approval of existing owners.

The income tax distinctions between partnerships and corporations may also be diminished for some types of manufacturing and service enterprises. A "small business deduction" exists for income tax purposes. This has the effect of taxing small corporations at a lower rate.

Distinctive Features of Partnership Accounting

There are relatively few differences between accounting for a proprietorship or partnership and a corporation. What differences there are relate primarily to the owners' equity accounts. Although in this section we shall deal exclusively with partnerships rather than proprietorships, the points made will generally apply to proprietorships as well. For accounting purposes the proprietorship may be viewed as a special case of a partnership — a "partnership" with only a single partner.

The owners' equity section of a partnership balance sheet usually consists of one capital account for each partner. Each capital account is credited (increased) by the amount of a partner's contributions to the firm and by his share of partnership profits. It is debited (decreased) by a partner's withdrawals from the firm and by his share of partnership losses.

EXAMPLE Lee and Grant decide to form a partnership. Lee contributes $200,000 cash, and Grant contributes a building, which has been appraised at $150,000 but on which there is a mortgage of $50,000. The building had been carried on Grant's personal books at a value of $75,000. The partnership agrees to assume the liability for the mortgage. The following entry would be required to establish the partnership:

(a)

Cash	$200,000	
Building	150,000	
Mortgage note payable		$ 50,000
Capital, Lee		200,000
Capital, Grant		100,000
To record formation of the partnership.		

Property contributed is valued at its fair market value, regardless of the value at which it might have been carried on the books of the individual partners prior to being assigned to the partnership.

The partners agree to share profits and losses in the same ratio as their initial capital contributions, 2:1. (Under Canadian Provincial law the partners are encouraged to sign a partnership agreement; otherwise, in case of disputes among the partners, they may be required to share income equally).

During the first year of operations the partnership had revenues of $240,000 and expenses of $180,000 — income of $60,000. The following *closing entry* would be required, assuming that revenues and expenses were properly recorded throughout the year:

(b)

Revenues (various accounts)	$240,000	
Expenses (various accounts)		$180,000
Capital, Lee		40,000
Capital, Grant		20,000
To close the revenue and expense accounts.		

During the course of the year Lee withdrew $20,000 in cash, and Grant, $40,000. In addition, each partner was paid $25,000 in salaries, included in expenses above. At the time of withdrawal the appropriate entry would be:

(c)

Withdrawals, Lee	$20,000	
Withdrawals, Grant	40,000	
Cash		$60,000
To record withdrawals.		

Withdrawals can also exist in the form of assets, such as inventory. Quite likely the partners would agree to withdrawals at cost. Hence, the credit would be to inventory instead of to cash.

The "withdrawals" account is the equivalent of the "dividends" account maintained by corporations. At year end it would be *closed* to partners' capital:

(d)

Capital, Lee	$20,000	
Capital, Grant	40,000	
Withdrawals, Lee		$20,000
Withdrawals, Grant		40,000
To close withdrawals account.		

It is critical that a partnership agreement set forth any amounts that the individual partners are to receive in salaries apart from the shares of earnings to which they are entitled. Payments of salaries to partners may be accounted for as ordinary expenses, or as distributions of income (treated like dividends). Salaries have no direct impact on the withdrawals account or the individual capital accounts.

Lee, capital

	Debit	Credit	
(d)	20,000	200,000	(a)
		40,000	(b)
		220,000	

Grant, capital

	Debit	Credit	
(d)	40,000	100,000	(a)
		20,000	(b)
		80,000	

At the conclusion of the year, Lee would have a capital balance of $220,000, and Grant, $80,000. The capital balances would no longer be in the original ratio of 2:1. Whether or not a partner should be permitted to draw his capital account below a specified level is a question that must be addressed in the partnership agreement. Some partnership agreements provide for the payment of interest to any partner who maintains an *excess* capital balance in relation to those of his partners.

As stated earlier, whenever accountants encounter non-arm's-length transactions — such as salary, bonus, and interest to partners — even when there is little doubt about the fair market value of the amounts involved, separate disclosure of each non-arm's-length amount should be given in the financial statements. This improves the chances for consistency ("comparability") from year to year ***within*** the firm and may help in comparability among firms (if a banker, for example, wants between-firm comparisons).

Partnership AB, for instance, may not show partners' salaries, bonuses and interest as an expense, but could include them outside of the income statement as distributions of income. Using the figures for Lee-Grant, income before the distributions would be $110,000 ($240,000 less $180,000 plus the two salaries of $25,000 each). The partners' financial statements could contain a separate "Statement of Partners' Capital" (which is a subdivision of the balance sheet, much like a retained earnings statement) which would show:

		Lee	*Grant*	*Total*
Opening balance		$200,000	$100,000	$300,000
Distribution of Income:				
Salary		25,000	25,000	
Remainder		40,000	20,000	110,000
		265,000	145,000	410,000
Withdrawals	— cash	20,000	40,000	60,000
	— salaries	25,000	25,000	50,000
		45,000	65,000	110,000
Closing balance		$220,000	$80,000	$300,000

We have illustrated distributions with salaries only; the same treatment could be given to bonuses and interest.

Whereas Lee-Grant showed the salaries to partners as an expense (reducing income to $60,000), AB did not, and had income of $110,000. Canadian GAAP requires disclosure — and this could be on the income statement ("Salary to partners, $50,000") or on the "Statement of Partners' Capital," as shown above, or in notes to financial statements. It is assumed that the reader is aware that alternative accounting treatments exist, and that financial statements must be read in their entirety. A straight comparison of the incomes — $110,000 for AB, versus $60,000 for Lee-Grant — would be unfortunate.

Corporate Capital Accounts

Throughout the book we have used the word "constraints" and have indicated that there are times when accounting and reporting are not strictly governed by facts and objectives. At times, constraints or rules overpower the importance of objectives and facts because the constraints have the weight of law behind them. For many years accounting education in Canada has concentrated extensively on teaching constraints — that is, it explains the accounting method required to comply with a Companies Act, Securities Act, or the *CICA Handbook*. The minimum type of reporting — a condensed form of stewardship disclosure — focuses on constraints and little else. In a few businesses, such as small owner-manager enterprises, this minimum reporting may be satisfactory. Fortunately for us, constraints or rules are not extensive but many topics require judgment and thoughtful analysis. Nevertheless, as users/readers we must be on guard for financial statements produced by preparers who pay attention primarily to constraints.

The following discussion of accounting for corporate capital is heavily laced with constraints or matters which must be adhered to carefully, providing little reporting choice. This "rules" approach may seem to contrast sharply with the flexibility which we have commented upon throughout the previous chapters. It may be helpful, as we explain the rules, to appreciate that they exist in large part because a corporation has been granted limited liability. In turn, therefore, some protection must be offered to creditors. They must, for instance, know how much security (the type, but not its net realizable value) exists for loans.

In addition, the separation of owners from managers is given special attention in corporate law. Stewardship financial reports, as a minimum, are required for owners. Also, corporate directors must state whether dividends are being paid out of income (a return *on* capital) or are merely a return of one's investment (return *of* capital). You will observe similar requirements as we proceed.

Types of Owners' Equity

Unlike partnership accounting, which has one continuing capital account for each partner, limited companies have accounts for:

1. Each type of share which is authorized and issued;
2. Amounts received in excess of "par value." (This applies only in those jurisdictions which permit par value shares);
3. Net income in excess of dividends. (Retained earnings);
4. Other equity amounts, such as appraisal increases. (Land may be debited, and an appraisal account may be credited.)

Some important differences exist between the federal and various provincial Companies Acts. For example, the Canada Business Corporations Act (federal) does not allow "par value" common shares whereas some provinces do. Legislators felt that "par value" could be confused with market value, and had other limitations. Our illustrations focus on federal legislation because the provinces in time will adopt its provisions. But our concern is also with users/readers of financial statements; accordingly, brief explanations of a few provincial requirements are necessary from time to time in order that financial statements based on them can be understood.

The Labatt's financial statements in Chapter 2 show three classes of shares authorized (by the Act under which Labatt's is incorporated, the Canada Business Corporations Act):

1. Preferred shares, of which 4,000,000 are authorized;
2. Class A common shares;
3. Class B common shares.

Note 4 to their financial statements (page 59) indicates the rights or entitlements of each class of shares. The distinction between the two classes of common shares is based on income tax legislation, which at one time permitted special tax privileges for certain earnings generated prior to changes in the income tax legislation. The distinction between common and preferred shares is more fundamental. The preferred ones are convertible into Class A common shares. This means that initially they are entitled to dividends (of $1 per share per year) before the common shareholder receives any dividend. However, these convertible shares may be switched to common shares at the option of the holder.

Labatt's also has a retained earnings account. Through this separation of equity accounts, creditors therefore clearly know that the "protection" for their investment lies in the net assets which exist after dividends are paid to eliminate all of retained earnings. In short, under the double-entry mechanism, the protection for creditors represents the common and preferred share balances. Similarly, the ultimate protection for preferred shareholders is the balance in the common share accounts. Preferred, in this case, is assumed to mean priority in the event of liquidation. Common share balances cannot be reduced without permission of the creditors.

In practice, the protection in the event of liquidation is often more or less than that just described. The reasons are:

1. Liquidation values differ from book values.
2. Liquidators receive fees for winding up a company, and rank ahead of most other creditors.
3. Bankruptcy legislation places creditors into one of three categories: preferred, secured, and unsecured. Preferred creditors may be governments or employees; they receive payment first. Secured creditors, such as bondholders, come next in a bankruptcy because the debt is secured by specific assets. Unsecured creditors are next, then preferred shareholders (generally speaking), and finally, common shareholders.

The word "preferred" implies preferred over common shareholders as to dividends and in the event of liquidation. Since many organizations are going concerns, except for dividend entitlements the distinction is often academic. Common shareholders are the *residual claimants*; they receive what is left in a liquidation. The risk of loss of their investment is higher; hence, in theory they should be entitled to a higher rate of return on their investment, after income taxes, than preferred shareholders and creditors.

A company such as Labatt's, which is governed by the Canada Business Corporations Act, must follow the various sections or provisions of the Act when preparing financial statements. One of these provisions is that it must comply with the *CICA Handbook*.

Shares Compared

Although above we have separated shares into two categories, preferred or common, there are really many types of shares. Prior to issuing shares, company officials (on the advice of underwriters, lawyers, and accountants) examine such features as: income tax status of the shares; general preference of investors/creditors; guidelines as to a suitable debt to equity balance for the company; the period of cash need of the company; current receptivity of investors to a particular type of security; and voting control of the company.

In recent years, income tax legislation as it affects shares and investor yields on shares has changed several times. During the middle and late 1970s the market was not overly receptive to share issues; in general, common share prices were depressed by an uncertain economy. In order to help Canadian companies balance their equity to debt ratios, the federal government altered the income tax rate on dividends so as to increase yields on shares. No doubt other income tax changes will occur during the 1980s; investors therefore must investigate income tax effects carefully before purchasing shares.

Two features which are of special concern to company officials are control and cash needs. When common shares are issued to outsiders (as opposed to the present shareholders) the ownership of the company shifts. The group with the largest block of outstanding common shares tends to control the company and decide its direction. Some officials may be reluctant to issue more *voting* common shares (some "common" shares may not carry a vote when there is more than one class of common) if there is a risk of losing control. Cash needs are important when a company can forecast a short-run requirement for cash and plenty of opportunity to repay. In such situations bonds or redeemable preferred shares would probably be issued. University-level finance courses will cover this subject in greater depth.

Issuing Shares

The journal entries made on issuing shares are much the same whether a company is closely owned or a large, publicly owned organization. Before proceeding to the entries, it seems worthwhile to review some relevant matters mentioned periodically in the book.

A nonpublic limited company has fewer legal concerns than does a public company which wishes to sell shares. Many nonpublic companies have been incorporated primarily to save or postpone income taxes and secondarily to obtain limited liability. The shares are issued to a few owners who are well aware of any non-arm's-length relationships and the general worth of assets contributed in exchange for shares. In the simple case, where cash is received in exchange for shares the entry would be:

Cash	$100,000	
Common shares		$100,000
To record the issue of common shares.		

The entire credit is to "common shares" because we have assumed that the company has been incorporated under the Canada Business Corporations Act.

If the company were incorporated under legislation which permitted par value common shares, and 6,000 shares with a par value of $10 each were issued, the journal entry would be:

Cash	$100,000	
Common shares		$60,000
Contributed surplus — premium on common shares		40,000

Although the account title of the latter line could simply be "premium on common shares" the *CICA Handbook* recommends that the balance sheet description — within the owners' equity section of the balance sheet — be "contributed surplus." The Canada Business Corporations Act does not permit shares to be issued at a discount below their par value.

If the shares were issued, say on incorporation of a partnership, and assets-less-liabilities were received as consideration for the shares, the entry might be:

Accounts receivable	$55,000	
Inventory	25,000	
Land	20,000	
Building and equipment	60,000	
Goodwill	15,000	
Accounts payable		$ 25,000
Common shares		150,000
To record issue of shares in consideration for the net assets of the A-B Partnership.		

Each of the assets and liabilities would be recorded at fair market value. That is why *no* accumulated depreciation would be carried forward from the partnership. (For income tax purposes, if there is a non-arm's-length transaction, such as when the owners of the partnership and limited company are the same, special rules apply, which are covered in income tax courses). Goodwill would represent the difference between the value of the business *as a whole* and the recorded fair market value of the assets less liabilities. Goodwill in effect represents those assets (such as people) not measured by accountants and reported on accounting financial statements.

The situation for publicly owned companies is a little more involved. They can sell securities such as bonds or preferred shares (probably without the right to convert to common shares) to insurance companies in what is called a "*private placement*." Such a placement does not require that financial statements be examined by one of the Provincial Securities Commissions. The issuer prepares (as a kind of "special purpose" accounting report) whatever the prospective purchaser wants to see, with few limits.

However, if the publicly owned company wishes to sell to the general public, the services of an underwriter/stockbroker are usually contracted for, along with those of the firm's lawyer and public accountant. A *prospectus* has to be prepared. This document contains the following types of information: description of the company, including its history and current sources of revenue; names and addresses of the directors and management; what the funds are to be used for; description of the security offered; details about the other securities which were previously sold; the financial statements (a recent balance sheet plus income, retained earnings and statements of changes in financial position for the previous five years); and certificates about the completeness of the document signed by officials of the company and others. A prospectus is a selling document which attempts to convince people that the securities are sound. One or more Provincial Securities Commission(s) reads the document for accuracy, but does not comment upon (recommend) the worth of the security.

The underwriter (and any underwriting partners) then either (1) agree(s) to sell as many of the securities as possible for a commission (called an agency agreement); or (2) directly buys *all* the shares or bonds for cash (called an underwriting). The latter arrangement guarantees that all of the securities will be sold — presumably at a higher price than that received by the issuing company so as to "guarantee" revenue for the underwriter. In both situations the underwriter advises the issuer as to an appropriate selling price.

In the case of an underwriting, the journal entry on sale to the underwriter would be:

Cash	$1,000,000	
Common shares		$1,000,000
To record sale of the shares.		

The credit to common shares is therefore less than what the public would pay the underwriter(s). In the case of an agency agreement, what happens to the commission? It theoretically could be recorded as a debit (deferred asset) and later charged to retained earnings; but the easiest way to handle it would be as for the underwriting, which credits common shares for the *net* cash received. Any deferred asset would *not* be amortized to income for two reasons:

1. What would be the amortization period? The shares, after all, extend over the life of the company, which could be forever.
2. An issue of shares is a *capital transaction*, and not an income statement transaction. That is, share capital is needed to operate the business; income is earned *on* the capital, and the cost of this capital is paid as dividends, which are distributions of income, not expenses. (In contrast, if bonds were being sold to an underwriter at a discount from face value, the discount could be deferred and amortized to income over the life of the bonds. You will observe that this is in accordance with our discussion of objectives of accounting and the treatment of interest noted in Chapter 10).

An Example

Moore decides to incorporate his existing business. The fair market value of all assets to be contributed to the corporation is $400,000. The corporation will also assume liabilities of the business, which amount to $50,000. As part of his incorporation plan, Moore will sell shares to outside investors, who have agreed to contribute $336,000 cash. Moreover, an attorney has agreed to accept shares in exchange for legal and other services connected with the organization of the company. The services have a fair market value of $14,000. The charter of the new company authorizes the issue of 20,000 common shares of no par value. The promoter (in this case, Moore) decides, however, to issue only 10,000 shares.

The net amount contributed to the corporation will be $700,000 — $350,000 contributed by Moore, $336,000 contributed by the other investors, and $14,000 contributed by the attorney. The new company will issue one share of common for each $70 of contributed value. The following entry would record its initial capitalization:

Various assets	$400,000	
Cash	336,000	
Organizational costs	14,000	
Various liabilities		$ 50,000
Common shares		700,000
To record formation of the limited company.		

The various assets and liabilities, including any intangible assets, would be classified and recorded in separate accounts as appropriate. Each shareholder would receive a number of shares indicative of his percentage contribution. Thus,

	Contribution	*Percentage*	*No.shares*
Moore	$350,000	50%	5,000
Other investors	336,000	48	4,800
Attorney	14,000	2	200

The important consideration is that each shareholder receives an ownership interest reflective of the fair market value of his contribution. Prior to the enactment of protective legislation, it was not unusual for the promoters to overvalue their own contribution and thereby take for themselves a disproportionate number of shares to be issued. But even today, because of the subjective nature of the valuation process, an investor who purchases shares of a newly formed corporation should carefully review the assets contributed by the promoters to make certain that they have not been overstated.

Should a firm issue additional shares subsequent to its formation, similar entries would be in order. The resultant increase in owners' equity would be reflected in the common shares account.

The price at which additional shares may be issued would be dependent on the market value as opposed to the book value of the company's existing shares outstanding.

Another Example

If the shares are issued in a province which permits par value common shares, any excess over par value is credited to a "premium" or "contributed surplus" account. Suppose that a firm has reported assets of $100,000, liabilities of $50,000, and owners' equity of $50,000. Owners' equity is composed of the following accounts:

Common shares, $1 par value, 10,000 shares issued and outstanding	$10,000
Contributed surplus	25,000
Retained earnings	15,000
Total owners' equity.	$50,000

The book value per share is $50,000 divided by 10,000 shares — $5 per share.

The company wishes to raise $100,000 in capital. The market price of the company's shares is $20 per share. (Large discrepancies between book value and market value are not uncommon. Book value is based on historical costs; market value is based on investor expectations as to future earnings.) Assuming that the market price is unaffected by the impending issue of the new shares (a major financial event may itself affect investor expectations of future earnings), the company could acquire the $100,000 in needed capital by issuing an additional 5,000 shares at $20 per share.

The journal entry to record the issue would be

Cash	$100,000	
Common shares, par value		$ 5,000
Contributed surplus		95,000
To record the issue of additional shares.		

Owners' equity would now be made up as follows:

Common shares $1 par value, 15,000 shares issued and outstanding	$ 15,000
Contributed surplus	120,000
Retained earnings	15,000
	$150,000

Book value per share would now be $10 ($150,000 divided by 15,000 shares) compared to $5 prior to the sale of the additional shares.

The increase in book value can be attributed to the willingness of the new investors to pay $20 per share for shares that had a book value of only $5 per share. The new investors contributed $100,000 in return for a one-third interest (5,000 shares out of 15,000 shares) in a company that will have *reported* net assets of $150,000.

Issue of Preferred Shares

Preferred shares (generally this means preferred over common shares as to dividends up to a stated rate, and preferred as to cash re-payment in the event of liquidation of the business) have some characteristics of bonds and some of common shares. Preferred shares generally have a fixed rate of dividend payment. Unlike bonds, they generally are not issued for a specific duration, but are redeemable at the option of the issuer. Often a redemption premium is paid if the shares are redeemed within several years of being issued.

Preferred shares issued prior to proclamation of the Canada Business

Corporations Act (December 1975) or issued in a province which permits par value shares would be recorded as noted. Assume that 100,000 shares with a par value of $20 each were issued for $21 each:

Cash	$2,100,000	
Preferred shares		$2,000,000
Contributed surplus — premium on preferred shares		100,000
To record issue of $20 par value preferred shares at $21 each.		

If these shares are not convertible into common and are later redeemed by the issuer for $22.50 each, the journal entry on redemption would be:

Preferred shares	$2,000,000	
Contributed surplus — premium on preferred shares	100,000	
Retained earnings	150,000	
Cash		$2,250,000
To record redemption of preferred shares at $22.50 each.		

Observe that the original "contributed surplus" on issue, of $100,000, is eliminated, and the loss of $150,000 — which is a capital transaction — is debited directly to retained earnings.

If the shares were convertible and were converted on a one-common-for-one-preferred-share basis, instead of being redeemed, the journal entry might be as follows, assuming the common shares were of no par value:

Preferred shares	$2,000,000	
Contributed surplus — premium on preferred shares	100,000	
Common shares		$2,100,000
To record conversion of preferred shares into common.		

Convertible preferred shares would have been issued initially because: (1) the potential buyers were not interested in preferred shares without conversion privileges unless the dividend rate were raised substantially; and/or (2) the issuing company believed that it would eventually need more common share equity so that it would have an equity base to enable it to issue more debt. Holders would convert to common when their investment yield on the common shares exceeded that for the preferred.

When preferred shares are issued without par value, the "contributed surplus — premium on preferred shares" account would not exist and the full credit would go to "preferred shares." On redemption or conversion, the full credit would be eliminated.

Common Shares Versus Preferred Shares Versus Bonds

As suggested in Chapter 10, in the discussion pertaining to interest, corporations view the issuance of shares and bonds as alternative means of acquiring long-term capital. The question whether the interests of the company would be better served by issuing shares or bonds is a complex one; it involves consideration of the present mix of debt and equity securities, anticipated earnings of the company, various technical features of the existing capital markets, and *control* of the company which rests with *common* shareholders.

Essentially, however, the choice among common shares, preferred shares, and bonds is generally analyzed in terms of the benefits that would accrue to the present owners of the company — the *existing common shareholders*: Would their earnings per share of common shares be higher or lower if additional common shares, rather than preferred shares or bonds, were issued? The example that follows indicates the *type* of evaluation that a company might undertake.

EXAMPLE

A company wishes to raise an additional $1 million in capital. Currently the company has 100,000 common shares issued and outstanding. It has three options under consideration:

1. Issue bonds. Bonds can be sold at a price to yield 5 percent per year.
2. Issue preferred shares. The company can issue 10,000 shares at a par value of $100. The shares would bear a dividend rate of $5.50 per share and would be sold at par.
3. Issue common shares. The present market price of the firm's common shares is $40 per share. To raise $1 million, it would have to issue an additional 25,000 shares ($1 million/$40 per share). The firm currently pays dividends of $2 on each of its common shares; such rate is expected to remain constant in the future.

The company anticipates that it will be able to earn $100,000 per year (after taxes) on the additional $1 million of funds it receives. The applicable income tax rate is 40 percent.

The three alternatives can be evaluated in terms of the advantages to common shareholders — that is, on the *increase* in earnings per common share, being the amount above the required interest and dividend payment on bonds and preferred, and the $2 current dividend on common — as follows:

	Bonds	*Preferred shares*	*Common shares*
Anticipated earnings	$100,000	$100,000	$100,000
Required payment of dividends or interest	$ 50,000	$ 55,000	$ 50,000
Less: Tax saving, 40% of interest	20,000[a]	—	—
Net cost of additional capital	$ 30,000	$ 55,000	$ 50,000
Earnings after cost of additional capital (i.e., return to common shareholders)	$ 70,000	$ 45,000	$ 50,000
Number of common shares outstanding	÷ 100,000 sh.	÷ 100,000 sh.	÷ 125,000 sh.[b]
Earnings in excess of the $2 per share common dividend	$.70	$.45	$.40

[a]A tax saving results only when bonds are issued, since interest, but not dividends, is deductible for income tax purposes.
[b]Only when additional common shares are issued will the number of common shares outstanding increase. Thus, the available earnings have to be divided among a larger number of shares. To the extent that the additional shares are sold to outsiders, the proportionate share of earnings available to each existing shareholder is reduced.

Given the specific assumptions of the example, the issuance of $1 million in bonds will result in the greatest increase in earnings per common share. The sale of either bonds or preferred shares enables the existing shareholders to *leverage* their investment. They are able to take advantage of other people's money to earn a return that exceeds the cost of obtaining such funds. Earnings above the cost of obtaining the funds — a cost which is fixed — accrue entirely to the existing common shareholders. The sale of common shares, however, requires the existing common shareholders to share any earnings in excess of the direct cost of obtaining the additional funds with the additional shareholders. *Leverage* enables existing common shareholders to reap the benefits of all earnings in excess of the cost of acquired capital, but it also requires them to bear the full burden of all deficiencies of earnings below such cost. In the event of a return less than the cost of capital, the financial *advantage* of leverage would operate to the detriment of the common shareholders.

The relative advantages of issuing the three types of securities depend on the anticipated earnings, the interest and dividend rates, and the market price of the common shares (i.e., the number of shares that must be issued to acquire a given amount of capital). If, for example, the market price of the common shares is relatively high with respect to anticipated earnings, then the appeal of common shares is greatly enhanced. The reader is encouraged to work through the same example with alternative assumptions.

Transactions in a Limited Company's Common Shares

Under the Canada Business Corporations Act and Regulations a limited company may acquire its own common shares if they are to be cancelled on acquisition. The Department of Consumer and Corporate Affairs that administers the Act can monitor any illegal trading in a company's own common shares because it requires corporations to disclose any acquisitions other than for redemption and cancellation.

Common shares which are acquired but not yet cancelled are normally shown on the balance sheet as a deduction from owners' equity. Note disclosure probably should explain the company's intentions about the acquired shares.

Summary

In this chapter we have focused on the equity accounts of proprietorships, partnerships, and corporations. Although there are important legal and organizational differences among proprietorships, partnerships, and corporations, form of organization is often of less significance in the operations of the enterprise than is first apparent. Many of the distinctions have been diminished by both statute and business practice. From the accounting standpoint, the differences among the various forms of organization are most evident on the income statement (non-arm's-length salary, bonuses, and interest of a proprietor or partner) and in the equity section of the balance sheet. Proprietorships and partnerships maintain separate equity accounts for each owner. Corporations, on the other hand, maintain separate equity accounts for each class of shares, for contributed surplus (where this is permitted by corporate legislation), and for earnings retained in the business.

Corporations can raise capital by issuing bonds, preferred shares, or common shares. Bonds have an advantage over preferred shares or common shares in that interest payments, unlike dividend payments, are deductible from earnings in computing taxable income. By issuing both bonds and preferred shares the company is able to leverage the investment of the common shareholders —to increase their return by making use of funds contributed by parties other than owners. The relative advantages of the three types of financing, however, depend on anticipated earnings of the company, prevailing interest and dividend rates, the prices at which the various securities may be sold, income tax implications, and risk considerations.

This chapter has dealt extensively with *constraints* or rules imposed by either the Federal or Provincial Corporations Acts. The requirements with respect to issuing, redeeming, and reporting transactions in shares is based on providing information in order to help creditors who are confined by limited liability given to shareholders.

In the chapter to follow we shall deal with additional issues with respect to capital accounts.

Questions, Problems, and Cases

Questions

11-1 Distinguish, in your own words, among the following:
a. proprietorship
b. partnership
c. cooperative
d. business corporation
e. special incorporation
f. charitable organization

*11-2 In what way are the requirements of legislation referred to as constraints in this chapter? Give several examples where such legislation might govern the method of accounting or disclosure selected.

11-3 The risks of being a *silent* partner (one who takes no active role in management) of a business organized as a partnership are far greater than being a silent shareholder of a firm organized as a corporation. Do you agree? Explain.

11-4 It is often pointed out that the limitation on liability afforded shareholders of a corporation makes it easier for a corporation as opposed to a partnership to raise capital. Cite an example of a situation where the limitation on liability may, in fact, make it more difficult for a corporation to acquire needed funds.

11-5 A corporation, it is said, is a legal "person". Why is a corporation, not a partnership or a proprietorship, so described?

11-6 a. Assume one partnership records partners' salaries as an expense, while another partnership records them as withdrawals from partners' capital balances. Explain which approach you think is more appropriate. Indicate the accounting principles, concepts, and the objectives of financial reporting you have used.

b. Would the financial statements of the two partnerships in Part a above be comparable? Explain. How might note disclosure facilitate comparability in this instance? What does this assume about the sophistication of readers of statements?

c. How would your answers to Parts a and b change if the transactions involved were interest payments on partners' loans?

11-7 a. Common shareholders are referred to in this chapter as "residual claimants." Explain. Does this mean that "net income" and "basic earnings per share" are of little interest to preferred or creditor interests as a measure of protection or performance?

b. Can you think of some financial statement ratios which might be relevant to preferred or creditor interests to portray protection or performance? (Note: Students may wish to contact a broker and other sources.)

11-8 An incoming partner is willing to pay $400,000 for a one-third interest in a partnership that will after his admission have recorded owners' capital of $900,000, if no revaluation of assets is made. Why would he be willing to pay such a *premium* price? What accounting issues are raised by his willingness to pay such a price?

11-9 What makes *preferred* shares preferred? What preferences attach to them?

11-10 A friend wants to purchase "safe" securities for a period of two to three years. He wants assurance that the original amount of his investment will remain intact. Assume that you are satisfied that the company in which he is considering investing is sound, and that it is highly unlikely that it will be unable to pay required preferred share dividends or interest. Would you necessarily suggest to him that the preferred shares of the company are safer investments than the common shares? What factors are most likely to influence the market price of the preferred shares, assuming that they are not convertible into common shares?

11-11 What critical accounting problems are involved in the formation of a corporation? What warnings would you give to someone who is about to purchase the common shares of a newly organized corporation?

11-12 A company has to raise an additional $1 million in capital. The earnings of the company fluctuate widely from year to year; often it incurs losses. What are the advantages (or disadvantages) of acquiring the necessary capital by issuing common shares as opposed to preferred shares?

11-13 Explain how and why an underwriter's commission paid on the issue of common shares is accounted for differently than an underwriter's commission paid on the issue of bonds. How is this in accordance with the objectives of accounting?

11-14 Should organization costs (legal and other costs connected with the incorporation of a company) be recognized as an asset? Should they be amortized over time to income? Explain.

11-15 Distinguish in your own words among:
(a) bonds; (b) preferred shares; (c) convertible preferred shares; (d) common shares. How does each differ in terms of "risk"?

Problems

P11-1 You have recently been offered the opportunity to purchase 1,000 common shares of Computer Service Co. Ltd. at a price of $15 per share (a price well below its book value). The company has just been formed; it has not yet commenced operations. It was organized by three computer-systems analysts, who are presently the only shareholders. The company intends to lease office space and computers; it will provide automated bookkeeping services to small businesses.

A balance sheet provided to you by the company reveals the following:

Cash	$100,000
Inventories and supplies	20,000
Goodwill	50,000
Common shares (20,000 shares authorized, 10,000 shares issued and outstanding)	$170,000

A footnote to the financial statements indicates that the $50,000 of goodwill represents the accumulated expertise of the founders of the corporation. All have had extensive experience with a leading computer manufacturer and have held management positions with other computer service companies. The goodwill was authorized by the firm's board of directors.

Required:

a. What reservations might you have about purchasing the shares of the company?

b. Assume instead that you were an independent public accountant called upon to audit the company shortly after its formation. What adjusting journal entry might you propose? Why?

P11-2 The 19x3 annual report of a company incorporated under provincial legislation (i.e. legislation which permits the issue of par value shares) contains the following note:

Preferred shares — The Company's preferred shares are issuable in series and are entitled to one vote per share. The outstanding $5 Cumulative Convertible Preferred shares, which is the only designated series, is convertible at the rate of 3.888 shares of common for each share of preferred and is redeemable at $105 per share, and in decreasing amounts from June 30, 19x6, to $100 after June 30, 19x8.

The shareholders' equity section of the balance sheet indicates the following:

Preferred shares — authorized 1,825,000 shares, par value $1 per share: $5 cumulative convertible preferred shares; outstanding 561,164 shares	$ 561,164
Common shares — authorized 20,000,000 shares, par value $1 per share; issued 10,748,462 shares	10,748,462
Contributed surplus — premium on common and preferred shares	42,930,965
	54,240,591
Retained earnings	122,696,044
	$176,936,635

Suppose that at the beginning of 19x4 all 561,164 preferred shares were converted (exchanged) into common shares. The company received no cash in the exchange.

Required:

a. Prepare a journal entry to record the exchange. Be sure that as the result of your entry the balance in the common shares, par value account is reflective of the new number of shares outstanding. Indicate the assumptions you have made.

b. Explain the meaning of the terms "cumulative," "convertible," and "redeemable," contained in the note's description of the preferred shares.

P11-3 Woolley Co. Ltd. has decided to issue 100,000 preferred shares that will pay an annual dividend of $6 per share. The preferred shares will have a stated value of $100 per share. At the date of issue, similar grades of preferred shares are being sold to provide a return to investors of 7 percent.

Required:

a. At what price is the issue of Woolley likely to be sold?

b. Prepare a journal entry to record the sale of the preferred shares. (Assume legislation permits the issue of preferred shares with a stated value).

c. Prepare an entry to record the payment of the first annual cash dividend.

d. Repeat Part b assuming that the shares are issued without stated (or par) value.

P11-4 Filmore and Francis are partners in a firm that operates a chain of drug stores. They decide to incorporate their business. Filmore has a 60 percent interest in the partnership and Francis a 40 percent interest.

The net assets (assets less liabilities) of the partnership are recorded on the books of the partnership at $8 million. However, after considerable study and consultation with independent appraisers, the partners decide that the fair market value of their business is $12 million. Indeed, just prior to their decision to federally incorporate their company, they received an offer to sell their entire business to an independent party for that amount.

The partners intend to issue 200,000 common shares. They plan to keep 100 percent of such shares for themselves.

Required:

a. To what might the excess of fair market value over book value be attributable? How should this excess be accounted for?

b. Prepare any journal entries required to record the formation of the new company.

P11-5 Simmons and Ross decide to form a partnership to engage in the sale of real estate. Simmons contributes land that has an appraised value of $400,000; Ross contributes cash of $100,000. The land is subject to a liability of $100,000, which the partnership agrees to assume. The land had been recorded on the personal books of Simmons at a value of $200,000. The partners agreed that profits and losses would be shared in proportion to the initial contributions of the owners. In addition, however, Ross would be paid a management fee of $10,000 per year.

During its first year of operations the partnership purchased additional land for $800,000, paying $150,000 cash and giving a note for the balance. It sold for $300,000 land that it had acquired for $200,000. The buyers paid cash of $90,000 and agreed to assume liabilities of $210,000 that the partnership had incurred when it had acquired additional land.

During the first year the partnership borrowed $80,000 from Simmons. It agreed to pay Simmons interest at the rate of 6 percent per year. As of year end the loan had been outstanding for six months, but the partnership had neither paid nor accrued any interest.

At year end, Ross withdrew $30,000 cash from the partnership and, in addition, was paid his management fee; Simmons withdrew nothing.

Required:

a. Prepare all necessary journal entries to record the formation of the partnership and to summarize all transactions in which it engaged during its first year of operations. Prepare also any required adjusting and closing entries.
b. Prepare a balance sheet as of year end.
c. Explain your treatment of the interest on the partnership loan and the management fee in Parts a and b above. Can you relate this treatment to your assumed objectives for the financial statements of the partnership?

P11-6 Alliance Department Stores Ltd. has agreed to purchase McKay Bros. Discount Store. McKay Bros. is operated as a partnership. The owners' equity accounts on the books of the partnership indicate that each of the two partners has a recorded capital balance of $100,000. An independent appraiser has determined that the value of the individual assets of the company (there are no significant liabilities) is $250,000. The partners, however, have had several offers to sell the entire business for $300,000.

Alliance Department Stores Ltd. has offered to purchase McKay Bros. with its common shares. The number of shares to be issued is currently being negotiated between the two parties. Alliance currently has 50,000 common shares outstanding. The company has $400,000 in share capital and $600,000 in retained earnings. The current market price for common shares of Alliance is $25 per share.

Six possible ways of determining the number of shares to be issued to the McKay Bros.' partners are under consideration. The value of a share to be issued by Alliance might be based on either its *book* or its market value. The value of the interest to be purchased by Alliance might be based on the book value of McKay Bros.' assets, the appraised value of its assets, or its market value as a going concern.

Required:

a. Determine the number of shares to be issued by Alliance under each of the six combinations:
   - Value of Alliance shares based on (1) book value *or* (2) market value, *and*
   - Value of McKay Bros. based on (1) book value, (2) appraised value, *or* (3) market value as a going concern.
b. How do you account for the difference among book value, appraised value, and market value as a going concern?
c. On which basis do you recommend that the number of shares should be determined?

P11-7 Bryan and Moore are partners in a retail stereo business. After several successful years of operation as a partnership, the two decide to federally incorporate their business as MacDonald Co. Ltd. Bryan and Moore share profits and losses in the ratio of 3:1. Prior to the liquidation of the partnership and its subsequent incorporation, the balance sheet of the partnership indicated the following:

Assets		
Cash		$ 12,000
Accounts receivable		26,000
Inventory		83,000
Furniture and fixtures	$ 75,000	
Less: Allowance for depreciation	22,000	53,000
Land		18,000
Building	102,000	
Less: Allowance for depreciation	60,000	42,000
Total assets		$234,000
Liabilities and owners' equity		
Accounts payable		$ 29,000
Notes payable		80,000
Capital, Bryan		93,750
Capital, Moore		31,250
Total liabilities and owners' equity		$234,000

Prior to transferring the assets to the corporation, the partners decided to adjust the books of the partnership to reflect current market value.

The building had a current market value of $85,000; the land, $26,000; and the furniture and fixtures, $30,000.

The firm had not previously provided for uncollectible accounts. However, it was estimated that $4,000 of the accounts would be uncollectible. It was also determined that $8,000 of inventory was obsolete. The new corporation was to assume the liabilities of the partnership except as noted below.

The new corporation was authorized to issue 100,000 common shares without par value. Common shares were to be issued at a price of $10 per share and in proportion to the fair market value of one's contribution. In addition to the partners, common shares were to be issued to the following parties:

To an attorney for providing services pertaining to the organization of the corporation. The fair market value of the services was $8,000.

To the party holding the note payable. He agreed to accept common shares in full payment of his $80,000 note.

To a relative of one of the partners. He agreed to invest $50,000 cash in the new corporation.

Required:

a. Prepare journal entries to revalue the partnership, to transfer the assets to the new corporation in exchange for common shares and to distribute the common shares to the partners.

b. Prepare journal entries to organize the new corporation.

c. Indicate the number of shares each investor would receive.

d. Suppose that an error occurs such that the estimates of current market value of the partnership are *understated*, and that this error is undetected. Explain in what sense the partners are unfairly treated on incorporation as a result. If the error resulted in an overstatement, explain how the other parties are unfairly treated upon incorporation. What does this tell you about the objective(s) of the accounting information in this instance?

P11-8 After 10 years, Freeman Brothers Men's Shop is going out of business. Freeman Brothers is operated as a partnership. Just prior to liquidation, its balance sheet reflected the following:

Cash	$ 20,000
Merchandise inventory	80,000
Total assets	$100,000
Current liabilities	$ 5,000
Capital, J. Freeman	45,000
Capital, L. Freeman	50,000
Total liabilities and owners' equity	$100,000

The two Freeman brothers share profits and losses equally.

The firm holds a going-out-of-business sale and sells its entire merchandise inventory for $100,000. It pays its creditors and distributes the remaining cash between the two partners.

Required:

a. Prepare the required journal entries to record the sale of the merchandise and to pay the liabilities. (Prepare any closing entries that might be required with respect to any revenues and expenses associated with the sale of the merchandise.)

b. Determine the balances in the partners' capital accounts immediately prior to the final distribution of cash between the partners. How do you explain that although the partners share profits and losses equally, their capital balances are not equal?

c. How much cash should be distributed to each of the partners? Prepare a journal entry to record the final distribution to the partners.

P11-9 The Frost Co. Ltd. was federally incorporated on June 1, 19x6. According to the terms of its charter, the firm was authorized to issue share capital as follows:

Common Shares: 100,000 shares without par value
Preferred Shares: $5 dividend rate, 10,000 shares without par value

During the first year of operation the following transactions, which affected share capital accounts, took place:

1. The corporation issued for cash 50,000 common shares at a price of $30 per share.

2. The corporation issued for cash 10,000 preferred shares at $90 per share.
3. The company purchased a building, giving the seller 10,000 common shares. At the time of the purchase, the common shares of the company were being traded in the open market at $25 per share.
4. The firm's advertising agency agreed to accept 3,000 common shares, rather than cash, in payment for services performed. At the time of payment the market price was $28 per common share.
5. The company sold 2,000 common shares to one shareholder at a price of $28 per share, and at a later date 1,000 common shares to another shareholder at a price of $31 per share.

Required:

a. Prepare journal entries to record the above transactions.
b. Suppose in 3 and 4 above that the fair market value of the building and advertising services were readily attainable by appraisal. Which measure of "fair market value" would you use to record the transactions and why? Before deciding, recall that the objectives of accounting are important in this instance. Think of who "gains" and who "loses" depending on the valuation decided upon.

P11-10 A firm wishes to construct a new plant. The estimated cost of the plant is $5 million. The firm is undecided as to whether to raise the required capital by issuing bonds or preferred shares. The current prevailing yield on bonds of similar grade is 7 percent, and that on preferred shares is 9 percent.

Required:

What would the minimum earnings that the firm would have to realize before taxes be under both alternatives, if it were to break even on the proposed project? The current tax rate is 40 percent.

P11-11 A corporation has decided to construct an addition to its plant. The cost of the addition is $5 million; it is expected to increase earnings by $900,000 per year before taking into account income taxes.

The firm is considering three alternatives to acquire the needed $5 million capital:

1. Sell bonds. Current yield rates are 8 percent per year.
2. Issue preferred shares. Current yield rates are 12 percent per year.
3. Issue common shares. The firm currently has 600,000 shares outstanding. It estimates that additional shares could be sold at a price of $10 per share. The company has not paid any dividends on common shares in recent years and does not plan to do so in the foreseeable future. The current tax rate is 48 percent.

Required:

a. Which alternative do you think the company ought to select if impact on earnings per share of common shares is to be the most important criterion?
b. Suppose that anticipated earnings from the new addition were $1.5 million per year. Which alternative do you think the firm ought to select? (You need not recompute earnings per share; simply use judgment.)

c. Suppose that estimated additional earnings were $900,000 per year but that the market price of the firm's common shares was $20 per share. Which alternative should now be favored?

P11-12 As of the end of 19x6, the KLM partnership had assets of $1 million, liabilities of $400,000, and partners' capital of $600,000 as follows:

Partner K	$200,000
Partner L	150,000
Partner M	250,000

The three partners share profits and losses equally.

Partner K has decided to sell his entire one-third interest in the partnership to P. P has agreed to pay, *directly* to K, $250,000 for his interest.

Required:

a. Prepare a journal entry to record the sale of the interest on the books of the partnership. (Assume that the sale will *not* be used as an occasion to revalue *partnership* assets.)

b. Suppose instead that the offer of $250,000 will be considered indicative of the value of partnership assets and that prior to the sale of K's interest the increase in value of partnership assets will be given accounting recognition. Prepare the journal entries that would be required to effect the revaluation of the assets and the transfer of interest. Indicate the balances in the partners' capital accounts immediately following the sale.

c. Indicate briefly the arguments in favor of each of the two approaches. Support your arguments with reference to current accounting principles, concepts, and objectives.

Cases

C11-1 Mr. Z, although a major partner, has less than a 50 percent interest (i.e., proportion of owners' equity) of X Co., a partnership. X Co. discovers during the year that it requires an audit for credit purposes.

The controller informed Mr. Z that in order to comply with generally accepted accounting principles, partners' salaries and interest on loans must be reported separately in the financial statements and not hidden in the income statement figures as presently done. On hearing the controller's comment, Mr. Z became very upset and gave the controller the following arguments on why he did not favor separate disclosure:

1. Separate disclosure is only necessary when salary and interest are not at fair values of services provided or at current interest rates.
2. The banker is not interested in "earnings" and if he were, he could get this information easily from Mr. Z over the telephone.
3. Materiality should be considered. In some years, Mr. Z has taken only a small withdrawal in salary and interest and in other years none at all. In these years, Mr. Z argues that no disclosure is necessary.
4. Separate disclosure would not be required if X Co. were incorporated.
5. Such salary and interest payments are "objective" because they are negotiated by several partners dealing with each other at arm's length.

6. Such disclosure is an annoying constraint which does not suit the facts at hand or the objectives of X Co.'s financial statements. Mr. Z argues that neither he nor his partners benefit from this kind of information.

Required:

Assume the role of the controller and give a reply to Mr. Z concerning each of the arguments raised. *(CICA adapted)*

C11-2 Several years ago two brothers, Dave and Gord, decided to go into business manufacturing popular brands of soft drinks and selling them directly to customers, using their rented warehouse as a retail outlet.

Business has flourished and the two brothers have decided to incorporate their business, and take advantage of limited liability and the lower corporate tax rate (25 percent for small business).

An excerpt from the most recent balance sheet of Soda Shoppes Co. is as follows:

Soda Shoppes Co.
Balance Sheet
December 31, 19x7

Assets		
Current assets:		
Accounts receivable, less doubtful accounts		$ 24,000
Inventories of raw materials		66,000
Total current assets		90,000
Long-term assets:		
Equipment, at cost	$42,000	
Less accumulated depreciation	10,000	32,000
		$122,000
Liabilities and Partners' Capital		
Current liabilities:		
Accounts payable		$ 31,000
Loan by Gord, at 12% per annum		15,000
Partners' capital:		
Dave	$38,000	
Gord	38,000	76,000
		$122,000

The two partners always kept their capital accounts in a ratio of 1:1 and any excess above this ratio was credited to a partner loan account, at 12 percent per annum.

The partners agree that assets are not carried on the books at fair values. Specifically, they note that:

1. According to a court-appointed trustee, an account receivable of $1,000 (previously written off) is now collectible in full.

2. Included in inventories is $5,000 of slow-moving stock which will have to be scrapped. The replacement cost of saleable inventory is $70,000.
3. The replacement cost of the used equipment is estimated to be $50,000.
4. There is unrecorded goodwill, due to the warehouse location and customer loyalty. As evidence of this, they point out that they were recently offered $150,000 for their business by Un-Cola Ltd. They declined the offer.

The partners agree that each should be issued 50 percent of the voting share capital of their new corporation, Soda Shoppes Ltd. However, they are unsure how to settle Gord's partnership loan account. They want to convert this to some form of equity or senior debt to facilitate later bank borrowing. Some suggestions by their lawyers are:

1. Unsecured debentures yielding 12 percent per annum.
2. Cumulative preferred shares (par value $100) having a dividend rate of $15 per share. (Assume legislation permits the issue of par value preferred shares).
3. Nonvoting common shares. Soda Shoppes Ltd. will pay common dividends using a fixed payout rate of 40 percent of net income. A growth rate of 20 percent per annum in the market value of common share equity is possible, the partners feel.

Required:

a. Prepare journal entries to (i) wind up the partnership's books and (ii) record the opening of Soda Shoppes Ltd. Also, prepare the opening balance sheet (December 31, 19x7) of Soda Shoppes Ltd. Carefully explain your decisions regarding valuation of partnership assets. Assume here that the partnership loan is converted to nonvoting common share equity.

b. Write a letter to the partners containing your thoughts, analyses, and recommendations regarding the form of equity or debt to be issued to Gord in exchange for his loan to the partnership. Consider the needs of the company in addition to those of Gord, and state any assumptions you make. (Ignore personal tax implications for Gord).

C11-3 Commencement Company Limited ("CCL" or the company) is a federally incorporated company owned entirely by Mr. Gunn. Business over the past few years has been extremely good and the company has been operating at full capacity. There is every likelihood that the demand for CCL's product will increase in the future. Rather than turn down orders in the future, Mr. Gunn has decided that it would be an appropriate time for the company to expand its operations. In this way the company could benefit more fully from the increased demand for its product.

Mr. Gunn realizes that expansion requires funds for investment in a plant expansion, new equipment and higher receivable and inventory levels because of higher sales. He has reviewed a number of alternative ways to finance the company's expansion program and has decided to sell shares to the general public.

He understands from the company's controller Ms. Briscoll that:

1. The company recognizes revenue on long-term contracts on a "com-

pleted contract" basis. This is because the "completed contract" basis is acceptable for tax purposes and thus minimizes the company's tax payments.

2. The company depreciates its fixed assets in accordance with the rates stipulated in the Income Tax Act. Since there are no other major uses of the financial statements, the company has found it easier to maintain one set of books for tax purposes only.
3. The company values its inventory of raw materials at the lower of FIFO cost and net realizable value. It has considerable work in process representing the work performed on long-term projects.
4. The company expenses supplies in the years they are purchased.
5. All other accounting treatments are in accordance with generally accepted accounting principles.

Required:

Assume the role of an accounting advisor, and prepare a report addressed to the president outlining the accounting implications to the company of selling shares to the public. Include in your report all relevant considerations such as possible changes in accounting principles, additional information that would be required and the accounting treatment you would recommend for the issue of shares.

12 *Capital Accounts, II*

This chapter will highlight some additional types of transactions and financial events that have an impact upon the owners' equity section of the balance sheet. First we shall consider the use of share rights and options as a means of acquiring additional capital. We shall deal next with distributions of earnings — dividends in cash, *in kind*, and shares — and with other types of financial events that have an effect upon retained earnings. We shall conclude with a discussion of key problems with respect to reports of earnings — those relating to calculation of earnings per share, to determination of earnings for an *interim* period, or for a segment of a business, and for future periods (forecasts).

Share Rights

If a corporation desired to raise capital by issuing additional shares, it could simply sell the shares to the general public. As a consequence of the sale, however, the proportionate ownership of existing shareholders might be diluted. If an existing shareholder owned 1,000 of 10,000 shares outstanding, then he would hold a 10 percent interest in the corporation. If the company were to sell an additional 5,000 shares to the general public, however, his interest would be reduced to 6.66 percent (one fifteenth). To prevent such dilution, many companies grant their shareholders *preemptive rights* to any new shares to be issued.

When a corporation decides to issue new shares, rights to purchase the shares normally would be mailed to all existing shareholders. Commonly, a right would permit the shareholder to purchase one or more shares at a price below that at which the share was currently being traded. If, for example, the shares were presently being traded at $50 per share, each right might provide for the purchase of one share for $48. This practice ensures that a large percentage of rights will be exercised. If the shareholder did not wish to exercise the right to purchase the stock at $48, then he could usually sell it in the open market. The price that a buyer would be willing to pay for the right would be represented by the difference between the market price and the exercise price (less any commission payable to brokers for trading the rights). A right that could be exercised at $48 would probably be traded, at a time when the market price was $50, for $50 minus $48 — $2. A purchaser would be willing to pay approximately $2 for the right since he would have to pay only $48 (directly to the company) to acquire the share. He would be as well off as if he had bought the share in the open market for $50 per share. Rights commonly expire within a short period of time, often no more than 30 days.

A company need not make any entries to record the issue of the rights. No additional capital is received until the rights are exercised. When a share right is exercised and new shares are issued, it would record the issue just as it would if there were no rights associated with the sale.

Warrants

Warrants are a special type of rights. Warrants, like rights, are options to purchase a stated number of shares at a stated price. Warrants, however, are usually issued by companies in connection with the sale of bonds in order to make the bonds more attractive to prospective purchasers. They are often called *sweeteners*. The issuing company guarantees the purchaser of the bond the opportunity to acquire an equity interest in the company at a fixed price. As a consequence, it is often able to reduce the interest rate it would otherwise have to pay. Warrants conventionally may be exercised over a longer period than rights; and, since it is anticipated that the market price of the shares will increase over time, the exercise price often is above, rather than below, the prevailing market price at the times the options are granted. Holders of warrants can be expected to exercise them, however, only at such time as the market price climbs above the exercise price. Warrants, like rights, can generally be freely traded apart from the securities with which they were initially associated.

Employee Share Options

In recent years, share options have become a popular means of compensating executives and other employees. Share options are a form of share rights. Share options permit the recipient to purchase shares of his employer's common share capital at a fixed price. Although the employee will have to pay for his shares, the price he pays remains constant regardless of fluctuations in market value. Should the market value of the shares increase above the set price (the exercise price), he could acquire the shares at a considerable savings over what he would otherwise have to pay. Should the market price fall below the exercise price, then he need not exercise his option and could allow it to lapse.

Share options are a means of compensating employees. Although the compensation does not require a direct cash outlay, the employer is nonetheless giving up something of value. Any shares issued to the employees at less than their market price represent an opportunity foregone to sell the shares to other investors at the market price.

The Labatt's financial statements (page 59) explain their employee share option plans. A typical plan might operate as follows: On January 1, 19x0, when a company's common shares are selling for $20 each, options are granted to senior employees so that they may purchase a specified number (say 100,000) of the company's shares for $20 each until December 31, 19x9. When the option is granted, a note (much like the Labatt's note) would appear in the company's financial statements. If the employee exercises her option (say for 10,000 shares) prior to the expiry date, the journal entry under the Canada Business Corporations Act is simply:

Cash	$200,000	
Common shares		$200,000
To record exercise of an employee's 10,000 share options.		

Even though the market price of the shares may have been $500,000 ($50 per share) at the time the options were exercised, the credit part of the entry is based on the figure for cash receipts. Clearly, under these circumstances the employee has been granted a $300,000 ($500,000 – $200,000) "bonus."

Observe that the "bonus" does not appear as an expense, even though the $300,000 can be viewed as a form of executive compensation. The employee's hard work helped to increase the market price of the common shares from $20 to $50. The senior employees, as compensation, received both a salary plus the gain on the common shares, yet only the salary appeared as an expense.

Does this violate the matching concept? Technically, share issues are *capital transactions*. Also, it can be reasoned that the share "bonus" is more than compensation — perhaps a form of gambling. Matching *could* be accommodated, but only with some difficulty. *If* the options were granted and exercised in the same financial year, the entry might be:

Cash	$200,000	
Salary expense	300,000	
Common shares		$500,000
To record the issue of common shares.		

That is, the common shares would be issued at market value.

Unfortunately, the situation becomes more complex if the increase of $30 ($50 – $20) occurs over many years. During this period the market price of the shares could be fluctuating. Is it possible to accrue an expense, with an entry such as this:

Salary expense	$100,000	
Accrued liability (?) or equity (?)		$100,000
To accrue a possible liability.		

What if the market price drops, and the employee does not exercise the option? Should salary expense be *credited* in a *subsequent* period? If it is, matching would not occur. Also, what is the offsetting credit when salary is debited? Obviously, the above approach is not satisfactory. Hence, in Canada, when options are exercised share capital is credited with the amount of cash received and not the current market value.

Compensation could be recorded under a *different set of facts*. *If*, the market price were $22 when the options were granted at $20, a "gift" of $2 per option has been granted to employees. Generally, however, the amounts involved are *not* material. Hence, the compensation is not likely to be recorded in Canadian companies.

Two other matters affecting share options are worth remembering. First, income tax legislation deals with the topic in depth; thus, share options are not a simple way of avoiding income tax. Second, if options are granted at option prices below market price at the date of granting, special approval of the transaction may be required from other shareholders. This is to prevent the directors from watering down (lowering) the value of each of the company's shares. Directors and officers must always be on guard about receiving adequate value for any shares which they issue for other than cash.

Retained Earnings

Retained earnings represent the total accumulated earnings of a corporation less amounts distributed to shareholder as dividends and any amounts transferred to other capital accounts.

Dividends are distributions of assets (or common shares) which serve to reduce retained earnings. They are *declared* by a formal resolution of a firm's board of directors. The announcement of a dividend would indicate the amount per share to be distributed, the *date of record* (that on which the share records will be closed and ownership of the outstanding shares determined), and the *date of payment*. A typical announcement might read as follows: "The board of directors of the XYZ Corporation, at its regular meeting of December 9, 19x6, declared a quarterly dividend of $2 per share payable on January 24, 19x7, to shareholders of record on January 3, 19x7."

The entry to record the declaration of a dividend is straightforward. On the date of declaration, when the liability for payment is first established, the entry (in this case to record a dividend of $2 per share on 100,000 shares outstanding) would be

Retained earnings	$200,000	
Dividends payable		$200,000
To record declaration of the cash dividend on common shares.		

When payment is subsequently made it would be recorded as follows:

Dividends payable	$200,000	
Cash		$200,000
To record payment of the dividend.		

Although conventional non-share dividends are charged to retained earnings, they are paid in cash or other tangible assets. It does not follow that merely because a company has a balance in retained earnings it has the wherewithal to make dividend payments. Retained earnings are a part of owners' equity. Owners' equity corresponds to the excess of assets over liabilities. It cannot be associated with specific assets or groups of assets to which shareholders have claim.

The nature of retained earnings is a common source of misunderstanding — a misunderstanding that can be attributed in large measure to the widespread use, until recently, of the term *earned surplus* in place of retained earnings. *Surplus* implies something extra — an amount over and above what is needed. Retained earnings may not, in fact, represent *surplus*. Rather, a balance in retained earnings may be indicative of earnings that have been reinvested in the corporation. By not distributing its earned assets to shareholders, the corporation may have internally financed expansion. The retained earnings, therefore, may not denote the availability of cash or other assets that can readily be distributed to shareholders; instead the company may have used its available resources to acquire land, buildings, and equipment.

Decisions as to when and how much of a dividend to declare are ordinarily made with primary reference to the corporation's current cash position, anticipated cash flow, whether the company can fruitfully reinvest any cash, and the attitude of investors. With regard to the latter factor, investors may consider the nondeclaration of a dividend to be very serious if the company has paid one regularly for many years. Also, the failure to declare a dividend may affect the credit-rating and bond-rating status of a company, thereby making subsequent borrowing of funds more expensive.

The company must also determine whether the available and projected cash is sufficient to meet its other operating requirements — the need to meet payrolls, maintain inventories, replace worn-out equipment, etc. In addition, however, the corporation must consider also the interests of shareholders. To the extent that assets are not distributed to shareholders, the shareholders are being forced to increase their investment in the corporation. Whether they wish to increase their investment will ordinarily depend in large measure on the return they could obtain from competing investment opportunities. If the funds to be retained in the corporation are likely to provide a return greater than shareholders could obtain elsewhere, then shareholders are often willing to permit the company to retain all or a portion of its assets. In fact, many corporations, particularly *growth* companies, omit payment of dividends for years at a time. Shareholders of such companies are willing to forego immediate cash returns for long-term corporate expansion and enhancement of their investment.

When the company's directors decide to declare a dividend they must also consider any restrictions which might be contained in bond or preferred-share indentures or agreements, or in corporate legislation. When bonds or preferred shares are sold to the general public a trustee is appointed on behalf of the bondholders or preferred shareholders. The trustee and the underwriter may agree that, in order to make the securities attractive and saleable, no dividends can be paid to common shareholders unless certain restrictions are met. One such restriction might be that retained earnings cannot drop below, say, $500,000 as a result of declaring a dividend.

Companies' legislation requires disclosure of the type of account debited when dividends are declared and, depending on the jurisdiction, there might be other restrictions. Permission of creditors might be needed to declare dividends out of other-than-retained earnings. In Canada, which has a large number of mining companies, capital such as the original common share investment can be returned to shareholders when the mine has exhausted the ore body, and funds are no longer needed. The specific wording of the governing legislation must be read carefully and legal advice should be obtained when "dividends" are to be debited to share capital.

Dividends in Kind

Although dividends are conventionally paid in cash, occasionally a company will distribute noncash assets. In 1979 The Hudson's Bay Co. offered to buy the voting common shares of Simpsons, which in turn held voting shares in Simpsons-Sears. Another company sought for a few days to compete with the Bay in bidding for Simpsons shares but eventually lost interest in buying the shares. During the process of negotiations with the two potential buyers, the directors of Simpsons tried to complicate negotiations and discourage a potential take-over of their company. They declared a dividend of their shares in Simpsons-Sears. This forced the Bay, who eventually gained control of Simpsons, to also acquire shares of Simpsons-Sears.

The journal entry on declaration of a dividend "in kind" would be:

Dividends (an account which is "closed" to retained earnings) or		
Retained earnings (equity −)	$40,000,000	
Investment in shares of Simpsons-Sears Limited (asset −)		$40,000,000
To record payment of dividend in kind.		

Observe that the credit to the "Investment in shares" account is for the *cost* of the asset, and not its fair market value. Accountants would not normally write up the asset to buying or selling market price, thereby recognizing a gain, before declaring a dividend. The reason is that an arm's-length transaction has not occurred. A dividend in kind has important income tax implications; it means shareholders must split the original cost of their shares into two parts — one for Simpsons (without Simpsons-Sears) and the other for Simpsons-Sears alone.

Share Splits

Corporations will sometimes *split* their shares. That is, they will issue additional shares for each share outstanding. A firm might, for example, split its shares three for one, meaning that for each one share presently held a shareholder will receive an additional two. Share splits are ordinarily intended to reduce the market price per share, to obtain a wider distribution of ownership, and to improve the marketability of the outstanding shares. The common shares of a corporation might be trading at $300 per share. The board of directors determines that at such a high price the share is less attractive to investors than it would be at a lower price. Many investors like to acquire shares in round lots of 100 shares since brokerage commissions are relatively high when fewer shares are purchased. The board might, therefore, vote a three-for-one share split. Each shareholder will end up with three times as many shares as he had previously, but the market price per share could be expected to fall to one third its previous price. Neither the corporation nor the individual shareholder would be intrinsically better or worse off as the result of the split.

Commonly, the corporation would reduce the par value (if any) of the common shares to reflect the split and would so notify shareholders. If the share previously had a par value of $1, it would subsequently have a new par value of $.33⅓. As a consequence, no accounting entries are required to effect the split. Common shares, par value, will in total remain unchanged. So, too, will contributed surplus and retained earnings. No par value shares would not have to undergo a modification because of their inherent flexibility.

Share or Stock Dividends

Shares may also be "split" by declaring a share (or stock) dividend, which increases the number of issued shares. Ordinarily the ratio of new shares to outstanding shares is decidedly lower for a share dividend than for a share split. Seldom would the number of new shares to be issued exceed 20 percent of previously outstanding shares. More significantly, the motivation underlying a share dividend is considerably different from that of other types of share splits. A corporation would issue a share dividend not to increase the marketability of its shares but rather to provide its shareholders with tangible evidence of an increase in their ownership interest. A company may view a share dividend as a substitute for a dividend in cash or other property. Lacking the available cash, it will distribute to each shareholder, on a *pro rata* basis, additional common shares. Sometimes, for example, a company that has consistently paid cash dividends will be caught in a *cash squeeze*. Rather than omitting the dividend entirely, the company will distribute additional shares instead of cash. A share dividend may also provide a means for a company to *capitalize* a portion of accumulated earnings. The company will transfer a portion of accumulated earnings from the retained earnings account (which may sometimes be viewed as a temporary capital account) to the common share account (which is considered to be of a more permanent nature). Such a transfer provides formal evidence that a portion of accumulated earnings has been invested in the business and is no longer available for the payment of dividends.

A share dividend, like other types of share splits, has no effect on the intrinsic worth of either the corporation or the shareholder. It leaves both parties neither better nor worse off than previously. A share dividend has no effect on corporate assets and liabilities. As a consequence of the dividend, additional common shares are outstanding. But since the net worth of the corporation remains the same, each common share represents a proportionately smaller interest in the corporation.

Suppose, for example, that a corporation, *prior* to declaration of a share dividend, had net assets of $100,000 and 1,000 common shares outstanding. A shareholder who owned 100 shares would have held a 10 percent interest in a company with a book value of $100,000. If the corporation declared a 3 percent share dividend, then the shareholder would receive 3 additional shares. He would now own 103 shares out of a total of 1,030 shares — still a 10 percent interest in a company with a book value of $100,000. Insofar as the market price for the shares is determined in a rational manner, then the market price per share could be expected to be reduced proportionately.

An interesting question arises as to whether share (stock) dividends are to be debited to retained earnings and credited to common share capital accounts at fair market value of the shares issued, *or* for something less (perhaps, par value if the jurisdiction of incorporation permits such type of shares). The *CICA Handbook* is silent on the subject of share dividends. In the U.S., fair market value would be used as the amount credited to common shares for each share issued as a dividend. In Canada the accounting treatment is governed by the constraints (corporate legislation). Some jurisdictions indicate that all shares must be issued at fair market value; otherwise, the directors who approved issue of the shares might be personally liable for the difference between issue price and fair market value in the event of bankruptcy. Most jurisdictions seem to allow share dividends to be issued at less than fair market value. After all, a share dividend depletes retained earnings and lessens the opportunity for cash dividends; it also credits more to the share capital account, which exists to "protect" creditors. (Technically the assets serve as protection. Under the double entry system the existence of equity signifies the existence of net assets).

Share dividends can have complicated income tax implications, if dividends are debited to some special income-tax-regulated sections of retained earnings. Directors of companies often seek income tax advice about the effects of different types of dividends (cash, in kind, or in shares) on shareholders and the company.

Appropriations of Retained Earnings

Occasionally a firm may wish to designate a portion of retained earnings for a specific purpose. It can do so by segregating and reporting separately the required amount and thereby notify shareholders that dividends will not be paid out of such accounts.

Retained earnings may be set aside for retirement of debt, for expansion, for *contingencies* such as losses from natural disasters, for foreign expropriations of property, for plant modernization, or for a variety of other activities.

The appropriation of retained earnings for specific purposes can be effected by a journal entry such as the following:

Retained earnings	$3,000,000	
Retained earnings appropriated for plant modernization		$3,000,000
To designate a portion of retained earnings for plant modernization.		

In the equity section of the balance sheet retained earnings would be divided into two or more categories: one or more for the specially appropriated amounts and one for the unappropriated balance. Retained earnings might be reported as in the following illustration:

Retained earnings:	
Unappropriated	$12,980,000
Appropriated for bond retirement	1,000,000
Appropriated for plant modernization	3,000,000
Appropriated for contingencies	200,000
Total	$17,180,000

When the firm makes the expenditure for which the appropriation was established it would simply restore the appropriated amount back to the unappropriated balance. Upon modernizing the plant for $3 million, the amount previously appropriated, the following entries would be made:

Plant	$3,000,000	
Cash (or notes payable)		$3,000,000
To record modernization of the plant.		
Retained earnings appropriated for plant modernization	$3,000,000	
Retained earnings		$3,000,000
To restore to retained earnings amounts previously appropriated.		

Observe that the appropriation account has to be restored to retained earnings; it cannot, for example, be debited and cash be credited. Also an appropriation account cannot be used to avoid a debt to expense. To illustrate, an appropriation of retained earnings may have been made for a *possible* expropriation of a firm's assets held in a foreign country. If the expropriation of the assets by a foreign government becomes more obvious (in which case a loss would be accrued) or occurs, the entry would be:

Expropriation loss (or expense)	$2,965,000	
Various assets		$2,965,000
To record expropriation.		

The debit to "expropriation loss" would be closed to income summary and then to retained earnings. If the appropriation of retained earnings originally was for $2,850,000, it would be returned by this entry:

Appropriated for possible expropriation	$2,850,000	
Retained earnings		$2,850,000
To record restoration to retained earnings.		

The entry thereby restores a large portion of retained earnings which had just been reduced by the actual expropriation loss. The debit to loss (expense) is shown directly on the income statement, and is not hidden by a direct offset to an appropriation account. Overall, retained earnings decreases by $2,965,000 from what it was before first being appropriated.

Appropriations of retained earnings are of little economic or accounting significance. They are probably harmless as long as they are properly interpreted; the danger is, however, that they may easily be misunderstood and thereby provide shareholders with an unwarranted sense of financial security.

Appropriations of retained earnings, although commonly referred to as *reserves*, do not, in fact, represent reserves at all. They do not insure that the firm will have the financial ability to carry out the activities for which they were intended.

Retained earnings, as has previously been stressed, cannot be associated with particular assets. The appropriation of retained earnings does *not* result in the establishment of a cash reserve or in any way increase the ability of the firm to make cash payments. It does not cause specific assets to be set aside for specific purposes. It represents nothing more than a bookkeeping entry — a reclassification of retained earnings. It is indicative of no substantive financial transaction. To the extent that investors believe that the existence of the reserve (appropriation) is evidence that the firm has the financial means to meet the need for which it was established, they will have been seriously deceived.

However, the existence of the reserve does provide an indication that management does not *intend* to pay dividends in an amount that would reduce retained earnings below the amount that has been set aside in the reserve. As a practical matter, however, the designation of retained earnings for specific purposes is unlikely to have an impact on dividend policy. As previously noted, the determining factors in the declaration of dividends are such factors as the availability of cash, the competing demands for cash, and the alternative investment opportunities open to shareholders.

None of these factors will be affected by the appropriations of retained earnings.

Provisions for Contingencies

Provisions or estimated liabilities for contingencies raise particularly provocative accounting questions. A contingency is a situation involving uncertainty as to possible losses that might result in the future should certain events occur or fail to occur. The critical accounting issues with respect to contingencies center around the accounting period in which potential losses should be charged to earnings.

One means of establishing a reserve for contingencies is simply to set aside a portion of retained earnings to accommodate losses as they actually occur. Suppose, for example, in 19x6 a firm becomes concerned that certain of its properties may be expropriated by a foreign government. It might, in that year, set up a reserve for contingencies as follows:

Retained earnings	$5,000,000	
Retained earnings appropriated for possible expropriation of foreign property		$5,000,000
To establish a reserve for expropriation of foreign properties.		

If in 19x8 $5 million of property is actually expropriated, then the balance in the reserve account would be restored to retained earnings and the loss charged against earnings of that year:

Retained earnings appropriated for possible expropriation of foreign properties	$5,000,000	
Retained earnings		$5,000,000
To restore to retained earnings amount previously appropriated so that actual loss can be charged to current earnings.		
Expropriation losses (expense +)	$5,000,000	
Plant and other assets		$5,000,000
To record the loss from expropriation of foreign property.		

"Expropriation losses" would be *closed* to income summary and then to retained earnings at year end.

Another means of establishing a contingency reserve is to charge the loss against earnings in the period in which it is first anticipated and then when it actually occurs to write it off against the estimated liability previously established. If in 19x6 the company first anticipated the loss, it would establish the estimated liability as follows:

Expropriation losses (expense +)	$5,000,000	
Estimated liability for expropriation of foreign properties		$5,000,000
To establish a liability for expropriation losses.		

In 19x8 when the loss actually occurred, it would write off the property expropriated against the estimated liability. Thus,

Estimated liability for expropriation of foreign properties	$5,000,000	
Plant and other assets		$5,000,000
To record the expropriation of property.		

In this situation the "estimated liability for expropriation" account can be debited and "plant" credited because the account was initially set up by a debit to expense. If an appropriation account was set up by debiting retained earnings, the appropriation account could *not* be reduced by directly crediting "plant and other assets."

The key distinction between the two methods is that under the second method the loss is recognized as a charge to income in 19x6, when it is first anticipated. Under the first method, the loss may not be charged to income until it actually occurs.

The second method is the more conservative of the two. It results in a charge to earnings prior to the period in which the value of an asset has been impaired or a liability incurred. But it is deficient in that it leaves to the discretion of management the period in which the loss should be charged and the amount of the loss to be charged. A corporation must always face an uncertain future. Possibilities of losses do not usually appear within a single accounting period; they develop over a number of years. Under the second method, management is afforded the opportunity to *manipulate* income by charging the loss to the period in which the effect on earnings would be least detrimental. Recognition of the loss is based on managerial judgment as opposed to specific transactions or events.

The Accounting Research Committee (ARC) of the CICA recognized the problem described above and acted in a manner similar to that of the U.S. Financial Accounting Standards Board (FASB). According to the ARC an expense account can be charged only if:

1. "it is likely that a future event will confirm that an asset had been impaired or a liability incurred at the date of the financial statements;"
2. "the amount of the loss can be reasonably estimated."

Nevertheless the pronouncement by the ARC does not eliminate the need for managerial and accounting judgment in determining when the value of an asset has actually been impaired or when there is a reasonable probability that the firm will have a liability to outside parties. Many losses do not occur at a single point in time. They occur over several accounting periods. Suppose, for example, a firm is sued for damages resulting from the manufacture of an allegedly faulty and dangerous product. The legal proceedings which lead to final resolution of the suit may take place over several accounting periods. The best estimate of the most likely outcome of the litigation may change from one period to another as the initial judgment is rendered and the case goes through several levels of appeal. The specific period in which the impairment of corporate net worth becomes sufficiently certain to warrant a charge to income is unlikely to be clear and must necessarily be determined on the basis of subjective opinion.

"Self-Insurance"

A special question of when to recognize losses arises when a firm *self-insures* a portion of its assets. An airline, for example, may self-insure for the first $1,000,000 of losses to its aircraft. You may self-insure for the first $100 of collision damage to your automobile. Most firms, like individuals, carry insurance to protect themselves against losses too great for them to bear at any one time. To the extent that a firm is likely to incur an estimable number of losses over a period of years, the effect of the insurance is that the cost of the losses is spread over a period of years (as the insurance premiums are paid) rather than charged in the years in which the losses actually take place. A few firms that self-insure may actually set aside a cash reserve to cover potential losses. Others do not specifically segregate any assets but make certain that they do not declare dividends to an extent which would impair their ability to cover possible losses. Most firms do not self-insure against major catastrophes. Instead, they self-insure against losses that occur with reasonable regularity — damage to automobiles or trucks, for example. Insurance rates are established by independent insurance companies on the basis of the actual or anticipated loss experience of the insured. Premiums are designed to cover actual losses plus costs of administering the policy and, in addition, to provide the insurer with a profit. By maintaining its own insurance coverage a firm is able to restrict its costs to the actual losses.

The accounting issue with respect to self-insurance asks whether firms that self-insure should properly charge to expense each year an amount approximately equal to what they would pay in insurance premiums had they insured their assets with outside companies. Suppose, for example, a firm estimates that, on the average, it can expect to incur $30,000 in property losses every five years. Each year it *might* make the following entry:

19x2:

Self-insurance expense	$6,000	
Estimated liability for self-insurance		$6,000
To establish an estimated liability for anticipated property losses.		

As it actually incurs a loss and has to repair or replace damaged property it would charge the loss against the estimated liability. Thus, assuming that it had to pay $12,000 to repair a truck, it would record the expenditure as follows:

19x9:

Estimated liability for self-insurance	$12,000	
Cash		$12,000
To record the expenditure to repair a damaged truck.		

Both the ARC and the FASB have stated that a debit to expense and credit to an estimated liability are *not* acceptable under current practice. Self-insurance is another form of contingency and must meet the two tests just described under the section "Provision for Contingencies." The ARC has added the comment that a firm which lacks adequate insurance *may* (but does not have to) disclose this fact in its financial statements.

The firm that self-insures is not prevented from making an appropriation of retained earnings — i.e., by debiting the retained earnings account and crediting "appropriation for self-insurance." However, when a loss occurs the entry would be:

Loss (from accident or fire) (expense +)	$152,500	
Assets		$152,500
To write-down assets damaged in an accident.		

The appropriation account might then be reduced and retained earnings would be credited.

Income Statement: All-inclusive versus Current Operating Performance

The income statement presents the revenues and expenses of a period. There is a diversity of opinion, however, on whether the income statement should focus upon the normal, recurring operations of the firm or upon all transactions that affect the equity of owners (excluding capital transactions such as dividends or gains and losses on retirement of shares).

Under one viewpoint, only those transactions which are indicative of the *current operating* performance of an enterprise should be taken into account in calculating net income. This viewpoint might be held by those who wish to predict cash flows (enroute to establishing a current worth of a firm) or evaluate management's current performance. Other transactions, those of an unusual, nonrecurring nature, should be segregated from the ordinary transactions and reported separately. The income statement should be a report on the normal operations of the firm.

Proponents of the current operating performance approach assert that net income for a given period is useful primarily in that it can serve as a basis for making comparisons among firms and among accounting periods for the same firm. To the extent that net income is "contaminated" by transactions that are highly unusual and unlikely to recur, its utility is diminished.

Those who favor the alternative approach, the *all-inclusive* income statement, maintain that the income statement should provide a complete record of *all transactions*, excluding dividend distributions, that have an impact upon the retained earnings of a business. They argue that the aggregate of periodic net incomes should provide a complete history of the earnings of the enterprise. They point out that the all-inclusive concept avoids the necessity of making highly subjective judgments as to what constitutes a charge or credit sufficiently unusual as to warrant exclusion from net income. Although proponents of the all-inclusive concept recognize the importance of distinguishing between recurring and nonrecurring revenues and expenses, they believe that the needs of analysts can best be served by providing in footnotes to the financial statements full disclosure of the nature of any unusual items affecting income.

This view coincides with research on the efficiency (called efficient markets research) of trading in company shares which are listed on the major stock exchanges. That is, with adequate disclosure (and assuming that costs of preparation and interpretation are comparable between competing accounting methods) investors are able to sort out what is relevant to them. The figures need *not* be shown directly on one particular financial statement, such as an income statement, in order to receive due consideration from investors.

Over the past several decades the accounting profession has wavered between the two concepts of the income statement. In recent years, however, there has been a decided swing toward the all-inclusive concept; the most recent opinions of authoritative bodies reflect the view that, with few exceptions, net income should include all items of gain and loss recorded during the period. Dividends and capital transactions, though, would be excluded from income determination.

Extraordinary and Unusual Items

Over the last decade the accounting profession has tended to require disclosure whenever measurement problems are complex and one, sensible solution is not evident, or when the managements of Canadian companies as a group are not yet ready to accept one particular measurement method. Disclosure — as a separate income statement item — has been invoked as a guiding principle in the case of transactions which do not appear to be recurring; they may fall into one of three categories: (1) extraordinary items; (2) unusual items; and (3) prior period adjustments.

The reporting approach in Canada differs slightly from that of other countries, especially the U.S., with respect to the first two items. The ARC of the CICA has defined extraordinary items as "gains, losses, and provisions for losses which, by their nature, are not typical of the normal business activities of the enterprise, are not expected to occur regularly over a period of years and are not considered as recurring factors in any evaluation of the ordinary operations of the enterprise." In order to apply this general guideline an accountant needs considerable judgment and advice from operating officers of the company. Whether or not accountants possess the required skills to apply the guidelines consistently for the same sets of facts is a question which the readers/users must ask themselves.

Accounting practitioners in Canada have refined the extraordinary category somewhat by excluding what they call "unusual items." Unusual items require separate disclosure on an income statement and consist of gains and losses (or provisions for losses) which are abnormal in size but affect accounts which are part of the company's normal operations. Examples include very large bad debts or write-downs of inventory. By giving separate disclosure, accountants let the readers decide for themselves whether or not such write-downs will occur again.

The financial statement presentation of extraordinary items would be, (the illustration excludes the top part of an income statement):

Income taxes	$800,000
Income before extraordinary items	955,600
Extraordinary loss on expropriation of assets located in [a foreign country], less deferred income taxes of $450,000 thereon	510,000
Net income	$445,600

Note that the extraordinary item is net of income tax effects. This occurs because of the location of extraordinary items below the deduction for income taxes. Some extraordinary items may be subject to capital gains income tax rates (which are half of the regular income tax rate for the company), and thus merit separate disclosure for this reason.

Prior Period Adjustments

Prior period adjustments involve corrections of earnings of a previous period. They are charges or credits made directly to retained earnings and are thereby excluded from the determination of income of a current year.

From a broad, theoretical point of view, prior period adjustments are required in a number of circumstances. In practice, the situations in which prior period adjustments are permissible have been severely restricted. They should theoretically (though *not* in practice) be made any time an estimate used in the determination of revenue or expense turns out to be less than 100 percent correct. If, for example, a firm has based depreciation of a long-lived asset on an anticipated useful life of 10 years but in fact has to retire the asset after 6 years, then income of each of the 6 years in which the asset has been used will have been overstated (as depreciation expense will have been understated) and should properly be corrected. Income of the year of retirement should not be burdened with the loss attributable to the premature disposition of the asset.

Prior period adjustments should also be made when the accounting effects of certain events or transactions that could not be determined with certainty in a prior period are finally resolved. As the result of a settlement with income tax authorities a firm might be required to pay back taxes on income earned in a previous period. The tax expense should properly be charged against income of the period to which it is related.

Similarly, if a firm changes an accounting principle, then it might also have to make a prior period adjustment. If, for example, a firm switches from a policy of recognizing revenue on long-term construction contracts on a percentage of completion basis to one of recognizing revenue at time of delivery, then it might be necessary to adjust accumulated earnings of prior years. Otherwise, revenue on the same project might be recognized twice.

To avoid the confusion that would result from frequent adjustments of prior period earnings, the ARC set forth specific criteria as to when prior period adjustments should be made. Adjustments should be limited to those items which (1) can be specifically identified with and directly related to the business activities of a particular prior period, (2) are not attributable to economic events occurring after the prior period, (3) depend primarily on determinations by persons other than management, *and* (4) were not susceptible of reasonable estimation prior to such determination. Prior period adjustments, according to the ARC, should be rare. Examples of events that require prior period adjustments are settlements of income taxes and settlements of litigation that relate to a previous period. But gains or losses resulting from changes in the useful lives of fixed assets do not, according to the ARC, warrant adjustment of prior period earnings.

EXAMPLE

A firm had reported net income for 19x6 of $1.5 million and retained earnings as of December 31, 19x6 of $8 million. In 19x7, as the result of an audit by the Department of National Revenue, the firm was required to pay additional income taxes, applicable to earnings of 19x6, of $200,000. The following journal entry in 19x7 would give effect to the payment of the additional taxes:

Retained earnings	$200,000	
Cash		$200,000
To record the payment of taxes applicable to income of 19x6.		

If, at the end of 19x7, the firm were to present comparative income statements for the years 19x6 and 19x7, then income of 19x6 would be adjusted to reflect the additional $200,000 in tax expense.

A comparative *statement of retained earnings* for the two years is presented below. A statement of retained earnings summarizes all activity in the retained earnings account for a period. It is included in corporate annual reports either as a separate statement or as a part of the income statement. (Assume that for 19x7 income was $2 million and that the firm paid dividends of $400,000 in each of the two years. Assume also that retained earnings at the beginning of 19x6 was previously reported to be $6.9 million.)

Statement of Retained Earnings
Years Ended December 31, 19x7 and 19x6

	19x7	*19x6*
Retained earnings at beginning of year:		
As previously reported	$8,000,000	$6,900,000
Adjustments (to be explained in a footnote)	(200,000)	—
As restated	$7,800,000	$6,900,000
Net income	2,000,000	1,300,000
Retained earnings prior to declaration of dividends	$9,800,000	$8,200,000
Cash dividends on common shares	400,000	400,000
Retained earnings at end of year	$9,400,000	$7,800,000

Although income for 19x6 was originally reported in the financial statements of 19x6 as $1.5 million, it would be restated in the comparative statements of income and retained earnings which would appear in the 19x6 annual report at $1.3 million. Beginning in 19x8, the January 1, 19x7, balance in retained earnings (previously reported in the 19x6 annual report at $8 million) would be reduced by $200,000 to $7.8 million.

Earnings per Share

If any one single measure of corporate performance is of primary concern to common shareholders and potential investors, it is unquestionably earnings per share (EPS). In its simplest form, calculation of earnings per share is straightforward:

$$\frac{\text{Net earnings} - \text{Preferred share dividends}}{\text{Number of common shares outstanding}}$$

Net earnings should be those after income taxes. Preferred share dividends must be deducted from earnings, since preferred dividends generally reduce the equity of common shareholders. An exception would occur when the preferred share dividends are *not cumulative* (something which is rare today) and have not been declared. *Cumulative* means that if the directors fail to declare the (usually) quarterly preferred dividend, then common shareholders would not receive a dividend until unpaid, outstanding preferred share dividends have been paid.

The number of shares outstanding should be based on the average number of shares outstanding during the year. This average would be weighted by the number of months the shares may have been outstanding. The average number of shares outstanding, rather than simply the number outstanding at year end, must be used in the denominator. This takes into account that the corporation may have had the use of the capital associated with any additional shares issued during the year for only a part of the year. The company's opportunity to generate earnings on the additional capital would have been limited by the number of months it had the use of such capital.

EXAMPLE

A firm had earnings after taxes of $800,000. It paid preferred share dividends of $200,000. It had 200,000 common shares outstanding since January 1. On October 1, it issued an additional 100,000 common shares.

Earnings available to common shareholders would be $600,000 (earnings after income taxes less preferred dividends declared). The average number of shares outstanding would be

200,000 shares × 9 months	1,800,000
300,000 shares × 3 months	900,000
	2,700,000
Divided by 12 months	÷ 12
	225,000 shares

Earnings per common share would be

$$\frac{\$600,000}{225,000} = \$2.67.$$

As a consequence of the complex capital structures of many firms, the straightforward computation of earnings per share may be misleading. Although the average number of shares actually outstanding during a year is, by year end, a historical fact, many firms have *already incurred commitments* (by having already granted warrants or options or sold convertible bonds or preferred shares) to issue additional shares in the future. If earnings per share are to have predictive value — if they are to be a useful guide toward future earnings per share — then the number of shares already committed to be issued in the future must also be taken into account. Otherwise earnings per share may take a precipitous drop in the period in which the additional shares are issued.

It is important to recognize that the obligation to issue the additional common shares stems from commitments contained in contracts or in other securities that may be outstanding: share rights, warrants, and options as well as bonds and preferred shares that might be converted into common shares. Earnings per share, as it is computed by accountants in Canada, does *not* attempt to account for the effect of new share issues made after the company's year end. An exception to this occurs only when (1) any share issues made shortly after the year end are as a result of commitments (such as share options or convertible debt or preferred shares) made prior to the year end, *and* (2) the shares sold *replace* bonds or other shares which existed prior to the year end. By following such an approach, accountants avoid engaging in forecasting. They merely reshuffle the EPS figure based on an already-known numerator, net income (after preferred dividends), plus hindsight about the denominator. This would include bond and share changes made up until the financial statements are finalized (which often is two weeks to four months after the year end).

When a firm has a complex capital structure — one that includes such securities that could potentially result in the *dilution* of earnings per share — the calculation of earnings per share becomes both subjective and complicated: subjective because it must necessarily be based on a number of estimates and assumptions, and complicated because the issue of the additional shares will affect not only the number of shares outstanding but overall corporate earnings as well.

The ARC became concerned in the late 1960s about the diversity of EPS computations which were being made by various analysts and accountants. The general public at that time seemed to be losing faith not only in the various EPS computations but in many other accounting figures as well. Hence, the ARC felt obligated to issue a pronouncement (or constraint according to the terms in this book) on the subject in an attempt to restore faith.

Before proceeding with a description of portions of their pronouncement it is important to place the entire matter of EPS in perspective. First, we have noted many times that net income as computed by accountants is a rough figure subject to considerable variation depending upon which accounting principles are chosen. Second, EPS is a ratio which in turn is used in the computation of another ratio, called the price/earnings ratio, having crude implications. The latter indicates the number of years of current earnings which one is paying for a share, based on its current market price. For example, if the current market price of one share is $10 and the EPS is $2, you are paying for five years of future earnings. There are many rough edges in such a computation. One, which you recall from Chapter 6, is that a dollar earned five years from now is not worth the same as a dollar earned today.

Nevertheless, the EPS and price/earnings ratios are widely quoted by stockbrokers. If used within the same company over a period of years these ratios may have merit. There are dangers in using them to compare two or more companies.

Canadian Practice

The ARC, unlike FASB in the U.S., recommended the use of as many as five different EPS computations per year for a company with a complex capital structure and particular types of financing. Since these computations could be based both on income before and after extraordinary items, a company might have to report as many as 10 different EPS figures each year. In one sense the existence of 10 different EPS figures for one year seems ludicrous. Yet, it also may provide the caution which users/readers should have towards the entire EPS exercise. Observe that Labatt's income statement in Chapter 2 shows only two EPS figures: basic, and fully diluted.

We intend to illustrate only the basic and fully diluted EPS computations, which are most frequently seen in practice. The others are fairly complex and can be saved for later courses for those who wish to major in accountancy.

Suppose that a company has the following capital structure as of December 31, 19x10:

Bonds payable, 10% due December 31, 19x25, convertible into five common shares for each $100	$2,000,000
Preferred shares, 12% dividend, cumulative	3,000,000
Common shares; issued 500,000	5,000,000
Retained earnings	2,600,000

In addition, 100,000 share options have been granted to employees to purchase common shares at $10 each. No shares were issued during 19x10. The current income tax rate is 40 percent. Net income for 19x10 was $1,100,000. Finally, the company anticipates that it will earn 8 percent after income taxes on new funds which come into the company.

Our *basic EPS* computation is therefore:

$$\frac{\text{Net income} - \text{Preferred dividends}}{\text{Average number of common shares outstanding}}.$$

$$\frac{\$1{,}100{,}000 - (12\% \times 3{,}000{,}000)}{500{,}000 \text{ shares}} = \$1.48 \text{ per share.}$$

Clearly the $1.48 basic earnings per share is not of much use to those whose objective is to predict future cash flows of the company and estimate the per share worth of the company at various future dates. Why? One reason is that the company has *already* issued *dilutive* securities which cause the common shareholders to have to share income at some future date. A dilutive security has the effect of lowering basic EPS.

In our illustration both the bond payable and the share options are dilutive at a $1.48 per share basic EPS:

(1) Bonds payable: The annual interest expense is $200,000 (10 percent × $2,000,000), which has the effect after income taxes of 40 percent of causing net income to be $120,000 ($200,000 − $80,000) lower than if the bonds did not exist. However, if they did not exist — that is, they were converted into 100,000 ($2,000,000/$100 × 5) common shares — they would raise net income but earn only $1.20 ($120,000 ÷ 100,000 shares) per share — which is below $1.48 and is therefore dilutive.

(2) Share options: Each share option brings $10 additional cash into the company. If on an after-income-tax basis the $10 generates only 80¢ ($10 @ 8%) of net income, the effect on EPS is $0.80. This, too, is below the $1.48; and there are 100,000 options outstanding.

Hence, when we recalculate the EPS after assuming that (1) all of the bondholders converted their bonds into common shares, and (2) all holders of the share options exercised them, *even though neither group did*, the EPS is:

	$	*Shares*	*EPS*
Basic	$740,000	500,000	$1.48
Bonds payable	120,000	100,000	
Share options	80,000	100,000	
	$940,000	700,000	$1.34

The ARC calls the $1.34 *fully diluted EPS*.

The $1.34 reflects a pessimistic view, from the common shareholder's **stand-point**, because it assumes, perhaps unjustifiably, that all holders of dilutive securities will acquire common shares immediately. The justification for the pessimism is interesting. Fully diluted earnings per share is an *outer boundary*. That is, it provides the worst possible result (assuming, of course, that net income remains at $1,100,000). Future "reality," presumably, lies somewhere between basic and fully diluted.

To repeat, with the exception of the 8 percent which we *imputed* as an investment yield on the share options (which amount is usually not *material*), the foregoing EPS computations are anchored to the 19x10 net income figure of $1,100,000. We have not forecast next year's income; nor have we forecast next year's sales of bonds or shares and imputed a net income or interest rate thereon. What we did juggle for our EPS computations was potential changes in the *current* capital structure.

As a result, the fully diluted EPS and the other three which we did not illustrate (called adjusted basic, pro forma basic, and pro forma fully diluted) are *not* forecasted EPS. Therefore they are not overly useful to those interested in the prediction objective of accounting, though they might serve as a starting point for predictions. Given the assumptions, the EPS figures may also not be of much use to those interested in stewardship — unless the company's capital structure (debt-equity mix) were fairly simple. They are, however, a rough guide or approximation and to many are better than no indicator.

Canadian accounting practitioners introduced their standardized computations in a period of corporate expansion with considerable creativity of new types of shares and bond sweeteners among underwriters. At that time accounting responded to the changing environment. In the past decade the environment has altered again. Maybe the approach to EPS should undergo revisions. It will, when current methods are sufficiently annoying to preparers and users.

Interim Financial Reports

Publicly traded corporations are required, and many other firms elect, to issue interim financial reports. Interim financial reports are those that cover less than a full year; commonly they cover a quarter year. The interim reports of most companies are not nearly so detailed as their annual reports; sometimes they provide only a few key indicators of performance such as sales or net income and earnings per share — often they include comparative income statements and statements of changes in financial position for the most recent quarter and the financial year to date.

The accounting principles to be followed in calculating income for a period of a quarter or half year are the same as those followed for a full year. Nevertheless, meaningful determination of income for short periods presents inherent difficulties. In an earlier chapter it was pointed out that over the life of an enterprise determination of income is relatively simple. Most accounting problems arise because of the need for financial information on a periodic basis. Revenues and expenses must be assigned to specific accounting periods long before the full consequences of a transaction are known with certainty. Prepaid and deferred costs must be *stored* in asset and liability accounts pending allocation to earnings of particular years. To the extent that interim periods are shorter than annual periods, the related problems of income determination and asset valuation are correspondingly greater. It becomes considerably more difficult to associate revenues with productive effort and to match expired costs with revenues.

The problems of preparing interim financial reports are compounded by the fact that whereas a period of a year will often correspond to a firm's natural business cycle, periods shorter than a year may be characterized by seasonal fluctuations in both revenues and expenses. Indeed, some revenues and expenses (such as bonuses to key personnel) are determined on an annual basis; they cannot readily be calculated for a period less than a year until results for the entire year are known. As a consequence, meaningful interim reports cannot be prepared for any one period without consideration of anticipated financial activities in subsequent periods. For example, a company typically could have losses in the first quarter, but four times out of five it could generate a profit for the entire year.

Some firms permit customers quantity discounts based on cumulative purchases during the year. The discount may not take effect until the customer has reached a specified level of purchases — a level not likely to be attained until the third or fourth quarter of the year. Prices — and revenues — will appear to be higher in the earlier quarters than the later ones. Unless an adjustment to revenues is made to take into account the discounts to be granted in the future, the interim reports will overstate earnings. In the same vein, firms may traditionally incur certain major costs in a particular season. Major repairs, for example, may be undertaken during a firm's "slow" season, but they benefit the entire year. Unless these expenditures are taken into account and spread over the entire year, the interim reports for each individual period may be misleading.

A pronouncement of the ARC deals specifically with issues of interim reports. It emphasizes that each interim period should be viewed as an integral part of an annual period and that, as appropriate, adjustments should be made to expenses and revenues to take into account benefits received or costs incurred in other periods. Although the pronouncement helped provide for greater uniformity of practice among firms, it did not (and, of course, could not) eliminate the underlying weaknesses of interim reports. Interim reports necessarily are based on an even greater number of subjective assumptions, estimates, and allocations than annual reports. They provide financial information for a relatively short period of time; if a business is seasonal, they cannot be relied upon as predictors of earnings for the remaining periods of the year. If carefully prepared, they can serve as a useful means of comparing performance in one quarter with that in a corresponding quarter of a prior year, though usually not among quarters of the same year. Interim reports unquestionably provide information that is of value to investors and other users of financial reports — but only if the users are aware of their inherent limitations.

Diversified Companies

In the next chapter we become involved with the problems of preparing consolidated (and other sorts of combined) statements for companies which hold voting shares of other companies. The consolidated statements require the aggregation or combining of net asset and income data. When we aggregate figures, by definition we both provide total, and destroy detailed, information and perspectives. What we destroy by consolidating is a look at the profitability of different, perhaps widely different, operating segments or divisions of the company. For instance, a large company with ownership in several other companies (using CPR as an example), could be involved in such diverse activities as real estate development, pulp and paper, rail transportation, air transportation, shipping, and steel making.

An investor needs more than interim or quarterly reports, and the annual financial statements prepared on an aggregate basis, as is seen in the Labatt's statements shown in Chapter 2. This need would especially apply to those outside readers whose objectives are to evaluate the performance of management or to predict (future) cash flows. A person interested in a pure stewardship objective may not care. Someone interested in evaluation or prediction would want to know the relative profitability of steelmaking versus air transportation. What would happen to overall profits if there were a strike in the shipping division?

The accounting profession's response to the difficulty of trying to predict from aggregated data is to suggest the use of divisional or segment reporting of *separable* income and net assets. That is, when the net assets are *not* common to all divisions (eg. head office assets are common to all), and revenue and costs can be separated by division or segment this information would be reported: total segment revenue, segment operating profit and segment identifiable assets. Unfortunately, the segment tabulations may not be complete because of the existence of assets which are common to several divisions, and because of non-arm's-length transfers between divisions. The real estate division may lease office and plant space to the airline division. Unless the lease calls for "market value" rental payments, the relative profitability of each segment or division may be artificial.

A divisional reporting for Labatt's in 1978 may appear as follows: (in thousands of dollars):

	Consolidated	*Brewing*	*Consumer Products*	*Agri Products*
Gross sales	$997,263	$512,351	$256,739	$28,173
Income before income taxes and interest expense	$ 66,679	$ 46,946	$ 7,749	$ 11,984
Interest expense	$ 14,499			
Income before income taxes	$ 52,180			
Assets employed in each division	$403,781	$182,092	$136,423	$ 78,266
Return on investment (or assets employed) *after* income taxes	10.3%	15.4%	3.5%	9.5%

Observe that Labatt's has not tried to break down by division items below the line "income before income taxes and interest expense." The figures may be too intertwined to be separable and informative. Labatt's has also shown the historic cost of the net assets used to generate the "income" and has computed a rate of return (income before income taxes and interest expense divided by assets employed in each division). As we observe in Chapter 16, the rate of return on current values may be much different.

A caution is in order. Accountants are sometimes not able to convince corporate managers of the need for greater disclosure to satisfy some groups of users. Diversified or segment reporting is such an example. The ARC, because of resistance from industry, does not forcefully push the idea of extensive, quarterly segment reporting; however, it does require publicly traded enterprises to provide segment data on an annual basis.

Forecast Figures

From time to time, the public and some accountants advocate external reporting of expected future (budgeted) income statements and balance sheets. They feel this information would be of immense help to some users of financial statements, (such as those interested in predicting corporate cash flows for the next several years). Both management and many accountants have resisted such suggestions because (1) they fear law suits (from those who use the information and suffer losses) and (2) they may not be confident of their estimates.

The ARC of the CICA is moving towards optional disclosure of budgeted or next year's condensed financial data and results. This probably means that only a few companies will exercise the option in the early 1980s. In order to do so they will have to disclose a considerable amount of detail about the economic and environmental assumptions which they have made in preparing the forecast. For example, what inflation rate, unemployment rate, and change in gross national expenditure are they expecting? When the assumptions are given and hindsight shows them to be slightly inaccurate, the user is still able to revise the forecast data to suit her needs.

All three of the subjects we have just discussed — interim, segment, and forecast reporting — are attempts to provide more timely and detailed information which helps readers/users to assess the *risk* (among other factors) of their investment. Such an exercise in reporting also can have beneficial results for preparers. First, a sound assessment of risk by investors might help the company in borrowing at more favorable interest or dividend rates. Second, detailed reporting can prevent needless speculations about a company, and the needless losses of human energy which occur during speculative periods. Third, the search for information for external reporting might encourage management of some companies to improve their internal or management accounting systems — and thereby improve management and profitability.

Summary

To a large extent in this chapter we have dealt with the relationships between a corporation and its shareholders. The manner in which a corporation raises additional capital and distributes it is obviously of critical concern to existing shareholders. It is likely to have an important impact upon both their absolute and proportionate interests in the corporation. But so also is the manner in which capital transactions are accounted for. The accounting practices of a firm may affect not only the legal and economic interests of shareholders but also may influence the policies of management.

In this chapter we have also explored selected problems of reporting earnings to shareholders and other interested parties. We have attempted to demonstrate that as a consequence of complex capital structures the computation of earnings per share is likewise complex. The difficulties of measuring income are compounded several fold as the period of measurement is reduced from one year to a few months.

Yet, there can be benefits to both preparers/management and users/readers from continuing efforts to improve interim, segment and forecast reporting in spite of technical, legal, and attitudinal problems on the horizon.

Notes

[1]See W. Beaver and D. Morse, "What Determines Price-Earnings Ratios?," *Financial Analysts Journal* (July–August 1978), pp. 65–76.

Questions, Problems, and Cases

Questions

12-1 Distinguish, in your own words, among the following:
a. Dividends in kind
b. Share dividends
c. Share splits
d. Share options
e. Share rights
f. Share warrants
Briefly describe how each transaction is recorded in the accounts.

12-2 A 100 percent share dividend is in effect a share split. Explain. Why is the accounting for both transactions not the same?

12-3 Some people argue that share dividends merely represent a reclassification of existing shareholders' equity. Others would argue that they have potential benefits for both the company and its shareholders. Explain the reasoning underlying each argument and indicate which one you agree with, giving your reasons and assumptions.

12-4 Share capital is legally regarded in some jurisdictions as protection for creditors, more than retained earnings which are available for dividends. Does this make economic sense? Explain how the requirement to record the issue of share dividends at fair market value, in some jurisdictions, stems largely from this legal view. Is it an objective, a fact, or a constraint that determines accounting treatment in this instance?

12-5 Dividends are sometimes said to be "paid out of retained earnings." Yet for many corporations, especially those that have been in existence for, and have expanded over, a period of several years, the balance in retained earnings is of little consequence in the decision as to the amount of dividends that can be declared. Why?

12-6 A firm owns 10,000 shares of another corporation. It wishes to distribute the shares to its shareholders as a dividend in kind. The shares were purchased by the company at a price of $4 per share. They have a present market value of $10 per share. If the company were to distribute the shares to its shareholders, how much gain on the transaction would the company report? If alternatively the company were to sell the shares first and then distribute the cash to the shareholders, how much gain on the transaction would the company report? How much revenue would the individual shareholders realize? How do you account for the inconsistency? What characteristic of the conventional accounting model allows for this inconsistency?

12-7 What information useful for decision-making is lost to readers when, upon exercise of a share option by an employee, the share capital is credited with the amount of cash received and not current market value? Similarly, what information is lost to readers when dividends in kind are recorded by the issuer at cost of the asset, rather than the asset's fair market value? Do you have suggestions in each case for getting this information to readers of financial statements? In what way does this illustrate the basic theme that the objectives of accounting are sometimes in conflict?

12-8 The following excerpt of a conversation was overheard in a crowded elevator: "I just heard that IBM is going to split its shares two for one. The announcement will be made later this week so you'd better purchase a few hundred shares before everyone else hears about it and the price skyrockets." Assuming that the tip is reliable, is there any rational reason for the price of IBM to "skyrocket?" Why do companies split their shares?

12-9 Is accounting recognition given to executive share options in the period that they are first issued? If not, why not and when does accounting recognition come into play?

*12-10 In calculating earnings per share, why is it necessary to make assumptions as to what a firm will do with any cash received when options are exercised? Does this amount to forecasting on the part of the accountant? Why not simply add the potential number of shares to be issued to the number of shares currently outstanding?

12-11 Distinguish between the *current operating* and the *all-inclusive* concepts of income. What types of events are likely to be accounted for differently if one, as opposed to the other, concept were accepted? In what sense does the research into stock market efficiency suggest that it doesn't matter all that much to public company shareholders which concept is used?

12-12 "The deficiencies and limitations of financial statements are magnified many times when such reports are prepared on a quarterly rather than an annual basis." Do you agree? Explain. In what sense do quarterly reports facilitate the prediction objective of accounting?

12-13 *Reserves for contingencies* are an indication of prudent and sound management. Their presence on the balance sheet assures investors that the company has "saved for a rainy day." Do you agree? Explain.

12-14 It has been observed that earnings per share is the only financial ratio that accountants compute for statement users. Why did the Accounting Research Committee choose to standardize this computation and not others involving ratios? What does this seem to assume about user preferences?

12-15 Explain, in your own words, the distinction between basic earnings per share and fully diluted earnings per share. For which objectives of accounting are each calculated? Explain.

Problems

P12-1 The balance sheet of Cannon Industries Ltd. reports the following amounts:

Cash		$ 1,000,000
Marketable securities		4,000,000
Other assets		15,000,000
Total assets		$20,000,000
Liabilities		$ 7,000,000
Common shares (500,000 shares issued and outstanding)	$4,000,000	
Retained earnings	9,000,000	13,000,000
Total liabilities and shareholders' equity		$20,000,000

Marketable securities include 300,000 shares of Consolidated Industries Ltd., which were purchased at a cost of $6 per share.

In past years the company has paid annual dividends of $4 per share. This year the company is considering two other alternatives to a cash dividend which it hopes will have "equal value" to shareholders:

1. A dividend in kind of shares of Consolidated Industries Ltd. The market value of the shares is $8 per share. The company would distribute to shareholders one share of Consolidated for each two shares of Cannon owned — a total of 250,000 shares.
2. A share dividend. The market value of Cannon Industries' shares is $80 per share. The company would distribute one additional share for each 20 shares presently owned — a total of 25,000 shares.

Required:

a. Prepare journal entries that would be required if the company were to issue (i) the dividend in kind, (ii) the share dividend, (iii) the cash dividend of $4 per share.

b. Which transaction leaves (i) the shareholder (ii) the company better off? Ignore tax considerations.

P12-2 Three firms in the same industry adopted different policies with respect to casualty insurance. Firm A purchased insurance from an outside company for $10,000 per year. Firm B *self-insured* against losses. Each year it contributed $10,000 to a special insurance fund (e.g., a bank account designated for the purpose). Firm C established a *reserve for insurance*. Each year it set aside $10,000 of retained earnings and added it to the reserve. The charge to retained earnings was made directly; it was not initially charged as a current expense (i.e., it was treated as an appropriation of retained earnings).

Each of the three firms estimated that, over a long period of time, it would incur a major loss (estimated to be in the range of $40,000 to $60,000) on the average of once every five years.

Assume that each of the three firms incurred a loss of $50,000 in the third year after having adopted its policy with respect to insurance.

Also, assume that Firms A, B, and C have incomes before tax of $500,000, $100,000, and $1,000,000 respectively.

Required:

a. Prepare journal entries for all three firms to record the events described, including the loss. Briefly explain the reasons for your entries.

b. Compare the impact of the policies on earnings of the three firms during the three-year period.

c. Comment on the relative abilities of the firms to sustain the losses.

P12-3 As of January 1, 19x7, the shareholders' equity section of Arrow Industries Ltd. contained the following balances:

Common shares (12,500,000 shares issued and outstanding)	$255,000,000
Retained earnings	300,000,000
	$555,000,000

In 19x7 the company had earnings of $20,000,000.

In 19x6 the company had declared cash dividends of $1.50 per share. In 19x7, however, the board of directors wished to use all available cash to pand facilities. It decided instead to issue a share (stock) dividend "equivalent in value" (based on market prices) to the cash dividend.

The market price of the firm's common shares on December 31, 19x7 was $60 per share.

Required:

a. How many additional common shares should the company issue?

b. Prepare a journal entry to record the distribution of the additional shares.

c. Comment on whether the shareholders are equally well off having received the share rather than the cash dividend.

P12-4 The Warwick Co. Ltd. had adopted a share option plan which entitles selected executives to purchase its common shares at $40 per share, the price at which the shares were being traded in the open market on the date the plan was adopted.

The plan provides that the options may be exercised one year after being received provided that the executive is still employed by the company. The options lapse, however, 2½ years after they have been issued.

Each option entitles the executive to purchase one common share. Common shares are without par value.

The following transactions or events with respect to the option plan took place over a period of years:

12/31/x1: The company issued 1,000 options to its executives. Market price of the shares on that date was $52.

12/31/x2: The company issued an additional 2,000 options. Market price of the shares was $35.

7/1/x3: Executives exercised 800 of the options issued in 19x1. Market price of the common shares was $42.

3/6/x4: Executives exercised 1,000 of the options issued in 19x2. Market price of the common shares was $48.

6/30/x5: The remaining 200 of the options issued in 19x1 lapsed. Market price of the common shares was $47.

Required:

a. Prepare journal entries, as required, to record the above transactions and events. Justify your entries with respect to the objectives for accounting information.

b. What information should be disclosed in a note to the company's annual statements each year? Why?

c. Suppose the options could be freely bought and sold. How much would a rational buyer be willing to pay for the options at the dates they were issued?

P12-5 The Mineral Wells Mining Co. Ltd. was organized in 19x7 for the sole purpose of extracting ore from a deposit that the company intended to purchase. It is anticipated that after the property is mined, the company will be dissolved.

The company issued 10,000 common shares at a price of $110 per share. It purchased the property for $1 million cash.

During its first year of operations the company extracted 25 percent of the available ore. It had sales revenue of $400,000 and operating expenses and taxes of $100,000, *excluding* depletion. All revenues were received, and all operating expenses were paid, in cash.

The company estimates that it requires an operating cash balance of $100,000.

Required:

a. Prepare an income statement and a balance sheet which would reflect the results of operations for the first year. State your assumptions.
b. Based entirely on the cash requirements of the firm, what is the maximum cash dividend it can afford to pay?
c. Prepare a journal entry to record payment of such "dividend." (Debit shareholders' equity accounts directly rather than "dividends.")
d. The statutes of many jurisdictions prohibit companies from paying dividends in amounts greater than the existing balance in retained earnings. The purpose of the restriction is to assure that distributions of corporate assets are not made to shareholders at the expense of creditors. Do you think that such restrictions should apply to companies organized to extract minerals from specific properties? What would be the impact, over time, of such restrictions on the assets of the companies?

P12-6 As of January 1, 19x7, the owners' equity section of Active Equity Ltd. contained the following balances:

Common shares, (100,000 shares issued and outstanding)	$1,000,000
Retained earnings	800,000
	$1,800,000

During 19x7 the following events took place:

1. On January 7, the company issued to executives options to purchase 2,000 common shares at a price of $25 per share. The market price of the common shares on that date was $28 per share.
2. On February 10, the company declared a cash dividend of $.50 per share. The dividend was paid on February 23.
3. On March 7, executives exercised options to purchase 2,000 shares. The market price of the common shares on that day was $26 per share.
4. On May 10, in lieu of its usual quarterly cash dividend, the company declared and paid a dividend in kind. The company distributed to shareholders 5,000 common shares of Temporary Investment Ltd. The prevailing market price for the shares was $10 per share; they had been purchased previously, and recorded on the books of Active Equity Ltd. at a price of $2 per share.
5. On August 10, the company declared and paid a share dividend equal in value (based on the current market price of the shares issued) to the $.50 per share of its traditional quarterly dividend. The market price of the shares on that date was $25.
6. On December 17, the company declared a share split. For each old share owned, shareholders would be given *two* new shares.

7. On December 28, the company issued to executives the options to purchase 4,000 common shares at a price of $12.50 per share. The market price of the shares on that date was $10 per share.

Required:

Prepare journal entries to record the above events. (Debit any dividends directly to the shareholders' equity accounts affected rather than to "dividends".) State your assumptions.

P12-7 Beedle Industries Ltd. is a company whose shares are actively traded on several Canadian security exchanges.

Beedle Industries Ltd. decided in 19x5 to divest itself of one of its divisions, which contributed 30 percent of sales, due to continued losses over the past few years.

The sequence of events is as follows: (Assume all amounts are very material.)

19x5: The shareholders approved a plan to sell the division. Management's best estimate of the loss on disposal is in the range of $500,000 to $1,000,000.

19x6: An agreement is signed with a buyer of the division and actual losses turn out to be $900,000.

Required:

a. Assume you are the controller of Beedle and you are finalizing the 19x5 financial statements, with no knowledge of the 19x6 events. What accounting treatment would you recommend for the anticipated loss? Be specific.

b. Assume you are the auditor of Beedle. What treatment would you like to see in the 19x5 statements? You have no knowledge of 19x6 events.

c. Prepare journal entries to record the 19x6 events. State your assumptions.

d. Would the 19x6 loss meet the requirements for a prior period adjustment? Explain.

e. Would the 19x6 loss be shown on the income statement as an extraordinary item? Explain.

P12-8 The question of how best to report upon pending litigation and final settlement of claims resulting from such litigation has always been a troublesome one to accountants. Assume the following facts:

In 19x4 a major manufacturer of electrical equipment is charged by a group of customers with engaging in pricing practices that are in violation of antitrust statutes. The alleged illegal activities took place in the years 19x1 to 19x3. The customers file suit in federal court; they seek damages totaling $36 million.

Attorneys for the defendant confidentially advise their client to "be prepared for a final judgment between $10 million and $20 million."

In 19x7, after a lengthy trial, the company is found liable to the plaintiffs for $20 million in damages. The company announces its intention to appeal.

In 19x8, an appeals court reverses the decision of the lower court and orders a new trial.

In 19x9, the company agrees to an out-of-court settlement with the plaintiffs. The firm will pay damages of $6 million.

In 19x10, the company pays the agreed upon amounts to the plaintiffs.

Required:

How, in your judgment (irrespective of any official pronouncements on the subject), do you think the company ought to account for the litigation? Indicate any specific journal entry that you think the company should make during or at the end of each of the years in question. Consider the possibility of making supplementary disclosures in footnotes to the financial statements. Bear in mind that the financial statements will be public documents, available to the plaintiffs and their attorneys.

P12-9 In 19x1, Southern Telephone Company Ltd. reported earnings of $6.5 million.

In 19x2, however, as a consequence of a suit filed by a consumer action group, a court ruled that the rates charged by the company were improperly high. The company was ordered to refund to customers $400,000 in overcharges applicable to 19x1. The net cost of the refunds to the company after taxes was $240,000.

In 19x2, the company had earnings after taxes (prior to taking into account refunds paid to its customers) of $6.4 million. Retained earnings as of January 1, 19x1 were $25.2 million. In 19x1 the company declared dividends of $4 million, and in 19x2, $4.2 million.

Required:

Prepare a comparative statement of retained earnings for 19x1 and 19x2. Be sure your statement gives effect to any prior period adjustments that might be required. Explain the reasoning underlying the prior period adjustments you make.

P12-10 In 19x6, the Convertible Company Ltd. had earnings after taxes and before dividends of $300,000. The company has 100,000 common shares issued and outstanding. The corporate income tax rate may be assumed to be 40 percent.

In addition, the company has outstanding $500,000 of bonds that are convertible into common shares. Each $1,000 of bonds may be converted into 40 common shares.

The company also has outstanding 3,000 convertible preferred shares. Each preferred share may be exchanged for five common shares. The preferred shares carry a dividend rate of $10 per share.

Required:

a. Determine basic earnings per share.
b. Determine fully diluted earnings per share.
c. What is the purpose of fully diluted earnings per share?

P12-11 Options Ltd. had earnings after taxes in 19x2 of $800,000. The company had 200,000 common shares outstanding. The current market price of the common shares at the company's year end was $25 per share.

In 19x1, the company adopted a share option plan. Currently outstanding are 50,000 options which enable the holder to purchase one share each at $20 per share and 10,000 options which may be exercised for one share each at $10 per share. The company expects to earn 10 percent after income taxes on new funds. The company has 10,000 convertible preferred shares outstanding, which carry a dividend rate of $8 per share. Each share is convertible into three common shares.

Required:

a. Determine basic earnings per share.
b. Determine fully diluted earnings per share.
c. Do you feel fully diluted earnings per share is more informative than basic earnings per share for Options Ltd.'s shareholders? Why?

P12-12 For the first three months in 19x1, the Timely Company Ltd. according to its president, had earnings before income taxes of $140,000, determined as follows:

Sales		$420,000
Cost of goods sold	$200,000	
Other expenses	80,000	280,000
Income before income taxes		$140,000

The following additional information has come to your attention:

1. The company gives quantity discounts to its customers based on total purchases for the year. No quantity discounts have been allowed to date. The firm estimates that total sales for the year, at *gross* sales price, will be $2 million. After taking into account quantity discounts, $200,000 of the sales will be at 95 percent of gross sales price (a discount of $10,000) and $400,000 will be at 90 percent of gross sales price (a discount of $40,000).
2. The company uses the LIFO inventory method and determines year-end inventory and the annual cost of goods sold on the basis of a periodic inventory count, which is taken on December 31 of each year. The cost of goods sold for the quarter ending March 31 was calculated as follows:

Goods on hand 1/1/x1: 30,000 units @ $5	$150,000	
Production, 1st quarter: 10,000 units @ $10	100,000	$250,000
Estimated goods on hand 3/31/x1: 10,000 units @ $5		50,000
Cost of goods sold, 30,000 units		$200,000

   The company estimates that it will complete the year with an inventory of 30,000 units. As a consequence, the ending inventory will be stated at $5 per unit. The firm will not have to "dip" into its LIFO stock. The cost of goods sold for the entire year will be based on current production costs of $10 per unit.
3. The company overhauls its plant once a year in July at a cost of $20,000. The cost of the overhaul has not been taken into account in computing first-quarter expenses.
4. Each December the company gives its salaried employees a bonus equal to approximately 10 percent of their annual salaries. First-quarter salaries (included in other expenses), without taking into account the bonus, amounted to $75,000. The bonus has not been included in first-quarter expenses.
5. Assume that the current federal income tax rate is 25 percent on the first $25,000 of taxable income and 46 percent on all earnings above

that amount. The company estimates that taxable income for the entire year will be $80,000.

Required:

a. Determine earnings after taxes for the first quarter of 19x1 as you believe they should be reported to the general public.

b. Do you feel the interim report of Timely Company Ltd. helps users predict earnings for the entire year? Explain. What are some of the inherent limitations of Timely's interim report?

P12-13 Conglomerate Ltd. presents consolidated statements to its shareholders but has decided this year for the first time to report segmented information in a note to its financial statements. Conglomerate allocates head office charges to each of its divisions at a rate of 10 percent of divisional sales, which Conglomerate figures roughly recovers the costs of central research and development, bond interest, and office and administrative overhead. Head office admits that some divisions are overcharged, some are undercharged, and that the charge is somewhat arbitrary. Divisional managers are paid a bonus based on divisional results.

Required:

a. Do you feel reporting, as segmented data, divisional earnings before income taxes makes sense for Conglomerate Ltd.? If not, how would you suggest reporting divisional results?

b. On what figure should the annual bonus for divisional managers be based? Why?

c. In general, what is the purpose of reporting segmented information to users? What are some of the inherent limitations of this information?

Cases

C12-1 Crystall Ball Ltd. is an established company whose shares are actively traded on a major Canadian securities exchange. The company has a sophisticated internal budgeting system which has been used for several years. On average, the forecasting error of net income (actual for year compared to budget) has been in the range of ± 10 percent.

The President of Crystall Ball is interested in disclosing forecasted net income in the President's Report section of the upcoming annual report, but wonders whether to forecast one net income figure or give a range, say $10,000,000 ± $1,000,000. He is concerned about the reliance users will place on this forecast, his legal liability in the event the forecast is wrong, and the tolerance of users for forecast errors. He would like to share some of this responsibility by getting the auditors of Crystall Ball Ltd. to attest to his forecast.

Required:

Assume the role of the controller of Crystall Ball Ltd. Prepare a report to the President addressing the concerns he has expressed regarding forecast figures.

C12-2 Foggy Limited's ("FL" or the company) main source of revenue is from the sale of "no brand" soft drinks to supermarket chains. With generic goods in the supermarkets, FL's profit has significantly improved during the past year. Volume is critical to the success of FL and therefore major attention has been directed at securing new contracts with supermarkets. The supermarkets have indicated they would prefer to deal with suppliers who can be relied upon for a steady source of supply. Accordingly, they avoid financially weak suppliers or new companies with no proven history of success.

Aside from the dramatic increase in profits, this past year, 19x1, has been an unusual one in that the following occurred:

1. FL is involved in litigation at the close of its fiscal year ending December 31, 19x1, and information available indicates that an unfavorable outcome is probable. Subsequently, after a trial on the issues, a verdict unfavorable to the enterprise is handed down, but the amount of damages remains unresolved at the time the financial statements are to be issued. Although the enterprise is unable to estimate the exact amount of the loss, its reasonable estimate at the time is that the judgement will be for not less than $300,000 or more than $900,000.
2. FL at December 31, 19x1, has an investment of $1,000,000 in the debentures of a concentrate supplier. The debentures are secured by the machinery and equipment (which is only a year old) of the supplier. The supplier recently declared bankruptcy. FL had loaned the supplier the money in the hopes of keeping the company going, as other brands of concentrate had proven to be inferior. FL is considering using the machinery to manufacture the concentrate itself, but is not sure it can match previous quality.
3. Effective January 2, 19x1, the anniversary date of its insurance policies, the company cancelled all its fire insurance coverage to "save" needed cash. The estimated total premium avoided was debited to an expense called "self-insurance provision."

Required:

a. Assume the role of an auditor. What would you recommend?
b. Assume the role of the controller of the company. What would you recommend?

C12-3 Mitchell Limited ("ML" or the company) is a Canadian public company incorporated under the Canada Business Corporations Act. It is successfully engaged in the manufacture of auto parts. While ML has a number of product lines, its most important line is auto bodies. The company's customers are primarily the three large car manufactuers — General Motors, Ford and Chrysler. Approximately 40 percent of the company's sales are made to plants in the United States. ML is listed on several Canadian stock exchanges and its shares are widely held and actively traded.

ML had, in 19x1, expanded its productive capacity in order to meet anticipated volume increases resulting from a contract signed with Ford. The equipment had cost $2,000,000 and was being depreciated on a straight-line basis over 20 years, the estimated life of the Ford contract. Without the Ford contract, the equipment would likely sit idle. Being very specialized, it has a low scrap value.

During the year 19x5, the company experienced the following major events:

1. On June 1, 19x5, ML acquired a piece of property consisting of land and a building from a company terminating its operations. This was a major change for ML. Previously, the company had leased its manufacturing facilities, but had decided to buy in order to make way for a planned plant expansion in anticipation of another large contract from Ford. The property had a list price of $1,000,000 and the building was insured for $500,000. ML acquired the property by issuing 100,000 common shares and assuming a first mortgage on the property in the amount of $150,000. On June 1, the common shares of ML were actively traded at $8⅜. Shortly after acquiring the property, real estate prices went soft and ML had an offer to buy the property from a large hotel chain for $800,000 cash.
2. In September, 19x5, the company learned that it had lost its contract to supply Ford with auto bodies effective January 1, 19x6.
3. In early October 19x5, ML announced it would be laying off 50 percent of its work force in response to losing all contracts with Ford. It indicated that it was actively seeking new contracts with other car manufacturers and that it was optimistic about the company's future.
4. In November 19x5, ML received a cheque for $3,000,000 from the Receiver General, the proceeds from a successful income tax appeal. ML had launched the appeal in 19x3 following a rather large reassessment on 19x2's taxable income as filed.

Required:

Assume the role of the controller of the company attempting to finalize the accounts of ML for the year ended December 31, 19x5, and:

a. identify the accounting problems facing the company.
b. indicate alternative accounting treatments which exist.
c. make recommendations including detailed disclosure for external financial statements, for the problems you have identified. Explain your recommendations, by referring to the accounting objectives, constraints, principles, etc., which you have used.

13 *Investments in Other Corporations*

This chapter examines the accounting and reporting issues that arise when a limited company acquires common shares of another company with the intention of keeping them for the longer term. It explains a number of "rules" made by professional accountants in the 1970s to reduce the number of alternative accounting treatments which might otherwise have been available. Some students may find a few of these rules difficult; others may lose sight of the larger picture, and become bogged down in the rules. Expect to read several paragraphs three or four times in order to grasp an important point. We are not trying to frighten readers with these comments, but are attempting to alert you so that you may draw upon your full resources from the outset of our examination of the topic.

The subject is important because many Canadian and non-Canadian companies invest in the common shares of a variety of other companies. Hence, we tend to encounter many "consolidated" financial statements, such as Labatt's as reproduced in Chapter 2. Labatt's owns a portion of many companies such as Ogilvie Flour Mills, Laura Secord, Catelli, Casabello Wines, and the Toronto Blue Jays of the American Baseball League. Yet, the accounting for some of them may differ as a result of the percentage of ownership which is held by Labatt's. The Toronto Blue Jays, for example, are less than 50 percent owned; hence, the current accounting "rules" indicate that the ball club's assets are not to be consolidated but are handled on what is called the "equity reporting basis" (which we shall explain later).

This differing accounting treatment therefore has potentially significant implications to readers of financial statements. In Chapter 12 we touched on the importance of segment reporting in diversified companies (to offset consolidated reports) for those persons whose objective is predicting cash flows. A banker who has loaned money to Laura Secord without guarantees from other companies in the Labatt's group wants to see Laura Secord's financial statements — not Labatt's consolidated statements. A long-term creditor or investor, however, may primarily want to see consolidated financial statements. We therefore, reencounter a principal theme of this book — different accounting for different users/*objectives*. Later we shall observe how *facts* (such as percent of ownership) and *constraints* enter into the topic of what is called *intercorporate investments* (i.e., investments in the common shares of other companies).

Unfortunately, the topic is full of traps which we will have to point out as we proceed. For instance, observe that we have stressed the words "common share" investment. We have excluded from our definition of intercorporate investments any investments in bonds or in preferred shares (except when the preferred shares are really common shares because they do not have a fixed dividend rate or upper dividend limit, and as a result, they "fully participate" or participate equally in any dividend along with common shareholders). The exclusion occurs because these types of securities normally do not share in the residual ownership of the company. (They also do not carry rights to vote and elect directors, except in special circumstances such as when the company is approaching bankruptcy.) When residual ownership and voting rights do not exist, as with bonds and preferred shares, control or influence cannot generally be exerted over the company whose securities are being held. A situation of influence in accounting occurs when a company does not have direct power or authority (as conveyed by law or binding contracts) over another company, but has to rely upon persuasion or convincing argument. A shareholder with few shares may have little influence with a board of directors, but one who also holds a lease on the company's plant assets could have much greater influence. The importance of influence or control will become clearer later in this chapter. As was noted in Chapter 6, investments in bonds and preferred shares are normally carried at cost (unless market value is lower) and, depending on the intentions of corporate management, may or may not be current assets.

Another important point to remember is that a *short-term* investment in common shares of another company does not qualify for intercorporate investment status. Thus, consolidated statements, or equity accounting, would not result.

A third point which we must warn you about in advance is to watch for very important distinctions between methods used for recording on a company's *books* (ledgers) and those used in *reporting* on the external financial statements. The books may record investments in common shares at cost. The external financial statements might expand disclosure of cost. This will be explained later.

To summarize, this chapter is similar to the previous two because it is heavily laced with constraints. From an educative viewpoint your authors thus face a slight dilemma. We have to tell you what the crucial constraints are, so that you will be able to understand current financial statements. This takes up more space than we would prefer to devote. But, we must warn you that the constraints or rules of today may not be the rules of tomorrow. In the past decade, a large percentage of CICA "constraint" material has had a short life because it has been replaced as objectives, facts, and education/awareness levels have changed.

Background Information

A corporation may acquire an equity interest (ownership of common or preferred shares) in another company for a number of reasons. A company may have cash that is temporarily idle. It may, therefore, purchase a relatively small number of the shares of another company in order to obtain a short-term return — as an alternative, perhaps to purchasing short-term government notes or certificates of deposits. Such securities are categorized on the books of the acquiring corporation as "marketable securities"; accounting for marketable securities was discussed in Chapter 6. On the other hand, a company may purchase the shares of another corporation as a long-term investment. It may do so because it believes that the securities will provide a long-term return equivalent to, or greater than, that which could be obtained by internal use of available funds. Or, it may seek to obtain a sufficient number of shares to exercise a measure of influence and control over the other corporation in order to gain entry into new markets or new industries, to develop sources of raw materials, or to integrate its own operations with those of the other company.

A company may acquire the shares of another company by purchasing them for cash or other assets. Or, especially if it intends to get possession of all, or almost all, of the outstanding shares, it may exchange its own common shares for those of the company it seeks to acquire. Moreover, a firm may obtain shares of another company simply by its organizing such a company and retaining all, or a portion, of the shares issued. To satisfy various legal requirements, to obtain certain income tax advantages, or to enhance organizational efficiency, many companies divide their operations into several subsidiary corporations, of which the *parent* corporation will hold controlling interest in each. Each subsidiary corporation may represent only a manufacturing or sales division or even a branch office. To take an extreme example, a well-known commercial loan company maintains separate corporations not only for each of its numerous branch offices but for each major type of loan made within a branch office. The parent corporation owns 100 percent of the common shares of all of the individual corporations.

The real estate industry tends to incorporate each of its office buildings, apartment blocks, and shopping centres separately, so as to (1) achieve limited liability, (2) arrange mortgages which are associated only with the specific property of the limited company, or (3) ease future sharing of ownership if this becomes useful to management.

Level of Influence

The critical determinant of the means by which intercorporate investments are reported in financial statements is the *degree* of control or influence that the investor corporation exerts over the acquired company. To the extent that the investor corporation exerts relatively minor influence, the investment would generally be reported by the *cost* method; to the extent that it exerts substantial influence, it would be reported by the *equity* method. (Both of these methods will be defined and evaluated shortly.) Insofar as the investor company is able to *control* the other company (control ordinarily being defined as ownership of over 50 percent of the voting common shares), the investment is commonly reported by means of *consolidated financial statements.* Consolidated financial statements report the financial position and earnings of two or more corporations as if they were a single entity. The three methods of *reporting* intercorporate investments — the cost, the equity, and the consolidated statement methods — are not, it should be emphasized, categorically consistent.

Since each corporation is a separate legal entity, a separate set of accounting records must, by law, be maintained for each. On the *books* (accounting journals and ledgers) of the investor corporation the shares of the other company must be accounted for (in contrast to reported) by *either* the cost or the equity method. If, however, the investor company has control over another corporation, then, for *purposes of reporting,* the individual financial statements of the two companies can be combined into a single, consolidated, set of statements. The relationships and distinctions among the methods will be brought out in the next several sections.

Degree of Influence

Where an investor corporation is unable to maintain significant influence over the company in which it owns an interest because of the small proportion of its holdings, it should *report* its investment on the cost basis. Evidence of an ability to influence significantly the key financial and operating policies over an investee company may be manifest by several factors: percentage of shares owned, representation on the corporate board of directors, membership on key policy-making committees, interchange of managerial personnel, material purchases or sales between the two companies, and exchanges of technological information. Even though a company may not own a majority of a corporation's outstanding common shares, it may nevertheless exercise a predominant impact on that company's policies. While recognizing that degree of influence cannot be readily measured, the ARC of the CICA, in order to achieve a greater degree of uniformity of practice, prescribed that an investment of 20 percent or more of the voting common shares of an investee should lead to a presumption that the investor has the ability to exercise significant influence over the investee. It directed, therefore, that, *in general*, investments of less than 20 percent of voting shares should be reported by the cost method and investments of between 20 and 50 percent should be reported by the equity method.

Note clearly that the 20 percent figure is strictly arbitrary. It was chosen by ARC primarily to mirror the U.S. position which promotes the highly elusive and questionable objective of forcing perhaps false (because facts may differ) uniformity of accounting treatment *among* companies. For instance, it may be possible to exert significant influence when 15 percent of the common shares are owned *if* the other 85 percent are scattered among thousands of shareholders, none of whom owns more than one percent of the shares. Similarly, a company owning 25 percent of the voting common shares may have little influence when another company (called the *investor*) owns 45 percent and can elect a majority of its own people to the board of directors of the *investee* company.

As a result of these obvious factual exceptions to the rule, the ARC allows companies to exercise some judgment in choosing their financial *reporting* methods. The company owning 25 percent might therefore report on the cost basis when the company with 45 percent ownership exerts significant influence or control. Conversely, equity basis reporting might be used with 15 percent ownership given conditions of widespread ownership of the remaining 85 percent.

Cost Method

Under the cost method, a company records its investment in the shares of another company at cost — the amount paid to acquire the shares. It recognizes revenue from its investment only to the extent that the investee company actually declares dividends. In the absence of unusual declines in market values, the investment would be maintained on the *books* of the investor at original cost. The carrying value of the investment would generally be unaffected by changes in the market value of shares owned or in the net worth of the company owned. The external financial statements would *report* the investment at cost *if* neither the equity nor consolidation methods of reporting are used, as was described in Chapter 6.

EXAMPLE

On January 1, 19x7, Adams Limited purchases 10,000 of 100,000 (10 percent) common shares of Cain Limited. It pays $30 per share. The following entry would be required on the *books* of the *investor* company, Adams Limited:

Investment in Cain Limited	$300,000	
Cash		$300,000
To record the purchase of 10,000 common shares of Cain Limited.		

On December 31, 19x7, Cain Limited announces that earnings for the year were $500,000 ($5 per common share).

No entry is required to record the announcement of the annual earnings. Adams Limited recognizes income from its investment only upon the actual declaration of dividends by the company whose shares it owns.

On the same date, December 31, 19x7, Cain Limited declares dividends of $2 per share, payable on January 20, 19x8. The accrual entry on December 31, 19x7 would be:

Dividend receivable	$20,000	
Dividend income from Cain Limited		$20,000
To record dividend receivable from Cain Limited.		

The cost method of maintaining investments was illustrated in previous chapters in connection with marketable securities and recognition of revenue/income from dividends. Dividends are recognized as revenue/income when declared.

Observe that this illustration is concerned with how the books (journals and ledgers) of the investor would be kept. Companies which *report* on a consolidated or equity accounting basis (to be described shortly) could maintain their books on a cost basis. The ARC's pronouncements (i.e., the constraints) apply to *reporting*, not to how a company maintains its internal books.

Using the cost basis of *reporting* a large, long-term investment in common shares of another company can severely limit the usefulness of the financial statements for various users/readers. For instance, if Adams controlled Cain (that is, through over 50 percent ownership the directors of both companies were mainly the same people), Adams could influence its dividend income, and hence its net income, by declaring or not declaring a dividend of a large size by influencing the board of directors of Cain. Income manipulation was only one of the ARC's reasons for attempting to restrict *reporting* at cost. Other reasons are explained later.

Equity Method

Under the equity method, a company records its purchases of shares in another company at cost (same as under the cost method), but it periodically adjusts the carrying value of its investment (ledger account) to take into account its proportion of the investee's earnings subsequent to the date it acquired its shares. It recognizes its proportion of increases or decreases in the net worth of the investee as soon as they are known to it. If net worth increases as the result of investee corporate earnings, then the investor company recognizes promptly on its own books revenue in the amount of its proportionate share of such earnings; it does not wait until such earnings are declared in the form of dividends. Since earnings of the investee company serve to increase the equity of the investor company in the investee company, the investor company will concurrently increase the carrying value of its investment by the amount of revenue recognized.

If net worth of the investee corporation decreases, then the investor will also recognize such decreases. Net worth will decrease as a consequence of operating losses. But it will also decrease whenever dividends are declared (a liability for the payment of a dividend is established; retained earnings are decreased). Hence, as the investee company declares a dividend, the investor company recognizes the dividend receivable and at the same time adjusts the carrying value of its investment to reflect the decline in the net worth of the investee. An example may help to clarify the accounting entries made on the *books* of the investor.

EXAMPLE

Assume the same facts as in the previous example, except that this time, on January 1, 19x7, Adams Limited purchases 20,000 of 100,000 outstanding common shares of Cain Limited. Again, it pays $30 per share. This time, however, since Adams has acquired 20 percent of the shares outstanding, we will assume that it exerts significant influence over Cain Limited; hence, it is appropriate to account for, and report, the investment by the equity method.

(a)

Investment in Cain Limited	$600,000	
Cash		$600,000
To record the purchase of 20,000 of Cain Limited's common shares.		

This entry is identical in form to that illustrated previously in connection with the cost method.

On December 31, Cain Limited announces that earnings for the year were $500,000 ($5 per common share).

(b)

Investment in Cain Limited	$100,000	
Income/revenue from investment in Cain Limited		$100,000
To record our proportionate (20%) share of 19x7 net income of Cain Limited.		

The net worth of Cain Limited increased by $500,000 as a consequence of 19x7 net income. Adams Limited may recognize 20 percent of that amount as its own revenue. Since Adams Limited receives no cash or other assets as a direct result of Cain Limited having realized the income, its share of the earnings would be reflected by an increase in the carrying value of its investment.

When Cain Limited declares a dividend of $2 per share, Adams Limited would establish a receivable account for the dividends but would recognize a corresponding *decrease* in the carrying value of its investment.

(c)

Dividends receivable	$40,000	
Investment in Cain Limited		$40,000
To record dividends to be received from Cain Limited.		

Upon learning that Cain Limited had declared a dividend, Adams Limited would *not*, under the equity method, recognize revenue. Revenue representing the earnings of Cain Limited had been recognized at the time it was first reported. To recognize it again when it is distributed to shareholders in the form of dividends would be to count it twice. The carrying value of the investment in Cain Limited would be reduced by the amount of the dividend received because, as a result of cash distributions to its shareholders, Cain Limited has reduced both its assets and its retained earnings. The share of Adams Limited in such retained earnings has thereby been proportionately reduced.

As indicated in the accompanying T accounts, the net effect of the last two entries [(b) and (c)] has been to increase the assets of Adams Limited by $100,000 (investment in Cain Limited, $60,000; dividends receivable, $40,000). Correspondingly, Adams Limited recognized $100,000 in revenue from its investment in Cain Limited. The $100,000 represents, of course, 20 percent of the reported earnings of Cain Limited.

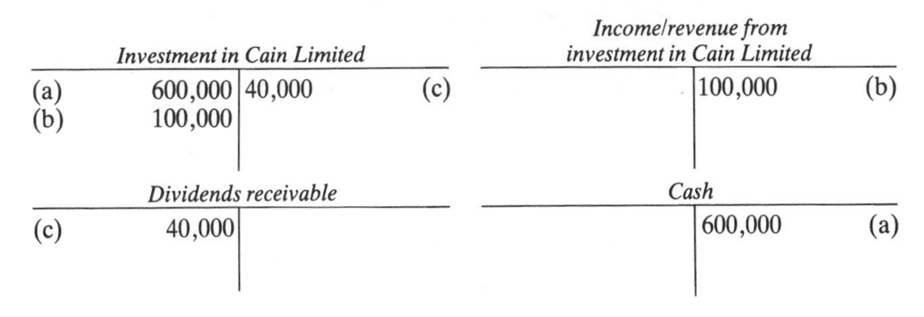

Cost and Equity Methods Compared

The differences between the cost and equity methods of recording on the *books* of the *investor* (Adams Limited) can be depicted as in Exhibit 13-1.

EXHIBIT 13-1

	Cost Method (10% of Common Shares Acquired)			*Equity Method (20% of Common Shares Acquired)*		
(1) Original investment	Investment in Cain Limited	$300,000		Investment in Cain Limited	$600,000	
	Cash		$300,000	Cash		$600,000
	To record purchase of common shares of Cain Limited.			To record purchase of common shares of Cain Limited.		
(2) Cain earns net income of $500,000	No journal entry			Investment in Cain Limited	$100,000	
				Income of Cain Limited		$100,000
				To record our proportionate share of Cain's net income.		
(3) Cain declares a dividend of $200,000 (If this is more than the increase in retained earnings since the shares were acquired, any excess represents a return *of* capital.)	Cash	$ 20,000		Cash	$ 40,000	
	Dividend income from Cain Limited		$ 20,000	Investment in Cain Limited		$ 40,000
	To record receipt of dividend — *assuming* that it was paid directly in cash).			(Same assumption as for cost method.)		

Aside from the dollars, the two differences worth noting are:

1. No entry is made under the cost method when the investee (Cain Limited) earns net income. (If Cain had made a loss that decreased the market value of the shares, the investment account might be written down, as was described in earlier chapters.)
2. When a dividend is declared by Cain the credit portion of the journal entry is quite different. Under the cost method the dividend is income or revenue (depending on one's point of view as to whether the amount is gross or net of expenses). Under the equity method the credit reduces the investment account to reflect the reduced equity of Cain Limited.

Let us now consider for the next several pages some of the external financial *reporting* (as opposed to recording or bookkeeping) implications of the two methods.

Justification for the cost and the equity methods and the distinctions between them can readily be appreciated when the two methods are viewed within the context of issues of revenue recognition. A company owns shares in another company. If the investee company is profitable, the investor company is obviously better off than if the investee company is not. Since, in the long run, earnings of a company represent revenue to its owners, earnings of the investee company signify revenue to the investor company. The question facing the accountant of the investor company relates to the point in time at which such revenue should be recognized.

Under the cost method the investor company recognizes as revenue its share of investee corporation earnings only as the investee corporation actually declares dividends — that is, as it announces its intention to distribute to shareholders the assets corresponding to the earnings available for distribution. The cost method is thereby more conservative than the equity method. Revenue is recognized by the investor company only as cash (assuming that the dividend is to be paid in cash) is about to be received. The cost method makes sense when an investor company has but little influence on the dividend or other operating policies of the company in which it owns shares, for although the investee company may be profitable, it need not necessarily declare dividends, and the investor company cannot require it to do so. It may be many years, therefore, before earnings of the investee company are translated into liquid assets of the investor company.

Under the equity method, the investor company recognizes as revenue its share of investee company earnings as soon as such earnings are reported, regardless of when such earnings are likely to be distributed to shareholders in the form of dividends. The equity method is appropriate when the investor company does have significant impact on the dividend policy of the investee firm. The rationale for the equity method can easily be understood if the consequences of *not* using the method are considered. If the investor had sufficient influence on the investee so that it could control if and when the investee could declare dividends, then it could readily control its own earnings. If the investor firm otherwise had an unprofitable year, it could direct that the investee firm increase its dividend payout. Its share of the dividends would be reflected immediately in higher reported revenues. If the investor firm otherwise had an unusually profitable year and did not "need" additional revenues in order to report satisfactory earnings, it could request that the investee firm delay payment of dividends until future periods. In Chapter 5 it was pointed out that under the stewardship objective of accounting revenue should be recognized only when it can be objectively measured and when eventual collection of cash can reasonably be assured. When a firm is able to exert substantial influence over the company in which it maintains an interest, then the two criteria are reasonably satisfied at the time the investee company reports its earnings. The equity method is thereby considered more appropriate. When the firm is unable to exert such influence, then the criteria are not reasonably satisfied until the investee company declares its intention to distribute cash or other assets. Hence, the cost method is more appropriate.

Consolidated Reports

When a company is able to control absolutely (this means that it holds over 50 percent of the voting common shares), as opposed to merely influence, the financial and operating policies of another company, then the interests of investors as well as some other users of financial statements could be better served by the preparation of consolidated financial statements. Consolidated financial statements report the financial position and results of operations of two or more corporations, each a separate legal entity, as if they were a single economic entity. They are designed to give effect to economic substance as opposed to legal form of the corporate relationship. They combine the assets, liabilities, revenues, and expenses of the two or more companies into a single balance sheet and income statement.

Consolidated statements are a means of *reporting*. The preparation of consolidated financial statements does not preclude the preparation of individual financial statements for specific purposes. For example, separate financial statements have to be prepared for income tax purposes. Separate statements of each entity may be requested by bankers. Indeed, each member of a group of corporations whose financial statements may be combined into a single consolidated set of statements must maintain separate accounting records. An investor corporation must, therefore, account for its ownership in other companies by either the cost or the equity method — although, as will be seen shortly, choice of method becomes immaterial since both the investment accounts and the revenue from investment accounts are eliminated in the process of consolidation.

The usual condition for consolidated statements is voting control of one company by another — that is, ownership of more than 50 percent of the voting shares. There are, however, exceptions to this rule, in both directions. For example, consolidation might be chosen if corporate legislation in the jurisdiction of the investor company permits such disclosure when 50 percent or less of the voting shares are owned. In the other direction, consolidated statements would not generally result in the most informative presentation and are, therefore, not required when the two or more companies are not, in fact, a single economic entity (if, for example, voting control is likely to be only temporary). Similarly, if a subsidiary company (even though it may be 100 percent owned) is in a specialized industry, one in which unique accounting practices are adhered to, the presentation of individual reports might be more useful to investors than a consolidated report.

As a general rule, if an investor company owns less than 20 percent of the voting shares of another company, it would *report* its investment on the cost basis; if it owns 20 percent or more, then it would *report* its investment on an equity basis; if it owns over 50 percent, it would *report* to shareholders on a consolidated basis, unless because of special circumstances consolidation is deemed inappropriate. As we noted before, there are also exceptions to the 20 percent ownership guideline.

A company that has control (over 50 percent ownership) of another company is referred to as a *parent*; the controlled company is known as a *subsidiary*.

An alternate name for the parent is *investor*; an alternate name for the subsidiary or company being "significantly influenced" is *investee*.

Principles of Consolidation — Balance Sheet

In their simplest form consolidated statements represent the sum of the balances in accounts of the individual companies which are to form the consolidated entity. However, as will be demonstrated in the series of short examples to follow, certain eliminations and adjustments are required to avoid double counting.

The objective of consolidated statements is to depict the financial position and results of operations of two or more companies as if they were a single economic entity. It is necessary, therefore, to adjust for the effect of certain intercompany transactions on both the income statement and the balance sheet. Consider the following illustration: If a parent company sells merchandise for $100 to a subsidiary company, which in turn sells it to outsiders for $120, then the sum of the sales of the two companies would be $220. But if the two companies were viewed as a single entity, then the sale from the parent to the subsidiary would be accounted for as an internal transfer as opposed to a sale. Total sales — those to outsiders — would be only $120. Elimination of the sale from parent to subsidiary is thereby required in the external financial statements. (We do *not* alter the books of either company.) Similarly, the cost of the goods sold by the parent to the subsidiary would have to be eliminated, when *reporting*, and if the subsidiary is still indebted to the parent for the goods which it purchased, so also would the account receivable (on the books of the parent) and the account payable (on the books of the subsidiary) be eliminated for *reporting* purposes. (Again, we do not alter the books of either the parent or the subsidiary. Alterations take place on separate work sheets which are not part of each company's books.)

The examples to follow will center first upon the effects of consolidation on the balance sheet and then on the income statement.

EXAMPLE 1

100 Percent Ownership; Consolidation Immediately upon Acquisition

A parent company purchases 100 percent of the common shares outstanding of a subsidiary company. Immediately after acquisition, the trial balances of the two individual companies appear in condensed form, as follows:

	Parent co.	*Subsidiary co.*
Cash	$ 20,000	$10,000
Account receivable (from subsidiary)	10,000	
Investment in subsidiary	40,000	
Other assets	80,000	40,000
	$150,000	$50,000
Account payable (to parent)		$10,000
Common shares	$ 30,000	10,000
Retained earnings	120,000	30,000
	$150,000	$50,000

Since the balances indicated are those immediately following acquisition, it is clear that the parent company must have paid $40,000 to acquire the subsidiary — the amount indicated in its investment in subsidiary account. From a consolidated standpoint, a company cannot have an investment in itself. At the same time, if the two sets of statements are to be combined, it would be inappropriate to report $40,000 owners' equity (common shares, $10,000, plus retained earnings, $30,000) of the subsidiary, since it is the parent company which is the sole owner of the subsidiary and which has such equity in the subsidiary. To effect a consolidation, it would be necessary to eliminate *both* the investment in the subsidiary *and* the equity of the owners. For convenience, the eliminations can be expressed in journal entry form:

(a)

Common shares (of subsidiary)	$10,000	
Retained earnings (of subsidiary)	30,000	
Investment in subsidiary (by parent)		$40,000
To eliminate the investment in subsidiary and corresponding subsidiary owners' equity accounts.		

The trial balance indicates that the subsidiary company owes the parent company $10,000. From the standpoint of the combined enterprise, both accounts receivable and payable would be overstated if assets and liabilities were simply added together; a company cannot have a payable and receivable from itself. The payable and receivable must be eliminated:

(b)

Account payable (to parent)	$10,000	
Account receivable (from subsidiary)		$10,000
To eliminate intercompany payable and receivable.		

The two entries would be posted to the books of *neither* the parent nor the subsidiary. They are nothing more than *work-sheet* eliminations to effect a combination of the two individual sets of statements. Thus,

	Original statements		*Adjustments*		*Combined statements*
	Parent co.	*Subsidiary co.*	*Debit*	*Credit*	
Cash	$ 20,000	$10,000			$30,000
Account receivable (from subsidiary)	10,000			(b) $10,000	
Investment in subsidiary	40,000			(a) 40,000	
Other assets	80,000	40,000			120,000
	$150,000	$50,000			$150,000
Accounts payable (to parent)		$10,000	(b) $10,000		
Common shares	$ 30,000	10,000	(a) 10,000		$ 30,000
Retained earnings	120,000	30,000	(a) 30,000		120,000
	$150,000	$50,000	$50,000	$50,000	$150,000

The consolidated balance sheet would appear as indicated in the far right-hand column.

EXAMPLE 2

Consolidation Immediately upon Acquisition; Existence of Minority Interest

Assume facts similar to those in Example 1, but this time suppose that the parent purchased only 80 percent of the common shares of the subsidiary. The parent paid $32,000 for its interest in the subsidiary, an amount which, in this example, happens to be equivalent to 80 percent of the *book value* of the subsidiary. In addition, assume that the retained earnings of the parent are only $112,000, rather than $120,000 as in Example 1. The individual statements of the two companies immediately following acquisition are presented in the first two columns of the work sheet below:

	Original statements		*Adjustments*		*Combined statements*
	Parent co.	*Subsidiary co.*	*Debit*	*Credit*	
Cash	$ 20,000	$10,000			$ 30,000
Account receivable (from subsidiary)	10,000			(c) $10,000	
Investment in subsidiary	32,000			(a) 32,000	
Other assets	80,000	40,000			120,000
	$142,000	$50,000			$150,000
Account payable (to parent)		$10,000	(c) $10,000		
Common shares	$ 30,000	10,000	{(a) 8,000; (b) 2,000}		$ 30,000
Retained earnings	112,000	30,000	{(a) 24,000; (b) 6,000}		112,000
Minority interest in subsidiary				(b) 8,000	8,000
	$142,000	$50,000	$50,000	$50,000	$150,000

As in Example 1, it is necessary to eliminate the investment of the parent company ($32,000) and the corresponding owners' equity of the subsidiary. Thus,

(a)

Common shares (of subsidiary)	$ 8,000	
Retained earnings (of subsidiary)	24,000	
Investment in subsidiary (by parent)		$32,000
To eliminate investment in subsidiary and corresponding amounts in subsidiary's owners' equity accounts.		

In this example, however, only 80 percent of the owners' equity of the subsidiary has been eliminated by the entry. The remaining 20 percent represents the equity of the *minority* shareholders — those who hold the remaining 20 percent interest in the firm. Consolidated financial statements are prepared from the perspective of the *majority* shareholders, those of the parent company. From the standpoint of a majority shareholder, it would be both confusing and misleading to report on the balance sheet common shares and retained earnings in two companies — those of the parent and those of the subsidiary. Hence, the minority interest in each of the owners' equity accounts (the amounts that remain after the majority interest has been eliminated) are reclassified into a single account, "minority interest in subsidiary":

(b)

Common shares (of subsidiary)	$ 2,000	
Retained earnings (of subsidiary)	6,000	
Minority interest in subsidiary		$8,000
To reclassify the equity of minority shareholders in the subsidiary.		

The minority interest in the subsidiary account represents the equity of the minority shareholders in the consolidated corporation. It is, in a sense, the portion of the residual interest in the subsidiary that may be assigned to the minority rather than the majority shareholders. As a consequence, some corporations report minority interest in subsidiaries among long-term liabilities. The amounts reported in the owners' equity section of the consolidated balance sheet represent only the equity of the parent company shareholders.

As in the previous example, it is necessary also to eliminate from both current assets and liabilities the entire amounts owed by the subsidiary to the parent:

(c)

Account payable (to parent)	$10,000	
Account receivable (from subsidiary)		$10,000
To eliminate intercompany payable and receivable.		

The column on the work sheet "Combined Statements" gives effect to the adjusting entries. Such entries, as indicated previously, are made only on the work sheet; they are *not* made on the books of either of the two companies.

One reason that the entire 100 percent (instead of 80 percent) of the "cash" and "other assets" balances of the subsidiary appear in the consolidated balance sheet is *control.* The parent company, through its election of the directors (who in turn appoint management) of the subsidiary, is able to control 100 percent of the assets and liabilities. [*If* the parent could only control 80 percent of the assets of the subsidiary, it would be possible to eliminate the minority interest of $8,000 by reducing "other assets" by $8,000 (20 percent of $40,000). This logically assumes that the subsidiary's "cash" of $10,000 would be used to pay off the account payable to the parent of $10,000. However, our "*if*" is not realistic; hence, the minority interest account description would appear on consolidated balance sheets whenever subsidiaries are less than 100 percent owned.]

EXAMPLE 3

Acquisition Price in Excess of Proportionate Share of Book Value

In the two preceding examples, the price paid by the parent to acquire its investment in the subsidiary was exactly equal to its proportionate share of the *book value* (which is equal to the owners' equity) of the subsidiary. If the parent company acquires its interest at an amount greater than the book value of the assets acquired, then such excess must be accounted for and reported in a manner indicative of its nature.

	Original statements		*Adjustments*		*Combined statements*
	Parent co.	*Subsidiary co.*	*Debit*	*Credit*	
Cash	$ 20,000	$10,000			$ 30,000
Account receivable (from subsidiary)	10,000			(c) $10,000	
Investment in subsidiary	37,000			(a) 37,000	
Other assets	80,000	40,000			120,000
Excess of cost over book value			(a) $ 5,000		5,000
	$147,000	$50,000			$155,000
Account payable (to parent)		$10,000	(c) 10,000		
Common shares	$ 30,000	10,000	(a) 8,000 (b) 2,000		$ 30,000
Retained earnings	117,000	30,000	(a) 24,000 (b) 6,000		117,000
Minority interest in subsidiary				(b) 8,000	8,000
	$147,000	$50,000	$55,000	$55,000	$155,000

Assume the same facts as in Example 2, except that the parent company paid $37,000 to acquire an 80 percent interest in the subsidiary — an 80 percent interest that has a book value of only $32,000 — and that the retained earnings of the parent are only $117,000. The first two columns of the work sheet indicate the financial position of the two individual companies immediately upon the acquisition of the subsidiary company by the parent company.

As in the previous examples, if the financial positions of the two individual companies are to be shown as if they were a single economic entity, then both the investment of the parent and its corresponding owners' equity as recorded on the books of the subsidiary must be eliminated. This time, however, although the investment is recorded on the books of the parent at $37,000, the corresponding equity is recorded on the books of the subsidiary at only $32,000. It is necessary, therefore, to reclassify the difference. Pending determination of the reason for the difference (see the discussion to follow), it may be classified *temporarily* as "excess of cost over book value":

(a)

Common shares (of subsidiary)	$ 8,000	
Retained earnings (of subsidiary)	24,000	
Excess of cost over book value	5,000	
Investment in subsidiary (by parent)		$37,000
To eliminate investment in subsidiary and corresponding amounts in subsidiary's owners' equity accounts.		

The interests of the minority shareholders are ordinarily considered to be unaffected by the decision of the parent company to pay an amount in excess of its book value for shares of the subsidiary. Owners' equity of the minority shareholders may be reclassified as in Example 2:

(b)

Common shares (of subsidiary)	$2,000	
Retained earnings (of subsidiary)	6,000	
Minority interest in subsidiary		$8,000
To reclassify the equity of minority shareholders in the subsidiary.		

And, as previously, the offsetting payable and receivable must be eliminated:

(c)

Account payable (to parent)	$10,000	
Account receivable (from subsidiary)		$10,000
To eliminate intercompany payable and receivable.		

Excess of cost over book value

The excess of cost over book value is often a source of confusion and misunderstanding. There are at least three reasons why an investor may pay an amount in excess of book value for a portion of ownership of a subsidiary (or investee) company. First, the book value of individual assets (and hence the recorded owners' equity) is based on historical cost — the amount initially paid to acquire the assets, less amortization and depreciation. Book value, as frequently emphasized throughout this text, is not necessarily indicative of fair market value. Thus, the price paid by the company to acquire its shares in the subsidiary may be indicative of the fair market value of the individual assets represented by such shares. If such is the case, then the excess of cost over book value should be assigned to the particular assets acquired. Consistent with the historical cost basis of accounting, assets should be valued at purchase price. Because the parent company may not have purchased the assets directly, but instead acquired the common shares of the company that has title to the assets, does not change the substance of the transaction. Nor should it change the manner in which the assets are to be accounted for. The following additional adjustment would be required insofar as the excess of cost over book value is to be allocated to specific assets:

(d^1)		
Other assets (that is, specific tangible assets such as land, inventory, buildings and equipment)	$5,000	
Excess of cost over book value		$5,000
To allocate the excess of cost over book value to specific tangible assets.		

Note: Entries (d^1) to (d^3) have not been posted to the work sheet; they represent alternative means of reclassifying the excess of cost over book value. It is important to re-emphasize that entry (d^1) does not get posted to the ledgers of the subsidiary. Cost to the subsidiary company remains the same (other assets of $40,000). *However*, cost to the *parent*, the new owner of the subsidiary, is $5,000 higher, and it is this higher amount which should appear as a cost on the consolidated financial statements. After all, typically it is only the consolidated statements which are sent to the shareholders of the parent.

Subsequent to the acquisition, the consolidated enterprise should base its charge for depreciation on the amounts at which the assets are recorded on the consolidated balance sheet. Depreciation charges, as a consequence, may be greater on the consolidated income statement than the sum of the depreciation charges on the financial statements of the two individual companies. The acquired subsidiary, on its own financial statements, will maintain its assets and continue to base depreciation at the initial values of the assets.

Second, a firm may pay for an interest in a subsidiary an amount in excess of the book value of such interest because the subsidiary possesses certain intangible assets which it does not have recorded on its own books. The subsidiary, for example, may have title to patents, copyrights, or trademarks which, because they have been developed internally (as opposed to purchased from outsiders), have not been given accounting recognition. When such assets are obtained in connection with the purchase of a subsidiary, they should properly be recorded at their fair market values. If the excess of cost over book value can be ascribed to specific intangibles, then it should be so reclassified:

(d²)		
Specific intangible assets (patents, copyrights, etc.)	$5,000	
Excess of cost over book value		$5,000
To allocate the excess of cost over book value to specific intangible assets.		

The values assigned to the specific intangibles should be amortized, *if* they have a limited life, and periodic charges reflected on the consolidated income statement, over their estimated useful lives. The amortization charges would not be recorded on the books of either the parent or the subsidiary — only on the statements of the two companies combined.

Third, a firm may pay to acquire another company an amount in excess of recorded book value because the company possesses certain intangible assets that cannot be specifically identified, or are not generally measured by accountants. Such assets may arise because of favorable customer attitudes toward the company, unusual talents of corporate managers, advantageous business locations, or special monopolistic or political privileges. Or they may arise because the individually identifiable assets when used together are worth considerably more than the fair market value of any of the assets employed independently. Whatever may be the attributes of such assets, however, they enable the firm to earn amounts in excess of "normal" returns. Such assets — that is, the amount in excess of book value that cannot be specifically allocated to other assets — may be classified as *goodwill*:

(d³)		
Goodwill	$5,000	
Excess of cost over book value		$5,000
To allocate the excess of cost over book value to goodwill.		

Goodwill

Goodwill, in a sense, is a residual. It represents that portion of the cost of acquiring a subsidiary that cannot be assigned directly to any specific assets. Goodwill is one asset that arises out of the consolidation process resulting from one company buying the common shares of another. (We have also seen goodwill arise when a partnership is incorporated.)

Although firms may over a number of years develop the attributes that comprise goodwill, they may not, under conventional stewardship accounting principles, give recognition to them. Goodwill may be recorded only when one firm purchases another and the excess of cost over book value cannot be specifically assigned to other assets.

The conventional practice of recording goodwill only to the extent purchased, however, has by no means been beyond criticism. In the example at hand, a company purchased for $37,000 an 80 percent interest in a company that has a book value of $40,000. The 80 percent interest, therefore, has a book value of $32,000, and the maximum amount of goodwill that can be recognized is $5,000. Many observers contend that it is illogical to record goodwill of only $5,000. They assert that if 80 percent of the company is worth $37,000, then 100 percent would be worth $46,250 — $37,000/.80. Recognition should be given to the entire $6,250 of goodwill ($46,250 less book value of $40,000 *or* $5,000/.80). To record less than the full $6,250 is to pretend that the 80 percent share of the subsidiary owned by the parent company has increased as a result of the development of the goodwill but that the share of the minority has not. Such an approach thereby leads to an undervaluation of the assets of the acquired company. The arguments of the critics, however, have not been accepted by the Accounting Research Committee (ARC). Their rejection stems, no doubt, in large measure from their desire to avoid giving accounting recognition to any assets not specifically acquired and paid for in an arm's-length exchange transaction. Also, it is not always obvious that the remaining 20 percent of the shares would be worth one quarter of the 80 percent. Control (that is, obtaining the first 50 percent plus one share) could easily be worth more than the remaining 49 percent.

As a consequence of the very nature of goodwill — it is a residual asset — its useful life is not readily determinable. Nevertheless, the ARC has prescribed that firms should make their best efforts to estimate the useful lives of all intangible assets, including goodwill, and that such assets should be amortized over their useful lives. In no event, however, should the amortization period exceed 40 years. To the extent, therefore, that a consolidated entity records goodwill, it must each year reduce the balance in the goodwill account (a credit to goodwill) and increase expenses by a like amount (debit to amortization of goodwill) by no less than one fortieth of the initial amount recorded. Both the goodwill itself and the charge for amortization would appear only on the consolidated statements, not on those of either the parent or the subsidiary by itself.

This ARC requirement to amortize goodwill has some important implications, which merit brief comment. The ARC found itself in a difficult position with regard to pronouncing on the amortization or non-amortization of goodwill. If it did *not* require amortization of goodwill, then two effects might occur:

1. The goodwill account (on consolidation) could build up unchecked as company after company was acquired by the parent. Although, such an event may first appear unlikely (because of the concept of conservatism) it is a greater possibility than one might think. The amount of a write-down — per conservatism — could be difficult to estimate because goodwill could represent assets which accountants do not measure (e.g., worth of people). If so, how does one measure what one would prefer not to measure?
2. Management of companies might be inclined to charge the "excess of cost over book value" to goodwill, instead of to an account such as the acquired building — which requires amortization.

As a result, both the ARC and the U.S. accounting profession settled on the 40-year amortization period. One fortieth of a number could easily not be material, and therefore would not upset many corporate managements. Thus, the ARC found a rule to get around the problem. But, the rule may ignore the facts for a particular company whose goodwill does not vanish over 40 years.

EXAMPLE 4

Consolidation in Years Subsequent to Acquisition

Characteristic of the first three examples was the assumption that the consolidated statements were prepared immediately upon the acquisition of the subsidiary by the parent. As a consequence, any amounts paid by the parent in excess of the book value of the subsidiary could readily be determined. Retained earnings of both the parent and the subsidiary as well as the investment of the parent in the subsidiary remained uncontaminated by profits or losses of the subsidiary subsequent to acquisition.

Example 4 extends Example 3 (with 80 percent ownership) for a period of one year after acquisition. Assume that the subsidiary company has had earnings of $6,000 in the first year after controlling interest was purchased by the parent company. Assume also, for simplicity, that the parent company had *zero earnings* during that period *except* insofar as it took into account its dividend from the subsidiary company. The subsidiary company paid $1,000 of dividends during the year; on its books, the parent company recorded its investment in the subsidiary company on the *cost* basis.

During this first year subsequent to the acquisition, the parent company — in accordance with the cost basis — would *not* have recorded its share of the $6,000 (or $4,800) of earnings, but *would* have recorded 80 percent of the $1,000 dividend. This means that cash and retained earnings increased by $800 ($1,000 @ 80 percent) in the parent.

In order to avoid double counting, the dividend of $800 will therefore have to be reversed (debited) out of retained earnings of the investor. The offsetting credit is *not* to cash (a warning we expressed in Chapter 4 on adjusting entries). The dividend will have to be replaced for consolidation purposes with the $4,800, which is the parent's proportionate share of the subsidiary's net income *unadjusted* for the $5,000 "excess of cost over book value." Let us assume that the $5,000 excess arises because current replacement cost of the building in a used condition (i.e., its "fair market value") exceeds its book value; the $5,000 therefore should be added to a "building" account and amortized over the building's *remaining* life of 10 years.

The work sheet elimination entries which are necessary to prepare a consolidated balance sheet are provided below. They are posted to the work sheet in Exhibit 13-2.

(a)

Account payable	$10,000	
Account receivable		$10,000
To eliminate the intercompany payable and receivable.		

(b)

Retained earnings (Parent)	$800	
Minority interest	200	
Retained earnings (subsidiary)		$1,000
To restore the parent's share of the $800 dividend and charge minority shareholders for the $200 which they received.		

Entry (b) may appear a little odd at first glance. However, to avoid double counting in the next entry (c), we must get into the habit of reversing the subsidiary's common share *dividend when the parent uses the cost basis*. Observe that $800 of the subsidiary's dividend came to rest in retained earnings of the parent, after passing through its dividend revenue/income account. When we are consolidating both the balance sheet and the income statement, the elimination debit would be to "dividend revenue." Entry (b) makes sense since the dividend ultimately was declared out of the retained earnings of the subsidiary. The two accounts which ultimately were affected were the two retained earnings. Hence, the elimination entry's debit and credit to retained earnings makes sense if we grasp that other accounts ("dividends declared" in the subsidiary, and "dividend revenue" in the parent) would normally be credited in a full consolidation of the income statement and the balance sheet. The $200 debit to minority interest merely recognizes that *their* 20 percent share of retained earnings (which we *report* on the consolidated balance sheet as minority interest) has decreased as a result of the dividend which they have already received. Minority interest can be viewed as a type of liability (in the common shareholder's eyes); the debit reduces the liability.

EXHIBIT 13-2

	Original Statements		*Adjustments*		*Combined (Consolidated) Statements*
	Parent	*Subsidiary*	*Debit*	*Credit*	
Cash	$ 20,800	$ 9,000			$ 29,800
Accounts receivable (from subsidiary)	10,000			(a) $10,000	
Investment in subsidiary	37,000			(d) 37,000	
Other assets (including building)	80,000	46,000	(d) 5,000	(e) 500	130,500
	$147,800	$55,000			$160,300
Accounts payable (to parent)		$10,000	(a) 10,000		
Common shares	$ 30,000	10,000	(d) 10,000		$ 30,000
Retained earnings	117,800	35,000	(b) 800 (c) 6,000 (d) 30,000 (e) 500	(b) 1,000 (c) 4,800	121,300
Minority interest in subsidiary			(b) 200	(c) 1,200 (d) 8,000	9,000
	$147,800	$55,000	$62,500	$62,500	$160,300

(c)

Retained earnings (subsidiary)	$6,000	
Retained earnings (parent)		$4,800
Minority interest		1,200

To divide the majority (parent company) and minority share of the subsidiary's net income of $6,000.

Entry (c) is similar in appearance to (b) in that we are primarily shuffling around $4,800 of retained earnings. It, too, would make more sense if we were dealing with an income statement. Yet, entries (b) and (c) as they now stand have great educational merit in that they proceed to the crux of the matter — which is moving the subsidiary's share of income less dividends into the parent's retained earnings account, for purposes of consolidation.

(d)

Common shares (of subsidiary)	$10,000	
Retained earnings (of subsidiary)	30,000	
Building	5,000	
Investment in subsidiary		$37,000
Minority interest		8,000
To eliminate unnecessary accounts and record minority interest plus the parent's share of the extra building cost.		

Entry (d) is not as complicated and confusing as it may first appear. When the parent employs the *cost basis* of bookkeeping for the investment in the subsidiary, we have to eliminate the investment account's cost balance by reverting to matters as they existed at the *date of acquisition* of the subsidiary (when the cost was incurred). At this date the parent paid $5,000 above cost on the subsidiary's books; thus, we record the $5,000 debit to building.

As noted earlier in the discussion of goodwill, the replacement cost used, or the market value of the building is really $6,250 above its net book value. But because the parent acquired only 80 percent of the shares, we record, under Canadian rules, only 80 percent of the $6,250, or $5,000. *If* the rules allowed us to record the full $6,250, the additional $1,250 would have to be credited to minority interest.

Similarly, retained earnings at the date of acquisition was $30,000. It has jumped to $35,000 as of the year end through net income of $6,000 and dividends of $1,000. The credit to minority interest is 20 percent of the common shares ($10,000) and retained earnings ($30,000) at the date of acquisition.

(e)

Retained earnings (parent)	$500	
Building (net of accumulated depreciation)		$500
To amortize the $5,000 increase in building over the remaining life of 10 years.		

Entry (e) recognizes that the $5,000 extra that we paid for the building will disappear at the end of 10 years, when the building becomes fully depreciated. The full $500 is charged against the *parent's* retained earnings because we initially recorded only the parent's share of cost of $5,000 (not the $6,250).

Let us prove two of the figures in the "combined (consolidated) statements" column of Exhibit 13-2:

(1) Retained earnings of $121,300:

Balance, on acquisition of company (see Example 3)		$117,000
Net income:		
Of parent	$ Nil	
Of subsidiary — 80% of $6,000	4,800	
Less amortization of $5,000 extra cost of land (not shown on subsidiary's books)	(500)	4,300
Closing balance		$121,300

(2) Minority interest of $9,000:

Balance, on acquisition of company: 20% of common shares and retained earnings	$ 8,000
Net income: 20% of $6,000	1,200
Dividend: 20% of $1,000	(200)
Closing balance	$ 9,000

Principles of Consolidation — Income Statement

In essence, the consolidated income statement, like the consolidated balance sheet, presents the sum of the balances in the accounts of the component corporations. However, as with the balance sheet, numerous adjustments and eliminations may be necessary to give effect to transactions among the individual companies.

The consolidated income statement provides an indication of the change in enterprise welfare between two points of time as if the various components of the enterprise were a single economic entity. Principles of revenue and expense recognition must be applied as if the individual companies whose statements are to be consolidated were, in fact, combined into a single company. As a consequence, revenues and expenses, if they are to be recognized, must be the result only of arm's-length transactions with parties *outside* of the *consolidated* entity.

Many of the eliminations and adjustments which affect the income statement directly affect the balance sheet also. It is generally convenient, therefore, to make the elimination and adjustment entries on a work sheet in which the initial positions of the individual companies are drawn from their respective trial balances and thereby include both income statement and balance sheet accounts. Such a work sheet is illustrated in Exhibit 13-3.

Intercompany transactions take many forms; the specific eliminations and adjustments that might be required must be determined in light of the particular nature of the transactions. Some typical intercompany transactions, on which the trial balances as contained in Exhibit 13-3 are based, may be used to provide an insight into the general approach to consolidations. In Exhibit 13-3 it may be assumed that the parent company owns an 80 percent interest in the subsidiary. Consolidated statements are to be prepared for the first year of combined operations.

Interest

The individual components of a company may enter into arrangements which result in revenues to one company and expenses to another but involve no transactions with outsiders. Suppose, for example, that a parent

EXHIBIT 13-3

Consolidated Work Sheet

	Preclosing trial balances debit (credit)		*Adjustments*		*Combined preclosing trial balance debit (credit)*
	Parent	*Subsidiary*	*Debit*	*Credit*	
Inventory	$ 40,000	$ 12,000		(b) $ 4,000	$ 48,000
Land	50,000	45,000		(c) 6,000	89,000
Investment in subsidiary	200,000			(d) 200,000	
Other assets	600,000	218,000			818,000
Excess of cost over book value (goodwill)			(d) $ 20,000	(f) 500	19,500
Liabilities	(30,000)	(20,000)			(50,000)
Minority interest in subsidiary				(e) 45,000	(45,000)
Common shares	(80,000)	(50,000)	(d) 40,000 (e) 10,000		(80,000)
Retained earnings	(687,000)	(175,000)	(d) 140,000 (e) 35,000		(687,000)
Sales	(400,000)	(300,000)	(b) 100,000		(600,000)
Gain on sale of fixed assets	(6,000)		(c) 6,000		
Interest revenue	(7,000)		(a) 7,000		
Cost of goods sold	240,000	210,000		(b) 6,000 (b) 90,000	354,000
Interest expense		7,000		(a) 7,000	
Other expenses	80,000	53,000			133,000
Amortization of goodwill			(f) 500		500
	$ 0	$ 0	$358,500	$358,500	$ 0

company makes a loan to its subsidiary. Interest on the loan would be recognized as a revenue to the parent and as an expense to the subsidiary. From the standpoint of the consolidated entity, the "loan" is nothing more than an intracompany transfer of funds from one "division" to another. Just as any intercompany payable and receivable outstanding at year end would be eliminated from the consolidated balance sheet, so too must the interest revenue and expense be eliminated from the income statement. If $7,000 of the interest revenue and expense reported on the individual statements were intercompany interest, then the following elimination would be required:

(a)

Interest revenue	$7,000	
Interest expense		$7,000
To eliminate intercompany interest.		

In Exhibit 13-3, no intercompany payable or receivable is indicated on the trial balance. It may be assumed that all loans had been repaid by year end.

Sales and cost of goods sold

From the standpoint of a consolidated enterprise, a sale of merchandise by one member of a consolidated group to another is not an event worthy of revenue recognition. A sale takes place only when merchandise is sold to a party outside of the consolidated enterprise. Intercompany sales should, of course, be given accounting recognition on the books of the individual companies; they must, however, be eliminated when reporting on the operations of the companies as a consolidated economic entity.

Assume, for example, that included in the revenues of the parent are $100,000 in sales to the subsidiary. The goods sold to the subsidiary were manufactured by the parent at a cost of $80,000. The subsidiary company in turn sold the goods to outsiders at a price of $120,000. The transactions would be reflected in the books of the two companies as follows:

	Parent	*Subsidiary*
Sales revenue	$100,000	$120,000
Cost of goods sold	80,000	100,000

From the standpoint of the consolidated entity, sales to outsiders were $120,000 and the cost of goods sold only $80,000. It is necessary to eliminate $100,000 in both sales revenue (the sale by the parent to the subsidiary) and cost of goods sold (the cost of the goods sold by the subsidiary to outsiders):

Sales revenue	$100,000	
Cost of goods sold		$100,000
To eliminate intercompany sales.		

Note: This entry has not been posted to the consolidated work sheet in Exhibit 13-3. Instead the alternative sales entry below has been used in the illustration.

Suppose alternatively that the parent had $100,000 in sales to the subsidiary which cost the parent $60,000 to manufacture. This time, however, assume that the subsidiary sold only 90 percent of such goods to outsiders. The other 10 percent of the goods remained in the inventory of the subsidiary. Subsidiary sales to outsiders were only $108,000; the cost of goods sold was only $90,000; the ending inventory was $10,000.

	Parent	*Subsidiary*
Sales revenue	$100,000	$108,000
Cost of goods sold	60,000	90,000
Ending inventory	—	10,000

Sales revenue — that is, sales revenue attributable to sales to outsiders — should properly be recorded at $108,000 and cost of goods sold represented by such sales at $54,000 (90 percent of the $60,000 that it cost to manufacture them). Ending inventory should properly be valued at $6,000 — the cost of the parent company to manufacture them (10 percent of the parent company's cost of goods sold *or* $60,000/$100,000 of $10,000 in inventory on hand). Sales revenue must thereby be reduced by $100,000 (the sales of the parent to the subsidiary), and cost of goods sold must be reduced by $96,000. [$60,000 cost to parent plus $90,000 (90 percent of $100,000) cost to subsidiary, less $54,000 (90 percent of $60,000 paid by parent) "real" cost of goods sold of the consolidated entity]. The $96,000 reduction in cost of goods sold may also be interpreted as a $90,000 elimination of the cost of the goods sold by the subsidiary to outsiders (already accounted for in parent company cost of goods sold) and a $6,000 reduction of cost of goods sold by the parent to the subsidiary. The latter reduction is required because 10 percent of the goods sold by the parent to the subsidiary is still in inventory; these goods have not been sold to outsiders.

The inventory of the subsidiary must also be reduced by $4,000. It did not cost the consolidated enterprise $10,000 as recorded on the books of the subsidiary but rather only $6,000 — the manufacturing cost to the parent. The required adjustment is

(b)

Sales revenue (of parent)	$100,000	
Cost of goods sold (of subsidiary)		$90,000
Inventory (of subsidiary)		4,000
Cost of goods sold (of parent)		6,000
To eliminate intercompany sales and adjust ending inventory for profit which had been recognized on intercompany sales.		

The cost of goods sold has been credited in two parts in order to show the component elements of the total amount.

A word of caution is in order for those who will proceed to further accounting courses. You may have observed that we have illustrated what is called a "downstream" sale (sale by parent to the subsidiary or investee) and not an "upstream" sale (sale by the subsidiary to the parent). In the upstream sale we might eliminate only 80 percent of the intercompany profit, because, from the minority shareholders' viewpoint, the 20 percent *may* be viewed as a sale to outsiders. Hence, the 20 percent might be considered earned in the minority shareholders' eyes. Present ARC rules require 80 percent elimination against the parent and 20 percent against minority shareholders in the subsidiary.

Sales of fixed assets

Fixed assets must be reported on the consolidated statements on the basis of their initial cost to the consolidated enterprise. If a fixed asset has been sold by one member of the consolidated group to another, then the amount at which the asset is carried on the books of an individual company may be greater or less than that based on original cost.

Assume, for example, that the $6,000 in the account of the parent company, "gain on sales of fixed assets" represents in its entirety the gain on the sale of land to the subsidiary. The land was sold to the subsidiary at a price of $45,000 (and represents the entire balance in the "land" account of the subsidiary). It had been purchased for, and had previously been carried in the accounts of the parent, at $39,000.

To report the consolidated results of operations and financial positions of the two companies, it is necessary to eliminate the effects of transactions that would be considered nothing more than internal transfers if the two companies were viewed as a single economic entity. Thus,

(c)

Gain on sale of fixed assets (by parent)	$6,000	
Land (of subsidiary)		$6,000
To adjust for intercompany sale of land.		

The intercompany sale of land will have to be accounted for in the preparation of consolidated statements in years subsequent to that in which the sale took place — in fact, for as long as the asset remains on the books of the subsidiary. The land will continue to be "overvalued" by the amount of the gain recognized by the parent. Since, on the books of the parent, the gain will have been *closed* at year end to retained earnings, retained earnings will be permanently overstated in subsequent years.

The complexities of adjusting for the sale of fixed assets are substantially compounded when the assets transferred are subject to depreciation. From the standpoint of the consolidated enterprise, depreciation charges must be determined on the basis of the original cost of the asset to the first member of the consolidated group that acquired it. On the books of the company on which the asset is presently recorded, however, it would be maintained on the basis of the price paid to the company, albeit a related company, from which it was purchased. If, for example, the fixed asset sold were equipment rather than land, then the subsidiary would properly depreciate, on its own books, an asset that had cost $45,000. If the useful life were 10 years, annual depreciation charges would be $4,500. For purposes of consolidated reporting, however, the asset initially cost only $39,000. Hence annual depreciation charges would be only $3,900. Adjustment would be required to reduce depreciation charges by $600. But, in addition, adjustments would also be required in each year after the first to "correct" for the cumulative effect on "accumulated depreciation" attributable to the previous "overstatements" of depreciation charges.

Elimination of investment in subsidiary; amortization of goodwill

The trial balances presented are those for the first year after acquisition of the subsidiary. The balances are *preclosing* balances. The revenue and expense accounts have not yet been closed to retained earnings, and the parent company has not yet recognized its share of subsidiary earnings. Hence, the balance in the investment in subsidiary account represents the amount paid by the parent to acquire its 80 percent interest in the subsidiary. Similarly, the balance in the subsidiary's retained earnings account is also that at the time of acquisition. The parent company must have paid, therefore, $200,000 for an 80 percent interest in a company that had a total book value of $225,000 (common shares of $50,000 plus retained earnings of $175,000). The excess of cost over book value — assumed in this case to represent goodwill — was, at the time of acquisition, $20,000 ($200,000 acquisition price, less $180,000, which is 80 percent of $225,000 book value). The following entry would eliminate the initial investment:

(d)

Common shares (of subsidiary)	$ 40,000	
Retained earnings (of subsidiary)	140,000	
Excess of cost over book value (goodwill)	20,000	
Investment in subsidiary (by parent)		$200,000
To eliminate investment in subsidiary and corresponding amounts in owners' equity accounts, and to establish goodwill.		

And the following entry would reclassify the minority interest:

(e)

Common shares (of subsidiary)	$10,000	
Retained earnings (of subsidiary)	35,000	
Minority interest in subsidiary		$45,000
To reclassify the equity of minority shareholders in the subsidiary at the time of acquisition.		

If it were decided to amortize the goodwill over 40 years, the maximum amortization period permitted by current professional pronouncements, then the following additional adjustment, one that affects directly the income statement, would have to be made:

(f)

Amortization of goodwill (expense)	$500	
Excess of cost over book value (goodwill)		$500
To amortize goodwill.		

Consolidated earnings can readily be determined from the combined preclosing trial balances:

Sales		$600,000
Cost of goods sold	$354,000	
Other expenses	133,000	
Amortization of goodwill	500	487,500
"Consolidated" income		$112,500

The $112,500 is *not* what would be reported on the consolidated income statement because the 20 percent minority shareholder interest in the subsidiary is viewed as an *expense* through the eyes of the majority shareholders, to whom consolidated financial statements are primarily directed.

The minority interest in earnings would be 20 percent of the earnings *only of the subsidiary*. The majority share would be total earnings less those ascribed to the minority:

Sales of subsidiary		$300,000
Cost of goods sold	$210,000	
Interest expense	7,000	
Other expenses	53,000	270,000
Subsidiary income		$ 30,000
Minority share of consolidated income (20% of $30,000):		$ 6,000
Majority share of consolidated income ($112,500 less $6,000):		106,500
Total		$112,500

A consolidated balance sheet can also be prepared from the combined trial balance. Since, however, the amounts reported in both the retained earnings accounts and the minority interest in subsidiary accounts represent *preclosing* balances, it is necessary to adjust both accounts to give effect to current year earnings:

	Retained earnings	*Minority interest in subsidiary*
Per preclosing trial balance	$687,000	$45,000
Share of current year income	106,500	6,000
Adjusted balance	$793,500	$51,000

Consolidated Financial Statements

Parent Limited
Consolidated Balance Sheet
As of End of First Year of Operations

Assets	
Inventory	$ 48,000
Land	89,000
Other assets	818,000
Excess of cost over book value (goodwill)	19,500
	$974,500
Equities	
Liabilities	$ 50,000
Minority interest in subsidiary	51,000
Common shares	80,000
Retained earnings	793,500
	$974,500

Parent Limited
Consolidated Income Statement
For First Year of Operations

Sales		$600,000
Cost of goods sold		354,000
Gross profit		246,000
Expenses:		
Other	$133,000	
Amortization of goodwill	500	133,500
		112,500
Minority interest in subsidiary		6,000
Net income (ignoring income tax)		$106,500

Reporting on the Equity Basis

Besides handling the books of the parent on the equity basis, we can also *report* to majority shareholders on the equity basis. In a consolidation we in effect replaced the "investment in subsidiary" account on the unconsolidated balance sheet with the individual assets less liabilities of the subsidiary. Also, on the unconsolidated income statement we replaced the "dividend revenue" account (if the parent used the cost basis) or the "revenue/income of the subsidiary" account (if the parent employed the equity basis of reporting and bookkeeping) with the individual revenue and expense figures for the subsidiary.

In equity *reporting* the amount of detail of disclosure is much less than for a consolidation. But by following the same process of making intercompany eliminations and fair (market) value costing (or amortizing goodwill), we arrive at exactly the same annual income and retained earnings of the parent plus its investee (or subsidiary) — that is, the majority shareholder's income — *as if we had consolidated.* For both equity and consolidation reporting we make exactly the same type of intercompany eliminations for such matters as intercompany interest revenue/expense transactions. However, under equity reporting, instead of debiting or crediting the individual revenue/expense accounts of the investee for eliminations in the work sheet, we debit or credit a one-line income figure called "income of investee." Similarly, we do not debit or credit the individual assets and liabilities of the investee on the work sheet; instead we debit or credit the "investment in investee" line of the balance sheet on the work sheet. The reason is that (at least in the simple case where there are no extraordinary and other complex transactions by the investee) the entire investment in the investee is shown on the external balance sheet as one line:

Equity in 40% owned company	$1,234,567

The income is also shown as one line:

Earnings of 40% owned company accounted for on the equity basis	$34,567

Equity reporting is sometimes called a "one line consolidation."

Equity *reporting* of the financial information in Exhibit 13-3 (which we previously used to illustrate a consolidation) would appear as follows:

Parent Limited
Balance Sheet
End of First Year of Operations

Inventory		$ 40,000
Land		50,000
Other assets		600,000
Investment in Subsidiary Limited, at equity		213,500
		$903,500
Liabilities		$30,000
Common shares		80,000
Retained earnings:		
Beginning of year	$687,000	
Add net income	106,500	
End of year		793,500
		$903,500

Parent Limited
Income Statement
First Year of Operations

Sales		$400,000
Cost of goods sold		240,000
Gross profit		160,000
Expenses:		
Other	$80,000	
Less:		
Gain on sale of assets	(6,000)	
Interest revenue	(7,000)	67,000
		93,000
Equity in income of Subsidiary Limited*		13,500
Net Income (ignoring income tax)		$106,500

*Normally this line would appear below income tax expense.

A comparison of equity reporting and consolidation reporting (page 580) for Parent Limited shows the following:

1. The net income of $106,500 is the same under both methods!
2. Equity reporting picks up Parent Limited's figures only (see trial balance in Exhibit 13-3) except for the one line on the balance sheet ("Investment in Subsidiary Limited, at equity") and one line on the income statement ("Equity in income of Subsidiary Limited").
3. The "Investment in Subsidiary Limited, at equity" account has increased by $13,500, the amount shown on the income statement.
4. Under equity reporting the statements are not labelled "consolidated" (unless some other subsidiary has been consolidated).

Where did the $13,500 come from?

Majority shareholders' equity of $30,000 *unadjusted* net income of subsidiary (80% x $30,000)	$24,000
Less:	
Amortization of goodwill (Consolidation journal entry "f", page 578)	(500)
Gain on sale of assets (Consolidation journal entry "c", page 576)	(6,000)
Unsold inventory (Consolidation journal entry "b", page 576)	(4,000)
Adjusted net income	$13,500

If we refer to the Labatt's financial statements in Chapter 2 we can note that Labatt's reports some of its investments (the Toronto Blue Jays, for instance, which is 45 percent owned) on an equity basis. On the income statement (page 52) Labatt's uses the one-line description "equity in net earnings of partly-owned businesses." On the balance sheet (page 53) the one-line description is "investment in partly-owned businesses".

Amortizations of goodwill arising on "consolidation" and the "extra" cost of assets (such as depreciation of the building's extra $5,000 cost in Example 4), although absorbed entirely by the parent, should be subtracted in arriving at the "equity in net earnings of companies reported on the equity basis." However, they may be included elsewhere on the income statements of some Canadian corporations. The important point is that the overall equity-accounted *earnings* of all companies would be the same as if consolidation had occurred.

Implications for Readers

If the "bottom line" — net income — is the same no matter whether equity reporting or consolidation reporting is chosen, who cares which reporting basis is used? The matter at issue is aggregation of figures, and the consequences for different types of decisions. Sometimes aggregation is an aid; at other times it can be a hindrance in forming judgments.

Consolidation accounting is usually employed when the parent has voting control (over 50 percent ownership) over a subsidiary. As a result the parent can move assets around its various controlled companies, almost at will. It could, for example, arrange a poor liquid asset position in a company which (in the absence of tough accounting rules) might be reported on the equity basis. This liquidity deficiency would not show up under one-line equity reporting (which is a net of liquid and non-liquid items), but some of the effects would net with other assets and liabilities in a consolidated balance sheet. But, to what degree? The consolidated figures group all similar assets and liabilities; thus we will probably learn little about any one company's impact on the overall figures. *However*, we will learn from consolidated statements whether the entire consolidated group of companies has a liquidity problem.

Similarly, a consolidated income statement gives us a clearer idea of individual revenue and expense amounts for the entire group of companies. But it, too, has its limitations. We are not told how much *each* of the companies which are reported on the equity basis contribute to income. Maybe we need divisional or segment reporting, if our objective is to predict. Maybe we need separate financial statements for each company in the group. A review of Labatt's financial statements in Chapter 2 tells us almost nothing about The Toronto Blue Jay Baseball Club, if that is our concern.

Business Combinations

The term "business combinations" does not have one clear, universal definition in Canada, although the CICA has attempted to define it well. The difficulty is caused by the definitions in some corporate legislation which, under some sets of facts, differs from the CICA's choice. A fairly well accepted one defines a business combination as occurring when:

1. One company buys over 50 percent of the common shares of another company. (i.e., an intercorporate investment exists); *or*
2. One company buys the *assets* and *liabilities* (not shares) of an *operating* division of another company. (This differs from buying a few assets — such as land and buildings. For example, in the late 1970s Westinghouse sold the net assets of its appliance division, as opposed to its entire company, to two other companies who continued to produce the same types of products).

In situation 1 we have both an intercorporate investment and a business combination. Situation 2 is a business combination, but is not an intercorporate investment. Business combinations can be accounted for in a variety of ways; two are permitted in current practice: (a) purchase-basis accounting, and (b) pooling-of-interests accounting. In the illustrations earlier in the chapter which employed the market value basis of determining cost of individual assets and liabilities on acquisition of a company (i.e., when we added $5,000 to the building value in Example 4) we were using purchase-basis accounting. Under this basis (i) the parent's share of the investee's assets and liabilities are recorded at "fair market value" (often replacement cost or net realizable value); and (ii) the minority interest share of investee net assets are shown at cost per the investee's books, on the consolidated balance sheet prepared at the date of acquisition. The fair market value is cost to the investor. Subsequent to the acquisition date, the fair market value costs would differ from the market values.

The alternative, now rarely permitted in Canada, is pooling-of-interests accounting, which uses *book values* of the investee in the consolidated financial statements prepared at the date of acquisition, and subsequently. Pooling-of-interests accounting was used in Canada and the U.S. in the 1960s and early 1970s to generate some highly questionable income figures. It was severely criticized, and the accounting profession acted to prevent its widespread use. Arbitrary guidelines were set by the CICA to circumscribe a set of facts under which book values (pooling-of-interest basis) might be used. The CICA purposely made the guidelines tough for a company to comply with, thereby severely limiting use of the pooling-of-interests basis of consolidation.

Instant Earnings

Let us illustrate the pooling-of-interests basis of consolidation, and some of its implications. First, we will show some possible implications. Suppose, for example, Alpha Limited acquired 500,000 common shares of Beta Limited at a price of $10 per share. In exchange for the shares, Alpha Limited issued to Beta Limited's shareholders 50,000 of its own common shares, each share having a market value of $100. The common shares do not have a par value. The following journal entry would be in order:

Investment in Beta Limited	$5,000,000	
Common shares		$5,000,000
To record purchase of 500,000 shares of Beta Limited.		

Such an acquisition may have a striking impact on the reported earnings of the parent company. Indeed, acquisitions may result in instant increases in reported profits even in the absence of any substantive improvements in the operations of either the parent or the subsidiary company. Consider the following additional information pertaining to the acquisition of Beta by Alpha:

Selected Financial Data Immediately Prior to Acquisition

	Alpha	*Beta*
Net assets	$1,000,000	$5,000,000
Common shares	$ 100,000	$ 500,000
Retained earnings	$ 900,000	$4,500,000
Number of shares outstanding	100,000 shares	500,000 shares
Book value per share	$ 10	$ 10
Latest annual income	$ 200,000	$ 500,000
Latest earnings per share	$ 2	$ 1
Market price of common shares	$ 100 per share	$ 10 per share

Alpha Limited is the smaller of the two companies in terms of assets and total earnings, but not in terms of market value. Yet investors obviously consider its prospects for future earnings to be relatively more promising than those of Beta. The price/earnings ratio (market price of common shares to earnings per share) of Alpha is 50 to 1 and that of Beta is only 10 to 1. Suppose that the exchange of shares were to be based on the market prices of the shares of the two companies. The 500,000 shares of Beta Limited have a total market value of $5 million (500,000 shares at $10 per share). Since each share of Alpha has a market value of $100, the number of shares that Alpha would be required to issue would be $5 million divided by $100 — 50,000.

If Alpha Limited were to issue 50,000 additional shares to the owners of Beta Limited, then it would have outstanding a total of 150,000 shares. Consolidated earnings, assuming no substantive improvement in the operations of either firm, would be the sum of the earnings of the two individual companies — $700,000 ($200,000 plus $500,000). No amortization of excess of cost over book value is required since the total market price of Beta Limited's shares is exactly equal to its book value. Earnings per share of Alpha Limited, reported on a consolidated basis, would now be $4.66 ($700,000 divided by 150,000 shares) — an increase of 133 percent over previously reported earnings of $2 per share.

The ramifications of this simplified example are critical to an understanding of the merger movement of the 1960s. In that period numerous firms acquired subsidiaries. Frequently, the acquired companies were in industries totally unrelated to those of the parents. Commonly the acquisitions were made for common shares rather than cash, and sometimes, a whale of a firm was swallowed up by a minnow.

The acquisition in the example, as is common in practice, was facilitated by the substantial difference in the price/earnings (P/E) ratios of the two firms. The P/E ratio of Alpha was considerably higher than that of Beta. Stock market prices tend to be based, at least in part, on reported earnings — but most particularly on expected future earnings (or cash flow), and on the trend in earnings over a number of years. The relatively high P/E ratio of Alpha would likely be accounted for, at least in part, by a trend of rapidly increasing earnings. The acquisition of Beta may help sustain that trend or even accentuate it. The P/E ratio of Alpha *might* remain high, but only if: (1) investors were naive and did not fully appreciate the finance and accounting methods which were employed to obtain "instant earnings," or (2) a change in prospects (net income) is expected for Beta. For example, a main reason for the recent low P/E ratio in Beta may have been poor management of the company, which will be replaced by far better managers who are expected to dramatically improve net income.

For those who believe in the efficiency of behavior of share prices on stock markets (efficient market hypothesis), Reason (1) above would not carry much weight or credibility *if* investors had adequate access to information about the two companies and their income prospects prior to the business combination (merger). Most supporters of the "hypothesis" agree with what is called its semi-strong form. This means in simple terms that on the average: (a) the market price of the shares fully reflects all *publicly available* information and (b) that investors as a group react quickly and in an unbiased manner to incorporate any newly released information into share market prices. This hypothesis should *not* be interpreted to mean that (a) *no one* loses or wins by investing in the market after acting at a later date upon "old" publicly available information; (b) accounting reports are not needed because people already know necessary financial information; (c) costs of preparing and interpreting financial reports are unimportant; (d) financial analysts are not necessary; (e) there are no exceptions to the general case; and (f) the so-called "efficient market" sets the one and only "true" market value.

It is possible that, even though Beta was a public company prior to the acquisition by Alpha, inadequate information about Beta's operations had been disclosed to investors. Without having adequate information publicly available the efficient (or naive) market may have guessed incorrectly about Beta's prospective earnings and the risk associated with the business. Accordingly, *if* as a result of the proposed combination the market receives new, favorable information about the company, the P/E ratio of Alpha combined with Beta could remain high. But if no new information comes to light (and the prospects for improved management are slim), the P/E ratio of combined Alpha-Beta could settle to around a weighted average of the two P/E ratios before the business combination. Hence, the instant earnings would be discounted by the stock market which would choose a lower P/E ratio.

However, if some stock markets are not efficient (presumably in part because many *naive* investors buy and sell through that market) the P/E ratio of combined Alpha-Beta could remain (unrealistically) high. In order for this to occur the investors would have to blindly attach the same P/E ratio to Beta's earnings that they did to Alpha's prior to the combination. Somehow these naive investors would have had to be uninformed about why Beta's earnings previously sold at a low P/E ratio — which may have been because of sound reasons such as limited growth prospects for the company and various business risks.

In brief, "instant earnings" computations are plagued with many questions as to their implications. The computation may be no more than a silly arithmetic exercise, if the market then lowers the P/E multiple of the combined companies. The P/E multiple may drop so that after combination, it simply represents a weighted average of what existed before the combination:

Before

	Market price
Alpha: 100,000 shares @ $100 per share	$10,000,000
Beta: 500,000 shares @ $10 per share	5,000,000
Total market values before combination	$15,000,000

After

Alpha (consolidated to include Beta) would have 150,000 common shares outstanding. *If* the market price of the total company remained the same, the market price of Alpha would still be $100, because $100 × 150,000 shares =	$15,000,000

However, at a new earnings per share of $4.66, the P/E ratio becomes $100/4.66 = *21.46* times. This is a considerable drop from the 50 times which Alpha had prior to the business combination.

However, if the accounting profession believes (1) that many naive investors exist, (2) that these investors cannot grasp the range of P/E implications about business combinations, and (3) that the profession has a responsibility to protect such naive investors, a clarification of accounting rules *is* necessary when business combinations occur. The ARC of the CICA obviously believed enough in the above three points that they acted to virtually eliminate pooling-of-interests accounting, which may, in part, contribute to naive investor misunderstanding. The risk, as always, is that the ARC could have forced "the accounting tail to wag the (business/economic) dog." Otherwise sound decisions to engage in business combinations *may* have been soured and prevented by "purchase accounting" rules. Such rules force fair market valuing of the acquiree's (such as Beta's) assets and liabilities, amortizations of goodwill and, for several assets and liabilities, amortizations of the excess of fair market value above book value, per the acquiree. [Remember amortization of the $5,000 building in Example 4 (page 571). This had the effect of lowering the parent's consolidated net income.][1]

Pooling-of-Interests Further Illustrated

In several of the discussions of business combinations to this point it has been assumed that one company acquires another. The combinations have been accounted for as purchase-type transactions — one company purchases, either for cash or common shares, the outstanding common shares of another. (The previous discussion of *instant earnings* used as an example a situation where book value and market value of Beta were identical, and thereby avoided "purchase accounting", and implicitly assumed pooling-of-interests accounting).

In those instances where a business combination is effected by an exchange of common shares — where one company, be it a new or existing company, acquires substantially all of the voting shares of another in return for its own common shares — the transaction *may* be accounted for as an alternative type of business combination — a pooling-of-interests. The financial consequences of accounting for a business combination as a pooling-of-interests rather than a purchase may be profound; reported earnings as well as values assigned to assets may be significantly different.

Underlying the pooling-of-interests method of accounting for business combinations is the rationale that two firms join together to operate as a single economic enterprise. Neither purchases the other, and both owners of the component companies are granted a proportionate interest in the combined enterprise. The combination represents a marriage of equals, or if not exactly of equals, then at least a situation where one party does not clearly dominate the other.

The key feature of the pooling-of-interests method involves each of the component companies' retaining its former basis of accounting. That is, the assets and liabilities of neither company are revalued at the time of combination. The recorded assets and liabilities of both companies are carried forward to the consolidated enterprise at their previously recorded amounts. So too are their retained earnings. No accounting recognition is given to new goodwill. Retention of the former basis of accounting is justified on the grounds that there has been no sale of the assets of one firm to another; there has merely been a fusion of two companies into one.

The pooling-of-interests method has had great appeal to firms effecting business combinations in that it commonly allows the consolidated enterprise to report higher earnings than if the combination were accounted for as a purchase. The pooling-of-interests method may result in higher reported earnings because it does not require the consolidated enterprise to increase the carrying values of the assets of the acquired firm so that they reflect an excess of purchase price over book value. No goodwill need be recorded. Therefore, the firm does not have to charge either depreciation or amortization on the amounts when the fair market values of either of the two firms exceed their book values.

An example can be used to illustrate the pooling-of-interests approach and to highlight the differences between the pooling-of-interests and the purchase methods of accounting for business combinations. Selected information about two firms, Delta Limited and Echo Limited, prior to their merger is indicated below:

	Balance sheets	
	Delta Limited	*Echo Limited*
Miscellaneous assets	$1,500,000	$6,000,000
Miscellaneous liabilities	$ 500,000	$1,000,000
Common shares, no par value	400,000	1,200,000
Retained earnings	600,000	3,800,000
	$1,500,000	$6,000,000
Number of shares outstanding	100,000	500,000
Net income, in year prior to merger	$ 200,000	$ 500,000
Earnings per share	$ 2	$ 1
Recent market price per share	$ 100	$ 20

Delta and Echo agree to combine their operations. Delta Limited will issue to the current shareholders of Echo Limited new common shares in exchange for their existing shares in Echo Limited. The number of shares to be issued by Delta will be based on the relative market prices of the shares just prior to the negotiations leading to the merger. Since the shares outstanding of Echo Limited have a current market value of $10 million (500,000 shares at $20 per share), Delta Limited will have to issue 100,000 shares ($10 million divided by $100, the market price of Delta Limited's shares).

Although the two firms may be combined into a single economic entity for reporting purposes, they are still independent legal entities; hence each firm must keep separate sets of accounting books and records. The firm which issues the shares may have to record them at either fair market value or at a lesser price, (such as the book value of the net assets obtained) as specified by the Companies Act under which it is incorporated. If the shares have to be issued at fair market value, (i.e. debit "Investment in Echo Limited", credit "Common shares" for the market price of shares issued) but under pooling-of-interests accounting the assets less liabilities are consolidated using book value of Echo Limited, an excess of credits over debits exists (as long as fair market value exceeds book value). This causes a minor problem; in brief, the excess of share price over book value of Echo is deducted from total owners' equity on consolidation, and the consolidated balance sheet balances. Subsequent to the merger the individual balance sheets of the two firms would appear as follows:

	Balance sheets	
	Delta Limited	*Echo Limited*
Miscellaneous assets	$1,500,000	$6,000,000
Investment in Echo Limited	5,000,000	—
	$6,500,000	$6,000,000
Miscellaneous liabilities	$ 500,000	$1,000,000
Common shares	5,400,000[a]	1,200,000
Retained earnings	600,000	3,800,000
	$6,500,000	$6,000,000

[a]Reflects the issue of 100,000 additional shares. The book value of Echo Limited is $5 million (assets less liabilities). Each share is considered to be issued at a price of $50 ($5 million divided by 100,000 shares).

To prepare a balance sheet on a consolidated basis, it is necessary to eliminate the "Investment in Echo Limited" and the corresponding owners' equity accounts of Echo Limited. Under pooling-of-interests accounting the specific elimination entry is sometimes a bit tricky. We have simplified matters in the example, and the entry is:

Common shares	$5,000,000	
Investment in Echo Limited		$5,000,000
To eliminate the investment account against common shares of Echo with the remainder charged to Delta.		

The consolidated balance sheet would appear as follows:

Miscellaneous assets	$7,500,000
Miscellaneous liabilities	$1,500,000
Common shares	1,600,000
Retained earnings	4,400,000
Total liabilities and owners' equity	$7,500,000

The assets and liabilities are stated on the same basis as on the books of the component companies. In contrast to the purchase method no adjustment has been made to asset values — either by revaluation of specific assets or by the addition of goodwill — to reflect the difference between the market value of the common shares issued by Delta Limited ($10 million) and the value at which the assets were recorded on the books of Echo Limited ($5 million).

If there were no substantive increase in the earnings of the two firms as a consequence of the merger, then earnings after the merger would be the sum of the earnings of the two individual firms — $200,000 contributed by Delta, $500,000 contributed by Echo, a total of $700,000. The earnings per share, based on 200,000 shares of Delta Limited's shares outstanding, would be $3.50. The earnings per share of Delta Limited, the firm whose shares remain outstanding, would thereby have increased as the result of the merger by $1.50 from what they were prior to the merger — an increase that can be attributed entirely to the *instant earnings* effect described earlier.

By contrast, if the combination had been accounted for as a purchase, then the combined entity would have reported either goodwill of $5 million, or specific assets would have been increased in carrying value by that same amount. If the $5 million in additional assets or in goodwill were depreciated or amortized over a period of, say, 20 years, then earnings would be $250,000 per year lower than under the pooling method. If earnings after the merger were the same as those prior to the merger, then consolidated earnings, if the combination were accounted for as a purchase, would be only $450,000 as opposed to $700,000 if accounted for as a pooling. Hence, earnings per share would be only $450,000 divided by 200,000 shares — $2.25.

Under pooling-of-interests accounting it would still be necessary to make work-sheet elimination entries for intercompany transactions. For example, if Echo has sold inventory to Delta at a profit, and the inventory remained on Delta's shelves at the year end, the entire intercompany profit (assuming that no minority shareholders exist) would have to be eliminated on consolidation.

Foreign Currency Translation

Often, the consolidation process is complicated by the location of one or more of the subsidiaries in a foreign country, and its financial statements are expressed in other than Canadian dollars. For our purposes, two basic interrelated questions arise in such cases:

1. For purposes of consolidation, should the assets and liabilities of the foreign subsidiary be translated from the foreign currency to Canadian dollars at:
   (a) the currency exchange rate in effect on the balance-sheet date (e.g., $1 Canadian = $0.88 U.S.)?
   (b) the currency exchange rate in effect when the asset was acquired, or liability incurred — which may have been many years ago (e.g., $1 Canadian = $1.03 U.S.)?
   (c) some combination of (a) and (b) (Cash at $0.88; land at $1.03)?
2. Does our response to Point 1 depend upon our objectives of financial reporting? (Many people would say "yes").

We raise the issue because it is a very important one for readers of financial statements. The choices can have dramatic effects on the balance sheet figures and net income. The methods chosen may simply not suit your objective of accounting if you are a user/reader. Unfortunately, the subject is too complex to explain in detail in an introductory book.

We can, however, give a few glimpses of the implications by selecting a related situation involving foreign currency translation. Suppose that a domestic Canadian company needing $10 million decides to borrow the funds in the New York market when $1 Canadian = $1 U.S. The loan is for 20 years at an interest rate of 9 percent per annum. At the balance sheet date one year later, assume that the exchange rate has changed so that $1 Canadian = $0.90 U.S. This means that *if* the Canadian company chose to pay off the U.S. debt on this date the cost would be $11,111,111 Canadian dollars ($10,000,000 divided by .90).

What should the Canadian company show on its balance sheet one year after borrowing the U.S. money? The choices are: (1) $10,000,000 (the amount of Canadian dollars which it received one year ago); (2) $11,111,111 (the amount of Canadian dollars it would take to pay off the U.S. debt as of the balance sheet date); (3) $11,055,556 ($11,111,111 less a 20-year straight-line amortization of the "premium" of $1,111,111); or (4) something else. Different assumptions can be made to support each of the choices. For instance, the $11,111,111 figure could be supported by assuming either: (a) the debt will be repaid shortly and will cost that amount; or (b) management erred in borrowing the U.S. debt a year early; hence the $1,111,111 should be charged to income in the year of "error":

Loss on currency translation (expense +)	$1,111,111	
Debt payable (liability +)		$1,111,111
To record debt at the current foreign exchange rate.		

For a management evaluation objective of accounting the $11,111,111 debt figure and $1,111,111 loss could be useful. But perhaps management did not err in borrowing one year ago. Maybe it had a very appealing investment opportunity and needed the funds. We are thus describing only the tip of a huge iceberg.

Choosing suitable methods of accounting is not an easy task, however, because of the conflicting objectives of accounting and reporting. Someone interested in predicting cash flows of a company may want consolidated statements, separate statements for each large investee, and statements for each operating division.

Summary

Intercorporate ownership may take a variety of forms. The objective of the accountant is to give effect to the economic substance of the relationship between the parties involved.

We have explained current *constraints,* requirements, or rules of both corporate law and the ARC of the CICA in this and the last two chapters.

This was necessary so that readers would be able to read with comprehension many financial statements which are being prepared in practice today. It is important to remember that constraints, like facts and objectives, will change over time. They are certainly not set in concrete for one's lifetime.

As a general rule, the manner of reporting the interest of one company in voting shares of another is determined by the degree of control that it is able to exercise. If an investor company is unable to exert substantial influence over the company whose shares it owns, it would report its interest on the *cost basis*. If it is able to exercise substantial or significant influence, it would report its interest on the *equity basis*.

When a corporation has control over another, then the information needs of the shareholders of the controlling company may best be served by combining the financial position and results of operations into a single set of *consolidated* financial statements. If the business combination were effected entirely by an exchange of common shares, then the consolidated statements might be prepared on a pooling-of-interests basis. If, on the other hand, one company acquired for cash or other assets the outstanding shares of another, the combination would be reported as a purchase.

Notes

[1]A further discussion of the efficient market hypothesis and its implications for accounting is provided in J.R.E. Parker, "Financial Reporting and Market Hypothesis," *CA magazine,* April 1979 and June 1979, and S. Basu, *Inflation Accounting, Capital Market Efficiency and Security Prices* (Hamilton: The Society of Management Accountants of Canada, 1977).

Questions, Problems, and Cases

Questions

*13-1 Under what circumstances should a firm report its investment in another company by the cost method? By the equity method? When should it prepare consolidated financial statements?

13-2 Why is the cost method considered inappropriate for investments in which the investor company can exert significant influence over the operating policies of the investee?

13-3 Why, under the equity method, does a firm *reduce* its balance in its investment account upon receipt (or declaration) of a dividend by the investee?

13-4 When under the equity method does an investor recognize revenue attributable to the earnings of the company in which it maintains an investment? When under the cost method? When is revenue recognized if consolidated statements are prepared?

13-5 In what way is the equity method of accounting for long-term investment an extension of the accrual concept? In what way are consolidated statements an extension of the entity concept (defined in Chapter 5)?

13-6 Equity reporting of long-term investments is sometimes called a "one-line consolidation." Why? Explain why consolidation is not regarded as appropriate for an investor who has significant influence yet does not have voting control of the investee.

13-7 Explain how consolidated statements are more informative than statements prepared on an equity basis, keeping in mind the various objectives of financial statements.

13-8 Consolidated statements aggregate and therefore hide information potentially useful to readers of financial statements who want to predict cash flows. Discuss how this is so and suggest a remedy.

13-9 From the standpoint of which group of shareholders — those of the parent, those of the subsidiary, or those of both — are consolidated statements prepared? Explain.

13-10 Why do consolidations relate only to corporate *reports* rather than to the underlying corporate books and records? On which set of books, those of the parent or the subsidiary, those of both, or those of neither, are consolidation adjustments made?

13-11 Explain the difference in consolidation worksheet entries between a parent company that uses the cost basis versus the equity basis for recording in its books the investment in a subsidiary. Why would the parent want to use the equity method for recording transactions on its company books if consolidated statements were going to be prepared anyway?

13-12 Under what conditions may a company improve its earnings per share simply by acquiring controlling interest in another company? How would this increase be interpreted by potential investors in the company? (Hint: Consider the efficient market hypothesis.)

13-13 What is *goodwill*? When is it recorded? From what does it arise? Suppose a firm acquires an interest in a subsidiary for an amount in excess of its book value. What difference might it make on consolidated net income if such excess were classified as goodwill rather than assigned to specific assets?

13-14 What is the underlying rationale of a pooling-of-interests? What critical differences arise in terms of asset valuation and income determination if a business combination is accounted for as a pooling rather than as a purchase? Why did the Accounting Research Committee (ARC) of the CICA discourage the pooling method? What assumption in this instance might have been made by the ARC about investors?

13-15 Some people have argued that goodwill should not be amortized unless there is proven diminution in value. Comment on the merit of this position. Explain why the ARC of the CICA settled on a 40-year amortization period.

13-16 Distinguish between an intercorporate investment and a business combination.

Problems

P13-1 On January 2, 19x8, the Alberta Company Limited purchased for $60 per share (cash) 2,000 of the 10,000 outstanding common shares of Calgary Ltd.

On July 5, 19x8, Calgary Ltd. reported earnings of $40,000 for the first half of the year.

On July 15, the board of directors of Calgary Ltd. declared and paid a $1 per share cash dividend.

On December 31, 19x8 Calgary Ltd. reported a loss of $15,000 for the second half of the year.

Required:

a. Prepare journal entries to account for the investment of the Alberta Company Limited in Calgary Ltd. using first the *cost* method and then the *equity* method.

b. Compare total revenues of the Alberta Company Limited attributable to its investment under the two alternative methods. Compare the year-end carrying value of the investment.

P13-2 On January 1, 19x1, the Eagleton Co. Ltd. purchased for $80,000 a 40 percent interest (4,000 out of 10,000 shares) in the common shares of Alexander Co. Ltd.

On December 31, 19x3, the Eagleton Co. Ltd. sold 1,000 of its shares at a price of $25 per share. It recorded a gain of $2,000 on the sale.

On December 31, 19x5, the remaining shares were reported on the books of Eagleton at a value of $78,000.

During the five-year period from 19x1 through 19x5 Alexander Co. Ltd. paid annual dividends of $1.50 per share.

Required:

a. Determine the earnings of Alexander Co. Ltd. during the period January 1, 19x1, to December 31, 19x3. (State your assumptions.)

b. Determine the earnings of Alexander Co. Ltd. during the period January 1, 19x4, to December 31, 19x5. (State your assumptions.)

P13-3 Wayside Ltd. purchased a piece of manufacturing equipment from its subsidiary, Gardner Ltd. Wayside Ltd. paid $40,000 for the equipment five years earlier. The equipment had been recorded on the books of Gardner Ltd. at a cost of $50,000 less accumulated depreciation of $25,000. Gardner Ltd. had been depreciating the asset over a period of 10 years. Wayside Ltd. will depreciate the asset over its remaining useful life of 5 years.

Required:

a. At what amount should Wayside Ltd. record the asset on its own books? How much depreciation should it charge each year?

b. At what amount should Wayside Ltd. report the asset on its consolidated balance sheet? How much depreciation should it report?

c. Suppose that depreciation charges on the equipment enter into computation of cost of goods sold. Explain the nature of any adjustments to cost of goods sold that might have to be made when a consolidated income statement is prepared. Suppose that not all goods manufactured in the course of a year are actually sold. Explain the nature of any adjustments to year-end inventory that might have to be made.

P13-4 Condensed balance sheets of three companies, A, B, and C, appear as follows:

	A	*B*	C
Miscellaneous assets	$500,000	$134,000	$90,000
Investment in B (80 percent)	190,000		
Investment in C (60 percent)		66,000	
	$690,000	$200,000	$90,000
Common shares	$ 50,000	$ 5,000	$10,000
Retained earnings	640,000	195,000	80,000
Total shareholders' equity	$690,000	$200,000	$90,000

B acquired its 60 percent interest in C at a time when the balance in the retained earnings account of C was $70,000. Company A just recently acquired its 80 percent interest in B.

Required:

a. Prepare any necessary journal entries to eliminate, for purposes of consolidation, the investment of B in C and to reclassify the interest of the minority shareholders.
b. Prepare any necessary journal entries to eliminate the investment of A in B and to reclassify the interest of the minority shareholders.
c. Combine the remaining balances into a consolidated balance sheet. Assign any excess of cost over book value to goodwill. (Assume book value of B and C's tangible net assets at date of acquisition equals their fair market value.)

P13-5 In 19x6, the National Products Company Ltd. acquired, for $200,000 in common shares, 100 percent control of Consumer Goods Co. Ltd. At the time of the acquisition the net assets (assets less liabilities) of Consumer Goods Co. Ltd. were recorded on its books at a value of $120,000. In 19x7 National Products Company Ltd. had earnings of $90,000, exclusive of earnings of Consumer Goods Co. Ltd. Consumer Goods Co. Ltd. had earnings of $20,000. There were no material intercompany transactions during the year.

Required:

Determine the consolidated earnings of National Products Company Ltd. and its subsidiary under the following alternative assumptions:

a. The combination is accounted for as a purchase, and the excess of acquisition cost over book value is allocated to various fixed assets that have an average remaining useful life of 10 years.
b. The combination is accounted for as a purchase, and the excess of acquisition cost over book value is allocated entirely to "goodwill". The goodwill is to be amortized over 40 years.
c. The business combination is accounted for as a pooling-of-interests.

P13-6 Indicated below are the condensed balance sheets of ABC Ltd. and DEF Ltd. as of December 31, 19x8. On that date, ABC Ltd. issued 25,000 new common shares in exchange for 100 percent of the outstanding shares of DEF Ltd. On the date of the exchange the market price of the ABC Ltd. shares was $50 per share.

	ABC Ltd.	*DEF Ltd.*
Assets	$2,500,000	$1,000,000
Common shares	$ 500,000	$ 250,000
Retained earnings	2,000,000	750,000
Total shareholders' equity	$2,500,000	$1,000,000

Required:

a. Prepare a journal entry to record the exchange of shares on the books of ABC Ltd. Assume that the exchange will be accounted for as a pooling-of-interests.

b. Make any entries that would be necessary for the preparation of a consolidated balance sheet, and prepare such a consolidated balance sheet.

c. Indicate any key differences in Parts a and b that would result if the transaction had been accounted for as a purchase rather than as a pooling.

P13-7 Parent Ltd. owns 100 percent of the outstanding stock of Sub Ltd. In 19x8 Parent Ltd. had earnings of $200,000 (exclusive of its share of Sub Ltd. earnings) and Sub Ltd. had earnings of $80,000.

Required:

a. Given the additional information that follows, determine consolidated earnings for the year (assume the book value of Sub Ltd.'s net assets at the date of acquisition equals their fair market value):

(i) Parent Ltd. sold merchandise to Sub Ltd. at a price of $150,000. The cost of such merchandise was $120,000. Sub Ltd. resold 60 percent of such merchandise at a price of $100,000. The remaining 40 percent is included in Sub Ltd. inventory.

(ii) Parent Ltd. made a loan of $100,000 to Sub Ltd. During the year, Sub Ltd. paid interest on the loan of $6,000.

(iii) Parent Ltd. purchased from Sub Ltd. a piece of equipment for $25,000. The equipment has a remaining useful life of 10 years and no anticipated salvage value. The equipment had a net value on the books of Sub Ltd. of $15,000 (cost of $30,000 less accumulated depreciation of $15,000). Sub Ltd. had been depreciating the equipment over a period of 20 years.

(iv) Sub Ltd. leased office space from Parent Ltd. In 19x8 Sub Ltd. made rent payments of $500 per month — a total of $6,000 during the year.

(v) Parent Ltd. paid for its interest in Sub Ltd. an amount that was $60,000 in excess of Sub Ltd.'s book value. The $60,000 was allocated entirely to goodwill and is being amortized over a period of 20 years.

b. State in words how the information in (iii) above would be recorded if Parent Ltd. owned 80 percent of the outstanding shares. (Hint: This is an "upstream" transaction.)

c. Why is the assumption that the book value of Sub Ltd.'s net assets at the date of acquisition equals their fair market value necessary?

P13-8 The Maine Corporation Ltd. owned 40 percent (10,000 shares) of the voting shares of the Bangor Corporation Ltd. and controlled a majority of seats on the latter's board of directors. Toward the end of 19x8, it was estimated by the controllers of the two firms that Maine Corporation Ltd. would have earnings for the year of approximately $10,000 (exclusive of earnings attributable to Bangor Corporation Ltd.) and that Bangor Corporation Ltd. would have earnings of approximately $50,000.

The president of Maine Corporation Ltd. was disappointed that his firm would earn only $10,000 plus its share of Bangor Corporation Ltd. earnings. Prior to 19x8 Maine Corporation Ltd. had increased its earnings by 10 percent each year; consistent with that trend Maine Corporation Ltd. would have to report total earnings in 19x8 of $45,000.

Required:

a. Maine Corporation Ltd. accounts for its interest in Bangor Corporation Ltd. on the equity basis. If Bangor Corporation Ltd. were to declare its usual dividend of $.50 per share, what would be the total reported income of Maine Corporation Ltd.?

b. The president of Maine Corporation suggested to his controller that Bangor Corporation Ltd. be directed to declare a special dividend of $3 per share. What impact would the additional dividend have on earnings of Maine Corporation Ltd.?

c. Suppose that Maine Corporation Ltd. accounted for its investment in Bangor Corporation Ltd. on the cost basis. What would the total reported earnings of Maine Corporation Ltd. be if the latter declared its regular dividend of $.50 per share? What impact would the additional dividend have on earnings of Maine Corporation Ltd.?

d. State why the equity rather than the cost method is considered appropriate for firms which can exert substantial influence over companies in which they have an interest. Is there an alternative way to disclose the same information and still achieve the desired objectives of financial accounting?

P13-9 The preclosing trial balances of Mann Ltd. and Rudolph Ltd. as of December 31, 19x8, are indicated below:

	Mann Ltd.	*Rudolph Ltd.*
Cash	$100,000	$ 20,000
Investment in Rudolph Ltd.	54,000	
Other assets	76,000	75,000
Common shares	10,000	10,000
Retained earnings	190,000	80,000
Sales	140,000	60,000
Cost of goods sold	95,000	50,000
Other expenses	15,000	5,000

Mann Ltd. owns 60 percent of the outstanding shares of the Rudolph Ltd. It acquired its investment in 19x4 for $30,000 at a time when the net worth of Rudolph Ltd. was $50,000. Mann maintains its investment in Rudolph on the equity basis. Mann Ltd. has not yet taken into account its share of Rudolph Ltd.'s 19x8 earnings.

Required:

a. Prepare a 19x8 income statement and balance sheet for Mann Ltd. assuming that it is deemed inappropriate to consolidate its accounts with those of Rudolph.
b. Prepare a *consolidated* income statement and balance sheet. Be sure that the last line of the income statement excludes the minority share of Rudolph Ltd.'s earnings.
c. Compare net worth and income under the two procedures. Why is the equity basis of accounting for business combinations sometimes referred to as a *one-line* consolidation?

P13-10 Stef Industries Ltd. recently purchased a 60 percent interest in Federal Electronics Ltd. Immediately following acquisition, the individual balance sheets of the two firms appeared as follows:

	Stef Industries Ltd.	*Federal Electronics Ltd.*
Cash	$ 20,000	$ 10,000
Other assets	200,000	185,000
Investment in Federal Electronics	120,000	
Total assets	$340,000	$195,000
Liabilities	$ 50,000	$ 20,000
Common shares	20,000	10,000
Retained earnings	270,000	165,000
Total liabilities and shareholders' equity	$340,000	$195,000

Required:

a. Stef Industries Ltd. can be presumed to have paid a market price for its acquisition. If a 60 percent interest in Federal Electronics Ltd. has a fair market value of $120,000, how much must the entire company be worth?
b. Assume that Stef Industries Ltd. was willing to pay an amount in excess of the book value because Federal Electronics Ltd. had developed patents on several electronic devices. The value of such patents is not recorded on the books of Federal. In preparing consolidated financial statements, what value should be assigned to the patents (i.e., what is the excess of cost over book value)?
c. If the book values of all other assets and liabilities of Stef Industries Ltd. approximate their fair market values, then what must be the fair market value of the patents?

d. How do you account for the fact that on the consolidated statements only 60 percent of the value of the patents will be recorded, whereas 100 percent of the value of the other assets of Stef Industries Ltd. will be recorded?

e. Prepare a consolidation entry — one in addition to those that would be conventionally made — to increase the value of patents to 100 percent of their presumed value. To which interest, majority or minority, did you assign the additional value? (Note that such entry would not ordinarily be made under present-day practice. It is one that many critics suggest *should* be made.)

P13-11 Octopus Ltd. a conglomerate, decided to acquire controlling interest in Meek Ltd.

The common shares of Octopus Ltd. had been trading at $20 per share and that of Meek Ltd. at $60 per share. Octopus had 1 million shares outstanding, and Meek had 300,000 shares outstanding.

The management of Meek was opposed to the takeover. To circumvent the opposition of management, Octopus offered to purchase all outstanding shares of Meek at a price of $80 per share — a price that was $20 greater than the market price prior to the announcement of its offer. Octopus would not, however, pay cash for the shares. Instead it would issue to Meek shareholders common shares of Octopus with a market value of $80 for each share that it received. Hence, it would issue four shares of Octopus shares for each share of Meek received.

In the year prior to the offer, Octopus had earnings of $50,000; Meek had earnings of $1 million. At the time of the offer, Meek had a book value (net worth) of $15 million.

Required:

a. Determine the earnings per share of Octopus in the year prior to the acquisition.

b. Determine the earnings per share of Octopus in the year immediately following the acquisition. Assume that Octopus will prepare consolidated financial statements and that the operating earnings of the two individual companies will remain unchanged. Any excess of cost over book value will be assigned to goodwill and amortized over a period of 40 years. Assume also that only 80 percent of the outstanding shares of Meek were tendered (sold) to Octopus. The remainder are being retained by minority shareholders.

c. Suppose an investor owned 1,000 shares of Meek. How much better off is he in terms of market value of his holdings after he sold his shares to Octopus than before?

d. How much better (or worse) off is he with respect to earnings that can be ascribed to his shares?

P13-12 Barry Industries Ltd. owns 80 percent of Debs Ltd. It purchased its interest in 19x4 at a price of $80,000. At the time of purchase, Debs had assets of $110,000 and liabilities of $20,000. Since 19x4 neither firm has issued additional shares or redeemed outstanding shares. Statements of position of the two firms as of December 31, 19x8 are presented below:

	Barry Industries Ltd.	*Debs Ltd.*
Cash	$200,000	$ 50,000
Fixed assets	600,000	100,000
Other assets	80,000	40,000
Investment in Debs Ltd.	112,000	—
Total assets	$992,000	$190,000
Accounts payable	$ 62,000	$ 10,000
Bonds payable	150,000	50,000
Common shares	100,000	40,000
Retained earnings	680,000	90,000
Total liabilities and shareholders' equity	$992,000	$190,000

Required:

a. On what basis, cost or equity, is it likely that Barry Industries Ltd. maintains its interest in Debs Ltd.?

b. By how much did the retained earnings of Debs Ltd. increase since Barry Industries acquired its interest in 19x4? How is such increase reflected in the accounts of Barry Industries Ltd.?

c. Prepare a journal entry, required for consolidation, to eliminate the increase in the "Investment in Debs Ltd." account that is attributable to the increase in Debs Ltd.'s retained earnings since the date of acquisition.

d. How much in excess of the book value of Debs Ltd. did Barry Industries Ltd. pay to acquire its interest in Debs Ltd.?

e. Prepare a journal entry to eliminate the remainder of the investment in the Debs Ltd. account.

f. Prepare a journal entry to assign the remaining balances in the shareholders' equity accounts of Debs Ltd. to the minority interests.

g. The entire excess of cost over book value can be attributed to goodwill. Prepare a journal entry to so reclassify it.

h. The goodwill is being amortized over a period of 20 years. Prepare a journal entry to reflect the fact that 5 years of goodwill have already been amortized.

i. Included in "other assets" of Barry Industries Ltd. is $50,000 in bonds issued by Debs Ltd. Prepare a journal entry to eliminate the intercompany payable and receivable.

j. Prepare a consolidated balance sheet.

P13-13 Indicated below are the preclosing 19x7 trial balances of X Ltd. and its subsidiary Y Ltd.

	X Ltd.		*Y Ltd.*	
	Dr.	*Cr.*	*Dr.*	*Cr.*
Cash	$ 15,000		$ 3,000	
Accounts and notes receivable	50,000		16,000	
Interest receivable	4,000		3,000	
Inventory	25,000		10,000	
Fixed assets	185,000		30,000	
Investment in Y Ltd.	34,200			
Accounts and notes payable		$ 44,000		$ 10,000
Interest payable		2,000		1,000
Common shares		60,000		30,000
Retained earnings		181,200		17,000
Sales		100,000		40,000
Interest and other revenues		12,000		2,000
Cost of goods sold and related expenses	80,000		32,000	
Interest expense	6,000		6,000	
	$399,200	$399,200	$100,000	$100,000

Other information:

1. X Ltd. owns 60 percent of the common shares of Y Ltd. X Ltd. acquired its interest in 19x4 at a cost of $30,000. At the time of acquisition Y Ltd. had retained earnings of $10,000.
2. X Ltd. was willing to pay an amount in excess of the book value of its investment in Y Ltd. because Y Ltd. owned land that was undervalued on its books.
3. In 19x7 X Ltd. had $20,000 in sales to Y Ltd. X Ltd.'s cost of the goods sold was $16,000. 25 percent of the goods sold to Y Ltd. have not yet been resold and are included in the inventory of Y Ltd.
4. Y Ltd. still owes X Ltd. $6,000 for the merchandise purchased.
5. In the course of the year X Ltd. made loans to Y Ltd. X Ltd. charged Y Ltd. $2,000 of interest on the loans. Although there was no outstanding balance on the principal of the loans at year-end, Y Ltd. was still indebted to X Ltd. for $1,000 in interest. Both companies have properly accrued the interest revenue or expense.
6. During the year X Ltd. sold some land to Y. Selling price was $6,000. The land had originally cost X Ltd. $3,000.
7. X Ltd. has not yet recognized its share of Y Ltd.'s 19x7 earnings.

Required:

a. Make all working paper journal entries necessary to prepare consolidated financial statements.

b. Prepare a consolidated income statement and balance sheet. Be sure to indicate the minority share of subsidiary earnings. You will probably find it useful to prepare a work sheet in which you establish columns for original balances, adjustments, and consolidated balances.

Cases

C13-1 I. Morris Limited (I.M.) is a Canadian public company which manufactures computer hardware equipment (e.g., printers, terminals, cathode ray tubes, etc.) for sale to a variety of customers. The company has had a long history of good earnings and high dividends. However, increasing competition in the industry has recently had an effect on company sales and I.M.'s inventory has been increasing.

Mr. Blaine, president of I.M., realized that major changes in the company's policies and operations would be required if I.M. were to maintain its excellent earnings performance. After consultation with a number of key company personnel the following proposals were being considered:

1. that I.M. begin to capitalize its advertising costs and amortize them over a five-year period rather than expensing them as incurred. This policy would increase reported earnings.
2. that I.M. retire its long-term debt in Canada, in which it is paying 12 percent per annum, and issue $5 million (U.S. dollars) in 20 year bonds at 9 percent per annum in the United States. Management reasons that, since the current foreign exchange rate is $1 Canadian = $1 U.S. and in one year's time is expected to be $1 Canadian = $0.97 U.S., the timing is right for an immediate U.S. issue and might have a favorable effect on earnings.
3. that I.M. increase its sales and reduce its inventory by selling surplus stocks of its products to Fastdata Ltd., a company in which I.M. owns 21 percent. I.M. is able to convince Fastdata to take unwanted stock "from time to time." This strategy would reduce inventory carrying costs and would permit I.M. to recognize full profits as soon as its product was delivered to Fastdata.
4. that I.M. issue its own shares (market value $100 each) and acquire 80 percent of the common shares of Canned Package Limited (CPL), a small private Canadian computer company with net assets of $800,000, which specializes in computer software. The purchase price would be $800,000 in cash, and since CPL has had average earnings of $100,000 over the past 5 years, I.M.'s reported earnings would increase by $80,000. The president anticipates that I.M.'s high P/E ratio (20 to 1) will prevail for the combined earnings and that I.M.'s shareholders will therefore be that much better off. I.M. and CPL currently have 150,000 and 100,000 common shares outstanding respectively. Public companies similar to CPL normally trade at a P/E ratio of 5 to 1, due to the riskiness of young new ventures in the market.

Before selecting an appropriate course of action, Mr. Blaine decided to consult his V.P. of Finance, Mr. J. Quill and obtain his opinions of the proposed strategies.

Required:

Assume the role of the V.P. of Finance. Identify the major accounting problems which this company faces. What would you recommend? Explain your position clearly stating the assumptions which you have made, the analysis you have performed and the logic you have employed. What general business advice would you have for the president?

C13-2 Clothes Limited (CL) operates a clothing factory and retail stores across Canada. The company is federally incorporated, having been formed over 60 years ago. At present 40 percent of CL's voting shares are held by a company listed on the Toronto Stock Exchange. The remaining 60 percent of the voting shares are owned by relatives of the founder of the company; they vote as a block and control CL, but allow the minority owner to influence decisions. The minority owner has an option to acquire control but it is not exercisable for another 6 years.

CL has just acquired an 80 percent interest in a clothing design-retail company, Star Wardrobes Limited (SWL). SWL specializes in designing and making high fashion clothes and retailing them through two stores, one in Montreal and one in Toronto. It has been able to compete successfully with international designers.

The chief financial officer of CL has asked your advice on how he should account for the purchase of SWL, in particular with respect to the following:

1. CL offered the majority shareholder of SWL $600,000 for her shares. Being 57 years old and not permitted by the contract to compete with SWL, she instead elected to receive $200,000 cash now and to receive $150,000 annually for the next 8 years, the annual amount being a management fee paid to her for her services as chief executive officer.
2. Just prior to the acquisition date, CL was able to persuade SWL to purchase an "unusally large amount" of CL's slow-moving stock, resulting in material profits for CL.
3. SWL, as a matter of policy, writes off all garment inventory over four months old. Net realizable value of this inventory is $12,000 at the date of acquisition.
4. SWL leases its two stores under contracts extending for another 30 years. Rental payments are 30 percent below current rates in the vicinity.

Required:

Advise the chief financial officer of CL.

C13-3 Three public accountants, A, B and C, were discussing various problems they encountered in their practices. The subject of the requirements of the ARC of the CICA for consolidated statements arose, and the following conversation took place:

A: "One thing that causes me a lot of problems is the requirement that any company with subsidiaries must consolidate. That means even small private companies. I don't think that's reasonable. Some of my clients don't want them, don't need them, don't understand them and don't want to pay for them."

B: "I can't understand why they say they don't need them. Surely they want one set of consolidated statements which portray one economic entity so that shareholders can assess their entire investment and evaluate management's performance in managing all assets at its disposal."

A: "Yes, but the shareholders of small private companies are typically close enough to daily operations that they know how their group of companies is doing, without having to see consolidated statements. Moreover, they typically only need financial statements for the bank and to file with income tax returns. For these two purposes, unconsolidated statements will suffice."

Required:

Discuss the viewpoints of each of A and B, relating your discussion to the various objectives of accounting and financial reporting.

(CICA adapted)

14 *Statement of Changes in Financial Position*

This chapter represents a major departure from the previous three. Whereas the previous three were filled with troublesome legal requirements and *CICA Handbook* constraints, the guiding principles for this chapter are *judgment* and *flexibility*. Our focus is strictly *reporting*. Assuming that the preparer is willing, the point of the exercise is to use the Statement of Changes in Financial Position (SCFP) to report (1) what is not already reported; or (2) what is not reported *well* by the balance sheet, income and retained earnings statements. In order to accomplish the task — which can differ from company to company and even from year to year for the same company — different statement designs or formats are essential. This chapter illustrates three types; many exist.

Basic Purposes

The SCFP is over 100 years old, and during its lifetime has experienced many format changes and variations of its purpose(s). In the past decade in Canada the SCFP has been designed by different preparers to accomplish one (and sometimes both) of two frequently conflicting purposes:

1. To report *changes* in the liquid assets less liquid liabilities of the entity, (often called the "liquidity" approach).
2. To report inter-entity (generally arm's-length) transactions (often called the "financing and investing" approach).

Supporters of the liquidity approach attempt to use the SCFP as an offsetting financial report to the income statement. That is, most businesses — especially smaller ones — have to be concerned with both profitability and liquidity. To avoid bankruptcy and provide a good return to investors, a balance must be maintained between having too many or too few "liquid" assets (such as cash and receivables), which tend to generate less income than non-liquid assets, such as land plus buildings. Whereas the income statement is concerned with measuring profitability, some statement should monitor changes in liquidity — especially for those businesses that might overextend their credit and risk bankruptcy. Some accountants feel that the SCFP can accomplish this task.

Supporters of the financing and investing approach are seeking to use the SCFP for additional or clearer disclosure of important transactions. An acquisition of land and buildings by issuing long-term debt does not appear on an income statement and only the closing balances of each account appear on a balance sheet. How does a reader tell whether two arm's-length transactions occurred (sell bonds for cash; buy land and buildings with cash)? The alternative might be that one non-arm's-length transaction occurred (the company president sold land and building which he owned and received a bond in exchange).

To the extent that a preparer is putting into an SCFP what would normally appear in footnotes, the purpose of the exercise supposedly is better communication. The assumption is that some people pay more attention to financial statements than to notes. Owners of small businesses and naive investors in larger companies might appreciate the "better" disclosure. However, believers in the semi-strong version of the efficient market hypothesis would argue that, ignoring costs, the effort was futile. Note disclosure would have been adequate for their purposes.

For large companies that encounter complex transactions, an SCFP based on the "financing and investing" approach could help to keep investors informed and interested in the company. If these same companies might also be subject to liquidity problems they may want a *second* SCFP, which in this case stresses liquidity. It is sometimes possible to structure one SCFP to accomplish both a liquidity and a financing and investing viewpoint. However, in recent years most Canadian companies do not appear to have accomplished both purposes well.

Liquidity

One of our greatest difficulties in designing an SCFP based on liquidity is to ascertain which assets and liabilities are liquid in a company and are significant in terms of accomplishing an important purpose — such as a warning of possible bankruptcy. For a bank, are the notes receivable from customers over the next two years liquid? For a public utility that generates hydro-electricity, are next year's billings to customers in effect a liquid asset? Is the cash balance the only liquid asset in a small business?

If we are attempting to predict liquidity, we should think in terms of a statement for the future, and not one for the past. Past trends of liquidity may or may not be helpful in forecasting. For many companies the assets that are very liquid fluctuate widely.

The most popular SCFP format in Canada in recent years has been the working capital format (that is, current assets minus current liabilities) as used by Labatt's in Chapter 2. To the extent that working capital represents the liquid position of a company, or to the extent that movements in working capital closely mirror movements in the "real" liquid state of the company, the working capital format is appropriate. However, let us examine the composition of working capital and speculate a little.

The accounts which make up working capital may differ from each other in two important respects: *valuation*, and *timing*. Inventory for example, is generally recorded at cost, not at net realizable or cash value. Also, inventory may have to be turned into accounts receivable first (through a sale on account) before cash is received, and the conversion to cash process could take two or more months.

In addition, to the extent that a company buys its equipment instead of renting it, subsequent to this acquisition a "form" of cash saving results. That is, when we have ownership, cash rentals need not be paid out. Hence, some might argue that next year's depreciation on the equipment (which might approximate a rental charge) could be viewed as a current asset. This is strange reasoning perhaps, but not necessarily off target for certain objectives or purposes of accounting.

A company that wants to compute the number of days it can survive a strike without having to borrow from a bank may wish to focus exclusively on cash flows over the *next* 60 to 90 days. In compiling cash receipts and disbursements figures, an accountant may observe thankfully that at least rental payments on equipment are not due.

Overall, working capital may be a suitable measure of liquidity in some firms; but for many others considerable doubt exists. A distiller of fine scotch whiskies may have a fairly non-liquid inventory, in a financial sense, if the aging process is not complete. Cash may be a better measure for immediate needs. At least the debts that are due can be paid if cash is at one's disposal.

Financing and Investing

Some transactions such as barters or noncash exchanges (debt issued for land and buildings) and switches of bonds into common shares are easily reported by an SCFP based on the financing and investing format. As well, the format can accommodate the problem caused by non-arm's-length (including bookkeeping) transactions. In earlier chapters we stressed the implications of assumptions made by accountants when they allocate costs — such as when fixed assets are depreciated or goodwill is amortized. Given that some users/readers (such as those outsiders who are interested in evaluating management and predicting cash flows) may not be interested in such bookkeeping transactions, we ought to devise a separate financial statement which excludes non-arm's-length bookkeeping.

The purpose of the income statement is strictly to measure income. As a result it is loaded with bookkeeping entries, such as depreciation expense, which are there as part of a matching process. These items could easily distract readers who want to learn about the recurring cash flow from "regular operations" — the regular transactions of the business excluding long-term financing and sales of long-lived assets.

Someone interested in prediction, for instance, would like to use the SCFP based on financing and investing for two broad purposes: (1) to ascertain whether the size of net assets and earnings will increase; and (2) to determine who is to share in these increased net assets and earnings. (More bondholders? Shareholders? The company's banker?) If the size of net assets and earnings increases by issuing more debt and expanding the plant, will the forecast increase in net revenue in the next few years exceed interest on the debt? How much is left for the shareholders? By focusing on changes in *financing* (or who furnished the funds) and changes in *investments* (or what type of asset was bought with the funds) the SCFP might very well meet the needs of some users.

Another Caution

We prefaced the foregoing discussion by stating that the preparer had to be willing to furnish the new information or new format, because corporate legislation and the *CICA Handbook* do not force or require disclosure on the SCFP of several of the concepts and transactions which we have discussed so far in this chapter. In contrast, the legislation or *Handbook* may force particular disclosure (but not of liquidity changes or some financing and investing transactions) on a balance sheet and income statement. In fact, in some jurisdictions and situations an SCFP may still not be required as part of the financial statement package — although mandatory use will surely appear by the mid 1980s.

A reluctant preparer may have to be influenced by users/readers, or more likely by the company's auditors. Such a process of influence takes time.

The Mechanics

Educators continually face a "no-win" situation: should the "whys" or should the "hows" be presented first? Both approaches have been used in this book. Now that some of the "whys" of the SCFP have been set forth, our attention must turn to the "hows." Then as the "hows" become clearer more "whys" can be given. One of the most troublesome parts of the "hows" for many people is in computing what are called "funds" from operations. Regardless of whether we use a liquidity or financing and investing approach in compiling our SCFP we have to compute the effect of funds from operations on an organization.

Suppose that an income statement for a retail company appears as follows:

Revenue		$10,000
Cost of goods sold*		6,000
Gross profit		$ 4,000
Expenses:		
Selling and administrative, paid in cash	$2,200	
Depreciation expense	1,500	3,700
Net income (ignoring income tax)		$ 300

*No depreciation is included.

Many people, including management, want to know the amount of "funds" (which could be defined as working capital, or as cash or as something between the two) generated by "operations." The term operations means the regular (not the unusual) purposes of the business, which in this example appears to be buying inventory and reselling it. The funds from operations figure lets us know what is available to pay dividends or to buy new equipment *without* having to sell other assets or incur more debt or equity to obtain "funds."

To begin, we will use a cash definition of funds. Let us assume for the moment that both the revenue and the cost of goods sold were cash transactions. If so, funds generated from operations is $1,800:

	Effect on Cash		
	Increase	*Decrease*	*Net Increase*
Revenue	$10,000		$10,000
Cost of goods sold		$ 6,000	4,000
Selling and administrative		2,200	1,800

We can arrive at the $1,800 another way (*backwards* method):

Net income	$ 300
Add depreciation expense (a charge to income which has no cash effect)	1,500
	$ 1,800

This latter method, which might be called the *backwards* method of arriving at funds from operations, is frequently seen in practice and in many books. As long as people remember that — with the double entry equation and mechanism — it is just *another* way of getting the result (funds from operations), confusion can be minimized. The most common point of confusion occurs when people see depreciation being included in the computation and then declare that depreciation is a source of funds! When funds means "cash," depreciation *clearly* is not a source of cash. Neither the debit nor the credit which sets up depreciation affects cash.

Our income statement equation is:

Cash revenue – (Cash cost of goods sold + selling and administrative) – Depreciation = Net income.

Transferring depreciation to the other side of the equation we get:

Cash revenue – Cash expenses
= Net income + Depreciation (a noncash cost).

When we make the example more realistic by assuming accrual accounting and define funds as working capital, depreciation is treated the same way. In order to credit revenue, we debit cash or accounts receivable or unearned revenue, all of which are part of working capital. When we debit costs of goods sold, we credit inventory, which is a part of working capital. When we debit selling and administrative expenses we credit accounts payable, cash or prepaid expenses — all of which are a part of working capital. Funds from operations, given our new assumptions, is still $1,800:

	Effect on working capital		
	Increase	*Decrease*	*Net Increase*
Revenue	$10,000		$10,000
Cost of goods sold		$ 6,000	4,000
Selling and administrative		2,200	1,800

Sources And Uses

The next step in the how-to-do-it process is clarifying what causes increases and what causes decreases in "funds." At this point we must choose between illustrating a liquidity or a financing and investing format. We have chosen liquidity to start with — what causes liquidity to increase or decrease. Let us commence by defining funds as working capital, and suppose that during a period the following transactions occurred:

1. A proprietorship was formed by putting $50,000 into a bank account.
2. Inventory costing $20,000 was acquired on account.
3. Inventory costing $12,000 was sold for $16,000 cash.
4. A truck was bought for $9,000 cash; depreciation of $800 was recorded.
5. Expenses of $2,300 were paid in cash.
6. Equipment was bought for $3,000 cash, but was found to be unsuitable and was sold for $2,650 cash; no depreciation was recorded.
7. The owner withdrew $2,000 of the original investment.

Items 2 through 6 involve working capital funds from operations, either wholly (2,3,5) or in part (4,6):

Revenue		$16,000
Cost of goods sold		12,000
Gross profit		4,000
Expenses:		
General	$ 2,300	
Depreciation	800	
Loss on sale of equipment	350	3,450
Net income (ignoring income tax, which is paid by the owner)		$ 550

Funds from operations would be computed as:

	–	+	*Net* +
Revenue		$16,000	$16,000
Cost of goods sold	$12,000		4,000
General expenses	2,300		1,700

The "backwards" way would be:

Net income		$ 550
Add items which lower income but which do not affect funds:		
Depreciation	$ 800	
Loss on sale of equipment	350	1,150
Funds generated by operations (i.e., a *source*)		$ 1,700

The loss on sale of $350 is like depreciation in its effect on funds. The entire entry to record the sale of equipment was:

Entry (6)

Cash (which is part of working capital)	$2,650	
Loss on sale of equipment	350	
Equipment		$3,000
To record disposal of equipment.		

If cash is involved in the transaction, how can we say that the loss did not affect working capital funds? Let us split the entry into its two parts:

(a)

Cash	$ 2,650	
Equipment		$ 2,650

(b)

Loss on sale of equipment	$ 350	
Equipment		$ 350

Entry (a) which increases working capital (cash, to be specific) but which credits equipment, a nonworking capital account, represents a source (increase) of liquidity (working capital funds). Entry (b) does not affect a working capital liquidity account, but it does lower income.

What else had an effect on working capital liquidity?

Entry (1)

Cash	$50,000	
Owner's capital		$50,000
To record commencement of a proprietorship.		

This transaction increased working capital (cash) by increasing owner's equity. It is therefore a *source* of funds to the company.

Entry (2)

Inventory	$20,000	
Accounts payable		$20,000
To record purchase of inventory on account.		

Entry (2) did not affect working capital (i.e. current assets minus current liabilities) in total; it did affect two of the accounts which make up working capital.

Entry (3)

Cash	$16,000	
Revenue		$16,000
To record cash sales.		
Cost of goods sold	$12,000	
Inventory		$12,000
To match expense to revenue.		

Both of these entries involve working capital and an income statement account. We have already captured their effect on liquidity in our computation of funds from operations. (We have to avoid duplication.)

Entry (4)

Truck	$9,000	
Cash		$9,000
To record purchase of a truck.		

Entry (4) reduces working capital liquidity and is therefore an "application" or *use* of working capital funds.

Entry (5)

Expenses	$2,300	
Cash		$2,300
To record cash expenses.		

Entry (5) is the same as (3) in its effect on working capital liquidity. Its impact is already incorporated into the funds from operations computations.

Entry (6) was analyzed, in part, previously. The entry to record purchase of the equipment is:

Equipment	$3,000	
Cash		$3,000
To record purchase of equipment.		

This entry is the same as Entry (4) and is a use of working capital.

Entry (7)

Owner's equity	$2,000	
Cash		$2,000
To record withdrawal of $2,000 of the original investment.		

Entry (7) is a *use* or an application of working capital funds caused by a decrease in owner's equity.

If we posted entries (1) to (7), as well as one for depreciation expense, and prepared a balance sheet, it would show:

Name of Proprietorship
Balance Sheet

Date

Cash		$52,350
Inventory		8,000
		60,350
Truck	$ 9,000	
Less accumulated depreciation	800	8,200
		$68,550
Accounts payable		$20,000
Owner's capital:		
Initial investment	$50,000	
Add net income	550	
	50,550	
Less withdrawal of investment	2,000	48,550
		$68,550

Working capital rose during the period from zero to $40,350 ($60,350 of current assets less $20,000 of current liabilities). An SCFP based on working capital funds is shown in Exhibit 14-1.

EXHIBIT 14-1

Name of Proprietorship
Statement of Changes in Financial Position
For the period ended ______

Sources of working capital:		
Funds from operations:		
Net income		$ 550
Add items which lowered income but which did not affect funds:		
Depreciation		800
Loss on sale of equipment		350
		1,700
Capital contributed by owner		50,000
Proceeds on sale of equipment		2,650
		54,350
Uses of working capital:		
Purchase of truck	$9,000	
Purchase of equipment	3,000	
Withdrawal of capital by owner	2,000	14,000
Increase in working capital		$40,350

Statement Interpretation

How do we interpret Exhibit 14-1? Its purpose is to show the *causes* of the $40,350 increase in working capital since commencement of the business. Summarizing, the sources and uses of working capital broadly speaking are:

Sources

- Sale of long-term debt, preferred and common shares, or their equivalent for unincorporated businesses, and receipt of working capital. (Increase working capital by increasing noncurrent liabilities or equity.)
- Sale of noncurrent asset, and receipt of working capital. (Increase working capital by decreasing noncurrent assets.)
- Funds generated from operations. (Increase working capital from income statement operations.)

Uses

- Redemption of long-term debt or equity, including payment of a dividend, out of working capital. (Decrease working capital by decreasing noncurrent liabilities or equity.)
- Purchase of a noncurrent asset out of working capital. (Decrease working capital by increasing a noncurrent asset.)
- Funds applied to operations. (This would occur when expenses exceed revenues for those accounts which are contras to working capital accounts, such as most revenue and cost of goods sold.)

An exhibit such as 14-1 does *not* show (if it is strictly concerned with items which directly affect working capital):

- Transactions solely between two or more working capital accounts. An example would be an increase in current assets (inventory) financed by an increase in current liabilities (accounts payable).

- Transactions solely between two or more noncurrent accounts. Examples would be conversions of convertible preferred shares into common shares, and acquisition of long-lived assets by directly issuing long-term debt or equity. The latter may be considered a barter-type (noncash) transaction.

Observe that the working capital SCFP very clearly focuses on the effects of what might be called the *non*operations or *non*income statement transactions. This occurs because it excludes transactions which are strictly between the current accounts (i.e., paying payables; buying inventory on account). By nonoperations we mean those perhaps infrequent transactions which are needed to finance the organization over the longer term and those perhaps infrequent investments in long-lived assets. In short, we are allowed to stand back from the day-to-day activities that are included in the income statement and individual accounts within working capital. We can therefore focus on the *overall* effects and trend of the financing and investing of the business.

Note clearly what we have just said. In spite of claims (such as the one we made earlier in explaining which type of SCFP we would illustrate first) that the SCFP based on working capital is a liquidity-type financial statement, in contrast, its greatest merit appears to be in focusing on the nonworking capital *causes* of a change in working capital. Thus, we may still need a liquidity-type financial statement for some businesses. (A cash SCFP format is illustrated later.)

Also observe that the working capital SCFP may have limitations in disclosing *all* financing and investing transactions if a company engaged in barters or conversions during the period. (A cure for this is illustrated later.) We might indicate the barters and conversions on the working capital SCFP, by showing the acquisition of a long-lived asset as an application or use of working capital and the increased debt given in exchange as a source. However, this can easily mislead readers into thinking that two arm's-length transactions occurred when, in fact, one non-arm's-length transaction might have been arranged.

In the case of Exhibit 14-1, the SCFP shows that, in broad terms, (1) a net of $48,000 was invested by the owner; and (2) $9,000 was used to buy a truck, but, broadly speaking, only $1,750 of this was financed by operations; and (3) $40,000 or so of working capital remains. No serious errors in investing or financing by the proprietorship appear, such as foolishly buying many long-lived assets and hoping to pay for them out of current assets (which might be low) or operations (which might generate few funds).

A Technique Illustrated

People who have not learned the difference between cash and accrual accounting will have considerable difficulty preparing an SCFP. Let us illustrate a technique, called the T account method, which may be helpful with the how-to-do-it.

Suppose that the proprietorship continues in existence for another year and the financial statements in Exhibit 14-2 are prepared at the end of its second year of operations.

EXHIBIT 14-2

	Balance Sheets at December 31	
	Year 2	*Year 1*
Cash	$ 3,100	$52,350
Accounts receivable	21,650	—
Inventory	21,150	8,000
	45,900	60,350
Truck, at cost	9,000	9,000
Equipment, at cost	21,600	—
	30,600	9,000
Less accumulated depreciation	3,600	800
	27,000	8,200
	$72,900	$68,550
Accounts payable	$14,000	$20,000
Long-term debt payable, on equipment	15,000	—
Owner's capital:		
Opening balance	48,550	—
Add:		
New capital	—	50,000
Net income	—	550
	48,550	50,550
Deduct:		
Net loss	2,650	—
Withdrawals	2,000	2,000
	4,650	2,000
Closing capital	43,900	48,550
	$72,900	$68,550

		Income Statement *Year ended December 31, Year 2*
Revenue		$78,250
Cost of goods sold		66,350
Gross profit		11,900
Expenses:		
Selling and administrative	$14,100	
Depreciation	3,000	
Gain on sale of equipment	(2,550)	14,550
Net Loss		$(2,650)

Further investigation of the activities of the proprietorship indicated that the following occurred in year 2:

(1) Equipment costing $18,000, on which $200 of depreciation had accumulated, was sold for $20,350 cash.

(2) Equipment costing $20,000 was financed by paying $5,000 cash and undertaking to pay the $15,000 remainder on January 15, year 4. (In strict terms the $15,000 is not a current liability at December 31, year 2.)

The "T account" method, which seems to have been pioneered primarily by Professor William Vatter, operates as follows:

Step 1: Special T accounts are set up for *each* noncurrent account (assuming that we are dealing with working capital SCFP); there is also one for working capital in total; and one for funds from operations (to represent the income statement's operating effects on funds). Whereas there are double horizontal lines for the working capital and noncurrent T accounts, there is only one for "funds from operations." The reason becomes clear later.

Working capital	
	$8,450

Truck	
nil	

Equipment	
$21,600	

Accumulated Depreciation	
	$2,800

Long-term debt	
	$15,000

Owner's capital	
$4,650	

Funds from operations	

Step 2: Between the two horizontal lines at the top of the T account we enter the *change* which occurred in that account during the period (except for "funds from operations"). For example, from an examination of the comparative balance sheets we can tell that working capital decreased by $8,450 during the period:

	End of Year	
	2	*1*
Cash	$ 3,100	$52,350
Accounts receivable	21,650	—
Inventory	21,150	8,000
Accounts payable	(14,000)	(20,000)
		40,350
Working capital	31,900	31,900
		$ 8,450

Step 3: A trial balance of the account differences is then prepared:

	Debit	Credit
Working capital		$ 8,450
Equipment	$21,600	
Accumulated depreciation		2,800
Long-term debt		15,000
Owner's capital	4,650	
	$26,250	$26,250

This allows us to catch any errors in preparing the T accounts.

Step 4: The point of the next two steps is to *reconstruct* as best we can the transaction journal entries which probably occurred during the year. Then, we post them to the T accounts *below* the lower of the two horizontal lines. The idea is to balance what is above to what is below the lower horizontal line in the T account. In this way we can ascertain what caused the decrease of $8,450 in working capital.

(A) Let us undertake the hardest part first. Whereas the other entries which we will have to prepare are original transaction entries, the one affecting funds from operations is a "closing" entry. It closes the net income or loss to retained earnings, or in this case, owner's capital.

(a)

Owner's capital	$2,650	
Funds from operations		$2,650
To close out the loss for the year.		

Observe that the credit goes to funds from operations because we do not have a T account for income statement items.

(B) We are told some information about the purchase of equipment; this can be journalized as follows:

(b)

Equipment	$20,000	
Cash (which is working capital)		$ 5,000
Long-term debt		15,000
To record purchase of equipment.		

(C) Some of the equipment was sold at a gain:

(c)

Cash (which is working capital)	$20,350	
Accumulated depreciation	200	
Equipment		$18,000
Gain on sale (which, under the backwards method, helps arrive at funds from operations)		2,550
To record sale of equipment.		

(D) Since a debit to equipment of $20,000 from entry (b) and a credit of $18,000 from (c) results in only a net debit of $2,000, and the change in the equipment T account is $21,600, we have to assume that another $19,600 of equipment was purchased. With no evidence to the contrary the safest assumption is that the credit was to working capital.

(d)

Equipment	$19,600	
Working capital		$19,600
To record purchase of equipment.		

(E) By posting journal entries to the T accounts as we proceed (something which is too space-consuming to do in a book) it is easier to ascertain which journal entries still have to be logically assumed. A look at the accumulated depreciation account after entry (c) would show a debit of $200 below the lower horizontal line. Yet we need an overall credit of $2,800. This means that the journal entry has to credit accumulated depreciation for $3,000. Fortunately, the income statement shows depreciation expense at $3,000; we therefore have our proof:

(e)

Funds from operations (depreciation expense)	$3,000	
Accumulated depreciation		$3,000
To record depreciation expense.		

Again, instead of a debit to an income statement account, the debit goes to funds from operations. It may now become a little more obvious that we intend to use the backwards method of arriving at funds from operations.

(F) The balance sheet tells us about the owner's withdrawal of $2,000:

	(f)	
Owner's capital	$2,000	
Working capital		$2,000
To record withdrawal.		

Step 5: Although posting would normally occur as we journalize in Step 4, the ledger accounts are set out separately at this stage for purposes of saving space in this book.

Working capital

	Dr		Cr
			8,450
(c)	20,350	(b)	5,000
		(d)	19,600
		(f)	2,000
		(g)	2,200
			8,450

Equipment

	Dr		Cr
	21,600		
(b)	20,000	(c)	18,000
(d)	19,600		
	21,600		

Accumulated depreciation

	Dr		Cr
			2,800
(c)	200	(e)	3,000
			2,800

Long-term debt

	Dr		Cr
			15,000
		(b)	15,000

Owner's capital

	Dr		Cr
	4,650		
(a)	2,650		
(f)	2,000		
	4,650		

Funds from operations

	Dr		Cr
(e)	3,000	(a)	2,650
		(c)	2,550
	3,000		5,200
(g)	2,200		
	nil		

You will observe that we have added entry (g):

Funds from operations	$2,200	
Working capital		$2,200
To balance the working capital account.		

The purpose of entry (g) is to total funds from operations and to transfer it to the working capital T account to ensure that the latter balances. That is, the $8,450 between the *top* two horizontal lines should balance to that between the *bottom* two horizontal lines. (Presumably we already balanced the noncurrent T accounts at Steps 4 and 5.)

Step 6: The SCFP can be prepared by concentrating on the information in the working capital T account:

EXHIBIT 14-3

Name of Proprietorship
Statement of Changes in Financial Position
For the Period Ended
December 31, Year 2

Uses of working capital:	
Funds used in operations:	
Net loss for the period	$ 2,650
Add gain on sale (which lowers the loss but does not affect working capital	2,550
	5,200
Deduct depreciation (which increases the loss but does not affect working capital)	3,000
	2,200
Acquisition of equipment ($19,600 plus $5,000)	24,600
Withdrawal by owner	2,000
	28,800
Source of working capital:	
Sale of equipment	20,350
Decrease in working capital	$ 8,450

Step 7: Step 7, if we are curious, would be to look at what has been produced in Step 6 and ensure that it makes sense. Working capital has dropped by $8,450 as a result of a use of funds to support operations, a withdrawal by the owner, and some transactions involving equipment. Does this give a complete picture of either (1) movements in liquidity; or (2) financing and investing activities?

SCFP Recast

A closer look at the SCFP prepared in Exhibit 14-3 and the financial statements in Exhibit 14-2 may indicate that Exhibit 14-3 is not as clear as it might be. Let us recast the results using first a financing and investing format, and second a cash format.

The financing and investing format is designed to portray all *significant* financing (changes in the right-hand side of the balance sheet) and investing (changes in the left-hand side of the balance sheet) activities to aid various users in understanding which transactions having longer-term implications occurred during the period. (As a matter of interest, some countries reverse the order. Assets may appear on the right hand side, and equities on the left — as is the case in the U.K. Also, public utilities and some real estate companies in Canada may show long-lived assets at the top and current ones at the bottom of a balance sheet.)

Emphasis in the case of some financing activities is placed on transactions initiated by outsiders (i.e., an attempt at disclosure of arm's-length events). For instance, stock (share) dividends and share (stock) splits may not be reported because they were initiated by management. However, a conversion of bonds to common shares would be reported because it would be initiated by the bondholders. Similar transactions are grouped to ease understanding. Large changes within working capital accounts would be reported separately.

Exhibit 14-4 provides one of several possible financing and investing formats for year 2 of the proprietorship. It was compiled by looking at the working capital T account and observing interesting journal entries or changes in the comparative balance sheets.

EXHIBIT 14-4

Name of Proprietorship
Statement of Changes in Financial Position
For the period ended December 31, Year 2

Investing:	
Acquisition of equipment ($20,000 + $19,600)	$ 39,600
Less long-term financing	15,000
	24,600
Less proceeds on sale of equipment	20,350
	4,250
Net* increase in accounts receivable	21,650
Net* purchase of inventory	13,150
Decrease in cash	(49,250)
	$(10,200)
Financing:	
Used to finance operations:	
Net loss for the period	$ 2,650
Add gain on sale of equipment	2,550
	5,200
Less depreciation	3,000
	(2,200)
Withdrawal by owner	(2,000)
Decrease in accounts payable	(6,000)
	$(10,200)

*For more complete disclosure these could be shown gross, less decreases. For example, both sales on account and cash collections might be provided, if informative, about accounts receivable.

Exhibit 14-4 may look very strange to accountants who are used to a working capital format. Exhibit 14-4 merely sets forth changes in the left-(investing) and right-(financing) hand sides of the balance sheet during a period. (It may, in fact, focus on this period too much. Perhaps the more important SCFP would be a two or three year cumulative one, which gets away from possible distortions caused by a one-year cut off.) The presentation style does not concern itself about figures being in brackets because there may be an important message in the fact that, outside of the $15,000 long-term financing, all the other financing items were *reductions* in funds.

The investing side need not show the $15,000 long-term financing. The two, equipment and its financing, were grouped to show *total* purchases of equipment, and how it was financed: less long-term debt, by selling other equipment, and by cash. Some people prefer to see the $15,000 on the financing side.

By splitting out the working capital accounts we obtain a better idea of how they are changing. Will sufficient cash funds be available to pay the accounts payable *and* the long-term financing coming due in just over one year? A cash format of SCFP might make this clearer.

Exhibit 14-5 recasts the information in Exhibits 14-2 and 14-3 into a cash SCFP. As a general rule it may be wise to prepare funds from operations on an accrual basis as is done in Exhibits 14-3 and 14-4. Many readers are probably accustomed to such a basis and could have difficulty understanding what other bases might be conveying.

EXHIBIT 14-5

Name of Proprietorship
Statement of Changes in Financial Position
For the period ended December 31, Year 2

Uses of cash:		
Acquisition of equipment		$ 24,600
Increase in inventory		13,150
Increase in accounts receivable		21,650
Withdrawal by owner		2,000
Payment of accounts payable		6,000
For operations:		
Net loss for period	$ 2,650	
Add gain on sale of equipment	2,550	
	5,200	
Less depreciation	3,000	3,200
		69,600
Sources of cash:		
Proceeds on sale of equipment		20,350
Decrease in cash		$ 49,250

Information which is netted in Exhibit 14-5 (such as the increase in inventory and receivables) may not be as useful as a gross-up. If we know that accounts receivable was debited for $70,000 and that all but $21,650 remains to be collected, this is different than if the original debits were for $21,650 and no sales on account were collected.

The prime purpose of Exhibit 14-5 is to trace liquidity movements. The focus on cash excludes some types of transactions, such as barters and conversions. The long-term financing of $15,000, for example, is not shown. The cash format would seem to be a better disclosure of liquidity movements for the proprietorship than are the working capital and financing and investing formats. But, as a general rule, for larger companies — except for those who deal extensively with liquid assets and liabilities, such as banks — the cash format may have a major shortcoming of not reporting barters and conversions.

Other formats

There are many possible statement designs, formats, and definitions of "funds." The theme mentioned on the first page of this chapter is to use whatever style or definition is necessary to convey a message about liquidity or financing and investing transactions. A good definition of liquidity for some companies is cash plus marketable securities. For another it might be cash plus marketable securities plus accounts receivable, less accounts payable.

Flexibility in format designs is somewhat hampered for limited companies by constraints of corporate law, which requires the presentation of two-year *comparative* SCFP. Some accountants may be reluctant to provide two different designs, side by side, in the financial statement package.

Some complications

Many complications can arise in preparing an SCFP using one of the designs and purposes which we have illustrated so far. A few are discussed in this section for those who seek more how-to-do-it.

Exhibit 14-6 is helpful to many (but not all) people who will spend the time learning how to use it. In preparing an SCFP based on the working capital format we might find that it is useful to know that there are only eight types of transactions. Students sometimes have difficulty in knowing which transactions affect "funds from operations," and which directly affect "funds." An analysis of journal entries can clear up this type of confusion.

EXHIBIT 14-6

CATEGORY	Account Debited	Account Credited	An Example	How Handled When Preparing a Working Capital SCFP	
1	Working Capital	Working Capital	Inventory Accounts Payable	Ignored	
2	Non-Working Capital	Non-Working Capital	Building Long-term debt	Ignored (A noncash or barter transaction *might* be reported. A financing and investing format *would* report important barter transactions.)	
3	Working Capital	Non-Working Capital	Accounts receivable Bonds payable	SOURCE OF FUNDS	
4	Non-Working Capital	Working Capital	Preferred shares Cash	USE OF FUNDS	
5	Income Statement	Working Capital	Selling expense Accounts payable	Ignored (see explanation)	"Forward" way of computing funds from operations.
6	Working Capital	Income Statements	Accounts receivable Revenue	Ignored (see explanation)	
7	Income Statement	Non-Working Capital	Depreciation expense Accumulated depreciation	Add debit to net income, or reduce net loss.	"Backwards" way of computing funds from operations.
8	Non-Working Capital	Income Statement	Deferred income tax Income tax "expense" (credit)	Deduct credit from net income, or increase net loss.	

Exhibit 14-6 may be used as follows after reconstructing journal entries that were thought to have occurred during the period. Before posting to T accounts, under the T account method, the entry may be analyzed to see into which of the eight categories it fits. For example, if common shares are sold for cash, the debit is to a working capital account and credit is to a nonworking capital account. This falls into Category 3 and is a source of funds. However, if the firm obtains cash by acquiring a bank loan, and the loan is payable on demand, the journal entry debits *and* credits a working capital account. This fits Category 1, but working capital in total (current assets minus current liabilities) is not affected. Hence, for reporting purposes, we can ignore the transaction in 1 because the SCFP based on working capital is not designed to disclose this type of activity.

Categories 5 and 6 duplicate 7 and 8; therefore we ignore (for purposes of SCFP reporting) transactions which involve 5 and 6. You will recall that "funds from operations" can be computed by either the "forward" (Categories 5 and 6) or the "backwards" (Categories 7 and 8) method. The T account way of learning how to handle SCFP mechanical problems employs the "backwards" method. Often classroom problems provide insufficient detail to use the "forward" method; and our starting point must be with classroom problems.

Some of the transactions which affect Categories 7 and 8 merit review. In our discussion of income tax allocation using the deferral method we split the overall journal entry into two parts, (A) cash portion, and (B) noncash portion:

	Year 1: Capital Cost Allowance exceeds Depreciation			*Year 2: Depreciation exceeds Capital Cost Allowance*		
(A) Cash Portion	Income tax expense	$6,000		Income tax expense	$10,000	
	Cash		$6,000	Cash		$10,000
(B) Non-Cash Portion	Income tax expense	$2,000		Deferred income tax	$ 2,000	
	Deferred income tax		$2,000	Income tax expense		$ 2,000

The (A) — Cash — portion of the above fits into Category 5 and can be ignored in both year 1 and year 2. The noncash portions (B) fit into Categories 7 and 8 (assuming that the deferred income tax amount is not a current liability). In year 1 we are making an entry much like depreciation (Category 7); that is, we are crediting a nonworking capital account. If there is a net *income* in year 1 the debit to income tax expense has the effect of lowering income but not affecting working capital. We thus add the amount to net income under the backwards method. If there is a net *loss* in year 1 we subtract the depreciation charge — income tax expense in portion B above — because it increased the loss but did not affect working capital.

Year 2 for the noncash portion (B) presents the opposite of year 1. The entry debits a noncurrent liability and credits the income statement; hence, it fits into Category 8. If there is a net *income* during the period, the amount involved is subtracted from net income to arrive at funds from operations because it raises net income but does not affect working capital funds. If there is a loss, the amount is added to net loss under the backwards method in order to compute funds from operations.

A situation where a parent company invests in a subsidiary or an investee (a significantly influenced company) presents another illustration of Categories 7 and 8. As noted in Chapter 13 the investor/parent may *record* and it may also *report* the investment on either the cost or the equity basis. (Note that the parent may *record* at cost but *report* on the equity basis.) When the cost basis is used by the investor to record, no entry is made when the investee earns net income. But when the dividend is received, the entry is:

Working capital (cash)	$5,000	
Funds from operations (dividend from investee)		$5,000
To record receipt of dividend.		

This entry fits into Category 6, and can be ignored. In contrast, when the equity basis of recording and reporting is used the journal entries are:

(a)

Investment in Waterhouse Limited	$12,000	
Funds from operations (re income of investee)		$12,000
To record accrual of investee's income.		

(b)

Working capital	$ 5,000	
Investment in Waterhouse Limited		$ 5,000
To record receipt of dividend.		

Entry (a) is Category 8, which adds back to a net loss or deducts from net income to compute funds from operations. Entry (b) is Category 3, which is a source of funds. The two could be reported as just described, *or* they may be treated as a group and shown as:

Funds from operations:	
Net income, *excluding* income from investee	$25,500
Dividend from Waterhouse Limited	5,000
	30,500

The ARC of CICA prefers the latter treatment, which includes the dividend in funds from operations. (This is consistent with the accounting treatment given to dividends received from a subsidiary when the parent records *and reports* its investment on the cost basis — which is rare.)

Extraordinary items may complicate disclosure in the SCFP. Both the Canadian and U.S. accounting professions have elected to commence the computation of "funds from operations" under the backwards method with the line "income before extraordinary items." To illustrate, assume that some unneeded land costing $100,000 is sold for $126,500 and that the $26,500 is regarded as an extraordinary gain:

Working capital (cash)	$126,500	
Land		$100,000
Extraordinary item — gain on sale of land		26,500
To record sale of land.		

The entry fits two categories of Exhibit 14-6:

(a)

Working capital	$126,500	
Land		$126,500

(b)

Land	$ 26,500	
Extraordinary item		$ 26,500

Part (a) is a source of funds (Category 3); and Part (b) would seem to be an "add back" to net loss (or subtract from net income) to arrive at funds from operations (Category 8). However, when we commence the computation of funds from operations with income *before* extraordinary items, there is no need to post any "add back" which is an extraordinary item. In using the T account solution approach, though, we must remember to journalize and post the extraordinary items separately. For instance, our net income before extraordinary items (but after income taxes) may be $505,000. This amount would be journalized as follows:

Funds from operations	$505,000	
Retained earnings		$505,000
To close to retained earnings.		

Obviously the $505,000 *credit* is not the full story if there is also an extraordinary gain on sale of land of $26,500. Somehow, a further $26,500 must be credited to retained earnings. This may be accomplished by this additional entry:

Extraordinary item — gain on sale of land	$26,500	
Retained earnings		$26,500
To close extraordinary item.		

Extraordinary items may encounter income tax effects. This is covered in the next section.

An Illustration

Another short example may help to pull the material together. Comparative, condensed financial statements, for Mann Limited, are as follows:

Balance Sheets:

	As of December 31	
	19x7	*19x6*
Current assets:		
Cash	$ 1,000	$ 8,920
Accounts receivable	155,600	142,850
Inventory	317,320	125,280
Prepaid expenses	18,230	23,600
	492,150	300,650
Investment in Chesley Limited, at cost	265,000	—
Buildings and equipment	2,787,210	2,655,000
Less accumulated depreciation	473,170	413,930
	2,314,040	2,241,070
Land	20,000	20,000
	$3,091,190	$2,561,720
Current liabilities:		
Bank loan	$ 273,000	$ 80,000
Accounts payable	103,200	109,965
Income tax payable	32,500	29,900
Other current liabilities	27,800	24,735
	436,500	244,600
Bonds payable, 12%, due 19x25 to 19x27	500,000	200,000
Preferred shares, 10%, convertible	600,000	800,000
Shareholders' equity:		
Common shares — no par value	700,000	500,000
Retained earnings	854,690	817,120
	1,554,690	1,317,120
	$3,091,190	$2,561,720

Income Statements:

	Year ended December 31	
	19x7	19x6
Revenue	$1,767,988	$1,675,250
Cost of goods sold	1,096,168	1,001,010
Gross profit	671,820	674,240
Expenses:		
Selling	140,627	135,655
Administrative	107,723	101,395
	248,350	237,050
Income before income tax and extraordinary item	423,570	437,190
Taxes on income	198,000	210,000
	225,570	227,190
Extraordinary item — loss due to fire, less $40,000 income tax saving thereon	58,000	—
Net income	$ 167,570	$ 227,190

Retained Earnings Statements:

	Year ended December 31	
	19x7	19x6
Balance at beginning of year	$ 817,120	$ 719,930
Add net income	167,570	227,190
	984,690	947,120
Deduct:		
Dividends — preferred	70,000	80,000
— common	60,000	50,000
	130,000	130,000
Balance at end of year	$ 854,690	$ 817,120

The company also engaged in the following transactions during 19x7:

1. A dividend of $20,000 was received from Chesley Limited (a 40 percent-owned company) and credited to administrative expense.
2. Equipment costing $38,500 upon which $6,230 of depreciation had accumulated was sold for $35,000 with the gain being credited to administrative expense.
3. The company negotiated an increase in its bank loan to $380,000 early in the year in order to acquire Chesley Limited. By year end, some of the loan had been repaid.
4. A $110,000 building was acquired by issuing a $100,000 bond, due in 19x27, to the previous owner plus paying $10,000 cash.

Before using the T account method of preparing an SCFP it is useful to examine the financial statements and accompanying information to form general impressions about the format of SCFP which might be useful. Observe that:

1. Although the change in working capital is minor, two of its accounts — bank loan, and inventory — have experienced large changes.
2. A barter transaction, involving building and bonds, occurred.
3. A preferred share conversion took place.

These three transactions are indicators pointing to the probable need for a financing and investing format. We can still accomplish our end by starting with a working capital T account, and adding some notations to the entries to jog our memory for when we prepare the SCFP.

The reconstructed journal entries are:

(a) Starting with the *additional information* provided below the income statement, we can observe that no entry is necessary to record the dividend from Chesley Limited. It is simply something which affects working capital and the income statement; its net effect is captured by funds from operations.

The sale of equipment requires an entry:

(a)

Working capital	$35,000	
Accumulated depreciation — equipment	6,230	
Equipment		$38,500
Funds from operations — gain on sale of equipment		2,730
To record sale.		

(b) The information about the bank loan is interesting and should be recalled for future use in preparing the SCFP. Rather than show only the net change in the bank loan — something which is readily ascertainable from comparative balance sheets — we can show the grossed-up situation: bank loan increase less repayment. This can provide useful information about two matters affecting the company: (i) its ability and power to negotiate higher loans, and (ii) its ability to repay the loans (from funds from operations, or from other borrowing). At this point, we need not make a journal entry.

The "partial" barter transaction requires a journal entry:

(b)

Building	$110,000	
Working capital — cash		$ 10,000
Bond payable		100,000
To record acquisition of building.		

(c) Switching to the *retained earnings* statement, we can reconstruct the income and dividends. First, the dividends:

(c)

Retained earnings	$130,000	
Working capital		$130,000
To record dividends.		

(d) The income statement contains an extraordinary item; hence, we need more than one entry to close to retained earnings.

(d)

Funds from operations	$225,570	
Retained earnings		$225,570
To record net income effect before extraordinary item.		

(e) The extraordinary item could be tricky. If uninsured inventory — that is, a working capital item — of $98,000 ($58,000 + $40,000) was destroyed, the entry is a debit to the income statement and a credit to working capital. Per Exhibit 14-6 (Category 5) we could ignore this item. But the ARC of the CICA suggests that it be reported as a separate item.

However, if the extraordinary item involved a building — that is, a noncurrent account — an entry is required. For simplicity, let us assume that an uninsured building upon which zero depreciation had accumulated was totally destroyed:

(e)

Extraordinary item — loss	$58,000	
Working capital	40,000	
Building		$98,000
To record fire loss.		

Observe that the income tax reduction of $40,000 has been debited to working capital. The entry may be split:

(e)(i) Extraordinary item	$58,000	
Building		$58,000
(e)(ii) Working capital	$40,000	
Building		$40,000

Since entry (e)(ii) involves working capital, per Exhibit 14-6, it is a source of funds. The extraordinary part of entry (e)(i) should be closed to retained earnings:

Retained earnings	$58,000	
Extraordinary item		$58,000

This combines the entry into a revised (e)(i):

(e)(i)

Retained earnings	$58,000	
Building		$58,000
To record disposal of building.		

Since both parts of (e)(i), revised, are nonworking capital, they do not appear on the SCFP. Entry (e)(i), revised, must be posted to indicate the reductions in each account. Entry (e)(ii) must also be posted as a source of funds (income tax effect of an involuntary disposal of a building).

(f) We may now shift our emphasis to the *balance sheet* information.

(f)

Investment in Chesley Limited	$265,000	
Working capital		$265,000
To record purchase of Chesley's common shares.		

(g) Entries involving the building and equipment account are next.

Asset, opening balance	$2,655,000
Less:	
Lost in fire (entries (e)(i), revised, and (e)(ii))	(98,000)
Sold (entry (a))	(38,500)
	$2,518,500
Add barter (entry (b))	110,000
	2,628,500
Assumed addition	158,710
Asset, closing balance	$2,787,210

(g)

Building and equipment	$158,710	
Working capital		$158,710
To record purchase of additional assets.		

(h) Accumulated depreciation — building and equipment:

Opening balance	$ 413,930
Less:	
Asset sold (entry (a))	6,230
	407,700
Assumed amount of depreciation	65,470
Closing balance	$ 473,170

(h)

Funds from operations	$65,470	
Accumulated depreciation		$65,470
To record depreciation.		

(i) Bonds payable has increased by $300,000 but $100,000 was from a non-cash exchange. The remainder must have been a separate sale.

(i)

Working capital	$200,000	
Bonds payable		$200,000
To record sale of bonds.		

(j) A noncash conversion of preferred shares occurred:

(j)

Preferred shares	$200,000	
Common shares		$200,000
To record conversion.		

The next step in the process is to prepare T accounts and post the above journal entries. The change in working capital is:

	19x7	*19x6*
Current assets	$492,150	$300,650
Current liabilities	436,500	244,600
	55,650	56,050
		55,650
Decrease in working capital		$ 400

Working Capital

Debit		Credit	
			400
(a) Disposal	35,000	(b) Building	10,000*
(e)(ii) Income tax	40,000	(c) Dividend	130,000
(i) Bonds	200,000	(f) Chesley	265,000
(k) Operations	288,310	(g) Building	158,710

Investment in Chesley Limited

Debit		Credit	
	265,000		
(f)	265,000		

Buildings and equipment

Debit		Credit	
	132,210		
(b)	110,000	(b)	38,500
(g)	158,710	(eii)	40,000
		(ei)	58,000

Accumulated Depreciation

Debit		Credit	
			59,240
(a)	6,230	(h)	65,470

Land

Debit	Credit
nil	

Bonds payable

Debit	Credit
	300,000
	(b) 100,000**
	(i) 200,000

Preferred shares

Debit	Credit
200,000	
(j) 200,000	

Common shares

Debit	Credit
	200,000
	(j) 200,000**

Retained earnings

Debit	Credit
	37,570
(c) 130,000	(d) 225,570
(ei) 58,000	

Funds from Operations

Debit		Credit	
(d) Net income	225,570	(a) Gain	2,730
(h) Depreciation	65,470		
	291,040		2,730
		(k)	288,310

*Indicates noncash exchange.
**Conversion with no cash or working capital effects.

A trial balance of the changes shows:

	+	−
Working capital		$ 400
Investment in Chesley Limited	$265,000	
Buildings and equipment	132,210	
Accumulated depreciation		59,240
Bonds payable		300,000
Preferred shares	200,000	
Common shares		200,000
Retained earnings		37,570
	$597,210	$597,210

The journal entry to close funds from operations to working capital is:

(k)

Working capital	$288,310	
Funds from operations		$288,310
To close to working capital.		

In order to assist in preparations of the SCFP, brief one or two-word reminders have been added to the working capital and funds from operations T accounts. Also the asterisk has been added to remind us to report the transaction as a separate item.

Two formats — both of which portray financing and investing — are provided in Exhibits 14-7 and 14-8. These two are assembled primarily by using the two T-accounts: working capital and funds from operations.

EXHIBIT 14-7

Mann Limited
Statement of Changes in Financial Position
Year ended December 31, 19x7

Uses of cash funds:		
Acquisition of building and equipment		$268,710
Less portion financed by bond payable		100,000
		168,710
Purchase of shares of Chesley Limited		265,000
Preferred and common share dividends		130,000
Additional investment in inventories		192,040
Change in working capital excluding bank loan and inventories		560
		$756,310
Sources of cash funds:		
From operations:		
Net income		$225,570
Add depreciation		65,470
		291,040
Deduct gain on disposal		2,730
		288,310
Preferred shares converted into $200,000 of common		—
Bonds sold		200,000
Income tax effect of loss due to fire		40,000
Proceeds on disposal of equipment		35,000
Increase in bank loan	$300,000	
Less portion repaid	107,000	193,000
		$756,310

Exhibit 14-7 attempts to stay fairly close to the sources and uses set forth in the working capital T account, but adds information concerning:

1. The net increase in inventory.
2. The bank loan increase less repayments.
3. The noncash acquisition of equipment.
4. The preferred share conversion.
5. Causes of changes in cash — the most liquid asset (and one which may be of concern to the company).

The balanced format also downplays any possible importance of working capital as such, and gives the separate disclosure to major changes within working capital.

EXHIBIT 14-8

Mann Limited
Statement of Changes in Financial Position
Year ended December 31, 19x7

Financing:		
Funds from operations		$288,310
Less preferred and common dividends paid		130,000
		158,310
Preferred shares of $200,000 converted to an equal amount of common shares		—
Bank loan increase	$300,000	
Less repayments	107,000	193,000
Bonds sold		200,000
		$551,310
Investing:		
Acquisition of building and equipment		$268,710
Less portion financed by bond payable		100,000
		168,710
Less proceeds on disposal ($35,000) and income tax refund on fire loss ($40,000)		75,000
		93,710
Additional investment in inventory		192,040
Acquisition of shares of Chesley Limited		265,000
Other		560
		$551,310

Exhibit 14-8 is structured on the changes in assets and liabilities approach. It deletes explanations of "funds from operations" and "other"; but these could be provided. It also groups accounts a little more, such as subtracting dividends from the funds from operations account. Funds is not defined in Exhibit 14-8, but it could represent a liquid definition, or simply purchasing power.

Many other formats or styles could be employed. The point of the exercise is communication: design to suit the needs of users.

A Compromise Design

The formats shown in Exhibits 14-7 and 14-8 are not yet popular in practice (and may never be). Much of the information — but not all — can be captured in a working capital format (Exhibit 14-9) which has been modified to accommodate transactions which do not directly affect working capital.

EXHIBIT 14-9

Mann Limited
Statement of Changes in Financial Position
Year ended December 31, 19x7

Application of working capital:		
Investment in Chesley Limited		$265,000
Preferred and common share dividends		130,000
Building and equipment acquired		268,710
		663,710
Sources of working capital:		
From operations (could give detail)	$288,310	
Bonds payable sold	300,000	
Proceeds on disposal of equipment	35,000	
Income tax effect of loss due to fire	40,000	663,310
Decrease in working capital		$ 400

Bearing in mind the purposes of an SCFP, which format would you choose (Exhibit 14-7, 14-8, or 14-9) for the given set of facts? Does your response change if you are a preparer instead of a user, or vice-versa? Why?

Summary

An SCFP is designed to report what is not reported, or not reported well, by the other formal financial statements. For some organizations the SCFP may be arranged to disclose changes in liquidity. The reason is that the income statement focuses on profitability and the balance sheet may not contain sufficient detail to learn of *flows* (increases and decreases) in liquid assets less liabilities. Other organizations may want the SCFP to report financing and investing transactions. Some users (such as those attempting to predict) may want information separated into arm's-length and non-arm's-length categories, so that they do not get confused by bookkeeping estimates (such as depreciation).

A preparer may not have any incentive to report detail which is not required by law, or by the *CICA Handbook* (should it apply because a chartered accountant, for example, is conducting an audit). If so, the SCFP could be skimpy. However, if the preparer wants to use the SCFP to its greatest degree there are few constraints. Flexibility and imagination apply.

Questions, Problems, and Cases

Questions

14-1 What purpose(s) does the Statement of Changes in Financial Position attempt to accomplish? How might the purpose(s) of the Statement of Changes in Financial Position affect your decision about its format or design (i.e., the definition of funds, the disclosure of barter transactions and so forth)?

14-2 "The Statement of Changes in Financial Position is superfluous. A sophisticated analyst can derive from comparative balance sheets and the income statement all the information contained in the statement." Do you agree? Explain.

14-3 A Statement of Changes in Financial Position, especially one based on the cash concept of funds, is sometimes said to be more "objective" than an income statement. Do you agree? Why?

*14-4 The working capital concept of funds is often used in Canada. Why do you suppose financial statement users are interested in changes, as well as reasons for the changes, in the working capital balance rather than the cash balance? Is working capital always a good measure of liquidity? Give examples to support your response.

14-5 Under what conditions would you use a cash concept of funds for a company's Statement of Changes in Financial Position?

14-6 Under what conditions would you use a financing and investing format for a company's Statement of Changes in Financial Position?

14-7 In a recent collective bargaining session, management argued that even though reported earnings were at record highs, the company was nevertheless unable to afford even a small increase in wages. In another session involving different companies and unions, the union asserted that even though the company incurred a severe loss, the company could well afford to grant a substantial wage increase. What do you think the two positions have in common? What argument with respect to reported earnings is likely to be made in both sets of negotiations?

14-8 Why must reported earnings be adjusted to determine funds from operations?

14-9 A magazine article contained the following comment with respect to a major corporation: "For the first time, the company's cash flow exceeded its income. The firm was basking in riches as depreciation write-offs poured a golden stream of cash into its treasury." In what way is such a statement misleading?

14-10 Why are some types of transactions (e.g., an exchange of bonds for preferred shares) reported as sources and uses of funds (defined as working capital) even though they resulted in neither an increase nor a decrease in working capital? Provide examples of such transactions.

14-11 In what way does the Statement of Changes in Financial Position based on a cash concept of funds differ from that based on a working capital concept? In preparing the statement based on the cash concept, what additional accounts must be analyzed?

14-12 This chapter advocates judgment and flexibility as guiding principles for selecting concepts, format, and design of the Statement of Changes in Financial Position. Why does the preparer have more flexibility when reporting information in the Statement of Changes in Financial Position? How would you judge which concept of funds and Statement of Changes in Financial Position design to use in a particular situation?

14-13 Distinguish between the user needs of a small privately-held company and a large company listed on a Canadian stock exchange. How might the needs of the users of these particular companies affect your selection of a concept of funds and a Statement of Changes in Financial Position design?

14-14 Previous chapters have discussed two important developments — (1) skepticism about the usefulness of cost allocations for some of the objectives of accounting (namely, cash prediction and management evaluation) and (2) research about the "efficiency" of the stock markets. What impact do you think these recent developments will have on the importance of the Statement of Changes in Financial Position?

Problems

P14-1 Indicate the impact that each of the following transactions will have on the working capital position of the company. Specify whether it would increase (I), decrease (D), or have no effect (NE) on working capital.

1. Declaration of a $150,000 stock dividend.
2. Declaration of a $150,000 cash dividend.
3. Purchase of marketable securities for $12,000.
4. Sale, for $15,000, of marketable securities that had initially cost $12,000.
5. Declaration of $8,000 in dividends by a firm in which the company has a 5 percent interest.
6. Declaration of $8,000 in dividends by a firm in which the company has a 40 percent interest.
7. Write-off of an uncollectible account of $3,000 against the allowance provided.
8. Acquisition of another company in exchange for $1 million in long-term notes.
9. Sale for $600 of merchandise that had cost $400.

P14-2 Described below are several transactions in which Feltham Ltd. engaged in 19x7:

1. Sold merchandise, on account, for $6,000. Cost of the goods sold, which had been included in inventory, was $5,000.
2. Collected $3,200 of the amount owed by customers.
3. Purchased additional inventory for $1,700 (on account).
4. Paid $1,500 of the amount owed to suppliers.
5. Purchased marketable securities for $700.
6. Sold the marketable securities for $500.
7. Recorded one month's interest on notes payable, $50.
8. Paid one month's interest on the notes payable, $50.

9. Recorded one month's rent due from tenant, $200.
10. Received payment of one month's rent from tenant.

Required:

a. Indicate whether the transactions would increase (I), decrease (D), or have no effect (NE) on the working capital of the corporation.
b. Indicate whether the transactions would increase (I), decrease (D), or have no effect (NE) on the cash balance of the corporation.

P14-3 The following account balances appeared on the financial statements of the Morrison Machine Co. Ltd.:

	19x8	*19x7*
Buildings and equipment	$475,000	$400,000
Accumulated depreciation	125,000	100,000
Depreciation	40,000	35,000
Gain on sale of equipment	2,000	57,000

During 19x8 the Morrison Machine Co. Ltd. purchased new equipment with $134,000 cash.

Required:

a. Compute the increase in funds (defined as working capital) attributable to the sale of equipment in 19x8.
b. Indicate the adjustments to 19x8 income that would be required to compute funds from operations.

P14-4 The Badlands Mining Co. Ltd. was organized to remove ore from a specific tract of land over a period of five years. In its second year of operations the company incurred a loss of $200,000, determined as follows:

Sales of ore		$2,000,000
Less: Depletion of ore	$1,000,000	
Depreciation on equipment	200,000	
Wages and salaries	400,000	
Other operating costs	600,000	2,200,000
Net loss		$ 200,000

In spite of the loss the president of the company recommended to the board of directors that it declare a dividend of $300,000. One member of the board declared the recommendation to be nonsense. "How can we justify declaring a dividend in a year when we 'took a financial beating?' "

Required:

a. How, in fact, might the board justify the declaration of a dividend?
b. Why would a Statement of Changes in Financial Position provide a better indication of the ability of the company to declare dividends than would a statement of income?
c. Suppose that the company planned to acquire $300,000 of equipment. Prepare a schedule which would support the position of the president that the company could "afford" to declare a dividend despite the required outlay for the equipment.

P14-5 The president of Fraser Ltd., Mr. Martian, is unhappy with company earnings for 19x5. Consequently he is considering changing several of the company's accounting principles and methods in order to improve 19x5 reported earnings. The changes he is considering are as follows:

1. Change from the LIFO to the FIFO method of accounting for inventories. (The prices of supplies, especially fuel, purchased by the company have been consistently increasing.)
2. Recognize revenue from the sale of tickets at the time a ticket is sold rather than at the time a passenger completes his flight. In 19x5 the number of tickets sold exceeded the number of flights taken.
3. Delay payments to certain suppliers until 19x6.
4. Delay until 19x6 required payments to the firm's pension fund.
5. Amortize (for reporting purposes) past service costs relating to pensions over a period of 20 years rather than 10 years, as is done currently.
6. Depreciate the company's fleet of 727 jets over a period of 15 years — the number of years over which a competitor depreciates similar planes — rather than 10 years, as is currently done.

Required:

a. Indicate the likely impact of each of the above suggestions on (i) reported earnings, (ii) flow of funds (defined as working capital) and (iii) flow of cash. Ignore any income tax implications.

b. Suppose that the company pays income tax at a rate of 40 percent. What would be the impact on reported earnings and the flow of working capital if the initial cost of the company's fleet of 727 jets was $30 million and the company uses a straight-line depreciation method? Assume that the depreciation charged for accounting purposes is also acceptable for tax purposes.

c. It is sometimes asserted that the Statement of Changes in Financial Position provides a more "objective" measure of financial performance than does the statement of income. Do you agree? Does it make a difference whether the Statement of Changes in Financial Position is based on working capital as opposed to cash? Comment.

d. If the major purpose of the Statement of Changes in Financial Position were to evaluate company liquidity, which definition of funds do you think better reflects the impact of the company's changes in accounting principles and methods?

P14-6 Ripstein Ltd. began operations in 19x2. Its income statement and balance sheet for its first year of operations are indicated below:

Ripstein Ltd.
Statement of Income
Year ended December 31, 19x2

Sales		$ 94,000
Less: Cost of goods sold	$48,000	
Depreciation	3,000	
Amortization of organizational costs	2,000	
Taxes	7,000	
Interest	1,000	
Other expenses	20,000	81,000
Net income		$ 13,000

Balance Sheet
As of December 31, 19x2

Assets		
Current assets		$ 37,000
Plant and equipment	$53,000	
Less: Accumulated depreciation	3,000	50,000
Land		20,000
Organizational costs		8,000
Total assets		$115,000
Equities		
Current liabilities		$ 19,000
Income taxes deferred until future years		2,000
Note payable	$40,000	
Less: Discount	6,000	34,000
Common shares		50,000
Retained earnings		10,000
Total liabilities and shareholders' equity		$115,000

Note: The reported interest expense of $1,000 represents, in its entirety, amortization of discount on note payable.

Required:

a. Reconstruct the transaction journal entries which probably occurred during the year.
b. Employ the T-account method illustrated in the chapter to prepare a Statement of Changes in Financial Position using a working capital definition of funds.
c. Assume the role of a creditor (i.e., the holder of the company's note payable). Explain how you would use the Statement of Changes in Financial Position.
d. What dangers exist in using a Statement of Changes in Financial Position based on a working capital definition of funds for assessing the liquidity of a company?

P14-7 Comparative income statements and balance sheets of Tomins Ltd. are presented below:

Tomins Ltd.
Statement of Income
Years Ending December 31

	19x7	*19x6*
Sales	$160,000	$146,000
Gain on sale of land sold	8,000	
	168,000	146,000
Less: Cost of goods sold	118,000	95,000
Other expenses	20,000	10,000
Income taxes	8,000	11,000
	146,000	116,000
Net income	$ 22,000	$ 30,000

Note: Included in cost of goods is depreciation expense of $10,000 in 19x7 and $9,000 in 19x6.

Balance Sheet
As of December 31

	19x7	19x6
Assets		
Current assets	$ 60,000	$ 47,000
Equipment	150,000	120,000
Less: Accumulated depreciation	(40,000)	(30,000)
	110,000	90,000
Land	35,000	50,000
Total assets	$205,000	$187,000
Equities		
Current liabilities	$ 20,000	$ 31,000
Income taxes deferred until future years	9,000	7,000
Notes payable	30,000	25,000
Common shares	100,000	100,000
Retained earnings	46,000	24,000
Total liabilities and shareholders' equity	$205,000	$187,000

Required:

a. Prepare a Statement of Changes in Financial Position using a working capital definition of funds.

b. Explain the uses which are made of the statement you prepared in Part a.

P14-8 Comparative income statements and balance sheets for the Rushmore Sales Co. Ltd. for the years ended December 31, 19x7 and 19x6 are indicated below:

Rushmore Sales Co. Ltd.
Balance Sheet
As of December 31

	19x7	19x6
Assets		
Cash	$ 40,000	$ 19,000
Accounts receivable	60,000	45,000
Inventories	20,000	28,000
Fixed assets (net of accumulated depreciation)	107,000	112,000
Total assets	$227,000	$204,000
Equities		
Accounts payable	$89,000	$85,000
Common shares	100,000	100,000
Retained earnings	38,000	19,000
Total equities	$227,000	$204,000

Income Statement
For Years Ending December 31

	19x7	*19x6*
Sales	$100,000	$ 85,000
Cost of goods sold	70,000	50,000
Depreciation	5,000	5,000
Other expenses	6,000	8,000
Total expenses	81,000	63,000
Net income	$ 19,000	$ 22,000

Required:

a. All sales were made on account. Determine the amount of cash collected during 19x7.

b. All "other expenses" were paid directly in cash. Indicate the amount of cash applied to the payment of the other expenses.

c. Determine the amount of inventory purchased during 19x7. Then determine the amount of cash payments made during the year in connection with purchases of inventory in 19x7 and prior years.

d. Indicate any other expenses not requiring an outlay of cash.

e. Prepare two Statements of Changes in Financial Position based on the cash concept of funds. In the first, indicate directly all sources and applications of cash (e.g., collections, purchases). In the second, start with net income as a source of cash and indicate any required adjustments (e.g., for changes in inventories, accounts receivable).

f. Explain the uses and limitations of the Statement of Changes in Financial Position based on a cash concept of funds.

P14-9 The records of Fleming Ltd. reflected the following data:

Balance Sheet Data

	December 31	
	19x7	*19x6*
Cash	$ 63,500	$ 64,000
Accounts receivable (net)	47,000	42,000
Inventory	44,000	46,000
Long-term investments	21,500	36,000
Fixed assets	128,000	110,000
Total debits	$304,000	$298,000
Accumulated depreciation	$ 69,000	$ 78,000
Accounts payable	42,000	49,000
Bonds payable	60,000	40,000
Common shares, no par	95,000	80,000
Retained earnings	38,000	51,000
Total credits	$304,000	$298,000

Additional data for the period January 1, 19x7 through December 31, 19x7:

1. Sales on account, $100,000.
2. Purchases on account, $70,000.
3. Expenses paid in cash, $39,000.
4. Decrease in inventory, $2,000.
5. Sold fixed assets for $6,000 cash; cost $21,000 and two-thirds depreciated (assume loss or gain is an extraordinary item).
6. Purchased fixed assets by issuing bonds payable of $30,000 and the remainder in cash.
7. Sold the long-term investments for $40,000 cash (assume this is not an extraordinary item).
8. Purchased long-term investments for cash, $21,500.
9. Retired bonds payable by issuing common shares, $10,000.
10. Collections on accounts receivable, $95,000.
11. Payments on accounts payable, $77,000.
12. Sold unissued common shares for cash, $5,000.

Required:

a. Prepare a Statement of Changes in Financial Position based on a cash concept of funds.
b. Prepare a Statement of Changes in Financial Position based on a working capital concept of funds.
c. Prepare a Statement of Changes in Financial Position using the financing and investing format.
d. Which Statement of Changes in Financial Position format would you recommend for Fleming Ltd.? Explain thoroughly.

P14-10 The accountant for Steel Ltd., Mr. F. Hintenberger, is having some difficulty deciding on the most meaningful Statement of Changes in Financial Position design for the company's financial statement readers. He has asked for your help and has provided you with the following comparative balance sheet and additional information:

Balance Sheet
December 31
(in thousands of dollars)

	19x5	*19x4*
Cash	$ 800	$ 1,500
Receivables	2,900	800
Inventories	1,650	1,600
Building and equipment	7,900	7,000
Accumulated depreciation	(1,800)	(2,400)
Land	4,500	3,000
Goodwill	450	500
	$16,400	$12,000

Accounts payable	$ 805	$ 800
Bank loan payable	3,000	900
Bonds payable	6,000	4,000
Preferred shares	500	2,000
Common shares	5,500	3,000
Retained earnings	595	1,300
	$16,400	$12,000

Additional information:

1. During the year the company negotiated a bank loan for $3,500 which it used in full temporarily and repaid some of it by December 31, 19x5.
2. In February 19x5 the company acquired an operating division ("X") of another company, recording it as follows:

Land	$ 700
Building and equipment	3,300
Goodwill	1,000
	$5,000

Consideration paid, at fair value	
Bonds payable	$4,000
Common shares	1,000
	$5,000

3. $1,500 par value of preferred shares were converted by holders into common shares.
4. Building and equipment costing $2,400 upon which $1,300 of depreciation had accumulated was sold for $1,350.
5. Net loss for the year was $280, yet dividends of $125 were paid on the preferred shares, and $300 were paid on the common shares.
6. $2,000 face value of bonds payable were redeemed during the year for $1,880.

Required:

a. Identify the transactions which would be excluded from a Statement of Changes in Financial Position disclosing only the changes in working capital.

b. Prepare a Statement of Changes in Financial Position using the financing and investing format.

c. Prepare a Statement of Changes in Financial Position based on a working capital definition of funds.

d. Assuming Steel Ltd. is a large public company, which Statement of Changes in Financial Position would you recommend? Why?

P14-11 Presented below are the balance sheets of McCracken Ltd. as of June 30, 19x5 and 19x4, and the income statement for 19x5:

McCracken Ltd.
Balance Sheet
As of June 30

	19x5	19x4
Assets		
Current		
Cash	$ 46,000	$ 13,000
Accounts receivable	65,000	12,000
Inventories	66,000	54,000
Total current assets	177,000	79,000
Noncurrent		
Property, plant, and equipment	925,000	1,090,000
Less: Accumulated depreciation	228,000	298,000
	697,000	792,000
Investment in subsidiary	230,000	219,000
Other assets	120,000	140,000
Total noncurrent assets	1,047,000	1,151,000
Total assets	$1,224,000	$1,230,000
Liabilities		
Current		
Accounts payable	$ 40,000	$ 35,000
Current portion of notes payable	145,000	15,000
Total current liabilities	185,000	50,000
Noncurrent		
Notes payable	74,000	280,000
Total liabilities	259,000	330,000
Shareholders' Equity		
Common shares	140,000	100,000
Retained earnings	825,000	800,000
Total shareholders' equity	965,000	900,000
Total liabilities and shareholders' equity	$1,224,000	$1,230,000

Statement of Income
Year Ending June 30, 19x5

Sales	$555,000	
Proportionate share of subsidiary earnings	26,000	$581,000
Less: Cost of goods sold	326,000	
Interest	20,000	
Taxes	30,000	
Other expenses	140,000	516,000
Net income		$ 65,000

Other information:

1. The company declared a *stock* dividend. Retained earnings of $40,000 ($40 per share) were transferred to "permanent" capital accounts.
2. Included in costs of goods sold and other expenses is a total of $90,000 in depreciation.
3. The company incurred an uninsured loss of its plant. Equipment that had a book value of $80,000 (original cost $240,000, accumulated depreciation $160,000) was destroyed. The loss is included among "other expenses." No other "property, plant, and equipment" was sold or retired.
4. Other assets include patents of $40,000 in 19x5 and $60,000 in 19x4. Amortization expense of $20,000 is included in other expenses.
5. The company owns a 30 percent interest in another company. It accounts for its investment by the equity method. The subsidiary paid dividends of $15,000 to McCracken Ltd. during 19x5.

Required:

a. Reconstruct the transaction journal entries which probably occurred during the year and post them to T-accounts.

b. Prepare a Statement of Changes in Financial Position using a working capital definition of funds.

P14-12 The consolidated balance sheets of Murphy Ltd. as of December 31, 19x2 and 19x1, are presented below. So also is the income statement for 19x2 and other information about the company.

Murphy Ltd.
Consolidated Balance Sheet
As of December 31

	19x2	*19x1*
Assets		
Current		
Cash	$ 88,000	$ 61,000
Accounts receivable	250,000	211,000
Inventory	269,000	245,000
Total current assets	607,000	517,000
Other assets		
Plant and equipment	950,000	958,000
Less: Accumulated depreciation	180,000	102,000
	770,000	856,000
Investment in unconsolidated subsidiary	50,000	—
Goodwill	65,000	74,000
Total other assets	885,000	930,000
Total assets	$1,492,000	$1,447,000

Equities		
Current liabilities		
Accounts payable	$ 218,000	$ 179,000
Other current liabilities	63,000	176,000
Total current liabilities	281,000	355,000
Other liabilities		
Deferred income taxes	24,000	20,000
Bonds payable	200,000	200,000
Less: Unamortized discount	13,000	14,000
	187,000	186,000
Total other liabilities	211,000	206,000
Total liabilities	492,000	561,000
Shareholders' equity		
Common shares	450,000	400,000
Retained earnings	550,000	486,000
Total shareholders' equity	1,000,000	886,000
Total liabilities and shareholders' equity	$1,492,000	$1,447,000

Murphy Ltd.
Consolidated Statement of Income
Year Ended December 31, 19x2

Sales		$883,000
Less expenses:		
Cost of goods sold	$596,000	
Depreciation	87,000	
Amortization of goodwill	9,000	
Interest	13,000	
Other expenses	8,000	
Income taxes	76,000	789,000
Net income		$ 94,000

Other information:

1. The company declared cash dividends of $30,000.
2. "Other expenses" includes a loss of $2,000 on equipment sold. The equipment had cost $17,000 and had a book value at time of sale of $8,000.
3. The bonds payable were 6 percent coupon bonds. They had been sold at a price to yield 7 percent.
4. The company acquired 20 percent interest in the subsidiary in exchange for 10,000 common shares.

5. The company credits the difference between taxes reported on the income statement and those actually payable to "deferred income taxes."

Required:
Prepare a Statement of Changes in Financial Position using a working capital definition of funds. Reconstruct journal entries as required and post them to a work sheet of T-accounts.

Cases

C14-1 In January 19x2 Chan Ltd. purchased an apartment building for $100,000. The company paid $10,000 in cash and gave a 10-year note for the balance. The company was required to pay only interest on the note at 6 percent per annum on December 31 for the first five years. In year 19x7 through 19x11 it was required to make principal payments of $18,000 per year.

In 19x2 the income statement of the company appeared as follows:

Revenues from rents		$20,000
Less: Depreciation	$ 9,000	
Interest	5,400	
Other expenses	6,000	20,400
Net loss		$ 400

Depreciation is based on 9% declining balance rate.

The president of the company, upon learning of the $400 loss, instructed his accountant to use the cash basis of reporting. In his opinion conventionally computed operating income was misleading in his company's situation and did not adequately measure the performance of real estate companies.

The accountant refused to adjust the statement. He told the president that the accounting profession required financial statements to be prepared on an accrual basis and that noncash as well as cash charges had to be matched against revenues in determining income.

The president could not understand how accountants could report a loss for a company which was successful. If this was the logic on which rules were based then he was obviously in the wrong business.

Required:

a. Do you believe the cash basis of accounting is a better measure for Chan Ltd.? Are there other ways to measure the performance of the company? How?

b. Why do you think the accounting profession adheres to matching and the accrual basis of accounting?

c. How might you help the president of Chan Ltd. and still adhere to generally accepted principles?

C14-2 Finney Limited (FL or the company) is a small, closely held retail store chain which sells shoes. Its five stores are located in shopping centers in a large Canadian city.

The company requires annual financial statements for the bank and must file an annual income tax return; otherwise, it has no special need for accounting. Cash and inventory control are facilitated by a cash register which provides data for direct feeding to a computer (owned by a financial institution). Reports of sales, purchases, and inventory levels are provided monthly for each store for a small fee by the computer owner. A public accountant prepares audited, annual financial statements and the company's income tax return.

The following conversation occurred recently between the president of FL and the company's public accountant:

President: What do you mean that your fee will increase 30 percent this year? I can't increase shoe prices 30 percent. If I did I wouldn't have any customers! I only need the financial statements to keep the bank happy — and the banker doesn't even want an audit; just statements.

Public Accountant: The banker wouldn't be very happy with unaudited statements. She wouldn't lend you as much money I guess — and you need a high loan in the autumn and spring when your inventory is high. . . . Besides, you wouldn't save that much having only unaudited statements. By the time we prepare unaudited ones we've had to do a large amount of verification. The additional cost is minor.

President: Let's get back to the 30 percent increase.

Public Accountant: Our costs are up. Your tax return is costlier to prepare because the regulations and legislation are more complex. In addition, we prepared a Statement of Changes in Financial Position for you this year.

President: Why did you do that? Our financial position didn't change during the year.

Public Accountant: The Statement of Changes in Financial Position is a new type of statement. Public accountants across the country are introducing it to clients to improve financial reporting.

President: I don't want something if it costs too much and doesn't tell me anything. What good does it do?

The following statements were prepared by the public accountant:

Finney Limited
Balance Sheet
January 31, 19x2
(with comparative figures for 19x1)

	19x2	*19x1*
Assets		
Current:		
Cash	$ 22,750	$ 1,800
Accounts receivable	76,200	29,600
Inventory	361,600	420,600
Prepaid expense	5,450	3,000
	466,000	455,000
Leasehold improvements and fixtures	162,000	160,000
Less accumulated amortization	128,000	124,000
	34,000	36,000
Deferred charges	19,000	22,000
	$519,000	$513,000
Liabilities and Equities		
Current		
Bank loan	$160,000	$200,000
Accounts payable	114,700	86,900
Income tax payable	16,000	17,000
Other current	26,300	2,950
	317,000	306,850
Deferred income tax	5,000	4,000
Debt payable — 12% due 19x2	—	120,000
Due to owners	23,850	20,000
Debt payable — 14% due 19x9	100,000	—
Owners' equity:		
Common shares	40,000	40,000
Contributed surplus	10,000	10,000
Retained earnings	23,150	12,150
	73,150	62,150
	$519,000	$513,000

Finney Limited
Income Statement
Year ended January 31, 19x2
(with comparative figures for 19x1)

	19x2	19x1
Revenue	$1,200,000	$1,100,000
Cost of goods sold	800,000	714,800
Gross profit	400,000	385,200
Expenses		
Depreciation	4,000	4,000
Selling and administrative	265,000	246,000
	269,000	250,000
Income before income tax	131,000	135,200
Income tax (deferred: 19x2 and 19x1 $1,000)	60,000	50,000
Net income	$ 71,000	$ 85,200

Finney Limited
Statement of Retained Earnings
Year ended January 31, 19x2
(with comparative figures for 19x1)

	19x2	19x1
Beginning of year	$ 12,150	$ 6,950
Net income	71,000	85,200
	83,150	92,150
Dividends	60,000	80,000
End of year	$ 23,150	$ 12,150

Finney Limited
Statement of Changes in Financial Position
Year ended January 31, 19x2

Sources:		
From operations:		
Net income		$ 71,000
Add: Leasehold amortization	$4,000	
Deferred charges	3,000	
Deferred income tax	1,000	8,000
		79,000

Debt payable	100,000
From owners	3,850
	182,850
Uses:	
Leasehold improvements	2,000
Dividend	60,000
Repay debt	120,000
	182,000
Increase in working capital	$ 850

Required:

a. Analyze and comment upon the strengths and weaknesses of the Statement of Changes in Financial Position (SCFP) prepared by the public accountant for Finney Limited.

b. Revise the SCFP as best you can to make it more informative to the president of FL.

c. Explain the purpose or uses of the SCFP you prepared in b. in language which the president of FL will likely understand.

C14-3 Knotty Pine Limited ("KPL" or the company) is a small closely held company. The owners do not take an active part in the management of the company. Instead, they rely heavily on the financial statements of the company as an indicator of KPL's performance. All operating decisions are made by Mr. Langdon, the president of the company.

KPL manufactures pine furniture and has a history of good profits. Until recently, the owners of KPL were very pleased with Mr. Langdon's performance. Now, however, some of the owners suspect Mr. Langdon is senile. This suspicion is not based on his age, since Mr. Langdon is thirty-one. Nor is it based on his background, since he has successfully completed an introductory accounting course and appears to be able to select accounting procedures to fit the situation. Their suspicions are based entirely on the following proposals which Mr. Langdon made at a recent Board of Directors meeting:

1. The cash dividend to shareholders should be reduced.
2. Inflation is making it harder for the company to operate.
3. The company requires additional capital investment from the owners to continue to survive and compete in the furniture market.

The owners find these proposals hard to accept especially since the company is profitable and in fact just completed one of its best years with net income of $120,000. They admit that the equipment is old but as long as the company is profitable they see no reason to replace it. In their opinion Mr. Langdon is jealous of the dividend they are receiving and is over-reacting to the problems of inflation. You have been hired by the owners of KPL to act as an accounting advisor. They want you to investigate the proposals made by Mr. Langdon. One of the owners heard about a Statement of Changes in Financial Position at a recent cocktail party and wondered if it would be of any use to KPL. The following data have been provided for you:

Balance Sheet Data

Debits	*19x8*	*19x7*
Cash	$ —	$ 20,000
Accounts receivable	200,000	100,000
Inventory	300,000	150,000
Long-term investments	—	50,000
Land	50,000	75,000
Fixed assets	500,000	530,000
Patents	8,000	10,000
Total debits	$1,058,000	$935,000

Credits	*19x8*	*19x7*
Accounts payable	$ 80,000	$ 40,000
Notes payable — short-term (nontrade)	20,000	10,000
Accrued wages	40,000	—
Accumulated depreciation	380,000	400,000
Notes payable — long-term	130,000	150,000
Common shares	300,000	250,000
Retained earnings	108,000	85,000
Total credits	$1,058,000	$935,000

Additional Data for 19x8:

1. Net income for the year was $120,000.
2. Depreciation recorded on the fixed assets was $25,000.
3. Purchased equipment costing $30,000 by issuing long-term notes payable.
4. Sold old machinery for $26,000 that originally cost $60,000.
5. Sold long-term investments for $85,000 cash.
6. Sales of $800,000 were on account.
7. Collections on accounts receivable were $700,000.
8. Retired $50,000 on long-term notes payable by issuing common shares.
9. Sold land for $45,000 cash.

Required:

Assume the role of an accounting advisor to the company. How might a Statement of Changes in Financial Position assist the owners of KPL? Prepare a Statement of Changes in Financial Position using a concept of funds and disclosure which you feel would be most meaningful to the owners of the company. Justify your response. Explain the importance of the information provided in your Statement of Changes in Financial Position to the owners of Knotty Pine Limited.

15 *Financial Statements: The Perspective of the Analyst*

Throughout the book we have emphasized a series of related themes. Some of the main ones are:

1. Preparers and users of financial statements can easily have *different objectives* or purposes of accounting in mind, resulting in a mismatch of information for a particular judgment by the user. Generally, unless the preparer violates a legal constraint, responsibility rests with the user to understand the strengths and limitations of accounting reports, and to absorb any personal financial losses caused in part by misinterpretations. Sometimes, especially for the larger public companies, an extensive amount of information is provided in the financial statements so that a variety of users can be accommodated. But, even then, a good grasp of accounting is needed to pick out what is relevant for a specific decision.
2. For many years, the accounting profession in Canada (Certified General Accountants, Chartered Accountants, Registered Industrial Accountants and others) faced the task of improving financial accounting and reporting with very little outside support, except from the management of some, mainly larger, companies. Until the early 1970s corporate and security legislation affecting financial reporting lagged (sometimes badly) in requesting those standards of reporting required by the *CICA Handbook*. Even today some jurisdictions in Canada do not actively demand disclosure required by the *CICA Handbook*. Unlike the U.S., Canada does not have a national government body promoting change and improvement in financial reporting practices.
3. Comparability *among* companies and consistency from year to year

within the *same* company are two quite different goals. The accounting concept of consistency aids readers in comparisons from year to year within the same company. Yet, the choice of an inappropriate accounting principle, even when applied consistently from year to year can hinder the free flow of timely information. Comparability among companies, especially those involved in a variety of ventures, may be no more than a "dream in color." Over and over we have seen that the accounting profession has not been able to spell out clearly circumstances where method A instead of B is appropriate. Differing objectives of preparers versus users, and the endless number of differing facts which one could encounter, render difficult the task of having detailed accounting pronouncements in many situations.

4. The system of corporate reporting which exists in Canada has some glaring deficiencies.[1] Managers of companies report on *themselves*; and auditors (supposedly appointed by shareholders but in practice often hired by management) may lack support in law to require management to change its disclosure. Auditors must try to influence their clients, but the effects of influence can easily fall far short of enforcement of legal requirements.
5. Accounting practice requires extensive use of professional judgment in order to sort out the substance of a transaction from its legal form. Some examples where substance and form might differ are with leases, pensions, and income taxation, but there are many others. If accountants can measure the substance of a transaction with sufficient objectivity then its effects will be included in a financial statement. When measurement is difficult, some words of disclosure might be provided. Consequently, notes to financial statements can be vital to readers. The numbers often cannot stand alone; hence, manipulation of the numbers (by ratio analysis, such as EPS) without reference to other nonquantitative analysis can be dangerous.
6. Accountants have only a limited understanding of how people make decisions from financial accounting data. As a result, a fair amount of "trial and error" accounting has taken place over the years, and will no doubt continue to occur. Accounting pronouncements may be made without full knowledge of facts, because of rapidly changing conditions. Preparers must be alert to changes in the business environment if they hope to make financial accounting relevant to diverse groups of users.
7. Future events are hard to predict because of considerable surrounding uncertainty. Any measurement system that deals with dynamic activities such as those which affect complex business organizations cannot distill these activities into a few accounting numbers. The numbers are bound to have serious limitations except for relatively stable or small firms.

Both future risk and rate of return on investment are important to investors. Financial statements may not capture sufficient information about future or current risk.

It is very important that we keep these themes in mind as we proceed through this chapter on financial analysis: they are especially needed to balance one's perspective in performing ratio analysis.

Labatt's and Molson's Compared

In order to provide a basis for comparison with Labatt's, we are reproducing, in Exhibit 15-1, the financial statements of The Molson Companies Limited for their year ended March 31, 1978. Molson's compete with Labatt's in the brewing industry in much of Canada. However, both companies have diversified into other industries. Labatt's financial statements and a listing of some of the other companies which they own or influence are noted in Chapter 2. Molson's has diversified into: (1) retail merchandising (Beaver Lumber Company Limited, which has stores from British Columbia to Quebec); (2) commercial products and services (Anthes Equipment Limited; Bennett Pump Company, and others); and (3) office and education products.

For the year ended March 31, 1978 the divisions or segments of Molson's made the following contributions to operating income. (Figures for Labatt's are provided on page 535 for their year ended April 30, 1978).

	In millions of dollars			
	Consolidated	*Brewing*	*Retail Merchandising*	*Other*
Sales and other revenue	$953.2	$490.4	$266.7	$196.1
Operating income (loss)	59.8	51.2	9.1	(0.5)
Income taxes thereon	22.8	20.7	2.9	(0.8)
Net operating income (before interest expense)	$ 37.0	$ 30.5	$ 6.2	$ 0.3
Capital employed at net book value	$354.7	$163.1	$110.2	$ 81.4
Return on capital employed (net operating income before interest divided by capital employed) at book value	10.4%	18.7%	5.6%	0.3%
Capital employed — measured at estimated *replacement* cost	$514.6	$299.5	$121.4	$ 93.7
Return on *replacement* capital	7.2%	10.2%	5.1%	0.3%

The brewing division therefore is a major contributor to net income.

The notes to Molson's financial statements should be reviewed along with the consolidated statements of earnings, balance sheet and the statement of changes in financial position (SCFP). Notes 8 and 10 are especially interesting.

EXHIBIT 15-1

The Molson Companies Limited

Consolidated Statement of Earnings

Year ended March 31	1978	1977
Revenues		
Sales and revenues	$951,919,000	$889,012,000
Investment income	510,000	439,000
Equity in earnings of other companies	791,000	1,288,000
	953,220,000	890,739,000
Costs and expenses		
Cost of sales, selling and administrative costs	724,966,000	675,032,000
Brewing excise and sales taxes	150,216,000	142,202,000
Depreciation	18,211,000	16,728,000
Interest on long-term debt	7,791,000	8,205,000
Other interest	2,920,000	4,054,000
	904,104,000	846,221,000
Earnings before income taxes	49,116,000	44,518,000
Income taxes	17,916,000	18,228,000
	31,200,000	26,290,000
Minority interest	256,000	259,000
Net earnings before extraordinary items	30,944,000	26,031,000
Extraordinary items	2,120,000	–
Net earnings for the year	$ 33,064,000	$ 26,031,000
Net earnings per share		
Before extraordinary items	$2.25	$1.90
After extraordinary items	2.41	1.90

The Molson Companies Limited

Consolidated Statement of Retained Earnings

Year ended March 31	1978	1977
Balance – beginning of year	$135,260,000	$120,621,000
Net earnings for the year	33,064,000	26,031,000
	168,324,000	146,652,000
Dividends	12,363,000	11,392,000
Balance – end of year	$155,961,000	$135,260,000

See Notes to Consolidated Financial Statements

The Molson Companies Limited

Consolidated Balance Sheet

As at March 31	1978	1977
Assets		
Current Assets		
Cash	$ 5,185,000	$ 2,632,000
Accounts receivable	83,555,000	77,265,000
Due from sale of a business and an investment	19,367,000	–
Inventories	141,825,000	148,333,000
Prepaid expenses	5,767,000	3,806,000
	255,699,000	232,036,000
Investments	13,226,000	11,818,000
Fixed Assets		
Land, buildings and equipment	359,724,000	340,510,000
Accumulated depreciation	170,371,000	150,899,000
	189,353,000	189,611,000
Other Assets – less amortization		
Intangible assets of acquisitions	3,330,000	3,421,000
Debenture discount and expenses	838,000	924,000
	4,168,000	4,345,000
	$462,446,000	$437,810,000
Liabilities		
Current Liabilities		
Bank indebtedness	$ 15,288,000	$ 21,421,000
Notes payable	30,284,000	29,951,000
Accounts payable	72,885,000	57,120,000
Income taxes	2,696,000	5,284,000
Excise and sales taxes	9,504,000	9,739,000
Dividends payable	3,122,000	2,934,000
Current instalments on long-term debt	2,792,000	2,821,000
	136,571,000	129,270,000
Long-term Debt	88,000,000	94,028,000
Minority Interest	3,606,000	3,723,000
Deferred Income Taxes	27,009,000	24,764,000
Deferred Income – less amortization	2,909,000	2,394,000
Shareholders' Equity		
Capital Stock	48,390,000	48,371,000
Retained Earnings	155,961,000	135,260,000
	204,351,000	183,631,000
	$462,446,000	$437,810,000

Signed on Behalf of the Board:

Director

Director

See Notes to Consolidated Financial Statements

The Molson Companies Limited

Consolidated Statement of Changes in Financial Position

Year ended March 31	1978	1977
Source of funds		
Net earnings before extraordinary items	$ 30,944,000	$ 26,031,000
Add (deduct) items not affecting working capital		
Depreciation	18,211,000	16,728,000
Deferred income taxes	3,648,000	4,056,000
Gain on sale of fixed assets	(2,430,000)	(2,233,000)
Equity in earnings of other companies (net of dividends received)	(526,000)	(1,059,000)
Other	365,000	(181,000)
Funds from operations	50,212,000	43,342,000
Proceeds on sale of –		
Fixed Assets	4,540,000	4,322,000
Investments	2,093,000	342,000
Extraordinary item – proceeds on sale of business and investment (less working capital sold of $5,681,000)	16,085,000	–
	72,930,000	48,006,000
Use of funds		
Dividends	12,363,000	11,392,000
Purchase of –		
Fixed assets	28,581,000	24,917,000
Investments	5,192,000	1,828,000
Business acquisitions (excluding working capital of $389,000; 1977 – $930,000)	2,537,000	1,923,000
Repayment and current portion of long-term debt	6,009,000	4,156,000
Extraordinary item – provision for estimated losses arising from planned disposal or discontinuance of businesses ($7,000,000 less items not affecting working capital)	1,886,000	–
	56,568,000	44,216,000
Working capital		
Increase in the year	16,362,000	3,790,000
At beginning of year	102,766,000	98,976,000
At end of year	$119,128,000	$102,766,000

See Notes to Consolidated Financial Statements

Notes to Consolidated Financial Statements

1. Accounting Policies

Consolidation: The accounts of all subsidiaries are consolidated. Purchase accounting principles are followed for subsidiaries acquired except for Anthes Imperial Limited in 1968 which was on the basis of pooling of interests.

Foreign Exchange: Earnings of foreign operations are translated at the average rate of exchange during the year. Current assets and current liabilities are translated at the rate at March 31 and other balance sheet accounts and related depreciation are translated at the rate on the date of acquisition. Net earnings in 1978 include translation gains of $1,142,000 ($380,000 in 1977).

Inventories: Inventories are valued at the lower of cost or net realizable value except for retail lumber inventories which are valued at the lower of cost or replacement cost. Cost is determined on a first-in, first-out basis.

Investments: Investments in effectively controlled companies are carried on the equity method. Other investments are carried on the cost basis.

Fixed Assets: Fixed assets are carried at cost. Depreciation is provided from the date assets are put into service on the straight-line method over their estimated useful lives, primarily at annual rates of 2½% for buildings and from 7% to 10% for equipment.

Intangible Assets of Acquisitions: Effective April 1, 1974, the amounts by which the purchase price exceeds the value of assets acquired in business combinations are carried as intangible assets and amortized on the straight-line basis over forty years.

Income Taxes: Deferred income taxes represent amounts deferred to future years due to the earlier deduction of certain expenses, principally depreciation, for tax purposes. Investment tax credits are reflected in earnings in the year they are claimed for tax purposes.

2. Business Combinations

The assets of a trucking company and a construction equipment company were acquired for cash and a note during the year and have been included on the basis of purchase accounting.

	1978	1977
Value of net tangible assets and goodwill acquired	$ 2,926,000	$ 2,853,000

3. Inventories

	1978	1977
Finished goods	$112,653,000	$113,291,000
Work in process	12,236,000	12,437,000
Raw materials and supplies	16,936,000	22,605,000
	$141,825,000	$148,333,000

4. Investments

	1978	1977
Mortgages and loans, at cost	$ 1,754,000	$ 3,790,000
Investments, at equity	4,279,000	6,570,000
Other investments, at cost	7,193,000	1,458,000
	$ 13,226,000	$ 11,818,000

Investments include marketable investments carried at $6,493,000 (1977—$6,099,000) which had a quoted value of $6,774,000 at March 31, 1978 (1977—$8,443,000).

5. Fixed Assets

	1978	1977
Land	$ 20,921,000	$ 21,721,000
Buildings	126,372,000	120,663,000
Equipment	212,431,000	198,126,000
	359,724,000	340,510,000
Accumulated depreciation	170,371,000	150,899,000
	$189,353,000	$189,611,000

6. Long-Term Debt

	1978		1977	
	Current	Total	Current	Total
Sinking Fund Debentures:				
8¼% maturing in 1991	-	$36,249,000	-	$ 38,769,000
8¼% maturing in 1995	$ 900,000	29,100,000	$ 900,000	30,000,000
6% maturing in 1982	-	1,710,000	$ 115,000	2,575,000
5¼% convertible maturing in 1989	-	2,194,000	-	2,213,000
8¾% maturing in 1988	-	1,000,000	-	1,000,000
Notes Payable:				
9% repayable by 1989	1,536,000	18,433,000	1,536,000	19,969,000
5¾% repayable by 1985	200,000	1,600,000	200,000	1,800,000
Sundry	156,000	506,000	70,000	523,000
	$2,792,000	90,792,000	$2,821,000	$ 96,849,000
Current instalments		2,792,000		2,821,000
		$88,000,000		$ 94,028,000

Sinking fund requirements and principal payments during the next five years are:
1979—$2,792,000; 1980—$3,012,000; 1981—$4,008,000; 1982—$5,860,000; 1983—$4,151,000.

7. Capital Stock

Authorized: Convertible common shares without par value — 15,000,000 Class "A", 7,000,000 Class "B", 7,000,000 Class "C", 15,000,000 Class "D".

Class "A" and "D" shares are interconvertible and Class "B" and "C" shares are interconvertible, on a one for one basis.

Class "A" and "D" shares are non-voting except, voting separately and as a class, the holders thereof are entitled to elect three members of the board of directors annually. Class "B" and "C" shares are fully voting.

Class "A" and "D" shares are entitled to a non-cumulative preferential dividend of 20¢ per share per annum. After the Class "B" and "C" shares receive dividends of 20¢ per annum, all shares rank equally as to dividends.

Dividends on Class "C" and "D" shares may be paid in cash out of tax-paid undistributed surplus on hand, or out of 1971 capital surplus on hand as defined in the Income Tax Act, until December 31, 1978.

Issued and Outstanding:	1978		1977	
	Shares	Amount	Shares	Amount
Class "A"	8,322,000	$37,977,000	8,306,600	$38,370,000
Class "B"	3,988,600	7,293,000	4,647,300	7,966,000
Class "C"	1,095,500	1,797,000	436,800	648,000
Class "D"	286,900	1,323,000	301,400	1,387,000
	13,693,000	$48,390,000	13,692,100	$48,371,000
Average number of shares outstanding	13,692,800		13,692,100	

During the year, the following shares were converted between the classes:	1978	1977
Class "A" to Class "D"	**117,900**	115,700
Class "D" to Class "A"	**132,400**	119,900
Class "B" to Class "C"	**748,200**	15,400
Class "C" to Class "B"	**89,500**	572,500

Convertible Debentures: Holders of the 5¼% debentures of a subsidiary may convert these debentures on or before May 1, 1979, into Class "A" shares on the basis of 47 shares for each $1,000 debenture. At March 31, 1978, 108,500 (1977–109,400) Class "A" shares were reserved for this purpose.

Stock Options: At March 31, the following options to employees to purchase shares on or before August 14, 1978 were outstanding:

	1978		1977	
	Option Price	**Shares**	Option Price	Shares
Class "A"	**$19.37**	**7,650**	$19.37	8,600
Class "B"	**17.50**	**7,650**	17.50	8,600
		15,300		17,200

Of the options outstanding at March 31, 1978, options covering 6,000 Class "A" shares and 6,000 Class "B" shares were held by officers, three of whom were also directors.

8. Extraordinary Items

Extraordinary items of $2,120,000 in 1978 (1977–nil) include the following:

Gain on sale of the John Wood division and the investment in The Rainier Companies, Inc. (net of deferred and current income taxes of $1,897,000 and $100,000)	$9,120,000
Provision for estimated losses arising from planned disposal or discontinuance of businesses (net of deferred income taxes of $3,300,000)	7,000,000
	$2,120,000

9. Additional Information

Pension Plans: The funding requirements for current service pension costs, based on actuarial determinations, are charged to earnings. Past service costs are being funded and charged to earnings equally over the next 16 years. The unfunded liability for past service pension costs which has not been recorded amounted to $27,000,000 at March 31, 1978 (1977–$25,300,000).

Commitments: Lease commitments which expire within thirty years require the following payments during the next five years: 1979–$11,800,000; 1980–$10,900,000; 1981–$9,900,000; 1982–$8,800,000; 1983–$8,400,000.

Properties leased are principally warehouses and retail stores.

Remuneration of Directors and Officers	**1978**	1977
Directors–number	**16**	16
–aggregate remuneration	**$ 73,000**	$ 72,000
Officers –number	**21**	22
–aggregate remuneration	**$1,338,000**	$1,263,000
Number of officers who are also directors	**5**	5

Classes of Business: The following are the proportions of consolidated sales by class of business:

	1978	1977
Brewing	**51%**	50%
Retail Merchandising	**28**	29
Other Businesses	**21**	21
	100%	100%

Anti-Inflation Legislation: The Canadian operations of the company are subject to federal legislation which became effective October 14, 1975 and established controls on prices, profit margins, compensation to employees and dividends to shareholders. Dividends are currently restricted to the present quarterly rate. These controls will phase out over the period from April 14 to December 31, 1978.

Income Taxes: Current income taxes for the year ended March 31, 1978, have been reduced by $2,050,000 resulting from the 3% inventory allowance which became effective on April 1, 1977.

Comparative Figures: Certain 1977 figures in the Consolidated Statement of Changes in Financial Position have been re-classified to conform with 1978 presentation.

10. Subsequent Event

On March 31, 1978, the Company was the beneficial owner of 140,600 common shares of The Diversey Corporation constituting approximately 7% of the total number outstanding, which the Company purchased at an aggregate cost of U.S. $2,471,555. During the period from March 31, 1978, through April 11, 1978, the Company purchased an additional 73,400 Diversey shares at an aggregate cost of U.S. $1,755,783, and is presently the beneficial owner of a total of 214,000 Diversey shares constituting approximately 10.6% of the total number outstanding. On May 19, 1978, the Company made a tender offer to purchase any and all outstanding Diversey shares at U.S. $30 per share in cash. Unless extended by the Company, the offer will expire on June 9, 1978. The total amount required to complete the cash tender offer at such price, assuming the acquisition of all Diversey shares remaining outstanding, and to pay all related fees and expenses, is estimated to be approximately U.S. $55,000,000. An unsecured bank loan, reducible by the proceeds of sales of certain businesses and investments, has been arranged to provide these funds.

Auditors' Report to the Shareholders

We have examined the consolidated balance sheet of The Molson Companies Limited as at March 31, 1978 and the consolidated statements of earnings, retained earnings and changes in financial position for the year then ended. Our examination was made in accordance with generally accepted auditing standards, and accordingly included such tests and other procedures as we considered necessary in the circumstances.

In our opinion, these consolidated financial statements present fairly the financial position of the company as at March 31, 1978 and the results of its operations and the changes in its financial position for the year then ended in accordance with generally accepted accounting principles applied on a basis consistent with that of the preceding year.

Coopers & Lybrand

Chartered Accountants May 19, 1978

Viewpoint of the Analyst

Rather than attempt to describe second hand what materials are studied by financial analysts, and what they provide to the public, we are reproducing a few of their shorter reports on companies. Needless to say analysts employed by insurance and brokerage companies conduct more extensive investigations than are reprinted here. In particular, reports on the outlook for the stock market in general are needed to complement the reports about specific companies. But these shorter reports capture many of the types of factors which the analyst investigates, and are therefore useful for us.

We have chosen reports from two different, large underwriting houses: Dominion Securities Limited and Wood Gundy Limited covering John Labatt Ltd. and its competitor in the brewing segment, The Molson Companies Limited. In viewing these reports, we might wish to concentrate on the following types of questions:

1. What sources of information were used by the analysts? (Can we tell for sure?)
2. What role did financial accounting statements probably have in assisting the analysts in their investigations?
3. Have the analysts missed any factors which you would have thought were important?
4. Have the analysts been naive and placed too much importance on accounting numbers? Or something else?
5. What would you suspect about the use of analysts' reports by the people who make considerable amounts of money "playing the stock market"? (Would they look at such reports? Would they have their own sources of information?)

First, let us reproduce the reports on Labatt's, dated December 1978 and March 1979 — for the period after release of the 1978 financial statements (see Chapter 2) in the summer of 1978. During this period stock prices for the market as a whole were moving upward. The recommendation on Labatt's, however, was less than positive and enthusiastic. Why?

Second, we are reprinting three reports on Molson's dated May 1978, September 1978, and February 1979. In contrast to Labatt's, the analysts are recommending the purchase of Molson's Class A common shares. Why? On the basis of what you have read — and assuming that the date is May 1978, or September 1978, or one of the other dates of the reports — *would you have purchased shares of Labatt's, Molson's, both or none*? If you *had* to choose one in which to invest, which would you pick? *Why?*

We cannot provide a "right" or "wrong" answer to the questions we have posed. Their educational value lies in the discussion among your colleagues and the instructor. When you have reached conclusions or responses to several of the questions, you should continue to the section on

"Hindsight." We are concerned here with the role of accounting in judgments — in this case the "invest or not" decision. Hence, in your analysis we would like you to concentrate on financial and accounting matters. Which pieces of information are useful to you? We recommend that you do not proceed to the next section, "Hindsight," until some thought has been given to a few of the questions posed under "Viewpoint of the Analyst." Otherwise, much of the benefit which might be derived from the section is lost.

EXHIBIT 15-2

Current Notes

JOHN LABATT LTD. ($20)

December 14th, 1978

	1978	1977	Percent Change
Six Months Ended October 31st			
Sales ($mil)	555.2	505.1	+9.9
Net Earnings ($mil)	14.4	19.3	-25.4
E.P.S. (S) Fully Diluted	1.08	1.42	-23.9
Second Quarter			
Sales ($mil)	284.2	253.3	12.2
Net Earnings ($mil)	5.0	8.4	-41.2
E.P.S. ($) Fully Diluted	.38	.63	-39.7

The Brewing Group

Labatt's domestic market share declined to 36.1% down 3.0% from a year earlier. These low levels have not been reached by the Company since 1975. The key reasons for the poor performance are: a) the strikes out West which affected Labatt the most severely due to strong market share in British Columbia and Manitoba relative to its competitors under normal conditions. The direct cost of the strike was approximately $7 mil after tax. b) the slow return to normal production after the labour settlements were reached (B.C. was the last to settle Sept. 3/78). For example a large shipment of U.S. beer, purchased by the B.C. Provincial Liquor Board just prior to settlement had to be sold, prior to Canadian beers attaining full distribution. c) Weakening market shares in Ontario and Quebec.

In the non-domestic brewery operations, relatively high start up costs of the new brewery plant in Sao Paulo, Brazil have inhibited any significant contribution to earnings from Skol-Caracu (41.2% owned by Labatt). As well, Labatt has not experienced the considerable buoyancy in the export sales to the States that the Canadian industry has enjoyed. We understand, though, that Labatt is planning to reposition its exported beer from a premium price beer into the super premium price category which should improve the bottom line for export sales.

The volume decline experienced by John Labatt has weakened operating margins considerably for the brewing operations. More normal market conditions should be the case for the second half of fiscal 1979. With the more stable Ontario market and Labatt's Special Light and John Labatt Extra Stock positioned in the relatively high growth segments of the beer industry, light beers and premium beers, respectively Labatt appears to have returned to number one position in Ontario. The introduction of a light ale, Cervoise, (5% alcohol content and 125 calories) into the Quebec market is clearly an attempt to recapture some of the lost market share in Quebec. Nevertheless, we do not anticipate a strong growth in sales in the second half, given the lack of buoyancy anticipated for the domestic industry and for export sales by Labatt.

Labatt recently announced the sale of Schwarz Services Ltd. a manufacturer of specialty brewing aids for $885,000 to Brent Chemical Corp. It is estimated that this division had sales of $3 1/2 mil. and was profitable, albeit a marginal contributor to Labatt's consolidated profit. This division did not fit into Labatt's operations and since the services were being sold to competitive breweries in the States it was difficult to operate as a subsidiary of John Labatt Ltd.

Consumer Products Group

This division should show good growth in sales and earnings for fiscal 1979. Casabello Wine Ltd in British Columbia enjoyed excellent sales growth due to the beer strikes out West and the wine operations in general are well positioned in the high growth table wine segment. Laura Secord and Catelli have experienced improvement in operations.

The future for LaMont wineries in California, purchased in June, is bright. The table wine volume growth in the U.S. is predicted to be approximately 10% in 1978 relative to 1977. However, to progress into establishing brand names from its original primary business of bulk sale, will demand large promotional expenditures and therefore we do not anticipate LaMont to be a major contribution to Labatt's earnings in the near future.

Agri Products Group

While Ault Products is showing improvement, the Feeds division and IGP are incurring losses. Part of the problem of the Feeds division was the shortage of wet grains, out West, as it is a by-product of beer. Strikes have hindered the starch operations of IGP and the high protein wheat crop in the States has inhibited sales of gluten into the U.S. as it is a source of protein used in baking, breakfast cereals and pet foods.

- 3 -

Earnings Estimates

For fiscal 1979, our fully diluted earnings estimate is in the range of $2.20 per share relative to $2.53 in fiscal 1978 reflecting the poor earnings performance from the brewery operations and lack of improvement in the Agri Products Group. For fiscal 1980, our range for earnings fully diluted is estimated to be $2.75 - $3.00. However for Labatt to attain the upper end of our range, there will have to be a considerable turnaround in market share performance in Canada, complemented by improvement in export sales, two factors in which Labatt still has to prove it can be successful. The past six months have indicated the vulnerability to weakening beer market share of too heavy a reliance on the two brand strategy.

Stock Comment

Until we see convincing evidence of a turnaround situation in the brewery operations or a major move by the Company via a new brand introduction or acquisition, we believe the shares of Labatt will move at best in line with the market over the next three to six months. It is doubtful we will see aggressive dividend increases by the Company, as we note the second dividend declared post AIB (payable Jan. 15) was not raised. Nevertheless, at recent prices, the share yield 6.0%.

Lea B. Hansen

Current Notes

JOHN LABATT LTD. ($20½)

March 16th, 1979

Nine Months Ended Jan. 31st	1979	1978	Percent Change
Sales ($mil)	883.2	755.9	+16.8
Net Earnings ($mil)	17.4	25.0	-30.4
E.P.S. ($) Fully Diluted	1.32	1.87	- 29.4
Third Quarter			
Sales ($mil)	278.0	249.8	+11.3
E.P.S. ($) (Fully Diluted)	.24	.44	-45.5

In light of the disappointing third quarter results, and an anticipated further decline in the fourth quarter earnings, our fiscal 1979 E.P.S. estimate is in the range of $1.90 fully diluted. Fiscal 1978 E.P.S. fully diluted was $2.53

The Brewing Operations

Having experienced substantial market share declines in the first half of fiscal 1979 due to the brewery strike out West, Labatt has improved market share by the third quarter to a level of 37.8%. Market share in British Columbia has been regained to around 50% levels; nevertheless pre-strike market share levels have not as yet been reached and there exists the possibility that there may perhaps be a permanent loss in market share to U.S. beer and/or wine on the West Coast due to the strike. In Ontario, having suffered from competitive brand introductions last year Labatt has regained number one position with their Special Light and Extra Stock introductions. Ontario beer sales, as a point of interest, increased 3.5% in calender 1978, buoyed to a large extent by new brand introductions. Labatt's Cervoise introduction has helped to shore up the previous weakening market share in Quebec.

Despite a recovery in market share by Labatt's, we remain concerned about: 1) the ability of Labatt to gain upward momentum in market share and 2) the impact on operating margins of the new brand introductions, since Labatts has historically been a two brand company. While on the one hand the two brand strategy was vulnerable from a market share point of view, margins could suffer in the near term with the move to a five brand company.

- 2 -

A significant negative factor to Labatt's nine month results was the $3.5 million loss or $.25 per share loss incurred by Labatts in the Brazilian brewery operation, Skol-Caracu (45% owned by Labatts). These losses are expected to continue into the fourth quarter resulting in an estimated total loss of $4.4 million or $.31 per share for Labatt's fiscal 1979 year. Start up costs with the $38 million new brewery plant, lower than expected operating income, exchange losses, and heavy interest expense are the key problems. It remains to be seen whether Labatt's management will be able to improve the bottom line and capitalize on the very buoyont growth in volume of beer of 6%-8% in Brazil.

Labatt appears to still be in the process of planning to reposition its U.S. exported beer into the super premium price category, so that in the near term little growth should be forthcoming for Labatts from the export market. In light of the above comments on both the international and domestic brewery operations, we do not anticipate strong growth in brewery earnings from Labatt's in the near term.

Consumer Products Group

This division should enjoy a solid increase in earnings in fiscal 1979. Laura Secord, with cocoa prices on the downtrend, should finally be able to capitalize on its successful new product introductions at the wholesale level. Combined with a profit contribution from Laura Secord in fiscal 1979, Catelli and U.S. Foods are enjoying earnings growth.

Agri Products Group

While Ault Products and Ogilvie Mills are contributing to earnings growth, IGP remains in a loss position due to the increase in the price of the wheat supply. As well, we note that plans to construct a starch and gluten plant in South Caroline have been postponed indefinitely in light of the unfavourable fundamentals.

Market Comment

Fiscal 1979 earnings, estimated in the order of $1.90 per share fully diluted, do include substantial non-recurring losses, such as the loss of approximately $.49 due to the Western brewery strike and a large portion of the $.31 per share loss to be reported associated with the Brazilian brewery operations. Our estimate for fiscal 1980, therefore is in the order of $2.75-$3.00 fully diluted.

The shares do yield an above market yield of 5.9% and trade at a 6.8X-7.4X multiple on fiscal 1980 earnings estimate. While the multiple is slightly undervalued, it is likely the shares will perform, at best, in line with the market.

Lea B. Hansen

Summary Report

THE MOLSON COMPANIES LIMITED

Listed - MOL.A - Montreal, Toronto, Vancouver

K. McAsey, C.F.A.
J. Cameron
Toronto
May 19, 1978

Current Price	1978 High	1978 Low	Indicated Dividend	Current Yield	Earnings Per Share 1977	Earnings Per Share 1978E	Earnings Per Share 1979E	P/E on 1978E
$17 3/4	$18 1/4	$15	$0.9125	5.1%	$1.70	$2.30	$2.50	7.7x

Summary and Recommendation

The share price of Molson has lagged behind those of major competitors despite the Company's strong earnings per share increase, estimated at 21% in fiscal 1978, and a further 9% in fiscal 1979. In addition to this growth, we believe that once the AIB controls are lifted, Molson's dividend rate should rise at least 15% to $1.05 per share, and could reach $1.15 based on historical payouts. However, despite these positive factors, Molson's price/earnings multiple is relatively low compared to its competitors. Purchase is recommended for capital appreciation over the next 6-12 months, accompanied by attractive current income.

The Company

Through its subsidiaries and divisions, Molson is engaged in the brewing of ales and beers and retail merchandising of home hardgoods. In addition, Molson owns the Anthes-Imperial group of companies whose operations include office and educational products, home furniture, construction products and services, and petroleum marketing equipment.

Technical Opinion

Molson's chart progression over the past 18 months is that of a potential double-bottom formation. An advance above $18 3/4 would clear the air for a move to the low twenties. Support exists at $15-14 1/2. (Chart courtesy of Graphoscope.) H.M.

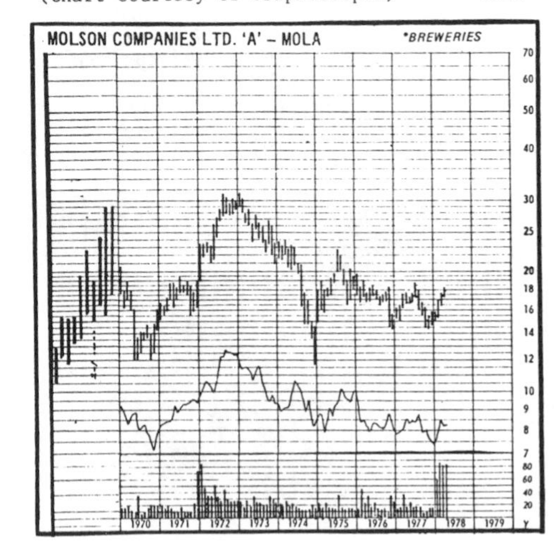

Outlook

During fiscal 1977, Molson's sales revenue from the brewing division rose 8% over 1976, and comprised half of total sales revenue. Given that the Canadian beer market experienced only a slight increase of 0.6% in volume growth during 1976, Molson's performance demonstrates its ability to increase its market share despite poor industry conditions. For fiscal 1978, Molson will continue to surpass expected market growth of about 2% in Canada, with brewing profits anticipated to increase 30% as a result of lower malt costs, a pronounced slowing in the escalation of wage and packaging costs, price increases of 8.9% for calendar 1977, rising market share and the effect of the inventory allowance on taxes. A further improvement is expected in fiscal 1979 although it will not match last year's extraordinary performance.

In recent years, Molson has entered the U.S. market through its subsidiary of Marlet Importing Co. which is now the second largest importer of beer in the U.S. During fiscal 1977, Molson's U.S. exports increased 73% over fiscal 1976, and are expected to have risen at least a further 30% in fiscal 1978. These exports are comprised of premium-priced brands, with the biggest seller being Molson Golden. Business is conducted in 18 states, with considerable future potential still existing as Molson continues to penetrate an increasing number of new markets.

Profits from the retail operations of Beaver Lumber rose more than 15% over fiscal 1977 levels, on a projected sales increase of 9%. This solid performance was masked by weakness in manufactured home operations, especially in Western Canada. However, during fiscal 1979, Beaver's profits are forecast to rise as much as 25% in this area over fiscal 1978 levels, based on our projections of farm incomes and retail sales in the West. With a total of 251 retail stores as of the end of fiscal 1977, Beaver has accomplished its primary goal of penetrating most principal market areas in Canada. The Company is now developing a franchise system to increase its exposure in markets where Beaver, as yet, is not fully represented.

Other operations consist principally of the old Anthes-Imperial group of companies which has been a drag on profits since 1975 due to over-capacity in a number of industries, competitive pressures and eroding profit margins. Reorganization and new management have turned around some companies, such as Willson Office Equipment and Moyer-Vico. However, it is Molson's policy to dispose of businesses which are unprofitable or only marginally profitable, such as Rainier Cos. and John Woods.

Over the past 11 years Molson's strategy has been one of diversification through acquisitions which tend to complement existing strengths in distribution and marketing. The underlying principle behind this was Molson's foresight in recognizing the limited growth potential in the Canadian brewing industry. The Company is financially strong, with total borrowings at the lowest point in three years, and is in a position to finance all but large acquisitions internally. If Diversey Corp. of Chicago is acquired, it would increase earnings per share by $0.10 in fiscal 1979, after carrying costs. Molson believes its strengths in marketing and distribution fit Diversey's needs and feels that the specialty chemical industry, in which Diversey specializes, has attractive growth potential. It should be noted that acquisitions, such as Diversey, have not been factored into our 1979 estimates. Nor has the probability that proceeds from past and future divestments will be applied to reduce current interest expense and/or carrying costs on future acquisitions.

* * * * * * * * * *

Earnings Per Share

	Q1 June	Q2 Sept.	Q3 Dec.	Q4 Mar.	Total	Dividends
1976	$0.50	0.66	0.40	0.16	$1.72	$0.80
1977	0.59	0.72	0.42	0.17	1.90	0.832
1978	---1.48----		0.57		2.30E	0.912

E.P.S. Growth Rate: 1967 - 77 : 3.8%
1972 - 77 : 4.7%

Capitalization ($000's)
(as of March 31, 1977)

Long-Term Debt	$ 94,028	30.5%
Minority Interest	3,723	1.2
Deferred Income & Taxes	27,158	8.8
Shareholders' Equity *	183,631	59.5
	$308,540	100.0%

* 13,692,100 Class A, B, C, and D common shares outstanding, on the average.

The Molson Companies Limited

September 30, 1978

We continue to recommend the purchase of *Molson 'A' ($20½)* shares, which we initially suggested in April. Earnings are projected to rise sharply from $2.25 last year to $2.75 this year, and to $2.95 and $3.25 in the following two years. The improvement will be due in large part to the elimination of most operations outside of Brewing and Retail, and their replacement by Diversey Corp., a U.S.-based producer of specialty chemicals.

The companies to be disposed of are mostly marginal or unprofitable. They have held back *Molson's* growth over the past five years. Proceeds from their disposal will amount to $40-45 million, which will provide about two-thirds of the $65 million required to buy Diversey. The latter is one of the four largest U.S. companies manufacturing specialty cleaning chemicals, primarily for the food industry. Diversey's earnings growth and return on equity have averaged close to 15 percent over the past 5 years. This growth has been financed by internally generated funds, and is much more stable than for most companies in the chemical business which are very sensitive to cyclical influences.

In its most recent quarter, *Molson* increased its market share of brewing by much more than the usual amount. This trend appears to be continuing. Raw material and wage costs are relatively stable. Thus, a further increase in brewing profits is expected for this year, despite higher marketing costs.

Operating profit of the Retail Group last year rose 14 percent despite a weak retail environment and a loss from the Manufactured Homes operation which was vulnerable to weakness in the B.C. and prairie economies. This year retail sales are better and manufactured homes will be profitable. We expect that profits will rise far more than they did last year.

At $20½, *Molson 'A'* shares are selling at a P/E of 7.0x our 1979 estimate. Carrying a worthwhile yield of 4.4%, we recommend the shares as excellent value.

— K. McAsey, reprinted from *Invest* (a Wood Gundy publication).

Current Notes

THE MOLSON COMPANIES LIMITED ($24½)

February 15th, 1979

	1978	1977	Percent Change
Nine Months Ended Dec. 31st			
Sales ($mil)	932.0	758.0	+23.0
Net Earnings ($mil)	40.7	28.5	+42.8
E.P.S. ($)	2.97	2.08	+42.9
Third Quarter			
Sales ($ mil)	316.2	242.9	+30.1
E.P.S. ($)	.77	.57	+35.1

Molson's excellent earnings growth in the third quarter exceeded our expectations. Strength was attributed to buoyant volume growth in the domestic beer industry and continued strength in export sales to the United States. For example the domestic beer industry in the quarter ended December 1978 grew, in volume terms, at a rate of 2.4%. Molson, due to market share improvement and strong export sales enjoyed volume growth of 5.6% in the comparable quarter. Beaver Lumber on the basis of strong sales growth of 16% in the third quarter and improved operating margins is enjoying good growth in earnings. Finally, Diversey, now fully consolidated, is estimated to have enjoyed close to 20% earnings growth and is estimated to have contributed approximately 5¢ per share before interest expense of acquisition to Molson's third quarter and approximately 20¢ per share for the nine months ended December.

We note that Molson is continuing their divestiture programme, having announced the sale of Anthes Equipment Ltd. and Bennett Pump since we last reported.

Our earnings per share estimate for Molson for fiscal 1979 is in the range of $3.15 - $3.20 assuming a flat to slight improvement in the fourth quarter. On the basis of strong growth in earnings from Diversey, continued improvement in Beaver Lumber, and continued improvement in market share in the domestic beer industry, we estimate higher earnings for fiscal 1980 to the range of $3.65-$4.00 per share.

The shares of Molson have appreciated approximately 11% since our buy recommendation in November 1978. With the substantial dividend increase to an annual rate of $1.20, the shares now yield an above market return of close to 5%. On the basis of fiscal 1979 estimated earnings, the shares are trading at a multiple of approximately 7.7x and on fiscal 1980 earnings, 6.7x - 6.0x. We feel that based on these multiples the shares are still undervalued and at recent trading prices we recommend a BUY.

Hindsight

By January, 1980, Labatt's A common shares were selling for just over $22 per share, up over 10 percent over the past year, but still a slight increase for investors after paying brokerage charges on acquisition of shares. Molson's, in contrast, was selling for between $25 and $26 per Class A common share — a significant increase above the price of $17.75 noted in the May 1978 analyst's report. What are the shares of each company selling for today? (Check the price quotes in a financial, or your local, newspaper.)

What caused the increase in Molson's share prices? The share price increase may have been brought about by favorable income prospects outside of the brewing business. As the analysts state, growth in the brewing industry is limited. Appendix 15-A contains abbreviated financial statements for Molson's for the year ended March 31, 1979. This information allows you to obtain some feedback on predictions which you may have made.

Observe clearly that even though we tried to locate a close competitor of Labatt's for the sake of comparability, the two companies differ significantly when one examines how each has diversified. Acquisition of successful companies outside of the brewing industry has been crucial to the overall success or failure of each company.

Ratio Analysis

Some analysts, such as bankers and employees of credit bureaus, compile a series of financial ratios to assist in their assessment of the credit worthiness of an applicant seeking a loan. Ratios are also used to check compliance with restrictive covenants set forth in long-term debt or preferred share issues. As long as ratios are interpreted with care they can be useful in detecting *crude* trends or overall problems needing further investigation.

However, it is useful to remember these points:

1. The balance sheet is a "snapshot" of an instant in time. The figures used in a ratio may be very different from those that existed a few days before or after the balance sheet date.
2. Balance sheets may be "window dressed," so that an artificial transaction — such as a one-week duration bank loan — may be arranged over the year end just to increase the company's cash position. Auditors try to convince clients to avoid window dressing, but some may occur. As a result, the balance sheet, the SCFP (perhaps), and the current ratio are not as informative as they might otherwise be. (You will recall in discussions of the

SCFP that the disclosure of flows of funds — increases and decreases — instead of *net* changes is recommended so as to minimize misinterpretation.)
3. A ratio is affected by the numerator (top) and/or denominator. A closer look at the component figures is therefore needed before sound conclusions may be drawn.

Bankers who are engaged in lending money to the public tend to have "loan limits" — the maximum they may lend without consulting a senior officer of the bank. Someone engaged as a loan officer in a branch bank in a small shopping center may be allowed to loan no more than $2,000 per customer without having to obtain approval from the bank's district office. A more experienced bank manager in a suburban branch might have a loan limited of $25,000, but may have to file a periodic report to head office on loans over, say, $20,000 (the "reporting limit"). Head office personnel might also have loan limits of $500,000 or $1,000,000 but would be required to compile financial reports on the lender for review by more senior officers.

These reports, prepared by bank personnel both before and after a loan is approved, include the following types of information:

1. Financial statements, which may or may not be audited, for recent periods.
2. Description of the business including its history, main products, customers, sales territories, number of employees and locations of factories.
3. Changes in the company's operations since the previous report to the bank.
4. Background about the principal management personnel.
5. Ratio analysis, perhaps for eight years if data is available.

Banks place considerable (possibly too much) faith in ratio analysis to locate potential trouble spots in a company. Much of this computation of ratios is performed by junior personnel who forward ratios to head office for review by officials who are more skilled in identifying loans that may not be repayable promptly. Ratio analysis of small, fairly stable businesses that encounter few complex transactions can be informative to bankers, who are quite concerned about liquidity and trends. Banks pay special attention to receivables (and sometimes to inventory) because these assets are security for many of their loans to small business.

The following are typical of the ratios compiled by bankers:

1. Number of days of sales in accounts receivable.
2. Number of days of sales in inventory, or inventory turnover.
3. Gross profit, and net income to sales.
4. Trends in income statement accounts, which are expressed as a percentage of sales.
5. Aged accounts receivable.
6. Number of days of sales in trade accounts payable (mainly meaning for purchases of inventory).

Number of days of sales in accounts receivable

This is an overall measure of the age of sales on account:

$$\frac{\text{Accounts receivable at year end}}{\text{Sales on account in year}} \times 365 \text{ (or } 360^{*}\text{) days}$$

Example:

$$\frac{\$\ 30{,}000}{\$365{,}000} \times 365 = 30 \text{ days.}$$

*Although there are 365 or 366 days in a year, many Canadian banks and credit bureaus appear to use the 360-day figure for convenience (12 months × 30 days = 360).

In general, *if* the sales on account and collections occur evenly throughout the year receivables are collected 30 days after the sale on account. Credit terms to customers of this firm must therefore require payment within 30 days; otherwise, the receivables would tend to be outstanding for a longer period than 30 days. In practice, if the figure for sales on account is difficult to obtain, total sales would be used. A company with large cash sales would therefore have a low number of days' sales in accounts receivable. Bank officials would compare this ratio to those for previous years of this company, and to other companies in the same line of business. If the ratio seemed too high or low the lender would be asked to explain why.

Number of days of sales in inventory (or inventory turnover)

This ratio is a mixture of valuations because inventory is generally measured at buying market price (cost) whereas sales are measured in selling market terms (net realizable value).

$$\frac{\text{Inventory at year end}}{\text{Sales}} \times 365 \text{ days}$$

Example:

$$\frac{\$\ 45{,}000}{\$365{,}000} \times 365 = 45 \text{ days.}$$

The ratio tells us that year-end inventories will produce, on average and roughly-speaking, 45 days of sales in the next year. Is the 45 days figure high or low? Good or bad? If it is high, is this because inventory is up? Or because sales are down? Such questions can be answered by further investigation. The ratio, when compared to that for another company or a previous period, is merely an aid in locating matters which might require further analysis.

The ratio might be refined by using cost of goods sold (which are priced at buying market) in place of sales:

$$\frac{\text{Inventory at year end}}{\text{Cost of goods sold}} \times 365 \text{ days}$$

A high figure *may* indicate the presence of obsolete inventory, or could simply be typical for the type of business.

Gross profit and net income to sales

These two ratios describe mark ups to selling price on purchases (or cost of goods manufactured) and the amount of net income earned for each dollar of sales. A food supermarket may have a low gross profit and net income for each dollar of sales:

$$\frac{\text{Gross profit}}{\text{Sales}} \times 100\%$$

Example:

$$\frac{\$\ 18{,}000}{\$100{,}000} = 18\%$$

$$\frac{\text{Net income}}{\text{Sales}} \times 100\%$$

Example:

$$\frac{\$\ \ 1{,}000}{\$100{,}000} = 1\%$$

Yet, it may be successful because its sales volume is high for the amount it has invested by way of owners' equity.

The financial statements of Labatt's and Molson's show the following net income to sales ratios:

Molson's:

$$\frac{\text{Net earnings before extraordinary items}}{\text{Sales and revenues}}$$

$$\frac{\$\ 30{,}944{,}000}{\$951{,}919{,}000} = 3.25\%$$

Labatt's:

$$\frac{\text{Net earnings}}{\text{Gross sales}}$$

$$\frac{\$\ 33{,}895{,}000}{\$997{,}263{,}000} = 3.40\%$$

Observe that the two companies give different disclosure to excise and sales taxes, and that we used gross sales. Also we did not include the extraordinary gain in Molson's in net earnings.

Trends for income statement accounts

This analysis is an extension of the previous two ratios which expressed a line on the income statement (such as gross profit or net income) as a percentage of sales. *If* costs vary in relation to sales, an analysis over several periods which is expressed as a percentage of the sales dollar could point out expenses which are getting out of control or are off trend. *But*, some expenses (such as types of rental charges, property taxes, depreciation, and amortization) are fixed in amount and do not vary with sales dollars. Hence, results of the analysis have to be interpreted with care.

A typical analysis would be:

	19x9	*19x8*	*19x7*
Sales	100.00%	100.0%	100.0%
Cost of goods sold	60.0	58.4	56.1
Gross profit	40.0	41.6	43.9
Selling expense	20.0	18.3	16.7
Administrative expense	10.0	10.9	12.0
	30.0	29.2	28.7
Income before income taxes	10.0	12.4	15.2
Taxes on income	4.7	5.9	7.3
Net income	5.3%	6.5%	7.9%

Observe that cost of goods sold and selling expense is increasing as a percentage of sales over the three years whereas administrative expense is decreasing. Why? Again we must check both the numerator and denominator (sales) of the ratio — which in this case is expressed as a percentage — to learn what happened. Administrative expense as a percentage of sales may have dropped because it is somewhat fixed, and sales dollars may have increased. On the other hand, if sales had dropped, and some fixed costs are included in cost of goods sold and selling expense, this would explain the rise in each cost percentage. Maybe inefficiencies have crept into the cost of goods sold and expense categories. The changing percentages may be false alarms, or something to be concerned about.

Aged accounts receivable

An aged list of accounts receivable is shown on page 298 of this book.

Number of days of sales in trade accounts payable.

This ratio might indicate whether the company is becoming slower in paying trade accounts for the purchase of inventory, is consistent, or is paying faster than in previous years. Fast payment is not necessarily wise because payment of accounts before they are due could result in an increase in the firm's bank loan, which increases interest expense.

$$\frac{\text{Trade accounts payable at year end}}{\text{Sales}} \times 365$$

Example:

$$\frac{\$\ 40{,}000}{\$365{,}000} \times 365 = 40 \text{ days.}$$

This ratio suffers from the same valuation problems as does inventory expressed as a percentage of sales. The denominator would be consistent with the numerator if cost of goods sold were used in place of sales.

Other Ratios

From time to time several other ratios, such as earnings per share, book value per share, the price-earnings ratio, and return on investment have been mentioned. These ratios are of greater interest to long-term creditors and investors than are the ratios mentioned in the previous section of this chapter.

Earnings per share and the price-earnings ratio were explained earlier. Book value per share can be tricky to compute under some sets of facts. For example, a special situation arises when a company has preferred shares outstanding which carry a redemption premium and on which cumulative dividends are in arrears (i.e., dividends have not been declared on the normal dividend due dates and are therefore not a balance sheet liability). Cumulative preferred share dividends that are in arrears have to be paid before common shareholders receive a dividend. Hence, cumulative, preferred dividends in arrears are a deduction from retained earnings when computing the book value of common shares. The same would apply to redemption (not issuance) premiums.

Example:

$$\frac{\text{Common shares + retained earnings + contributed surplus (if any)} - \text{preferred dividend in arrears} - \text{redemption premium on preferred shares}}{\text{Number of common shares}}$$

$$= \text{Book value per common shares.}$$

The book value of a company which has been in existence for some time would probably be very different from market value per share as quoted on a stock exchange.

Book value of a preferred share would include the redemption premium. If preferred dividends are in arrears these would be included as well.

Return on investment (ROI) can be computed in several different ways. The basic ratio is:

$$\frac{\text{Net income}}{\text{Investment}}$$

This divides into two components:

$$\frac{\text{Net income}}{\text{Sales}} \times \frac{\text{Sales}}{\text{Investment}}$$

These two could be broken down even further. For example, investment could be split into working capital and long-term assets net of liabilities.

Net income and investment could be measured by such methods as:

	Possible "Net income" or numerator	*Possible "Investment" or denominator*
(1)	Net income	Owners' equity
(2)	Net income	Total assets, less accumulated depreciation
(3)	Net income	Total assets, excluding accumulated depreciation
(4)	Dividends	Market price of shares

Many other possibilities exist. As well, different buying market and selling market measures (see Chapter 16) could be selected. In all, the term ROI needs careful defining because people use it in many different ways.

Ratio Restrictions

Ratios are sometimes referred to in short-term loan agreements and contracts between a company and its bondholders and preferred shareholders. Generally, the reference is to *not* declaring a dividend to common shareholders or not issuing further debt unless certain conditions are met. These "restrictive covenants," as they are commonly called, might include working capital, the number of times interest has been earned, and debt to equity position.

Using Molson's 1978 financial statements:

$$\text{Working capital ratio} = \frac{\text{Current assets}}{\text{Current liabilities}}$$

$$= \frac{\$255{,}699{,}000}{\$136{,}571{,}000} = \underline{\underline{1.87}}$$

$$\text{Times bond interest earned} = \frac{\text{Earnings before income tax + interest on long-term debt}}{\text{Interest on long-term debt}}$$

$$= \frac{\$49{,}116{,}000 + \$7{,}791{,}000}{\$7{,}791{,}000} = \underline{\underline{7.30}}$$

$$\text{Debt to equity percentage} = \frac{\text{Long-term debt}}{\text{Shareholders' equity}} \times 100\%$$

$$= \frac{\$\ 88{,}000{,}000}{\$204{,}351{,}000} \times 100\% = \underline{\underline{43\%}}$$

$$\text{Debt as a percentage of debt plus equity} = \frac{\text{Long-term debt}}{\text{Long-term debt + shareholders' equity}} \times 100\%$$

$$= \frac{\$88,000,000}{\$88,000,000 + \$204,351,000} \times 100\% = \underline{\underline{30\%}}$$

A restrictive covenant concerning working capital may not permit declaration of a dividend unless the ratio is, say, 1.3 to 1 *after* declaration of a dividend. Such a convenant is popular but highly questionable as a protection under some sets of circumstances. For example, a company on the verge of bankruptcy could sell its long-term assets, thereby increasing its working capital and working capital ratio.

The times-bond-interest-earned computation is tricky. Observe that in computing the times that interest is earned we must include the *one* time that it has already been paid and included in interest expense. That is why we add the interest expense in the numerator. The thought behind the computation is that a long-term creditor can see roughly how much income before income taxes exists to cover interest on debt.

The debt to equity ratios are a measure of leverage (on equity) and of risk to debtholders. A high debt to equity ratio indicates that in the event of a downturn in business sales, losses might be suffered by more than the common shareholder — perhaps the debtholders.

Other Considerations

Although some lenders or investors concentrate on *one* company's return on investment and risk, many money managers must consider a *portfolio* of several companies. For instance, one company which suffers when the economic outlook is poor (perhaps a construction company) may be combined with one (perhaps a gold mining company) which benefits during an economic downturn. The earnings of the two companies *combined* are therefore not subject to the wide swings in income which would occur when all the investor's money was used to buy shares in the construction company.

Ratio analysis must therefore be evaluated through the eyes of different users. A banker interested in lending to one company may give far greater attention to ratios than the manager of, say, a mutual fund, which holds shares in many companies.

Summary

Potentially, many different types of users wanting to form different judgments could read financial statements. Several of these users and their objectives were described throughout the book, especially in Chapter 5.

Although ratio analysis has limitations because: (1) of valuation differences among assets and liabilities; (2) the balance sheet reports an instant in time, and figures shortly before or after could differ substantially; (3) both the numerator and denominator affect a ratio; and (4) other difficulties, the analysis also has benefits. A trend meriting further investigation can come to light from the analysis. Contracts for the sale of bonds or preferred shares may require a trustee for the buyers to compute ratios.

Stock brokers use far more than financial statements when analyzing a company and recommending purchase or sale of its shares. Future earnings are important to analysts, and past financial data may not indicate expected future earnings or cash flows.

Notes

[1]See T.R. Archibald, "A Shareholder's Perspective on External Accounting Reports," *Canadian Chartered Accountant* (February 1971), pp. 105-110.

Questions, Problems and Cases

Questions

*15-1 In order to interpret financial statements wisely it is important to know the objectives of financial accounting used and to understand the limitations of the accounting reports. Explain.

15-2 "An analyst who understands a firm's accounting reports and knows how to calculate all the financial statement ratios understands just about all there is to know about a company." Do you agree? Explain your position through the use of specific examples.

15-3 One financial analyst recently commented to another, "As you can see, over each of the last three years, company A has had a higher rate of return on investment than company B. Since both firms are in the same industry, it seems pretty clear that company A is the better managed of the two." Cite five examples of how the difference in return on investment may be attributable entirely to choice among accounting alternatives.

15-4 Both John Labatt Ltd. and The Molson Companies Limited disclose accounting policies in their first note to the financial statements. Why do companies disclose this type of information? Is it necessary for an understanding of the financial statements? How would you decide which accounting policies to explain in a note to the financial statements?

15-5 What is meant by *quality* of earnings? What are the major characteristics of *high-quality* earnings?

15-6 The specific manner in which a ratio is determined should depend on the specific decision at hand. Illustrate this statement by comparing return on investment as computed using total investment with that computed using shareholders' equity. Can you think of another example?

15-7 Why do normal ranges for most ratios and percentages vary from industry to industry? Provide an example.

15-8 From the standpoint of the shareholders, the lower the debt to equity ratio, the better, since there are smaller claims against the resources of the firm on the part of creditors. Do you agree? Explain.

15-9 "The notes to the financial statements are a critical part of the financial statement package." Do you agree? Give examples to support your position.

15-10 Why is it desirable for a corporation to relegate certain types of financial data to footnotes rather than including them in the main body of the financial reports?

15-11 One of the "key accounting concepts" is full disclosure. Why don't companies disclose "everything" in the notes to the financial statements? What factors would you consider in deciding whether information should be disclosed in the notes to the financial statements? Give examples of how disclosure of information might lead to potential conflicts between financial statement user groups.

15-12 Some creditors may insist that companies requesting loans have their financial statements audited. Why do you suppose they do this? Of what value is an auditors' report?

15-13 Define what is meant by "stock market efficiency." If the market is efficient, then how would this affect the way in which you prepared accounting information?

15-14 Identify potential differences in the decisions made by investors and creditors. How might these differences result in different types of information being required (i.e., information about the environment, ratio analysis and so forth)?

15-15 "Accounting should be relevant to the needs of users. However, one of the difficulties with this concept is that it requires knowledge about the needs of users and how they make decisions. This knowledge is difficult to acquire." Explain the quotation. Does this mean that accounting should not attempt to serve the needs of users?

Problems

P15-1 Review the reports prepared on John Labatt Ltd. and The Molson Companies Limited by Dominion Securities Limited and Wood Gundy Limited respectively, included in the chapter.

Required:

a. What sources of information were used by the analyst?
b. Does the information appear to be future- or past-oriented? Or a mixture?
c. What role did financial accounting statements probably have in assisting the analysts in their investigation?

d. Has the analyst missed some factors which you would have thought were important?

e. Has the analyst been naive and placed too much importance on accounting numbers? Or something else?

f. What would you suspect about the use of such analyst's reports by the people who make considerable amounts of money "playing the stock market"?

P15-2 The president of a company, in requesting a renewal of an outstanding loan, wrote to an officer of a bank: "In spite of a decline in sales and earnings, we were able to strengthen our working capital position." He went on to cite the increase in the current ratio as evidence of the improvement.

The balance sheet of the company reported the following current assets and liabilities:

	December 31, 19x6	*December 31, 19x5*
Cash	$ 60,000	$120,000
Accounts receivable	270,000	190,000
Inventories	420,000	300,000
Total current assets	$750,000	$610,000
Accounts payable	$370,000	$330,000
Notes payable	140,000	140,000
Total current liabilities	$510,000	$470,000

The income statement (in summary form) revealed the following:

	19x6	*19x5*
Sales	$1,400,000	$1,560,000
Cost of goods sold	840,000	936,000
Other expenses	240,000	260,000
Total expenses	1,080,000	1,196,000
Net income	$ 320,000	$ 364,000

Required:

a. Determine the current ratio for both years.

b. Calculate the number of days' sales in accounts receivable.

c. Provide a possible explanation for the increase in accounts receivable and inventories that would undermine the contention of the president that the firm's working position has improved. Has the current position of the company really improved?

d. Why might the officer of the bank be interested in the calculations performed in Parts a and b? Why must care be taken in the use of these measures?

P15-3 Laughlin Ltd. has $30 million in total assets. It has $10 million in current liabilities outstanding and $20 million in shareholders' equity. There are presently 100,000 common shares outstanding. After-tax earnings over the past several years have averaged $2.1 million per year.

The company has decided to expand its operations by constructing a new plant. The new plant will cost $6 million, and it is estimated that it will increase earnings by $360,000 after taxes, not taking into account costs of financing.

The company has two options available to it to finance the plant. First, it can issue additional common shares. The additional shares could be sold for $400 per share.

Alternatively, it can raise the required $6 million by issuing bonds. The bonds would be sold to yield purchasers 10 percent per year. The interest costs would be tax deductible by the company. The applicable tax rate is 48 percent.

Required:

a. Assume that the company will construct the new plant. For each of the alternatives determine anticipated (i) return on investment (all capital), (ii) return on investment (shareholders' equity), and (iii) earnings per share.

b. After reviewing the figures just computed, the president of the company stated, "It is obvious that we are better off financing expansion with debt rather than equity. In the future, let's finance all additions by issuing bonds rather than shares." Comment on the logic of the president.

P15-4 Greer Ltd. was founded in January, 19x6. The company issued 300,000 common shares at $10 per share.

The company acquired trucks at a total cost of $3 million. The useful lives of the trucks were estimated to be ten years, with zero salvage value.

During its first year of operations the revenues of the firm, less all expenses other than depreciation and income taxes, were $1.3 million. The applicable income tax rate is 40 percent. The company uses the tax allocation basis of accounting for taxes; that is, reported tax expense is based on *reported* (book) income; it is not indicative of the required current tax payment.

For income tax purposes a 30 percent declining balance rate may be used.

Required:

a. Determine the first year's return on investment (on shareholders' equity) under each of the following assumptions:
   (i) The firm uses straight-line depreciation for book purposes and 30 percent declining balance for income tax purposes.
   (ii) The firm uses 30 percent declining balance depreciation for book purposes and 30 percent declining balance depreciation for tax purposes.

   Base your computation on year-end shareholders' equity as opposed to average shareholders' equity.

b. Why might there be a difference between the depreciation rate used for book purposes and that used for income tax purposes?

c. Comment on any substantive (i.e., "real" economic) differences in rate of return under each of the two methods.

d. Assuming that the users of the financial statements understand accounting principles what information should be disclosed in the notes to the financial statements in order that they are not misled?

P15-5 What effect would each of the following transactions have on a firm's (a) current ratio, and (b) debt to equity ratio? Indicate whether each transaction would cause the ratio to increase (I) or decrease (D) or whether it would have no effect (NE). Assume that any transactions involving revenues or expenses have an immediate impact upon retained earnings. Assume that all ratios were initially *greater* than 1:1.

1. The firm sells goods on account. Assume that the firm maintains its inventory records on a perpetual basis and that the price at which the goods are sold is greater than their initial cost.
2. The firm collects the amount receivable from the customer to whom it made the sale.
3. The firm issues long-term bonds.
4. The firm issues preferred shares in exchange for cash.
5. The firm declares, but does not pay, a dividend on common shares.
6. The firm pays the previously declared dividend.
7. The company purchases merchandise inventory on account.
8. The company pays for the merchandise previously purchased.
9. The firm purchases equipment, giving the seller a three-year note for the entire amount payable.
10. The firm recognizes depreciation for the first year.
11. The company writes off an uncollectible account receivable against the allowance for uncollectibles.
12. The firms writes off inventory as obsolete.

P15-6 A friend, who is president of Statistical Software Co. Ltd., asked you to invest in his company. In explaining to you the advantages of such an investment, he pointed to the firm's profitability as evidenced by a high rate of return on shareholders' equity and the security of the investment as measured by *times interest earned*.

The firm develops and sells customized computer programs to industrial firms. The programs are intended to enable a firm to generate statistical information about its operations.

The president of Statistical Software Co. Ltd. provided you with the company's 19x7 financial statements. The statements of income and of changes in financial position (cash basis) are presented below:

Statement of Income
Year Ended December 31, 19x7

Sales	$540,000	
Other revenues	260,000	$800,000
Cost of programs developed	530,000	
Other expenses	90,000	
Interest	20,000	
Taxes	40,000	680,000
Net income		$120,000

Statement of Changes in Financial Position
Year Ended December 31, 19x7

Sources of cash		
From operations		
Income	$120,000	
Add: Depreciation and amortization	60,000	
Subtract: Gain on sale of land	(160,000)	$ 20,000
Sale of land		220,000
Total sources of cash		240,000
Uses of cash		
Increase in accounts receivable		170,000
Increase in advertising and promotion costs expected to benefit future periods		30,000
Increase in program development costs applicable to software to be delivered in future		120,000
Total uses of cash		320,000
Decrease in cash		(80,000)
Cash balance beginning of year		410,000
Cash balance end of year		$330,000

The balance sheet reveals that average shareholders' equity during the year was $600,000.

Required:

a. Determine the rate of return on shareholders' equity and the times interest earned measure of coverage of fixed interest charges.

b. Review carefully the two statements presented. Recognizing that no investment decisions can be made on the basis of statements for a single year, what questions would you raise (or what reservations would you have) pertaining to the firm's *quality* of earnings?

P15-7 The president of Burgstahler Ltd. is faced with the decision whether to expand the corporation by acquiring a new plant. The cost of the new plant would be $500,000. The necessary capital could be acquired by issuing bonds which would provide a return to lenders of 12 percent per year. The new plant would increase corporate pretax earnings by $70,000 prior to taking into account required interest payments of $60,000.

Burgstahler Ltd. in recent years has had annual pretax income, after deducting $50,000 in interest payments, of $250,000. The firm, as of December 31, 19x6, has outstanding debt of $500,000 and shareholders' equity of $1.5 million.

The financial vice-president favors acquisition of the new plant, arguing that corporate earnings would be increased by $10,000. The corporate controller opposes the acquisition, maintaining that it would result in reduction of the firm's return on total invested capital.

Required:

a. Why do you suspect the controller is concerned about a reduction in the firm's return on invested capital? What assumption about the sophistication of the financial statement readers is he making? What arguments might you provide to him to allay his fears?

b. Determine return on investment (all capital) if (i) the plant is not acquired and (ii) the plant is acquired. Assume that earnings on the old facilities will be the same in the future as they have been in the past. Disregard income taxes, and base your computations on invested capital as of the beginning of 19x7.

c. Determine return on investment (shareholders' equity) under the two alternatives.

d. Calculate earnings per share under the two alternatives. The company has 10,000 common shares outstanding.

e. Do you think the company should acquire the plant? Explain.

f. Comment on the potential dangers of using return on investment as a criterion for making management decisions.

P15-8 The financial statements of the Yorkville Bottling Co. Ltd. revealed the following data for 19x6:

Current assets	$ 420,000
Other assets (property, plant and equipment)	6,580,000
Current liabilities	670,000
Other liabilities	2,308,000
Sales	11,500,000
Interest expense	350,000
Net income	1,400,000

Required:

a. Determine the following relationships (based on year-end balances):
   (i) Return on investment (all capital).
   (ii) Current ratio.
   (iii) Debt to equity.
   (iv) Plant and equipment turnover.

b. Investigation reveals that included in current assets are marketable securities that are recorded at a cost of $100,000. Their current market value is $350,000. Moreover, the company's plant is located on land that had originally cost $500,000. The land currently has a fair market value of $1 million. Recompute the above relationships to take into account the additional information. Which set of relationships do you think is more relevant to most decisions required by both managers and investors?

c. Comment on how the revised ratios may affect the analyst's view of both financial position and operating performance.

P15-9 The financial statements as of January 31, 19x4 and 19x5, of the Caldwell Clearance Co. Ltd. are presented below. The Caldwell Clearance Co. Ltd. operates a chain of low-priced department stores located throughout

Canada. Most of its merchandise is priced under $10, but the stores also carry a line of major appliances. The company opened its first store in 19x1.

Caldwell Clearance Co. Ltd.
Consolidated Balance Sheet as of January 31
(000's omitted)

	19x5	*19x4*
Assets		
Current		
Cash and equivalent	$ 79,642	$ 45,952
Accounts receivable (net)	431,191	540,802
Inventories	407,357	450,636
Other current assets	6,591	7,299
Total current assets	924,781	1,044,689
Noncurrent		
Property and equipment (net)	101,932	100,983
Investment in subsidiaries	49,764	44,251
Other assets	5,790	5,063
Total noncurrent assets	157,486	150,297
Total assets	$1,082,267	$1,194,986
Liabilities and shareholders' equity		
Current		
Accounts payable	$ 50,067	$ 58,192
Notes and other payables	600,995	453,096
Miscellaneous accruals	79,144	46,691
Taxes payable	19,700	103,078
Total current liabilities	749,906	661,057
Noncurrent		
Notes payable	99,005	100,000
Bonds payable	117,336	120,336
Other liabilities	2,183	18,845
Total noncurrent liabilities	218,524	239,181
Shareholders' equity		
Preferred shares	7,465	7,464
Common shares	68,698	67,812
Retained earnings	37,674	219,472
Total shareholders' equity	113,837	294,748
Total liabilities and shareholders' equity	$1,082,267	$1,194,986

Caldwell Clearance Co. Ltd.
Consolidated Statement of Income
(000s omitted)

	Years ended 1/31/19x5	1/31/19x4
Net sales	$1,761,952	$1,845,802
Other revenues	10,700	15,617
Total revenues	1,772,652	1,861,419
Cost of goods sold	1,303,267	1,282,944
Selling and other expenses	726,420	546,202
Interest	37,771	18,082
Income tax expense (refund)	(117,466)	3,289
Total expenses	1,949,992	1,850,517
Net income (loss)	$ (177,340)	$ 10,902

Required:

a. Explain as best you can the reason for the decline in earnings in 19x5.
b. Compare the liquidity of the company in 19x5 with that of 19x4.
c. Compare the debt to equity ratio of 19x5 with that of 19x4.
d. Comment on the firm's ability to meet fixed interest charges.
e. Comment on the critical problems that the firm will face in the following year. Do you see any bright spots? Do you believe that the ability of the firm to survive is in question?
f. What information about the company would you require before you could complete your evaluation of its ability to survive?

P15-10 Return on investment (ROI) can be computed in several different ways. For instance income and investment could be measured by such methods as:

Possible "Income" or numerator	*Possible "Investment" or denominator*
1. Net income	1. Shareholders' equity
2. Net income + interest	2. Total assets, less accumulated depreciation
3. Net income – preferred share dividends	3. Equity of common shares

Required:

a. Compute the various ROI measures indicated above for John Labatt Ltd. and The Molson Companies Limited for 1978.
b. Explain the use you would make of each of the above measures of ROI. Compare the results of your calculations in Part a. What conclusions can you make?
c. What are the limitations of each of these ROI measures?
d. What additional information would you require to evaluate the adequacy of a company's ROI?

P15-11 Creditors often use ratio analysis to monitor the performance of companies to which they have loaned funds or to check a company's compliance with various restrictive covenants that may be contained in the loan agreement.

The following are typical ratios compiled by bankers:

1. Number of days of sales in accounts receivable.
2. Number of days of sales in inventory, or inventory turnover.
3. Net income to sales.
4. Number of days' sales in trade accounts payable.
5. Trends in income statement accounts.
6. Working capital ratio.
7. Times interest earned.
8. Debt as a percentage of debt plus equity.

Required:

a. Compute each of the above ratios for John Labatt Ltd. and The Molson Companies Limited for 1977 and 1978.

b. Compare your calculations in Part a. As a creditor, what conclusions would you make?

c. What are the limitations of each of the measures you performed in Part a?

d. If you were contemplating investing in one of the two companies how might you use the ratios computed in Part a?

e. Evaluate the suitability of each company's Statement of Changes in Financial Position design.

P15-12 Both John Labatt Ltd. and The Molson Companies Limited have not capitalized their lease commitments. Suppose that the companies had purchased the property that they presently rent. Assume that both companies could borrow funds to finance their purchase at a rate of 10 percent per year.

Required:

a. Is there sufficient information disclosed in the financial statements to enable you to capitalize their leases? What information is missing?

b. As best you can, determine the present value of the lease commitments for each company. State your assumptions.

c. Calculate the debt to equity ratio and return (defined as net income + interest) on total assets as at the year end before and after your capitalization of lease commitments. What is your conclusion?

d. Why might some companies decide it is in their interest to capitalize lease commitments?

P15-13 Examine the notes to the financial statements of both John Labatt Ltd. and The Molson Companies Limited.

Required:

a. Identify differences in the accounting policies of the companies and the potential impact these differences would have on reported earnings.

b. Identify the different objectives of accounting which are fulfilled by the information disclosed in the notes to the financial statements of each company. (For the purpose of this part of the question it may be assumed that the stewardship objective is fulfilled.)

Example:

Objective	*Molson's*	*Information*
Cash prediction	Note 9	Annual lease commitments for the next five years indicate future cash outflows of the company which are fixed at March 31, 1978.

c. Identify the conditions necessary for the accounting treatment given investments, extraordinary items, pension plans, and lease commitments by each of John Labatt Ltd. and The Molson Companies Limited.

d. Which company's financial statements do you feel are more informative? Why?

e. Suggest possible improvements to the notes to the financial statements. Explain your reasoning.

Cases

C15-1 You have just been hired as an investment analyst for a large underwriting house, Good Company Limited. Your first assignment is to evaluate two companies in the same industry and recommend which one is the best buy. You have been provided with the following data:

1. Both companies have total assets of $5,000,000 and liabilities of $3,000,000;
2. The companies have the following income statements:

	Company A	*Company B*
Sales	$500,000	$500,000
Cost of goods sold	300,000	200,000
Gross margin	200,000	300,000
Selling and administrative expenses	75,000	125,000
Income before tax	$125,000	$175,000

3. Both companies are engaged in the manufacture of chemicals.

Required:

Which company is the best buy? Identify the information you would require, together with the reasons for the additional information, in order to decide which company is the best investment.

C15-2 Hardwood Furniture Company ("HFC or the company") is a public company that has been in the furniture-making business for a number of years. As a result of its emphasis on manufacturing a quality product at a reasonable price, it has been able to develop a wide customer base. Consequently, it has never been seriously affected by changes in consumer tastes or incomes. Until recently, it has been able to coast on its fine reputation, and shareholders have become accustomed to receiving "healthy" dividends.

However, early in 19x6, other companies began to offer a similar quality product to that of HFC and at a lower price. This competition had an immediate effect on HFC's sales and it became evident to HFC's president and major shareholder, Mr. Marshall, that the company would have to reevaluate its strategy.

After a careful review of market conditions, Mr. Marshall decided that the key to HFC's survival would be a major modernization of its equipment. With this in mind during 19x6 the company:

1. Disposed of equipment that had an original cost of $100,000 and accumulated depreciation of $80,000 (i.e., a net book value of $20,000) for $30,000 cash. (Note: Assume no tax is applied to this transaction.)
2. Acquired new equipment for $400,000 cash.

According to Mr. Marshall the $400,000 of new additions is only a beginning. He estimates that an additional $500,000 of new equipment is required to restore HFC's competitive edge in the industry.

In order to buy this additional equipment, HFC needs cash and therefore Mr. Marshall has come to you requesting a $500,000 loan. He would like to borrow this money for a five-year term at a 15 percent rate of interest (i.e., the going rate of interest for a medium-risk loan). He has left the following financial statements for your review and would like to have your decision concerning the loan as soon as possible.

Hardwood Furniture Limited
Balance Sheet

	October 31 19x6	19x5
Assets		
Cash	$ —	$ 50,000
Marketable securities at cost (market: 19x6 — $75,000, 19x5 — $60,000)	60,000	60,000
Accounts receivable, net	300,000	300,000
Inventories at lower of cost and market	500,000	350,000
Total current assets	860,000	760,000
Property, plant and equipment, at cost (note 2)	1,200,000	900,000
Less accumulated depreciation	410,000	400,000
	790,000	500,000
Organization costs, at cost	20,000	30,000
	$1,670,000	$1,290,000

Liabilities		
Bank indebtedness	$ 240,000	$ —
Accounts payable and accrued liabilities	350,000	300,000
Dividends payable	50,000	—
Income taxes payable	2,000	80,000
Total current liabilities	642,000	380,000
Long-term debt:		
10% note payable due November 1, 19x8	300,000	300,000
12% note payable due November 1, 19x15	100,000	—
	400,000	300,000
Deferred income taxes	48,000	40,000
Shareholders' Equity		
Common shares (Note 3)		
Authorized:		
1,000,000 common shares, no par value		
Issued:		
120,000 common shares	150,000	120,000
Retained earnings	430,000	450,000
Total shareholders' equity	580,000	570,000
	$1,670,000	$1,290,000

Hardwood Furniture Limited
Income Statement

	For the Year Ended October 31, *19x6*	*19x5*
Revenue:		
Sales	$1,000,000	$1,500,000
Costs:		
Cost of goods sold	800,000	1,000,000
Marketing and distribution	10,000	50,000
Administrative and general	90,000	60,000
Interest	60,000	30,000
	960,000	1,140,000
	40,000	360,000
Income taxes:		
Current	12,000	170,000
Deferred	8,000	10,000
	20,000	180,000

Net income before extraordinary item	20,000	180,000
Gain on sale of property, plant and equipment, net of taxes	10,000	—
Net income	30,000	180,000
Retained earnings, opening	450,000	320,000
	480,000	500,000
Less dividends	50,000	50,000
Retained earnings, closing	$ 430,000	$ 450,000

Hardwood Furniture Limited
Notes to Financial Statements

1. Summary of significant accounting policies:

   Inventories:
   Inventories are stated at the lower of LIFO cost and net realizable value.

   Property, Plant and Equipment:
   Depreciation is recorded generally on the straight-line basis over the estimated service lives of the assets.

   Organization Costs:
   Organization costs are amortized on a straight-line basis of $10,000 per year. This policy was commenced in 19x5.

   Income Taxes:
   Income taxes are accounted for on the tax allocation basis for all timing differences between accounting and taxable income.

2. Property, Plant and Equipment:

	19x6		*19x5*	
	Cost	*Accumulated Depreciation*	*Cost*	*Accumulated Depreciation*
Land	$ 100,000	$ —	$100,000	$ —
Buildings	600,000	270,000	600,000	240,000
Machinery	500,000	140,000	200,000	160,000
	$1,200,000	$410,000	$900,000	$400,000

   Total depreciation for 19x6 was $90,000 (19x5 — $50,000). The long-term debt is secured by the company's property, plant and equipment.

3. Common Shares:
   During the year the company issued an additional 20,000 shares for cash at a value of $1.50 per share.

4. Contingent Liabilities:
   The company is a defendant in an action brought in the Supreme Court of Ontario for damages in the amount of $200,000 for an alleged breach of contract. Legal counsel is of the opinion that there is no reason to concede any liability or to assume that the result of the action will adversely affect the financial position of the company.

Required:

Assume the role of a creditor and:

a. Prepare a Statement of Changes in Financial Position for the company for the year ended October 31, 19x6 based on the working capital concept of funds.
b. Indicate whether you would loan Hardwood Furniture Company the $500,000 which they have requested. Explain your position clearly by stating the assumptions which you have made, the financial statement analysis you have performed and the logic you have employed.
c. What additional information would you require to assist your decision?

C15-3 Three years ago your uncle, Mr. Galvin, was forced to sell his business because of poor health. He realized $500,000 on the sale of his business which he invested in government bonds yielding 8 percent per annum.

The other night, January 31, 19x8, your uncle was over for dinner. During a lull in the conversation, he expressed a keen desire to get back into business. He had completely recovered and over the past two months had been investigating numerous private companies.

He was anxious to use his $500,000 to purchase a business in the same industry in which he had spent his last 20 business years. He had narrowed his choice down to two companies, S Ltd. and B Ltd., which generally satisfied his requirements. He was under the impression from some of the stories you had told him about your accounting course that you were a sharp interpreter of financial statements. He therefore wanted you to assist him in his decision.

S Ltd. is wholly owned by Mr. S; Mr. S and his wife are directors of the company. Mr. S is retiring shortly and will sell all his common shares for $500,000. Mr. S desires to retain his preferred shares as a source of retirement income. B Ltd. is wholly owned by Mr. B, his wife and their son. Mr. and Mrs. B are the directors of the company. Mrs. B is not active in the company's operations and is not drawing any salary. The Bs wish to sell all their common and preferred shares for $500,000. Both sets of prospective vendors require cash for their shares.

He left you with a summary of financial data for the last four years. He has also determined that the accounting practices of the two companies are similar and both companies operated at approximately 70 percent capacity during 19x7.

Required:

Analyze the facts and financial data presented to you in the attached financial statements and prepare a summary of the comments which you would discuss with your uncle at your next meeting together with your recommendation. State all assumptions that you feel are required to make your recommendation. (Ignore any tax implications.)

(CICA adapted)

Balance Sheets (in thousands of dollars)

	S Ltd. as at June 30				B Ltd. as at November 30			
	19x7	19x6	19x5	19x4	19x7	19x6	19x5	19x4
Assets								
Current Assets								
Cash	$ 10	$ 12	$ 5	$ 9	$ 50	$ 40	$ 35	$ 30
Accounts receivable	92	80	80	70	262	237	208	185
Inventories — at lower of cost or net realizable value	215	197	188	176	203	190	166	148
Prepaid expenses	8	6	7	5	5	8	6	8
	325	295	280	260	520	475	415	371
Fixed assets								
Land, building and equipment, at cost (S Ltd.)	1,638	1,571	1,510	1,443				
Equipment and leasehold improvements, at cost (B Ltd.)					375	331	277	288
Less accumulated depreciation	630	525	424	326	177	144	116	87
	1,008	1,046	1,086	1,117	198	187	161	201
Other assets								
Goodwill, at cost	50	50	50	50	—	—	—	—
	$1,383	$1,391	$1,416	$1,427	$ 718	$ 662	$ 576	$ 572
Liabilities								
Current liabilities								
Bank loan	—	—	—	$ 15	$ 100	$ 100	—	—
Accounts payable and accrued liabilities	$ 211	$ 193	$ 185	147	88	76	$ 51	$ 63
Income taxes payable	9	7	5	3	20	—	4	7
Instalments due within one year on long-term debt	50	50	50	50	—	—	—	—
	270	250	240	215	208	176	55	70
Long-term debt (8%), non-current portion	400	450	500	550	—	—	—	—
Shareholders' equity								
Share capital:								
Preferred — 5% (S Ltd.)	300	300	300	300				
Preferred — 7% (B Ltd.)					200	200	200	200
Common	150	150	150	150	75	75	75	75
Retained earnings	263	241	226	212	235	211	246	227
	$1,383	$1,391	$1,416	$1,427	$ 718	$ 662	$ 576	$ 572

Statements of income and retained earnings (in thousands of dollars)

	S Ltd.				B Ltd.			
	Years Ended June 30				Years Ended November 30			
	19x7	19x6	19x5	19x4	19x7	19x6	19x5	19x4
Sales	$ 900	$ 810	$ 792	$ 774	$ 495	$ 330	$ 480	$ 405
Cost of sales	578	513	505	505	157	112	150	135
Gross profit	322	297	287	269	338	218	330	270
Selling and variable operating expenses	37	30	25	24	22	18	18	15
Depreciation and other fixed expenses (Notes 1 and 2)	181	177	174	161	210	214	222	219
	218	207	199	185	232	232	240	234
Income (loss) before income taxes	104	90	88	84	106	(14)	90	36
Income taxes	52	45	44	42	36	—	35	8
Net income (loss) for the year	52	45	44	42	70	(14)	55	28
Retained earnings at beginning of year	241	226	212	200	211	246	227	220
	293	271	256	242	281	232	282	248
Deduct dividends on – Preferred shares	15	15	15	15	14	14	14	14
– Common shares	15	15	15	15	32	7	22	7
	30	30	30	30	46	21	36	21
Retained earnings at end of year	$ 263	$ 241	$ 226	$ 212	$ 235	$ 211	$ 246	$ 227

Notes: (1) Fixed expenses include directors' remuneration ($30,000 per year for S Ltd. and $50,000 per year for B Ltd.).
(2) For B Ltd. only, fixed expenses also include lease payments of $100,000 per year. B Ltd. leases its premises under a 15-year lease expiring in 19x20.

Appendix 15-A

The Molson Companies Limited 1979 Financial Report

The Molson Companies Limited financial report for the year ended March 31, 1979 is included in this Appendix. This information has been segregated from the 1978 results included in this chapter to encourage readers to: (1) initially, focus on the investment decision and comparison between Labatt's and Molson's; and (2) receive some feedback on their judgments and those of the analysts whose reports were reprinted in the chapter. Does the following information help to explain the share-price rise in Molson's? In whole? In part?

EXHIBIT 15A-1

Consolidated Statement of Earnings ($000's)

The Molson Companies Limited

Year ended March 31	1979	1978
Revenues		
Sales and revenues	$1,196,859	$951,919
Investment income	2,251	510
Equity in earnings of other companies	1,218	791
	1,200,328	953,220
Costs and expenses		
Cost of sales, selling and administrative costs	912,597	724,966
Brewing excise and sales taxes	171,595	150,216
Depreciation	20,881	18,211
Interest on long-term debt	12,491	7,791
Other interest	5,517	2,920
	1,123,081	904,104
Earnings before income taxes	77,247	49,116
Income taxes	31,939	17,916
	45,308	31,200
Minority interest	1,232	256
Net earnings before extraordinary items	44,076	30,944
Extraordinary items	—	2,120
Net earnings for the year	$ 44,076	$ 33,064
Net earnings per share		
Before extraordinary items	$3.20	$2.25
After extraordinary items	3.20	2.41

Consolidated Statement of Retained Earnings ($000's)

The Molson Companies Limited

Year ended March 31	1979	1978
Balance – beginning of year	$155,961	$135,260
Net earnings for the year	44,076	33,064
	200,037	168,324
Dividends	14,535	12,363
Balance – end of year	$185,502	$155,961

(See Notes to Consolidated Financial Statements)

Consolidated Balance Sheet ($000's)

The Molson Companies Limited

As at March 31	1979	1978
ASSETS		
Current Assets		
Cash and short-term investments	$ 30,925	$ 5,185
Accounts receivable	116,172	83,555
Due from sale of businesses	1,195	19,367
Inventories	172,033	141,825
Prepaid expenses	9,486	5,767
	329,811	255,699
Investments	23,945	13,226
Fixed Assets		
Land, buildings and equipment	396,567	359,724
Accumulated depreciation	169,988	170,371
	226,579	189,353
Other Assets – less amortization		
Intangible assets of acquisitions	49,025	3,330
Debenture discount and expenses	742	838
	49,767	4,168
	$630,102	$462,446
LIABILITIES		
Current Liabilities		
Bank indebtedness	$ 34,554	$ 15,288
Notes payable	23,989	30,284
Accounts payable	120,137	72,885
Income taxes	11,643	2,696
Excise and sales taxes	13,179	9,504
Dividends payable	4,159	3,122
Current instalments on long-term debt	21,510	2,792
Deferred revenue	3,393	–
	232,564	136,571
Other Liabilities		
Long-term Debt	113,080	88,000
Minority Interest	6,816	3,606
Deferred Income Taxes	32,758	27,009
Deferred Income – less amortization	4,432	2,909
Deferred Liabilities	2,584	–
	159,670	121,524
SHAREHOLDERS' EQUITY		
Capital Stock	52,366	48,390
Retained Earnings	185,502	155,961
	237,868	204,351
	$630,102	$462,446

Signed on Behalf of the Board: Director [signature]

Director [signature]

(See Notes to Consolidated Financial Statements)

Consolidated Statement of Changes in Financial Position ($000's)

The Molson Companies Limited

Year ended March 31	1979	1978
Source of funds		
Net earnings before extraordinary items	$ 44,076	$ 30,944
Add (deduct) items not affecting working capital—		
Depreciation	20,881	18,211
Deferred income taxes	2,794	3,648
Amortization of intangible assets	1,308	89
Gain on sale of fixed assets	(4,241)	(2,430)
Equity in earnings of other companies (net of dividends received)	(745)	(526)
Other	578	276
Funds from operations	64,651	50,212
Proceeds from —		
Sale of fixed assets	7,007	4,540
Sale of investments	298	2,093
Sale of businesses (less working capital of $11,282; 1978 — $5,681)	14,014	16,085
Long-term borrowing	46,889	—
Issue of common stock	3,976	—
	136,835	72,930
Use of funds		
Dividends	14,535	12,363
Purchase of —		
Fixed assets	40,812	28,581
Investments	7,458	5,192
Business acquisitions (excluding working capital of $26,897; 1978 — $389)	63,657	2,537
Repayment and current portion of long-term debt	32,254	6,009
Extraordinary item — provision for estimated losses arising from planned disposal or discontinuance of businesses ($7,000 less items not affecting working capital)	—	1,886
	158,716	56,568
Working capital		
Increase (Decrease) in the year	(21,881)	16,362
At beginning of year	119,128	102,766
At end of year	$ 97,247	$119,128

(See Notes to Consolidated Financial Statements)

Notes to Consolidated Financial Statements

1. Accounting policies

Consolidation: The accounts of all subsidiaries are consolidated.

Foreign exchange: Earnings of foreign operations are translated at the average rate of exchange during the year. Current assets and current liabilities are translated at the rate at March 31 and other balance sheet accounts and related depreciation are translated at the rate on the date of acquisition. Net earnings in 1979 include translation gains of $587,000 ($1,142,000 in 1978).

Inventories: Inventories are valued at the lower of cost or net realizable value except for retail lumber inventories which are valued at the lower of cost or replacement cost. Cost is determined on a first-in, first-out basis.

Investments: Investments in effectively controlled companies are carried on the equity method. Other investments are carried on the cost basis.

Fixed assets: Fixed assets are carried at cost. Depreciation is provided from the date assets are put into service on the straight-line method over their estimated useful lives, primarily at annual rates of 2½% for buildings and from 7% to 10% for equipment.

Intangible assets of acquisitions: Intangible assets of acquisitions after April 1, 1974 are being amortized by charges to earnings on a straight-line basis over periods not exceeding forty years, except for $12 million of hockey franchises which are not amortized as the Company believes there has been no decrease in their value.

Income taxes: Deferred income taxes represent amounts deferred to future years due to the earlier deduction of certain expenses, principally depreciation, for tax purposes. Investment tax credits are reflected in earnings in the year they are claimed for tax purposes.

2. Business combinations

During the year, four businesses (two in 1978) were acquired for cash and have been included on the basis of purchase accounting.

($000's)	The Diversey Corporation (Effective June 1, 1978)	Club de Hockey Canadien Inc. (Effective July 1, 1978)	Wheatley & Wilson Ltd. (Effective Aug. 1, 1978)	Biltrite (Effective March 31, 1979)	1979	1978
Net tangible assets acquired	$28,071	–	$1,177	$5,770	$ 35,018	$2,926
Assigned to fixed assets	11,396	–	–	–	11,396	–
Intangible assets of acquisitions	26,880	*$20,052	–	–	46,932	–
Purchase price	$66,347	$20,052	$1,177	$5,770	$93,346	$2,926

*Includes $15,500 of hockey franchises and other contract rights.

3. Inventories ($000's)	1979	1978
Finished goods	$138,486	$112,653
Work in process	6,361	12,236
Raw materials and supplies	27,186	16,936
	$172,033	$141,825

4. Investments ($000's)	1979	1978
Mortgages and loans, at cost	$ 3,777	$ 1,754
Investments, at equity	8,630	4,279
Other investments, at cost	11,538	7,193
	$ 23,945	$ 13,226

5. Fixed assets ($000's)	1979	1978
Land	$ 25,575	$ 20,921
Buildings	146,442	126,372
Equipment	224,550	212,431
	396,567	359,724
Accumulated depreciation	169,988	170,371
	$226,579	$189,353

6. Long-term debt ($000's)

	1979 Current	1979 Total	1978 Current	1978 Total
Sinking Fund Debentures:				
8¼% maturing in 1991	–	$ 35,655	–	$36,249
8¼% maturing in 1995	$ 900	28,200	$ 900	29,100
6% maturing in 1982	–	1,696	–	1,710
5¼% convertible maturing in 1989	–	537	–	2,194
8¾% maturing in 1988	–	–	–	1,000
Notes Payable:				
9% repayable by 1989	1,536	16,897	1,536	18,433
5¾% repayable by 1985	200	1,400	200	1,600
Other(1)	89	2,015	–	–
Term loan maturing June 1981, currently bearing interest at 9 9/16% ($32,000 U.S.)	18,550	36,438	–	–
Loan bearing interest at prime bank rate plus ¼%	–	10,000	–	–
Sundry	235	1,752	156	506
	$21,510	$134,590	$2,792	$90,792
Current instalments		21,510		2,792
		$113,080		$88,000

(1) – Note payable in equal annual instalments from June 1980 to June 1983, with interest at 1¼% to 1½% over the prevailing London interbank rate, 14.4% at March 31, 1979 – £600,000;
– 8⅝% note payable in equal quarterly instalments from December 1978 to September 1988, secured by certain properties – 1,344,000 Deutchmarks.

Sinking fund requirements and principal payments during the next five years are: 1980–$21,510; 1981–$18,237; 1982–$20,192; 1983–$4,488; 1984–$4,172.

7. Capital stock

Authorized: Pursuant to supplementary letters patent dated October 4, 1978, the authorized share capital of the Company was altered, effective as of January 1, 1979, to:
30,000,000 Class "A" common shares without par value, and
14,000,000 Class "B" common shares without par value.

Also by virtue of such supplementary letters patent, effective as of January 1, 1979, the then authorized, issued and outstanding, Class "C" and Class "D" interconvertible common shares without par value were reclassified as, respectively, Class "B" and Class "A" common shares without par value.

The Class "A" shares are non-voting except, voting separately and as a class, the holders thereof are entitled to elect three members of the Board of Directors annually. The Class "B" shares are fully voting.

The Class "A" shares are entitled to non-cumulative preferential dividends aggregating 20¢ per share per annum. No further dividend can be paid until the Class "B" shares receive a dividend or dividends aggregating 20¢ per share per annum, and thereafter the Class "A" and Class "B" shares rank equally as to dividends.

Issued and Outstanding at March 31:	1979 Shares	1979 Amount	1978 Shares	1978 Amount
Class "A"	8,781,500	$43,184,000	8,322,000	$37,977,000
Class "B"	5,089,300	9,182,000	3,988,600	7,293,000
Class "C"	–	–	1,095,500	1,797,000
Class "D"	–	–	286,900	1,323,000
	13,870,800	$52,366,000	13,693,000	$48,390,000
Average number of shares outstanding	13,743,900		13,692,800	

During the year, the following shares were issued for cash:	1979 Shares	1979 Amount	1978 Shares	1978 Amount
Class "A"–Employee stock option purchases	94,700	$2,227,000	–	–
Class "B"–Employee stock option purchases	5,200	92,000	–	–

During the year, the following shares were converted between the classes:	1979 (1)	1978
Class "A" to Class "D"	64,000	117,900
Class "D" to Class "A"	71,800	132,400
Class "B" to Class "C"	556,400	748,200
Class "C" to Class "B"	586,900	89,500

(1) During the nine months ended December 31, 1978.

Stock options: At March 31, the following options to employees to purchase shares were outstanding:

	Expiry date	1979 Option price	1979 Shares	1978 Option price	1978 Shares
Class "A"	August 14, 1980	$19.375	1,950	$19.375	7,650
Class "B"	August 14, 1980	$17.50	1,950	$17.50	7,650
			3,900		15,300
Class "A"	November 27, 1983(2)	$23.75	80,500	–	–

(2) Granted during the year from 400,000 Class "A" shares reserved under employee stock option plan adopted by the Board of Directors on November 20, 1978.

Of the options outstanding at March 31, 1979, options covering 58,600 (1978 – 6,000) Class "A" shares and 1,100 (1978 – 6,000) Class "B" shares were held by officers, two (1978 – three) of whom were and are also directors, and a director who was and is a senior officer of a Company subsidiary, as a group.

At March 31, 1979, 312,400 (1978 – 11,400) Class "A" shares and 1,900 (1978 – 11,400) Class "B" shares remained reserved for this purpose.

Convertible debentures: Holders of the 5¼% debentures of a subsidiary may, on or before May 1, 1979, convert these debentures into Class "A" shares on the basis of 47 shares per $1,000 debenture. During the year, 77,900 (1978 - 900) Class "A" shares were issued upon the conversion of $1,657,000 (1978 – $19,000) aggregate principal amount of debentures. At March 31, 1979, 30,600 (1978 - 108,500) Class "A" shares remained reserved for this purpose.

Shareholders' Optional Stock Dividend Plan: During the year, the Board of Directors adopted the plan and reserved a total of 100,000 Class "A" shares for issuance thereunder as optional stock dividends in lieu of cash. The plan became effective with the dividend paid on April 1, 1979.

8. Additional information

Pension plans: The funding requirements for current service pension costs, based on actuarial determinations, are charged to earnings. Past service costs are being charged to earnings and funded over periods not exceeding 15 years. The unrecorded unfunded liability for past service pension costs amounted to $26,000,000 at March 31, 1979 (1978 – $27,000,000).

Commitments: Lease commitments, which expire within thirty years, require the following payments during the next five years:

1980–$18,100,000; 1981–$16,400,000; 1982–$15,100,000; 1983–$13,600,000; 1984–$12,800,000.

Properties leased include warehouses, retail stores and sports arenas.

Remuneration of Directors and Officers	1979	1978
Directors–number	16	16
–aggregate remuneration	$ 82,800	$ 73,000
Officers –number	19	21
–aggregate remuneration	$1,326,000	$1,338,000
Number of officers who are also directors	5	5

Classes of business: The following are the proportions of consolidated sales by class of business:

	1979	1978
Brewing	48%	51%
Retail merchandising	25	28
Specialty chemicals	13	–
Other businesses	14	21
	100%	100%

Anti-inflation legislation: Under the terms of the Anti-Inflation Act and Regulations the Canadian operations of the Company were subject to restraint of profit margins, prices and compensation until December 31, 1978, and restraint of dividends until October 13, 1978.

Income Taxes: Current income taxes for the year ended March 31, 1979 have been reduced by $1,852,000 ($2,050,000 in 1978) resulting from the 3% federal inventory allowance.

Auditors' Report to the Shareholders

We have examined the consolidated balance sheet of The Molson Companies Limited as at March 31, 1979 and the consolidated statements of earnings, retained earnings and changes in financial position for the year then ended. Our examination was made in accordance with generally accepted auditing standards, and accordingly included such tests and other procedures as we considered necessary in the circumstances.

In our opinion, these consolidated financial statements present fairly the financial position of the company as at March 31, 1979 and the results of its operations and the changes in its financial position for the year then ended in accordance with generally accepted accounting principles applied on a basis consistent with that of the preceding year.

Coopers & Lybrand

Chartered Accountants May 25, 1979

Shortly before official release of the 1979 financial report of The Molson Companies Limited, the following story appeared in *The Globe and Mail* (June 4, 1979):

Molson unlikely to match high growth

Molson Cos. Ltd. of Montreal should perform very well in fiscal 1980 but is unlikely to match the high rate of earnings growth achieved in fiscal 1979, A.G. McCaughey, corporate vice-president, finance, said in a Canadian Dow Jones interview.

In the year ended March 31, 1979, the diversified brewing company earned $44.1-million or $3.20 a share on revenue of $1.2-billion, up from $30.9-million or $2.25 a share on revenue of $951.9-million in fiscal 1978. Results for the year-ago period excluded a $2.1-million gain on the sale of subsidiaries.

Although the group is unlikely to match the 42 per cent earnings growth achieved in fiscal 1979 — aided by the acquisition of Diversey Corp., the earlier sale of less profitable subsidiaries and good performances by the company's beer and retail divisions — Mr. McCaughey said "we've now really assigned our resources to the business that we want to be in. Apart from one business that's yet to prove its profitability — our office products division — we're happy with the outlook for others."

Mr. McCaughey said Molson Breweries has been able to achieve a steady, modest increase in its market share, which together with exports enables it to sustain growth slightly ahead of the industry's rate of about 1.5 per cent a year.

Molson, the second largest brewer in Canada with about 35 per cent of the Canadian market, sold 6.9 million barrels of beer in fiscal 1979, of which somewhat over 500,000 barrels went in exports to the United States.

The company's sales to the United States are growing at a faster rate than its domestic sales but Molson has no plans to follow other foreign breweries in setting up plants in the United States because Molson brands "would probably lose their magic as an import beer."

Mr. McCaughey said the company is very happy with the performance of Diversey Corp., acquired last July for $66-million. He said the Chicago-based specialty chemicals company "has had a 20 per cent growth rate since we bought it with a parallel growth in earnings and has contributed more to the group than we expected when we bought it."

Molson's recent extensive program of acquisitions and divestitures "is just about at the end of the road for the time being. We have had a few smaller businesses that are still being sold off, as part of the earlier program, but we're now basically positioned the way we want to be." But he added that Molson is "always alert to the possibility of expansion in the fields we're already in."

The company's Beaver Lumber Co. retail business had satisfactory sales and earnings in fiscal 1979 but its office products division "has a long way to go before we're happy with its profit."

The company is selling off some of the division's manufacturing facilities, expanding its retail outlets, bringing in new people and generally streamlining the operation.

"We're confident it can be made to pay."

Mr. McCaughey declined to comment in detail on financial aspects of the Montreal Canadiens hockey team, acquired for $20-million last July, other than to say the team is a major promotional asset and that the team and Molson's lease on the Montreal Forum contribute modestly to the group in direct earnings.

Referring to recent reports that Molson is considering buying the Rochester Lancers, a professional soccer team based in Rochester, N.Y., Mr. McCaughey said "we're talking with the owners but only about the possibility of acquiring advertising and promotional rights. I doubt that there's any thought or discussion going on in the direction of acquiring the team."

Molson already has an agreement for advertising rights to the Toronto Blizzard professional soccer team.

16 *General Price Level Restatements and Current Value Accounting*

Throughout the book we have noted the strengths and weaknesses of a few measurements for the different, and sometimes conflicting, objectives or purposes of financial accounting. Mainly, though, we have focused upon traditional historic cost accounting. We have observed that additional disclosure directly on the financial statements, or in the notes thereto, can supplement the historic cost measurements, and perhaps help to meet the differing needs of users/readers. We have seen attempts to reduce diversity of accounting methods so as to move towards a (probably unattainable) goal of having one method of accounting for one set of objectives-facts-constraints. We have also recognized the importance of judgment in choosing measurements and disclosure, because considerable choice still exists in the process of selecting "suitable" accounting principles. Above all, we can now better understand the comments in Chapter 1 about the dynamic nature of financial accounting *and* the need for accounting to change in order to meet changing environmental conditions and information needs of users of financial statements.

A considerable amount of information about a company can be gleaned from notes to financial statements; notes are not restricted to one main system of measurement — historic costs, one of the members of the current value family, or something else. However, the messages which we may seek about the financial strength and trends of a company might still be observed by utilizing *one* system of measurement or financial statements with their accompanying notes.

This chapter examines two alternative measurement systems to the basic historic cost system used by Labatt's, Molson's and other Canadian companies, and illustrated in the early chapters. Each of these alternatives with accompanying notes could be viewed by some people as able to stand alone. However, the current thrust in most countries is towards reporting only *some* of the figures which these other measurement systems generate. But the reporting would be *supplementary* information to the basic historic cost system. Our approach will be to illustrate the mechanics of each system in its entirety. If the resulting information is then considered useful, in whole or in part, it can be reported in whatever way seems informative to users.

Some Basics

Before proceeding to the techniques or how-to-do-it, some broader observations are in order. Important distinctions exist between a reporting format that must stand alone and one that is designed to supplement another system. Reporting a supplementary figure requires greater benefit-cost justification on the part of the preparer than a figure that might only be needed to "balance" the prime measurement system. This is because preparers often are subject to pressure from owners and higher management to avoid needless costs. Preparers should ensure that a supplementary figure is provided *only when it conveys new, otherwise unavailable, information*.

Although the foregoing cost-benefit point may seem obvious to some, it certainly does not appear to be obvious to many others. During the second half of the 1970s Canadian accountants have spent considerable time debating the merits of alternative, *supplementary* measurements to a historic cost system. One of these alternatives, called a general price-level restatement of historic cost (to be described shortly) would seem to duplicate much (but not all) of the information included in a historic cost financial statement package.

Why would some accountants advocate such duplication? Many reasons could exist, a few of which are:

1. Prestige of the accounting profession in Canada.
2. Attempts, through duplication and contrast, to influence the federal and provincial governments of Canada so that they might allow greater recognition in the income tax system for the effects of inflation. (The impact of different objectives or purposes of financial accounting on our accounting and reporting methods appears "front and center" in the picture.)
3. Misunderstanding.

The prestige of accountants in Canada is at stake when the U.S. and other countries, such as U.K. and Australia, are attempting to respond to the effects of changing prices on accounting reports, while Canada might be viewed as moving slowly.[1] Some accountants want to end the debate and choose a simple approach — perhaps one which is "too simple" and lacking in credibility.

Some company officials — such as those with huge investments in long-lived depreciable assets, which are subject to rising replacement costs — believe that they are over-taxed. They want greater relief from the effects of inflation than income tax legislation currently provides. They reason that an alternative measurement system to historic cost might provide relief from income taxation.

With reference to the misunderstanding issue, we can eliminate its distracting effects only by further education. Clearly, different people have different objectives of accounting in mind. If a historic cost system with its accompanying notes does not meet their needs, they will favor an alternative. When several alternatives are available, it is not surprising that different preparer and user groups may elect different alternatives. One group may favor replacement cost, another net realizable value, while another will want both figures.

Some people resist change. They will go to great lengths to criticize something new, often because the new system has not "proven itself" yet. How a new system can prove itself without being given a chance is a point overlooked by these critics.

In keeping with the role of a university/college we intend in this chapter to investigate some alternatives to historic cost both from a "how-to-do-it" and "why-do-it" perspective. We will attempt to fit the material into the objectives-facts-constraints framework simply for analytical purposes. It would *not* be wise to assume that we are seeking the "*best*" measurement system under all circumstances. Rather, we are seeking to identify the specific circumstances where each system seems sensible and where it does not. For example, would a small owner-managed company need a complex system based on both buying market (replacement costs) and selling market (net realizable value) prices? Do the costs of preparing the data exceed benefits in decision-making? If the small business does not need the different system, which companies might?

Alternatives Compared

The two alternatives to historic cost which have received the most attention in Canada in recent years are:

1. A general price level restatement of historic cost financial statements (GPL); and

2. A form of current value accounting (CVA) — either buying or selling market prices or some combination thereof.

Other alternatives exist, but we only have space to deal with the two above.

GPL accounting restates the traditional historic cost financial statements by employing a price index which measures *general* inflation (general or average price changes) in Canada. The federal government department in Canada which is charged with preparing such a price index is Statistics Canada. Of the many indexes that it prepares, the closest to the needs for accounting purposes is called the Gross National Expenditure Implicit Price Deflator (GNE deflator). It measures price changes in many, but not all, goods and services on which a *dollar* is spent in Canada. Price movements in the GNE deflator often are similar to those for the Consumer Price Index (CPI), which measures price changes in food, clothing, shelter, health care, transportation, and other items on which people spend their disposable income. To simplify discussions in this chapter we will use the CPI, even though it is second-best, because it is easier for people to identify with. *However, it is important to remember that the only conceptually-sound index for GPL is the GNE deflator. It is the only one which is broad enough to track changes in the purchasing power of the Canadian dollar. Less broad prices indexes are likely to be useful for CVA, not for GPL.*

In one very crude sense, inflation is the result of having larger increases in the money supply than in the output of goods and services. (We will ignore why the increases in money supply occur because economics courses explain inflation, international trade implications, and other important factors.) As a result more dollars are "chasing" the goods, and selling prices of food, clothing, or other goods are forced upwards by those possessing the dollars. This means that on the average during inflation the dollar buys less than it did a few months or years ago. That is, the average *purchasing power* of the *dollar* has dropped.

Accounting figures on historic cost financial statements therefore do not reflect current *general* or overall average purchasing power. (We already know that most figures on historic cost financial statements do not reflect current *specific* purchasing power for that particular asset or liability. By specific purchasing power we mean current buying or current selling market prices of an asset or liability.) Some accountants believe that the accounting figures should reflect *purchasing power* and that it, not dollars, should be the yardstick used in measuring financial statements.

Let us return to our example of a house, which was used earlier in the book. Suppose that you bought a house on January 1, 19x1 for $50,000, when the Consumer Price Index (CPI) was 150. On January 1, 19x10 the CPI was 225. The selling price of the house on January 1, 19x10 was $80,000. Balance sheets prepared on different measurement scales as of January 1, 19x10 would show:

Historic cost	$50,000
General price level restatement of historic cost (GPL):	
$\$50,000 \times \frac{225}{150}$	$75,000
Selling market price	$80,000

The GPL restatement follows the same accounting principles and concepts (see Chapter 5) as the historic cost system, even including "lower of cost and market." For instance, if the selling market price were $65,000 instead of $80,000, the GPL restatement would have to be reduced to $65,000 from $75,000. (Under these facts, GPL and current value are equal with regard to "objectivity" of the measurements.) The basic technique of GPL is quite simple:

$$\text{Historic cost} \times \frac{\text{General price index at date of financial statements}}{\text{General price index on date the house was bought}} = \text{GPL figure.}$$

Only through coincidence would the GPL figure represent buying or selling market price.

Exhibit 16-1 provides another way of contrasting GPL with one of the current value measures, buying market or selling market price, during a period of inflation.

The GPL line theoretically represents the weighted *average* price change for all goods and services exchanged in Canada. Some goods would obviously increase more, while others would increase less, than the average. When we are referring to the current prices of specific or individual commodities we are referring to current value accounting. The *average* price change for *all* goods and services in the economy is inflation, which can be accounted for by general price level accounting (GPL).

Capital Maintenance

The pricing or valuation of assets and liabilities is only half the picture. We must also specify what we wish our *capital* (owners' equity, roughly speaking) to be. *Then, and only then, can we compute an income figure.* Under the historic cost concept we implicitly assumed that capital was maintained (capital maintenance) at the money or dollar (not purchasing power) contributions of owners, plus retained earnings.

EXHIBIT 16-1

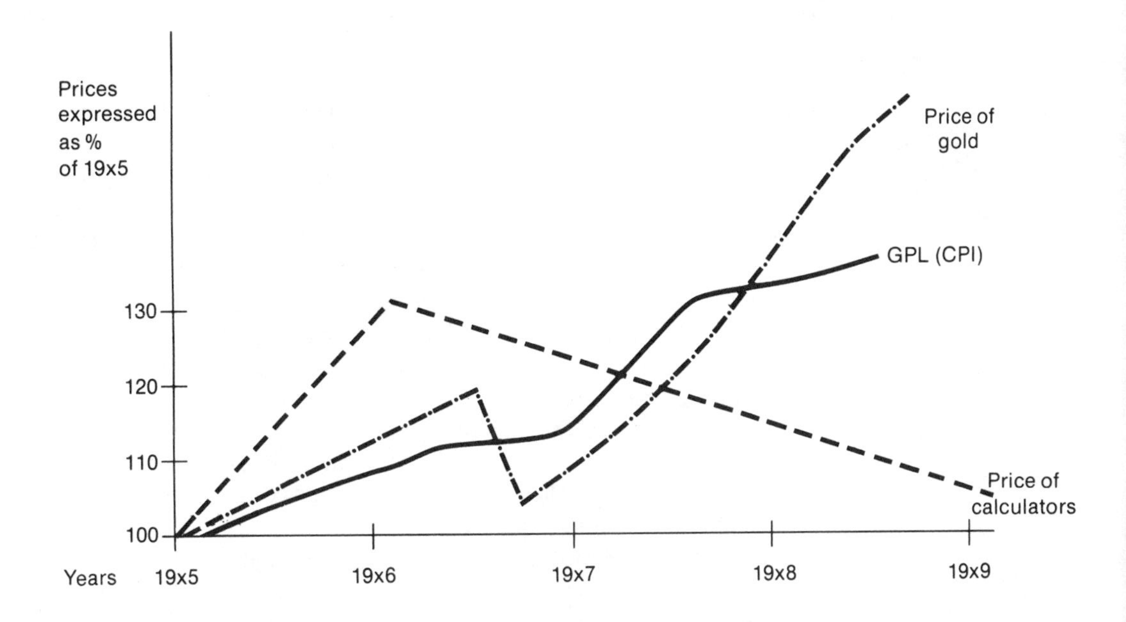

Suppose that we sold the aforementioned house for $80,000. How much was our income or profit? Let us choose three possibilities:

	(1)	(2)	(3)
Asset valuation basis chosen:	Historic cost	GPL	Selling price
Capital maintenance:	Historic money	GPL	Selling price (physical capacity)
Revenue	$80,000	$80,000	$80,000
Cost of house sold	50,000	75,000	80,000
Income	$30,000	$ 5,000	$ —

The rationale for using historic money capital maintenance (1) — the basis implied in traditional financial statements — could simply be that this accomplishes the stewardship objective of accounting. It is inexpensive to compute from a bookkeeping standpoint, and if no one demands anything else, why not select it if one of the three had to be chosen?

Category (2) assumes that people invest in a business in the hope of receiving a return on their investment which enables them to be "better off tomorrow." Specifically, Category (2) suggests that when people invest, they in effect postpone consumption of *general* goods, or some composite of all goods and services in Canada. Do they? This might include machinery, equipment, all imports, and exports, if we apply the GNE deflator. Alternatively, using the CPI assumes that investors postpone the consumption of consumer goods. The latter index would make sense if we performed the GPL restatement for the original owner of the business who might well have postponed the consumption of consumer, as opposed to all, goods. But, few larger businesses operate for several years with the same owners. Thus, a GPL restatement of the money investment of the original owner could be of little interest to someone who buys ownership at a later date, when the GPL index has shifted.

The use of "selling price" capital maintenance (or one of the other current value measures) is tied to a *continuity* assumption about the company. We have previously explained continuity in connection with a house example as meaning that if the occupant needed another place to live, then capital maintenance probably should be thought of in terms of a physical item, a house. Generally we do not refer to selling price capital maintenance, but to *physical* or *operating* capacity.

No *one* of the capital maintenance concepts is always the "best." Each makes sense under some identifiable circumstances. Mostly, we need more than one measure to draw informative conclusions about the operations of a complex organization. For example, should transit fares within a town or city be based on the original cost of the buses and other equipment, or on the replacement cost? If you chose original cost, explain why. How would you defend it? Identifiable assumptions are present in your choice. Let us see whether we can identify some.

Suppose that a transit company owned by a city bases its fares on cost of operation, less a subsidy from the city's general property tax receipts. The transit company bought a new fleet of buses early in 19x1 which would operate for 10 years, when they would have to be replaced. Annual operating cost for 19x1 to 19x10 are expected to be:

Wages, and all costs except depreciation	$ 8,000,000
Depreciation on original cost of buses	2,000,000
	10,000,000
Less subsidy	3,000,000
Net cost	$ 7,000,000
Expected number of riders	14,000,000
Ticket price	50¢ each

Assume that the buses, costing a total $20,000,000, were paid for in cash in 19x1. The funds were obtained from the city, on a long-term basis. Assume also that wages and related costs were constant from 19x1 to 19x10, and that fares remained at 50¢ each for the 14,000,000 riders per year. Finally, assume that at the end of 19x10 the cost of replacing the buses is $55,000,000. (Normally the price rise from $20,000,000 would occur over 10 years. To keep the example simple we are ignoring reality somewhat. Suppose that the rise to $55,000,000 from $20,000,000 occurs early in year 19x1.)

Where will the $35,000,000 ($55,000,000 – $20,000,000) come from to acquire the new buses at the end of 19x10 (or beginning of 19x11)? Maybe it could be borrowed for a 10-year period and interest expense charged to riders from 19x11 to 19x20. (If so, we are treating the riders in 19x11 to 19x20 differently from those who rode in 19x1 to 19x10 and did not pay interest on $20,000,000 capital provided by the city.) Maybe we should charge the riders in 19x1 to 19x10 sufficiently to pay for the replacement cost of what they are using up each year.

What should the fare be for 19x11 to 19x20, assuming that wages and other costs remain at $8,000,000, the subsidy is still $3,000,000, and 14,000,000 riders per year use the service?

Wages and all costs except depreciation	$ 8,000,000
Depreciation on new buses	5,500,000
	13,500,000
Less subsidy	3,000,000
Net cost	$10,500,000
Expected number of riders	14,000,000
Ticket price	75¢ each

If we charge a 75¢ fare from 19x1 to 19x10, this will generate enough cash to replace the buses in 19x11:

Per year:	Revenue: 14,000,000 × 75¢	$10,500,000
	Costs, less subsidy ($8,000,000 – $3,000,000)	5,000,000
	Net cash received	$ 5,500,000
	Times 10 years	$55,000,000

However, if we charge a 50¢ fare we will generate 25¢ (75¢ – 50¢) × 14,000,000 × 10 years or $35,000,000 *less*.

Which fare should we choose for 19x1 to 19x10? If our choice is 50¢ then we are assuming that the additional $35,000,000 would be "borrowed" from someone and that any "borrowing" cost (interest most likely, or dividends) would be charged to riders in 19x11 to 19x20. We are also assuming that riders *in 19x1 to 19x10* should benefit in late 19x1 through 19x10 from the company managers' ability to purchase buses below replacement cost.

In contrast, if we choose 75¢ fares from 19x1 to 19x10 we are favoring a continuity approach whereby the bus company is to be in business forever (or at least until 19x20 when the replacement buses wear out). That is, our capital maintenance is a physical concept — a fleet of buses capable of handling 14,000,000 passengers per year. We are also assuming that the current user ought to pay for what is used up year-by-year on a replacement cost basis, and that the date of purchase of an asset and its original cost are not relevant in such a decision on fares.

The points noted are only a few of those which might be considered. Which fare would you pick: 75¢ or 50¢ for 19x1 to 19x10? Why? If the company were to cease operations at the end of 19x20 what fare would you choose for the second 10-year period (19x11 – 19x20)?

General Price Level Accounting

More could be said about the strengths and weaknesses of the alternatives to historic cost, but it is useful to illustrate the "how-to-do-it" first, in order to aid understanding the "why." General price level accounting has existed in books since the 1930s, and perhaps before. Variations have been practised in countries with high inflation rates, such as in South America.

The steps in restating from historic cost dollars to dollars of general purchasing power are as follows:

Step 1: Separate what are called the "monetary" from the "nonmonetary" assets and liabilities on the balance sheet. These two differ from current assets and current liabilities. An item is *monetary*, roughly speaking, when it is fixed in amount by some type of contract, although the definition of "monetary" can differ under a current value accounting system. A dollar bill is fixed by law; what it buys in purchasing power varies, but the amount — $1 — remains unchanged over time. Accounts receivable is fixed (usually); the company receives a specified number of dollars from the debtor. Accounts payable, and bonds payable are similarly fixed and consequently, monetary items; the company pays the creditors a specified amount of money, not an unchanging amount of general purchasing power.

Nonmonetary items are free to float with inflation (or deflation). Inventory which is not yet sold may rise in price with inflation. It is not important for purposes of the nonmonetary definition that the amount of price rise be the same as inflation, which is an average. Land, plant, equipment, goodwill and other long-lived assets are nonmonetary because their price is not fixed by a contract.

Some variations might occur. Rent might, at some future time if inflation persists, be indexed to the CPI. If so, rent receivable that is indexed to increase in amount to correspond to inflation rate increases becomes, by definition, a nonmonetary asset because it floats in price.

Step 2: The nonmonetary items are restated by the formula:

$$\text{Historic cost} \times \frac{\text{General price index at balance sheet date}}{\text{General price index when asset was acquired}} = \text{GPL restatement.}$$

The numerator (top) index is as of the balance sheet date simply because this is the date closest to when the financial statements are being read. (Economists would use some *past* base year if they were restating a series occurring over time.)

Step 3: The income statement accounts are similarly restated. Depreciation expense would be restated as in Step 2 because depreciation is an allocation of original cost. Selling expense, in contrast, would be restated to the year end (numerator) from the date when cash (or a monetary item) was expended.

Step 4: A gain or loss on general purchasing power is computed and credited or charged (generally) to the income statement. This gain or loss item arises because net monetary assets (which signify a loss) or net monetary liabilities (which signify a gain) are held by a company during inflation. Being fixed by contract the assets lose general purchasing power. Receivables, for instance, may be received in cash three months after a sale. If the receivable were for $1,000 and the CPI rose 5 percent during this time, a loss of $50 (measured in end-of-period dollars) would result:

$1,000 + 5% =	$1,050
Received	1,000
Loss of purchasing power	$ 50

That is, at the end of three months we require $1,050 to buy general goods which we could have bought for $1,000 three months ago. The debtor gained $50 over the three months by paying us in dollars of less purchasing power.

We see this same concept at work every day in Canada. Someone buys a house with a huge mortgage. The house asset is nonmonetary and its price tends to rise over time with inflation, sometimes more, sometimes less, depending on its location. The mortgage is a monetary liability and as the years pass the home buyer pays it off with dollars of diminished purchasing power. The home buyer gains purchasing power on the mortgage payable. The mortgage company probably breaks even on inflation, because it borrowed the money from others to lend to the home buyer. The mortgage company gains interest revenue, which exceeds interest expense, and tries to avoid being caught by inflation. (The mortgage company may gain from inflation if it, in effect, borrows for longer periods than it lends during inflation. This might occur if cash payments are due to it monthly but it repays in a lump sum to lenders at the *end* of five years.)

The restatement process can be illustrated by two examples. We will commence with a simple one. Suppose that a company opens for business on January 1, 19x1 with $100,000 cash. At midyear it buys some land costing $60,000 paying cash of $40,000 and agreeing to pay the remainder one year later. With no other transactions, the company's historic cost balance sheet at December 31, 19x1 shows:

Cash	$ 60,000
Land	60,000
	$120,000

Accounts payable	$ 20,000
Capital	100,000
	$120,000

However, during this one-year period the price index (CPI) rose as follows:

January 1, 19x1	100
Mid year, 19x1	105
December 31, 19x1	110

When we GPL restate the historic cost balance sheet to *dollars of general purchasing power* at December 31, 19x1 we obtain the following:

Cash (a monetary asset) $60,000 $\times \frac{110}{110} =$	$ 60,000
Land (a nonmonetary asset) $60,000 $\times \frac{110}{105} =$	62,857
	$122,857

Accounts payable (a monetary liability) $20,000 $\times \frac{110}{110} =$	$ 20,000
Capital (a nonmonetary equity) $100,000 $\times \frac{110}{100} =$	110,000
Deficit (figure needed to balance)	(7,143)
	$122,857

No restatement is necessary for monetary items because they already are stated in dollars of general purchasing power at December 31, 19x1 — meaning in numerator 110.

Where did the $7,143 come from? It is the net loss in general purchasing power (measured in December 31, 19x1 dollars of general purchasing power) which arose from two factors:

1. The holding of a monetary asset (in this case cash) while the general price index rose, which earned a purchasing power loss.
2. A purchasing power gain resulted from holding a monetary liability while the price index rose.

	Net Loss
Cash:	
(a) $100,000 was held from January 1 to midyear. This resulted in a loss *measured* at midyear in *dollars of general purchasing power at midyear* of:	
$\left(\$100{,}000 \times \frac{105}{100}\right) - \$100{,}000 = \underline{\underline{\$5{,}000}}$	
[Midyear − Beginning of year]	
This $5,000 is measured in numerator index of 105, whereas we want it measured in numerator 110 (year-end dollars). Hence,	
$\$5{,}000 \times \frac{110}{105} =$	$5,238
(b) $60,000 was held from midyear until year end. The loss measured in index 110 is therefore	
$\left(\$60{,}000 \times \frac{110}{105}\right) - \$60{,}000$	2,857
	8,095
Accounts payable:	
The *gain* from midyear until year end is	
$\left(\$20{,}000 \times \frac{110}{105}\right) - \$20{,}000$	952
Net loss in general purchasing power measured in index 110 dollars	$7,143

Another Example

Exhibit 16-2 provides a slightly more complex example to bring out the difficulties which arise when transactions are occurring regularly throughout the year. The object is to restate the historic cost financial statements in Exhibit 16-2 to dollars of general purchasing power at December 31, 19x4.

EXHIBIT 16-2

Bolla Limited
Balance Sheets

	December 31	
	19x4	*19x3*
Cash	$ 1,000	$ 800
Accounts receivable	4,100	3,200
Inventory	4,900	4,600
	10,000	8,600
Building and equipment	6,000	6,000
Less accumulated depreciation	1,800	1,200
	4,200	4,800
	$14,200	$13,400
Accounts payable	$ 4,650	$ 4,200
Owners' equity:		
Capital	8,000	8,000
Retained earnings	1,550	1,200
	$14,200	$13,400

Income Statement
Year ended December 31, 19x4

Revenue		$14,000
Cost of goods sold		11,050
Gross profit		2,950
Expenses:		
Selling and administration	$2,000	
Depreciation	600	2,600
Net income (income tax is ignored)		$ 350

Retained Earnings Statement
Year ended December 31, 19x4

Opening balance	$ 1,200
Add net income	350
Closing balance	$ 1,550

Additional Information:

(1) Consumer Price Index (CPI):

January 1, 19x1 (when business commenced)	150
January 1, 19x2 (when $6,000 of building and equipment acquired)	160
When $4,600 of inventory on hand at January 1, 19x4 was acquired	175
When $11,350 of inventory was acquired; $4,900 of which is on hand at December 31, 19x4	185
January 1, 19x4	180
December 31, 19x4	200

(2) The selling and administrative expenses were paid in cash over the year, when the CPI averaged 190. Similarly, revenue arose evenly during the year and the CPI on average was 190.

(3) Inventory acquisitions (reflected in accounts payable) were paid as follows:

(a) $4,200, payable at December 31, 19x3 was paid when the CPI stood at	185
(b) The $6,450 that was paid from the $11,350 purchase occurred when the CPI was	190

Restatement Process: The simplest starting point is with the *closing* balance sheet. The object of the exercise is to restate the comparative balance sheets and the income statements to CPI 200 (dollars of general purchasing power at December 31, 19x4).

		CPI Index 200
Cash	$1,000 × $\frac{200}{200}$	$ 1,000
Accounts receivable	$4,100 × $\frac{200}{200}$	4,100
Inventory (nonmonetary)	$4,900 × $\frac{200}{185}$	5,297
Building (nonmonetary)	$6,000 × $\frac{200}{160}$	7,500
Accumulated depreciation (nonmonetary)	$1,800 × $\frac{200}{160}$	(2,250)
		$15,647
Accounts payable	$4,650 × $\frac{200}{200}$	$ 4,650
Capital (nonmonetary)	$8,000 × $\frac{200}{150}$	10,667
Retained earnings (balancing figure)		330
		$15,647

Next, we restate the opening balance sheet. This can be done in two steps or through a one-step shortcut. We will handle this the longer way, which involves:

1. Restating the balance sheet to dollars of general purchasing power as of the beginning of the period (Index 180).
2. Moving the restated balance sheet from index 180 to index 200.

First, the restatement to index 180:

Cash	$\$800 \times \frac{180}{180}$	\$ 800
Receivables	$\$3{,}200 \times \frac{180}{180}$	3,200
Inventory (nonmonetary)	$\$4{,}600 \times \frac{180}{175}$	4,731
Building and equipment (nonmonetary)	$\$6{,}000 \times \frac{180}{160}$	6,750
Accumulated depreciation (nonmonetary)	$\$1{,}200 \times \frac{180}{160}$	(1,350)
		\$14,131
Accounts payable	$\$4{,}200 \times \frac{180}{180}$	4,200
Capital	$\$8{,}000 \times \frac{180}{150}$	9,600
Retained earnings (balancing figure)		331
		\$14,131

Second, the entire balance sheet is rolled forward to index 200:

		CPI Index 200
Cash	$\$\ 800 \times \frac{200}{180}$	\$ 889
Receivables	$3{,}200 \times \frac{200}{180}$	3,556
Inventory	$4{,}731 \times \frac{200}{180}$	5,257
Building and equipment	$6{,}750 \times \frac{200}{180}$	7,500
Accumulated depreciation	$(1{,}350) \times \frac{200}{180}$	(1,500)
		\$15,702

Accounts payable	$\$4,200 \times \frac{200}{180}$	$ 4,667
Capital	$9,600 \times \frac{200}{180}$	10,667
Retained earnings	$331 \times \frac{200}{180}$	368
		$15,702

Restatement of the income statement is trickier. No dividends were declared; hence, the restated net income (in index 200) has to be:

Opening retained earnings	$368
Closing retained earnings	330
Loss for the period	$ 38

The difficult parts are:
1. Computation of cost of goods sold.
2. Computation of the loss in general purchasing power.

			CPI Index 200
Revenue	$\$14,000 \times \frac{200}{190}$		$14,737
Cost of goods sold: Opening inventory	$4,600 \times \frac{200}{175}$	$ 5,257	
Purchases	$11,350 \times \frac{200}{185}$	12,270	
		17,527	
Closing inventory	$(4,900) \times \frac{200}{185}$	(5,297)	12,230
	11,050		
Gross profit			2,507
Expenses: Selling and administration	$\$2,000 \times \frac{200}{190}$		2,105
Depreciation	$600 \times \frac{200}{160}$		750
			2,855
Net loss before gain of general purchasing power			348
Gain of general purchasing power			310
Net loss (income taxes are ignored)			$ 38

The gain of general purchasing power during 19x4, measured in dollars of general purchasing power as of December 31, 19x4, is computed as follows:

Monetary assets — monetary liabilities during 19x4 (at historic cost):

	Index	+	−	*Net Asset (liability)*
Opening balance (cash + receivables − payables)	180			$ (200)
Payables paid (no net effect)	185	$ 4,200	$ 4,200	(200)
Inventory acquired (credit to payables)	185		11,350	(11,550)
Revenue less selling and administration	190	14,000	2,000	450
Payment of payables (no net effect)	190	6,450	6,450	450
End of period	200			450

Components of the overall gain are:

(a) $200 of net liabilities held while the index rose from 180 to 185:

$$\left(\$200 \times \frac{185}{180}\right) - \$200 = \qquad \$\ 6.$$

(b) $11,550 of net liabilities held while the index rose from 185 to 190:

$$\left(\$11{,}550 \times \frac{190}{185}\right) - \$11{,}550 = \qquad \$312.$$

(c) $450 of net assets held while the index rose from 190 to 200:

$$\left(\$450 \times \frac{200}{190}\right) - \$450 = \qquad \$(24).$$

Restating them to index 200 (dollars of general purchasing power as of December 31, 19x4):

	Gain in Index 200
(a) $\left(\$6 \times \frac{200}{185}\right)$	$ 6
(b) $\left(\$312 \times \frac{200}{190}\right)$	328
(c)	(24)
Overall gain for the period	$310

Note that we have computed the gain or loss whenever there is a change in the index number. In practice this computation may occur monthly or quarterly.

Reconstruction of the net monetary asset account in historic dollars is similar to a working capital SCFP computation. Some items, such as collecting receivables or paying payables, do not affect the total position.

GPL Interpreted

If the GPL financial statements are accompanied by the usual footnotes (similar to those for Labatt's in Chapter 2), what do the GPL financial statements tell users? How much is repetition of historic cost financial statements? How much is new information?

As with historic cost, there is a danger that "unlike" companies could be made to look "alike." For example, two companies might have bought $1,000,000 worth of land in 1930. Today one piece may have a net realizable value of $100,000,000 (in the center of a large city) but the other may have a net realizable value of $40,000,000. A general price level restatement, however, may show $32,000,000 for both parcels of land. The balance sheet figures derived under GPL usually do not represent a current buying or selling market price; yet, people may not interpret them that way.

The GPL income statement shows a new piece of information — gain or loss of general purchasing power, although some accountants do not agree with showing the entire gain or loss on the income statement. By itself the sum does not mean much; however, it might be compared to other effects. For example, a bank might incur a general purchasing power loss of $10,000,000; yet, it may have an interest revenue increase of well over $10,000,000. In brief the bank raised interest rates on its loans receivable (a monetary item) to compensate for purchasing power losses due to inflation.

Purchasing power gains can be increased by having huge amounts of debt outstanding. However, huge amounts of debt can be risky and in poor years for a company may hasten bankruptcy. A balance between profitability and liquidity has to be struck.

Given the above somewhat inconclusive merits to GPL why do people advocate it? Some possible (yet questionable) reasons are:

1. It is not difficult to apply, and makes few alterations in the historic cost system. As such it is easier to audit than, say, a current buying or selling market value system.
2. For some companies (not having huge amounts of monetary debt) income is lowered by GPL restatements. Perhaps, managers of these com-

panies reason, if many companies report on a GPL basis, the governments may at some future date use GPL as a basis for assessing income taxes. Although the total tax revenue required by government may not change, some companies may pay less (and others would have to pay more, or individuals would have to pay more).

Some other reasons were noted earlier.

The main merits of the GPL concept may lie in comparing its balances with other figures. For instance, we may have invested in land costing \$100,000. The land may have a GPL restatement of \$180,000 and a net realizable value of \$205,000. The comparison of the \$205,000 with the \$180,000 tells us that by investing in land we did \$25,000 (\$205,000 – \$180,000) better than general inflation. We could sell the land and buy more general goods than we could have bought with the \$100,000 investment (or postponed consumption).

Another possibility is to GPL restate current value figures of previous years to make them somewhat comparative. This topic is covered in advanced courses.

Current Value

The term "current value," like "market value," lacks precision. Current value is a broad term which might mean any one of the following:

Buying market price:
- Reproduction cost (cost today of an identical item)
- Replacement cost
- Perhaps, discounted future cash costs

Selling market price:
- Net realizable value
- Discounted future cash receipts

These terms tend to apply to the valuation or pricing of assets and liabilities. When equity is to be measured (or capital maintained) on a "current value" basis, it is usually called physical or operating capacity.

From time to time we have stressed the need for two or more pieces of information in order to form judgments. Someone, such as a potential creditor, who is interested in management evaluation may desire to separate and assess management's behavior into at least two functions: *buying* or purchasing goods, and *selling* goods. How is this separation accomplished in the following situation?

January 1: Commenced business with \$3,000,000.
January 2: Bought 10,000 tons of raw sugar at \$300 per ton.

May 1:	Processed the 10,000 tons of raw sugar; replacement cost is now $400 per ton.
June 30:	(Year end of company) Sold the 10,000 tons of processed sugar for $500 per ton. Processing costs are $60 per ton. Replacement cost is still $400 per ton.

An income statement prepared under the traditional historic cost basis would show:

Revenue:		
10,000 tons @ $500 per ton		$5,000,000
Cost of goods sold:		
Purchased sugar:		
10,000 tons @ $300 per ton	$3,000,000	
Processing cost	600,000	3,600,000
Gross profit		$1,400,000

Has management performed well? We may compare the $1,400,000 to last year's figure of, say, $400,000 and assume that management's "ability" is improving. But is it? Maybe during last year raw sugar prices were constant. As we saw in Chapter 8 the use of historic cost for the pricing of assets has limitations if the objective of accounting is to permit assessment of the performance of current management by investors.

If we charge cost of goods sold at replacement cost of $400 per ton, cost of goods sold becomes $4,600,000 ($400 times 10,000 tons, plus $600,000) and gross profit would be $400,000 — the same as last year. This means that from a *selling* (as opposed to buying) viewpoint management's behavior is constant. (Observe that the two figures which we used for our comparison were net realizable value revenue, and replacement cost of goods sold.)

But, from a *buying* standpoint the company *may* by better off by $1,000,000 ($400 less $300 per ton, times 10,000 tons) due to buying practices. Why do we say *may*? In order to respond we must turn to considering our "capital maintenance" concept. If capital is defined as original money capital, the $1,000,000 would appear in income. Income equals revenue less historic cost of goods sold under the money capital maintenance concept. If management were simply lucky by buying when they did, the appearance of the $1,000,000 on the income statement makes them look better than they probably are. If the buying at $300 per ton was the result of careful planning, then the appearance of $1,000,000 in income seems justified — *from an evaluation of management point of view.* But from a *prediction* point of view, misleading results might occur unless the $1,000,000 is reported on a separate line. Then, those interested in prediction could exclude the $1,000,000 from their thinking if it is not thought to be a recurring item.

Suppose, instead, that prices of raw sugar are expected to rise for some years, and that the company needs a basic tonnage of raw sugar, somewhere around the 10,000 ton level, in order to ensure its continuity. Under such circumstances a physical-capacity capital maintenance concept and a replacement-cost asset price basis could provide useful information. Income would be $400,000 because replacement cost of goods sold would be $4,000,000 (not $3,000,000), excluding processing costs. That is, the write-up of inventory to replacement cost would occur with this journal entry:

Inventory	$1,000,000	
Capital maintenance increment		$1,000,000
To write up 10,000 tons of inventory from $300 to $400 per ton.		

(Unless the company's journals and ledgers were maintained on a replacement cost/physical capacity basis, the entry would be made on work sheets — as was the case with consolidation and equity reporting.)

A company applying the replacement cost (asset valuation) and physical capacity (capital maintenance) combination would show the following (partial) financial statements:

Income Statement:		
Revenue		$5,000,000
Cost of goods sold:		
Materials purchased and used	$4,000,000	
Processing expenses	600,000	4,600,000
Gross profit		$ 400,000
Balance Sheet:		
Cash ($5,000,000 less $600,000)		$4,400,000
Owners' equity:		
Original capital		$3,000,000
Capital maintenance increment		1,000,000
Retained earnings (assuming no other expenses or income tax exist)		400,000
		$4,400,000

If detailed changes in the "capital maintenance increment" account are reported from year to year this could assist those who wish to predict and maybe those who wish to evaluate management. We state "maybe" because readers must be able to sort good luck from good management if they want to form a sound assessment. Such a sorting may be very difficult or impossible. (Observe that the capital maintenance increment and inventory write-up represent the difference between the two figures, historic cost and replacement cost.) In a more sophisticated system the difference could be between replacement cost and possibly general price-level restated historic cost.

Human behavior

By changing the asset valuation basis and capital maintenance concept away from historic cost not only do we alter income from year to year and over the life of the company, but *we might easily change people's behavior.* People can be amazingly flexible, and might adjust to new rules when they know that their performance is being evaluated on a new, different basis. However, they may first have to be educated to understand how to process the new information in their minds and convert it into actions.

Suppose that salesmen are paid a commission which is a percentage of gross profit (revenue less historic cost of goods sold). Suppose further that the company involved buys steel in bulk from the various Canadian steel mills and distributes it in small quantities to a variety of construction companies. When the economy is booming, the steel mills may not have adequate production volumes to satisfy demand and prices of steel could rise. The opposite can occur during an economic slowdown.

If the salesmen receive a commission based on historic cost gross profit they could cause problems for the company. When steel prices are rising historic cost will lag replacement cost. Hence, the following could occur:

	Historic Cost Asset Pricing	*Replacement Cost Asset Pricing*
Revenue	$25,000	$25,000
Cost of goods sold	21,000	24,500
Gross profit	4,000	500
Income tax @ 55% (The income tax legislation taxes on *historic* profit but permits an inventory allowance which we will ignore)	2,200	2,200
Income (ignoring selling expense)	$ 1,800	Loss $(1,700)

In the mid 1970s in Canada this was not an uncommon situation — to be selling at a loss based on replacement cost. Once we deduct the salesman's commission, the loss based on replacement cost of goods sold would be even higher than the $1,700. In summary, the commission system *motivated* salesmen to cause losses.

When steel prices are declining in general, historic cost (unless written down to replacement cost — something which is not likely to occur daily or weekly in practice in a historic cost financial accounting system) likely exceeds replacement cost. How does this affect sales personnel? Unless they have permission to sell at a loss based on historic cost, and are rewarded by other than commissions based on historic cost, sales may cease. More likely, though, sales will cease on those items with huge drops in replacement cost because salesmen will exert more effort towards selling items which provide them with a commission — products where replacement and historic cost are similar.

How might the behavior of people be changed? A *management* accounting system might be set up to separate the purchasing and selling functions of a business. When the system is operational for management purposes it could be extended to external or financial accounting. In theory using the foregoing wholesaling illustration, salesmen would receive a commission based on replacement cost gross profit. Buyers of commodities such as steel would be judged primarily on their performance in ordering the required quantity at the desired price. Thus, if a government removed a manufacturing tax and the replacement cost fell, salesmen would *not* be required to sell at the historic cost including tax. Any differences between historic cost and replacement cost would be charged or credited to whoever requested the commodity.

In practice, facts may differ. In this book we have occasionally mentioned the discounted present value concept of valuation. Yet we know that we give this concept little attention when we make most of our major personal purchases. In business we have to give the concept more attention than for our personal purchases; but how much more? A replacement cost system has similar soft spots. If, when replacement costs are rising, a competitor continues to base selling prices on historic cost, we are not going to sell much if our selling prices are considerably higher. We may have to strike a balance between holding onto inventory and selling it at less than we would like to obtain.

What do we do in practice? We might want to pay salesmen on some combination of gross profit based on historic cost plus gross profit based on replacement cost. Somehow we must use the accounting system to *motivate* people in the ways felt necessary to achieve corporate and personal success.

Ethics

From time to time we have touched upon but not adequately dealt with a troublesome consideration — ethics. Do accounting reports and financial statements *manipulate people*? If so, should they?

Accounting information is not neutral; it is full of judgments. These judgments are made by preparers who bring their life-long experiences, knowledge, biases, and even prejudices to their judgments. The task of an auditor is to surface these biases and try to neutralize or disclose them; but how successful auditors are in this duty is unknown. Evidence of negotiations between client and auditor is not publicly available and is hard, if not impossible, to gather.

A change from historic cost to a current value system will not alter the potential for manipulation, which can be defined as causing people to behave in a way desired by the preparer. One of the prime reasons for choosing another measurement system is to provide a different point of view. However, some less informed people will worry about multiple measures. "Which is the correct number?" Others will appreciate the different views being presented and be able to sort out the measurement biases a little better. The more information reported (a costly choice) the harder it can become to manipulate people.

Successful analysts are those who can understand, albeit only broadly, the personality of the preparer. Some preparers are cautious; others overly optimistic. Some may manipulate intentionally, others unintentionally. Analysts must keep their eyes and ears open.

Replacement Cost Example

A two-year example may help to pull together some of the *net asset value* (basis of pricing assets and liabilities) and *capital maintenance* (basis of pricing long-term equity) concepts mentioned in the book. We intend to use historic cost or replacement cost for net asset values. Capital maintenance will be either historic money capital or physical capacity. In practice, companies might use more than one basis of net asset valuation in supplementary reports provided to shareholders.

Suppose that a company engages in the following transactions:

1. The business commences January 1, 19x1 with $3,000 of cash and capital.
2. Next day 30 tons of inventory are bought for $100 per ton.
3. No other transactions occur until December 31, 19x1, at which time the replacement cost of inventory is $115 per ton.
4. On December 31, 19x1 (the year end of the company) 20 tons are sold for $140 per ton.
5. On January 2, 19x2, 25 tons are bought for $115 per ton.
6. No other transactions occur until December 30, 19x2, at which time the replacement cost of inventory is $90 per ton.
7. On December 31, 19x2, 25 tons are sold for $102 per ton.

We will show the results on *four* different bases:

Net Asset Valuation	*Capital Maintenance*
1. Historic cost (HC)	Money Historic Capital (MHC)
2. Replacement cost (RC)	Money Historic Capital (MHC)
3. Replacement cost (RC)	Physical capacity — method 1 (PC 1)
4. Replacement cost (RC)	Physical capacity — method 2 (PC 2)

Other bases could be used, such as general price-level restated owners' equity (capital maintenance).

Exhibits 16-3 and 16-4 provide a response. We have split the computations into 19x1 and 19x2 for reasons which become obvious later. Income taxes and other expenses are ignored in the illustration.

EXHIBIT 16-3 *19x1:*

	(1)	(2)	(3)	(4)
Net asset valuation	HC	RC	RC	RC
Capital maintenance	*MHC*	*MHC*	*PC 1*	*PC 2*
Income Statements:				
Revenue	$2,800	$2,800	$2,800	$2,800
Cost of goods sold	2,000	2,300	2,300	2,300
	800	500	500	500
Gross profit				
Holding gain: 30 tons @ $15 ($115–$100)		450		
Income	$ 800	$ 950	$ 500	$ 500
Balance Sheets:				
Cash	$2,800	$2,800	$2,800	$2,800
Inventory	1,000	1,150	1,150	1,150
	$3,800	$3,950	$3,950	$3,950
Original capital	$3,000	$3,000	$3,000	$3,000
Capital maintenance increment	—	—	450	450
Retained earnings	800	950	500	500
	$3,800	$3,950	$3,950	$3,950

Exhibit 16-3 requires some explanation. A holding gain arises in (2) for the entire *30* tons because this tonnage was held all year. The holding gain in (2) is replacement cost less historic cost money capital. Some people may split the $450 into two parts: (a) $300 representing the 20 tons which were sold @ $15 (sometimes called "realized" holding gain); and (b) $150 representing the unsold tonnage (sometimes called "unrealized holding gain"). Columns (3) and (4) credit the "holding" effect to capital maintenance increment. Both show $3,450 of equity ($3,000 plus $450) — which represents 30 tons of inventory @ $115 per ton.

Exhibit 16-4 portrays 19x2. In 19x2 replacement prices drop, and holding losses, or capital maintenance debits, occur. A distinction can be drawn between Column PC 1 and PC 2. PC 1's definition of physical capital is tied to 30 tons of steel. That is, management believes that in order to stay in business for a long time, capital must be maintained at 30 tons times current replacement cost. PC 2's definition of physical capital "floats" and represents the tonnage quantity on hand at any time. (In 19x1 thirty tons are on hand for most of the year, whereas in most of 19x2 thirty-five tons are on hand). PC 2 is more practical for businesses which are continually expanding and contracting.

EXHIBIT 16-4 *19x2:*

	(1)	(2)	(3)	(4)
Net asset valuation	HC	RC	RC	RC
Capital maintenance	MHC	MHC	PC 1	PC 2
Income Statements:				
Revenue	$2,550	$2,550	$2,550	$2,550
Cost of goods sold(FIFO)	2,725	2,250	2,250	2,250
Gross profit (loss)	(175)	300	300	300
Holding loss on 35 tons		(875)		
Write-down of closing inventory to replacement cost	(250)			
Loss on 5 tons in excess of 30			(125)	
Income (loss)	$ (425)	$ (575)	$ 175	$ 300
Balance Sheets:				
Cash	$2,475	$2,475	$2,475	$2,475
Inventory	900	900	900	900
	$3,375	$3,375	$3,375	$3,375
Capital—original	$3,000	$3,000	$3,000	$3,000
Capital maintenance (debit) increment	—	—	(300)	(425)
Retained earnings	375	375	675	800
	$3,375	$3,375	$3,375	$3,375

Exhibit 16-4 requires more than one reading to grasp fully. A good starting point is the balance sheet. The cash figure represents sales in years 19x1 and 19x2 less purchases of 25 tons @ $115 per ton. In all four cases the inventory has to be written down to replacement cost. (Basis (1), we will assume, employs lower of FIFO cost or replacement cost.) The capital maintenance debit in (3) is the sum required to represent, together with original capital, 30 tons at the current replacement cost of $90 per ton ($2,700). Column (4) is a little trickier because under the floating capital maintenance system 35 tons existed in the year 19x2. Hence, 35 tons @ $25 ($115 less $90) is debited to capital maintenance. This lowers the $450 credit at the end of 19x1 to a net debit of $425 at the end of 19x2.

Turning to the income statement of Exhibit 16-4 we can observe that the inventory write-down in Column (1) is shown below the gross profit line; it could be part of cost of goods sold. The $875 holding loss in Column (2) could be split into realized and unrealized portions. In Column (3), which we have defined as a company with a physical-capacity capital maintenance of 30 tons, a write-down *to income* is needed because we held 35 tons — 5 over normal — during a period when replacement cost dropped $25 per ton. In column (4) price changes go through the capital maintenance account.

Results Interpreted

Who could fruitfully use financial statements based on columns (2), (3), or (4)? In a major sense, much of Column (2) is already in use in Canada by open-end mutual fund companies. Such companies hold shares of other companies as their principal assets. Corporate law (constraints) requires that capital be based or maintained on a form of historic money capital. Yet, the common shares of these funds are bought and sold on the basis of a current value (often plus a salesmen's commission on the purchase side). Shareholders are interested in seeing the net assets valued at a current value; not at original cost. The actual (in practice) income statements of open-end mutual funds differ from those in Exhibits 16-3 and 16-4 in that separation of holding gains between items which are sold and unsold is provided.

Column (3) can aid evaluation of management by outsiders. If management bought an extra 5 tons above its normal of 30 — presumably in the hope of making additional profits — the effects of this decision are income or loss items (not capital). In contrast, column (4) obscures the effect of the purchase of additional tonnage.

None of the four columns by itself gives a complete picture of several of the possible objectives or purposes of financial accounting. Someone interested in prediction would like to know both cash receipts (net realizable value) and cash payments (replacement cost) for all assets for many years into the future. This requires not only multiple measures, but forecasting. On the other hand owners of a small business with rapid turnover of assets might be well served by historic cost accounting.

Summary

Two types of alternatives to the historic cost measurement system — general price level restatements (GPL), and current value accounting (CVA) — have been introduced and explained briefly in this chapter. In some circumstances, where individual commodity prices are changing rapidly, or a general inflationary trend is occurring, these "alternatives" might provide an additional helpful perspective. GPL could apply for the latter (inflation) and CVA for the former. Viewing disclosure in cost-benefit terms, we have to observe that these additional measures likely would be reported only when they provide otherwise unavailable information, or help accomplish an objective which is not well-served under present accounting. (Some people may hope that extensive use of GPL may serve as a lobby to the Federal Government and encourage more recognition of inflationary effects in the income tax system.)

GPL restatements of historic cost are an accounting response to general inflationary trends only, and make no attempt to reflect individual changes in asset and liability prices. Many people question whether they provide any information which cannot be approximated from historic cost financial statements. The income statement based on GPL may show a gain or loss on general purchasing power which arises from holding net monetary liabilities or assets. This may be useful information for analysts of banks and other companies with huge monetary balances. But it must be used with care. By its nature of using one general price-index for restatements, GPL might make unlike situations look alike to a partially informed reader.

CVA financial statements can take many forms and are dependent upon which bases are chosen for net asset valuation and capital maintenance. When used in management accounting systems, the CVA alternatives can help motivate managers in ways which differ from the effects of historic cost. Replacement cost net asset values, for instance, may help separate purchasing from selling functions of a (wholesaling or manufacturing) business that buys well in advance of selling its inventory. This separation may assist those who wish to assess judgments by senior management. Two or more current value figures may aid in prediction. Return on current investment requires both net asset and capital maintenance measures and different combinations might aid investors in judging the relative profitability of businesses.

CVA has drawbacks, which have been mentioned from place to place in the book. CVA requires greater estimation than, say, historic cost accounting. At the present time in Canada, the concepts are not well understood by a large group of preparers and users. For those who believe in one of the efficient market hypotheses, CVA might not be adding information which is not already known to investors. Many investors (see Chapter 15) have sources outside of financial statements, such as direct interviews with corporate management.

The theme which might be drawn from this chapter is that each of the different measures has its place. Our role as preparers or users is to apply and interpret the measurement system where it makes sense, and not nonsense. Historic cost figures clearly have limitations when the purchasing power of the dollar (inflation) is dropping and prices of individual commodities are fluctuating. No single alternative will meet the approval of all preparers or users.

Notes

[1]The accounting profession in Canada has produced some material for public review starting with a CICA study in 1972: L.S. Rosen, *Current Value Accounting and Price Level Restatements* (Toronto: CICA), some guidance on general price level accounting in 1974, and position papers on current value accounting in 1976 and 1979. See also two important publications of The Society of Management Accountants of Canada: J.R. Hanna, *Accounting Income Models: An Application and Evaluation* (Hamilton, 1974); and S. Basu and J.R. Hanna, *Inflation Accounting: Alternatives, Implementation Issues and Some Empirical Evidence* (Hamilton, 1975).

Questions, Problems, and Cases

Questions

16-1 Distinguish between general price level restatements of historic cost and current value accounting.

16-2 Increases in the prices of goods and services can be attributable to at least two fundamental economic forces. What are these forces? With which of the two do price level adjustments attempt to deal?

16-3 Price level adjustments in no way undermine the historical, transaction-based underpinning of financial accounting. Price level adjusted statements must be distinguished from those in which assets are recorded at current market values in that the former are firmly rooted in historical costs, while the latter are not. Do you agree? Explain.

16-4 Canadian companies should logically oppose price level adjustments because in a period of inflation they result in lower reported earnings. Does such a statement make any sense? Do price level adjustments necessarily reduce reported earnings? Explain.

16-5 What is the difference between monetary and nonmonetary items? Why is it generally unnecessary to convert monetary items into current dollars?

16-6 What are purchasing power gains or losses? How are they computed?

16-7 What are the major determinants of the difference between price level adjusted earnings and conventional earnings?

16-8 "A general price level adjustment to historic cost accounting is like prescribing an aspirin to relieve pain — it treats the symptom, not the cause." Do you agree? Why?

16-9 The term "current value," like "market value," lacks precision. Identify specific measures of "current value." Explain how each of these measures when used as a basis for valuing assets and liabilities might assist the readers of financial statements.

*16-10 What is meant by the "capital maintenance" concept? How does it affect the determination of income? Identify alternative measures of capital maintenance. Explain when each of these measures might "make sense."

16-11 "By changing the asset valuation base and capital maintenance concept away from historic cost we might easily change people's behavior." Explain.

16-12 In order to make judgments, two or more pieces of information are required. Give examples of how the measurement of assets and liabilities on more than one basis (i.e., replacement cost, net realizable value, discounted cash flow and so forth) might improve the judgments of the readers of financial statements.

16-13 "In the search for practical answers to the problem of how financial reporting should be changed as a result of an inflationary environment, it is important to ask the right questions. If, for example, one asks only how financial statements can be adjusted to reflect a change in the purchasing power of money, one can obtain a solution that ignores many facets of the problem of the impact of inflation on business." Do you agree? Explain your position logically.

16-14 A noted political columnist has referred to accountants as being "intellectually stunted" seemingly because he feels that the objectives of accounting, as seen by accountants, are too narrow. What do you see as being "reasonable" objectives or purposes of financial accounting? Explain your beliefs thoroughly.

16-15 "One of the main criticisms of the user orientation in accounting (i.e., trying to ascertain what users want and need) is that users do not know for sure what they need and want, and their needs vary over time. Accounting should be concerned instead with measuring facts that everyone can agree on, and where there is little uncertainty of measurement." Comment in specific terms on this quotation.

Problems

P16-1 Indicate whether each of the following items should be considered a monetary (M) or a nonmonetary (N) item:

1. Cash on hand.
2. Cash in bank.
3. Marketable securities (e.g., shares)
4. Accounts and notes receivable.
5. Inventories.
6. Refundable deposits.
7. Property, plant and equipment.
8. Accumulated depreciation.
9. Goodwill.
10. Patents, trademarks, licenses.
11. Accounts and notes payable.
12. Dividends payable.
13. Bonds payable.
14. Common shares.
15. Retained earnings.

P16-2 In 19x2, a certain grade of lumber sold for $115 per 1,000 board feet. In 19x7, the same grade of lumber sold for $165 per 1,000 board feet. In 19x2 the Consumer Price Index was at 135; in 19x7 it was 188. By how much did the price of lumber actually increase, after taking into account the decline in the overall value of the dollar? Express your answer in terms of 19x7 dollars.

P16-3 The only assets of Equipment Rental Co. Ltd. are equipment that is on lease to outsiders. As of January 1, 19x1, the terms of existing lease contracts provide for payments to the company of $10,000 at the end of each of the next five years.

On December 31, 19x1, and on December 31, 19x2, the company received $10,000 in rentals. It immediately distributed the same amount to shareholders in the form of both a dividend and a return of their invested capital. Moreover, on December 31, 19x2, the firm was able to renegotiate the terms of outstanding leases so as to increase rentals for the remaining three years to $12,000 per year.

Required:

a. Determine the value of the enterprise as of January 1, 19x1, 19x2 and 19x3. Value is to be defined as the present value of anticipated cash receipts discounted at a rate of 8 percent.
b. Determine income for 19x1 and 19x2. Income is to be defined as the amount of cash distributed to shareholders less the change in the value of the enterprise.
c. What are the problems with using a discounted cash flow basis of valuing assets (e.g., equipment) of a manufacturing company?

P16-4 As of December 31, 19x8, a company reported a balance in its truck account of $106,000 and a balance of $62,800 in the related accumulated depreciation account. Supporting documentation reveals the following:

Year	*Number of trucks acquired*	*Cost per truck*	*Balance in truck account*	*Balance in accumulated depreciation account*
19x5	3	$12,000	$ 36,000	$ 28,800
19x6	2	15,000	30,000	18,000
19x7	2	20,000	40,000	16,000
19x8	0	—	—	—
			$106,000	$ 62,800

Depreciation is recorded on a straight-line basis. The useful life of a truck is assumed to be five years; salvage value is considered to be zero.

For the years 19x5 to 19x8, the Consumer Price Index was at the following levels:

19x5	148
19x6	159
19x7	178
19x8	188

Required:

a. Determine depreciation charges for 19x8 on both a conventional and a general price level restated basis.

b. Suppose that on December 31, 19x8, after 19x8 depreciation has been recorded, one of the trucks acquired in 19x5 was sold for $3,000. Determine the gain or loss to be recognized under both conventional and a general price level restated basis of accounting. (State your assumptions.)

P16-5 The balance sheet of the Byrd Flying Service Co. Ltd. as of December 31, 19x6, appears as follows:

Byrd Flying Service Co. Ltd.
Balance Sheet as of December 31, 19x6

Assets

Cash		$ 5,000
Accounts receivable		6,000
Inventories		9,000
Planes and equipment	$320,000	
Less: Accumulated depreciation	80,000	240,000
Total assets		$260,000

Liabilities and Shareholders' Equity

Accounts payable	$ 7,000
Wages payable	2,000
Tickets sold for trips not yet taken	1,000
Notes payable	150,000
Common shares	40,000
Retained earnings	60,000
Total liabilities and shareholders' equity	$260,000

The inventory was acquired throughout 19x6. The average Consumer Price Index for 19x6 was 170.

The planes and equipment were acquired in 19x2 at a time when the Consumer Price Index was at 135.

Accounts receivable, accounts payable, wages payable, and tickets sold for trips not yet taken arose from transactions that took place during the third and fourth quarters of 19x6. The average Consumer Price Index for those quarters was 175.

The notes payable were issued in connection with the purchase of the planes and equipment in 19x2. (Consumer Price Index, 135.)

The common shares were sold in 19x1 when the Consumer Price Index was at 128.

The Consumer Price Index as of December 31, 19x6 was at 178.

Required:

Prepare a general price level restated balance sheet expressed in terms of year end 19x6 dollars.

P16-6 Two companies, firm A and firm B, are in different industries. Both, however, are of the same size and do the same volume of business. The 19x5 income statements and balance sheets for the two firms are presented below:

Income Statements
For the Year Ending December 31, 19x5

	Firm A	*Firm B*
Sales	$1,000,000	$1,000,000
Cost of goods sold (excluding depreciation)	700,000	850,000
Depreciation	200,000	50,000
	900,000	900,000
Net income	$ 100,000	$ 100,000

Balance Sheets as of December 31, 19x5

	Firm A	*Firm B*
Inventory	$ 200,000	$ 800,000
Fixed assets	800,000	200,000
Total assets	$1,000,000	$1,000,000
Owners' equity	$1,000,000	$1,000,000

The fixed assets of both firms were acquired in 19x1 at a time when the Consumer Price Index was at 144.

Ending inventory was acquired in the fourth quarter of 19x5 at a time when the Consumer Price Index was at 178.

Sales and all merchandise may be assumed to have been made and purchased evenly throughout 19x5. The average for 19x5 was 170.

Required:

a. Prepare general price level restated income statements for each of the two companies.

b. Comment on the reason for the differences in general price level restated earnings.

P16-7 As of the beginning of 19x7 an investor had $200,000 in cash. On the first day of the year he placed $100,000 in a savings bank and purchased, for $50 per share, 2,000 common shares (a nonmonetary asset) of a well-known company.

In the course of the year, the investor earned interest of $6,000 on the money placed in the savings account. He earned dividends of $3,000 on the common shares which he held. At year end, he sold the 2,000 common shares at a price of $52 per share.

The Consumer Price Index at the start of 19x7 was at a level of 159. On average during the year it was at 170, and at year end it was at 178.

Required:

a. Determine income for the year on a conventional historic cost basis.
b. Determine the gain or loss in purchasing power for the year.
c. Determine the gain or loss, on a price level adjusted basis, on the sale of the common shares.
d. Determine price level adjusted earnings for the year, including the gains or losses in purchasing power on the sale of common shares.
e. Reconcile, on a price level adjusted basis, the equity of the investor at the start of the year with that at the end.

P16-8 Presented below are the 19x7 comparative balance sheet and income statement for Crunch Limited.

Balance Sheet
As of December 31

	19x7	*19x6*
Cash	$ 225,000	$ 152,000
Receivables	300,000	250,000
Inventory	535,000	518,000
Plant — Net	860,000	900,000
	$1,920,000	$1,820,000
Accounts payable	$ 143,200	$ 220,000
Bonds	860,000	800,000
Common shares	400,000	400,000
Retained earnings	516,800	400,000
	$1,920,000	$1,820,000

Income Statement
Year Ended December 31, 19x7

Sales		$1,400,000
Cost of goods sold	$ 900,000	
Depreciation	140,000	
Interest	60,000	
Other expenses	30,000	1,130,000
Income from operations		270,000
Taxes		135,000
Net income		$ 135,000

Additional Information:

1. Dividends paid during 19x7 were $18,200. The dividends were paid during the third quarter of 19x7.
2. Purchases during 19x7 were $917,000.
3. On January 1, 19x7, Crunch acquired a fixed asset for $40,000 cash and $60,000 of bonds. The asset is to be depreciated over five years on

a straight-line basis with a full year's depreciation to be recorded in 19x7.

4. The Consumer Price Index was as follows:
   100 at date of issue of common shares
   110 at date of issue of bonds outstanding at December 31, 19x6 and acquisition of fixed assets
   190 when the 19x6 year end inventory was acquired
   200 at January 1, 19x7
   210 average for 19x7
   217.5 when the 19x7 year end inventory was acquired; and
   220 at December 31, 19x7.

Required:

a. Prepare a general price level restated historic cost comparative balance sheet at December 31, 19x7 and a statement of income and retained earnings for 19x7.

b. How might the price level restated historic cost income statement be used to persuade the government that they are over-taxing companies?

P16-9 The following data relate to Progress Co. Ltd.:

	Balance Sheet December 31	
	19x6	*19x7*
Monetary assets	$ 5,000	$ 2,000
Inventory	4,000	8,000
Plant and equipment	20,000	30,000
Accumulated depreciation	(9,000)	(12,000)
	$20,000	$28,000
Current liabilities	$ 2,000	$ 6,000
Long-term debt	7,000	7,000
Common shares	9,000	9,000
Retained earnings	2,000	6,000
	$20,000	$28,000

	Income Statement — Year Ended December 31, 19x7
Sales (net)	$20,000
Cost of goods sold	12,000
Gross profit	8,000
Expenses	4,000
Net income	$ 4,000

Additional Information:

1. Plant and equipment was acquired on the following dates:

January 1, 19x1	$10,000
January 1, 19x4	$10,000
January 1, 19x7	$10,000

Depreciation on plant and equipment is 10 percent straight-line per annum.

2. The inventory at December 31, 19x6, was acquired when the general price index was 80. Additional purchases of inventory in 19x7 amounted to $16,000 and were made evenly throughout the year.
3. The common shares of the business were issued on January 1, 19x1.
4. The general price indexes were as follows:

January 1, 19x1	25
January 1, 19x4	75
December 31, 19x6	100
Average for 19x7	125
Average for last 6 months of 19x7	137
December 31, 19x7	150

Required:

a. Prepare a comparative balance sheet at December 31, 19x7 and an income statement for the year ended December 31, 19x7 in dollars of general purchasing power as of December 31, 19x7.

b. Clearly explain the uses and limitations of the financial statements which you prepared in Part a above.

P16-10 Crandall Limited commences business on January 1, 19x8 with $1,000 cash credited to capital. On January 2, 19x8 100 items of inventory are bought at $10 each. On January 15, 19x8 60 items are sold at $20 each. Current replacement cost of each unit of inventory on January 15, 19x8 is $13. The current replacement cost and the selling price of each unit of inventory on January 31, 19x8 are $16 and $25 respectively.

The remaining 40 items are sold on February 15, 19x8 at $30 each. The current replacement cost of each unit of inventory on February 15, 19x8 was $20.

Required:

a. Prepare income statements and balance sheets for January and February using the following valuation bases:
   1. historic cost
   2. current entry price (current replacement cost)
   3. current exit price (current selling price)

b. Given the general price indexes for 19x8 were as follows:

January 1	100	February 15	120
January 15	100	February 28	140
January 31	100		

Prepare a revised income statement and balance sheet for February using a general price level restated historic cost basis of valuation.

c. Evaluate the difficulties of implementing a current entry price basis of valuation for Crandall Limited.

d. What additional problems would be encountered in implementing a current value basis of valuation if Crandall had fixed assets?

e. Evaluate the usefulness of the statements you prepared in Part a.

P16-11 Knight Limited is a steel distributor. The company commenced business on January 1, 19x8 with $150 that it used to buy 5 tons of steel at $30 per ton.

No transactions occurred until December 31, 19x8 when the replacement cost rose to $45 per ton and one ton was sold for $65. During 19x8 general prices rose 10 percent.

Required:

Prepare an Income Statement for the year ended December 31, 19x8 for the following situations:

Case (1)	Net asset value	= general price level restated historic cost
	Capital maintenance	= general price level restated historic cost (purchasing power)
Case (2)	Net asset value	= replacement cost
	Capital maintenance	= money capital
Case (3)	Net asset value	= replacement cost
	Capital maintenance	= replacement cost (operating capacity)
Case (4)	Net asset value	= replacement cost
	Capital maintenance	= general price level restatement of historic cost

P16-12 Two companies, the FIFO Co. Ltd. and the LIFO Co. Ltd. engage in operations in an identical manner. The former, however, maintains its inventory on a FIFO basis and the latter on a LIFO basis.

As of the start of 19x4 each firm had 5,000 units of production on hand. The units of the LIFO Co. were assumed to have been acquired in 19x1 and were carried on the books of the company at a value of $170,000 ($34 per unit). Those of the FIFO Co. were assumed to have been acquired in 19x3 and were carried on the books at a value of $250,000 ($50 per unit).

In 19x4 each company purchased 24,000 units of product as follows:

1st quarter	6,000 units	@ $51 =	$ 306,000
2nd quarter	6,000 units	@ 52 =	312,000
3rd quarter	6,000 units	@ 54 =	324,000
4th quarter	6,000 units	@ 56 =	336,000
	24,000		$1,278,000

At the end of the year each company sold 21,000 units for $1,470,000; at year end each had 8,000 units remaining in inventory.

Relevant values for the general price level index are:

19x1	111 (when Lifo Co. acquired its opening inventory)	
19x3	159 (when Fifo Co. acquired its opening inventory)	
19x4	1st quarter	164
	2nd quarter	167
	3rd quarter	172
	4th quarter	178

Required:

a. Determine cost of goods sold and year-end 19x4 inventory for each of the two firms on a historical cost basis. Calculate income for the two companies.

b. Determine cost of goods sold and year-end 19x4 inventory for each of the two firms on a price level adjusted basis. Calculate income for the two companies.

c. Assume that the replacement cost of inventory was $50 per unit at the beginning of 19x4 and $58 at the end of 19x4 (when the company sold 21,000 units). If a replacement cost basis of valuing inventory is used determine cost of goods sold and year-end 19x4 inventory for each of the two firms. Calculate income for the two companies.

d. Which net asset valuation basis would you recommend? Be sure to indicate the use you intend to make of the information in order to justify your response.

e. If the stock markets are "efficient" and the method of inventory valuation is disclosed then how would investors interpret the difference in income of the two firms calculated in Part a?

P16-13 Fuecher Limited commenced business on January 1, 19x9 with $2,000 which it used to buy 10 units of inventory at $200 each. No transactions occurred until December, 19x9. On December 31, 19x9 the company sold 5 units for $300 each and purchased two more units for $250 each. During the year the general price rose 10 percent.

Required:

a. Prepare an Income Statement for the year ended December 31, 19x9 under each of the following assumptions:

Case (1) Net asset value = historic cost
Capital maintenance = operating or physical capacity (i.e., replacement cost)

Case (2) Net asset value = replacement cost
Capital maintenance = operating or physical capacity (i.e., replacement cost)

Case (3) Net asset value = replacement cost
Capital maintenance = general price level restated historic cost.

b. Explain where each of Cases (1), (2) and (3) would "make sense."

c. Indicate some of the problems in implementing the system described in Case (2) above.

Cases

C16-1 Electric Company Limited is a public utility company. It is subject to regulation by a commission which established rates such as that utilities within its jurisdiction are permitted to earn a return of 7 percent on total invested capital. A condensed balance sheet and income statement of Electric Company Limited for the year ending December 31, 19x1, the first year of its operations, appears as follows:

Balance Sheet as of December 31, 19x1

Assets		
Cash and accounts receivable		$ 1,500,000
Inventories and supplies		200,000
Plant and equipment	$12,000,000	
Less: Accumulated depreciation	850,000	11,150,000
Total assets		$12,850,000
Equities		
Current liabilities		$ 300,000
Long-term debt (at 10% interest)		9,000,000
Shareholders' equity		3,550,000
Total equities		$12,850,000

Statement of Income
For the Year Ending December 31, 19x1

Revenue		$ 5,149,500
Operating expenses	$ 2,500,000	
Depreciation	850,000	
Interest	900,000	4,250,000
Net income before taxes		$ 899,500

Return on investment is defined as net income before taxes divided by total assets. Thus $899,500/$12,850,000 equals 7 percent.

All assets except for plant and equipment represent fair market value, that is the cash and accounts receivable reflect cash the company either has or will receive in the near future and the book value of inventories and supplies equals the replacement cost of these items at December 31, 19x1. The plant and equipment consists of the following items:

	Historic Cost	*Replacement cost at December 31, 19x1*
Land	$ 500,000	$ 600,000
Building (depreciated on a straight-line basis over 25 years)	5,000,000	6,100,000
Equipment (depreciated on a straight-line basis over 10 years)	6,500,000	7,500,000
	$12,000,000	$14,200,000

The long-term debt and common shares were issued when the general price index was at 140. The fixed assets were acquired when the general price index was at the same level.

Revenues, operating expenses, and interest were incurred evenly throughout 19x1. The average general price index for 19x1 was 146.

The company paid dividends in 19x1 of $400,000. They may be assumed to have been paid evenly throughout the year.

At the start of 19x1 the company received $12,050,500 cash from the debt issue and the issue of common shares and paid $12,000,000 cash for plant and equipment.

Inventories and supplies were acquired at year end. The general price index at year end was 152.

Required:

a. Determine the actual rate of return for 19x1 on a general price level restated basis and on a current value basis.

b. Which base do you think the regulatory commission should use? Why?

C16-2 At a cocktail party, you happen to overhear the following conversation between a businessman and an accountant:

BUSINESSMAN: If my business is to be ongoing, I must generate enough money for the replacement of equipment when the equipment wears out or becomes obsolete. I don't see why accountants don't provide for this in their determination of profits.

ACCOUNTANT: Accountants cannot provide for future costs. Their job is to account for past costs. For instance, we record the actual cost of your equipment on your company's books, estimate how long it will be useful and what its salvage value might be and then match the original cost, through "depreciation," to revenue the equipment generates. In this way, we derive an objective and useful income figure.

BUSINESSMAN: (slightly annoyed) Your depreciation formula may be enshrined in professional standards, law and other impressive documents but it seems to me that the exercise is useless. It does not accurately reflect an important cost of doing business. I would say that the neat symmetrical depreciation charge you so laboriously calculate distorts the performance of a company. In addition, your judgments about the useful life, the salvage value and the likely revenue stream are all subjective. Therefore, how can you stand there and tell me the income figure you derive is objective? In my opinion it is subjective and useless.

ACCOUNTANT: (fidgeting somewhat) You have been talking about how to account for equipment from your own point of view. However, other people such as creditors, tax authorities and so forth use your financial statements. The Income Tax Act defines cost as the price paid at the acquisition date not the replacement date. Therefore, it is important to keep track of original cost.

In addition, creditors often compare your financial statements to those of other companies when making a lending decision. This comparability aspect is aided by historic cost accounting. While I admit some subjectivity does exist, at least we are dealing with one known amount — the original cost of an asset. Actually, I think the income figure would be even more useful to creditors if only one depreciation method was allowed.

BUSINESSMAN: (muttering while walking way) These accountants are so righteous about their accounting methods. If only they would wake up one day and realize the books are not the business!

Required:

Evaluate the arguments of both the businessman and the accountant. How would you have dealt with the businessman's concerns?

C16-3 Canadian Steel Limited ("CSL" or the company) is federally incorporated. Its common shares and debentures are held by the general public. CSL is a steel wholesaler engaged essentially in buying large volumes of steel at a discount, storing it and selling it in smaller units to customers.

Recently CSL increased their selling price of steel. Almost immediately articles appeared in the newspapers criticizing the price increase. The fact that the company reported earnings of $5.00 per share and had a 15 percent return on shareholders' equity received a lot of attention in the newspapers.

Management has decided to embark on a publicity campaign in order to explain to the public and their customers that the price increase was justified and that their return on investment before the price increase was inadequate.

In addition the president of the company would like to improve the performance evaluation and motivation of managers. Specifically he would like an accounting system which:

1. immediately motivates managers to raise the selling price when the replacement cost of steel changes.
2. motivates managers to sell in bulk to customers if selling prices exceed replacement cost.
3. gives credit to the purchasing department for bulk buying before price increases.
4. separates the efficiency of the selling departments from the buying and storing functions of the company.

Required:

What would you recommend? Consider potential implementation problems like the availability of the information you intend to use, the reaction of the company's auditors, etc.

Appendix

table 1

Future Value of $1

No. of periods	2%	3%	4%	5%	6%	7%	8%
1	1.0200	1.0300	1,0400	1.0500	1.0600	1.0700	1.0800
2	1.0404	1.0609	1.0816	1.1025	1.1236	1.1449	1.1664
3	1.0612	1.0927	1.1249	1.1576	1.1910	1.2250	1.2597
4	1.0824	1.1255	1.1699	1.2155	1.2625	1.3108	1.3605
5	1.1041	1.1593	1.2167	1.2763	1.3382	1.4026	1.4693
6	1.1262	1.1941	1.2653	1.3401	1.4185	1.5007	1.5869
7	1.1487	1.2299	1.3159	1.4071	1.5036	1.6058	1.7138
8	1.1717	1.2668	1.3686	1.4775	1.5938	1.7182	1.8509
9	1.1951	1.3048	1.4233	1.5513	1.6895	1.8385	1.9990
10	1.2190	1.3439	1.4802	1.6289	1.7908	1.9672	2.1589
11	1.2434	1.3842	1.5395	1.7103	1.8983	2.1049	2.3316
12	1.2682	1.4258	1.6010	1.7959	2.0122	2.2522	2.5182
13	1.2936	1.4685	1.6651	1.8856	2.1329	2.4098	2.7196
14	1.3195	1.5126	1.7317	1.9799	2.2609	2.5785	2.9372
15	1.3459	1.5580	1.8009	2.0789	2.3966	2.7590	3.1722
16	1.3728	1.6047	1.8730	2.1829	2.5404	2.9522	3.4259
17	1.4002	1.6528	1.9479	2.2920	2.6928	3.1588	3.7000
18	1.4282	1.7024	2.0258	2.4066	2.8543	3.3799	3.9960
19	1.4568	1.7535	2.1068	2.5270	3.0256	3.6165	4.3157
20	1.4859	1.8061	2.1911	2.6533	3.2071	3.8697	4.6610
21	1.5157	1.8603	2.2788	2.7860	3.3996	4.1406	5.0338
22	1.5460	1.9161	2.3699	2.9253	3.6035	4.4304	5.4365
23	1.5769	1.9736	2.4647	3.0715	3.8197	4.7405	5.8715
24	1.6084	2.0328	2.5633	3.2251	4.0489	5.0724	6.3412
25	1.6406	2.0938	2.6658	3.3864	4.2919	5.4274	6.8485
26	1.6734	2.1566	2.7725	3.5557	4.5494	5.8074	7.3964
27	1.7069	2.2213	2.8834	3.7335	4.8223	6.2139	7.9881
28	1.7410	2.2879	2.9987	3.9201	5.1117	6.6488	8.6271
29	1.7758	2.3566	3.1187	4.1161	5.4184	7.1143	9.3173
30	1.8114	2.4273	3.2434	4.3219	5.7435	7.6123	10.0627
31	1.8476	2.5001	3.3731	4.5380	6.0881	8.1451	10.8677
32	1.8845	2.5751	3.5081	4.7649	6.4534	8.7153	11.7371
33	1.9222	2.6523	3.6484	5.0032	6.8406	9.3253	12.6760
34	1.9607	2.7319	3.7943	5.2533	7.2510	9.9781	13.6901
35	1.9999	2.8139	3.9461	5.5160	7.6861	10.6766	14.7853
36	2.0399	2.8983	4.1039	5.7918	8.1473	11.4239	15.9682
37	2.0807	2.9852	4.2681	6.0814	8.6361	12.2236	17.2456
38	2.1223	3.0748	4.4388	6.3855	9.1543	13.0793	18.6253
39	2.1647	3.1670	4.6164	6.7048	9.7035	13.9948	20.1153
40	2.2080	3.2620	4.8010	7.0400	10.2857	14.9745	21.7245
41	2.2522	3.3599	4.9931	7.3920	10.9029	16.0227	23.4625
42	2.2972	3.4607	5.1928	7.7616	11.5570	17.1443	25.3395
43	2.3432	3.5645	5.4005	8.1497	12.2505	18.3444	27.3666
44	2.3901	3.6715	5.6165	8.5572	12.9855	19.6285	29.5560
45	2.4379	3.7816	5.8412	8.9850	13.7646	21.0025	31.9204
46	2.4866	3.8950	6.0748	9.4343	14.5905	22.4726	34.4741
47	2.5363	4.0119	6.3178	9.9060	15.4659	24.0457	37.2320
48	2.5871	4.1323	6.5705	10.4013	16.3939	25.7289	40.2106
49	2.6388	4.2562	6.8333	10.9213	17.3775	27.5299	43.4274
50	2.6916	4.3839	7.1067	11.4674	18.4202	29.4570	46.9016

9%	10%	11%	12%	13%	14%	15%
1.0900	1.1000	1.1100	1.1200	1.1300	1.1400	1.1500
1.1881	1.2100	1.2321	1.2544	1.2769	1.2996	1.3225
1.2950	1.3310	1.3676	1.4049	1.4429	1.4815	1.5209
1.4116	1.4641	1.5181	1.5735	1.6305	1.6890	1.7490
1.5386	1.6105	1.6851	1.7623	1.8424	1.9254	2.0114
1.6771	1.7716	1.8704	1.9738	2.0820	2.1950	2.3131
1.8280	1.9487	2.0762	2.2107	2.3526	2.5023	2.6600
1.9926	2.1436	2.3045	2.4760	2.6584	2.8526	3.0590
2.1719	2.3579	2.5580	2.7731	3.0040	3.2519	3.5179
2.3674	2.5937	2.8394	3.1058	3.3946	3.7072	4.0456
2.5804	2.8531	3.1518	3.4785	3.8359	4.2262	4.6524
2.8127	3.1384	3.4985	3.8960	4.3345	4.8179	5.3503
3.0658	3.4523	3.8833	4.3635	4.8980	5.4924	6.1528
3.3417	3.7975	4.3104	4.8871	5.5348	6.2613	7.0757
3.6425	4.1772	4.7846	5.4736	6.2543	7.1379	8.1371
3.9703	4.5950	5.3109	6.1304	7.0673	8.1372	9.3576
4.3276	5.0545	5.8951	6.8660	7.9861	9.2765	10.7613
4.7171	5.5599	6.5436	7.6900	9.0243	10.5752	12.3755
5.1417	6.1159	7.2633	8.6128	10.1974	12.0557	14.2318
5.6044	6.7275	8.0623	9.6463	11.5231	13.7435	16.3665
6.1088	7.4002	8.9492	10.8038	13.0211	15.6676	18.8215
6.6586	8.1403	9.9336	12.1003	14.7138	17.8610	21.6447
7.2579	8.9543	11.0263	13.5523	16.6266	20.3616	24.8915
7.9111	9.8497	12.2392	15.1786	18.7881	23.2122	28.6252
8.6231	10.8347	13.5855	17.0001	21.2305	26.4619	32.9190
9.3992	11.9182	15.0799	19.0401	23.9905	30.1666	37.8568
10.2451	13.1100	16.7386	21.3249	27.1093	34.3899	43.5353
11.1671	14.4210	18.5799	23.8839	30.6335	39.2045	50.0656
12.1722	15.8631	20.6237	26.7499	34.6158	44.6931	57.5755
13.2677	17.4494	22.8923	29.9599	39.1159	50.9502	66.2118
14.4618	19.1943	25.4104	33.5551	44.2010	58.0832	76.1435
15.7633	21.1138	28.2056	37.5817	49.9471	66.2148	87.5651
17.1820	23.2252	31.3082	42.0915	56.4402	75.4849	100.6998
18.7284	25.5477	34.7521	47.1425	63.7774	86.0528	115.8048
20.4140	28.1024	38.5749	52.7996	72.0685	98.1002	133.1755
22.2512	30.9127	42.8181	59.1356	81.4374	111.8342	153.1519
24.2538	34.0039	47.5281	66.2318	92.0243	127.4910	176.1246
26.4367	37.4043	52.7562	74.1797	103.9874	145.3397	202.5433
28.8160	41.1448	58.5593	83.0812	117.5058	165.6873	232.9248
31.4094	45.2593	65.0009	93.0510	132.7816	188.8835	267.8635
34.2363	49.7852	72.1510	104.2171	150.0432	215.3272	308.0431
37.3175	54.7637	80.0876	116.7231	169.5488	245.4730	354.2495
40.6761	60.2401	88.8972	130.7299	191.5901	279.8392	407.3870
44.3370	66.2641	98.6759	146.4175	216.4968	319.0167	468.4950
48.3273	72.8905	109.5302	163.9876	244.6414	363.6791	538.7693
52.6767	80.1795	121.5786	183.6661	276.4448	414.5941	619.5847
57.4176	88.1975	134.9522	205.7061	312.3826	472.6373	712.5224
62.5852	97.0172	149.7970	230.3908	352.9923	538.8065	819.4007
68.2179	106.7190	166.2746	258.0377	398.8813	614.2395	942.3108
74.3575	117.3909	184.5648	289.0022	450.7359	700.2330	1083.6574

table 2

Present Value of $1

No. of periods	2%	3%	4%	5%	6%	7%	8%
1	.9804	.9709	.9615	.9524	.9434	.9346	.9259
2	.9612	.9426	.9246	.9070	.8900	.8734	.8573
3	.9423	.9151	.8890	.8638	.8396	.8163	.7938
4	.9238	.8885	.8548	.8227	.7921	.7629	.7350
5	.9057	.8626	.8219	.7835	.7473	.7130	.6806
6	.8880	.8375	.7903	.7462	.7050	.6663	.6302
7	.8706	.8131	.7599	.7107	.6651	.6227	.5835
8	.8535	.7894	.7307	.6768	.6274	.5820	.5403
9	.8368	.7664	.7026	.6446	.5919	.5439	.5002
10	.8203	.7441	.6756	.6139	.5584	.5083	.4632
11	.8043	.7224	.6496	.5847	.5268	.4751	.4289
12	.7885	.7014	.6246	.5568	.4970	.4440	.3971
13	.7730	.6810	.6006	.5303	.4688	.4150	.3677
14	.7579	.6611	.5775	.5051	.4423	.3878	.3405
15	.7430	.6419	.5553	.4810	.4173	.3624	.3152
16	.7284	.6232	.5339	.4581	.3936	.3387	.2919
17	.7142	.6050	.5134	.4363	.3714	.3166	.2703
18	.7002	.5874	.4936	.4155	.3503	.2959	.2502
19	.6864	.5703	.4746	.3957	.3305	.2765	.2317
20	.6730	.5537	.4564	.3769	.3118	.2584	.2145
21	.6598	.5375	.4388	.3589	.2942	.2415	.1987
22	.6468	.5219	.4220	.3418	.2775	.2257	.1839
23	.6342	.5067	.4057	.3256	.2618	.2109	.1703
24	.6217	.4919	.3901	.3101	.2470	.1971	.1577
25	.6095	.4776	.3751	.2953	.2330	.1842	.1460
26	.5976	.4637	.3607	.2812	.2198	.1722	.1352
27	.5859	.4502	.3468	.2678	.2074	.1609	.1252
28	.5744	.4371	.3335	.2551	.1956	.1504	.1159
29	.5631	.4243	.3207	.2429	.1846	.1406	.1073
30	.5521	.4120	.3083	.2314	.1741	.1314	.0994
31	.5412	.4000	.2965	.2204	.1643	.1228	.0920
32	.5306	.3883	.2851	.2099	.1550	.1147	.0852
33	.5202	.3770	.2741	.1999	.1462	.1072	.0789
34	.5100	.3660	.2636	.1904	.1379	.1002	.0730
35	.5000	.3554	.2534	.1813	.1301	.0937	.0676
36	.4902	.3450	.2437	.1727	.1227	.0875	.0626
37	.4806	.3350	.2343	.1644	.1158	.0818	.0580
38	.4712	.3252	.2253	.1566	.1092	.0765	.0537
39	.4619	.3158	.2166	.1491	.1031	.0715	.0497
40	.4529	.3066	.2083	.1420	.0972	.0668	.0460
41	.4440	.2976	.2003	.1353	.0917	.0624	.0426
42	.4353	.2890	.1926	.1288	.0865	.0583	.0395
43	.4268	.2805	.1852	.1227	.0816	.0545	.0365
44	.4184	.2724	.1780	.1169	.0770	.0509	.0338
45	.4102	.2644	.1712	.1113	.0727	.0476	.0313
46	.4022	.2567	.1646	.1060	.0685	.0445	.0290
47	.3943	.2493	.1583	.1009	.0647	.0416	.0269
48	.3865	.2420	.1522	.0961	.0610	.0389	.0249
49	.3790	.2350	.1463	.0916	.0575	.0363	.0230
50	.3715	.2281	.1407	.0872	.0543	.0339	.0213

9%	10%	11%	12%	13%	14%	15%
.9174	.9091	.9009	.8929	.8850	.8772	.8696
.8417	.8264	.8116	.7972	.7831	.7695	.7561
.7722	.7513	.7312	.7118	.6931	.6750	.6575
.7084	.6830	.6587	.6355	.6133	.5921	.5718
.6499	.6209	.5935	.5674	.5428	.5194	.4972
.5963	.5645	.5346	.5066	.4803	.4556	.4323
.5470	.5132	.4817	.4523	.4251	.3996	.3759
.5019	.4665	.4339	.4039	.3762	.3506	.3269
.4604	.4241	.3909	.3606	.3329	.3075	.2843
.4224	.3855	.3522	.3220	.2946	.2697	.2472
.3875	.3505	.3173	.2875	.2607	.2366	.2149
.3555	.3186	.2858	.2567	.2307	.2076	.1869
.3262	.2897	.2575	.2292	.2042	.1821	.1625
.2992	.2633	.2320	.2046	.1807	.1597	.1413
.2745	.2394	.2090	.1827	.1599	.1401	.1229
.2519	.2176	.1883	.1631	.1415	.1229	.1069
.2311	.1978	.1696	.1456	.1252	.1078	.0929
.2120	.1799	.1528	.1300	.1108	.0946	.0808
.1945	.1635	.1377	.1161	.0981	.0829	.0703
.1784	.1486	.1240	.1037	.0868	.0728	.0611
.1637	.1351	.1117	.0926	.0768	.0638	.0531
.1502	.1228	.1007	.0826	.0680	.0560	.0462
.1378	.1117	.0907	.0738	.0601	.0491	.0402
.1264	.1015	.0817	.0659	.0532	.0431	.0349
.1160	.0923	.0736	.0588	.0471	.0378	.0304
.1064	.0839	.0663	.0525	.0417	.0331	.0264
.0976	.0763	.0597	.0469	.0369	.0291	.0230
.0895	.0693	.0538	.0419	.0326	.0255	.0200
.0822	.0630	.0485	.0374	.0289	.0224	.0174
.0754	.0573	.0437	.0334	.0256	.0196	.0151
.0691	.0521	.0394	.0298	.0226	.0172	.0131
.0634	.0474	.0355	.0266	.0200	.0151	.0114
.0582	.0431	.0319	.0238	.0177	.0132	.0099
.0534	.0391	.0288	.0212	.0157	.0116	.0086
.0490	.0356	.0259	.0189	.0139	.0102	.0075
.0449	.0323	.0234	.0169	.0123	.0089	.0065
.0412	.0294	.0210	.0151	.0109	.0078	.0057
.0378	.0267	.0190	.0135	.0096	.0069	.0049
.0347	.0243	.0171	.0120	.0085	.0060	.0043
.0318	.0221	.0154	.0107	.0075	.0053	.0037
.0292	.0201	.0139	.0096	.0067	.0046	.0032
.0268	.0183	.0125	.0086	.0059	.0041	.0028
.0246	.0166	.0112	.0076	.0052	.0036	.0025
.0226	.0151	.0101	.0068	.0046	.0031	.0021
.0207	.0137	.0091	.0061	.0041	.0027	.0019
.0190	.0125	.0082	.0054	.0036	.0024	.0016
.0174	.0113	.0074	.0049	.0032	.0021	.0014
.0160	.0103	.0067	.0043	.0028	.0019	.0012
.0147	.0094	.0060	.0039	.0025	.0016	.0011
.0134	.0085	.0054	.0035	.0022	.0014	.0009

table 3 **Future Value of an Annuity of $1 in Arrears**

No. of periods	*2%*	*3%*	*4%*	*5%*	*6%*	*7%*	*8%*
1	1.0000	1.0000	1.0000	1.0000	1.0000	1.0000	1.0000
2	2.0200	2.0300	2.0400	2.0500	2.0600	2.0700	2.0800
3	3.0604	3.0909	3.1216	3.1525	3.1836	3.2149	3.2464
4	4.1216	4.1836	4.2465	4.3101	4.3746	4.4399	4.5061
5	5.2040	5.3091	5.4163	5.5256	5.6371	5.7507	5.8666
6	6.3081	6.4684	6.6330	6.8019	6.9753	7.1533	7.3359
7	7.4343	7.6625	7.8983	8.1420	8.3938	8.6540	8.9228
8	8.5830	8.8923	9.2142	9.5491	9.8975	10.2598	10.6366
9	9.7546	10.1591	10.5828	11.0266	11.4913	11.9780	12.4876
10	10.9497	11.4639	12.0061	12.5779	13.1808	13.8164	14.4866
11	12.1687	12.8078	13.4864	14.2068	14.9716	15.7836	16.6455
12	13.4121	14.1920	15.0258	15.9171	16.8699	17.8885	18.9771
13	14.6803	15.6178	16.6268	17.7130	18.8821	20.1406	21.4953
14	15.9739	17.0863	18.2919	19.5986	21.0151	22.5505	24.2149
15	17.2934	18.5989	20.0236	21.5786	23.2760	25.1290	27.1521
16	18.6393	20.1569	21.8245	23.6575	25.6725	27.8881	30.3243
17	20.0121	21.7616	23.6975	25.8404	28.2129	30.8402	33.7502
18	21.4123	23.4144	25.6454	28.1324	30.9057	33.9990	37.4502
19	22.8406	25.1169	27.6712	30.5390	33.7600	37.3790	41.4463
20	24.2974	26.8704	29.7781	33.0660	36.7856	40.9955	45.7620
21	25.7833	28.6765	31.9692	35.7193	39.9927	44.8652	50.4229
22	27.2990	30.5368	34.2480	38.5052	43.3923	49.0057	55.4568
23	28.8450	32.4529	36.6179	41.4305	46.9958	53.4361	60.8933
24	30.4219	34.4265	39.0826	44.5020	50.8156	58.1767	66.7648
25	32.0303	36.4593	41.6459	47.7271	54.8645	63.2490	73.1059
26	33.6709	38.5530	44.3117	51.1135	59.1564	68.6765	79.9544
27	35.3443	40.7096	47.0842	54.6691	63.7058	74.4838	87.3508
28	37.0512	42.9309	49.9676	58.4026	68.5281	80.6977	95.3388
29	38.7922	45.2189	52.9663	62.3227	73.6398	87.3465	103.9659
30	40.5681	47.5754	56.0849	66.4388	79.0582	94.4608	113.2832
31	42.3794	50.0027	59.3283	70.7608	84.8017	102.0730	123.3459
32	44.2270	52.5028	62.7015	75.2988	90.8898	110.2182	134.2135
33	46.1116	55.0778	66.2095	80.0638	97.3432	118.9334	145.9506
34	48.0338	57.7302	69.8579	85.0670	104.1838	128.2588	158.6267
35	49.9945	60.4621	73.6522	90.3203	111.4348	138.2369	172.3168
36	51.9944	63.2759	77.5983	95.8363	119.1209	148.9135	187.1021
37	54.0343	66.1742	81.7022	101.6281	127.2681	160.3374	203.0703
38	56.1149	69.1594	85.9703	107.7095	135.9042	172.5610	220.3159
39	58.2372	72.2342	90.4091	114.0950	145.0585	185.6403	238.9412
40	60.4020	75.4013	95.0255	120.7998	154.7620	199.6351	259.0565
41	62.6100	78.6633	99.8265	127.8398	165.0477	214.6096	280.7810
42	64.8622	82.0232	104.8196	135.2318	175.9505	230.6322	304.2435
43	67.1595	85.4839	110.0124	142.9933	187.5076	247.7765	329.5830
44	69.5027	89.0484	115.4129	151.1430	199.7580	266.1209	356.9496
45	71.8927	92.7199	121.0294	159.7002	212.7435	285.7493	386.5056
46	74.3306	96.5015	126.8706	168.6852	226.5081	306.7518	418.4261
47	76.8172	100.3965	132.9454	178.1194	241.0986	329.2244	452.9002
48	79.3535	104.4084	139.2632	188.0254	256.5645	353.2701	490.1322
49	81.9406	108.5406	145.8337	198.4267	272.9584	378.9990	530.3427
50	84.5794	112.7969	152.6671	209.3480	290.3359	406.5289	573.7702

9%	10%	11%	12%	13%	14%	15%
1.0000	1.0000	1.0000	1.0000	1.0000	1.0000	1.0000
2.0900	2.1000	2.1100	2.1200	2.1300	2.1400	2.1500
3.2781	3.3100	3.3421	3.3744	3.4069	3.4396	3.4725
4.5731	4.6410	4.7097	4.7793	4.8498	4.9211	4.9934
5.9847	6.1051	6.2278	6.3528	6.4803	6.6101	6.7424
7.5233	7.7156	7.9129	8.1152	8.3227	8.5355	8.7537
9.2004	9.4872	9.7833	10.0890	10.4047	10.7305	11.0668
11.0285	11.4359	11.8594	12.2997	12.7573	13.2328	13.7268
13.0210	13.5795	14.1640	14.7757	15.4157	16.0853	16.7858
15.1929	15.9374	16.7220	17.5487	18.4197	19.3373	20.3037
17.5603	18.5312	19.5614	20.6546	21.8143	23.0445	24.3493
20.1407	21.3843	22.7132	24.1331	25.6502	27.2707	29.0017
22.9534	24.5227	26.2116	28.0291	29.9847	32.0887	34.3519
26.0192	27.9750	30.0949	32.3926	34.8827	37.5811	40.5047
29.3609	31.7725	34.4054	37.2797	40.4175	43.8424	47.5804
33.0034	35.9497	39.1899	42.7533	46.6717	50.9804	55.7175
36.9737	40.5447	44.5008	48.8837	53.7391	59.1176	65.0751
41.3013	45.5992	50.3959	55.7497	61.7251	68.3941	75.8364
46.0185	51.1591	56.9395	63.4397	70.7494	78.9692	88.2118
51.1601	57.2750	64.2028	72.0524	80.9468	91.0249	102.4436
56.7645	64.0025	72.2651	81.6987	92.4699	104.7684	118.8101
62.8733	71.4027	81.2143	92.5026	105.4910	120.4360	137.6316
69.5319	79.5430	91.1479	104.6029	120.2048	138.2970	159.2764
76.7898	88.4973	102.1742	118.1552	136.8315	158.6586	184.1678
84.7009	98.3471	114.4133	133.3339	155.6196	181.8708	212.7930
93.3240	109.1818	127.9988	150.3339	176.8501	208.3327	245.7120
102.7231	121.0999	143.0786	169.3740	200.8406	238.4993	283.5688
112.9682	134.2099	159.8173	190.6989	227.9499	272.8892	327.1041
124.1354	148.6309	178.3972	214.5828	258.5834	312.0937	377.1697
136.3075	164.4940	199.0209	241.3327	293.1992	356.7868	434.7451
149.5752	181.9434	221.9132	271.2926	332.3151	407.7370	500.9569
164.0370	201.1378	247.3236	304.8477	376.5161	465.8202	577.1005
179.8003	222.2515	275.5292	342.4294	426.4632	532.0350	664.6655
196.9823	245.4767	306.8374	384.5210	482.9034	607.5199	765.3654
215.7108	271.0244	341.5896	431.6635	546.6808	693.5727	881.1702
236.1247	299.1268	380.1644	484.4631	618.7493	791.6729	1014.3457
258.3759	330.0395	422.9825	543.5987	700.1867	903.5071	1167.4975
282.6298	364.0434	470.5106	609.8305	792.2110	1030.9981	1343.6222
309.0665	401.4478	523.2667	684.0102	896.1984	1176.3378	1546.1655
337.8824	442.5926	581.8261	767.0914	1013.7042	1342.0251	1779.0903
369.2919	487.8518	646.8269	860.1424	1146.4858	1530.9086	2046.9539
403.5281	537.6370	718.9779	964.3595	1296.5289	1746.2358	2354.9969
440.8457	592.4007	799.0655	1081.0826	1466.0777	1991.7088	2709.2465
481.5218	652.6408	887.9627	1211.8125	1657.6678	2271.5481	3116.6334
525.8587	718.9048	986.6386	1358.2300	1874.1646	2590.5648	3585.1285
574.1860	791.7953	1096.1688	1522.2176	2118.8060	2954.2439	4123.8977
626.8628	871.9749	1217.7474	1705.8838	2395.2508	3368.8380	4743.4824
684.2804	960.1723	1352.6996	1911.5898	2707.6334	3841.4753	5456.0047
746.8656	1057.1896	1502.4965	2141.9806	3060.6258	4380.2819	6275.4055
815.0836	1163.9085	1668.7712	2400.0182	3459.5071	4994.5213	7217.7163

table 4 **Present Value of an Annuity of $1 in Arrears**

No. of periods	2%	3%	4%	5%	6%	7%	8%
1	.9804	.9709	.9615	.9524	.9434	.9346	.9259
2	1.9416	1.9135	1.8861	1.8594	1.8334	1.8080	1.7833
3	2.8839	2.8286	2.7751	2.7232	2.6730	2.6243	2.5771
4	3.8077	3.7171	3.6299	3.5460	3.4651	3.3872	3.3121
5	4.7135	4.5797	4.4518	4.3295	4.2124	4.1002	3.9927
6	5.6014	5.4172	5.2421	5.0757	4.9173	4.7665	4.6229
7	6.4720	6.2303	6.0021	5.7864	5.5824	5.3893	5.2064
8	7.3255	7.0197	6.7327	6.4632	6.2098	5.9713	5.7466
9	8.1622	7.7861	7.4353	7.1078	6.8017	6.5152	6.2469
10	8.9826	8.5302	8.1109	7.7217	7.3601	7.0236	6.7101
11	9.7868	9.2526	8.7605	8.3064	7.8869	7.4987	7.1390
12	10.5753	9.9540	9.3851	8.8633	8.3838	7.9427	7.5361
13	11.3484	10.6350	9.9856	9.3936	8.8527	8.3577	7.9038
14	12.1062	11.2961	10.5631	9.8986	9.2950	8.7455	8.2442
15	12.8493	11.9379	11.1184	10.3797	9.7122	9.1079	8.5595
16	13.5777	12.5611	11.6523	10.8378	10.1059	9.4466	8.8514
17	14.2919	13.1661	12.1657	11.2741	10.4773	9.7632	9.1216
18	14.9920	13.7535	12.6593	11.6896	10.8276	10.0591	9.3719
19	15.6785	14.3238	13.1339	12.0853	11.1581	10.3356	9.6036
20	16.3514	14.8775	13.5903	12.4622	11.4699	10.5940	9.8181
21	17.0112	15.4150	14.0292	12.8212	11.7641	10.8355	10.0168
22	17.6580	15.9369	14.4511	13.1630	12.0416	11.0612	10.2007
23	18.2922	16.4436	14.8568	13.4886	12.3034	11.2722	10.3711
24	18.9139	16.9355	15.2470	13.7986	12.5504	11.4693	10.5288
25	19.5235	17.4131	15.6221	14.0939	12.7834	11.6536	10.6748
26	20.1210	17.8768	15.9828	14.3752	13.0032	11.8258	10.8100
27	20.7069	18.3270	16.3296	14.6430	13.2105	11.9867	10.9352
28	21.2813	18.7641	16.6631	14.8981	13.4062	12.1371	11.0511
29	21.8444	19.1885	16.9837	15.1411	13.5907	12.2777	11.1584
30	22.3965	19.6004	17.2920	15.3725	13.7648	12.4090	11.2578
31	22.9377	20.0004	17.5885	15.5928	13.9291	12.5318	11.3498
32	23.4683	20.3888	17.8736	15.8027	14.0840	12.6466	11.4350
33	23.9886	20.7658	18.1476	16.0025	14.2302	12.7538	11.5139
34	24.4986	21.1318	18.4112	16.1929	14.3681	12.8540	11.5869
35	24.9986	21.4872	18.6646	16.3742	14.4982	12.9477	11.6546
36	25.4888	21.8323	18.9083	16.5469	14.6210	13.0352	11.7172
37	25.9695	22.1672	19.1426	16.7113	14.7368	13.1170	11.7752
38	26.4406	22.4925	19.3679	16.8679	14.8460	13.1935	11.8289
39	26.9026	22.8082	19.5845	17.0170	14.9491	13.2649	11.8786
40	27.3555	23.1148	19.7928	17.1591	15.0463	13.3317	11.9246
41	27.7995	23.4124	19.9931	17.2944	15.1380	13.3941	11.9672
42	28.2348	23.7014	20.1856	17.4232	15.2245	13.4524	12.0067
43	28.6616	23.9819	20.3708	17.5459	15.3062	13.5070	12.0432
44	29.0800	24.2543	20.5488	17.6628	15.3832	13.5579	12.0771
45	29.4902	24.5187	20.7200	17.7741	15.4558	13.6055	12.1084
46	29.8923	24.7754	20.8847	17.8801	15.5244	13.6500	12.1374
47	30.2866	25.0247	21.0429	17.9810	15.5890	13.6916	12.1643
48	30.6731	25.2667	21.1951	18.0772	15.6500	13.7305	12.1891
49	31.0521	25.5017	21.3415	18.1687	15.7076	13.7668	12.2122
50	31.4236	25.7298	21.4822	18.2559	15.7619	13.8007	12.2335

9%	10%	11%	12%	13%	14%	15%
.9174	.9091	.9009	.8929	.8850	.8772	.8696
1.7591	1.7355	1.7125	1.6901	1.6681	1.6467	1.6257
2.5313	2.4869	2.4437	2.4018	2.3612	2.3216	2.2832
3.2397	3.1699	3.1024	3.0373	2.9745	2.9137	2.8550
3.8897	3.7908	3.6959	3.6048	3.5172	3.4331	3.3522
4.4859	4.3553	4.2305	4.1114	3.9975	3.8887	3.7845
5.0330	4.8684	4.7122	4.5638	4.4226	4.2883	4.1604
5.5348	5.3349	5.1461	4.9676	4.7988	4.6389	4.4873
5.9952	5.7590	5.5370	5.3282	5.1317	4.9464	4.7716
6.4177	6.1446	5.8892	5.6502	5.4262	5.2161	5.0188
6.8052	6.4951	6.2065	5.9377	5.6869	5.4527	5.2337
7.1607	6.8137	6.4924	6.1944	5.9176	5.6603	5.4206
7.4869	7.1034	6.7499	6.4235	6.1218	5.8424	5.5831
7.7862	7.3667	6.9819	6.6282	6.3025	6.0021	5.7245
8.0607	7.6061	7.1909	6.8109	6.4624	6.1422	5.8474
8.3126	7.8237	7.3792	6.9740	6.6039	6.2651	5.9542
8.5436	8.0216	7.5488	7.1196	6.7291	6.3729	6.0472
8.7556	8.2014	7.7016	7.2497	6.8399	6.4674	6.1280
8.9501	8.3649	7.8393	7.3658	6.9380	6.5504	6.1982
9.1285	8.5136	7.9633	7.4694	7.0248	6.6231	6.2593
9.2922	8.6487	8.0751	7.5620	7.1016	6.6870	6.3125
9.4424	8.7715	8.1757	7.6446	7.1695	6.7429	6.3587
9.5802	8.8832	8.2664	7.7184	7.2297	6.7921	6.3988
9.7066	8.9847	8.3481	7.7843	7.2829	6.8351	6.4338
9.8226	9.0770	8.4217	7.8431	7.3300	6.8729	6.4641
9.9290	9.1609	8.4881	7.8957	7.3717	6.9061	6.4906
10.0266	9.2372	8.5478	7.9426	7.4086	6.9352	6.5135
10.1161	9.3066	8.6016	7.9844	7.4412	6.9607	6.5335
10.1983	9.3696	8.6501	8.0218	7.4701	6.9830	6.5509
10.2737	9.4269	8.6938	8.0552	7.4957	7.0027	6.5660
10.3428	9.4790	8.7331	8.0850	7.5183	7.0199	6.5791
10.4062	9.5264	8.7686	8.1116	7.5383	7.0350	6.5905
10.4644	9.5694	8.8005	8.1354	7.5560	7.0482	6.6005
10.5178	9.6086	8.8293	8.1566	7.5717	7.0599	6.6091
10.5668	9.6442	8.8552	8.1755	7.5856	7.0700	6.6166
10.6118	9.6765	8.8786	8.1924	7.5979	7.0790	6.6231
10.6530	9.7059	8.8996	8.2075	7.6087	7.0868	6.6288
10.6908	9.7327	8.9186	8.2210	7.6183	7.0937	6.6338
10.7255	9.7570	8.9357	8.2330	7.6268	7.0997	6.6380
10.7574	9.7791	8.9511	8.2438	7.6344	7.1050	6.6418
10.7866	9.7991	8.9649	8.2534	7.6410	7.1097	6.6450
10.8134	9.8174	8.9774	8.2619	7.6469	7.1138	6.6478
10.8380	9.8340	8.9886	8.2696	7.6522	7.1173	6.6503
10.8605	9.8491	8.9988	8.2764	7.6568	7.1205	6.6524
10.8812	9.8628	9.0079	8.2825	7.6609	7.1232	6.6543
10.9002	9.8753	9.0161	8.2880	7.6645	7.1256	6.6559
10.9176	9.8866	9.0235	8.2928	7.6677	7.1277	6.6573
10.9336	9.8969	9.0302	8.2972	7.6705	7.1296	6.6585
10.9482	9.9063	9.0362	8.3010	7.6730	7.1312	6.6596
10.9617	9.9148	9.0417	8.3045	7.6752	7.1327	6.6605

Index

D

E

F

G

H

I

J

K

L

M

N

O

P